Collins Student Atlas

T0364487

MAP SKILLS

- iii Map symbols and Map types
- iv Graphs and Statistics
- 1 Latitude and Longitude
- 2 Scale
- 3 Projections
- 4 Aerial photographs
- 5 Introducing GIS
- 6 Satellite images

UNITED KINGDOM

- 7 UK and Ireland
- 8-9 Southeast England
- 10-11 Wales and Southwest England
- 12-13 Northern England
- 14-15 Northern Ireland and Southern Scotland
- 16-17 Northern Scotland
- 18 Ireland
- 19 Satellite Image
- 20-21 Political
- 22 Relief
- 23 Geology
- 24-25 Climate
- 26 Agriculture and Forestry
- 27 Agriculture and Fishing
- 28 Industry
- 29 Energy
- 30-31 Population and Migration
- 32 Transport
- 33 Tourism

EUROPE

- 34 Relief
- 35 Political
- 36 Climate
- 37 Tourism
- 38 Land Use and Economic Activity
- 39 European Union
- 40 Population
- 41 Cities
- 42 Netherlands, Belgium and Luxembourg
- 43 Scandinavia
- 44 France
- 45 Spain and Portugal
- 46-47 Central Europe
- 48-49 Mediterranean Basin
- 50-51 Southeast Europe
- 52-53 Eastern Europe
- 54-55 Russia

NORTH AMERICA

- 56 Relief
- 57 Political
- 58 Climate
- 59 Natural Hazards
- 60-61 Canada
- 62-63 United States
- 64 United States: Population
- 65 United States: Economy
- 66-67 Mexico and the Caribbean

SOUTH AMERICA

- 68 Relief
- 69 Political
- 70 Climate
- 71 Economy and Population
- 72-73 South America
- 74 Brazil: Population
- 75 Brazil: Migration, Economy and Trade
- 76-77 Brazil: Deforestation

AFRICA

- 78 Relief
- 79 Political
- 80 Climate
- 81 Land Use
- 82 Population and Wealth
- 83 Southern Africa
- 84-85 Northern Africa

ASIA

- 86 Relief
- 87 Political
- 88-89 Climate
- 90-91 Population and Cities
- 92 Land Use
- 93 Middle East: Oil and Gas
- 94-95 Middle East
- 96 Pakistan, India, Bangladesh and Myanmar
- 97 India and Bangladesh: Population
- 98-99 China
- 100 China: Population
- 101 China: Land Use and Trade
- 102-103 Southeast Asia
- 104 Japan: Relief and Land Use
- 105 Japan: Economic Activity, Population and Tectonics

- 108-109 Australia and New Zealand
- 110 Australia: Land Use, People and Natural Hazards
- 111 Australia: Minerals and Manufacturing

POLES

- 112 Arctic Ocean and Antarctica

WORLD

- 113 International Organizations
- 114-115 Political
- 116-117 Relief
- 118-119 Tectonics
- 120-121 Climatic Systems
- 122-123 Climatic Regions
- 124-125 Climate Statistics
- 126-127 Biomes, Soils and Soil Erosion
- 128 Agriculture
- 129 Inequalities
- 130-131 Population
- 132 Urbanization
- 133 Migration
- 134 Birth Rate, Death Rate and Infant Mortality Rate
- 135 Life Expectancy, Literacy and Doctors
- 136 HDI, Access to Safe Water and Nutrition
- 137 HIV, Poverty and Aid
- 138-139 Environmental Issues
- 140-141 Climate Change
- 142 Fuel Production and Energy
- 143 GNI, Employment and Trade
- 144-145 Ecological Footprint
- 146-147 Tourism
- 148 Communications
- 149 Air Transport and Time Zones

WORLD STATISTICS

- 150-157 Country Statistics
- 158-163 Regional Indicators

- 164-188 Index

Go to **collins.co.uk/StudentAtlasDictionary** for a free downloadable *Dictionary of Geographical terms*

Published by Collins
An imprint of HarperCollins Publishers
Westerhill Road
Bishopbriggs
Glasgow G64 2QT
www.harpercollins.co.uk

HarperCollins Publishers
Macken House, 39/40 Mayor Street Upper, Dublin 1, D01 C9W8, Ireland

Eighth edition 2024

© HarperCollins Publishers 2024
Maps © Collins Bartholomew Ltd 2024

Collins ® is a registered trademark of HarperCollins Publishers Ltd

All rights reserved. No part of this publication may be reproduced, stored in a retrieval system,
or transmitted, in any form or by any means, electronic, mechanical, photocopying, recording
or otherwise, without the prior permission in writing of the publisher or copyright owners.

The contents of this publication are believed correct at the time of printing. Nevertheless the
publisher can accept no responsibility for errors or omissions, changes in the detail given or
for any expense or loss thereby caused.

HarperCollins does not warrant that any website mentioned in this title will be provided
uninterrupted, that any website will be error free, that defects will be corrected, or that the
website or the server that makes it available are free of viruses or bugs. For full terms and
conditions please refer to the site terms provided on the website.

Dates in this publication are based on the Christian Era and the designations BC and AD are
used throughout. These designations are directly interchangeable with those referring to the
Common Era, BCE and CE respectively.

A catalogue record for this book is available from the British Library.

ISBN 978-0-00-865285-2

10 9 8 7 6 5 4 3 2 1

Printed in Malaysia

All mapping in this atlas is generated from Collins Bartholomew digital databases.
Collins Bartholomew, the UK's leading independent geographical information supplier,
can provide a digital, custom, and premium mapping service to a variety of markets.
For further information, e-mail: collinsbartholomew@harpercollins.co.uk
or visit our website at: www.collinsbartholomew.com

If you would like to comment on any aspect of this book,
please contact us at the above address or online.

www.collins.co.uk
e-mail: collinsmaps@harpercollins.co.uk

MIX
Paper | Supporting
responsible forestry
FSC™ C007454

This book contains FSC™ certified paper and other controlled
sources to ensure responsible forest management.

For more information visit: www.harpercollins.co.uk/green

Acknowledgements

Agriculture and Horticulture Development Board, UK
Airports Council International
Australian Government
Bathymetric data: The GEBCO Digital Atlas, published by the British Oceanographic Data Centre
  on behalf of IOC and IHO, 1994
BP Statistical Review of World Energy
Brazilian Institute of Geography and Statistics
British Geological Survey
Climate Change Vulnerability Index, 2023 © Verisk Maplecroft
Dartmouth Flood Observatory, USA
Global Footprint Network National Footprint Accounts, 2022 (http://data.footprintnetwork.org)
Intergovernmental Panel on Climate Change
International Telecommunication Union
IUCN Red List of Threatened Species™
Met Office, UK
NI Forest Service Copyright
Office for National Statistics, UK
UK Government (gov.uk) – public sector information licensed under the Open Government Licence v3.0
UN Commodity Trade Statistics
UN Department of Economic and Social Affairs, Population Division
UN Development Programme
UNESCO World Heritage Centre
UN Food and Agriculture Organization
UNHCR (UN Refugee Agency)
US Bureau of Labor Statistics
US Census Bureau
US Energy Information Administration
USGS Earthquake Hazards Program
USGS Mineral Resources Program
World Bank Group
World Resources Institute
World Tourism Organization

Image credits

p4 Richard Cooke/Alamy Stock Photo (vertical), A.P.S. (UK)/Alamy Stock Photo (oblique); **p5** MODIS Rapid Respose
Team, NASA/GSFC (Alps satellite image); **p6** NASA Earth Observatory (Hurricane Sandy), NOAA Remote Sensing Division
(New Jersey), NASA/Science Photo Library (Lake Chad); **p19** Planet Observer/Science Photo Library; **p25** daulon/
Shutterstock (Greenhouse gases diagram); **p59** NASA Earth Observatory/NOAA GOES Project; **p76-77** NASA/Earth
Observatory; **p91** NASA/Ron Beck, USGS Eros Data Center Satellite Systems Branch; **p132** NASA Earth Observatory.

Map symbols

symbols are used, in the form of points, lines
r areas, on maps to show the location of
nd information about specific features.
he colour and size of a symbol can give
n indication of the type of feature and its
elative size.

he meaning of map symbols is explained in
key shown on each page. Symbols used on
eference maps are shown here.

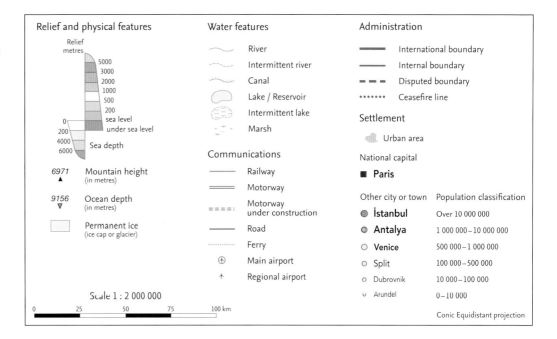

Relief and physical features

Relief metres
5000
3000
2000
1000
500
200
0 sea level
200 under sea level
4000 Sea depth
6000

6971 ▲ Mountain height (in metres)

9156 ▼ Ocean depth (in metres)

Permanent ice (ice cap or glacier)

Water features

River
Intermittent river
Canal
Lake / Reservoir
Intermittent lake
Marsh

Communications

Railway
Motorway
Motorway under construction
Road
Ferry
⊕ Main airport
✈ Regional airport

Scale 1 : 2 000 000

0 25 50 75 100 km

Administration

International boundary
Internal boundary
Disputed boundary
Ceasefire line

Settlement

Urban area

National capital

■ Paris

Other city or town | Population classification
● İstanbul | Over 10 000 000
● Antalya | 1 000 000 – 10 000 000
○ Venice | 500 000 – 1 000 000
○ Split | 100 000 – 500 000
○ Dubrovnik | 10 000 – 100 000
○ Arundel | 0 – 10 000

Conic Equidistant projection

Map types

Many types of map are included in the atlas to show different information. The type of map,
s symbols and colours are carefully selected to show the theme of each map and to make
hem easy to understand. The main types of map used are explained below.

olitical maps provide an overview of the
ze, location and boundaries of countries
n a specific area, such as a continent.
oloured squares indicate national capitals.
oloured circles represent other cities
r towns.

Physical or relief maps use colour to show
oceans, seas, rivers, lakes and the height of
the land. The names and heights of major
landforms are also indicated.

Reference maps bring together the
information provided in the two types
of map described on the left. They show
relief and physical features as well as
country borders, major cities and towns,
roads, railways and airports.

tract from page 69

Extract from page 78

Extract from page 98

istribution maps use different colours,
mbols, or shading to show the location and
stribution of natural or man-made features.
this map, symbols indicate the distribution
the world's largest cities.

Graduated colour maps use colours or
shading to show a topic or theme and a
measure of its intensity. Generally, the
highest values are shaded with the darkest
colours. In this map, colours are used to show
the number of fixed broadband subscriptions
per 100 people.

Isoline maps use thin lines to show the
distribution of a feature. An isoline passes
through places of the same value. Isolines
may show features such as temperature
(isotherm), air pressure (isobar) or height of
land (contour). The value of the line is usually
written on it. On either side of the line the
value will be higher or lower.

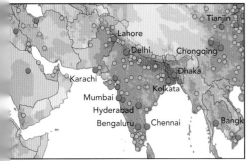

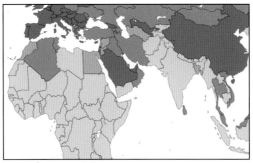

ract from page 131

Extract from page 148

Extract from page 36

Graphs and Statistics

Graphs are a visual way of presenting statistical information.
There are different kinds of graphs in this atlas.
Some graphs are designed to present a particular
kind of information.

Line graph
UK employment in agriculture, 2002 – 2022
from page 27

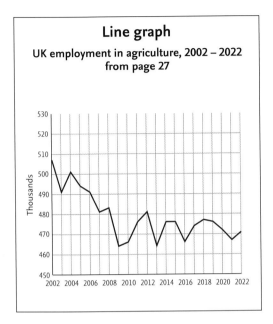

Bar graph
UK population by age group
from page 31

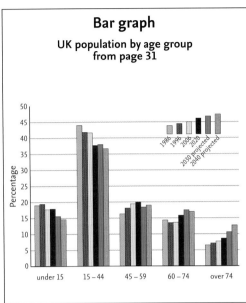

Climate graph
from page 36

A climate graph contains information about the average yearly
temperatures and average yearly rainfall for a particular
location. The graph below shows the average maximum and
minimum temperatures for Seville for one year.

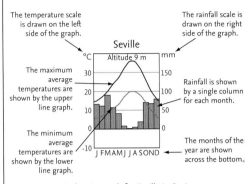

The temperature scale
is drawn on the left
side of the graph.

The maximum
average
temperatures are
shown by the upper
line graph.

The minimum
average
temperatures are
shown by the lower
line graph.

The rainfall scale is
drawn on the right
side of the graph.

Rainfall is shown
by a single column
for each month.

The months of the
year are shown
across the bottom.

A climate graph for Seville in Spain

Pie chart
Middle East oil production, 2022
from page 93

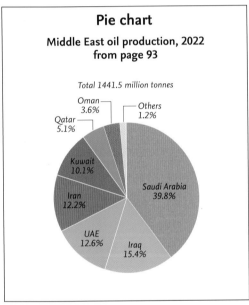

Stacked circles
extract from US largest urban
agglomerations, 2020, from page 64

Population pyramid
Singapore's population structure
from page 90

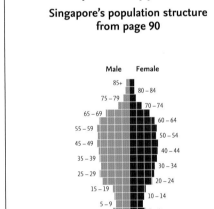

Each full square represents 1% of
the total population

Throughout this atlas there are sets of
statistics presented as tables showing values
or indicators related to the themes covered
on a map spread.

Climate statistics, population statistics,
country indicators, trade values etc are just
some of the tables found throughout the atlas.

Population by country, 2021

Country	Population (thousands)	Density (persons per sq km)
England	56 536	434
Wales	3105	150
Scotland	5480	70
Northern Ireland	1905	141
United Kingdom	**67 026**	**276**

Top 5 largest urban agglomerations, 2020

Urban agglomeration	Population
Tōkyō Japan	37 393 129
Delhi India	30 290 936
Shanghai China	27 058 479
Dhaka Bangladesh	21 005 860
Beijing China	20 462 610

Vancouver	Jan	Feb	Mar	Apr	May	Jun	Jul	Aug	Sep	Oct	Nov	Dec
Temperature - max. (°C)	5	7	10	14	18	21	23	23	18	14	9	6
Temperature - min. (°C)	0	1	3	4	8	11	12	12	9	7	4	2
Rainfall - (mm)	218	147	127	84	71	64	31	43	91	147	211	224

Flag	Country	Capital city	Population total 2022	Density persons per sq km 2022	Birth rate per 1000 population 2021
	St Vincent and the Grenadines	Kingstown	103 948	267	13
	Samoa	Apia	222 382	79	27
	San Marino	San Marino	33 660	552	6
	São Tomé and Príncipe	São Tomé	227 380	236	28

Latitude

Latitude is distance, measured in degrees, north and south of the Equator. Lines of latitude circle the globe in an east-west direction. The distance between lines of latitude is always the same. They are also known as parallels of latitude. Because the circumference of Earth gets smaller toward the poles, the lines of latitude are shorter nearer the poles.

Longitude

Longitude is distance, measured in degrees, east and west of the Greenwich Meridian (prime meridian). Lines of longitude join the poles in a north-south direction. Because the lines join the poles, they are always the same length, but are farthest apart at the Equator and closest together at the poles. These lines are also called meridians of longitude.

Finding places

When lines of latitude and longitude are drawn on a map, they form a grid, which looks like a pattern of squares. This pattern is used to find places on a map. Latitude is always stated before longitude (e.g. 42°N 78°W).

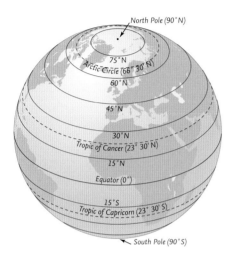

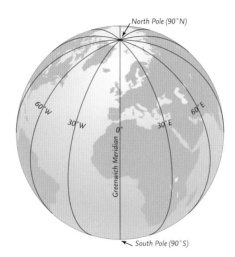

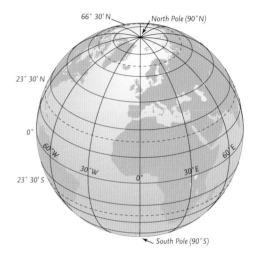

All lines of latitude have numbers between 0° and 90° and a direction, either north or south of the Equator. The Equator is at 0° latitude. The North Pole is at 90° north and the South Pole is at 90° south. The 'tilt' of Earth has given particular importance to some lines of latitude. They include:

- the Arctic Circle at 66° 30' north
- the Antarctic Circle at 66° 30' south
- the Tropic of Cancer at 23° 30' north
- the Tropic of Capricorn at 23° 30' south

The Equator also divides the Earth into two halves. The northern half, north of the Equator, is the **Northern Hemisphere**. The southern half, south of the Equator, is the **Southern Hemisphere**.

Longitude begins along the Greenwich Meridian (prime meridian), at 0°, in London, England. On the opposite side of Earth is the 180° meridian, which is the International Date Line. To the west of the prime meridian are Canada, the United States, and Brazil; to the east of the prime meridian are Germany, India and China. All lines of longitude have numbers between 0° and 180° and a direction, either east or west of the prime meridian.

The Greenwich Meridian and the International Date Line can also be used to divide the world into two halves. The half to the west of the Greenwich Meridian is the **Western Hemisphere**. The half to the east of the Greenwich Meridian is the **Eastern Hemisphere**.

By stating latitude and then longitude of a place, it becomes much easier to find. On the map (below) point A is easy to find as it is exactly latitude 58° north of the Equator and longitude 4° west of the Greenwich Meridian (58°N 4°W).

To be even more accurate in locating a place, each degree of latitude and longitude can also be divided into smaller units called **minutes** ('). There are 60 minutes in each degree. On the map (below) Halkirk is one half (or 30/60ths) of the way past latitude 58°N, and one-half (or 30/60ths) of the way past longitude 3°W. Its latitude is therefore 58 degrees 30 minutes north and its longitude is 3 degrees 30 minutes west. This can be shortened to 58°30'N 3°30'W. Latitude and longitude for all the places and features named on the maps are included in the index.

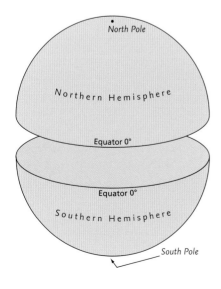

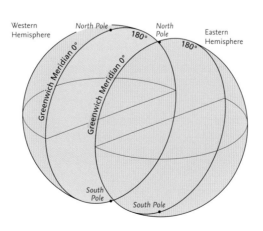

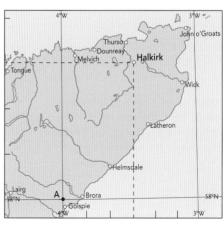

Scale

To draw a map of any part of the world, the area must be reduced, or 'scaled down,' to the size of a page in this atlas, a foldable road map, or a topographic map. The scale of the map indicates the amount by which an area has been reduced.

The scale of a map can also be used to determine the actual distance between two or more places or the actual size of an area on a map. The scale indicates the relationship between distances on the map and distances on the ground.

Ways of describing scale

Word scale: You can describe the scale in words e.g. one centimetre on the map represents 100 kilometres on the ground.

Line scale: A line with the scale marked on it is an easy way to compare distances on the map with distances on the ground.

Ratio scale: This method uses numbers to compare distances on the map with distances on the ground, e.g. 1:40 000 000. This means that one centimetre on the map represents 40 million centimetres on the ground. This number is too large to mean much to most people, so we convert centimetres to kilometres by dividing by 100 000 which equals 400 kilometres.

Scale and map information

The scale of a map affects how much information the map can show.

As the area shown on a map becomes larger, the amount of detail and accuracy of the map becomes less and less.

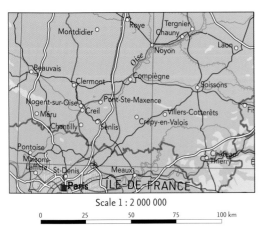

Scale 1 : 2 000 000

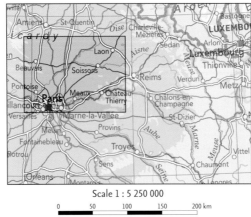

Scale 1 : 5 250 000

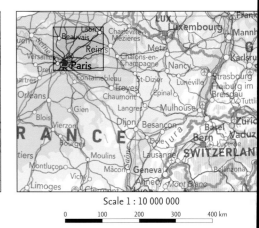

Scale 1 : 10 000 000

Measuring distance

The instructions below show you how to determine how far apart places are on a map, then using the line scale, to determine the actual distance on the ground.

Measuring straight-line distances:
1. place the edge of a sheet of paper on the two places on a map,
2. on the paper, place a mark at each of the two places,
3. place the paper on the line scale,
4. measure the distance on the ground using the scale.

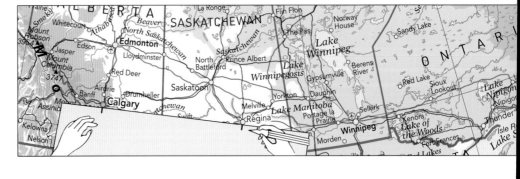

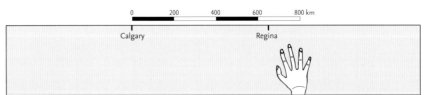

Measuring curved or road distances:
1. place a sheet of paper on the map and mark off the start point on the paper,
2. move the paper so that its edge follows the bends and curves on the map,
3. mark off the end point on the sheet of paper,
4. place the paper on the line scale and read the actual distance following a road or railroad.

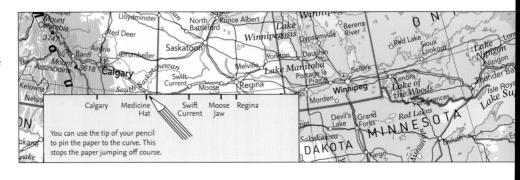

Representing a spherical Earth as a flat map has presented a number of challenges for map makers. A map projection is a way of showing the Earth's surface on a flat piece of paper. There are many types of map projections. None of them shows the Earth with perfect accuracy. All map projections distort either: area, direction, shape or distance.

Cylindrical projections

Cylindrical projections are constructed by projecting the surface of the globe or sphere (Earth) onto a cylinder that just touches the outside edges of that globe. Two examples of cylindrical projections are Mercator and Times.

Mercator Projection (see pages 102–103 for an example of this projection)

The Mercator cylindrical projection is useful for areas near the equator and to about 15 degrees north or south of the equator, where distortion of shape is minimal. The projection is useful for navigation, since directions are plotted as straight lines.

Eckert IV (see pages 116–117 for an example of this projection)

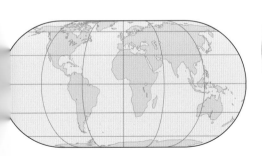

Eckert IV is an equal area projection. Equal area projections are useful for world thematic maps where it is important to show the correct relative sizes of continental areas. Eckert IV has a straight central meridian but all others are curved, which helps suggest the spherical nature of the Earth.

Conic projections

Conic projections are constructed by projecting the surface of a globe or sphere (Earth) onto a cone that just touches the outside edges of that globe. Examples of conic projections are Conic Equidistant and Albers Equal Area Conic.

Conic Equidistant Projection (see pages 54–55 for an example of this projection)

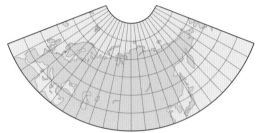

Conic projections are best suited for areas between 30° and 60° north and south of the equator when the east–west distance is greater than the north–south distance (such as Canada and Europe). The meridians are straight and spaced at equal intervals.

Lambert Conformal (see pages 60–61 for an example of this projection)

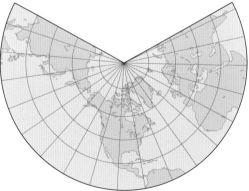

Lambert's Conformal Conic projection maintains an exact scale along one or two standard parallels (lines of latitude). Angles between locations on the surface of the Earth are correctly shown. Therefore, it is used for aeronautical charts and large scale topographic maps in many countries. It is also used to map areas with a greater east–west than north–south extent.

Azimuthal projections

Azimuthal projections are constructed by projecting the surface of the globe or sphere (Earth) onto a flat surface that touches the globe at one point only. Some examples of azimuthal projections are Lambert Azimuthal Equal Area and Polar Stereographic.

Polar Stereographic Projection (see page 112 for an example of this projection)

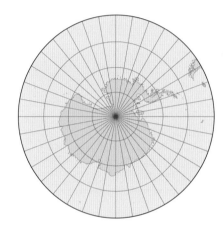

Azimuthal projections are useful for areas that have similar east–west and north–south dimensions such as Antarctica and Australia.

Lambert Azimuthal Equal Area (see pages 108–109 for an example of this projection)

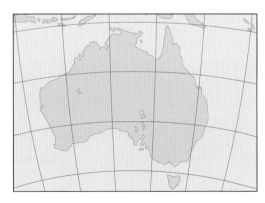

This projection is useful for areas that have similar east–west and north–south dimensions such as Australia.

Aerial photographs

Aerial photographs are images of the land usually taken from an aeroplane. There are two kinds of aerial photographs, vertical aerial photographs and oblique aerial photographs.

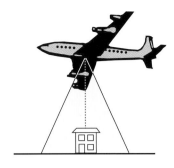 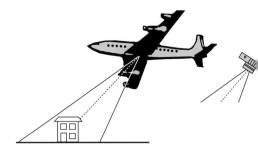

Camera position for a vertical aerial photograph

Camera position for an oblique aerial photograph

Vertical aerial photographs are taken from a digital camera fixed under an aeroplane. The camera points straight down at the ground. Objects are shown from above and may be difficult to identify.

Vertical aerial photographs show the same view of the land as a large scale map. Cartographers use vertical aerial photographs to help the make 1 : 50 000 topographic maps.

A vertical aerial photograph of Whitby, North Yorkshire

Oblique aerial photographs are taken from a camera that is positioned at an angle to the ground. Objects are more easily recognised in oblique aerial photographs. There are two kinds of oblique aerial photographs: high angle and low angle oblique aerial photographs. A high angle aerial photograph shows a large area of land. The horizon is usually visible. In low angle aerial photographs the horizon is not visible. The area of land shown is usually much smaller.

A low angle oblique aerial photograph of the same area of Whitby, North Yorkshire

GIS concepts

GIS stands for **Geographic Information System**. A GIS is a set of tools that can be used to collect, store, retrieve, modify and display spatial data. Spatial data can come from a variety of sources including existing maps, satellite imagery, aerial photographs or data collected from GPS (Global Positioning System) surveys.

GIS links this information to its real world location and can display this in a series of layers which you can then choose to turn off and on or to combine using a computer.

GIS can work with spatial information in three ways.
- A map made up of a collection of layers containing symbols. The illustration on the right shows a number of GIS layers.
- As geographic information called a database, stored on a computer.
- As a set of tools that create new datasets using existing stored geographic data.

Uses of GIS

GIS can be used in many ways to help solve problems, identify patterns, make decisions and plan development. A local government for example might want to build a new business area in a settlement. A GIS would be able to provide information on: the numbers of people who live in the area, transport routes, the average income of the population, and the kinds of goods people buy. A GIS could also be used to identify the number of houses built on a flood plain. This information could inform emergency planning or the relocation of the houses.

GIS terms

Spatial data: Spatial data describes the location and shape of features. You can see these features on a map or on a computer screen.

Attribute data: Attribute data describes or adds information about a feature, such as: population numbers, names of places, climate statistics. Attribute data may be stored in tables or as text within a GIS. Attribute data is made up of both raster and vector data.

Vector data: Represents map features as points, lines and area, e.g. mountain peaks, rivers, settlements.

Raster data: Represents map features as cells in a grid. Points, lines and areas can also be stored as cells of a grid. A satellite image is an example of raster data.

  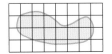

GIS layers

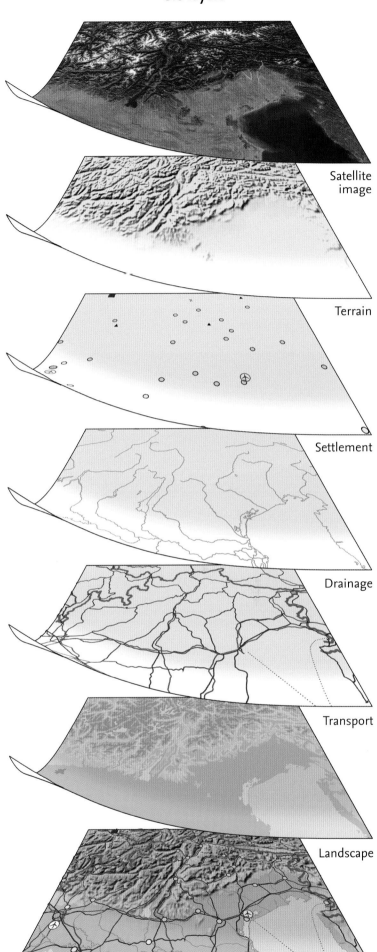

Satellite image

Terrain

Settlement

Drainage

Transport

Landscape

Atlas map

An example of different layers that can be stored and used in a GIS.

Satellite images

Satellite images

Images captured by a large number of Earth-observing satellites provide unique views of the Earth. The science of gathering and interpreting such images is known as remote sensing. Geographers use images taken from high above the Earth to determine patterns, trends and basic characteristics of the Earth's surface. Satellites are fitted with different kinds of scanners or sensors to gather information about the Earth. The most well known satellites are Landsat and SPOT.

Satellite sensors detect electromagnetic radiation – X-rays, ultraviolet light, visible colours and microwave signals. This data can be processed to provide information on soils, land use, geology, pollution and weather patterns.

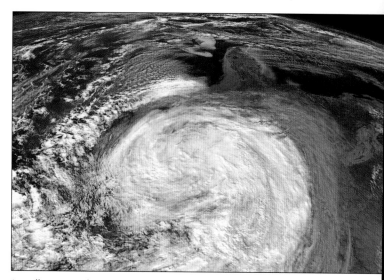

A satellite image showing Hurricane Sandy over northeastern US, in 2012. Satellite images help people to prepare for approaching natural disasters such as cyclones and floods. Weather scientists use satellite images to help them forecast the weather.

Natural disasters

Satellite images have many uses. One use is comparing two images to examine how conditions have changed over time. Satellite images taken before and after a natural event such as a flood or a violent storm can illustrate the extent of damage and help emergency planning.

In October 2012, the effects of Hurricane Sandy caused extensive damage and loss of life in the Caribbean and eastern US. The two satellite images above show part of the town of Mantoloking on the New Jersey coast before (left image) and after (right image) the storm struck.

Climate change

Satellite images taken over time can be used to identify the effects of climate change. For example, a series of satellite images can show how far ice sheets have retreated, or how the shorelines of lakes and seas have changed in a certain time period.

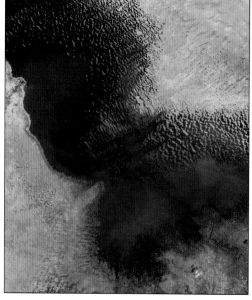
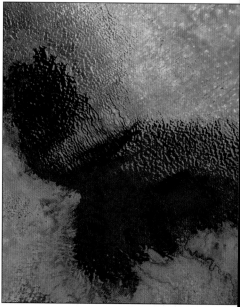

Satellite imagery showing the reduction in size of Lake Chad between 1973 (left) and 2007 (right).

A T L A N T I C
O C E A N

Shetland Islands

Orkney Islands

Outer Hebrides

S C O T L A N D

Aberdeen

Dundee

● Glasgow   ◻ Edinburgh

North Sea

NORTHERN IRELAND   ◻ Belfast

Newcastle upon Tyne

Sunderland

Middlesbrough

Irish Sea

Isle of Man
(British Crown Dependency)

Blackpool   Bradford   **Leeds**   Kingston upon Hull

Preston   Blackburn

Bolton   Huddersfield

IRELAND   ◻ Dublin   **Manchester**   Oldham   Rotherham

Liverpool   St Helens   Stockport   **Sheffield**

Birkenhead   E N G L A N D

Stoke-on-Trent

Derby   **Nottingham**

Telford   Norwich

Walsall   **Leicester**   Peterborough

Wolverhampton   Sutton Coldfield

Dudley   **Birmingham**   Cambridge

Cork   West Bromwich   Coventry   Ipswich

W A L E S   Northampton   Colchester

Milton Keynes

Gloucester   Luton   Southend-on-Sea

Oxford   Watford

Swansea   Newport   Swindon   Slough

◻ Cardiff   ● Bristol   Reading   ■ London

Woking   Crawley

Celtic Sea   Southampton   Portsmouth   Brighton

Exeter   Poole   Worthing   Eastbourne

● Bournemouth

Plymouth

English Channel

F R A N C E

Channel Islands (British Crown Dependency)

Legend

Water features
~ River
⬭ Lake / Reservoir

Administration
Boundaries
━━ International
── Internal

Settlement
Cities and towns in order of size
National capital
■ London
Administrative capital
◻ Belfast
Other city or town
● Glasgow
◉ Liverpool
○ Swansea

Scale 1 : 4 500 000
0   50   100 km

Conic Equidistant projection

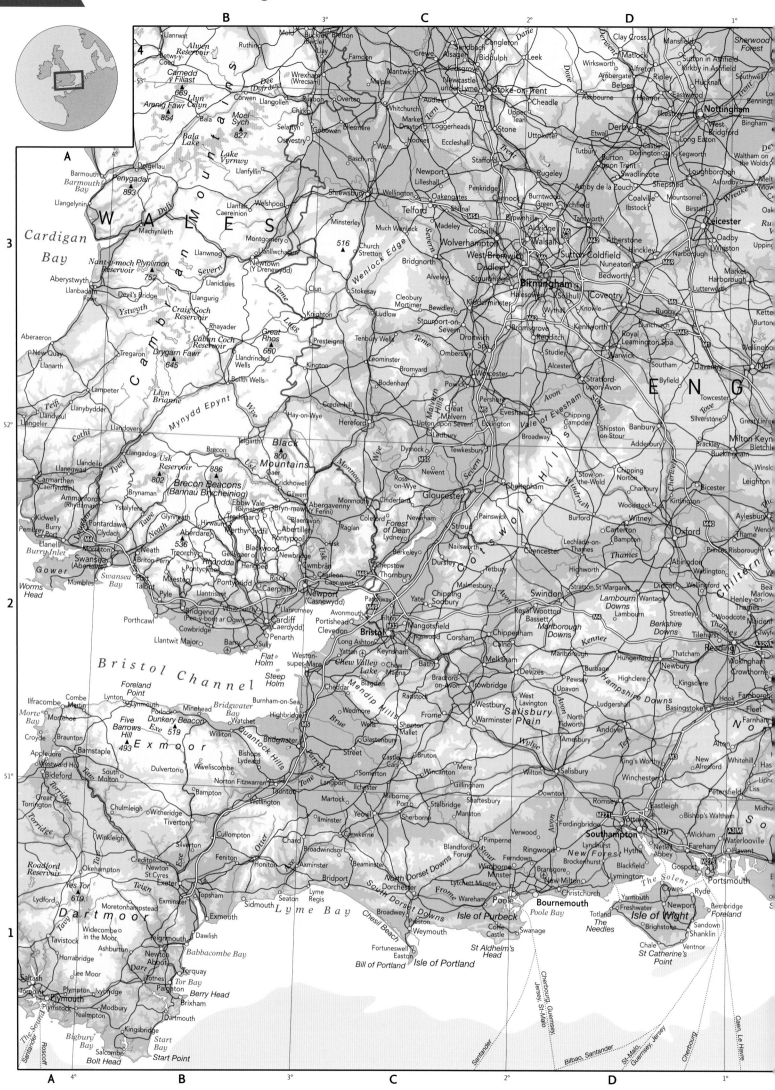

Relief and physical features

Relief
metres
1000
500
200
100
0 sea level
50 under sea level
100
200

1085 ▲ Mountain height
(in metres)

Water features

~~~~~~ River
~~~~~~ Canal
⬭ Lake / Reservoir

Communications

—————— Railway
—————— Motorway
—————— Road
··········· Car ferry
⊕ Main airport
✈ Regional airport

Administration
Boundaries

━━━━ International
———— Internal

Settlement
🏙 Urban area

Cities and towns in order of size

National capital   Other city or town

■ **London**   ◉ **Birmingham**
                       ◎ **Bristol**
                       ○ Oxford
                       ○ Colchester
                       ○ Wantage

Scale 1 : 1 200 000

0   10   20   30   40 km

Conic Equidistant projection

North Sea

English Channel

Strait of Dover

BELGIUM

WEST-VLAANDEREN

HAINAUT

FRANCE

HAUTS DE FRANCE

Greenwich (Prime) Meridian

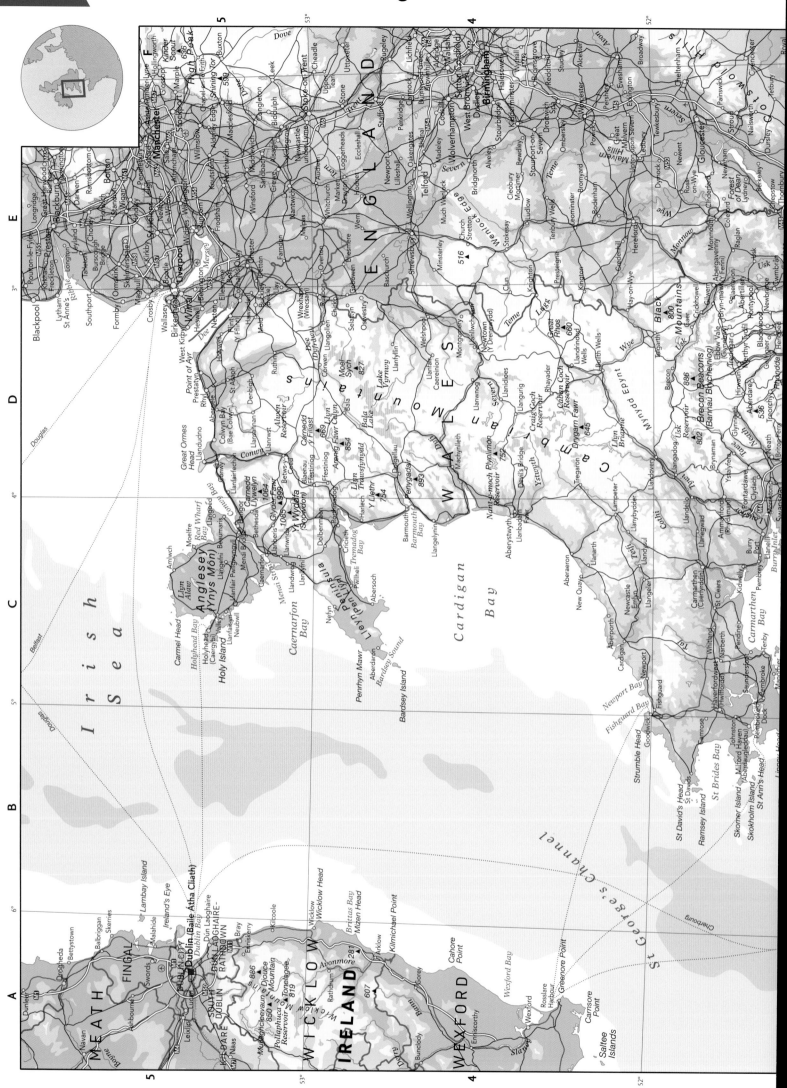

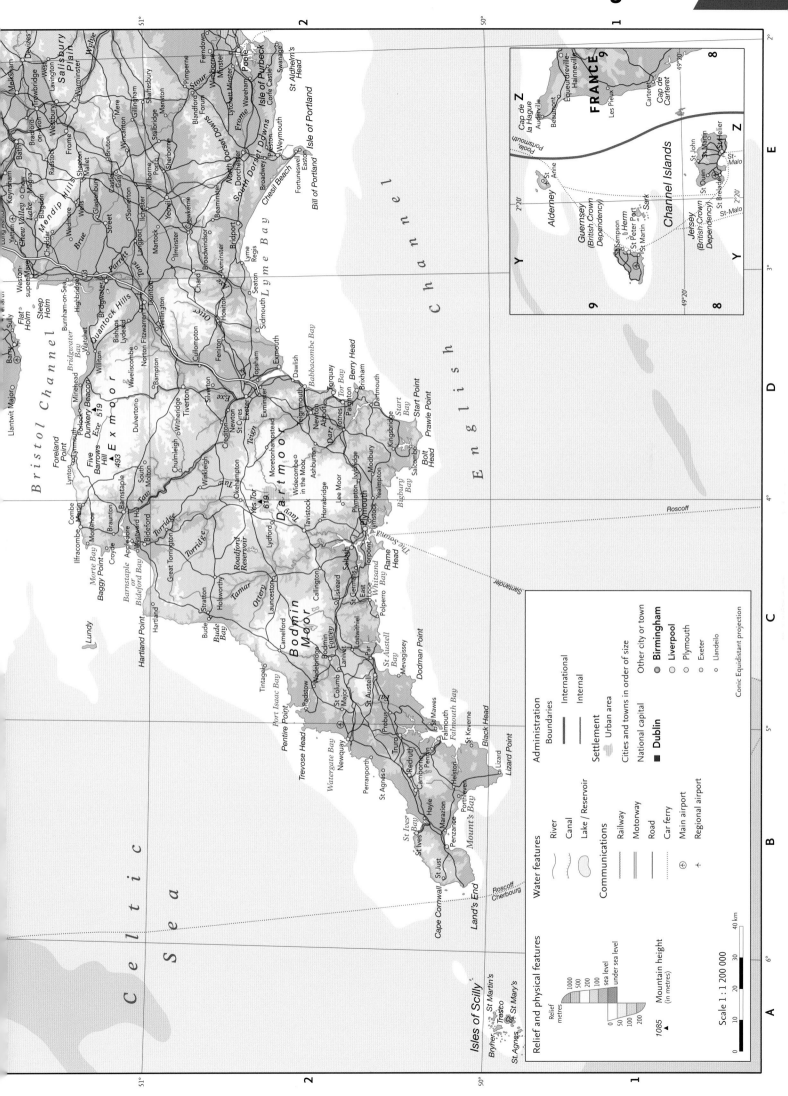

Isles of Scilly
St Martin's
Bryher
Tresco
St Agnes
St Mary's

Celtic Sea

Lundy

Cape Cornwall
Land's End
St Just
St Ives Bay
St Ives
Marazion
Penzance
Mount's Bay
Porthleven
Hayle
St Agnes
Camborne
Redruth
Perranporth
Newquay
Watergate Bay
St Columb Major
Truro
Probus
Helston
Lizard
Lizard Point
St Keverne
Black Head
Falmouth
Falmouth Bay
St Mawes
Mevagissey
St Austell
St Austell Bay
Par
Dodman Point
Lanvet
Fowey
Bodmin
Wadebridge
Padstow
Trevose Head
Pentire Point
Port Isaac Bay
Tintagel
Camelford
Bodmin Moor
Lostwithiel
Polperro
East Looe
St Germans
Callington
Liskeard
Stratton
Bude Bay
Bude
Holsworthy
Launceston
Whitsand Bay
Rame Head
Saltash
Plymouth
The Sound
Yealmpton
Plympton
Modbury
Bigbury Bay
Salcombe
Bolt Head
Kingsbridge
Start Point
Start Bay
Prawle Point
Dartmouth
Brixham
Berry Head
Paignton
Torquay
Tor Bay
Babbacombe Bay
Newton Abbot
Dawlish
Exmouth
Topsham
Exeter
Exminster
Sidmouth
Seaton
Lyme Regis
Lyme Bay
Bridport
West Bay
Chesil Beach
Bill of Portland
Isle of Portland
Easton
Weymouth
Fortuneswell
Broadway
Preston
Dorchester
Puddletown
Bere Regis
Wareham
Swanage
St Alban's Head
Corfe Castle
Isle of Purbeck
Poole
Wimborne Minster
Ferndown
Blandford Forum
Sturminster Newton
Stalbridge
Gillingham
Shaftesbury
Mere
Wincanton
Bruton
Castle Cary
Somerton
Langport
Ilminster
Chard
Axminster
Honiton
Cullompton
Tiverton
Wellington
Taunton
Bridgwater
Burnham-on-Sea
Highbridge
Weston-super-Mare

Bristol Channel
Foreland Point
Lynton
Lynmouth
Minehead
Watchet
Williton
Porlock
Combe Martin
Ilfracombe
Mortehoe
Morte Bay
Baggy Point
Braunton
Croyde
Barnstaple
Appledore
Bideford
Westward Ho!
Barnstaple or Bideford Bay
Hartland Point
Hartland
Great Torrington
Bideford
South Molton
Chulmleigh
Winkleigh
Okehampton
Crediton
Silverton
Bampton
Dulverton
Dunster
Bishops Lydeard
Norton Fitzwarren
Wiveliscombe
Dulverton

Exmoor
Dunkery Beacon 519
Five Barrows Hill 493

Dartmoor
Moretonhampstead
Widecombe in the Moor
Ashburton
Bovey Tracey
Lee Moor
Tavistock
Horrabridge
Lydford
Yes Tor 619
Roadford Reservoir

Torridge
Taw
Exe
Teign
Dart
Tamar
Ottery
Tavy
Lyd
Parrett
Tone
Brue
Culm
Otter

Quantock Hills
Steep Holm
Flat Holm
Sully
Barry
Llantwit Major
Llantwit Majoro

Mendip Hills
Cheddar
Wedmore
Glastonbury
Street
Wells
Shepton Mallet
Wedmore
Evercreech
Bruton
Frome
Radstock
Keynsham
Bath
Bradford-on-Avon
Trowbridge
Westbury
Warminster
Salisbury Plain
Wylye
Devizes
Melksham
Lavington
Calne
Marlborough

North Dorset Downs
South Dorset Downs
Yeovil
Sherborne
Yetminster
Beaminster
Broadwindsor
Crewkerne
Martock
Ilchester
Yeovilton

English Channel

St Austell
Probus
Feock
Carnon Downs

Channel Islands inset

FRANCE
Cap de la Hague
Equeurdreville-Hainneville
Beaumont
Les Pieux
Cherbourg
Audeville
Carteret
Cap de Carteret

Alderney
St Anne

Guernsey
(British Crown Dependency)
St Sampson
St Peter Port
Herm
Sark
St Martin

Jersey
(British Crown Dependency)
St Ouen
St John
St Martin
St Helier
St Brelade
St-Malo

Channel Islands

Poole
Portsmouth
Roscoff
St-Malo

Roscoff
Cherbourg
Santander
Roscoff

Legend

Relief and physical features

Relief
metres
1000
500
200
100
sea level
under sea level
50
100
200

1085 ▲ Mountain height (in metres)

Water features
River
Canal
Lake / Reservoir

Communications
Railway
Motorway
Road
Car ferry
⊕ Main airport
+ Regional airport

Administration
Boundaries
International
Internal

Settlement
Urban area

Cities and towns in order of size
National capital ■ **Dublin**
Other city or town
● **Birmingham**
◎ Liverpool
○ Plymouth
○ Exeter
○ Llandeilo

Scale 1:1 200 000

Conic Equidistant projection

0   10   20   30   40 km

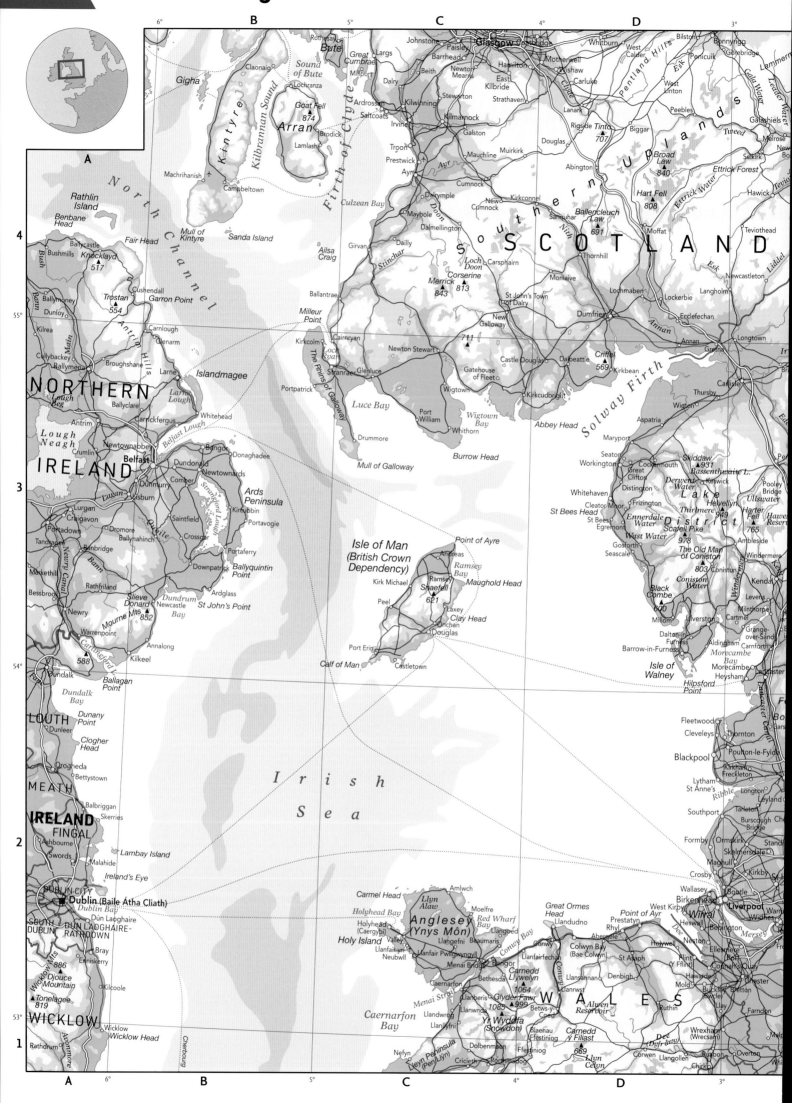

Northern England map. Place names include:

North Channel, Irish Sea, Firth of Clyde

SCOTLAND — Southern Uplands, Glasgow, Paisley, Johnstone, Barrhead, Hamilton, Motherwell, Wishaw, Carluke, Lanark, Biggar, Kilmarnock, Ayr, Prestwick, Troon, Irvine, Kilwinning, Ardrossan, Saltcoats, Largs, Millport, Dalry, Beith, Stewarton, Galston, Mauchline, Cumnock, New Cumnock, Kirkconnel, Sanquhar, Thornhill, Moffat, Dumfries, Lockerbie, Langholm, Newcastleton, Annan, Gretna, Longtown, Carlisle, Peebles, Galashiels, Melrose, Selkirk, Hawick, Teviothead, Ettrick Forest, Pentland Hills, West Linton, Penicuik, Gorebridge, Bonnyrigg, Whitburn, West Calder, Bilston, Broad Law 840, Hart Fell 808, Ballencleuch Law 691, Tinto 707, Merrick 843, Corserine 813, Loch Doon, Carsphairn, Maybole, Dalmellington, Dailly, Girvan, Ballantrae, Stranraer, Kirkcolm, Cairnryan, Loch Ryan, Portpatrick, The Rhins of Galloway, Newton Stewart, Glenluce, Wigtown, Whithorn, Port William, Drummore, Mull of Galloway, Burrow Head, Luce Bay, Wigtown Bay, New Galloway, St John's Town of Dalry, Gatehouse of Fleet, Castle Douglas, Dalbeattie, Kirkcudbright, Abbey Head, Criffel 569, Kirkbean, Solway Firth, Aspatria, Maryport, Workington, Seaton, Cockermouth, Keswick, Skiddaw 931, Bassenthwaite L., Wigton, Thursby, Milleur Point, Ailsa Craig, Culzean Bay, Stinchar, Momaive, Lochmaben, Dalrymple, Doon, Stewarton, East Kilbride, Newton Mearns, Strathaven, Douglas, Abington, Rigside, Broughshane

Lake District — Whitehaven, St Bees Head, St Bees, Egremont, Cleator Moor, Frizington, Distington, Great Clifton, Gosforth, Seascale, Wast Water, Ennerdale Water, Scafell Pike 978, Derwent Water, Thirlmere, Helvellyn 949, Ullswater, Pooley Bridge, Harter Fell 765, Hawes Water, Ambleside, Windermere, The Old Man of Coniston 803, Coniston, Coniston Water, Kendal, Black Combe 600, Millom, Ulverston, Dalton-in-Furness, Barrow-in-Furness, Isle of Walney, Morecambe Bay, Heysham, Hilpsford Point, Cartmel, Levens, Milnthorpe, Grange-over-Sands, Aldingham, Carnforth, Lancaster, Morecambe, Fleetwood, Cleveleys, Thornton, Poulton-le-Fylde, Blackpool, Kirkham, Freckleton, Lytham, St Anne's, Ribble, Longton, Leyland, Southport, Formby, Tarleton, Burscough, Ormskirk, Skelmersdale, Crosby, Bootle, Liverpool, Wallasey, Birkenhead, West Kirby, Wirral, Bebington, Neston, Heswall, Ellesmere Port, Chester

NORTHERN IRELAND — Rathlin Island, Benbane Head, Ballycastle, Bushmills, Knocklayd 517, Trostan 554, Cushendall, Garron Point, Ballymoney, Dunloy, Kilrea, Ballymena, Broughshane, Carnlough, Glenarm, Larne, Islandmagee, Larne Lough, Whitehead, Carrickfergus, Antrim, Crumlin, Lough Neagh, Lough Beg, Newtownabbey, Belfast, Belfast Lough, Bangor, Donaghadee, Newtownards, Dundonald, Comber, Dunmurry, Lisburn, Lurgan, Craigavon, Portadown, Tandragee, Banbridge, Dromore, Ballynahinch, Saintfield, Killyleagh, Crossgar, Downpatrick, Ards Peninsula, Kircubbin, Portavogie, Portaferry, Ballyquintin Point, Strangford Lough, St John's Point, Ballyquintin Point, Ardglass, Newtownhamilton, Markethill, Bessbrook, Newry, Rathfriland, Slieve Donard 852, Mourne Mts, Newcastle, Dundrum Bay, Annalong, Kilkeel, Warrenpoint, Carlingford Lough 588, Ballagan Point, Main, Bann, Lagan, Quoile, Newry Canal

IRELAND — Dublin (Baile Átha Cliath), Dún Laoghaire, Dún Laoghaire-Rathdown, South Dublin, Fingal, Ashbourne, Swords, Malahide, Lambay Island, Ireland's Eye, Bray, Enniskerry, Kilcoole, Wicklow, Wicklow Head, Rathdrum, Wicklow Mts, Djouce Mountain 886, Tonelagee 819, Dundalk, Dundalk Bay, Dunany Point, Clogher Head, Drogheda, Bettystown, Balbriggan, Skerries, LOUTH, MEATH, WICKLOW, Dunleer, Carlingford, Greenore

WALES — Anglesey (Ynys Môn), Holyhead (Caergybi), Holy Island, Holyhead Bay, Carmel Head, Amlwch, Moelfre, Red Wharf Bay, Llanfairfechan, Llangoed, Beaumaris, Menai Bridge, Bangor, Bethesda, Caernarfon, Carnedd Llywelyn, Llanberis, Glyder Fawr 999, Yr Wyddfa (Snowdon) 1085, Llanllyfni, Llandwrog, Caernarfon Bay, Nefyn, Llŷn Peninsula (Pen Llŷn), Criccieth, Porthmadog, Dolbenmaen, Blaenau Ffestiniog, Carnedd y Filiast 669, Betws-y-Coed, Afon Llŷn, Great Ormes Head, Llandudno, Colwyn Bay (Bae Colwyn), Rhos-on-Sea, Abergele, Rhyl, Prestatyn, Point of Ayr, Flint, Holywell, Mold, Buckley, Denbigh, St Asaph, Ruthin, Llanrwst, Llansannan, Corwen, Llangollen, Wrexham (Wrecsam), Ruabon, Chirk, Overton, Llanfair Pwllgwyngyll, Menai Strait, Carnedd 1064

Isle of Man (British Crown Dependency) — Point of Ayre, Andreas, Ramsey Bay, Ramsey, Maughold Head, Kirk Michael, Snaefell 621, Peel, Laxey, Onchan, Douglas, Clay Head, Port Erin, Calf of Man, Castletown

Relief and physical features

Relief
metres

1000
500
200
100
0 — sea level
50 — under sea level
100
200

▲ 1085 Mountain height
(in metres)

Water features

River
Canal
Lake / Reservoir

Communications

Railway
Motorway
Motorway under construction
Road
Car ferry
⊕ Main airport
✈ Regional airport

Administration

Boundaries
International
Internal

Settlement

Urban area

Cities and towns in order of size

National capital | Other city or town
■ Dublin | ● Manchester
 | ○ Liverpool
 | ○ Bradford
 | ○ Carlisle
 | ○ Keswick

Scale 1 : 1 200 000

0   10   20   30   40 km

Conic Equidistant projection

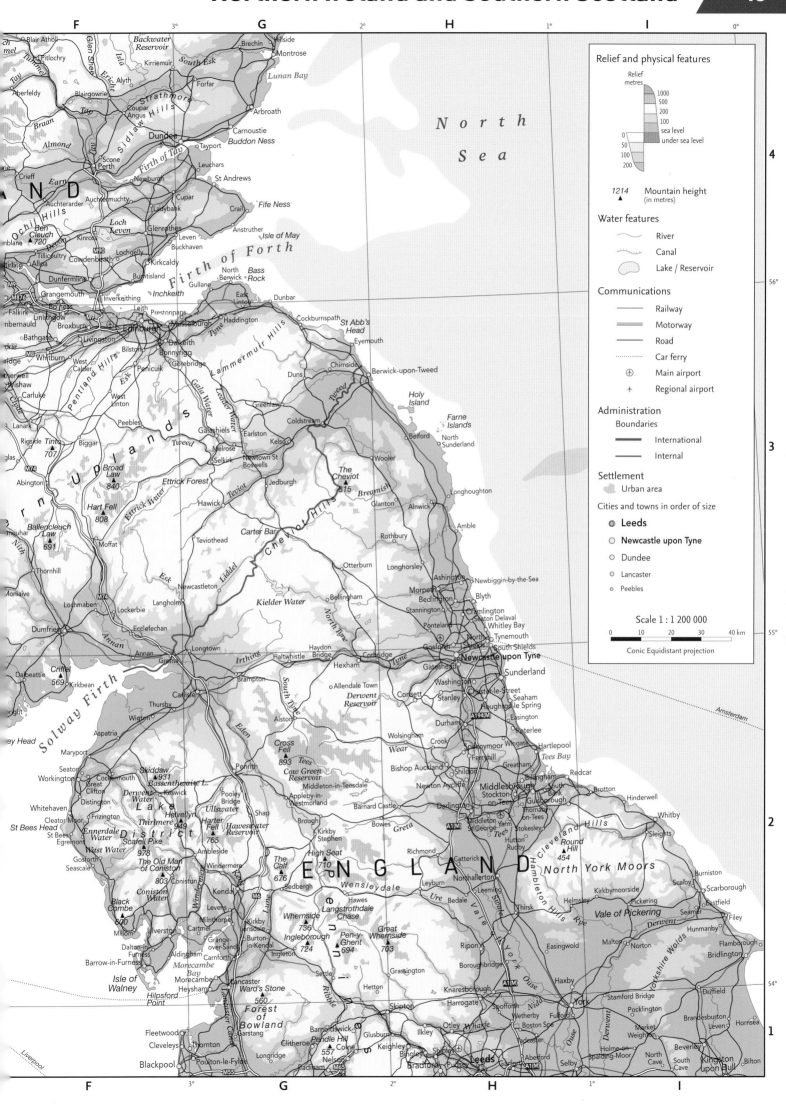

Relief and physical features

Relief metres

1000
500
200
100
sea level
under sea level

0
50
100
200

1214 Mountain height
▲ (in metres)

Water features

River

Canal

Lake / Reservoir

Communications

Railway

Motorway

Road

Car ferry

⊕ Main airport

✈ Regional airport

Administration

Boundaries

International

Internal

Settlement

Urban area

Cities and towns in order of size

● **Leeds**

◉ **Newcastle upon Tyne**

◎ Dundee

◌ Lancaster

∘ Peebles

Scale 1 : 1 200 000

0 10 20 30 40 km

Conic Equidistant projection

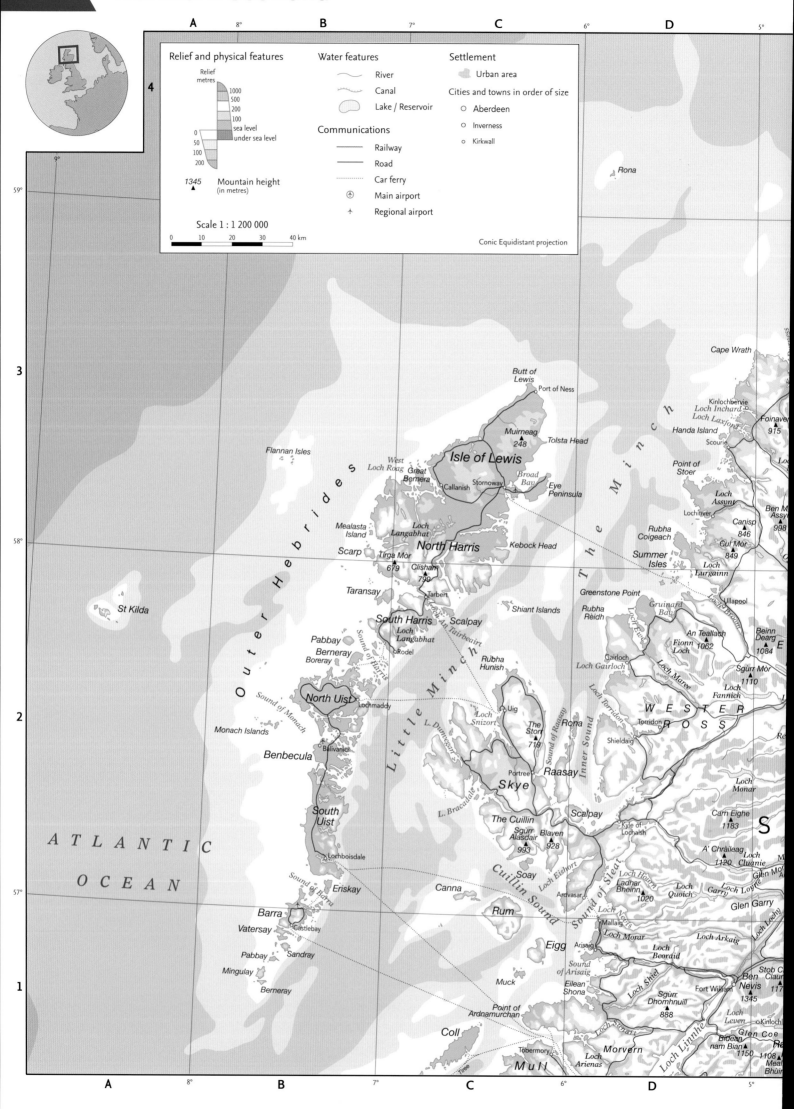

Relief and physical features

Relief metres

1000
500
200
100
0   sea level
50   under sea level
100
200

▲ 1345   Mountain height (in metres)

Scale 1 : 1 200 000

0   10   20   30   40 km

Water features

River
Canal
Lake / Reservoir

Communications

Railway
Road
Car ferry
⊕ Main airport
✈ Regional airport

Settlement

Urban area

Cities and towns in order of size

○ Aberdeen
○ Inverness
○ Kirkwall

Conic Equidistant projection

Orkney Islands

Mull Head
Papa Westray
North Ronaldsay
Noup Head
Westray
The North Sound
North Ronaldsay Firth
Eday
Sanday
Rousay
Loth
Sanday Sound
Brough Head
Birsay
Egilsay
Stronsay
Westray Firth
Stronsay Firth
Shapinsay
Loch of Harray
Finstown
Wide Firth
Auskerry
Loch of Stenness
Kirkwall
Stromness
Mainland
Gritley
Lerwick
Ward Hill
▲ 479
Scapa Flow
Copinsay
Hoy
Flotta
Burray
South Walls
St Margaret's Hope
South Ronaldsay
Burwick
Pentland Firth
Island of Stroma
Brough Ness
Pentland Skerries
Dunnet Head
Thurso Bay
John o'Groats
Duncansby Head
Strathy Point
Dounreay
Thurso
Dunnet Bay
Loch Heilen
Melvich
Halkirk
Loch Watten
Sinclair's Bay
Loch Tongue
Naver
Halladale
Thurso
Wick
Tongue
Loch Loyal
CAITHNESS
Wick
Klibreck
961
Loch Rimsdale
Latheron
SUTHERLAND
Helmsdale
Brora
Helmsdale
Lairg
Brora
Golspie
Bonar Bridge
Dornoch
Loch Glass
Dornoch Firth
Tarbat Ness
Invergordon
Tain
Nigg Bay
Cromarty
Balintore
Moray Firth
Black Isle
Fortrose
Cromarty Firth
Beauly Firth
Conon Bridge
Moray Firth
Inverness
Great Glen
Ness

Shetland Islands

Herma Ness
Unst
Baltasound
Point of Fethaland
Yell Sound
Yell
Fetlar
Isbister
Ronas Hill
▲ 450
Esha Ness
Out Skerries
St Magnus Bay
Hillswick
Toft
Muckle Roe
Voe
Whalsay
Papa Stour
Melby
Shetland Islands
Walls
Bressay
Foula
Scalloway
Lerwick
Isle of Noss
Burra
Sumburgh
Mousa
Sumburgh Head
Fair Isle

North Sea

Lossiemouth
Portknockie
Troup Head
Fraserburgh
Burghead
Buckie
Portsoy
Macduff
Loch of Strathbeg
Kinloss
Cullen
Banff
Crimond
Elgin
Fochabers
Rattray Head
Nairn
Forres
Isla
Aberchirder
Deveron
New Pitsligo
North Ugie
Rothes
Knock Hill
▲ 430
Turriff
Mintlaw
Peterhead
Lossie
Keith
Boddam
Findhorn
Dufftown
(Charlestown of Aberlour)
Huntly
Cruden Bay
Spey
STRATHBOGIE
Urie
Ellon
Grantown-on-Spey
Deveron
Bogie
Oldmeldrum
Strathspey
Hills of Cromdale
Insch
Inverurie
SCOTLAND
Càrn Mòr
804
Kemnay
Kintore
Don
Geal Charn
821
Dyce
Westhill
Aberdeen
Monadhliath Mountains
Cairn Gorm
▲ 1245
Avon
Càrn Dearg
945
Cairngorm Mts
Aboyne
Kingussie
Ben Macdui ▲ 1309
Dee
Portlethen
Newtonmore
Cairn Toul ▲ 1291
Ballater
Newtonhill
Braemar
Mount Keen
939
Stonehaven
Grampian Mountains
Lochnagar
1155
Beinn Dearg
1008
Carn nan Gabhar
Mayar
928
Inverbervie
Forest of Atholl 1121
Water of Saughs
Laurencekirk
Loch Ericht
Glen Shee
North Esk
Hillside
Loch Garry
Blair Atholl
Backwater Reservoir
Brechin
Loch Errochty
Pitlochry
Isla
South Esk
Montrose
Loch Tummel
Tummel
Kirriemuir
Alyth
Schiehallion 1083
Forfar
Lunan Bay
Loch Rannoch
Aberfeldy
Tay
Strathmore
Lyon
Blairgowrie
Arbroath

Relief and physical features

Relief
metres
1000
500
200
100
sea level
0
50 under sea level
100
200

▲ 1041 Mountain height (in metres)

Water features

~~ River

~~ Canal

Lake / Reservoir

Marsh

Communications

—— Railway

==== Motorway

—— Road

⊕ Main airport

Administration

Boundaries

—— International

—— Internal

Settlement

▣ Urban area

Cities and towns in order of size

National capital   Other city or town

■ Dublin   ○ Belfast

                          ○ Cork

                          ○ Killarney

Scale 1 : 2 000 000

0   25   50   75 km

Conic Equidistant projection

ATLANTIC OCEAN

UNITED KINGDOM

SCOTLAND

Colonsay
Scalasaig
Islay
Port Askaig
Portnahaven
Port Ellen
Mull of Oa
Machrihanish
Campbeltown
Kintyre
Mull of Kintyre
Gigha
Goat Fel 874
Brodi

NORTHERN IRELAND

Malin Head
Inishtrahull
Glengad Head
Giant's Causeway
Fair Head
Rathlin Island
Bloody Foreland
Tory Island
Inishowen
Slieve Snaght 615
Portrush
Bushmills
Ballycastle
Coleraine
Ballymoney
Trostan 554
Garron Point
Aran Island
Gweebarra Bay
Derryveagh Mts
Errigal 752
Londonderry (Derry)
Limavady
Antrim Hills
Carnlough
Larne
Letterkenny
Lifford
Buncrana
Dungiven
Magilligan
Maghera
Ballymena
Islandmagee
Carrickfergus

DONEGAL

Rossan Point
Killybegs
Donegal
Blue Stack Mts 676
Finn
Derg
Strabane
Sperrin Mts 683
Newtownstewart
Omagh
Cookstown
Magherafelt
Lough Neagh
Antrim
Newtownabbey
BELFAST
Belfast Lough
Bangor
Newtownards
Ards Peninsula
Dundrum
Strangford

Donegal Bay
Ballyshannon
Bundoran
Lough Derg
Lough Melvin
Lough Erne
Lower Lough Erne
Enniskillen
Dungannon
Portadown
Lurgan
Armagh
Banbridge
Lisburn
Portaferry
Ardglass
St John's Poin
Downpatrick

Inishmurray
Sligo Bay
Sligo
Manorhamilton
Upper Lough Erne
Lisnaskea
Monaghan
Clones
Newry
Mourne Mts
Slieve Donard 852
Newcastle
Kilkeel
Carlingford L.

Erris Head
Belmullet
The Mullet
Downpatrick Head
Killala Bay
Carrowmore Lake
Blacksod Bay
Achill Island
Slieve Car 772
Nephin 806
Lough Conn
Ballina
Foxford
Knocklalongey 542
SLIGO
LEITRIM
L. Allen
Boyle
Lough Key
Carrick-on-Shannon
Lough Gowna
CAVAN
Cavan
Bailieborough
Kingscourt
Carrickmacross
MONAGHAN
Castleblayney
Annalee
Lough Oughter

Tubbercurry
Charlestown
Moy
Lough Gara
LONGFORD
Longford
Lough Sheelin
MEATH
Kells
Navan
Athboy
Trim
Dundalk Bay
Dunany Point
Dunleer
Clogher Head
Drogheda
Balbriggan
Skerries

Clew Bay
Clare Island
Inishturk
Inishbofin
MAYO
Castlebar
Westport
Lough Carra
Lough Mask
Partry Mts
Claremorris
Ballyhaunis
Castlerea
ROSCOMMON
Roscommon
Lanesborough
Lough Ree
WESTMEATH
Mullingar
Kinnegad
Inny
Ashbourne
Swords
FINGAL
Malahide
Lambay Island
Ireland's Eye
DUBLIN
Dublin (Baile Átha Cliath)
Dublin Bay

Slyne Head
Connemara
Lough Corrib
GALWAY
Tuam
Clare
Athenry
Oranmore
GALWAY
Iar Connaught
Galway
Galway Bay
Inishmore
Aran Islands
Inishmaan
Inisheer
Ballinasloe
Suck
Athlone
Shannon
Clara
Tullamore
OFFALY
Banagher
Birr
Portumna
LAOIS
Leixlip
KILDARE
Naas
Newbridge
Kildare
Kilcullen
SOUTH DUBLIN
DÚN LAOGHAIRE-RATHDOWN
Dún Laoghaire
Bray
Liffey
Pollaphuca Reservoir
WICKLOW

Hag's Head
Liscannor Bay
Ennistymon
Donegal Point
CLARE
Slievecallan 391
Ennis
Gort
Loughrea
Scalp 327
Lough Derg
Roscrea
Devil's Bit Mountain 481
Nenagh
Templemore
Thurles
TIPPERARY
Kilcormac
Mountmellick
Mountrath
Abbeyleix
337
Carlow
CARLOW
Castlecomer
Muine Bheag
Bunclody
607
Arklow
Kilmichael Point
Wicklow
Wicklow Head
Rathdrum
Mizen Head
Cahore Point

Loop Head
Kilkee
Kilrush
Mouth of the Shannon
Ballybunnion
Rathkeale
Croom
LIMERICK
Newcastle West
Kilmallock
Tipperary
Cashel
Kilkenny
KILKENNY
Callan
Thomastown
New Ross
Enniscorthy
WEXFORD
Wexford Bay
Wexford
Rosslare Harbour

Kerry Head
Tralee Bay
Brandon Head
Brandon Mountain 952
Sybil Point
Great Blasket I.
Dingle
Castlegregory
KERRY
Killorglin
Carrauntoohil 1041
Macgillycuddy's Reeks 774
840
Knockaboy 707
Kenmare
Caha Mts
Bantry
Clonakilty
Bantry Bay
Dursey Head
Bolus Head
Bray Head
Cahersiveen
Dingle Bay
L. Leane
Killarney
Boggeragh Mts
Mallow
Fermoy
Blackwater
Bride
Lismore
Dungarvan
WATERFORD
Seefin 728
Comeragh Mts
Clonmel
Carrick-on-Suir
Slievenamon
719
Fethard
Knockmealdown Mts
Tar
Waterford
Tramore
Dunmore East
Hook Head
Saltee Islands

Mullaghareirk Mts
Abbeyfeale
Rathluirc
517
Mitchelstown
Buttevant
Castleisland
Feale
Listowel
Newcastle West
Galtee Mts
919
Limerick
Castleconnell
Brosna
Tullamore

CORK
CORK CITY
Cork (Corcaigh)
Cobh
Midleton
Youghal
Knockadoon Head
Blarney
Macroom
Lee
Bandon
Kinsale
Old Head of Kinsale
Seven Heads
Galley Head
Clear Island
Cape Clear
Skibbereen

IRELAND

Irish Sea

St George's Channel

1. Snow-covered mountains in Scotland.

2. The dark green areas are coniferous forests.

3. Mountains covered with heather and poor grass.

4. Large parts of Ireland are covered in rich grassland, shown in green.

5. Much of the land in the UK is used for agriculture. This is why so much of the image shows greens and browns.

6. Areas of grey represent built-up areas.

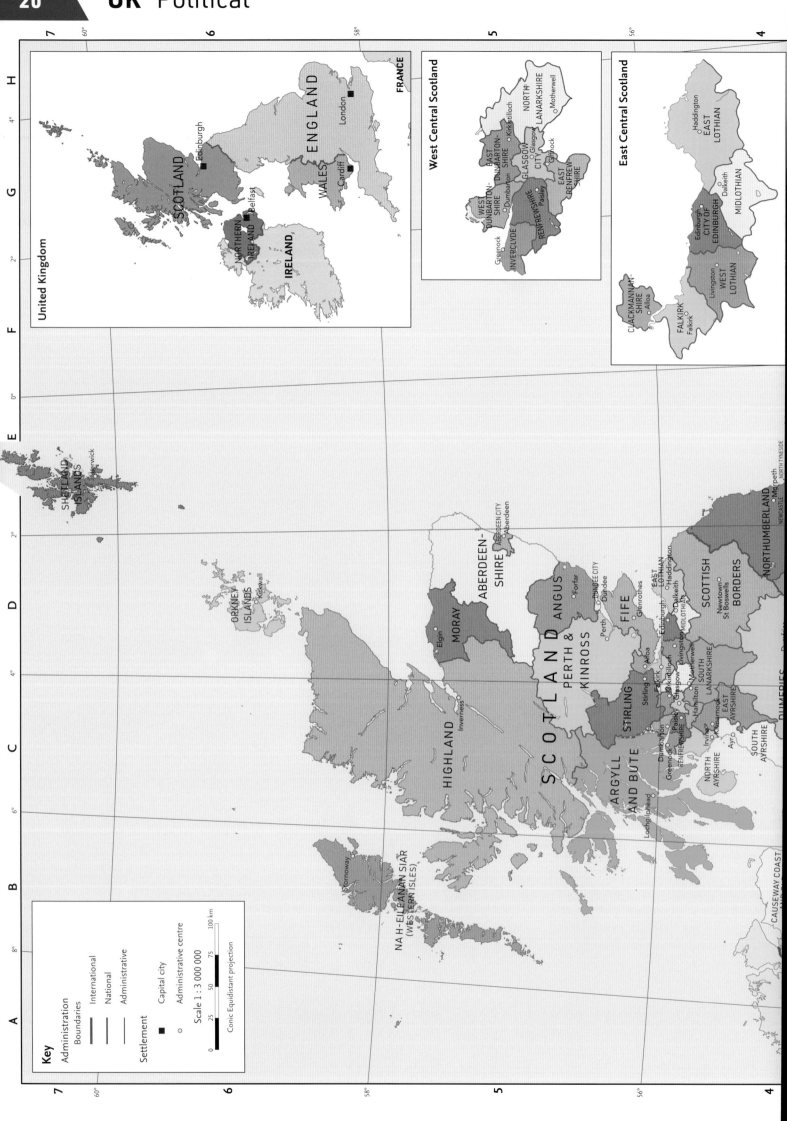

United Kingdom

SCOTLAND

Edinburgh

ENGLAND

London

WALES

Cardiff

NORTHERN IRELAND

Belfast

IRELAND

FRANCE

West Central Scotland

NORTH LANARKSHIRE

Kirkintilloch

Motherwell

WEST DUNBARTON-SHIRE

EAST DUNBARTON-SHIRE

Dumbarton

GLASGOW CITY

Glasgow

Greenock

Gourock

EAST RENFREW-SHIRE

RENFREWSHIRE

Paisley

Greenock

INVERCLYDE

East Central Scotland

EAST LOTHIAN

Haddington

MIDLOTHIAN

Dalkeith

CITY OF EDINBURGH

Edinburgh

CLACKMANNAN-SHIRE

Alloa

FALKIRK

Falkirk

WEST LOTHIAN

Livingston

Key

Administration

Boundaries

International

National

Administrative

Settlement

■ Capital city

○ Administrative centre

Scale 1 : 3 000 000

0   25   50   75   100 km

Conic Equidistant projection

SHETLAND ISLANDS

Lerwick

ORKNEY ISLANDS

Kirkwall

NA H-EILEANAN SIAR (WESTERN ISLES)

Stornoway

HIGHLAND

Inverness

MORAY

Elgin

ABERDEEN-SHIRE

ABERDEEN CITY

Aberdeen

S C O T L A N D

ANGUS

Forfar

PERTH & KINROSS

Perth

DUNDEE CITY

Dundee

FIFE

Glenrothes

STIRLING

Stirling

ARGYLL AND BUTE

Lochgilphead

Dumbarton

Greenock

RENFREW-SHIRE

Paisley

NORTH AYRSHIRE

Irvine

Kilmarnock

EAST AYRSHIRE

Ayr

SOUTH AYRSHIRE

Alloa

Falkirk

Kirkintilloch

Glasgow

Hamilton

Motherwell

SOUTH LANARKSHIRE

Livingston

Edinburgh

MIDLOTHIAN

Dalkeith

Haddington

EAST LOTHIAN

SCOTTISH BORDERS

Newtown

St Boswells

NORTHUMBERLAND

Morpeth

NEWCASTLE

NORTH TYNESIDE

DUMFRIES

CAUSEWAY COAST

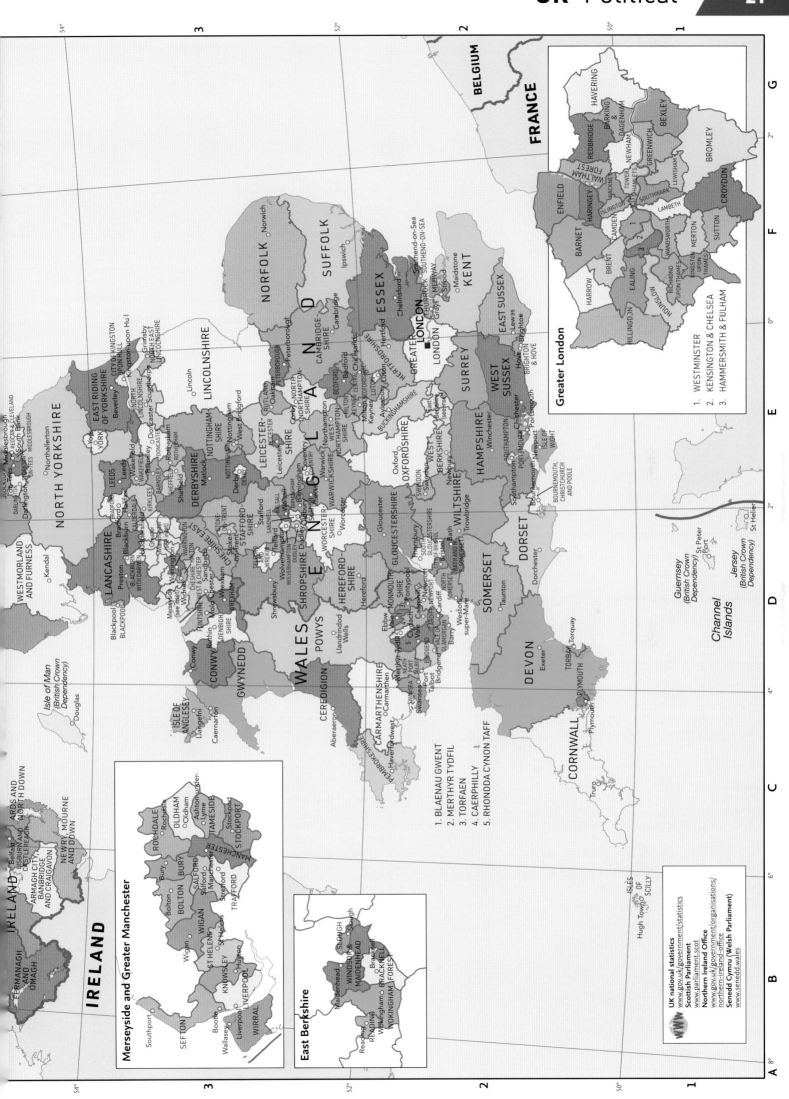

FRANCE

BELGIUM

Greater London

HAVERING
BARKING & DAGENHAM
NEWHAM
BEXLEY
REDBRIDGE
WALTHAM FOREST
GREENWICH
ENFIELD
TOWER HAMLETS
HACKNEY
HARINGEY
BROMLEY
LEWISHAM
SOUTHWARK
ISLINGTON
CAMDEN
LAMBETH
CROYDON
BARNET
1
2
WANDSWORTH
3
SUTTON
HARROW
BRENT
EALING
KINGSTON UPON THAMES
MERTON
RICHMOND UPON THAMES
HILLINGDON
HOUNSLOW

1. WESTMINSTER
2. KENSINGTON & CHELSEA
3. HAMMERSMITH & FULHAM

NORFOLK
Norwich

SUFFOLK
Ipswich

E N G L A N D

LINCOLNSHIRE
Lincoln

EAST RIDING OF YORKSHIRE
CITY OF KINGSTON UPON HULL
Kingston upon Hull
Beverley
Grimsby
NORTH LINCOLNSHIRE
NORTH EAST LINCOLNSHIRE
Scunthorpe

NORTH YORKSHIRE
York
Northallerton

REDCAR & CLEVELAND
Middlesbrough
STOCKTON-ON-TEES
Darlington
HARTLEPOOL
Stockton-on-Tees
South Bank
DARLINGTON

WESTMORLAND AND FURNESS
Kendal

LANCASHIRE
Blackpool
BLACKPOOL
Preston
Blackburn
BLACKBURN WITH DARWEN

LEEDS
BRADFORD
Bradford
Halifax
CALDERDALE
Wakefield
WAKEFIELD
KIRKLEES
Huddersfield
SHEFFIELD
Sheffield
Rotherham
ROTHERHAM
Barnsley
BARNSLEY
Doncaster
DONCASTER

NOTTINGHAMSHIRE
Matlock
DERBYSHIRE
Nottingham
NOTTINGHAM
Derby
DERBY

LEICESTERSHIRE
Leicester
LEICESTER
RUTLAND
Oakham

NORTHAMPTONSHIRE
NORTH NORTHAMPTONSHIRE
Northampton
WEST NORTHAMPTONSHIRE

CAMBRIDGESHIRE
Peterborough
PETERBOROUGH
Cambridge

BEDFORD
Bedford
CENTRAL BEDFORDSHIRE
MILTON KEYNES
Milton Keynes
LUTON
Luton

ESSEX
Chelmsford
Southend-on-Sea
SOUTHEND-ON-SEA
THURROCK
Grays
Strood
MEDWAY
Maidstone

GREATER LONDON
LONDON
LONDON
HERTFORDSHIRE
Hertford
St Albans
Hemel Hempstead
Aylesbury
BUCKINGHAMSHIRE
Oxford
OXFORDSHIRE

KENT
EAST SUSSEX
Lewes
Brighton
BRIGHTON & HOVE
Hove
Chichester
WEST SUSSEX

SURREY
Guildford

HAMPSHIRE
Winchester
SOUTHAMPTON
Southampton
PORTSMOUTH
Portsmouth
ISLE OF WIGHT
Newport

BERKSHIRE
Reading
Newbury
SWINDON
Swindon
WILTSHIRE
Trowbridge

BOURNEMOUTH, CHRISTCHURCH AND POOLE
Bournemouth
DORSET
Dorchester

SOMERSET
Taunton
BATH AND NORTH EAST SOMERSET
Bath
NORTH SOMERSET
Weston-super-Mare
BRISTOL
SOUTH GLOUCESTERSHIRE
Thornbury
GLOUCESTERSHIRE
Gloucester
WORCESTERSHIRE
Worcester

HEREFORDSHIRE
Hereford
SHROPSHIRE
Shrewsbury
Telford
TELFORD AND WREKIN
STAFFORDSHIRE
Stafford
STOKE-ON-TRENT
Stoke-on-Trent
WALSALL
SANDWELL
Wolverhampton
WOLVERHAMPTON
DUDLEY
Dudley
BIRMINGHAM
Birmingham
SOLIHULL
Coventry
COVENTRY
WARWICKSHIRE
Warwick
WORCESTER

CHESHIRE EAST
CHESHIRE WEST & CHESTER
Chester
Sandbach
WARRINGTON
HALTON
Widnes
Merseyside
(see inset)

DEVON
Exeter
TORBAY
Torquay

CORNWALL
Truro
Plymouth
PLYMOUTH

WALES
POWYS
Llandrindod Wells
CEREDIGION
Aberaeron
GWYNEDD
Caernarfon
ISLE OF ANGLESEY
Llangefni
CONWY
Conwy
DENBIGHSHIRE
Rhuthin
FLINTSHIRE
Mold
WREXHAM
Wrexham

CARMARTHENSHIRE
Carmarthen
PEMBROKESHIRE
Haverfordwest
SWANSEA
Swansea
NEATH PORT TALBOT
Port Talbot
BRIDGEND
Bridgend
VALE OF GLAMORGAN
Barry
CARDIFF
Cardiff
Newport
NEWPORT
MONMOUTHSHIRE
Ebbw Vale
Pontypool
1
2
3
4
5

1. BLAENAU GWENT
2. MERTHYR TYDFIL
3. TORFAEN
4. CAERPHILLY
5. RHONDDA CYNON TAFF

Isle of Man
(British Crown Dependency)
Douglas

IRELAND

FERMANAGH AND OMAGH
ARMAGH CITY, BANBRIDGE AND CRAIGAVON
NEWRY, MOURNE AND DOWN
ARDS AND NORTH DOWN
Belfast
LISBURN AND CASTLEREAGH

IRELAND

Merseyside and Greater Manchester

ROCHDALE
Rochdale
OLDHAM
Oldham
Ashton-under-Lyne
TAMESIDE
Bury
BURY
BOLTON
Bolton
SALFORD
Salford
Manchester
MANCHESTER
Stockport
STOCKPORT
Stretford
TRAFFORD
WIGAN
Wigan
ST HELENS
St Helens
KNOWSLEY
Huyton
LIVERPOOL
Liverpool
SEFTON
Southport
Bootle
Wallasey
WIRRAL

East Berkshire

SLOUGH
Slough
Maidenhead
WINDSOR & MAIDENHEAD
BRACKNELL FOREST
Bracknell
WOKINGHAM
Wokingham
READING
Reading

Channel Islands

Guernsey (British Crown Dependency)
St Peter Port
Jersey (British Crown Dependency)
St Helier

ISLES OF SCILLY
Hugh Town

UK national statistics
www.gov.uk/government/statistics
Scottish Parliament
www.parliament.scot
Northern Ireland Office
www.gov.uk/government/organisations/northern-ireland-office
Senedd Cymru (Welsh Parliament)
www.senedd.wales

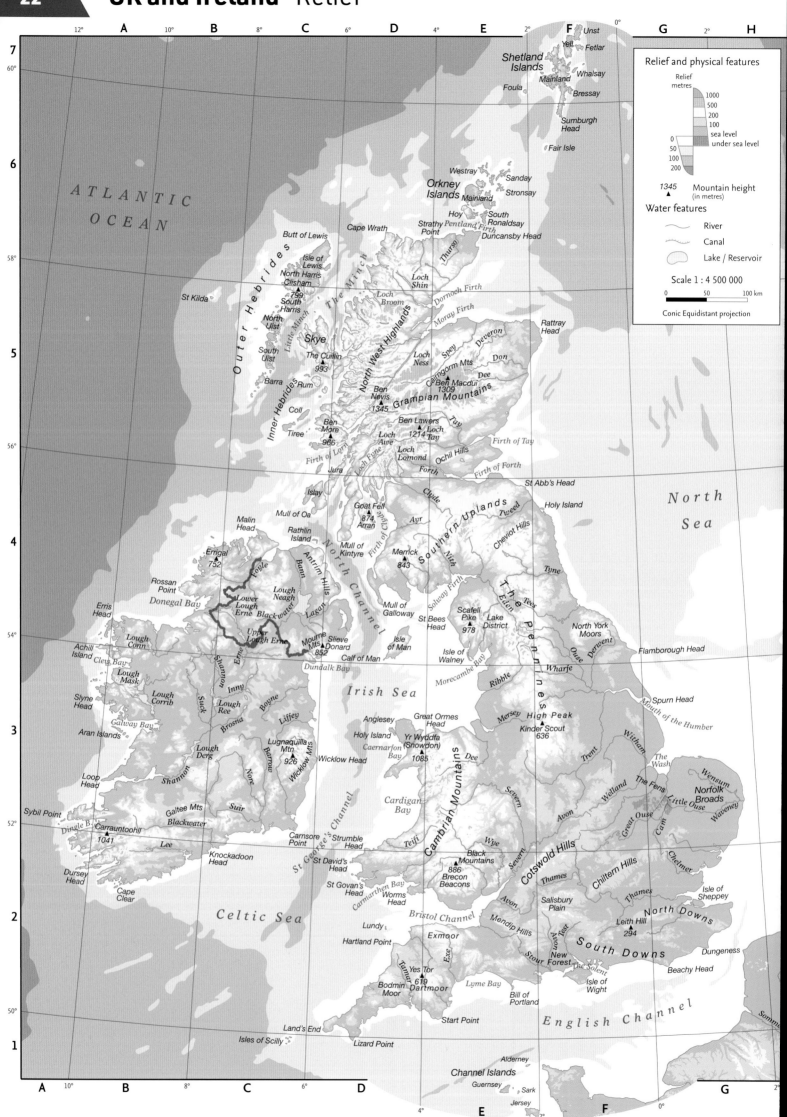

Relief and physical features

Relief
metres

1000
500
200
100
0 sea level
50
100 under sea level
200

▲1345 Mountain height (in metres)

Water features

⌇ River

⌇ Canal

◯ Lake / Reservoir

Scale 1 : 4 500 000

0   50   100 km

Conic Equidistant projection

ATLANTIC OCEAN

North Sea

Irish Sea

Celtic Sea

English Channel

St George's Channel

Bristol Channel

North Channel

Shetland Islands
Unst
Yell
Fetlar
Whalsay
Mainland
Foula
Bressay
Sumburgh Head
Fair Isle

Orkney Islands
Westray
Sanday
Stronsay
Mainland
Hoy
South Ronaldsay
Strathy Point
Duncansby Head
Pentland Firth

Cape Wrath
Thurso
Dornoch Firth
Butt of Lewis
Isle of Lewis
North Harris
Clisham
799
South Harris
North Uist
St Kilda
South Uist
Barra
Outer Hebrides
The Minch
Little Minch
Skye
The Cuillin
993
Loch Broom
Loch Shin
North West Highlands
Rum
Coll
Tiree
Ben More
966
Ben Nevis
1345
Inner Hebrides
Loch Ness
Spey
Cairngorm Mts
Ben Macdui
1309
Dee
Don
Deveron
Grampian Mountains
Rattray Head
Moray Firth
Ben Lawers
1214
Loch Tay
Tay
Loch Awe
Loch Fyne
Loch Lomond
Ochil Hills
Firth of Tay
Firth of Forth
Forth
Jura
Islay
Mull of Oa
Goat Fell
874
Arran
Firth of Clyde
Mull of Kintyre
Ayr
Clyde
Merrick
843
Nith
Southern Uplands
Tweed
St Abb's Head
Holy Island
Cheviot Hills
Tyne
The Pennines
Eden
Tees
Solway Firth
St Bees Head
Scafell Pike
978
Lake District
North York Moors
Derwent
Flamborough Head
Isle of Man
Calf of Man
Isle of Walney
Morecambe Bay
Ribble
Wharfe
Ouse
Spurn Head
Mouth of the Humber
Mersey
High Peak
Kinder Scout
636
Malin Head
Errigal
752
Rossan Point
Donegal Bay
Foyle
Bann
Antrim Hills
Rathlin Island
Lough Neagh
Lower Lough Erne
Blackwater
Lagan
Upper Lough Erne
Mourne Mts
Slieve Donard
852
Dundalk Bay
Mull of Galloway
Erris Head
Achill Island
Clew Bay
Lough Conn
Lough Mask
Lough Corrib
Slyne Head
Galway Bay
Aran Islands
Shannon
Erne
Inny
Lough Ree
Suck
Lough Derg
Brosna
Boyne
Liffey
Lugnaquilla Mtn
926
Wicklow Mts
Wicklow Head
Barrow
Nore
Loop Head
Shannon
Lough
Galtee Mts
Blackwater
Sybil Point
Dingle B.
Carrauntoohil
1041
Dursey Head
Cape Clear
Lee
Suir
Knockadoon Head
Carnsore Point
Strumble Head
St David's Head
St Govan's Head
Worms Head
Carmarthen Bay
Black Mountains
886
Brecon Beacons
Cambrian Mountains
Anglesey
Holy Island
Great Ormes Head
Yr Wyddfa (Snowdon)
1085
Caernarfon Bay
Cardigan Bay
Teifi
Dee
Wye
Severn
Avon
Cotswold Hills
Thames
Chiltern Hills
Thames
The Wash
Wensum
Norfolk Broads
Waveney
Little Ouse
Cam
Great Ouse
Welland
Witham
Trent
Nene
Chelmer
The Fens
Isle of Sheppey
North Downs
Leith Hill
294
South Downs
Dungeness
Beachy Head
Salisbury Plain
Mendip Hills
Avon
Test
New Forest
The Solent
Isle of Wight
Bill of Portland
Lyme Bay
Stour
Lundy
Hartland Point
Exmoor
Exe
Tamar
Yes Tor
619
Dartmoor
Bodmin Moor
Start Point
Land's End
Isles of Scilly
Lizard Point
Alderney
Channel Islands
Guernsey
Sark
Jersey
Somme

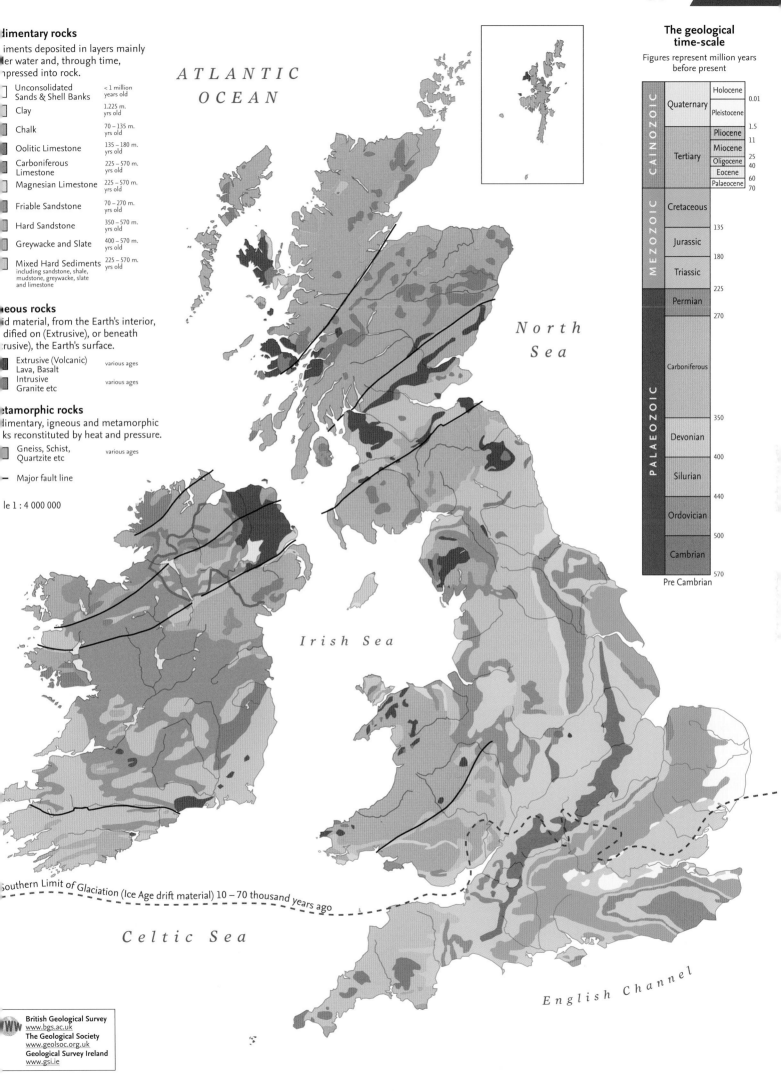

Sedimentary rocks

Sediments deposited in layers mainly under water and, through time, compressed into rock.

- Unconsolidated Sands & Shell Banks — < 1 million years old
- Clay — 1.225 m. yrs old
- Chalk — 70 – 135 m. yrs old
- Oolitic Limestone — 135 – 180 m. yrs old
- Carboniferous Limestone — 225 – 570 m. yrs old
- Magnesian Limestone — 225 – 570 m. yrs old
- Friable Sandstone — 70 – 270 m. yrs old
- Hard Sandstone — 350 – 570 m. yrs old
- Greywacke and Slate — 400 – 570 m. yrs old
- Mixed Hard Sediments including sandstone, shale, mudstone, greywacke, slate and limestone — 225 – 570 m. yrs old

Igneous rocks

Solid material, from the Earth's interior, solidified on (Extrusive), or beneath (Intrusive), the Earth's surface.

- Extrusive (Volcanic) Lava, Basalt — various ages
- Intrusive Granite etc — various ages

Metamorphic rocks

Sedimentary, igneous and metamorphic rocks reconstituted by heat and pressure.

- Gneiss, Schist, Quartzite etc — various ages
- — Major fault line

Scale 1 : 4 000 000

ATLANTIC OCEAN

North Sea

Irish Sea

Celtic Sea

English Channel

Southern Limit of Glaciation (Ice Age drift material) 10 – 70 thousand years ago

The geological time-scale
Figures represent million years before present

Era	Period	Epoch	
CAINOZOIC	Quaternary	Holocene	0.01
		Pleistocene	1.5
	Tertiary	Pliocene	11
		Miocene	25
		Oligocene	40
		Eocene	60
		Palaeocene	70
MEZOZOIC	Cretaceous		135
	Jurassic		180
	Triassic		225
PALAEOZOIC	Permian		270
	Carboniferous		350
	Devonian		400
	Silurian		440
	Ordovician		500
	Cambrian		570
	Pre Cambrian		

British Geological Survey
www.bgs.ac.uk
The Geological Society
www.geolsoc.org.uk
Geological Survey Ireland
www.gsi.ie

UK Climate

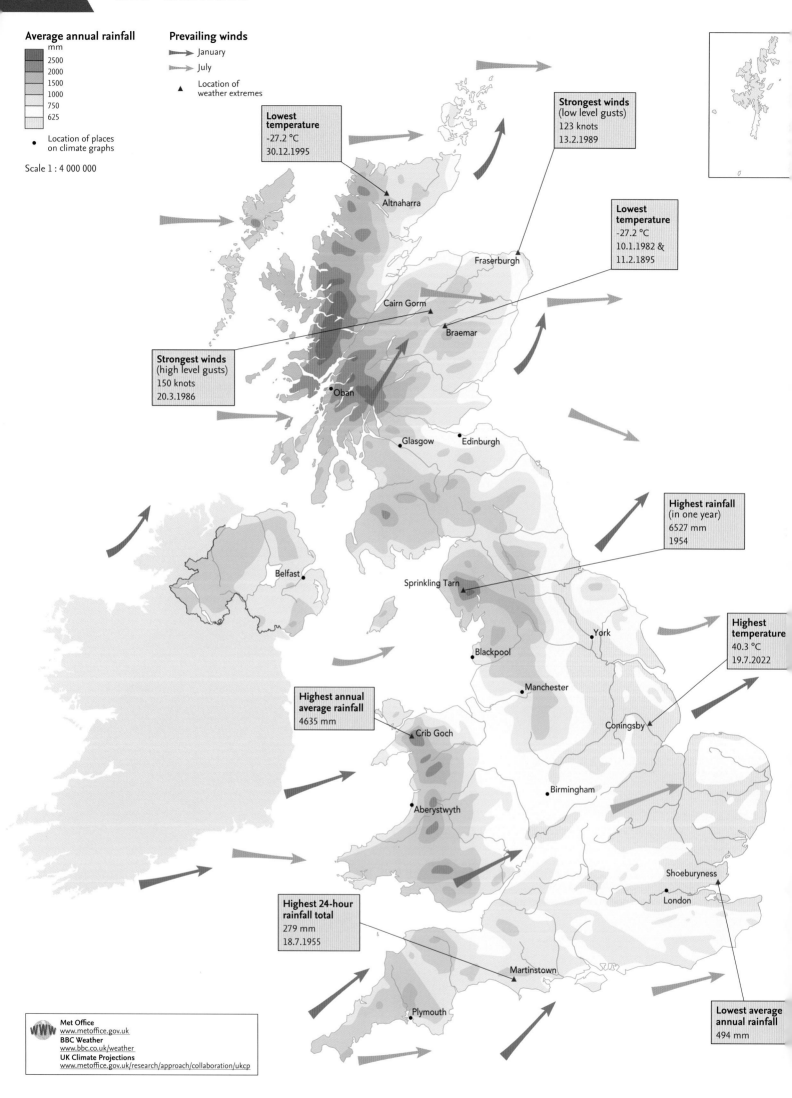

Average annual rainfall
mm
2500
2000
1500
1000
750
625

• Location of places
  on climate graphs

Scale 1 : 4 000 000

Prevailing winds
→ January
→ July
▲ Location of
  weather extremes

Lowest temperature
-27.2 °C
30.12.1995

Altnaharra

Strongest winds
(low level gusts)
123 knots
13.2.1989

Lowest temperature
-27.2 °C
10.1.1982 &
11.2.1895

Fraserburgh

Cairn Gorm

Braemar

Strongest winds
(high level gusts)
150 knots
20.3.1986

•Oban

Glasgow •Edinburgh

Highest rainfall
(in one year)
6527 mm
1954

Belfast

Sprinkling Tarn

York

Blackpool

Manchester

Highest annual average rainfall
4635 mm

Crib Goch

Highest temperature
40.3 °C
19.7.2022

Coningsby

Birmingham

Aberystwyth

Shoeburyness

London

Highest 24-hour rainfall total
279 mm
18.7.1955

Martinstown

Plymouth

Lowest average annual rainfall
494 mm

Met Office
www.metoffice.gov.uk
BBC Weather
www.bbc.co.uk/weather
UK Climate Projections
www.metoffice.gov.uk/research/approach/collaboration/ukcp

January temperature

°C
6
4
2
0

Currents
→ Warm
→ Cold

Scale 1 : 12 000 000

July temperature

°C
16
14
12
10

Currents
→ Warm
→ Cold

Scale 1 : 12 000 000

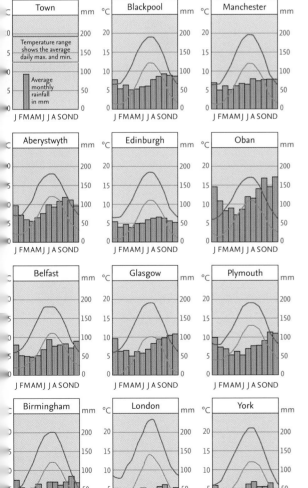

Climate graphs

Town
mm
200
150
100
50
0

Temperature range shows the average daily max. and min.

Average monthly rainfall in mm

J F M A M J J A S O N D

Blackpool
°C mm
20 200
15 150
10 100
5 50
0 0
J F M A M J J A S O N D

Manchester
°C mm
20 200
15 150
10 100
5 50
0 0
J F M A M J J A S O N D

Aberystwyth
°C mm
20 200
15 150
10 100
5 50
0 0
J F M A M J J A S O N D

Edinburgh
°C mm
20 200
15 150
10 100
5 50
0 0
J F M A M J J A S O N D

Oban
°C mm
20 200
15 150
10 100
5 50
0 0
J F M A M J J A S O N D

Belfast
°C mm
20 200
15 150
10 100
5 50
0 0
J F M A M J J A S O N D

Glasgow
°C mm
20 200
15 150
10 100
5 50
0 0
J F M A M J J A S O N D

Plymouth
°C mm
20 200
15 150
10 100
5 50
0 0
J F M A M J J A S O N D

Birmingham
°C mm
20 200
15 150
10 100
5 50
0 0
J F M A M J J A S O N D

London
°C mm
20 200
15 150
10 100
5 50
0 0
J F M A M J J A S O N D

York
°C mm
20 200
15 150
10 100
5 50
0 0
J F M A M J J A S O N D

Sea level rise

Projected flooding of land with the following rise in sea level (metres)

5
10
15
20
25

Land above 25 metres

Scale 1 : 12 000 000

Climate change

The Earth's climate has changed on many timescales in response to natural factors.

The Sun drives our climate

1. Most sunlight passes through the atmosphere and warms the Earth.

2. Infrared radiation is given off by the Earth. Most IR escapes through outer space and cools the Earth.

3. But some IR is trapped by gases in the air and this reduces the cooling effect.

This is known as the greenhouse effect.

The gases responsible for this are called greenhouse gases. These include:

 Carbon Dioxide CO_2

 Methane CH_4

 Ozone O_3

 Water vapour H_2O

Nitrous Oxide N_2O

Greenhouse gases are so effective at keeping the Earth warm that any changes will affect the Earth's temperature.

A changing climate

In the last century our climate has started to change rapidly. How can we tell if these changes are natural or down to us?

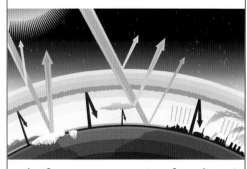

What factors cause a warming of our climate?

 More energy from the sun.

 Large natural events e.g. El Nino.

 Increased greenhouse gases.

There is evidence that the majority of warming seen over the last 100 years is due to increased amounts of greenhouse gases in the atmosphere

Greenhouse gases occur naturally but human activities have increased the amount of carbon dioxide, methane and some others.

 Burning of fossil fuels such as coal, gas and oil.

Changes in land use such as clearing forests for crop production.

 Carbon dioxide concentrations have increased by around 40% since 1750.

There is a natural carbon cycle in our climate. The increase in CO_2 in the atmosphere cannot be explained by this alone.

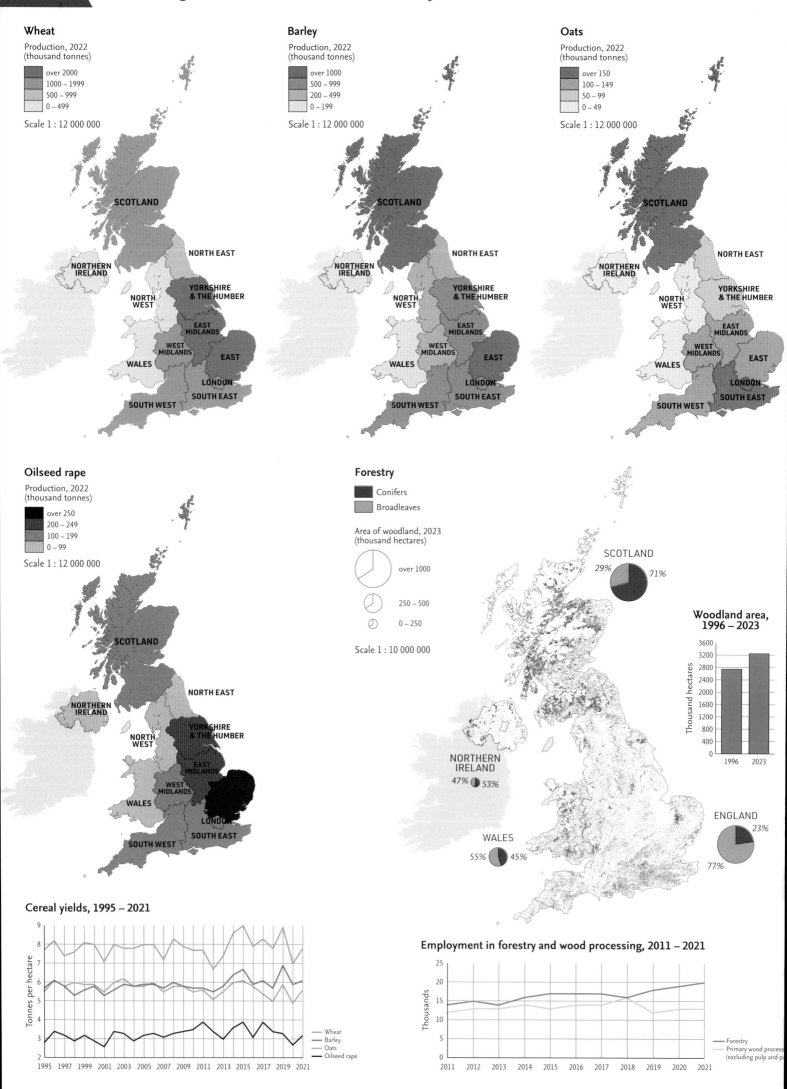

Wheat

Production, 2022
(thousand tonnes)

- over 2000
- 1000 – 1999
- 500 – 999
- 0 – 499

Scale 1 : 12 000 000

Barley

Production, 2022
(thousand tonnes)

- over 1000
- 500 – 999
- 200 – 499
- 0 – 199

Scale 1 : 12 000 000

Oats

Production, 2022
(thousand tonnes)

- over 150
- 100 – 149
- 50 – 99
- 0 – 49

Scale 1 : 12 000 000

Oilseed rape

Production, 2022
(thousand tonnes)

- over 250
- 200 – 249
- 100 – 199
- 0 – 99

Scale 1 : 12 000 000

Forestry

- Conifers
- Broadleaves

Area of woodland, 2023
(thousand hectares)

- over 1000
- 250 – 500
- 0 – 250

Scale 1 : 10 000 000

SCOTLAND 29% 71%

NORTHERN IRELAND 47% 53%

WALES 55% 45%

ENGLAND 23% 77%

Woodland area, 1996 – 2023

Cereal yields, 1995 – 2021

- Wheat
- Barley
- Oats
- Oilseed rape

Employment in forestry and wood processing, 2011 – 2021

- Forestry
- Primary wood processing (excluding pulp and p...)

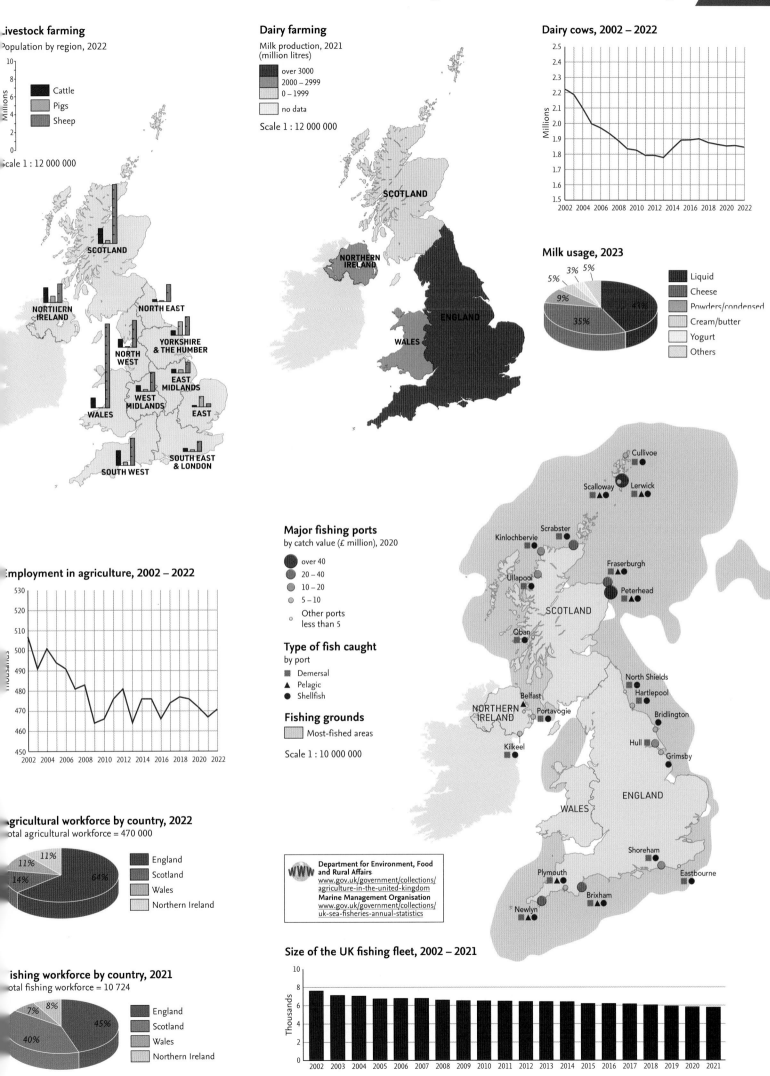

Livestock farming
Population by region, 2022

Millions
Cattle
Pigs
Sheep

Scale 1 : 12 000 000

SCOTLAND
NORTHERN IRELAND
NORTH EAST
NORTH WEST
YORKSHIRE & THE HUMBER
WEST MIDLANDS
EAST MIDLANDS
WALES
EAST
SOUTH WEST
SOUTH EAST & LONDON

Dairy farming
Milk production, 2021 (million litres)
- over 3000
- 2000 – 2999
- 0 – 1999
- no data

Scale 1 : 12 000 000

SCOTLAND
NORTHERN IRELAND
ENGLAND
WALES

Dairy cows, 2002 – 2022
Millions
2002 2004 2006 2008 2010 2012 2014 2016 2018 2020 2022

Milk usage, 2023
43% Liquid
35% Cheese
9% Powders/condensed
5% Cream/butter
3% Yogurt
5% Others

Employment in agriculture, 2002 – 2022
Thousands
2002 2004 2006 2008 2010 2012 2014 2016 2018 2020 2022

Major fishing ports
by catch value (£ million), 2020
- over 40
- 20 – 40
- 10 – 20
- 5 – 10
- Other ports less than 5

Type of fish caught
by port
- Demersal
- Pelagic
- Shellfish

Fishing grounds
Most-fished areas

Scale 1 : 10 000 000

Cullivoe
Scalloway
Lerwick
Scrabster
Kinlochbervie
Fraserburgh
Ullapool
Peterhead
SCOTLAND
Oban
North Shields
Hartlepool
Belfast
Bridlington
NORTHERN IRELAND
Portavogie
Hull
Kilkeel
Grimsby
ENGLAND
WALES
Shoreham
Plymouth
Eastbourne
Brixham
Newlyn

Agricultural workforce by country, 2022
Total agricultural workforce = 470 000
64% England
14% Scotland
11% Wales
11% Northern Ireland

Fishing workforce by country, 2021
Total fishing workforce = 10 724
45% England
40% Scotland
7% Wales
8% Northern Ireland

WWW Department for Environment, Food and Rural Affairs
www.gov.uk/government/collections/agriculture-in-the-united-kingdom
Marine Management Organisation
www.gov.uk/government/collections/uk-sea-fisheries-annual-statistics

Size of the UK fishing fleet, 2002 – 2021
Thousands
2002 2003 2004 2005 2006 2007 2008 2009 2010 2011 2012 2013 2014 2015 2016 2017 2018 2019 2020 2021

Employment by economic sector, 2023

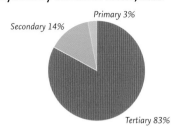

Primary 3%
Secondary 14%
Tertiary 83%

Primary employment by industry sector, 2023

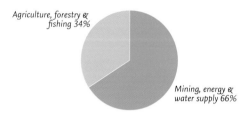

Agriculture, forestry & fishing 34%
Mining, energy & water supply 66%

Secondary employment by industry sector, 2023

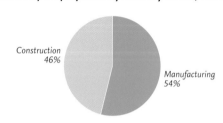

Construction 46%
Manufacturing 54%

Tertiary employment by industry sector, 2023

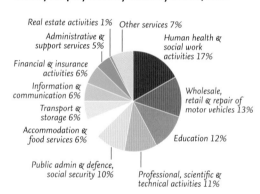

Real estate activities 1%
Administrative & support services 5%
Financial & insurance activities 6%
Information & communication 6%
Transport & storage 6%
Accommodation & food services 6%
Public admin & defence, social security 10%
Other services 7%
Human health & social work activities 17%
Wholesale, retail & repair of motor vehicles 13%
Education 12%
Professional, scientific & technical activities 11%

Unemployment, 2006 – 2022

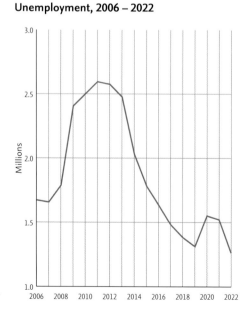

Agriculture, forestry and fishing

Employment compared to national average (index value 1.0), 2022

- over 1.5
- 1.0 – 1.5
- 0.5 – 1.0
- less than 0.5
- no data

Scale 1 : 14 000 000

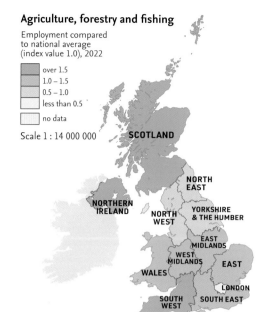

Retail

Employment compared to national average (index value 1.0), 2022

- over 1.5
- 1.0 – 1.5
- 0.5 – 1.0
- less than 0.5
- no data

Scale 1 : 14 000 000

Motor trades

Employment compared to national average (index value 1.0), 2022

- over 1.5
- 1.0 – 1.5
- 0.5 – 1.0
- less than 0.5
- no data

Scale 1 : 14 000 000

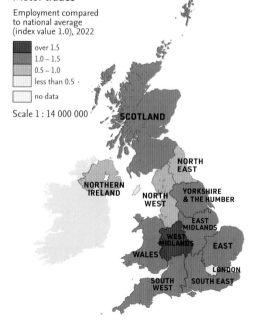

Construction

Employment compared to national average (index value 1.0), 2022

- over 1.2
- 1.0 – 1.2
- 0.8 – 1.0
- less than 0.8
- no data

Scale 1 : 14 000 000

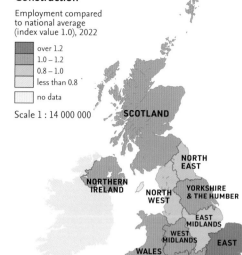

Professional, scientific and technical

Employment compared to national average (index value 1.0), 2022

- over 1.25
- 1.0 – 1.25
- 0.75 – 1.0
- less than 0.75
- no data

Scale 1 : 14 000 000

Finance and insurance

Employment compared to national average (index value 1.0), 2022

- over 2.0
- 1.5 – 2.0
- 1.0 – 1.5
- 0.5 – 1.0
- less than 0.5
- no data

Scale 1 : 14 000 000

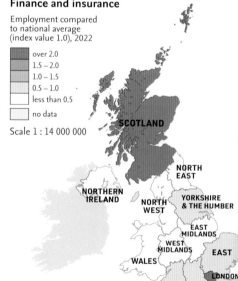

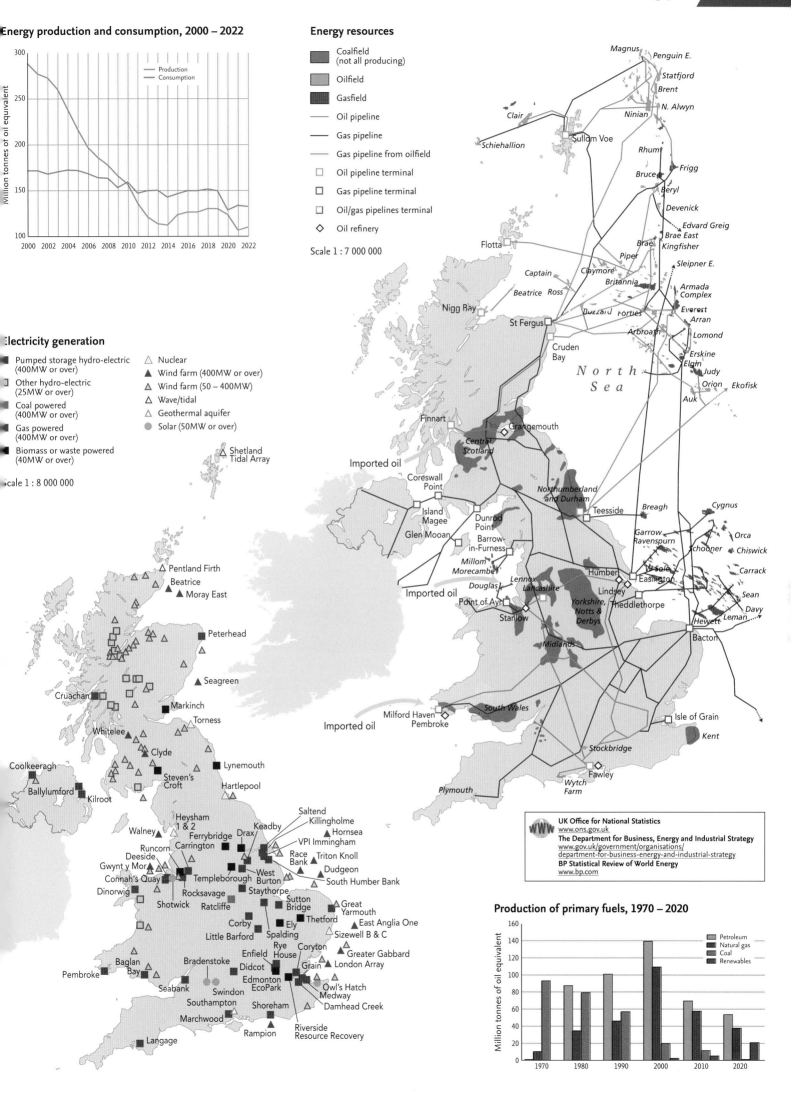

Energy production and consumption, 2000 – 2022

Million tonnes of oil equivalent

- Production
- Consumption

Energy resources

- Coalfield (not all producing)
- Oilfield
- Gasfield
- —— Oil pipeline
- —— Gas pipeline
- —— Gas pipeline from oilfield
- ☐ Oil pipeline terminal
- ☐ Gas pipeline terminal
- ☐ Oil/gas pipelines terminal
- ◇ Oil refinery

Scale 1 : 7 000 000

Electricity generation

- Pumped storage hydro-electric (400MW or over)
- Other hydro-electric (25MW or over)
- Coal powered (400MW or over)
- Gas powered (400MW or over)
- Biomass or waste powered (40MW or over)
- △ Nuclear
- ▲ Wind farm (400MW or over)
- △ Wind farm (50 – 400MW)
- △ Wave/tidal
- △ Geothermal aquifer
- ● Solar (50MW or over)

Scale 1 : 8 000 000

Map labels

Magnus, Penguin E., Statfjord, Brent, Clair, Ninian, N. Alwyn, Schiehallion, Sullom Voe, Rhum, Frigg, Bruce, Beryl, Devenick, Edvard Greig, Brae East, Brae, Kingfisher, Flotta, Piper, Sleipner E., Captain, Claymore, Britannia, Armada Complex, Beatrice, Ross, Everest, Arran, Nigg Bay, Buzzard, Forties, St Fergus, Arbroath, Lomond, Cruden Bay, Erskine, Elgin, North Sea, Judy, Orion, Ekofisk, Auk

Finnart, Grangemouth, Central Scotland, Imported oil, Coreswall Point, Northumberland and Durham, Breagh, Cygnus, Island Magee, Dunrod Point, Teesside, Garrow Ravenspurn, Orca, Glen Mooan, Barrow-in-Furness, Schooner, Chiswick, Millom, Morecambe, W Sole, Carrack, Imported oil, Douglas, Lennox, Lancashire, Humber, Easington, Sean, Point of Ayr, Lindsey, Davy, Stanlow, Yorkshire, Notts & Derbys, Theddlethorpe, Hewett, Leman, Midlands, Bacton

Milford Haven, Pembroke, South Wales, Isle of Grain, Imported oil, Kent, Stockbridge, Plymouth, Fawley, Wytch Farm

Production of primary fuels, 1970 – 2020

Million tonnes of oil equivalent

- Petroleum
- Natural gas
- Coal
- Renewables

1970, 1980, 1990, 2000, 2010, 2020

Electricity generation labels

Shetland Tidal Array, Pentland Firth, Beatrice, Moray East, Peterhead, Seagreen, Cruachan, Markinch, Torness, Whitelee, Clyde, Coolkeeragh, Lynemouth, Ballylumford, Kilroot, Steven's Croft, Hartlepool, Heysham 1 & 2, Saltend, Killingholme, Walney, Keadby, Drax, Hornsea, Ferrybridge, VPI Immingham, Runcorn, Carrington, Race Bank, Triton Knoll, Deeside, West Burton, Dudgeon, Gwynt y Mor, Templeborough, Connah's Quay, Rocksavage, Staythorpe, South Humber Bank, Dinorwig, Shotwick, Ratcliffe, Sutton Bridge, Great Yarmouth, Corby, Ely, Thetford, Little Barford, Spalding, East Anglia One, Enfield, Rye House, Coryton, Sizewell B & C, Baglan Bay, Bradenstoke, Didcot, Grain, Greater Gabbard, Pembroke, Seabank, Edmonton EcoPark, London Array, Swindon, Medway, Owl's Hatch, Southampton, Shoreham, Damhead Creek, Marchwood, Riverside Resource Recovery, Langage, Rampion

UK Office for National Statistics
www.ons.gov.uk
The Department for Business, Energy and Industrial Strategy
www.gov.uk/government/organisations/
department-for-business-energy-and-industrial-strategy
BP Statistical Review of World Energy
www.bp.com

Population density

Persons per sq km

- over 150
- 10 – 150
- under 10

Cities

- over 5 000 000
- 1 000 000 – 5 000 000
- 500 000 – 1 000 000
- 100 000 – 500 000
- 20 000 – 100 000

Scale 1 : 5 000 000

Population change

Percentage change, 2011 – 2021

- 15.0 and over
- 10.0 – 14.9
- 5.0 – 9.9
- 0.1 – 4.9
- 0 and under
- no data

Scale 1 : 10 000 000

UK Office for National Statistics
www.ons.gov.uk
England and Wales Census
www.statistics.gov.uk/census
Scotland's Census
www.scotlandscensus.gov.uk
Northern Ireland Census
www.nisra.gov.uk/statistics/census

Population statistics

Life expectancy	Birth rate	Death rate	Infant mortality	Unemployment rate	Not in education or employment
81 years (2019) Males **79**, Females **83**	**1.0%** (2021) 10 per 1000 people	**1.0%** (2021) 10 per 1000 people	**0.4%** (2021) 4 per 1000 live births	**3.7%** of workforce (2022)	**11.6%** of 16–24 year olds (2023)

Population under 15

Percentage, 2021

	20.0 and over
	18.0 – 19.9
	16.0 – 17.9
	14.0 – 15.9
	13.9 and under

Scale 1 : 10 000 000

Population over 65

Percentage, 2021

	27.0 and over
	22.0 – 26.9
	17.0 – 21.9
	12.0 – 16.9
	11.9 and under

Scale 1 : 10 000 000

Population structure

UK, 2020

Each full square represents
1% of the total population

UK, 2050

Each full square represents
1% of the total population

Internal migration

Number of people moving, 2020

	Moving into area
	Moving out of area

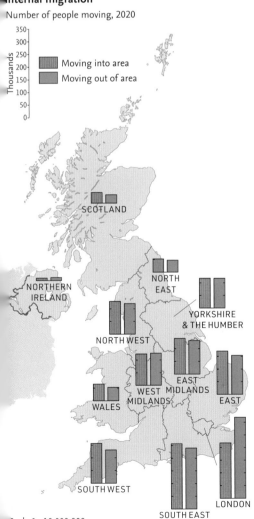

SCOTLAND

NORTHERN IRELAND

NORTH EAST

YORKSHIRE & THE HUMBER

NORTH WEST

WEST MIDLANDS

EAST MIDLANDS

WALES

EAST

SOUTH WEST

LONDON

SOUTH EAST

Scale 1 : 10 000 000

Reasons for immigration, 2010 – 2020

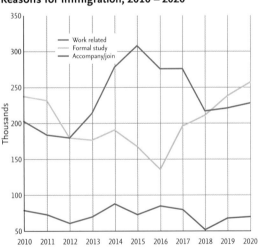

International migration, 2010 – 2020

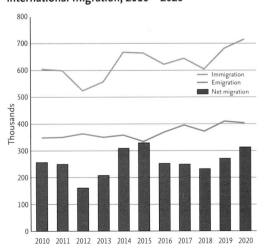

Population by ethnic group, 2021

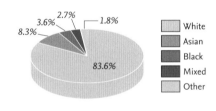

	White
	Asian
	Black
	Mixed
	Other

83.6% 8.3% 3.6% 2.7% 1.8%

Population by country, 2021

Country	Population (thousands)	Density (persons per sq km)
England	56 536	434
Wales	3105	150
Scotland	5480	70
Northern Ireland	1905	141
United Kingdom	**67 026**	**276**

Population by age group

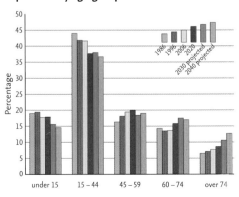

Road network

M1 — Motorway and number
A1 — Linking primary road and number

Scale 1 : 10 000 000

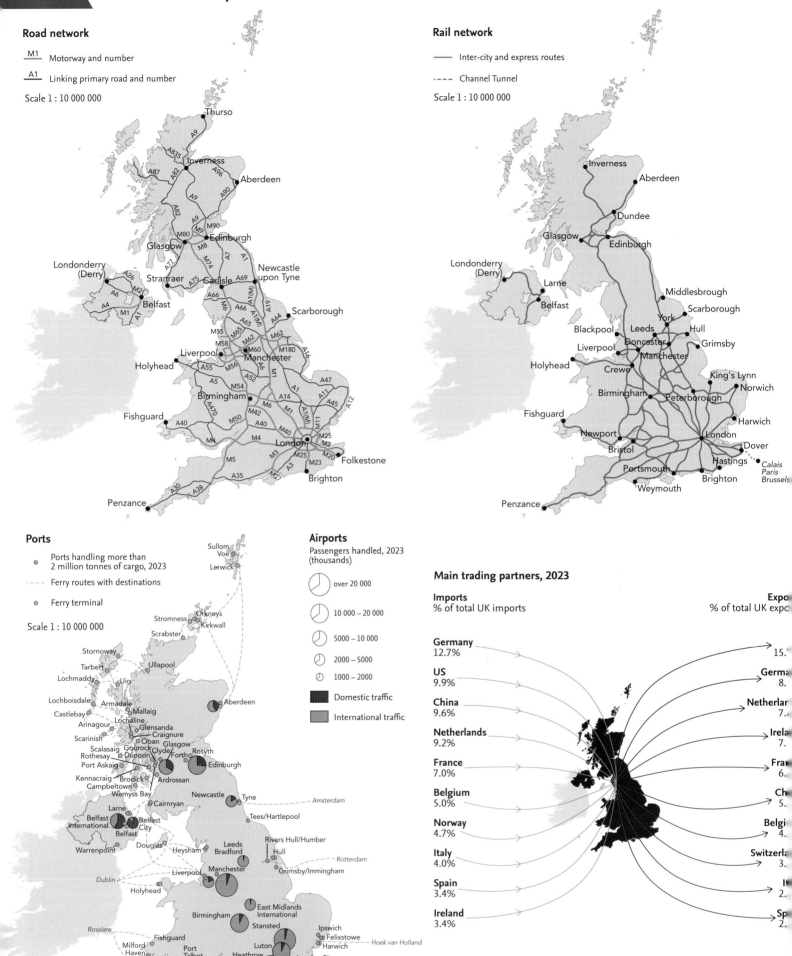

Rail network

—— Inter-city and express routes
- - - - Channel Tunnel

Scale 1 : 10 000 000

Ports

- Ports handling more than 2 million tonnes of cargo, 2023
- - - - Ferry routes with destinations
- Ferry terminal

Scale 1 : 10 000 000

Airports

Passengers handled, 2023 (thousands)

- over 20 000
- 10 000 – 20 000
- 5000 – 10 000
- 2000 – 5000
- 1000 – 2000

Domestic traffic
International traffic

Main trading partners, 2023

Imports
% of total UK imports

Germany 12.7%
US 9.9%
China 9.6%
Netherlands 9.2%
France 7.0%
Belgium 5.0%
Norway 4.7%
Italy 4.0%
Spain 3.4%
Ireland 3.4%

Expo
% of total UK expo

15.
Germa 8.
Netherlan 7.
Irela 7.
Fra 6.
Ch 5.
Belgi 4.
Switzerla 3.
I 2.
Sp 2.

Office for National Statistics
www.ons.gov.uk
Department for Transport
www.gov.uk/government/organisations/department-for-transport
National Highways (for England)
nationalhighways.co.uk

Transport Scotland
www.transport.gov.scot
Welsh Government Transpor
www.gov.wales/transport
Northern Ireland
Department for Infrastructur
www.infrastructure-ni.gov.uk

Legend

National Park

National Landscape (England, Wales & N. Ireland)
National Scenic Areas (Scotland)

Heritage Coast (England and Wales)

— Long distance footpath

▲ World Heritage site

● Major tourist attraction

○ Other tourist attraction

Scale 1 : 4 500 000

International arrivals to the UK, 2022

US 15%
France 9%
Ireland 8%
Germany 7%
Spain 6%
Netherlands 5%
Poland 4%
Italy 4%
Canada 3%
Switzerland 3%
Australia 2%
Belgium 2%
Romania 2%
Sweden 2%
Denmark 2%
Norway 2%
India 2%
Portugal 2%
Others 20%

London

London Zoo
British Library
Madame Tussauds
British Museum
Museum of London
National Portrait Gallery
Somerset House
St Paul's Cathedral
Serpentine Gallery
Royal Academy of Arts
Tate Modern
Tower of London
Science Museum
National Gallery
London Eye
Southbank Centre
Victoria and Albert Museum
Westminster Abbey / Palace of Westminster
Natural History Museum
Imperial War Museum
Tate Britain

Scotland key

1. Edinburgh Castle
2. Scottish National Gallery
3. St Giles' Cathedral
4. National Museum of Scotland

Map labels

Shetland Islands
Fair Isle
Orkney Islands
Heart of Neolithic Orkney
Lewis
Harris
St Kilda
North Uist
South Uist
Wester Ross
Speyside Way
Great Glen Way
Glen Affric
Loch Ness
Cairngorm Mountains
Skye
Kintail
Knoydart
Ben Nevis and Glen Coe
Loch Shiel
L. Tummel
Cairngorms
Mull
Rob Roy Way
Fife Coastal Path
Jura
Loch Lomond and The Trossachs
Antonine Wall
Forth Bridge
Old & New Towns of Edinburgh
Islay
Loch Lomond Shores
Riverside Museum
Kelvingrove Art Gallery & Museum
John Muir Way
New Lanark
Kintyre Way
Arran
Ayrshire Coastal Path
Southern Uplands Way
Northumberland
Giant's Causeway
Binevenagh
Antrim Coast and Glens
Hadrian's Wall
Beamish, the Living Museum of the North
Ulster Way
Sperrin
Titanic Belfast
Hadrian's Wall Path
North Pennines
Durham Castle & Cathedral
Cleveland Way
Fermanagh Lakeland
Lagan Valley
Strangford and Lecale
Lake District
North York Moors
Mourne
Windermere Lake Cruises
Yorkshire Dales
Flamingo Land
Ring of Gullion
Arnside & Silverdale
Fountains Abbey / Studley Royal Park
Raad ny Foillan Coastal Path
Forest of Bowland
Nidderdale
Yorkshire Wolds Way
Blackpool Pleasure Beach
Saltaire
York Minster
The Deep
Pleasureland Southport
The Lowry
Xscape Yorkshire
Lincolnshire Wolds
Merseyside Maritime Museum
World Museum
Cannon Hall Farm
Peak District
Anglesey
Tir Prince Fun Land
Chester Zoo
Jodrell Bank Observatory
Derwent Valley Mills
Peddars Way and Norfolk Coast Path
Castles & Town Walls of King Edward
Clwydian Range
Chester Cathedral
Alton Towers
Norfolk Coast
The Slate Landscape of Northwest Wales
Pontcysyllte Aqueduct
Cannock Chase
Drayton Manor
The Broads
Lleyn
Eryri (Snowdonia)
Ironbridge Gorge
Great Yarmouth Pleasure Beach
Offa's Dyke Path
Shropshire Hills
Midlands Arts Centre
Library of Birmingham
Ferry Meadows
Glyndwr's Way
Malvern Hills
Suffolk Coast and Heaths
Pembrokeshire Coast Path
Blenheim Palace
Dedham Vale
Bannau Brycheiniog (Brecon Beacons)
Wye Valley
Cotswolds
Ridgeway
Chilterns
River Lee Country Park
Colchester Zoo
Pembrokeshire Coast
Blaenavon Industrial Landscape
Cotswold Way
Thames Path
Royal Botanic Gardens, Kew
SEE INSET
Adventure Island
Gower
Wales Millennium Centre
The North Wessex Downs
Maritime Greenwich
Barry Island Pleasure Park
Bath
Roman Baths
Surrey Hills
N. Downs Way
Canterbury Cathedral
Kent Downs
Exmoor
Quantock Hills
Mendip Hills
Longleat Safari Park
Stonehenge
Avebury
South Downs
High Weald
Dorset
Poole Pottery
New Forest
S. Downs Way
Flamingo Park
Eastbourne Pier
Dorset & East Devon Coast
Isle of Wight
Brighton Pier
Eden Project
Dartmoor
Cornwall & West Devon Mining Landscape
South West Coast Path
Isles of Scilly

London inset key

5. Windsor Castle
6. Legoland
7. Thorpe Park
8. Hampton Court Palace
9. Chessington World of Adventures
10. RHS Garden Wisley

Office for National Statistics
www.ons.gov.uk
VisitBritain
www.visitbritain.com
VisitEngland
www.visitengland.com
VisitScotland
www.visitscotland.com
Visit Wales
www.visitwales.com
Discover Northern Ireland
discovernorthernireland.com

A 30° B 20° C 10° D 0° E 10° F 20° G 30° H 40° I 50° J 60° K 70° L

Jan Mayen

Barents Sea

Arctic Circle
Denmark Strait
North Cape
Sørøya
Ostrov Kolguyev
Arctic Circle
Gora Narodnaya
1894

Norwegian Sea

Dyrafjördur
Fontur
Iceland Snæfell
1833
Vatnajökull
Faxaflói

Lofoten Vesterålen
Inarijärvi
Sápmi
Kola Peninsula
Chëshskaya Guba
Poluostrov Kanin
Mezen

Vestfjorden
Luleälven
Kemijoki
White Sea
Northern Dvina
Pechora
Usa

Faroe Islands
Umeälven
Indalsälven
Gulf of Bothnia
Lake Onega
Pechora
Vychegda
Kama

ATLANTIC OCEAN
Shetland
Åland Islands
Lake Ladoga
Ural Mountains

Rockall
Orkney
Mälaren
Gulf of Finland
Rybinskoye Vodokhranilishche
Volga

Outer Hebrides
Vänern
Hiiumaa
Lake Peipus
Kuybyshevskoye Vodokhranilishche
Volga

Malin Head
Ben Nevis
1345
Saaremaa
Gotland
Gulf of Riga
Central Russian
Volga Upland
Ural

Donegal Bay
North Sea
Vättern
Öland
North European Plain
Upland

Galway Bay
Jutland
Zealand
Fyn
Bornholm
Pripet Marshes
Kyivske Vodoskhovyshche
Don

Ireland
Shannon
Irish Sea
Great Britain
The Wash
Frisian Islands
Elbe
Warta
Bug
Dnieper
Tsimlyanskoye Vodokhranilishche
Don

Cape Clear
Yr Wyddfa (Snowdon)
1085
Ijsselmeer
Weser
Oder
Vistula
Dniester
Caspian

St George's Channel
Land's End
Isles of Scilly
Thames
Maas
Rhine
Elbe
Ore Mountains
Sudeten
Vistula
Sea of Azov

Channel Islands
English Channel
Strait of Dover
Seine
Marne
Ardennes
Moselle
Taunus
Bohemian Forest
Carpathian Mts
Dnieper
Stavropol'skaya Vozvyshennost'

Brittany
Loire
Vienne
Saône
Jura
Danube
Inn
Danube
Lake Tisza
Balaton
Hungarian Plain
Transylvanian Alps
Crimea
Caucasus
El'brus
5642

Bay of Biscay
Allier
Mont Blanc
4806
Matterhorn
4478
Großglockner
3798
Po
Mures
Danube
Black Sea

Cape Finisterre
Puy de Sancy
1886
Massif Central
Rhône
Apennines
Dinaric Alps
Sava
Morava
Balkan Mts
Sea of Marmara
ASIA

Cantabrian Mts
Pyrenees
Aneto
3404
Gulf of Lions
Côte d'Azur
Corsica
Gulf of Genoa
Ligurian Sea
Adriatic Sea
Rhodope Mts
Mt Olympus
2911
Aegean Sea

Douro
Duero
Ebro
Balearic Sea
Sardinia
Vesuvius
1281
Pindus
Corfu
Evvoia

Tagus
Golfo de Valencia
Minorca
Majorca
Ibiza
Tyrrhenian Sea
G. of Taranto
Ionian Sea
Dodecanese
Naxos
Rhodes

Sierra Morena
Guadalquivir
Sierra Nevada
Balearic Is
Sicily Mount Etna
3357
Zakynthos Sea
Kythira
Crete

Cabo de São Vicente
Strait of Gibraltar
Mediterranean Sea
C. Passero

AFRICA

Relief and physical features

Relief metres
5000
3000
2000
1000
500
200
sea level
0
under sea level
200
4000
6000

5642 ▲ Mountain height (in metres)

Permanent ice (ice cap or glacier)

Scale 1 : 25 000 000

0   250   500 km

Conic Equidistant projection

Cross-section

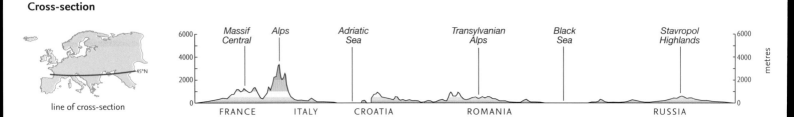

line of cross-section

6000
4000
2000
0

Massif Central
Alps
Adriatic Sea
Transylvanian Alps
Black Sea
Stavropol Highlands

6000
4000
2000
0
metres

FRANCE   ITALY   CROATIA   ROMANIA   RUSSIA

A 30° **B** 20° **C** 10° **D** 0° **E** 10° **F** 20° **G** 30° **H** 40° **I** 50° **J** 60° **K** 70° **L**

Arctic Circle

Jan Mayen (Norway)

ICELAND
■ Reykjavík

Barents Sea

White Sea

N O R W A Y

S W E D E N

F I N L A N D

Oslo

Stockholm

Gulf of Bothnia

Helsinki

○ St Petersburg

R U S S I A

■ Moscow

A T L A N T I C

O C E A N

Faroe Islands (Denmark)

North Sea

Edinburgh

Belfast

UNITED

KINGDOM

Dublin

IRELAND

London

English Channel

DENMARK

Copenhagen

Gulf of Finland

Tallinn

ESTONIA

Baltic Sea

Riga

LATVIA

LITHUANIA

Vilnius

Minsk

RUSSIA

Volgograd ○

A S I A

Caspian Sea

NETHERLANDS

Amsterdam

The Hague

Brussels

BELGIUM

Berlin

GERMANY

POLAND

Warsaw

BELARUS

Kyiv

U K R A I N E

LUXEMBOURG
Luxembourg

Paris

Prague

CZECHIA

SLOVAKIA

Bratislava

Vienna

MOLDOVA

Chișinău

Munich

F R A N C E

Bern

LIECHTENSTEIN

AUSTRIA

Budapest

HUNGARY

Odesa ○

SWITZERLAND

Lyon

SLOVENIA

Zagreb

ROMANIA

Bucharest

Milan

Ljubljana

CROATIA

Belgrade

Black Sea

SAN
MARINO

BOSNIA &
HERZEGOVINA

SERBIA

ANDORRA

Andorra
la Vella

Barcelona

MONACO

Adriatic Sea

Sarajevo

MONTENEGRO

Sofia

BULGARIA

VATICAN
CITY

I T A L Y

Podgorica

KOSOVO

Priština

Skopje

İstanbul

Lisbon

Madrid

Rome

Tirana

NORTH
MACEDONIA

Ankara

PORTUGAL

S P A I N

Balearic Islands

Corsica

Sardinia

Turrhenian Sea

ALBANIA

Aegean Sea

T U R K E Y

Palma

GREECE

Ionian Sea

Gibraltar (Uk)

Strait of Gibraltar

M e d i t e r r a n e a n

Sicily

S e a

Sea

Athens

AFRICA

MALTA

Crete

Rhodes

	International boundary
■	National capital
○	Important city

Russia and Turkey straddle the continents of Europe and Asia

Scale 1 : 25 000 000

0   250   500 km

Conic Equidistant projection

D 0° **E** 10° **F** 20° **G** 30° **H** 40° **I**

Facts about Europe

Total land area	**9 908 599 sq km**
Highest peak	**El'brus, 5642 m**
Longest river	**Volga, 3688 km**
Largest country	**Ukraine, 603 700 sq km** (excluding Russia)
Most populous country	**Germany, 83 369 843** (excluding Russia)

Population by country, 2022
top ten countries

Netherlands 17 564

Belgium 11 656

Romania 19 659

Ukraine 39 702

Germany 83 370

Poland 39 857

UK 67 026

Spain 45 132

France 64 627

Italy 59 037

Population in thousands

GNI by country, 2022
top ten countries

Sweden 660 554

Belgium 568 316

Poland 689 129

Switzerland 784 469

Netherlands 1 016 725

Germany 4 488 992

Spain 1 508 540

UK 3 273 921

Italy 2 218 620

France 3 115 319

Gross National Income in US $ millions

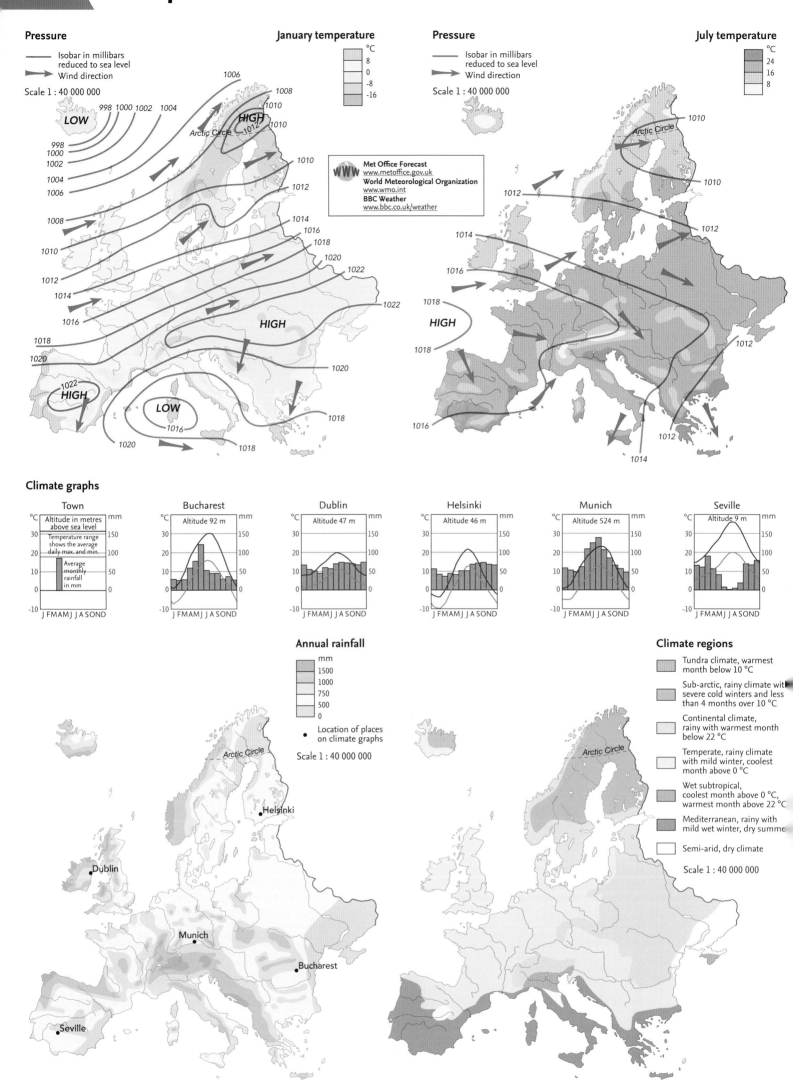

Pressure

Isobar in millibars
reduced to sea level
Wind direction

Scale 1 : 40 000 000

LOW

HIGH

Arctic Circle

HIGH

LOW

HIGH

January temperature

°C
8
0
-8
-16

WWW Met Office Forecast
www.metoffice.gov.uk
World Meteorological Organization
www.wmo.int
BBC Weather
www.bbc.co.uk/weather

Pressure

Isobar in millibars
reduced to sea level
Wind direction

Scale 1 : 40 000 000

Arctic Circle

HIGH

July temperature

°C
24
16
8

Climate graphs

Town

°C   mm
Altitude in metres
above sea level
30   150
Temperature range
shows the average
daily max. and min.
20   100
Average
monthly
rainfall
in mm
0   50

-10
J FMAMJ J A SOND

Bucharest
Altitude 92 m

Dublin
Altitude 47 m

Helsinki
Altitude 46 m

Munich
Altitude 524 m

Seville
Altitude 9 m

Annual rainfall

mm
1500
1000
750
500
0

• Location of places
on climate graphs

Scale 1 : 40 000 000

Helsinki

Dublin

Munich

Bucharest

Seville

Climate regions

Tundra climate, warmest
month below 10 °C

Sub-arctic, rainy climate with
severe cold winters and less
than 4 months over 10 °C

Continental climate,
rainy with warmest month
below 22 °C

Temperate, rainy climate
with mild winter, coolest
month above 0 °C

Wet subtropical,
coolest month above 0 °C,
warmest month above 22 °C

Mediterranean, rainy with
mild wet winter, dry summer

Semi-arid, dry climate

Scale 1 : 40 000 000

Arctic Circle

ICELAND

Tourist resorts

- Mountain/lake resort
- Coastal resort
- Cultural resort

Scale 1 : 20 000 000

NORWAY

SWEDEN

FINLAND

Fjords

Oslo

Stockholm

Helsinki

Tallinn

St Petersburg

ESTONIA

RUSSIA

Moscow

LATVIA

Rīga

DENMARK

Copenhagen

LITHUANIA

Vilnius

RUSSIA

Masurian Lakes

BELARUS

Edinburgh

UNITED

IRELAND Dublin

KINGDOM York

Stratford

Oxford

Bath London

NETH.

Amsterdam

Brugge

Berlin

Warsaw

Kyiv

GERMANY

Cologne

Dresden

POLAND

BELGIUM

Brussels

LUX.

Heidelberg

Rhine

Prague

Kraków

Lviv

UKRAINE

Paris

CZECHIA

Brittany

Strasbourg

Munich

Danube

SLOVAKIA

Vienna

FRANCE

Loire

SWITZ.

Salzburg

AUSTRIA

Budapest

MOLDOVA

Geneva

A

Italian Lakes

HUNGARY

ROMANIA

Perigord

Rhone

Venice

SLOVENIA

Caucasus

Santiago de Compostela

Nîmes

Avignon

CROATIA

Black Sea

Pyrenees

Carcassonne

Provence

Riviera

Florence

BOSNIA & HERZ.

SERBIA

ANDORRA

Côte d'Azur

Siena

Dubrovnik

MONT.

Oporto

Salamanca

Barcelona

Corsica

ITALY

KOS.

BULGARIA

PORTUGAL

Madrid

Costa Brava

Rome

NORTH MACEDONIA

İstanbul

SPAIN

ALBANIA

TURKEY

Lisbon

Minorca

Naples

Córdoba

Majorca

Seville

Ibiza

Sardinia

Corfu

Granada

Delphi

Algarve

Costa Blanca

Athens

Costa del Sol

Sicily

Greek Islands

Rhodes

GREECE

MALTA

Crete

WWW **World Tourism Organization**
www.unwto.org
UNESCO World Heritage Sites
whc.unesco.org
VisitEurope
www.visiteurope.com

Tourist arrivals, 2018

Countries with more than 2.5 million international arrivals
(including Russia and Turkey)

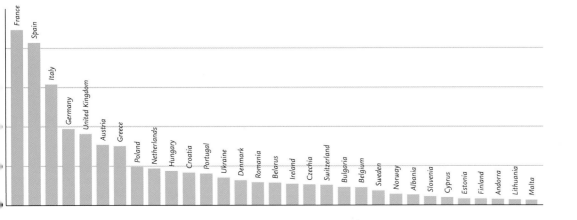

France, Spain, Italy, Germany, United Kingdom, Austria, Greece, Poland, Netherlands, Hungary, Croatia, Portugal, Ukraine, Denmark, Romania, Belarus, Ireland, Czechia, Switzerland, Bulgaria, Belgium, Sweden, Norway, Albania, Slovenia, Cyprus, Estonia, Finland, Andorra, Lithuania, Malta

Land use

- Industrial and urban area
- Cropland
- Cropland, grassland and woodland
- Grassland and grazing
- Grassland and woodland
- Temperate forest
- Coniferous forest
- Scrubland or desert
- Tundra

● Urban centre

Extractive industry

- Oil
- Gas
- Coal

Scale 1 : 25 000 000

Map labels

Perm, Helsinki, St Petersburg, Oslo, Stockholm, Tallinn, Kazan', Nizhniy Novgorod, Gothenburg, Riga, Moscow, Samara, Copenhagen, Vilnius, Minsk, Glasgow, Bremen, Hamburg, Gdansk, Manchester, Warsaw, Birmingham, Rotterdam, Berlin, Łódź, Volgograd, London, Essen-Dortmund, Dresden, Wrocław, Kyiv, Le Havre, Zwickau, Katowice, Donetsk, Paris, Saarbrücken, Prague, Lviv, Rostov-na-Donu, Metz, Strasbourg, Odesa, Bordeaux, Linz, Bratislava, Lyon, Vienna, Budapest, Grenoble, Milan, Graz, Oviedo, Ljubljana, Zagreb, Bilbao, Bologna, Belgrade, Bucharest, Madrid, Toulouse, Marseille, Rome, Sofia, İstanbul, Barcelona, Lisbon, Valencia, Naples, Bari, Thessaloniki, Seville, Cartagena, Piraeus

Oil production, 2021

Romania 2.1%
Italy 3.0%
Denmark 2.0%
Others 8.8%
UK 25.5%
Norway 58.6%

Total: 160.2 million tonnes

Natural gas production, 2021

Poland 1.9%
Germany 2.2%
Romania 4.0%
Netherlands 8.6%
Others 4.7%
Ukraine 8.8%
Norway 54.3%
UK 15.5%

Total: 181.0 million tonnes oil equivalent

Coal production, 2021

Others 10.6%
Romania 2.6%
Bulgaria 4.0%
Serbia 5.6%
Czechia 8.6%
Poland 35.1%
Ukraine 10.6%
Germany 22.9%

Total: 119.9 million tonnes oil equivalent

Energy consumption by fuel, 2021

Hydro electric 7.4%
Nuclear energy 9.7%
Coal 12.2%
Oil 33.5%
Renewables 12.3%
Natural gas 24.9%

Agricultural production by weight, 2021

Oats, Olives, Apples, Chicken, Tomatoes, Rapeseed, Grapes, Pig meat, Sunflower seed, Barley, Potatoes, Maize, Sugar beet, Milk, Wheat

0 50 100 150 200 250 300
Million tonnes

Agricultural production by value, 2021

Apples, Rapeseed, Eggs, Tomatoes, Barley, Olives, Potatoes, Chicken, Sunflower seed, Grapes, Maize, Beef, Pig meat, Wheat, Milk

0 20 40 60 80 100
Billion dollars

Employment in industry, 2021

Percentage of total employment

- 30.0 – 39.9
- 25.0 – 29.9
- 20.0 – 24.9
- 15.0 – 19.9
- 9.0 – 14.9
- No data

Scale 1 : 50 000 000

ICELAND, NORWAY, SWEDEN, FINLAND, ESTONIA, LATVIA, LITHUANIA, RUS., RUSSIA, UNITED KINGDOM, IRELAND, DENMARK, BELARUS, NETHERLANDS, GERMANY, POLAND, BELGIUM, LUX., CZECHIA, UKRAINE, FRANCE, SWITZ., AUSTRIA, SLOVAKIA, HUNGARY, MOL., SL., CROATIA, ROMANIA, PORTUGAL, ANDORRA, ITALY, B.H., SERBIA, BULGARIA, MON., KOS., SPAIN, ALBANIA, N.M., TURKEY, GREECE, MALTA

European Union members

Date joined

- 1958
- 1973
- 1981
- 1986
- 1995
- 2004
- 2007
- 2013

EU candidate

Non member

European Parliament

The UK joined the European Union in 1973 but left in 2020.

Scale 1 : 25 000 000

BEL.	BELGIUM
B.H.	BOSNIA & HERZEGOVINA
K.	KOSOVO
L.	LIECHTENSTEIN
LUX.	LUXEMBOURG
MO.	MONTENEGRO
NETH.	NETHERLANDS
N.M.	NORTH MACEDONIA
RUS.	RUSSIA
SL.	SLOVENIA
SW.	SWITZERLAND
V.C.	VATICAN CITY

European Union population by country, 2022

countries

Eurozone

Non Eurozone

Non EU member

1 : 40 000 000

Eurostat
ec.europa.eu/eurostat
European Union
europa.eu
European Parliament
www.europarl.europa.eu

Europe Population

ICELAND

Population per sq km

- over 500
- 251 – 500
- 101 – 250
- 26 – 100
- 1 – 25
- less than 1

Scale 1 : 25 000 000

ICELAND

NORWAY

SWEDEN

FINLAND

ESTONIA

RUSSIA

LATVIA

LITHUANIA

RUS.

DENMARK

BELARUS

UNITED KINGDOM

IRELAND

NETHERLANDS

POLAND

GERMANY

BELGIUM

LUX.

UKRAINE

CZECHIA

SLOVAKIA

FRANCE

SWITZ.

AUSTRIA

HUNGARY

MOL.

SL.

CROATIA

ROMANIA

ITALY

B.H.

SERBIA

PORTUGAL

ANDORRA

MON.

KOS.

BULGARIA

SPAIN

ALBANIA

N.M.

TURKEY

GREECE

MALTA

EUROSTAT
ec.europa.eu/eurostat/
United Nations Population Division
www.un.org/development/desa/pd

Population under 15, 2022

Percentage of total population

- over 19
- 17 – 18.9
- 16 – 16.9
- 14 – 15.9
- 12 – 13.9

Scale 1 : 45 000 000

Population 65 and over, 202

Percentage of total population

- over 23
- 21 – 22.9
- 19 – 20.9
- 16 – 18.9
- 8 – 15.9

Scale 1 : 45 000 000

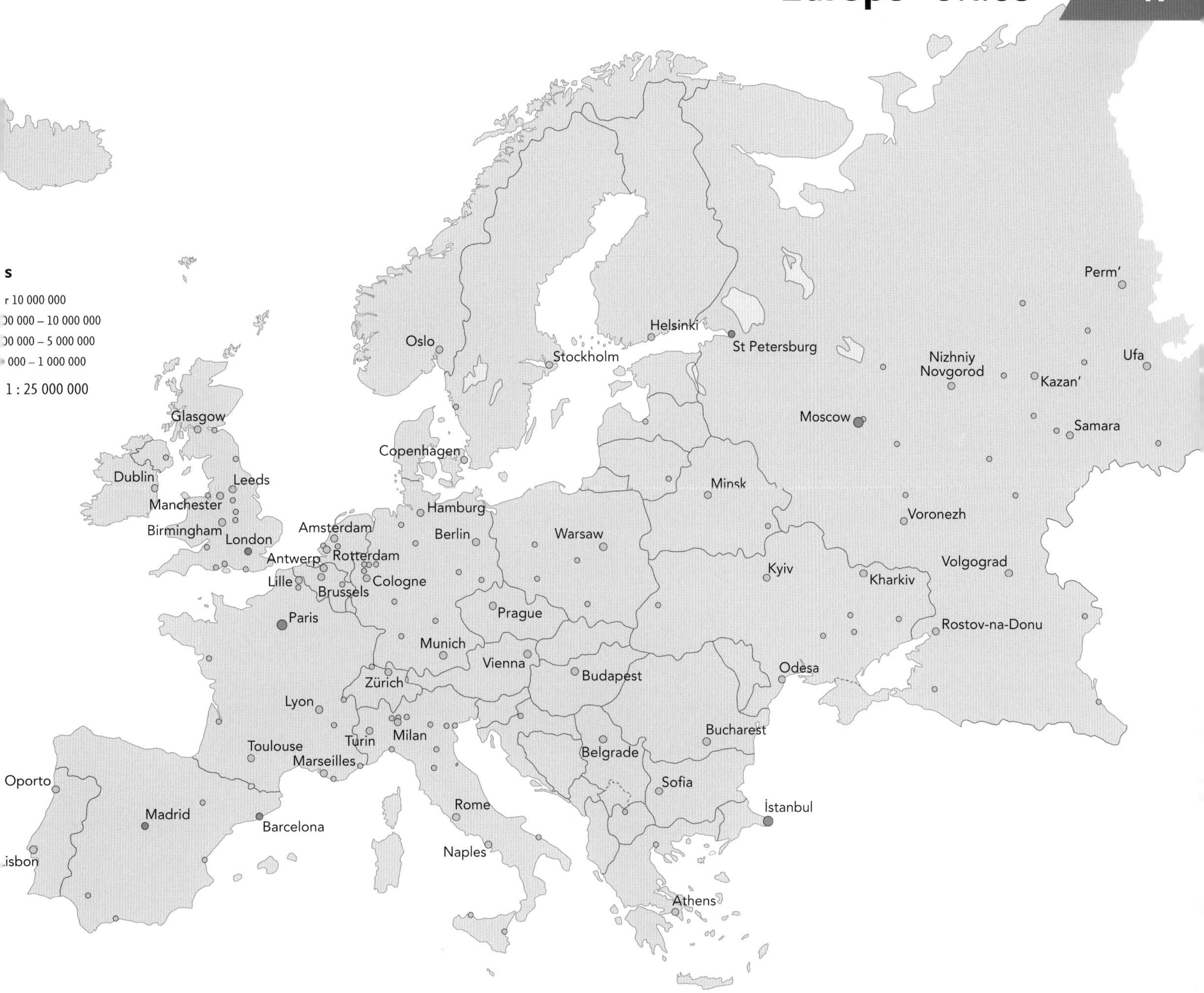
s
r 10 000 000
)0 000 – 10 000 000
)0 000 – 5 000 000
000 – 1 000 000
1 : 25 000 000
Perm'
Helsinki
St Petersburg
Oslo
Stockholm
Nizhniy Novgorod
Ufa
Kazan'
Glasgow
Moscow
Samara
Copenhagen
Dublin
Leeds
Minsk
Manchester
Hamburg
Birmingham
Amsterdam
Berlin
Warsaw
Voronezh
London
Antwerp
Rotterdam
Lille
Cologne
Brussels
Kyiv
Kharkiv
Volgograd
Paris
Prague
Rostov-na-Donu
Munich
Vienna
Budapest
Odesa
Zürich
Lyon
Bucharest
Turin
Milan
Toulouse
Marseilles
Belgrade
Oporto
Sofia
Rome
İstanbul
Madrid
Barcelona
Naples
isbon
Athens

Largest urban agglomerations, 2020

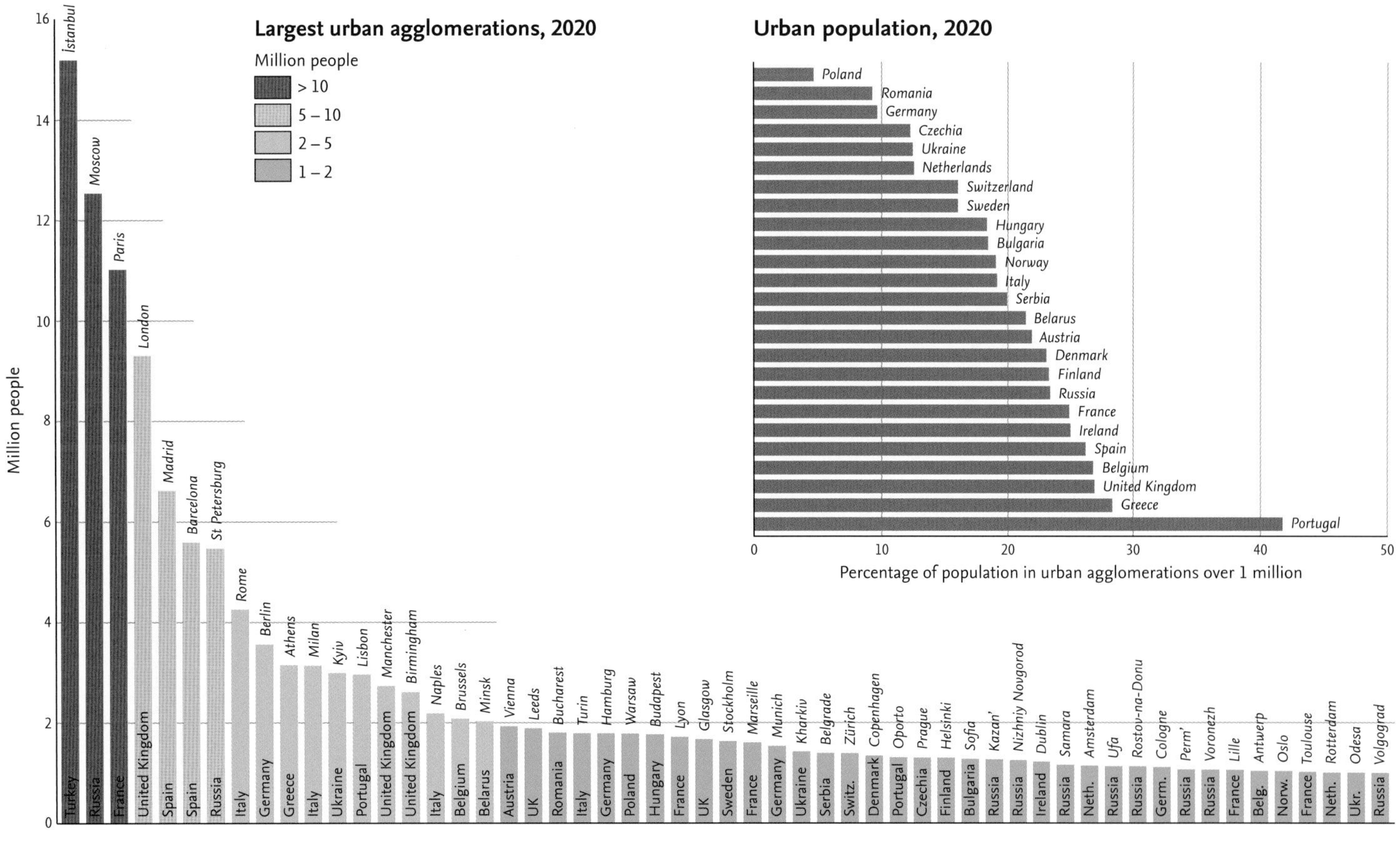
Million people
> 10
5 – 10
2 – 5
1 – 2
Million people
0
2
4
6
8
10
12
14
16
İstanbul Turkey
Moscow Russia
Paris France
London United Kingdom
Madrid Spain
Barcelona Spain
St Petersburg Russia
Rome Italy
Berlin Germany
Athens Greece
Milan Italy
Kyiv Ukraine
Lisbon Portugal
Manchester United Kingdom
Birmingham United Kingdom
Naples Italy
Brussels Belgium
Minsk Belarus
Vienna Austria
Leeds UK
Bucharest Romania
Turin Italy
Hamburg Germany
Warsaw Poland
Budapest Hungary
Lyon France
Glasgow UK
Stockholm Sweden
Marseille France
Munich Germany
Kharkiv Ukraine
Belgrade Serbia
Zürich Switz.
Copenhagen Denmark
Oporto Portugal
Prague Czechia
Helsinki Finland
Sofia Bulgaria
Kazan' Russia
Nizhniy Novgorod Russia
Dublin Ireland
Samara Russia
Amsterdam Neth.
Ufa Russia
Rostov-na-Donu Russia
Cologne Germ.
Perm' Russia
Voronezh Russia
Lille France
Antwerp Belg.
Oslo Norw.
Toulouse France
Rotterdam Neth.
Odesa Ukr.
Volgograd Russia

Urban population, 2020

Poland
Romania
Germany
Czechia
Ukraine
Netherlands
Switzerland
Sweden
Hungary
Bulgaria
Norway
Italy
Serbia
Belarus
Austria
Denmark
Finland
Russia
France
Ireland
Spain
Belgium
United Kingdom
Greece
Portugal
0
10
20
30
40
50
Percentage of population in urban agglomerations over 1 million

Netherlands, Belgium and Luxembourg

Relief and physical features

Relief
metres

5000
3000
2000
1000
500
200
sea level
0
under sea level
200
4000
6000

818 ▲ Mountain height
(in metres)

Permanent ice
(ice cap or glacier)

Water features

River
Canal
Lake / Reservoir
Marsh

Communications

Railway
Motorway
Motorway under construction
Road
⊕ Main airport

Administration
Boundaries

International
Internal

Settlement

Urban area

Cities and towns in order of size

National capital

■ **Brussels**

Other city or town

◉ **Lille**
○ **Saarbrücken**
○ Ghent
○ Leuven

Scale 1 : 2 000 000

Conic Equidistant projection

0   25   50   75   100 km

Scale 1 : 5 250 000

Lambert Conformal Conic projection

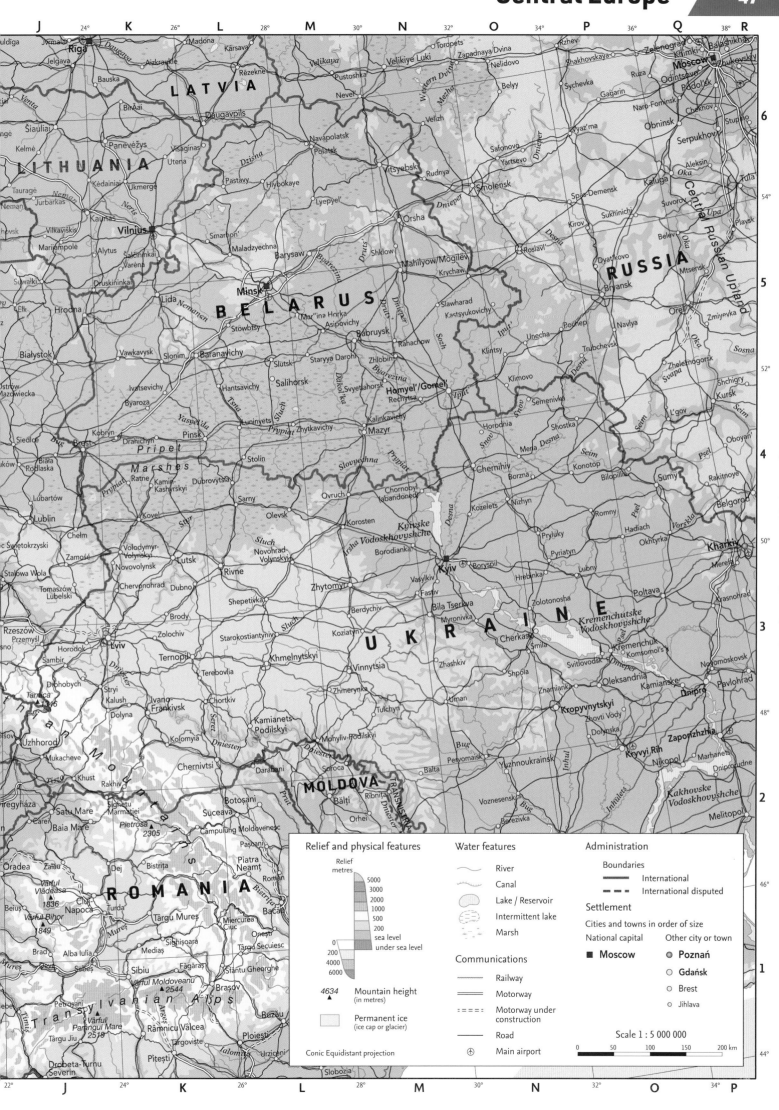

Relief and physical features

Relief metres
5000
3000
2000
1000
500
200
sea level
under sea level
0
200
4000
6000

4634 ▲ Mountain height (in metres)

Permanent ice (ice cap or glacier)

Conic Equidistant projection

Water features

~ River

~ Canal

◯ Lake / Reservoir

◯ Intermittent lake

◯ Marsh

Communications

Railway

Motorway

===== Motorway under construction

Road

✈ Main airport

Administration

Boundaries

International

International disputed

Settlement

Cities and towns in order of size

National capital   Other city or town

■ Moscow   ◉ Poznań

○ Gdańsk

○ Brest

○ Jihlava

Scale 1 : 5 000 000

0   50   100   150   200 km

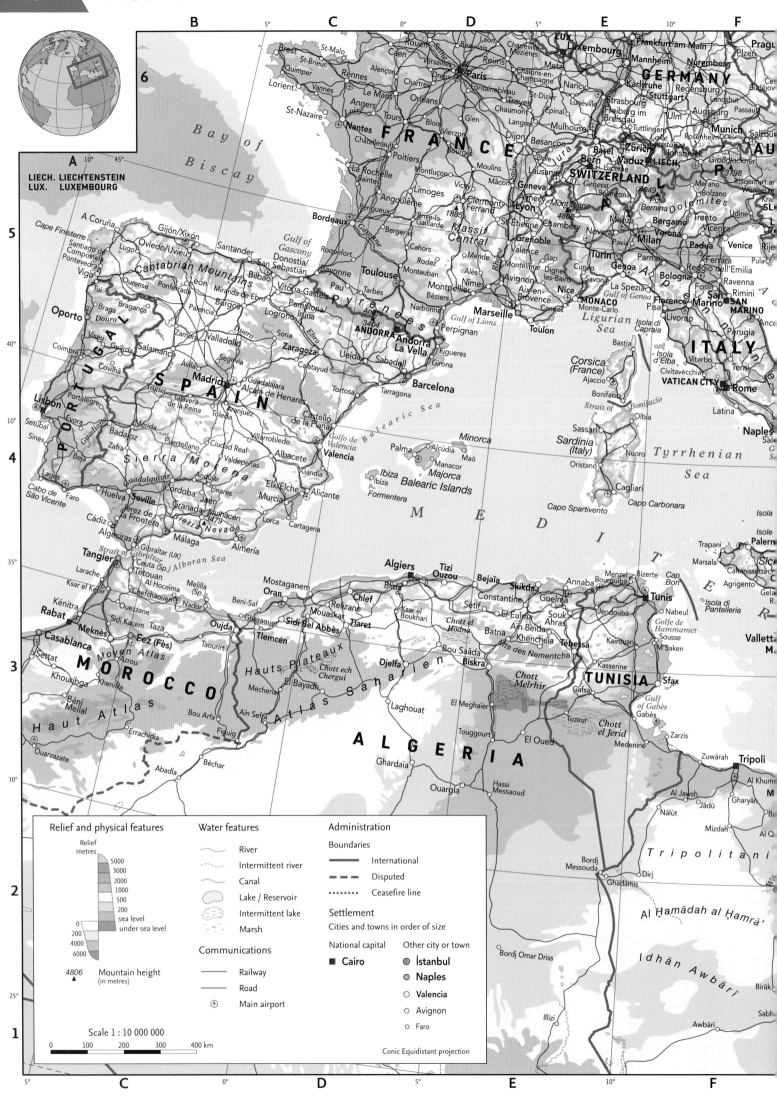

LIECH. LIECHTENSTEIN
LUX. LUXEMBOURG

Relief and physical features

Relief
metres

5000
3000
2000
1000
500
200
sea level
0
200
4000
6000
under sea level

▲ 4806 Mountain height
(in metres)

Water features

～ River
⌁ Intermittent river
⌇ Canal
⬭ Lake / Reservoir
⬭ Intermittent lake
⌇ Marsh

Communications

── Railway
── Road
⊕ Main airport

Administration

Boundaries

── International
── Disputed
⋯ Ceasefire line

Settlement

Cities and towns in order of size

National capital

■ Cairo

Other city or town

◉ İstanbul
◉ Naples
◯ Valencia
○ Avignon
○ Faro

Scale 1 : 10 000 000

0 100 200 300 400 km

Conic Equidistant projection

Relief and physical features

Relief
metres
5000
3000
2000
1000
500
200
sea level
0
under sea level
200
4000
6000

3917 ▲ Mountain height
(in metres)

Water features

~~~~ River
~~~~ Intermittent river
~~~~ Canal
Lake / Reservoir
Intermittent lake
Marsh

Communications

Railway
Motorway
Motorway under construction
Road
⊕ Main airport

Administration

Boundaries

International
Disputed
Ceasefire line

Settlement

Cities and towns in order of size

National capital   Other city or town
■ Athens   ● İstanbul
                    ● Bursa
                    ○ Krasnodar
                    ○ Split
                    ○ Dubrovnik

Scale 1 : 5 000 000

0   50   100   150 km

Conic Equidistant projection

Southeast Europe

H 30° I 32° J 34° K 36° L 38° M

Odesa

MOLDOVA

Comrat
Bolhrad
Artsyz
Bilhorod-
Dnistrovskyi
Tatarbunary
Cahul
Reni
Izmail
Babadag
Sulina
Tulcea
Danube Delta
Svodă
Constanţa
Mangalia
Nos Kaliakra
Kavarna

UKRAINE

Karkinitska Zatoka
Skadovsk
Novooleksiivka
Yany Kapu
Henichesk
Armiansk
Chornomorske
Dzhankoi
Nyzhnohirskyi
CRIMEA
Administered by Russia
Yevpatoriia
Simferopol
Sevastopol
Yalta
Sudak
Feodosiia
Kerch

Sea of Azov
Primorsko-Akhtarsk
Temryuk
Anapa
Novorossiysk
Krymsk
Slavyansk-na-Kubani
Kuban'
Krasnodar
Tshchikskoye Vodokhranilishche
Timashëvsk

RUSSIA

Khadyzhensk
Psebay
Tuapse
Caucasus
Sochi
Gagra
GEORGIA
Sokhumi

B l a c k   S e a

Eaada Burnu
Sinop
İnebolu
Bafra
Samsun
Terme
Rize

Zonguldak
Bartın
Kastamonu
Boyabat
Vezirköprü
Ordu
Giresun
Trabzon
Ereğli
Karabük
Devrez
Osmancık
Merzifon
Niksar
Gümüşhane
Sebinkarahisar
Bayburt
Pontic Mountains

Kandıra
Düzce
Gerede
Tosya
Kızılırmak
Çorum
Amasya
Turhal
Yeşilırmak
Tokat
Suşehri
Kelkit
Kelkit

İstanbul
Sarıyer
Beykoz
Bosporus
İzmit
Adapazarı
Bolu
Köroğlu Tepesi 2400
Beypazarı
Sungurlu
Akdağmadeni
Sivas
Divriği
Tunceli

Bakırköy
Kadıköy
Kartal
Körfez
Yalova
Gölcük
Geyve
Göynük
Mudurnu
Keçiören
Kalecik
Yıldızeli
Zara
Kızıl Dağı 3025
Erzincan
Euphrates

Sea of Marmara
Gemlik
Bursa
Uludağ 2493
Bilecik
İnegöl
Sakarya
Porsuk
Ankara ⊕
Çankaya
Kırıkkale
Yozgat
Delice
Boğazlıyan
Şarkışla
Kangal
Arapgir
Keban Barajı

Çırma
İnönü
Bozüyük
Eskişehir
Polatlı
Kızılırmak
Kaman
Kırşehir
Elazığ

Susurluk
Kemalpaşa
Tavşanlı
Sivrihisar
Yunak
Kaman
Avanos
Kayseri
Pınarbaşı
Malatya
Ergani

Esir
Kütahya
Sakarya
Emirdağ
Cihanbeyli
Lake Tuz
Nevşehir
Erciyes Dağı 3917
Siverek

Simav
Eski Gediz
A   n   a   t   o   l   i   a
Akşehir
Aksaray
Elbistan
Göksun
Adıyaman
Atatürk Barajı

Demirci
Uşak
Banaz
Sandıklı
T U R K E Y
Bor
Niğde
Demirkazık Tepe 3756
Kahramanmaraş
Viranşehir

Alaşehir
Afyonkarahisar
Çivril
Çivril
Gelincik Dağı 2799
Eğirdir
Dinar
Eğirdir Gölü
İsparta
Beyşehir Gölü
Beyşehir
Konya
Karapınar
Medetsiz Tepe 3524
Seyhan
Kozan
Kadirli
Osmaniye
Gaziantep
Nizip
Birecik
Akçakale
Euphrates
Şanlıurfa

Nazilli
Menderes
Gediz
Denizli
Burdur
Korkuteli
Serik
Geyik Dağ 2877
Karaman
Ereğli
Ceyhan
Ceyhan
Adana
Kilis
Kırıkhan

Yatağan
İğla
Dalaman
Elmalı
Antalya
Manavgat
Ermenek
Mut
Tarsus
Mersin
İskenderun Körfezi
İskenderun
Kırıkhan
Aleppo
Buhayrat al Asad
Ar Raqqah

Marmaris
Fethiye
3073
Kaş
Alanya
Antalya Körfezi
Alanya
Silifke
Erdemli
Antakya
Samandağ
İdlib
Balīkh

Rhodes
Lindos
Taurus Mountains
Anamur
Latakia
Jablah
Ma'arrat an Nu'mān

Cape Apostolos Andreas
Aigialousa
Jablah
Bāniyās
Ḥamāh
S Y R I A

CYPRUS
Kyrenia
Administered as Northern Cyprus
Famagusta
Latakia
Ṭarṭūs
Tadmur

Cape Arnauti
Polis
Nicosia
Olympos 1952
Larnaca
Homs
Qornet es Saouda 3088
Al Qaryatayn

Paphos
Limassol
Tripoli
An Nabk
Sab' Ābār

S E A
LEBANON
Zahlé
Beirut

H 30° I 32° J 34° K 36° L 38° M

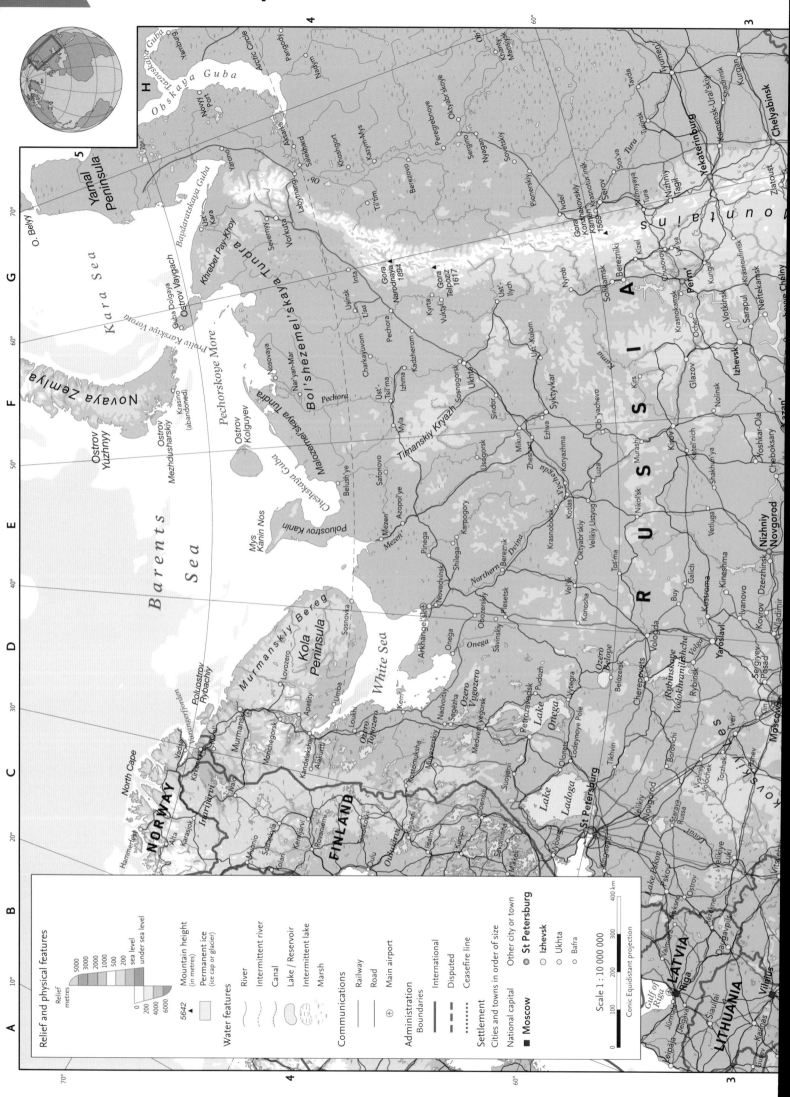

Relief and physical features

Relief
metres

5000
3000
2000
1000
500
200
sea level
under sea level
0
200
4000
6000

5642 ▲ Mountain height
(in metres)

Permanent ice
(ice cap or glacier)

Water features

River
Intermittent river
Canal
Lake / Reservoir
Intermittent lake
Marsh

Communications

Railway
Road
⊕ Main airport

Administration
Boundaries
International
Disputed
Ceasefire line

Settlement
National capital ■ Moscow
Cities and towns in order of size
● St Petersburg
◉ Izhevsk
○ Ukhta
○ Bafra
Other city or town

Scale 1 : 10 000 000
0   100   200   300   400 km
Conic Equidistant projection

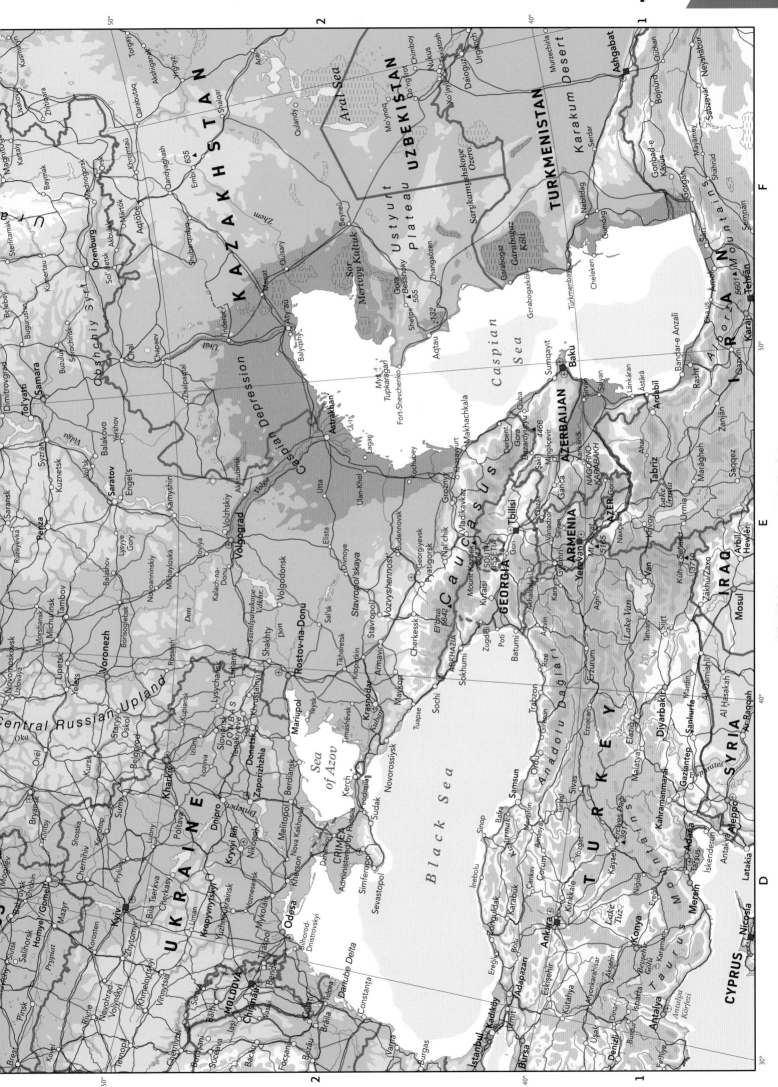

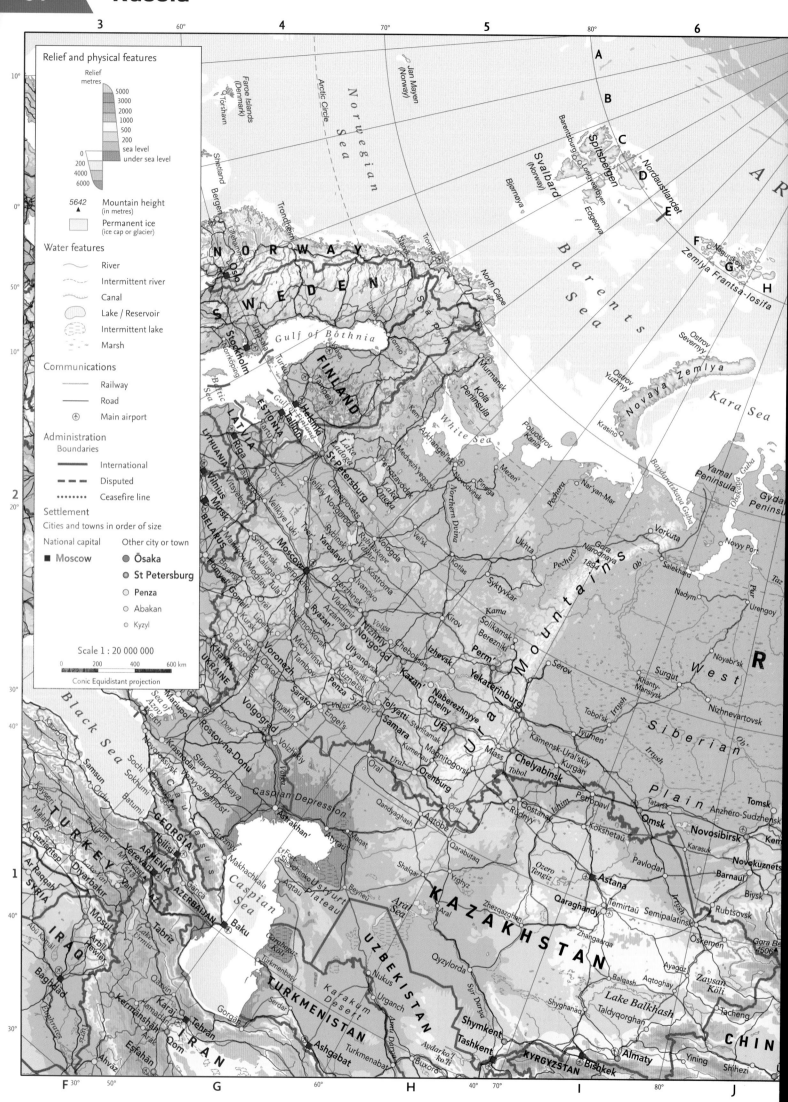

Relief and physical features

Relief
metres
5000
3000
2000
1000
500
200
sea level
0
200   under sea level
4000
6000

5642 ▲ Mountain height
(in metres)

Permanent ice
(ice cap or glacier)

Water features

~~~~ River

- - - - Intermittent river

===== Canal

Lake / Reservoir

Intermittent lake

Marsh

Communications

++++ Railway

──── Road

⊕ Main airport

Administration

Boundaries

──── International

- - - - Disputed

·········· Ceasefire line

Settlement

Cities and towns in order of size

National capital   Other city or town

■ Moscow   ● Ōsaka

      ● St Petersburg

      ○ Penza

      ○ Abakan

      ○ Kyzyl

Scale 1 : 20 000 000

0   200   400   600 km

Conic Equidistant projection

6 90° 80° 5 70° 4

U.S.

U
T
S
R
Q
P
O
N
M
L
K

ARCTIC OCEAN

Ostrov Komsomolets
Severnaya Zemlya
Ostrov Oktyabr'skoy Revolyutsii
Ostrov Bol'shevik
Proliv Vil'kitskogo

New Siberian Islands
Ostrov Kotel'nyy
Ostrov Novaya Sibir'
Ostrov Bol'shoy Lyakhovskiy

East Siberian Sea

Laptev Sea

Wrangel Island
Proliv Longa
Chukchi Sea

Chukotskiy Poluostrov
Uelen
Egvekinot
Anadyr'
Anadyrskiy Zaliv

Bering Strait
St Lawrence Island
St Matthew I.

Bering Sea

Taymyr Peninsula
Gory Byrranga
Ozero Taymyr
North Siberian Lowland
Khatangskiy Zaliv
Olenekskiy Zaliv
Ust'-Olenek
Olenek
Tiksi
Bulun
Kazach'ye

Yanskiy Zaliv
Verkhoyansk
Adycha
Khrebet Cherskogo
Mama
Gora Pobeda 3003

Belaya
Malyy Anyuy
Bol'shoy Anyuy
Srednekolymsk
Kolyma
Omolon

Seymchan
Balkan
Susuman
Strelka
Palatka

Gizhiga
Kamenskoye
Zaliv Shelikhova
Penzhinskaya Guba

Koryakskiy Khrebet
Olyutorskiy Zaliv
Karaginskiy Zaliv

Khrebet Kolymskiy

Palana
Kamchatka
Sopka Klyuchevskaya 4750
Ust'-Kamchatsk

Petropavlovsk-Kamchatskiy
Ozernovskiy

Kamchatka Peninsula

Gora Kamen' 1678
Norils'k
Ozero Khantayskoye
Kheta
Khatanga
Popigay
Anabar
Kotuy
Olenek
Muna
Vilyuy
Markha
Verkhnevilyuysk
Nyurba
Lena
Yakutsk
Ust'-Maya
Maya
Aldan
Allakh-Yun'
Okhotsk

Sea of Okhotsk

Siberia
Central Siberian Plateau
RUSSIA

Gora Kamen'
Tembenchi
Tura
Chernyshevskiy
Mirnyy
Chunya
Lensk
Olekminsk
Aldan
Uchur
Ayan
Shantarskiye Ostrova
Uda
Okha
Ostrov Sakhalin

Podkamennaya Tunguska
Angara
Ust'-Ilimsk
Lena
Vitim
Olëkma
Tynda
Stanovoy Khrebet
Khrebet Dzhugdzhur
Aleksandrovsk-Sakhalinskiy
Tatarskiy Proliv
Poronaysk
Uglegorsk

Kuril Islands
Administered by Russia Claimed by Japan

Kansk
Bratsk
Ust'-Kut
Lake Baikal
Kachug
Zeya
Skovorodino
Amur
Svobodnyy
Komsomol'sk-na-Amure
Yuzhno-Sakhalinsk
Korsakov
Wakkanai

Krasnoyarsk
Nizhneudinsk
Abakan
Usol'ye-Sibirskoye
Sretensk
Chita
Karymskoye
Zeya
Blagoveshchensk
Khabarovsk
Hokkaido
Asahikawa
Asahi-dake 2291
Kushiro

Vostochnyy Sayan
Irkutsk
Ulan-Ude
Yablonovyy Khrebet
Borzya
Argun'
Hulun Buir
Bei'an
Yichun
Jiamusi
Jixi
Sikhote-Alin'
Lake Khanka
Sapporo
Hakodate
Aomori

Kyzyl
Hövsgöl Nuur
Kyakhta
Bayan-Uul
Hulun Nur
Fuyu
Qiqihar
MANCHURIA
Daqing
Harbin
Mudanjiang
Ussuriysk
Vladivostok
Nakhodka
Akita
Yamagata
Sendai

Uvs Nuur
Ulan Bator
Choybalsan
Da Hinggan Ling
CHINA
Ulanhot
Jilin
Yanji
Ch'ongjin
Kimch'aek
Niigata

MONGOLIA
Altay
Bayanhongor
Arvayheer
Xilinhot
Chifeng
Shenyang
Fushun
Anshan
Changchun
Tonghua
NORTH KOREA
Dandong
P'yongyang
Tokyo
Yokohama
Kyoto
Osaka
Nagoya

JAPAN
Sea of Japan (East Sea)

K 100° L 110° M 120° 40° N 130° O

170° 60° 180° 3 170° 50° 160° 2 40° 1 140°

Relief and physical features

Relief
metres

5000
3000
2000
1000
500
200
sea level
under sea level
200
4000
6000

6190 ▲ Mountain height
(in metres)

Permanent ice
(ice cap or glacier)

Scale 1 : 45 000 000

0   500   1000 km

Lambert Azimuthal Equal Area projection

Cross-section

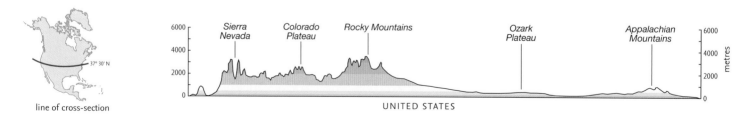

line of cross-section

Sierra Nevada · Colorado Plateau · Rocky Mountains · Ozark Plateau · Appalachian Mountains

UNITED STATES

International boundary
National capital
Important city

1 ST KITTS AND NEVIS
2 ST VINCENT & THE GRENADINES
3 BARBADOS

Scale 1 : 45 000 000

0   500   1000 km

Lambert Azimuthal Equal Area projection

Facts about North America

Total land area   **24 680 331 sq km**

Highest peak   **Denali (Mt McKinley), 6190 m**

Longest river   **Mississippi-Missouri, 5969 km**

Largest country   **Canada, 9 984 670 sq km**

Most populous country   **United States, 338 289 857**

Population by country, 2022 top ten countries

Cuba 11 212
Dominican Republic 11 229
Haiti 11 585
Guatemala 17 844
Canada 38 454
Honduras 10 433
Nicaragua 6948
El Salvador 6336
Mexico 127 504
United States 338 290

Population in thousands

GNI by country, 2022 top ten countries

Cuba 100 933
Dominican Republic 101 653
Mexico 1 327 006
Canada 2 061 750
Guatemala 92 915
Panama 73 866
Costa Rica 65 659
El Salvador 29 899
Honduras 28 607
United States 25 454 400

Gross National Income in US $ millions

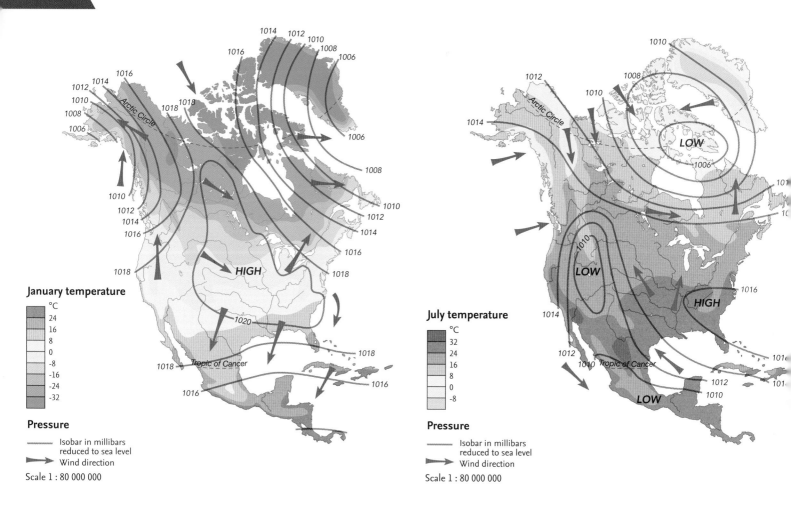

January temperature

°C
24
16
8
0
-8
-16
-24
-32

Pressure

— Isobar in millibars
 reduced to sea level
➤ Wind direction

Scale 1 : 80 000 000

July temperature

°C
32
24
16
8
0
-8

Pressure

— Isobar in millibars
 reduced to sea level
➤ Wind direction

Scale 1 : 80 000 000

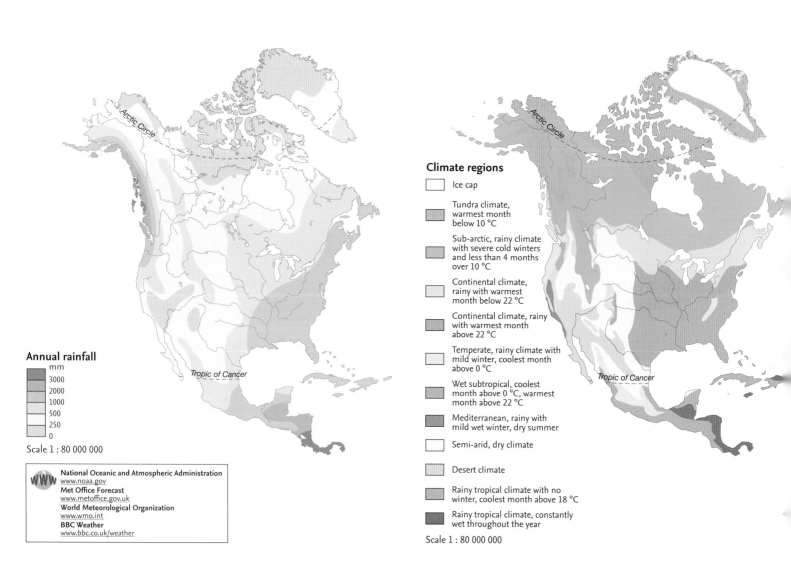

Annual rainfall

mm
3000
2000
1000
500
250
0

Scale 1 : 80 000 000

WWW **National Oceanic and Atmospheric Administration**
www.noaa.gov
Met Office Forecast
www.metoffice.gov.uk
World Meteorological Organization
www.wmo.int
BBC Weather
www.bbc.co.uk/weather

Climate regions

☐ Ice cap

Tundra climate,
warmest month
below 10 °C

Sub-arctic, rainy climate
with severe cold winters
and less than 4 months
over 10 °C

Continental climate,
rainy with warmest
month below 22 °C

Continental climate, rainy
with warmest month
above 22 °C

Temperate, rainy climate with
mild winter, coolest month
above 0 °C

Wet subtropical, coolest
month above 0 °C, warmest
month above 22 °C

Mediterranean, rainy with
mild wet winter, dry summer

Semi-arid, dry climate

Desert climate

Rainy tropical climate with no
winter, coolest month above 18 °C

Rainy tropical climate, constantly
wet throughout the year

Scale 1 : 80 000 000

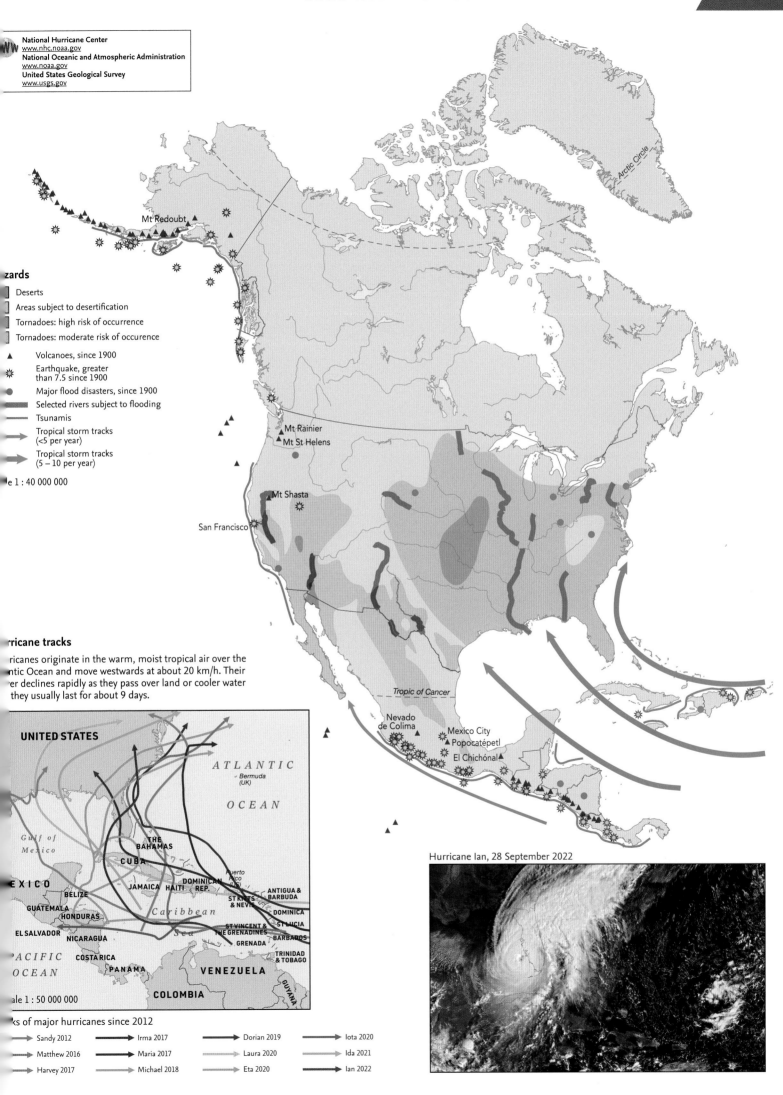

National Hurricane Center
www.nhc.noaa.gov
National Oceanic and Atmospheric Administration
www.noaa.gov
United States Geological Survey
www.usgs.gov

...zards

- Deserts
- Areas subject to desertification
- Tornadoes: high risk of occurrence
- Tornadoes: moderate risk of occurence
- ▲ Volcanoes, since 1900
- ✳ Earthquake, greater than 7.5 since 1900
- ● Major flood disasters, since 1900
- Selected rivers subject to flooding
- Tsunamis
- → Tropical storm tracks (<5 per year)
- → Tropical storm tracks (5 – 10 per year)

...e 1 : 40 000 000

...rricane tracks

...ricanes originate in the warm, moist tropical air over the ...ntic Ocean and move westwards at about 20 km/h. Their ...er declines rapidly as they pass over land or cooler water ...they usually last for about 9 days.

UNITED STATES

ATLANTIC
Bermuda (UK)
OCEAN

Gulf of Mexico

THE BAHAMAS

CUBA

...EXICO

BELIZE
GUATEMALA
HONDURAS
EL SALVADOR
NICARAGUA

JAMAICA HAITI DOMINICAN REP.

Puerto Rico (US)

ANTIGUA & BARBUDA
ST KITTS & NEVIS
DOMINICA
ST LUCIA
ST VINCENT & THE GRENADINES
GRENADA
BARBADOS
TRINIDAD & TOBAGO

Caribbean Sea

...ACIFIC
...OCEAN

COSTA RICA
PANAMA
VENEZUELA
COLOMBIA
GUYANA

...ale 1 : 50 000 000

...ks of major hurricanes since 2012

→ Sandy 2012	→ Irma 2017	→ Dorian 2019	→ Iota 2020
→ Matthew 2016	→ Maria 2017	→ Laura 2020	→ Ida 2021
→ Harvey 2017	→ Michael 2018	→ Eta 2020	→ Ian 2022

Mt Redoubt ▲

Arctic Circle

Mt Rainier
Mt St Helens

Mt Shasta

San Francisco

Tropic of Cancer

Nevado de Colima
Mexico City
Popocatépetl
El Chichónal

Hurricane Ian, 28 September 2022

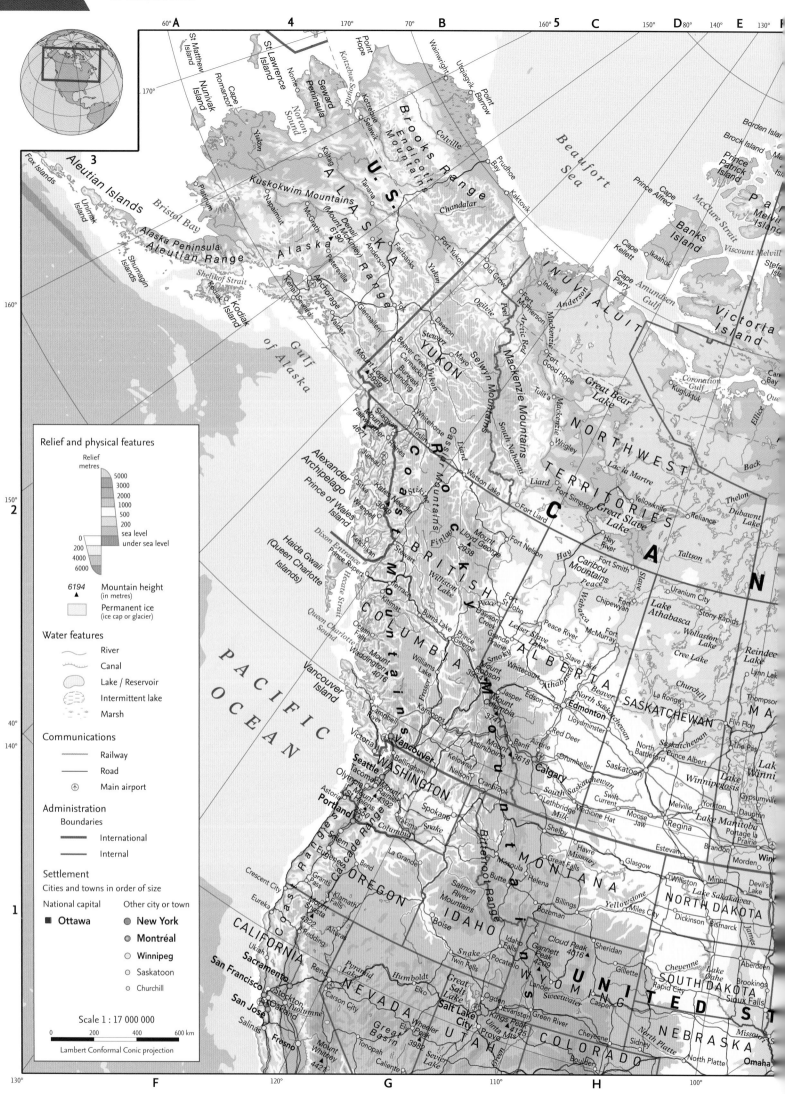

Relief and physical features

Relief
metres
5000
3000
2000
1000
500
200
sea level
0
200 under sea level
4000
6000

▲ 6194   Mountain height
(in metres)

Permanent ice
(ice cap or glacier)

Water features

River

Canal

Lake / Reservoir

Intermittent lake

Marsh

Communications

Railway

Road

⊕   Main airport

Administration

Boundaries

International

Internal

Settlement

Cities and towns in order of size

National capital   Other city or town

■ **Ottawa**   ● **New York**

                       ◉ **Montréal**

                       ◎ **Winnipeg**

                       ○ Saskatoon

                       ○ Churchill

Scale 1 : 17 000 000

0   200   400   600 km

Lambert Conformal Conic projection

Top coordinate labels: H 100° I 90° J 80° K 70° L 60° M 50° N 40° O 80° P 5 20° Q 70° 10° 4 R 60°

British Empire Range
North Geomagnetic Pole (2024)
Axel Heiberg Island
Ellesmere Island
Nares Strait
Amund Ringnes Island
Cape Parry
Thule
Melville Bay
Cape York
Greenland (Denmark)
Kangertittivaq
ICELAND
Arctic Circle
Siglufjörður
Akureyri
Höfn
Reykjavík
Ísafjörður
Faxaflói
Keflavík

Cornwallis Island
Devon Island
Resolute
Jones Sound
Lancaster Sound
Baffin Bay
Upernavik
Denmark Strait
Kong Christian IX Land
3700 Gunnbjørn Field
Tasiilaq

Somerset Island
Brodeur Peninsula
Arctic Bay
Bylot Island
Mittimatalik
Sisimiut
Disko
Qasigiannguit

Gulf of Boothia
Borden Peninsula
Baffin Island
Clyde River
Home Bay
Davis Strait
Kong Frederik VI Kyst

Boothia Peninsula
Taloyoak
Melville Peninsula
Sanirajak (Hall Beach)
Prince Charles Island
Penny Icecap
Pangnirtung
Cape Dyer
Cumberland Sound
Maniitsoq
Nuuk (Godthåb)
Paamiut
Cape Farewell

Naujaat
Foxe Basin
Nettilling Lake
Amadjuak Lake
Iqaluit
Frobisher Bay
Resolution Island
Labrador Sea
Ivittuut
Nanortalik

NUNAVUT
Manittuaq
Southampton Island
Coral Harbour
Foxe Channel
Foxe Peninsula
Mansel Island
Salluit
Kangiqsujuaq
Akpatok Island
Cape Chidley
ATLANTIC OCEAN

Arviat
Fisher Strait
Coats Island
Péninsule d'Ungava
Puvurnituq
Ungava Bay
Kangiqsualujjuaq
Kangirsuk
George
Nain
NEWFOUNDLAND AND LABRADOR

CANADA
Ottawa Islands
Inukjuak
Rivière aux Feuilles
Kuujjuaq
Rivière à la Baleine
Hopedale
Cape Harrison

Cape Churchill
Churchill
Hudson Bay
Belcher Islands
Caniapiscau
NUNATSIAVUT
Smallwood Reservoir
Labrador
Schefferville
Happy Valley-Goose Bay
Port Hope Simpson
St Anthony

Fort Severn
Lac à l'Eau Claire
Réservoir Robert-Bourassa
Lac Caniapiscau
Churchill
Labrador City
Wabush
Petit Mécatina
Strait of Belle Isle

Cape Henrietta Maria
James Bay
Chisasibi
Réservoir La Grande 4
Réservoir La Grande 3
Gagnon
Grand Falls
Windsor
Gander
Bonavista
St John's

Big Trout Lake
Winisk
Akimiski Island
Eastmain
QUÉBEC
Réservoir Manicouagan
Havre-St-Pierre
Corner Brook
Newfoundland
Cape Race

ONTARIO
Albany
Fort Albany
Waskaganish
Lac Mistassini
Mistissini
Sept-Îles
Île d'Anticosti
Channel-Port-aux-Basques
St Pierre and Miquelon (France)

Lake Sioux Lookout
Moosonee
Harricanaw
Lac Evans
Chibougamau
Baie-Comeau
Pén. de Gaspé
Gulf of St Lawrence
Cabot Strait
Sydney
Cape Breton Island

Sandy Lake
Missinaibi
Réservoir Gouin
Roberval
Chicoutimi
Gaspé
Rimouski
Bathurst
P.E.I.
Charlottetown

Frances Lake
Lake Nipigon
Longlac
Kapuskasing
La Sarre
Amos
Jonquière
Rivière-du-Loup
Edmundston
NEW BRUNSWICK
Moncton
Cape Breton

Woods
Thunder Bay
Nipigon
Timmins
Val-d'Or
Québec
Presque Isle
Fredericton
Saint John
Truro
NOVA SCOTIA
Sable Island

Isle Royale
Groundhog
Kirkland Lake
Trois-Rivières
MAINE
Bangor
Bay of Fundy
Halifax

DAKOTA
Duluth
Lake Superior
Chapleau
Sault Sainte Marie
Ottawa
Sherbrooke
Mount Washington 1918
Augusta
Yarmouth
Cape Sable

Minneapolis
St Paul
Eau Claire
Marquette
Escanaba
Sudbury
North Bay
Montréal
Portland
Cape Sable

WISCONSIN
Green Bay
La Crosse
Traverse City
MICHIGAN
Grand Rapids
Bay City
Georgian Bay
Lake Huron
Ottawa
Ottawa
Burlington
VER. 1918
N.H.
Concord
Boston
Cape Cod

Milwaukee
Cedar Rapids
Rockford
MICHIGAN
Flint
Lansing
Lake Michigan
Toronto
Hamilton
Lake Ontario
Kingston
Peterborough
Oshawa
Rochester
Syracuse
Albany
MASS.
Springfield
Hartford
R.I.
Providence
Long Island

Des Moines
Chicago
Gary
South Bend
Toledo
Detroit
London
Lake Erie
Erie
Buffalo
NEW YORK
Scranton
Allentown
Trenton
New York

Cleveland
Akron
PENN.

Bottom coordinate labels: 90° J 80° K 70° L 60° M

CO. — CONNECTICUT
MASS. — MASSACHUSETTS
N.H. — NEW HAMPSHIRE
P.E.I. — PRINCE EDWARD ISLAND
PENN. — PENNSYLVANIA
R.I. — RHODE ISLAND
VER. — VERMONT

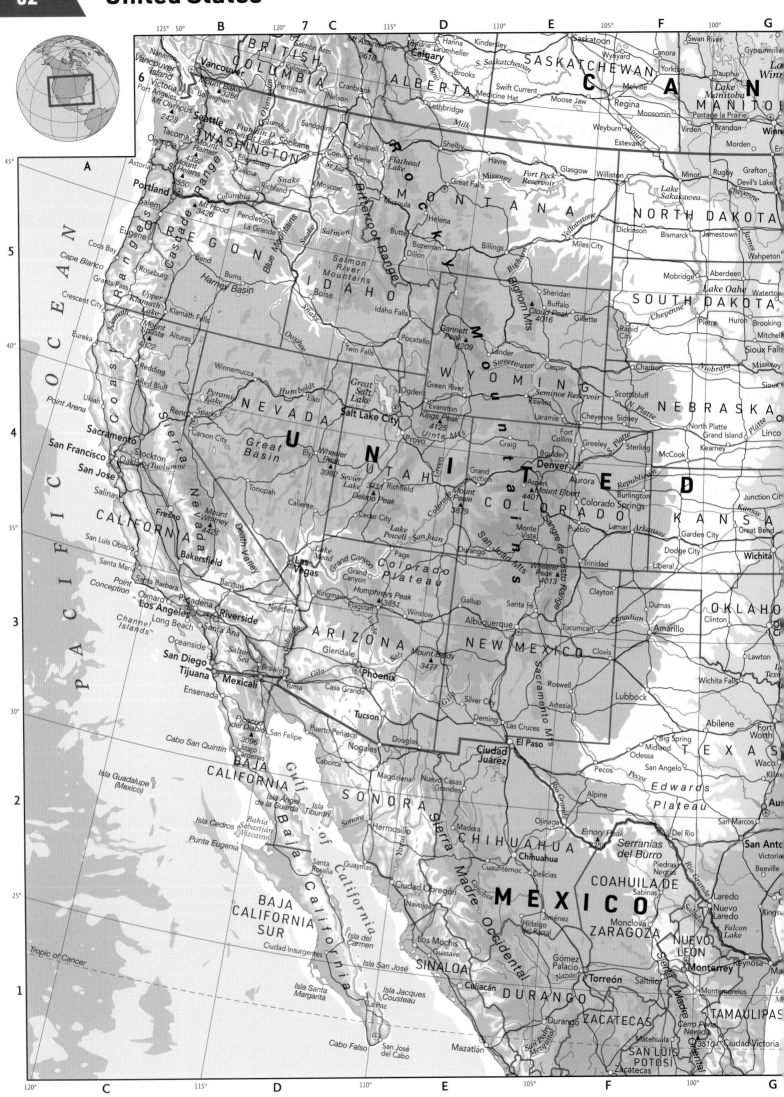

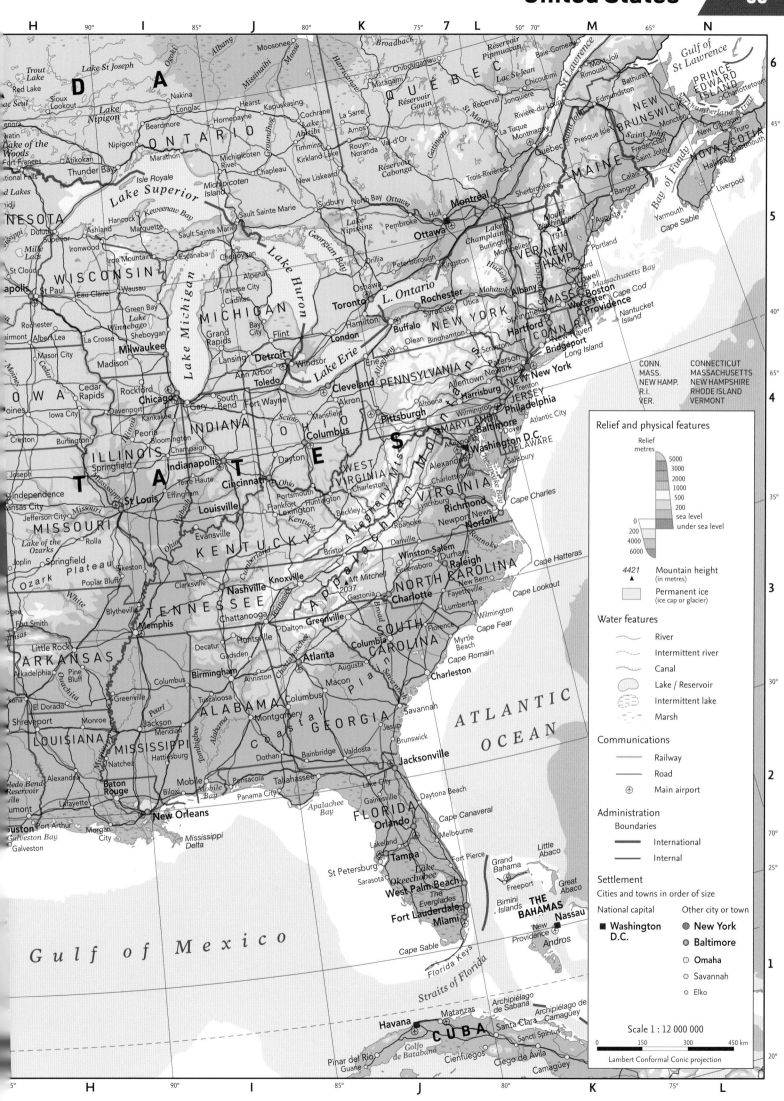

Relief and physical features

Relief
metres

5000
3000
2000
1000
500
200
0 sea level
under sea level
200
4000
6000

▲ 4421 Mountain height (in metres)

Permanent ice (ice cap or glacier)

Water features

~~~ River

Intermittent river

Canal

Lake / Reservoir

Intermittent lake

Marsh

Communications

Railway

Road

⊕ Main airport

Administration

Boundaries

International

Internal

Settlement

Cities and towns in order of size

National capital | Other city or town

■ Washington D.C. | ● New York
● Baltimore
○ Omaha
○ Savannah
○ Elko

Scale 1 : 12 000 000

0   150   300   450 km

Lambert Conformal Conic projection

United States Population

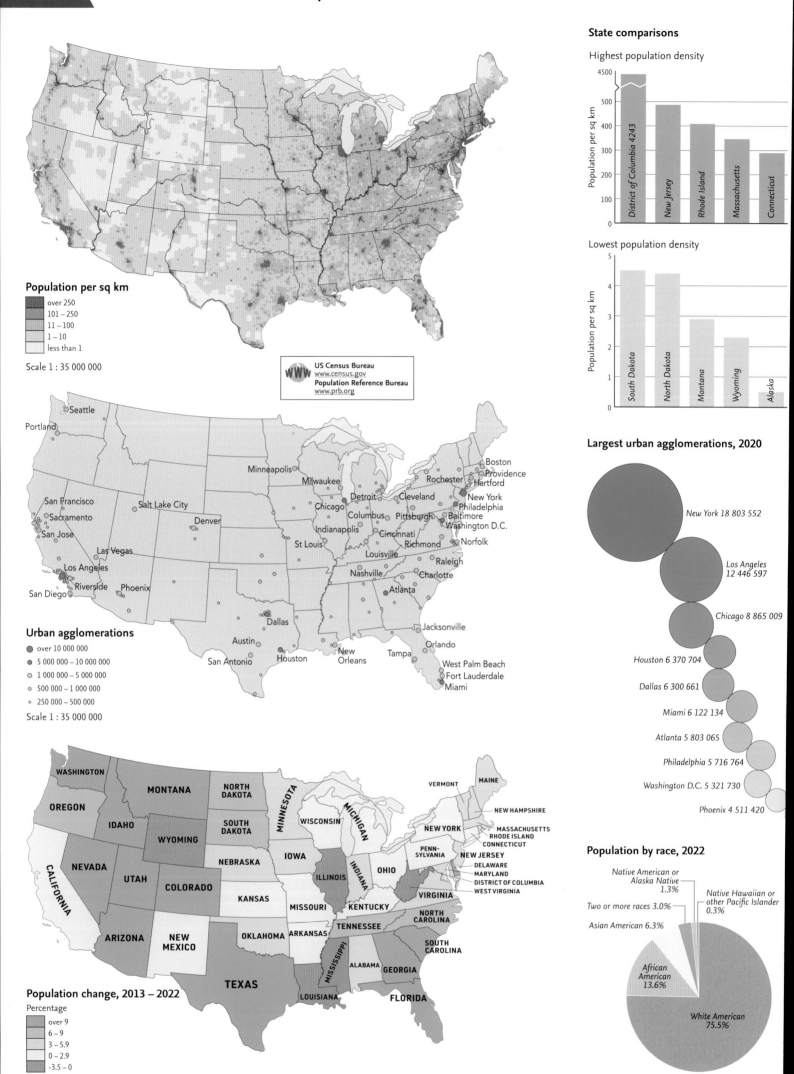

Population per sq km
- over 250
- 101 – 250
- 11 – 100
- 1 – 10
- less than 1

Scale 1 : 35 000 000

US Census Bureau
www.census.gov
Population Reference Bureau
www.prb.org

Urban agglomerations
- over 10 000 000
- 5 000 000 – 10 000 000
- 1 000 000 – 5 000 000
- 500 000 – 1 000 000
- 250 000 – 500 000

Scale 1 : 35 000 000

Population change, 2013 – 2022
Percentage
- over 9
- 6 – 9
- 3 – 5.9
- 0 – 2.9
- -3.5 – 0

Scale 1 : 35 000 000

State comparisons

Highest population density
Population per sq km

District of Columbia 4243, New Jersey, Rhode Island, Massachusetts, Connecticut

Lowest population density
Population per sq km

South Dakota, North Dakota, Montana, Wyoming, Alaska

Largest urban agglomerations, 2020

- New York 18 803 552
- Los Angeles 12 446 597
- Chicago 8 865 009
- Houston 6 370 704
- Dallas 6 300 661
- Miami 6 122 134
- Atlanta 5 803 065
- Philadelphia 5 716 764
- Washington D.C. 5 321 730
- Phoenix 4 511 420

Population by race, 2022

- White American 75.5%
- African American 13.6%
- Asian American 6.3%
- Two or more races 3.0%
- Native American or Alaska Native 1.3%
- Native Hawaiian or other Pacific Islander 0.3%

19.1% are Hispanic/Latino

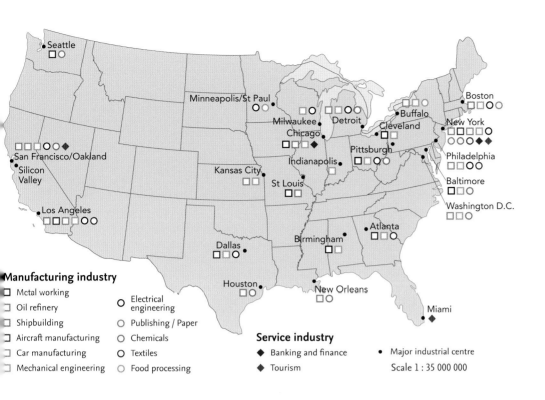

Manufacturing industry

- ☐ Metal working
- ☐ Oil refinery
- ☐ Shipbuilding
- ☐ Aircraft manufacturing
- ☐ Car manufacturing
- ☐ Mechanical engineering
- ◯ Electrical engineering
- ◯ Publishing / Paper
- ◯ Chemicals
- ◯ Textiles
- ◯ Food processing

Service industry

- ◆ Banking and finance
- ◆ Tourism
- • Major industrial centre

Scale 1 : 35 000 000

Manufacturing sales, 2011 – 2022

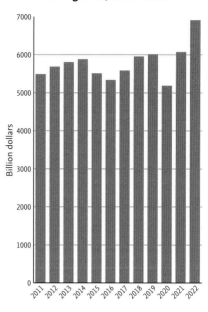

Billion dollars

Unemployment, 2008 – 2022

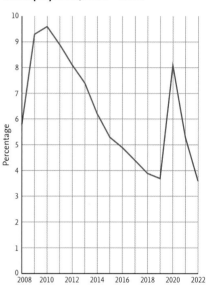

Percentage

Unemployment, 2023

Percentage
- 5 – 5.4
- 4 – 4.9
- 3 – 3.9
- 2.5 – 2.9
- 1.5 – 2.4

Scale 1 : 35 000 000

Main trading partners, 2022

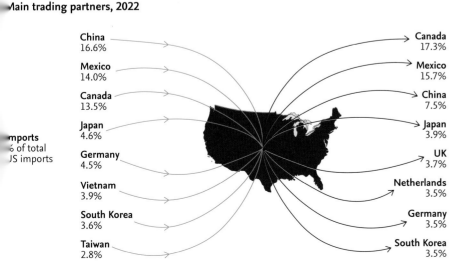

China 16.6%
Mexico 14.0%
Canada 13.5%
Japan 4.6%
Germany 4.5%
Vietnam 3.9%
South Korea 3.6%
Taiwan 2.8%

Imports
% of total
US imports

Canada 17.3%
Mexico 15.7%
China 7.5%
Japan 3.9%
UK 3.7%
Netherlands 3.5%
Germany 3.5%
South Korea 3.5%

Exports
% of total
US exports

Trade, 2022

Imports

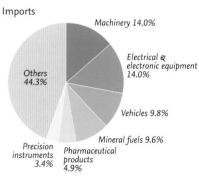

- Machinery 14.0%
- Electrical & electronic equipment 14.0%
- Vehicles 9.8%
- Mineral fuels 9.6%
- Pharmaceutical products 4.9%
- Precision instruments 3.4%
- Others 44.3%

Exports

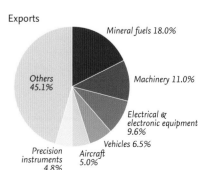

- Mineral fuels 18.0%
- Machinery 11.0%
- Electrical & electronic equipment 9.6%
- Vehicles 6.5%
- Aircraft 5.0%
- Precision instruments 4.8%
- Others 45.1%

ATLANTIC OCEAN

Dalton
Greenville
Florénce
Lumberton
Wilmington
Cape Fear
Atlanta
Columbia
Myrtle Beach
Augusta
SOUTH CAROLINA
Macon
Columbus
GEORGIA
Cape Romain
Charleston
Bainbridge
Valdosta
Brunswick
Savannah
Jesup
Tallahassee
Jacksonville
Lake City
Gainesville
Apalachee Bay
FLORIDA
Orlando
Daytona Beach
Lakeland
Melbourne
St Petersburg
Tampa
Fort Pierce
Sarasota
Lake Okeechobee
West Palm Beach
Fort Lauderdale
Cape Sable
Miami
Florida Keys
Straits of Florida

Bermuda (UK) Hamilton

ST LUCIA
Pointe du Cap
Gros Islet
Castries
Cap Marquis
Anse-la-Raye
Canaries
Dennery
Soufrière
Micoud
Choiseul
Laborie
Vieux Fort
Scale 1 : 2 000 000

BARBADOS
North Point
Speightstown
Holetown
Six Cross Roads
Bridgetown
Carlisle Bay
Oistins
South Point
The Crane
Scale 1 : 2 000 000

Scale 1 : 2 500 000
Chupara Point
Matelot
Galera Point
Diego Martin
VENEZUELA
Port of Spain
Tunapuna
Arima
Matura Bay
San Juan
Chaguanas
Caroni
Sangre Grande
Gulf of Paria
Couva
Tabaquite
Manzanilla Point
TRINIDAD AND TOBAGO
Trinidad
California
Cocos Bay
San Fernando
Rio Claro
Guatauaro Point
La Brea
Princes Town
Pierreville
Point Fortin
Penal
Ortoire
Mayaro Bay
Bonasse
Siparia
Galeota Point
Icacos Pt

Grand Bahama
Freeport
Great Abaco
Bimini Islands
Eleuthera
THE BAHAMAS
New Providence
Nassau
Cat Island
Andros
San Salvador
Exuma Cays
Rum Cay
Great Exuma

Tropic of Cancer

Havana
Matanzas
Archipiélago de Sabana
Crooked Island
Turks and Caicos Islands (UK)
Pinar del Río
CUBA
Santa Clara
Archipiélago de Camagüey
Acklins Island
Guane
Cienfuegos
Sancti Spíritus
Ciego de Ávila
Little Inagua Island
Cockburn Town
Turks Islands
Isla de la Juventud
Archipiélago de los Canarreos
Camagüey
Great Inagua
Archipiélago de los Jardines de la Reina
Las Tunas
Holguín
Baracoa
Hispaniola
Santiago
Golfo de Guacanayabo
Bayamo
Guantánamo
Port-de-Paix
Cap-Haïtien
1974
Sa Maestra
Santiago de Cuba
Gonaives
HAITI
Pico Duarte
Santo Domingo
San Juan
Virgin Is. (UK)
Anegada
Leeward Islands
Little Cayman
Cabo Cruz
Pico Turquino
3087
Mona Passage
Anguilla (UK)
Grand Cayman
Cayman Brac
Jérémie
Port-au-Prince
DOMINICAN REPUBLIC
Mayagüez
Ponce
Puerto Rico (US)
Virgin Is. (US)
Sint Maarten (Neth.)
St-Martin (Fr.)
St-Barthélemy (Fr.)
ANTIGUA AND BARBUDA
Cayman Islands (UK)
Montego Bay
Les Cayes
Jacmel
Isla Beata
Cabo Beata
Isla Mona
ST KITTS AND NEVIS
St John's
JAMAICA
Kingston
Isla Saona
Lesser Antilles
Montserrat (UK)
Basse-Terre
Guadeloupe (Fr.)
Marie-Galante
DOMINICA
Roseau
Martinique (Fr.)
Fort-de-France
Castries
ST LUCIA
Kingstown
Bridgetown
ST VINCENT AND THE GRENADINES
BARBADOS
GRENADA
St George's
Tobago

Laguna de Caratasca
Cayos Miskitos
Isla de Providencia (Colombia)
Aruba (Neth.)
Curaçao (Neth.)
Bonaire (Neth.)
Isla Blanquilla (Ven.)
Isla Orchila (Ven.)
TRINIDAD & TOBAGO
Coco
Rio Isabela
Isla de San Andrés (Colombia)
Punta Gallinas
Punto Fijo
Isla La Tortuga
Pen. de Paria
Port of Spain
Rio Grande
Punta de Perlas
Riohacha
Golfo de Venezuela
Coro
Güiria
NICARAGUA
Maicao
Maiquetía
Cumana
Punta Gorda
Barranquilla
Santa Marta
Maracaibo
Barquisimeto
Caracas
Barcelona
Maturín
Lake Nicaragua
Cartagena
Valledupar
Cabimas
Valencia
Maracay
San Juan
COSTA RICA
San José
Golfo de Morrosquillo
Lake Maracaibo
Acarigua
Valle de la Pascua
El Tigre
Cerro Chirripó
Sincelejo
Valera
Guanare
San Fernando de Apure
Ciudad Guayana
Bahía de Coronado
3818
Montería
Mérida
Barinas
Ciudad Bolívar
El Callao
Península de Osa
PANAMA
Panama City
Turbo
Pico Bolívar
4978
Orinoco
Embalse de Guri
Golfo de Chiriquí
David
Aguadulce
La Palma
Cúcuta
San Cristóbal
VENEZUELA
La Paragua
Punta Mala
Bucaramanga
Meta
Guiana Highlands
Golfo de Cupica
Medellín
Sierra Nevada del Cocuy
5120
Cerro Yaví
2285
La Gran Sabana
Quibdó
Tunja
Meta
Pakaraima Mountains
Manizales
Pereira
Bogotá
Sa Parima
Armenia
Ibagué
Villavicencio
Buenaventura
Guaviare
Orinoco
Cali
Neiva
COLOMBIA
BRAZIL
Palmira
Tumaco
Pico da Neblina
2995
Florencia
Equator

Caribbean Sea

Cross-section

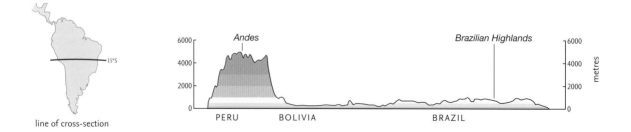

line of cross-section

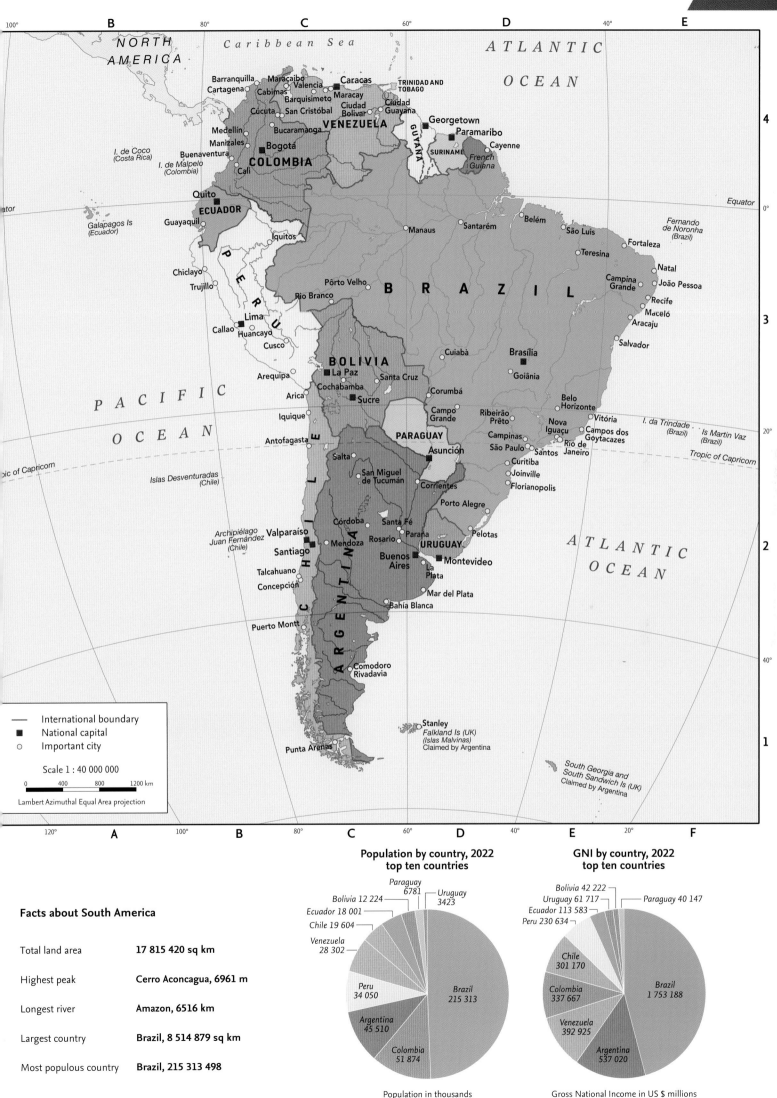

Facts about South America

Total land area	**17 815 420 sq km**
Highest peak	**Cerro Aconcagua, 6961 m**
Longest river	**Amazon, 6516 km**
Largest country	**Brazil, 8 514 879 sq km**
Most populous country	**Brazil, 215 313 498**

**Population by country, 2022
top ten countries**

Paraguay 6781
Uruguay 3423
Bolivia 12 224
Ecuador 18 001
Chile 19 604
Venezuela 28 302
Peru 34 050
Argentina 45 510
Colombia 51 874
Brazil 215 313

Population in thousands

**GNI by country, 2022
top ten countries**

Bolivia 42 222
Uruguay 61 717
Ecuador 113 583
Peru 230 634
Paraguay 40 147
Chile 301 170
Colombia 337 667
Venezuela 392 925
Argentina 537 020
Brazil 1 753 188

Gross National Income in US $ millions

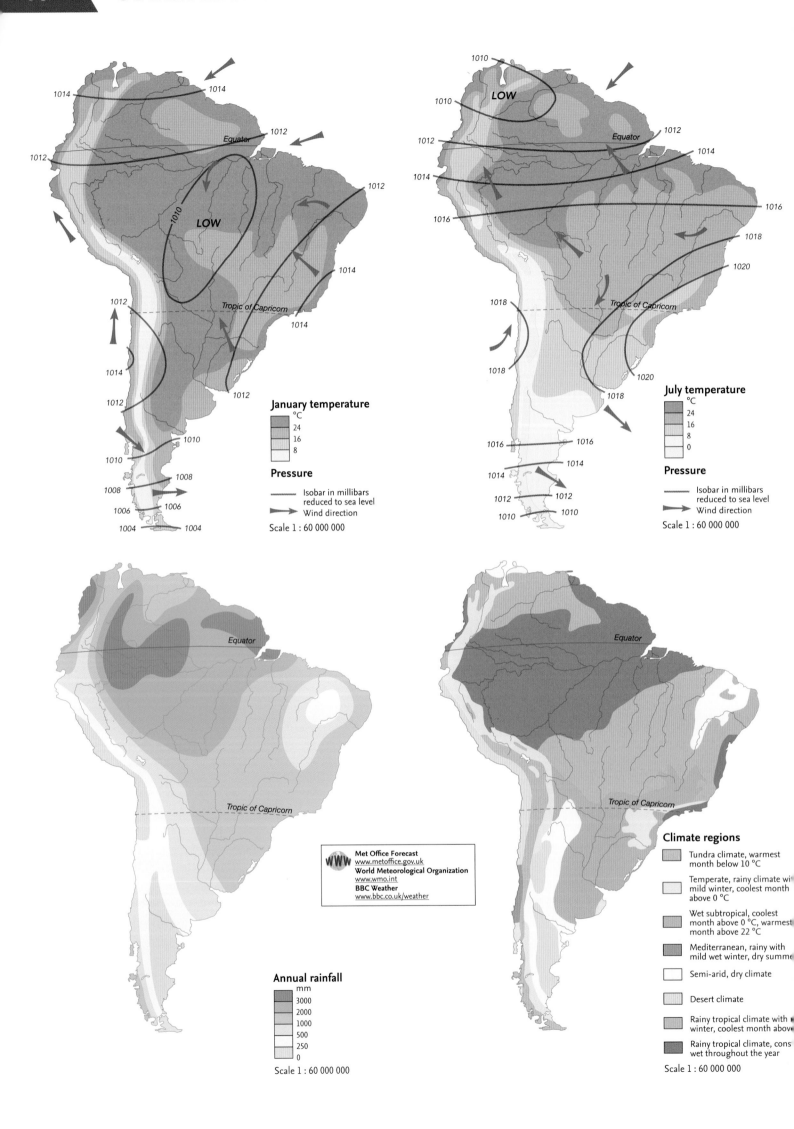

January temperature
°C
24
16
8

Pressure

——— Isobar in millibars
reduced to sea level

➤ Wind direction

Scale 1 : 60 000 000

July temperature
°C
24
16
8
0

Pressure

——— Isobar in millibars
reduced to sea level

➤ Wind direction

Scale 1 : 60 000 000

WWW Met Office Forecast
www.metoffice.gov.uk
World Meteorological Organization
www.wmo.int
BBC Weather
www.bbc.co.uk/weather

Annual rainfall
mm
3000
2000
1000
500
250
0

Scale 1 : 60 000 000

Climate regions

Tundra climate, warmest
month below 10 °C

Temperate, rainy climate wit
mild winter, coolest month
above 0 °C

Wet subtropical, coolest
month above 0 °C, warmest
month above 22 °C

Mediterranean, rainy with
mild wet winter, dry summe

Semi-arid, dry climate

Desert climate

Rainy tropical climate with
winter, coolest month above

Rainy tropical climate, cons
wet throughout the year

Scale 1 : 60 000 000

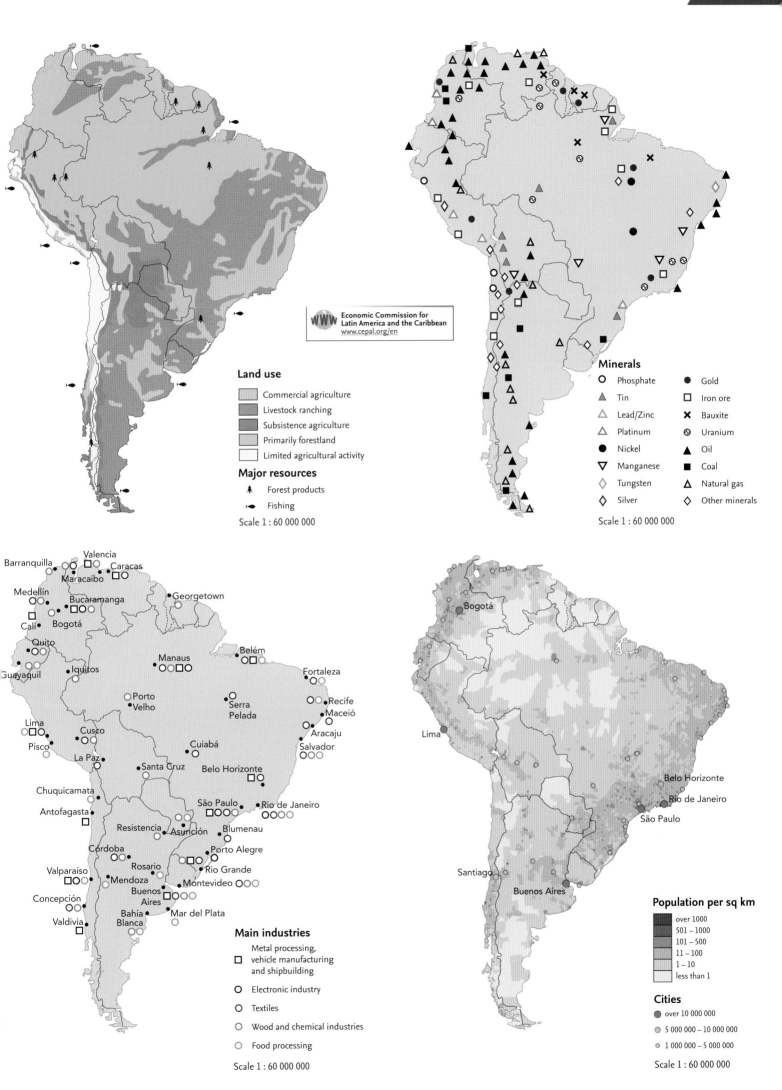

Economic Commission for Latin America and the Caribbean
www.cepal.org/en

Land use

- Commercial agriculture
- Livestock ranching
- Subsistence agriculture
- Primarily forestland
- Limited agricultural activity

Major resources

- ♣ Forest products
- ⊷ Fishing

Scale 1 : 60 000 000

Minerals

○ Phosphate	● Gold
▲ Tin	□ Iron ore
△ Lead/Zinc	✕ Bauxite
△ Platinum	⊗ Uranium
● Nickel	▲ Oil
▽ Manganese	■ Coal
◇ Tungsten	△ Natural gas
◇ Silver	◇ Other minerals

Scale 1 : 60 000 000

Main industries

- ▢ Metal processing, vehicle manufacturing and shipbuilding
- ○ Electronic industry
- ○ Textiles
- ○ Wood and chemical industries
- ○ Food processing

Scale 1 : 60 000 000

Barranquilla
Valencia
Caracas
Maracaibo
Medellín
Bucaramanga
Georgetown
Cali
Bogotá
Quito
Guayaquil
Iquitos
Belém
Manaus
Porto Velho
Fortaleza
Serra Pelada
Recife
Maceió
Lima
Cusco
Aracaju
Pisco
La Paz
Cuiabá
Salvador
Santa Cruz
Belo Horizonte
Chuquicamata
São Paulo
Rio de Janeiro
Antofagasta
Resistencia
Asunción
Blumenau
Córdoba
Porto Alegre
Valparaíso
Rosario
Rio Grande
Mendoza
Montevideo
Concepción
Buenos Aires
Mar del Plata
Valdivia
Bahía Blanca

Population per sq km

- over 1000
- 501 – 1000
- 101 – 500
- 11 – 100
- 1 – 10
- less than 1

Cities

- ● over 10 000 000
- ● 5 000 000 – 10 000 000
- ○ 1 000 000 – 5 000 000

Scale 1 : 60 000 000

Bogotá
Lima
Belo Horizonte
Rio de Janeiro
São Paulo
Santiago
Buenos Aires

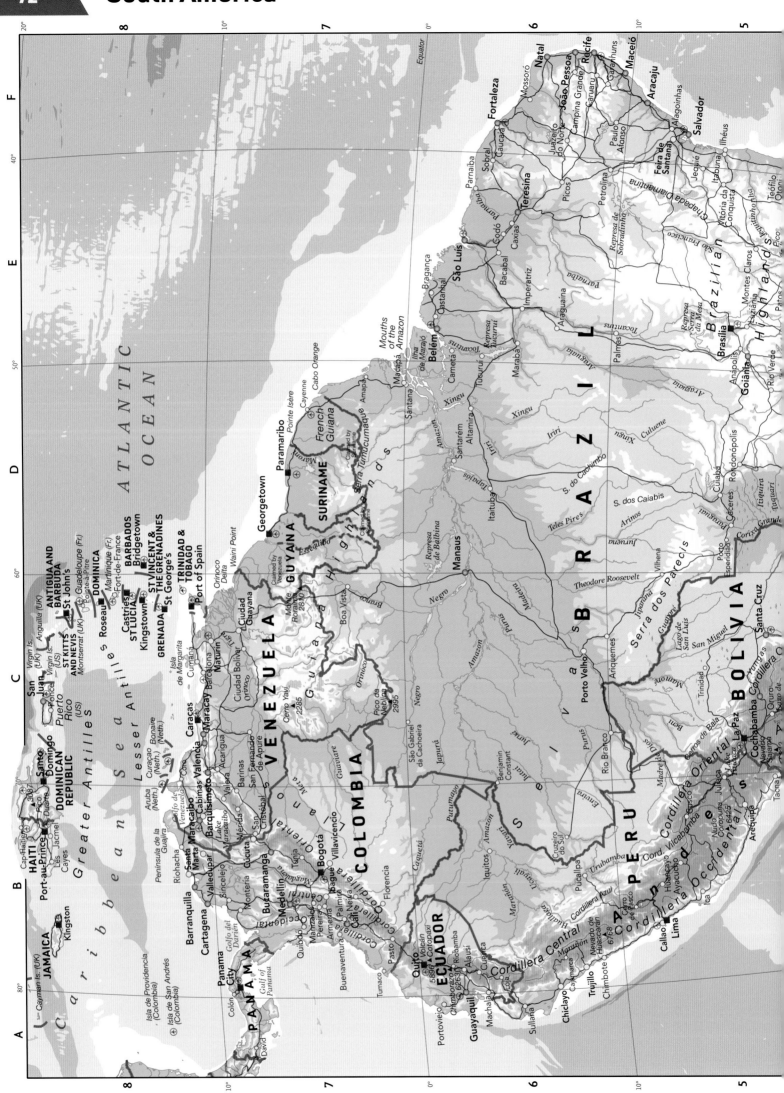

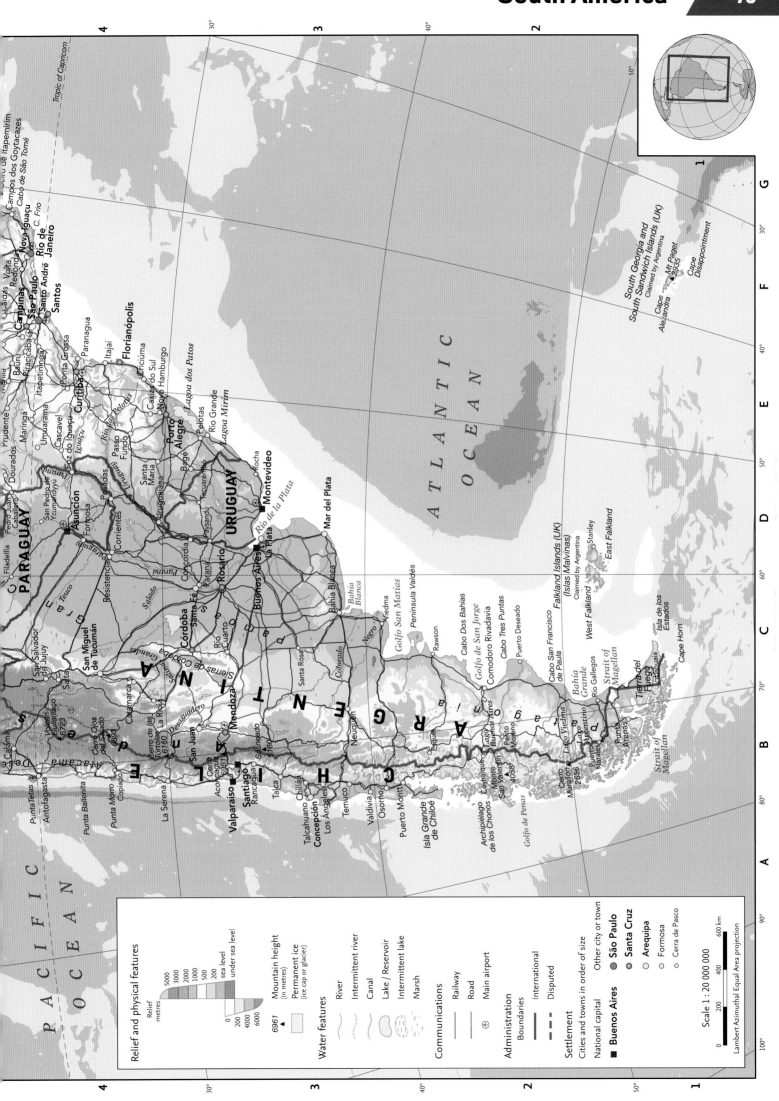

PACIFIC OCEAN

ATLANTIC OCEAN

PARAGUAY

URUGUAY

ARGENTINA

CHILE

São Paulo
Santos
Campinas
Rio de Janeiro
Nova Iguaçu
Santo André
Curitiba
Florianópolis
Porto Alegre
Montevideo
Mar del Plata
Buenos Aires
La Plata
Rosario
Santa Fé
Córdoba
San Miguel de Tucumán
Mendoza
Santiago
Valparaíso
Rancagua
Concepción
Asunción
Corrientes
Resistencia
Salta

Cerro Aconcagua 6961
Ojos del Salado 6893
Llullaillaco 6723

Bahía Blanca
Santa Rosa
Neuquén
Viedma
Rawson
Comodoro Rivadavia
Puerto Deseado
Río Gallegos
Punta Arenas
Puerto Natales
Ushuaia

Golfo San Matías
Península Valdés
Golfo de San Jorge
Cabo Dos Bahías
Cabo Tres Puntas
Cabo San Francisco de Paula
Bahía Grande
Strait of Magellan
Tierra del Fuego
Isla de los Estados
Cape Horn

Falkland Islands (UK)
(Islas Malvinas)
Claimed by Argentina
West Falkland
East Falkland
Stanley

South Georgia and
South Sandwich Islands (UK)
Claimed by Argentina
Cape Alexandra
Mt Paget 2935
Cape Disappointment

Lago Argentino
Lago Buenos Aires
Lago Viedma
Cerro San Valentín 4058
Monte San Valentín
Cerro Murallón 2656

Archipiélago de los Chonos
Golfo de Penas
Isla Grande de Chiloé
Puerto Montt
Osorno
Valdivia
Temuco
Los Ángeles
Talcahuano
Chillán
Talca
San Juan

Relief and physical features

	Relief metres
	5000
	3000
	2000
	1000
	500
	200
	sea level
	under sea level
	200
	4000
	6000

▲ 6961   Mountain height (in metres)

Permanent ice (ice cap or glacier)

Water features

〰 River
〰 Intermittent river
Canal
Lake / Reservoir
Intermittent lake
Marsh

Communications

—— Railway
—— Road
⊕ Main airport

Administration

Boundaries
—— International
‒ ‒ ‒ Disputed

Settlement

National capital
■ **Buenos Aires**   Other city or town
● **São Paulo**
● Santa Cruz
○ **Arequipa**
○ Formosa
○ Cerro de Pasco

Cities and towns in order of size

Scale 1 : 20 000 000

| 0 | 200 | 400 | 600 km |

Lambert Azimuthal Equal Area projection

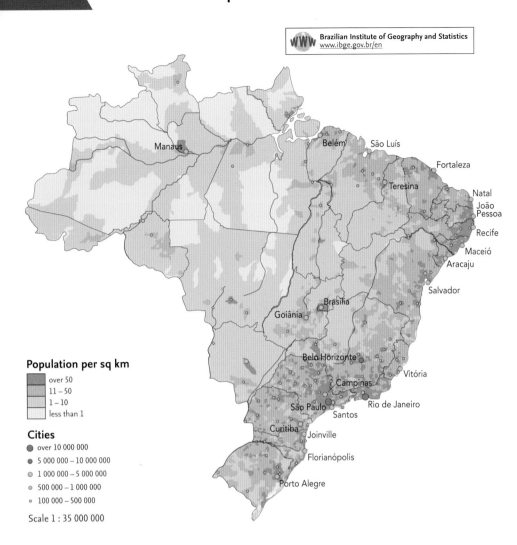

www Brazilian Institute of Geography and Statistics
www.ibge.gov.br/en

Population per sq km

- over 50
- 11 – 50
- 1 – 10
- less than 1

Cities

- over 10 000 000
- 5 000 000 – 10 000 000
- 1 000 000 – 5 000 000
- 500 000 – 1 000 000
- 100 000 – 500 000

Scale 1 : 35 000 000

Population growth, 2000 – 2060

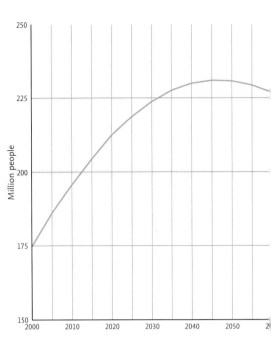

Urban and rural population, 1940 – 2022

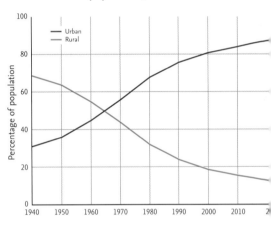

Largest urban agglomerations, 2020

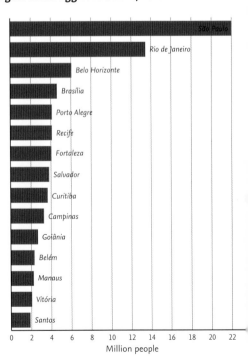

Metropolitan region density

Population per sq. km

- over 5000
- 2000 – 5000
- 1000 – 2500
- less than 1000
- Future area of metropolitan expansion

Scale 1 : 35 000 000

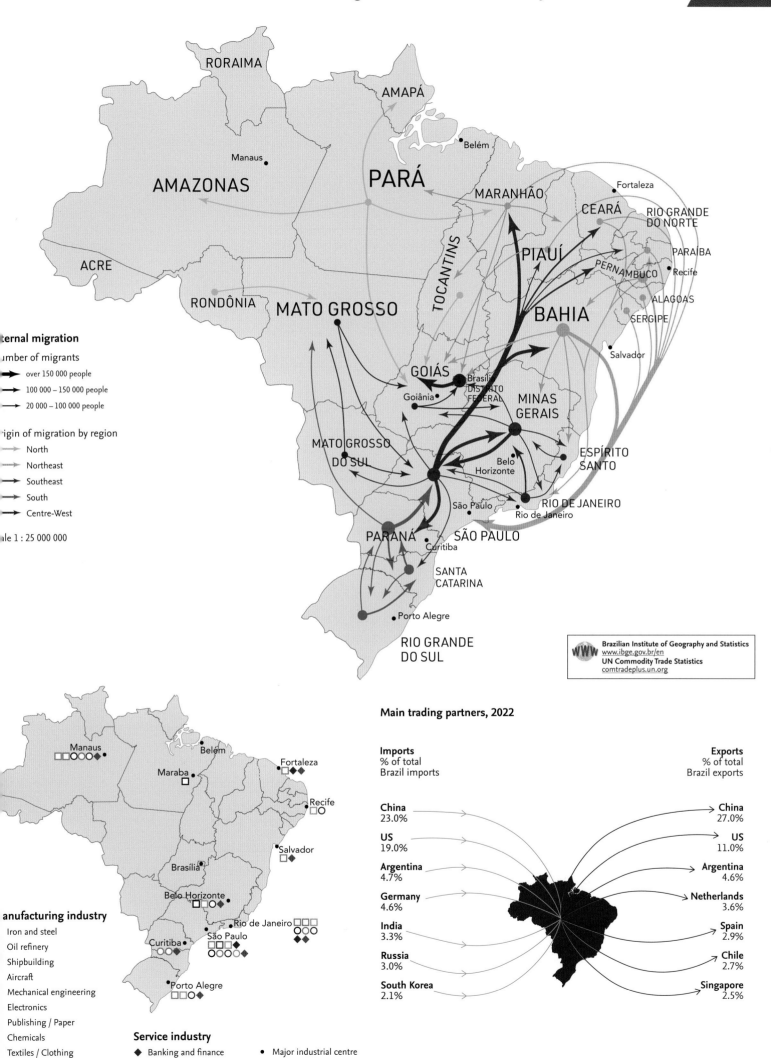

RORAIMA

AMAPÁ

• Belém

Manaus •

AMAZONAS

PARÁ

MARANHÃO

Fortaleza •

CEARÁ

RIO GRANDE
DO NORTE

PARAÍBA

• Recife

PERNAMBUCO

ALAGOAS

SERGIPE

PIAUÍ

ACRE

RONDÔNIA

MATO GROSSO

TOCANTINS

BAHIA

• Salvador

GOIÁS

Goiânia •

Brasília
DISTRITO
FEDERAL

MINAS
GERAIS

ESPÍRITO
SANTO

MATO GROSSO
DO SUL

Belo
Horizonte •

RIO DE JANEIRO

São Paulo •

Rio de Janeiro •

PARANÁ

SÃO PAULO

Curitiba •

SANTA
CATARINA

• Porto Alegre

RIO GRANDE
DO SUL

Internal migration

Number of migrants

over 150 000 people

100 000 – 150 000 people

20 000 – 100 000 people

Origin of migration by region

North

Northeast

Southeast

South

Centre-West

Scale 1 : 25 000 000

WWW **Brazilian Institute of Geography and Statistics**
www.ibge.gov.br/en
UN Commodity Trade Statistics
comtradeplus.un.org

Manufacturing industry

Iron and steel

Oil refinery

Shipbuilding

Aircraft

Mechanical engineering

Electronics

Publishing / Paper

Chemicals

Textiles / Clothing

Food processing

Service industry

◆ Banking and finance

◆ Tourism

• Major industrial centre

Scale 1 : 50 000 000

Manaus

Belém

Fortaleza

Marabá

Recife

Salvador

Brasília

Belo Horizonte

Rio de Janeiro

São Paulo

Curitiba

Porto Alegre

Main trading partners, 2022

Imports % of total Brazil imports		**Exports** % of total Brazil exports
China 23.0%		**China** 27.0%
US 19.0%		**US** 11.0%
Argentina 4.7%		**Argentina** 4.6%
Germany 4.6%		**Netherlands** 3.6%
India 3.3%		**Spain** 2.9%
Russia 3.0%		**Chile** 2.7%
South Korea 2.1%		**Singapore** 2.5%

Part of the Amazon rainforest in Rhôndonia, Brazil. The straight lines in the forest show where whole blocks of trees have been cut down.

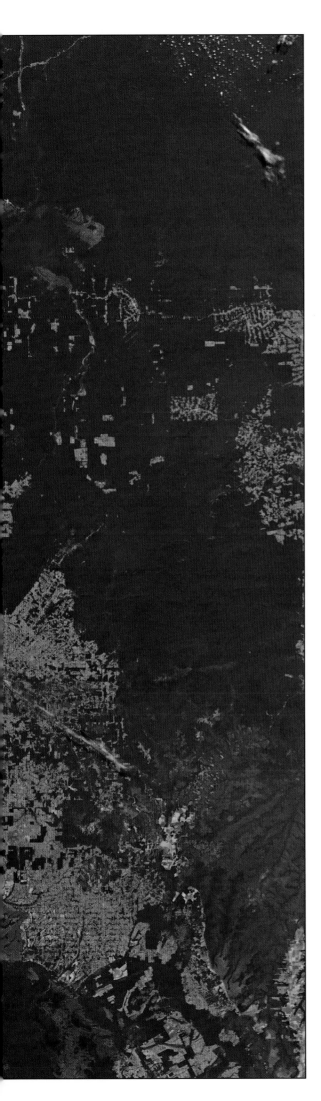

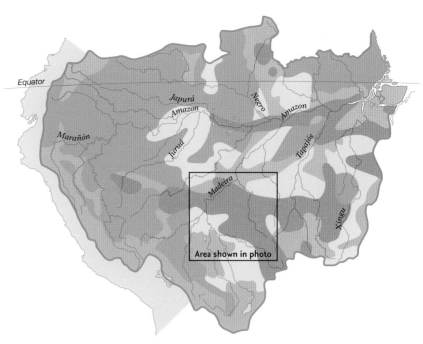

State of the Amazon rainforest

Rainforest

- Deforested by 2009
- High threat of deforestation
- Medium threat of deforestation
- Low threat of deforestation

Other vegetation

- Grassland or woodland
- No data
- ——— Boundary of Amazon Basin rainforest

Scale 1 : 35 000 000

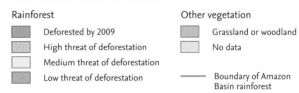

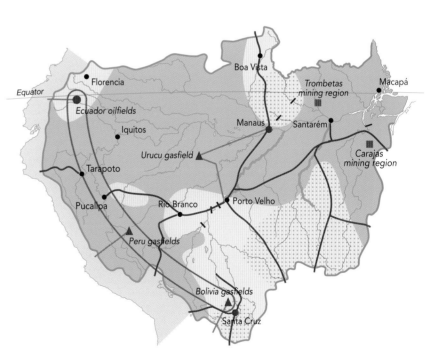

Threats to the Amazon rainforest

Extractive industry

- ● Oilfield
- ▲ Gasfield
- ▦ Mining region

- ——— Main highway
- —I— Major dam
- ——— Industrial waterway
- ——— Pipeline
- ——— Boundary of Western Amazon zone of oil and gas development

Main population centres

- ● over 1 000 000
- ● 100 000 – 500 000

Area of agricultural expansion

- Pasture for extensive cattle ranching
- Extensive cropping: for stock feed (soybeans, sorghum, maize), industrial crops (oil palm, sunflower, cotton) and biofuels (sugar cane, maize)

Scale 1 : 35 000 000

A
- 20°
- Tropic of Cancer
- Cape Verde
  - Santo Antão
  - Boa Vista
  - Fogo
  - Santiago
- Gambia

Madeira

Canary Islands

Jebel Toubkal ▲4167 Atlas Mountains

El Djouf

Sénégal

Niger

Bani

White Volta

Black Volta

Fouta Djallon

S a h e l

Lake Volta

Cape Palmas

Bight of Benin

Gulf of Guinea

Príncipe

São Tomé

Bioko

S a h a r a

Ahaggar
Mont Tahat ▲ 2918

Mt Gréboun ▲ 1944 Massif de l'Aïr

Plateau du Djado

Bodélé

Lake Chad

Chari

Jos Plateau

Benue

Niger

Cameroon Highlands
Mont Cameroun ▲ 4095

Mediterranean Sea

EUROPE

Gulf of Gabès

Gulf of Sirte

T i b e s t i
Emi Koussi ▲ 3415

Qattara Depression

Libyan Desert

Nile

Lake Nasser

Suez Canal
Sinai

Nubian Desert

Darfur
Jebel Marra ▲ 3088

Sudd

Uele

Ubangi

Sangha

Congo

Aruwimi

Lomani

Congo Basin

Lake Albert

Lake Edward

Mount Stanley ▲ 5109

Lake Victoria

Mount Kenya ▲ 5199

Kilimanjaro ▲ 5895

Masai Steppe

Blue Nile

Atbara

White Nile

Gezira

Ras Dejen ▲ 4550
Lake Tana

Ethiopian Highlands

Denakil

Gulf of Aden

Webi Shabeelle

Red Sea

ASIA

Tropic of Cancer

ATLANTIC OCEAN

Ascension

St Helena

Equator

Congo

Kasai

Kwilu

Cuango

Cuanza

Bié Plateau

Huíla Plateau

Cunene

Lake Tanganyika

Lake Mweru

Luapula

Chaîne des Mitumba

Muchinga Mts

Luangwa

Great Rift Valley

Rufiji

Lake Nyasa

INDIAN OCEAN

Pemba Island

Zanzibar Island

Mafia Island

Comoro Islands

Aldabra Islands

Namib Desert

Orange

Etosha Pan

Cubango

Zambezi

Victoria Falls

Makgadikgadi

Kalahari Desert

Lake Kariba

Zambezi

Matabele Upland

Save

Limpopo

Madagascar

Réunion

Tropic of Capricorn

Mozambique Channel

Vaal

Great Karoo

Drakensberg
Thabana Ntlenyana ▲ 3482

Cape of Good Hope

Cape Agulhas

Relief and physical features

Relief metres

| 5000 |
| 3000 |
| 2000 |
| 1000 |
| 500 |
| 200 |
| 0 sea level |
| under sea level |
| 200 |
| 4000 |
| 6000 |

5895 ▲ Mountain height (in metres)

Scale 1 : 42 000 000

0   500   1000 km

Lambert Azimuthal Equal Area projection

Cross-section

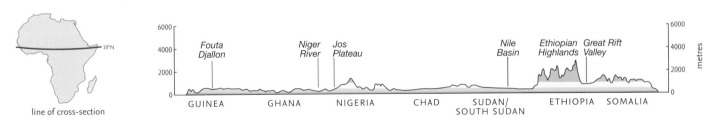

line of cross-section

10°N

| Fouta Djallon | Niger River | Jos Plateau | | Nile Basin | Ethiopian Highlands | Great Rift Valley |

6000 — 4000 — 2000 — 0

GUINEA   GHANA   NIGERIA   CHAD   SUDAN/SOUTH SUDAN   ETHIOPIA   SOMALIA

metres 6000 — 4000 — 2000 — 0

Legend

- International boundary
- ■ National capital
- ○ Important city

1 THE GAMBIA
2 GUINEA-BISSAU
3 TOGO
4 EQUATORIAL GUINEA
5 SÃO TOMÉ & PRÍNCIPE
6 RWANDA
7 BURUNDI

Scale 1 : 42 000 000

0   500   1000 km

Lambert Azimuthal Equal Area projection

Facts about Africa

Total land area	**30 343 578 sq km**
Highest peak	**Kilimanjaro, 5895 m**
Longest river	**Nile, 6695 km**
Largest country	**Algeria, 2 381 741 sq km**
Most populous country	**Nigeria, 218 541 212**

Population by country, 2022 top ten countries

- Algeria 44 903
- Sudan 46 874
- Uganda 47 250
- Kenya 54 027
- South Africa 59 894
- Tanzania 65 498
- Dem. Rep. Congo 99 010
- Egypt 110 990
- Ethiopia 123 380
- Nigeria 218 541

Population in thousands

GNI by country, 2022 top ten countries

- Tanzania 75 940
- Côte d'Ivoire 73 645
- Ghana 78 658
- Kenya 117 313
- Ethiopia 126 126
- Morocco 141 068
- Algeria 175 187
- South Africa 406 307
- Egypt 455 137
- Nigeria 468 653

Gross National Income in US $ millions

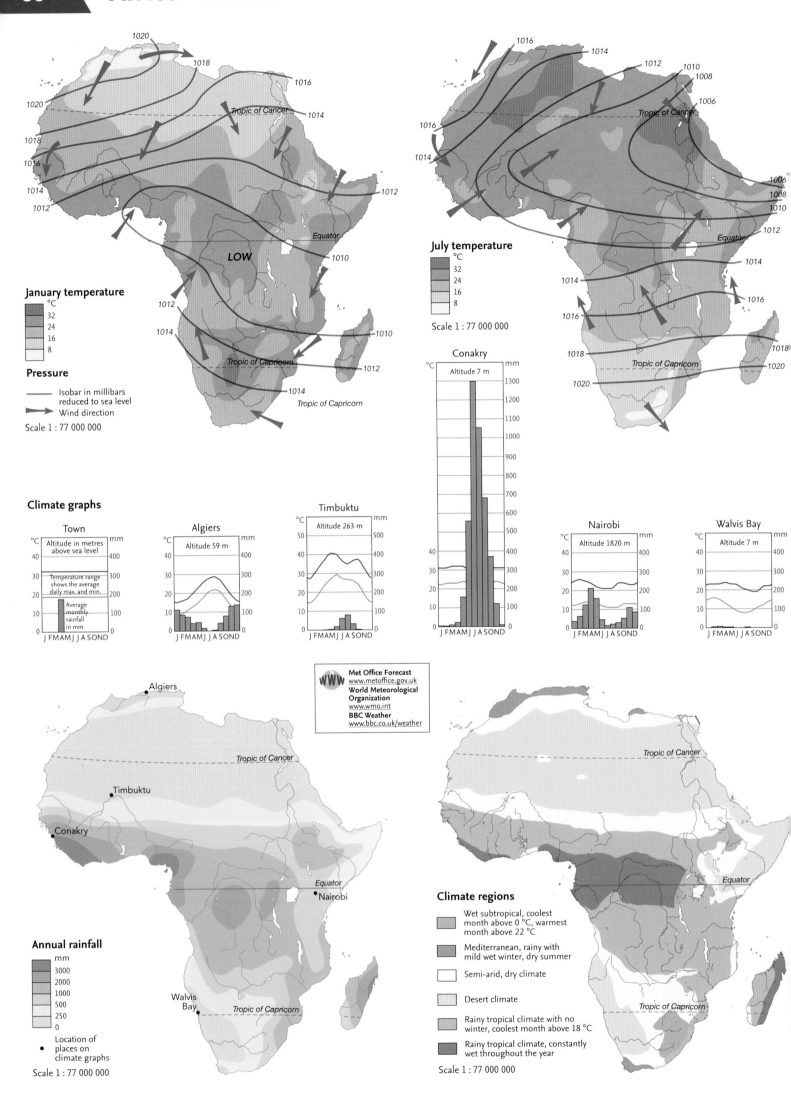

January temperature
°C
32
24
16
8

Pressure
Isobar in millibars reduced to sea level
Wind direction
Scale 1 : 77 000 000

July temperature
°C
32
24
16
8
Scale 1 : 77 000 000

Climate graphs

Town
°C   mm
40   Altitude in metres   400
     above sea level
30   Temperature range   300
     shows the average
     daily max. and min.
20   200
10   Average   100
     monthly
     rainfall
     in mm
0 J FMAMJ J A SOND   0

Algiers
Altitude 59 m

Timbuktu
Altitude 263 m

Conakry
Altitude 7 m

Nairobi
Altitude 1820 m

Walvis Bay
Altitude 7 m

Met Office Forecast
www.metoffice.gov.uk
World Meteorological
Organization
www.wmo.int
BBC Weather
www.bbc.co.uk/weather

Annual rainfall
mm
3000
2000
1000
500
250
0
● Location of places on climate graphs
Scale 1 : 77 000 000

Climate regions
Wet subtropical, coolest month above 0 °C, warmest month above 22 °C

Mediterranean, rainy with mild wet winter, dry summer

Semi-arid, dry climate

Desert climate

Rainy tropical climate with no winter, coolest month above 18 °C

Rainy tropical climate, constantly wet throughout the year

Scale 1 : 77 000 000

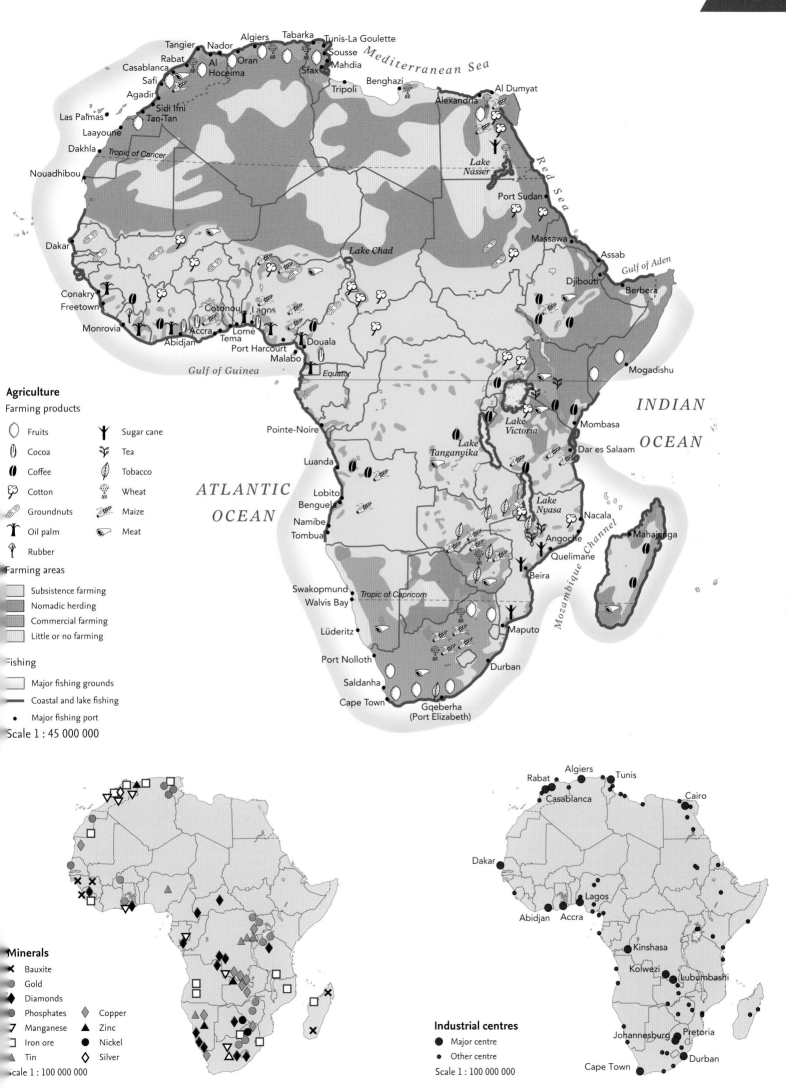

Mediterranean Sea

Tangier
Algiers
Tabarka
Tunis-La Goulette
Nador
Sousse
Rabat
Oran
Mahdia
Casablanca
Al Hoceima
Sfax
Safi
Tripoli
Benghazi
Agadir
Al Dumyat
Sidi Ifni
Alexandria
Las Palmas
Tan-Tan
Laayoune
Tropic of Cancer
Dakhla
Lake Nasser
Nouadhibou
Port Sudan
Massawa
Dakar
Assab
Gulf of Aden
Conakry
Djibouti
Freetown
Berbera
Monrovia
Mogadishu
Abidjan
Cotonou
Lagos
Accra
Lome
Tema
Port Harcourt
Douala
Malabo
Equator
Gulf of Guinea

Agriculture

Farming products

Fruits   Sugar cane
Cocoa   Tea
Coffee   Tobacco
Cotton   Wheat
Groundnuts   Maize
Oil palm   Meat
Rubber

Farming areas

Subsistence farming
Nomadic herding
Commercial farming
Little or no farming

Fishing

Major fishing grounds
Coastal and lake fishing
Major fishing port

Scale 1 : 45 000 000

Pointe-Noire
Luanda
ATLANTIC OCEAN
Lobito
Benguela
Namibe
Tombua
Swakopmund
Walvis Bay
Lüderitz
Port Nolloth
Saldanha
Cape Town
Gqeberha (Port Elizabeth)

Lake Tanganyika
Lake Victoria
Mombasa
Dar es Salaam
INDIAN OCEAN
Lake Nyasa
Nacala
Angoche
Quelimane
Beira
Tropic of Capricorn
Maputo
Durban
Mozambique Channel
Mahajanga

Minerals

Bauxite
Gold
Diamonds
Phosphates   Copper
Manganese   Zinc
Iron ore   Nickel
Tin   Silver

Scale 1 : 100 000 000

Industrial centres

Major centre
Other centre

Scale 1 : 100 000 000

Rabat
Algiers
Tunis
Casablanca
Cairo
Dakar
Lagos
Abidjan
Accra
Kinshasa
Kolwezi
Lubumbashi
Johannesburg
Pretoria
Cape Town
Durban

Africa Population and Wealth

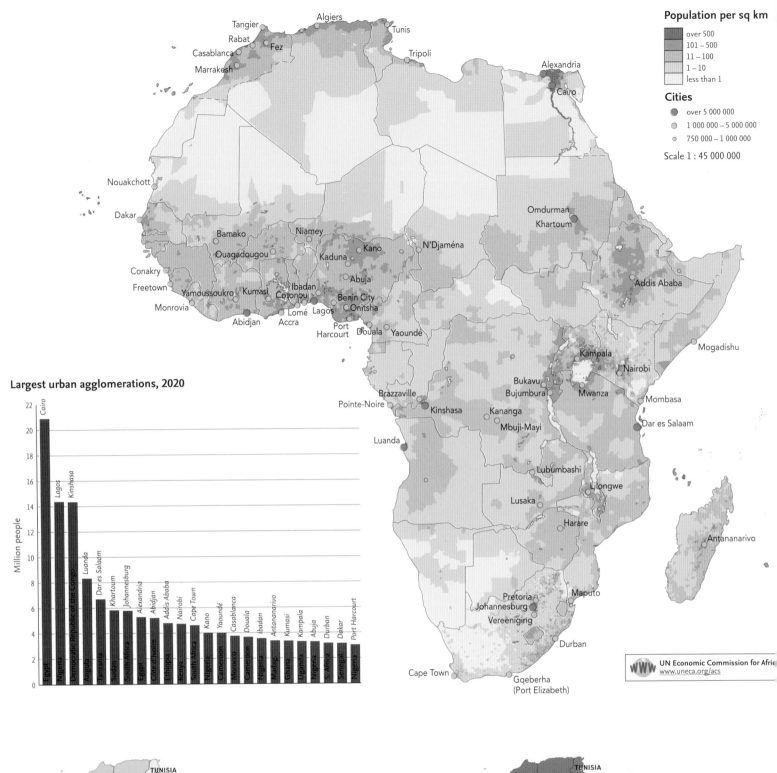

Population per sq km
- over 500
- 101 – 500
- 11 – 100
- 1 – 10
- less than 1

Cities
- over 5 000 000
- 1 000 000 – 5 000 000
- 750 000 – 1 000 000

Scale 1 : 45 000 000

UN Economic Commission for Africa
www.uneca.org/acs

Largest urban agglomerations, 2020

Million people (y-axis from 0 to 22)

Cities (left to right): Cairo (Egypt), Lagos (Nigeria), Kinshasa (Democratic Republic of the Congo), Luanda (Angola), Dar es Salaam (Tanzania), Khartoum (Sudan), Johannesburg (South Africa), Alexandria (Egypt), Abidjan (Côte d'Ivoire), Addis Ababa (Ethiopia), Nairobi (Kenya), Cape Town (South Africa), Kano (Nigeria), Yaoundé (Cameroon), Casablanca (Morocco), Douala (Cameroon), Ibadan (Nigeria), Antananarivo (Madag.), Kumasi (Ghana), Kampala (Uganda), Abuja (Nigeria), Durban (S. Africa), Dakar (Senegal), Port Harcourt (Nigeria)

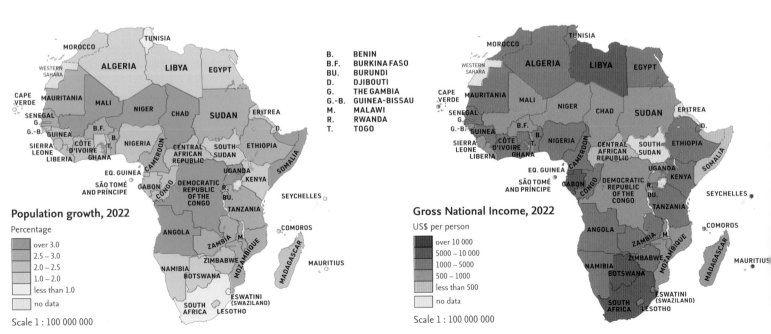

B. BENIN
B.F. BURKINA FASO
BU. BURUNDI
D. DJIBOUTI
G. THE GAMBIA
G.-B. GUINEA-BISSAU
M. MALAWI
R. RWANDA
T. TOGO

Population growth, 2022

Percentage
- over 3.0
- 2.5 – 3.0
- 2.0 – 2.5
- 1.0 – 2.0
- less than 1.0
- no data

Scale 1 : 100 000 000

Gross National Income, 2022

US$ per person
- over 10 000
- 5000 – 10 000
- 1000 – 5000
- 500 – 1000
- less than 500
- no data

Scale 1 : 100 000 000

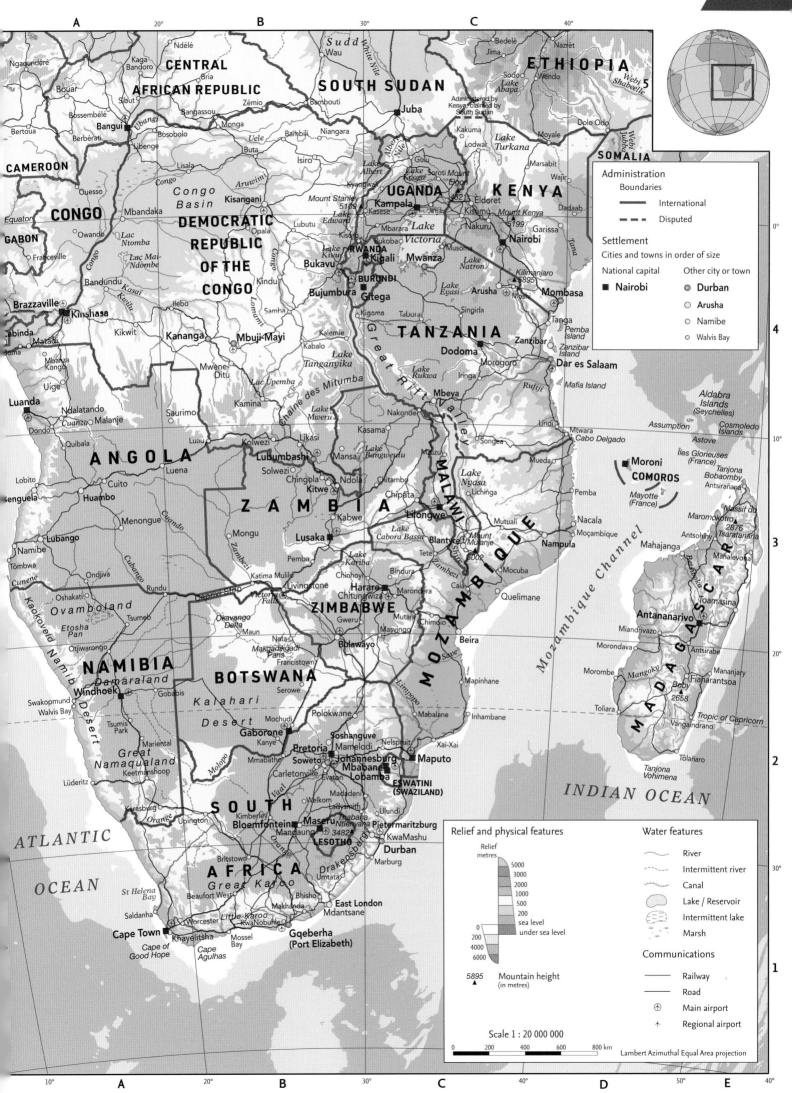

Administration

Boundaries

——— International

– – – Disputed

Settlement

Cities and towns in order of size

National capital | Other city or town
■ Nairobi | ● Durban
 | ○ Arusha
 | ○ Namibe
 | ○ Walvis Bay

Relief and physical features

Relief metres

5000
3000
2000
1000
500
200
sea level
0
under sea level
200
4000
6000

▲ 5895 Mountain height (in metres)

Water features

～～ River

- - - Intermittent river

～～ Canal

Lake / Reservoir

Intermittent lake

Marsh

Communications

——— Railway

——— Road

⊕ Main airport

✈ Regional airport

Scale 1 : 20 000 000

0   200   400   600   800 km

Lambert Azimuthal Equal Area projection

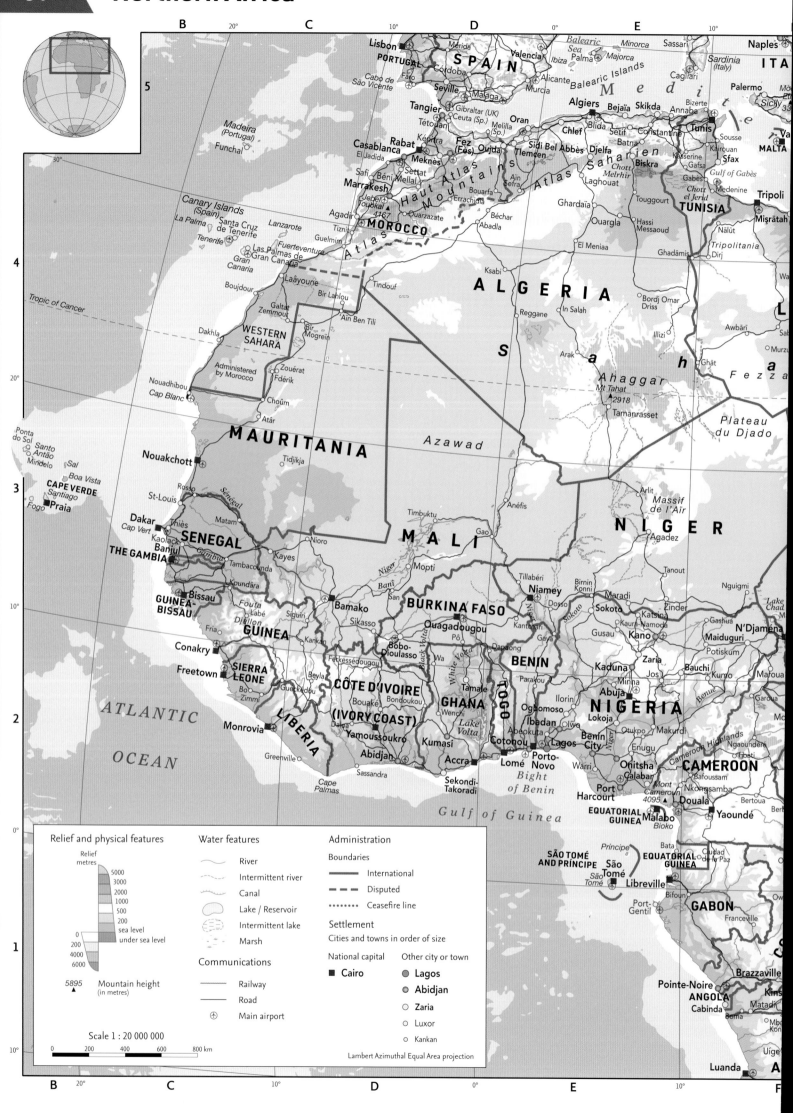

Relief and physical features

Relief
metres

5000
3000
2000
1000
500
200
sea level
0
under sea level
200
4000
6000

5895 △ Mountain height
(in metres)

Scale 1 : 20 000 000

0   200   400   600   800 km

Water features

~~~ River

~~~ Intermittent river

~~~ Canal

Lake / Reservoir

Intermittent lake

Marsh

Communications

—— Railway

—— Road

⊕ Main airport

Administration

Boundaries

——— International

– – – Disputed

········ Ceasefire line

Settlement

Cities and towns in order of size

National capital   Other city or town

■ Cairo   ● Lagos

● Abidjan

○ Zaria

○ Luxor

○ Kankan

Lambert Azimuthal Equal Area projection

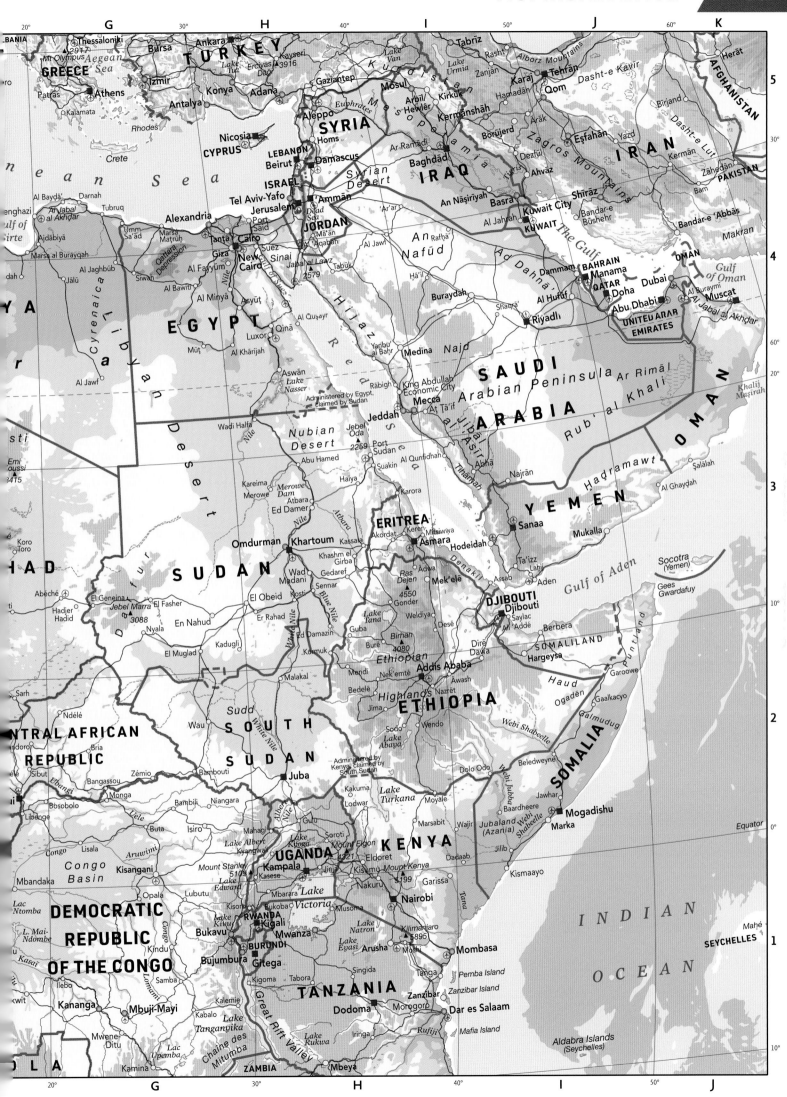

ALBANIA
GREECE
Thessaloniki
Mt Olympus
2917
Patras
Athens
Kalamata
Aegean Sea
Bursa
Izmir
Antalya
Rhodes
Crete
TURKEY
Ankara
Konya
Adana
Kayseri
Erciyas Daği 3916
Gaziantep
Aleppo
Homs
SYRIA
Damascus
LEBANON
Beirut
Nicosia
CYPRUS
ISRAEL
Tel Aviv-Yafo
Jerusalem
Mosul
Arbil
's Hewlêr
Kirkuk
Tabrīz
Lake Van
Lake Urmia
Zanjān
Rasht
Karaj
Qom
Kermānshāh
Hamadān
Borūjerd
Arāk
Esfahān
IRAQ
Baghdād
Ar Ramādī
An Nāşirīyah
Basra
Ahvāz
Dezful
Shīrāz
IRAN
Tehrān
Alborz Mountains
Dasht-e Kavir
Zāhjan
Yazd
Kermān
Bam
Birjand
Dasht-e Lut
AFGHANISTAN
Herāt
PAKISTAN
Zāhedān
Makran
Bandar-e Abbās
Bandar-e Būshehr
Kuwait City
KUWAIT
Al Jahrah
The Gulf
Dammam
BAHRAIN
Manama
QATAR
Doha
Dubai
Abu Dhabi
UNITED ARAB
EMIRATES
OMAN
Al Buraymi
Al Jabal al Akhdar
Muscat
Gulf of Oman

Mediterranean Sea
Al Baydā'
Darnah
Tubruq
Al Jabal al Akhdar
Benghazi
Gulf of Sirte
Ajdābiyā
Marsa al Burayqah
Jālū
LIBYA
Cyrenaica
Libyan
Desert
Al Jaghbūb
Jālū
Siwah
Qattara
Depression
Umm Sa'ad
Marsa Matrūh
Alexandria
Tanta
Cairo
Giza
New Cairo
Al Fayyūm
Al Minyā
Asyūt
Al Bawiti
Al Wāḥāt
EGYPT
Suez
Sinai
Jabal al Lawz 2579
Port Said
Damascus
JORDAN
Amman
Dead Sea
Ma'ān
Al 'Aqabah
Tabūk
'Ar'ar
Al Jawf
An Nafūd
Rafhā'
Hā'il
Buraydah
Ad Dahnā'
Shaqrā'
Riyadh
Al Hufūf
An Nafūd
Najd
SAUDI
ARABIA
Arabian Peninsula
Ar Rimāl
Rub' al Khali
OMAN
Gulf of Oman
Khalij
Maşīrah
Salālah
Al Ghaydah
Hadramawt

Al Jawf
Luxor
Al Quşayr
Qinā
Mūt
Al Khārijah
Aswān
Lake Nasser
Administered by Egypt, claimed by Sudan
Wadi Halfa
Nubian
Desert
Jebel Oda 2259
Port Sudan
Suakin
Abu Hamed
Kareima
Merowe
Merowe Dam
Atbara
Ed Damer
Haiya
Kassala
Karora
Al Qunfidhah
Rābigh
King Abdullah
Economic City
Mecca
Jeddah
At Tā'if
Medina
Yanbu'
al Bahr
Red Sea
Jibāl
al 'Asīr
Tihāmah
Abhā
Najrān
Sanaa
YEMEN
Mukalla
Aden
Ta'izz
Lahij
Al Hudaydah
Hodeidah
Mitsiwa
Denakil
Assab
Gulf of Aden
Socotra
(Yemen)
Gees
Gwardafuy

CHAD
Emi Koussi
3415
Koro Toro
Abéché
Hadjer Hadid
Jebel Marra
3088
El Geneina
El Fasher
Nyala
Kadugli
El Muglad
Darfur
SUDAN
Omdurman
Khartoum
Wad Madani
El Obeid
En Nahud
Er Rahad
Kosti
Sennar
Ed Damazin
Kurmuk
White Nile
Blue Nile
Khashm el Girba
Gedaref
Ras Dejen
4550
Gonder
Lake Tana
Birhan
4080
Adwa
Mek'elē
Weldiya
Desē
ERITREA
Asmara
Akordat
Keren
Hargeysa
SOMALILAND
Berbera
Garoowe
PUNTLAND
DJIBOUTI
Djibouti
Saylac
Aïl 'Addē
Dire Dawa
Harer
Ethiopian
Highlands
Addis Ababa
Nek'emtē
Nazrēt
ETHIOPIA
Āwash
Haud
Ogadēn
Gaalkacyo
Galmudug
Webi Shabeelle

CENTRAL AFRICAN
REPUBLIC
Ndélé
Sarh
Bria
Bangassou
Zémio
Bambouti
Niangara
Monga
Bambili
Isiro
Buta
Bondo
Bosobolo
Libenge
Ubangi
Uele
Congo
Lisala
Mbandaka
Kisangani
Aruwimi
Opala
DEMOCRATIC
REPUBLIC
OF THE CONGO
Congo Basin
Lac Ntomba
L. Mai-Ndombe
Ilebo
Kananga
Mbuji-Mayi
Kindu
Lubutu
Mahagi
Lake Albert
Lake
Kyoga
Kyangwali
Soroti
Mount Elgon
4321
Jinja
Kampala
Kasese
Mount Stanley
5109
Lake Edward
Mbarara
Bukoba
Lake Kivu
Lake Victoria
RWANDA
Kigali
BURUNDI
Bujumbura
Gitega
Kigoma
Lake Tanganyika
Chaîne des Mitumba
Kalemie
Kabalo
Kamina
Mwene Ditu
Lac Upemba
ANGOLA
ZAMBIA
Kindu
Mwanza
Musoma
Lake Eyasi
Lake Natron
TANZANIA
Dodoma
Tabora
Singida
Morogoro
Iringa
Mbeya
Lake Rukwa
Great Rift Valley

SOUTH
SUDAN
Malakal
Wau
Bentiu
Sudd
Bambouti
Juba
Bor
Gulu
Lodwar
Kakuma
Lake Turkana
Moyale
Administered by
Kenya, claimed by
South Sudan
Dolo Odo
Marsabit
Wajir
Dadaab
Baardheere
Jubaland
(Azania)
Webi Jubba
Beledweyne
SOMALIA
Jawhar
Mogadishu
Marka
Jilib
Kismaayo
INDIAN
OCEAN
Equator
Mahé
SEYCHELLES
Aldabra Islands
(Seychelles)

UGANDA
KENYA
Eldoret
Kisumu
Mount Kenya
5199
Nakuru
Nairobi
Garissa
Tana
Mombasa
Kilimanjaro
5895
Moshi
Arusha
Pemba Island
Tanga
Zanzibar
Zanzibar Island
Dar es Salaam
Mafia Island
Rufiji

Euphrates
Tigris
Nile
Red Sea
Hijaz
Syrian Desert
Mesopotamia
Zagros Mountains
Lake Tuz
Kuwait

Relief and physical features

Relief metres

5000
3000
2000
1000
500
200
0 — sea level
— under sea level
200
4000
6000

▲ 8849 Mountain height (in metres)

Permanent ice (ice cap or glacier)

Scale 1 : 57 000 000

0   500   1000   1500 km

Lambert Azimuthal Equal Area projection

Cross-section

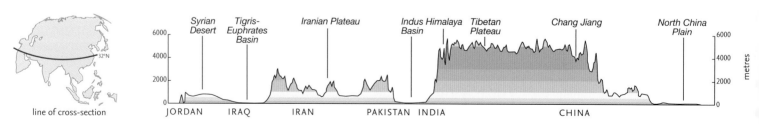

line of cross-section

Syrian Desert
Tigris-Euphrates Basin
Iranian Plateau
Indus Himalaya Basin
Tibetan Plateau
Chang Jiang
North China Plain

6000
4000
2000

metres

JORDAN   IRAQ   IRAN   PAKISTAN   INDIA   CHINA

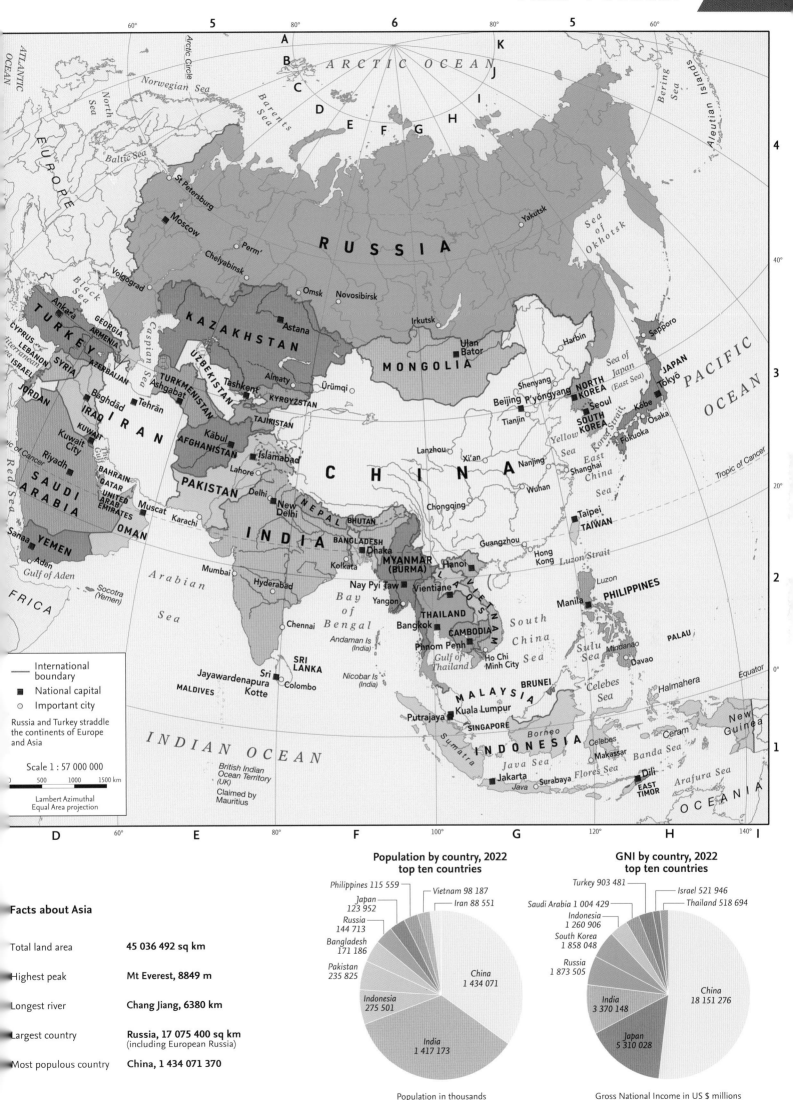

Facts about Asia

Total land area	**45 036 492 sq km**
Highest peak	**Mt Everest, 8849 m**
Longest river	**Chang Jiang, 6380 km**
Largest country	**Russia, 17 075 400 sq km** (including European Russia)
Most populous country	**China, 1 434 071 370**

Population by country, 2022 top ten countries

Philippines 115 559
Japan 123 952
Russia 144 713
Bangladesh 171 186
Pakistan 235 825
Indonesia 275 501
India 1 417 173
China 1 434 071
Vietnam 98 187
Iran 88 551

Population in thousands

GNI by country, 2022 top ten countries

Turkey 903 481
Saudi Arabia 1 004 429
Indonesia 1 260 906
South Korea 1 858 048
Russia 1 873 505
India 3 370 148
Japan 5 310 028
China 18 151 276
Israel 521 946
Thailand 518 694

Gross National Income in US $ millions

Scale 1 : 57 000 000

0 500 1000 1500 km

Lambert Azimuthal Equal Area projection

International boundary
National capital
Important city

Russia and Turkey straddle the continents of Europe and Asia

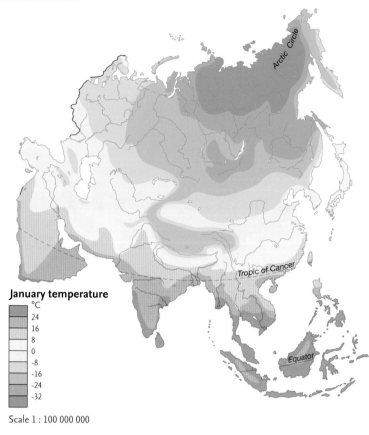

January temperature

°C
24
16
8
0
-8
-16
-24
-32

Scale 1 : 100 000 000

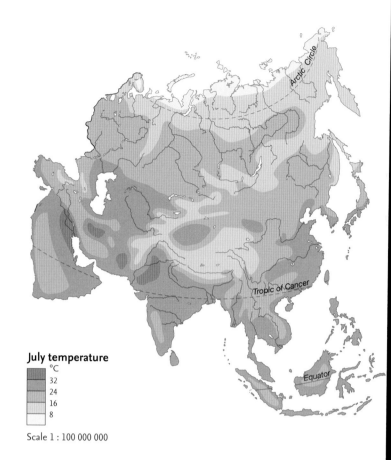

July temperature

°C
32
24
16
8

Scale 1 : 100 000 000

Climate graphs

Town

°C   mm
40   Altitude in metres   400
     above sea level
30   Temperature range   300
     shows the average
     daily max. and min.
20   200
             Average
10   monthly   100
             rainfall
0   in mm   0

-10
   J FMAMJ J A SOND

Makassar

°C   mm
        Altitude 2 m 700
                      600
                      500
                      400
                      300
                      200
                      100
                      0
   J FMAMJ J A SOND

Padang

°C   mm
50 Altitude   500
      7 m
40   400
30   300
20   200
10   100
0   0
   J FMAMJ J A SOND

Riyadh

°C   mm
50 Altitude 590 m 500
40   400
30   300
20   200
10   100
0   0
   J FMAMJ J A SOND

Shanghai

°C   mm
50 Altitude 7 m   500
40   400
30   300
20   200
10   100
0   0
   J FMAMJ J A SOND

Tomsk

°C   mm
30 Altitude 122 m 300
20   200
10   100
0   0
-10
-20
-30
   J FMAMJ J A SOND

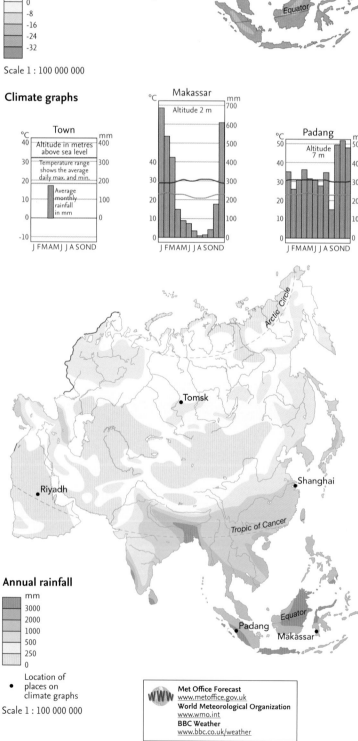

Annual rainfall

mm
3000
2000
1000
500
250
0

• Location of
  places on
  climate graphs

Scale 1 : 100 000 000

WWW **Met Office Forecast**
www.metoffice.gov.uk
World Meteorological Organization
www.wmo.int
BBC Weather
www.bbc.co.uk/weather

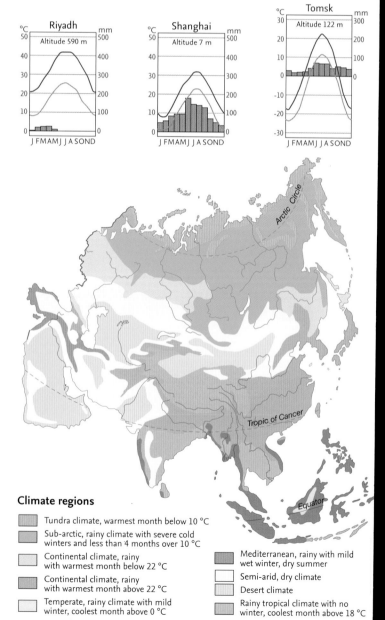

Climate regions

Tundra climate, warmest month below 10 °C

Sub-arctic, rainy climate with severe cold
winters and less than 4 months over 10 °C

Continental climate, rainy
with warmest month below 22 °C

Continental climate, rainy
with warmest month above 22 °C

Temperate, rainy climate with mild
winter, coolest month above 0 °C

Wet subtropical, coolest month
above 0 °C, warmest month above 22 °C

Mediterranean, rainy with mild
wet winter, dry summer

Semi-arid, dry climate

Desert climate

Rainy tropical climate with no
winter, coolest month above 18 °C

Rainy tropical climate, constantly
wet throughout the year

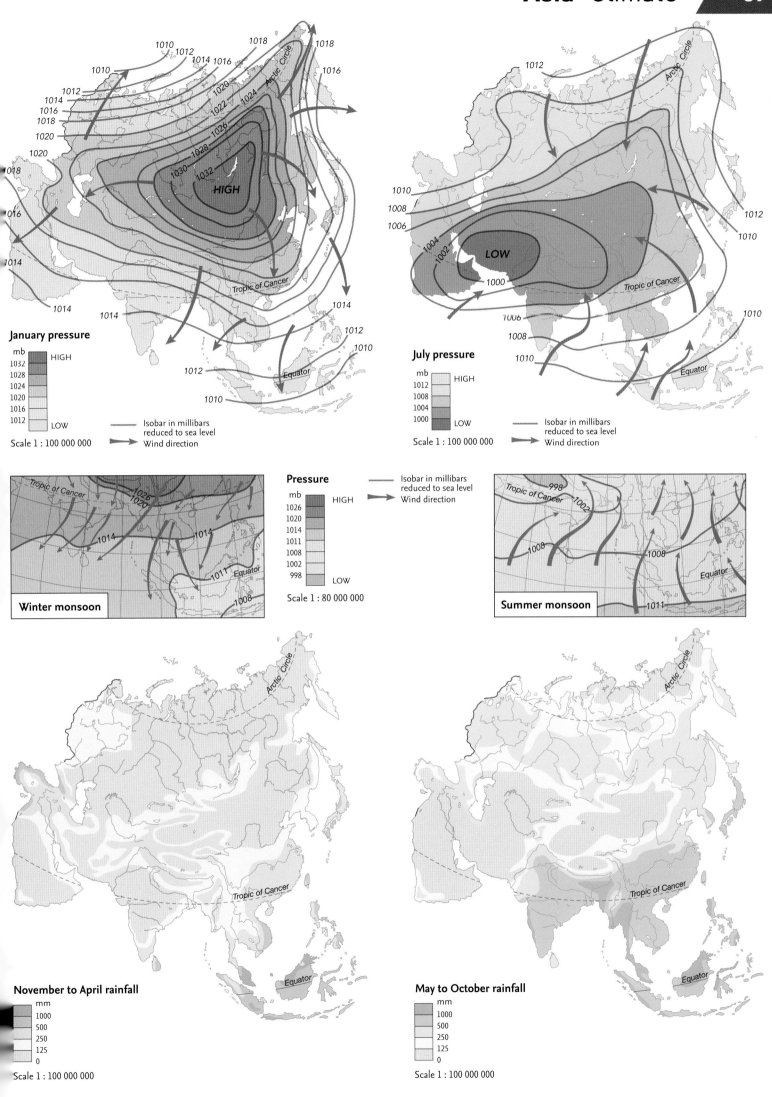

January pressure

mb
1032 HIGH
1028
1024
1020
1016
1012 LOW

Scale 1 : 100 000 000

——— Isobar in millibars
reduced to sea level
➤ Wind direction

July pressure

mb
1012 HIGH
1008
1004
1000 LOW

Scale 1 : 100 000 000

——— Isobar in millibars
reduced to sea level
➤ Wind direction

Winter monsoon

Pressure

mb
1026 HIGH
1020
1014
1011
1008
1002
998 LOW

Scale 1 : 80 000 000

——— Isobar in millibars
reduced to sea level
➤ Wind direction

Summer monsoon

November to April rainfall

mm
1000
500
250
125
0

Scale 1 : 100 000 000

May to October rainfall

mm
1000
500
250
125
0

Scale 1 : 100 000 000

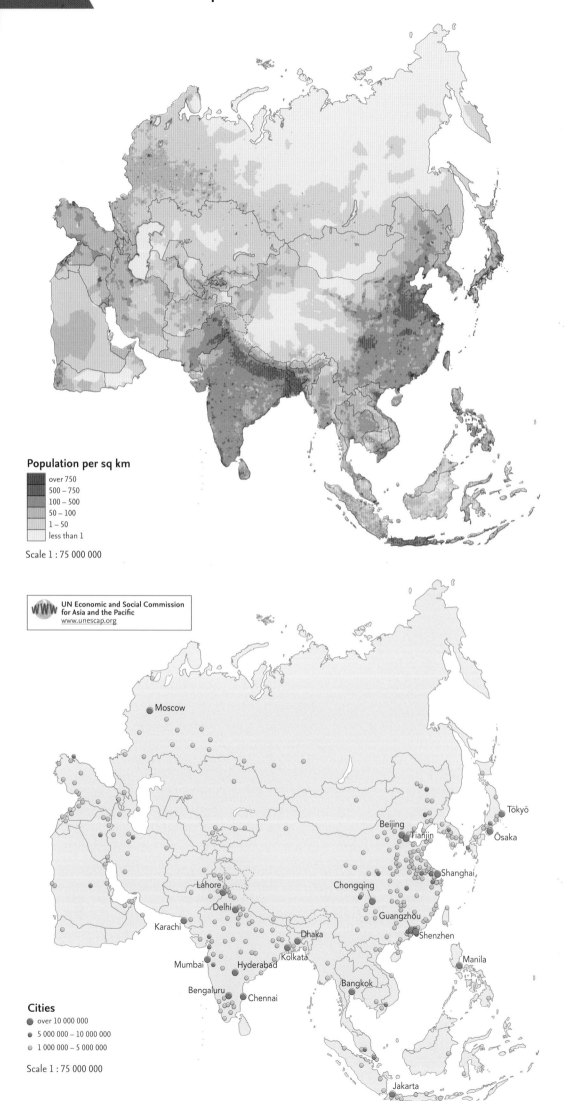

Population per sq km

- over 750
- 500 – 750
- 100 – 500
- 50 – 100
- 1 – 50
- less than 1

Scale 1 : 75 000 000

UN Economic and Social Commission
for Asia and the Pacific
www.unescap.org

Cities

- over 10 000 000
- 5 000 000 – 10 000 000
- 1 000 000 – 5 000 000

Scale 1 : 75 000 000

Top 10 densely populated countries, 202

Country	Population per sq km
Singapore	9352
Bahrain	2131
Maldives	1758
Bangladesh	1189
Taiwan	660
Lebanon	525
South Korea	522
India	448
Israel	409
Philippines	385

Population pyramids, 2020

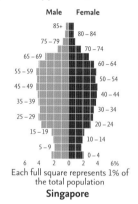

Each full square represents 1% of
the total population

Singapore

Each full square represents 1% of
the total population

Philippines

Population growth, 1950 – 2050

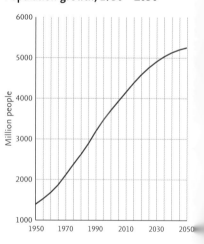

Top 5 largest urban agglomerations, 20

Urban agglomeration	Population
Tōkyō Japan	37 393 129
Delhi India	30 290 936
Shanghai China	27 058 479
Dhaka Bangladesh	21 005 860
Beijing China	20 462 610

Tōkyō, the capital of Japan, has been the world's most populous metropolitan area since 1970.

This false-colour Landsat 7 image shows this vast conurbation, situated on the eastern shore of the Japanese island of Honshū. Tōkyō Bay dominates the centre of this scene. The greater Tōkyō area fans out in a crescent shape around the western, northern, and eastern shores of Tōkyō Bay. Pressure on the land has led to major land reclamation projects in the bay – obvious from the angular shape of the coastline. Tōkyō International airport is built entirely on reclaimed land.

Asia Land Use

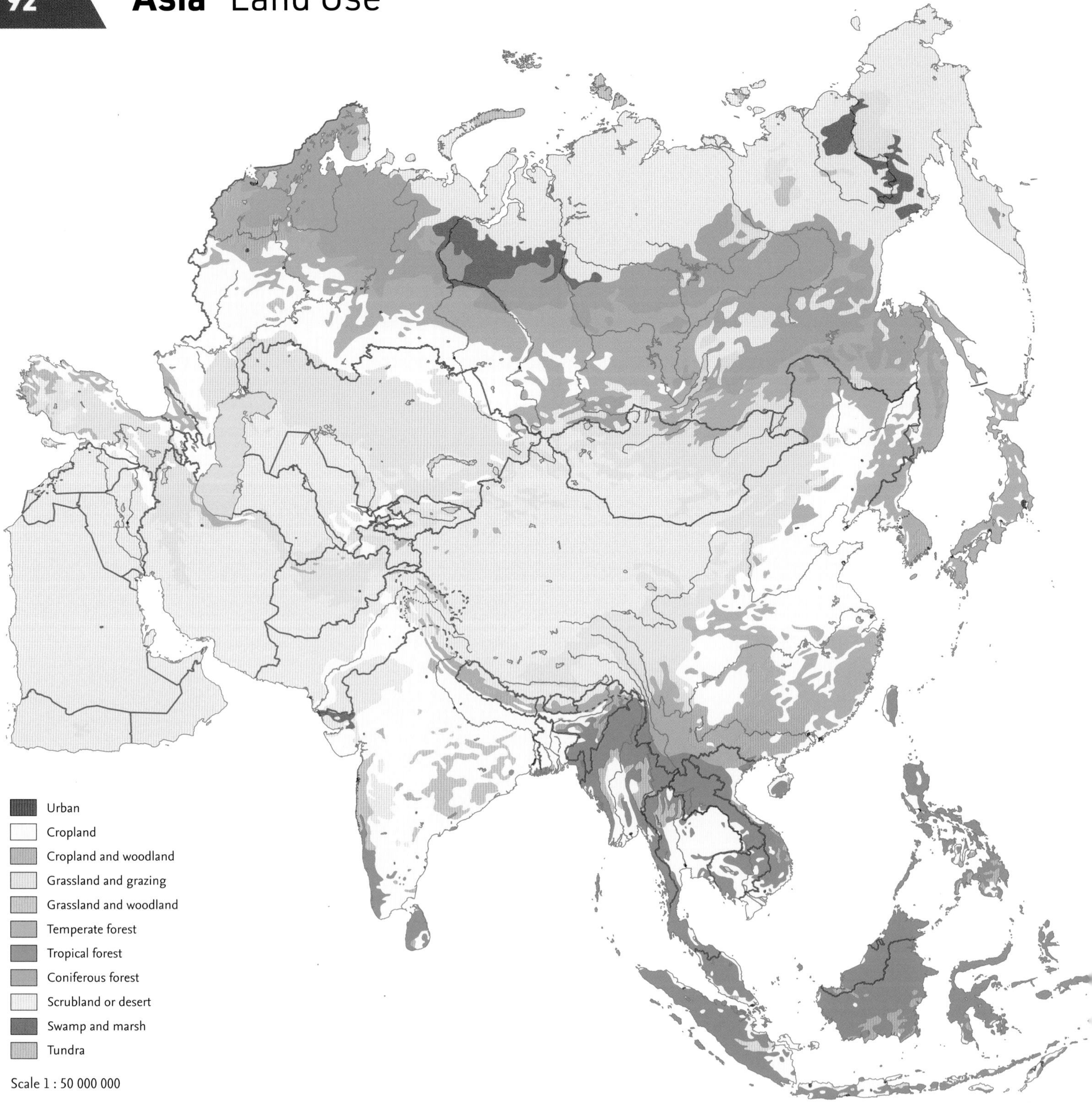

Urban
Cropland
Cropland and woodland
Grassland and grazing
Grassland and woodland
Temperate forest
Tropical forest
Coniferous forest
Scrubland or desert
Swamp and marsh
Tundra

Scale 1 : 50 000 000

Land use by region, 2018

Arable land
Permanent crops
Forest
Other

Russia
Central
Western
Eastern
Southern
Southeastern

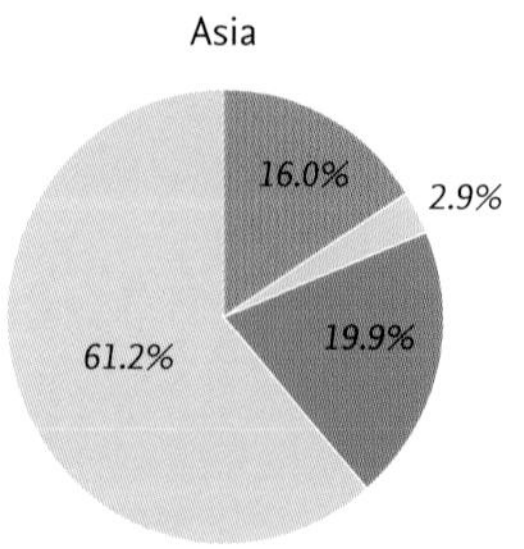

Asia

16.0%   2.9%
19.9%
61.2%

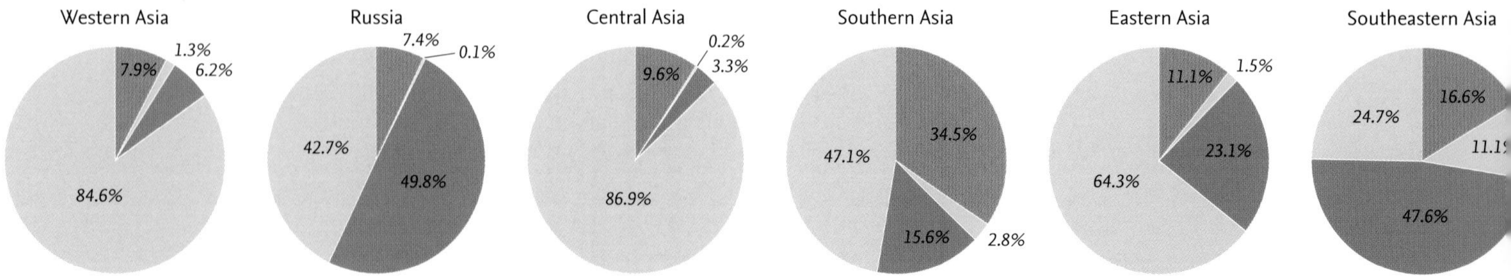

Western Asia

1.3%
7.9%   6.2%
84.6%

Russia

7.4%   0.1%
42.7%
49.8%

Central Asia

0.2%
9.6%   3.3%
86.9%

Southern Asia

34.5%
47.1%
15.6%   2.8%

Eastern Asia

11.1%   1.5%
64.3%
23.1%

Southeastern Asia

16.6%
24.7%
11.1%
47.6%

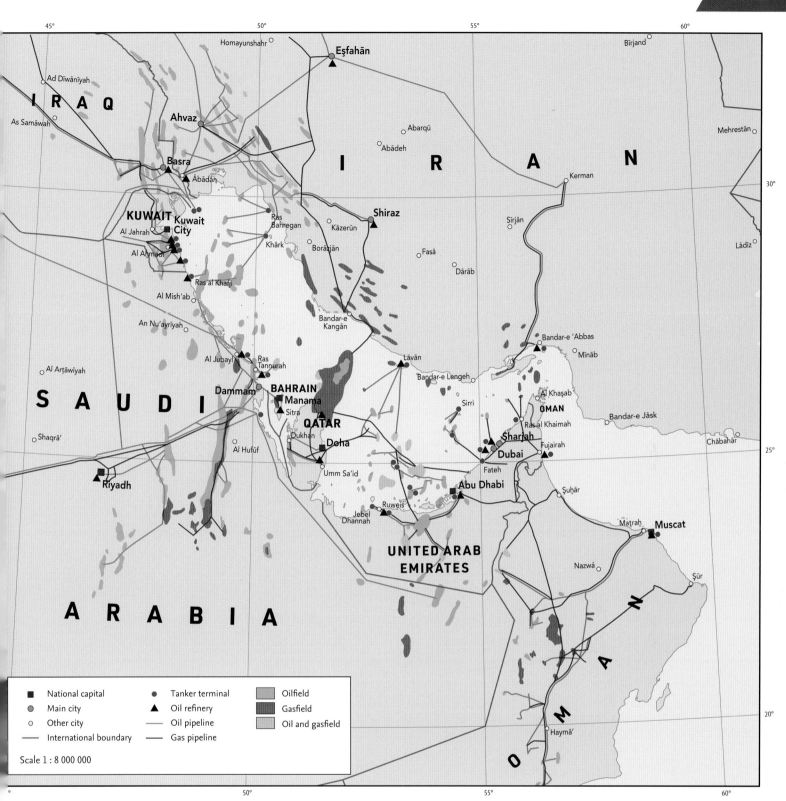

45°　　　　　50°　　　　　55°　　　　　60°

I R A Q

Ad Dīwānīyah

As Samāwah

Homayunshahr　　Eşfahān

Ahvaz

Abarqū

Ābādeh

I R A N

Basra

Ābādān

Kerman

Mehrestān

KUWAIT　Kuwait City

Ras Bahregan

Shiraz

Al Jahrah

Khārk

Kāzerūn

Sīrjān

Lādīz

Al Ahmadi

Borāzjān

Fasā

Ras al Khafji

Dārāb

Al Mish'ab

Bandar-e Kangān

An Nu'ayrīyah

Lāvān

Bandar-e 'Abbas

Mīnāb

Al Arţāwīyah

Al Jubayl

Ras Tannurah

Bandar-e Lengeh

Al Khaşab

Bandar-e Jāsk

S A U D I

BAHRAIN　Manama

Sirri

OMAN

Dammam

Sitra

Ras al Khaimah

Shaqrā'

Shariah

QATAR

Dukhān

Doha

Fujairah

Dubai

Chābahār

Al Hufūf

Umm Sa'id

Fateh

Şuḩār

A R A B I A

Riyadh

Jebel Dhannah

Ruweis

UNITED ARAB EMIRATES

Abu Dhabi

Maţraḩ　Muscat

Nazwá

Şūr

O M A N

Haymā'

Legend
- ■ National capital
- ◉ Main city
- ○ Other city
- — International boundary
- ● Tanker terminal
- ▲ Oil refinery
- — Oil pipeline
- — Gas pipeline
- ▢ Oilfield
- ▢ Gasfield
- ▢ Oil and gasfield

Scale 1 : 8 000 000

l and gas production

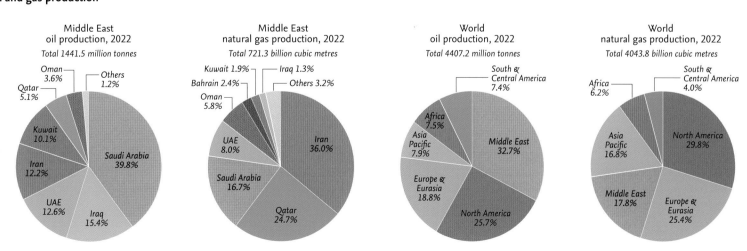

Middle East oil production, 2022
Total 1441.5 million tonnes

- Oman 3.6%
- Others 1.2%
- Qatar 5.1%
- Kuwait 10.1%
- Iran 12.2%
- UAE 12.6%
- Iraq 15.4%
- Saudi Arabia 39.8%

Middle East natural gas production, 2022
Total 721.3 billion cubic metres

- Kuwait 1.9%
- Iraq 1.3%
- Bahrain 2.4%
- Others 3.2%
- Oman 5.8%
- UAE 8.0%
- Saudi Arabia 16.7%
- Qatar 24.7%
- Iran 36.0%

World oil production, 2022
Total 4407.2 million tonnes

- South & Central America 7.4%
- Africa 7.5%
- Asia Pacific 7.9%
- Europe & Eurasia 18.8%
- North America 25.7%
- Middle East 32.7%

World natural gas production, 2022
Total 4043.8 billion cubic metres

- South & Central America 4.0%
- Africa 6.2%
- Asia Pacific 16.8%
- Middle East 17.8%
- Europe & Eurasia 25.4%
- North America 29.8%

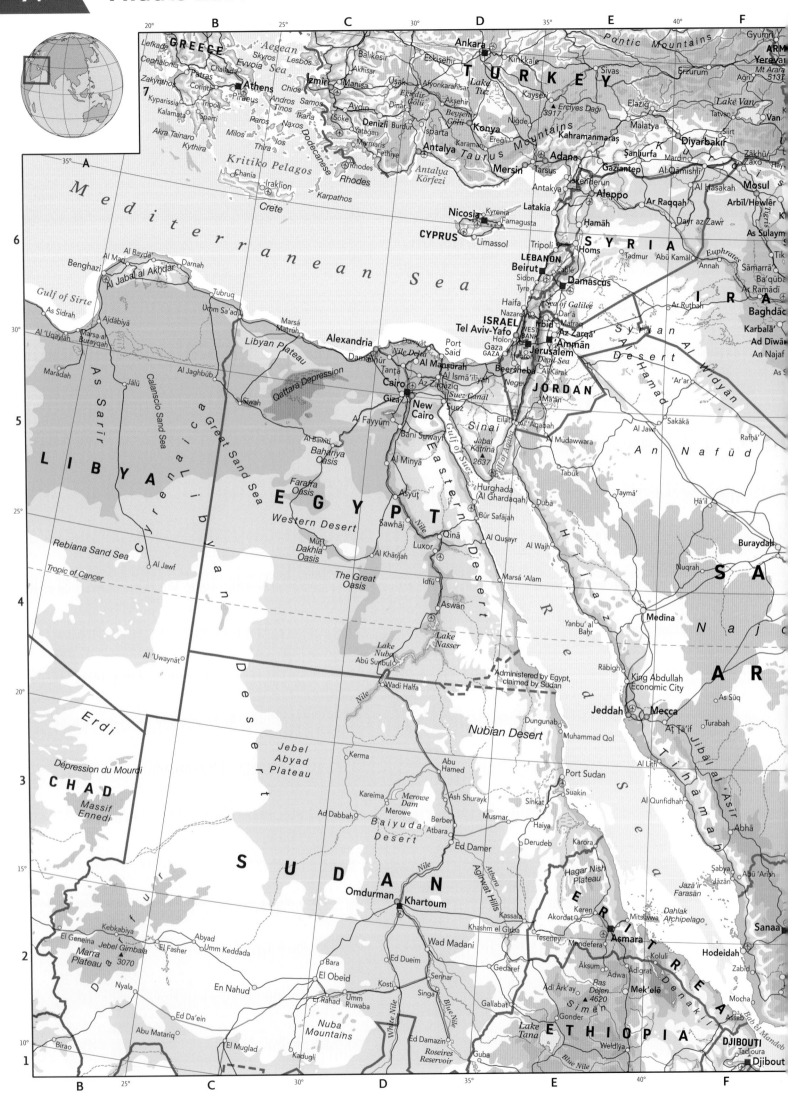

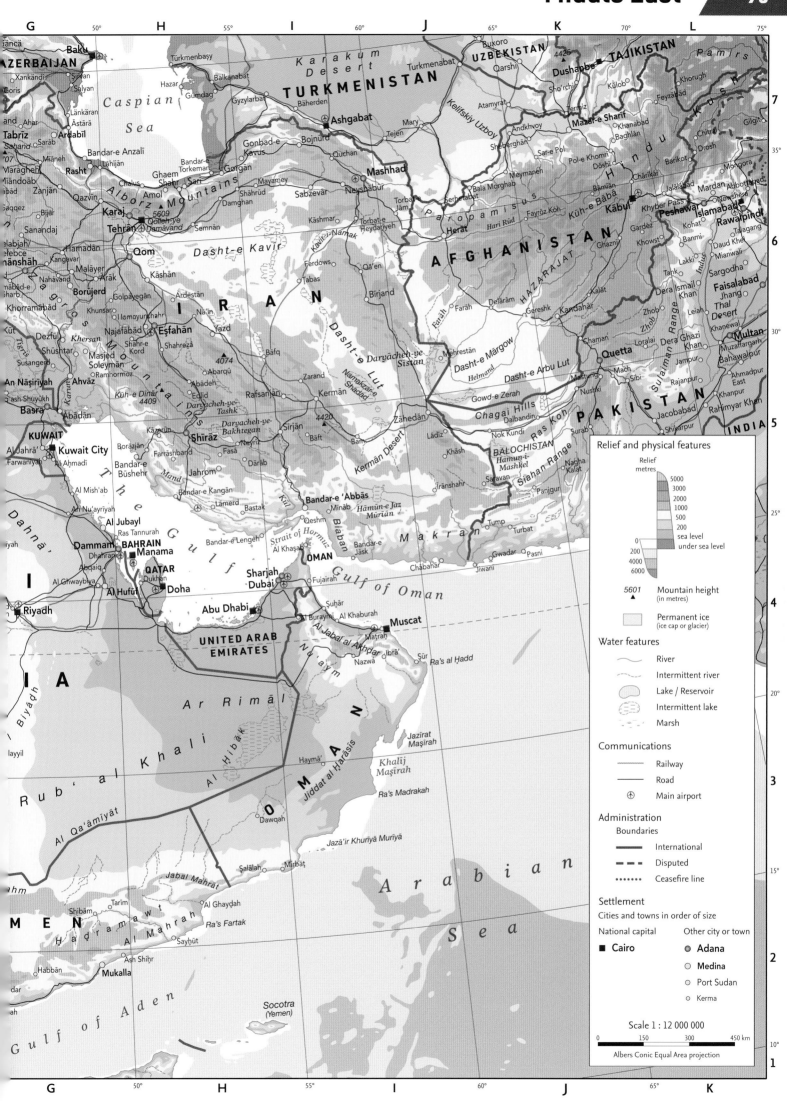

Relief and physical features

Relief
metres

5000
3000
2000
1000
500
200
0 sea level
under sea level
200
4000
6000

5601 ▲ Mountain height
(in metres)

Permanent ice
(ice cap or glacier)

Water features

~~~ River

~ ~ ~ Intermittent river

Lake / Reservoir

Intermittent lake

Marsh

Communications

Railway

Road

⊕ Main airport

Administration

Boundaries

International

Disputed

Ceasefire line

Settlement

Cities and towns in order of size

National capital | Other city or town
■ Cairo | ◉ Adana
 | ○ Medina
 | ○ Port Sudan
 | ○ Kerma

Scale 1 : 12 000 000

0   150   300   450 km

Albers Conic Equal Area projection

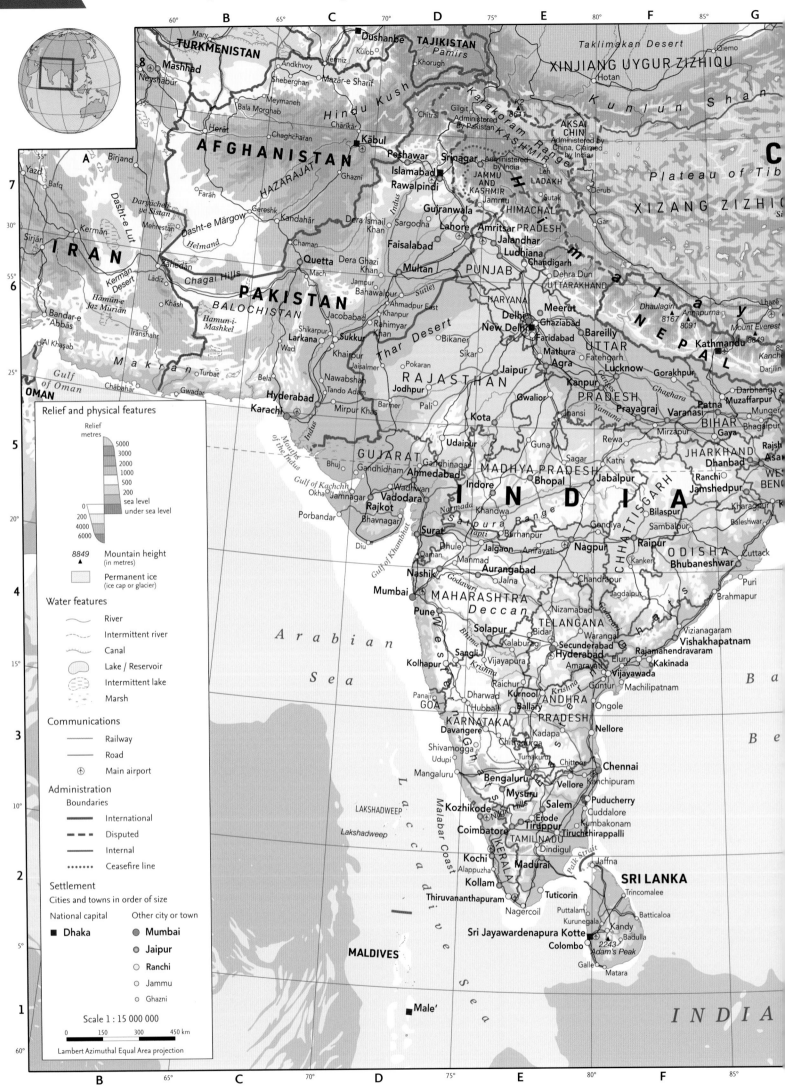

Relief and physical features

Relief metres

5000
3000
2000
1000
500
200
sea level
under sea level
200
4000
6000

8849 ▲ Mountain height (in metres)

Permanent ice (ice cap or glacier)

Water features

~~~ River
~ ~ ~ Intermittent river
~~~ Canal
Lake / Reservoir
Intermittent lake
Marsh

Communications

Railway
Road
⊕ Main airport

Administration

Boundaries

International
Disputed
Internal
Ceasefire line

Settlement

Cities and towns in order of size

National capital   Other city or town

■ Dhaka   ● Mumbai
            ◉ Jaipur
            ○ Ranchi
            ○ Jammu
            ○ Ghazni

Scale 1 : 15 000 000

0   150   300   450 km

Lambert Azimuthal Equal Area projection

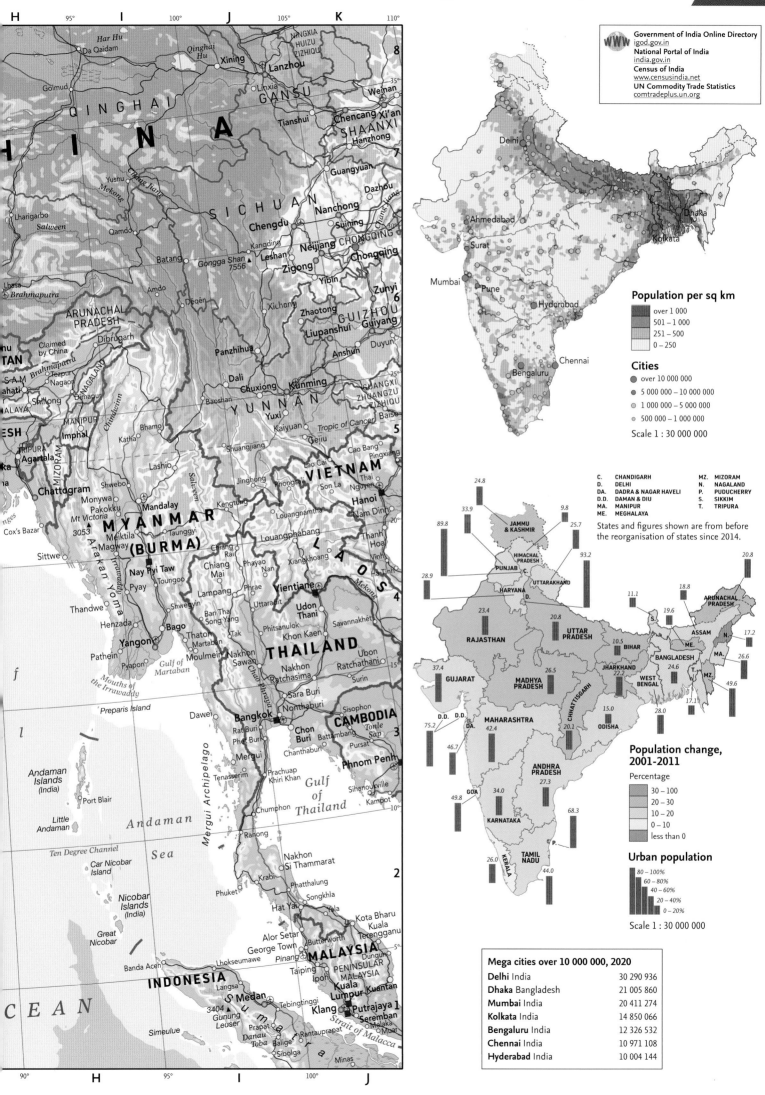

www Government of India Online Directory
igod.gov.in
National Portal of India
india.gov.in
Census of India
www.censusindia.net
UN Commodity Trade Statistics
comtradeplus.un.org

Population per sq km

over 1 000
501 – 1 000
251 – 500
0 – 250

Cities

over 10 000 000
5 000 000 – 10 000 000
1 000 000 – 5 000 000
500 000 – 1 000 000

Scale 1 : 30 000 000

C. CHANDIGARH
D. DELHI
DA. DADRA & NAGAR HAVELI
D.D. DAMAN & DIU
MA. MANIPUR
ME. MEGHALAYA
MZ. MIZORAM
N. NAGALAND
P. PUDUCHERRY
S. SIKKIM
T. TRIPURA

States and figures shown are from before
the reorganisation of states since 2014.

Population change, 2001-2011

Percentage

30 – 100
20 – 30
10 – 20
0 – 10
less than 0

Urban population

80 – 100%
60 – 80%
40 – 60%
20 – 40%
0 – 20%

Scale 1 : 30 000 000

Mega cities over 10 000 000, 2020

Delhi India	30 290 936
Dhaka Bangladesh	21 005 860
Mumbai India	20 411 274
Kolkata India	14 850 066
Bengaluru India	12 326 532
Chennai India	10 971 108
Hyderabad India	10 004 144

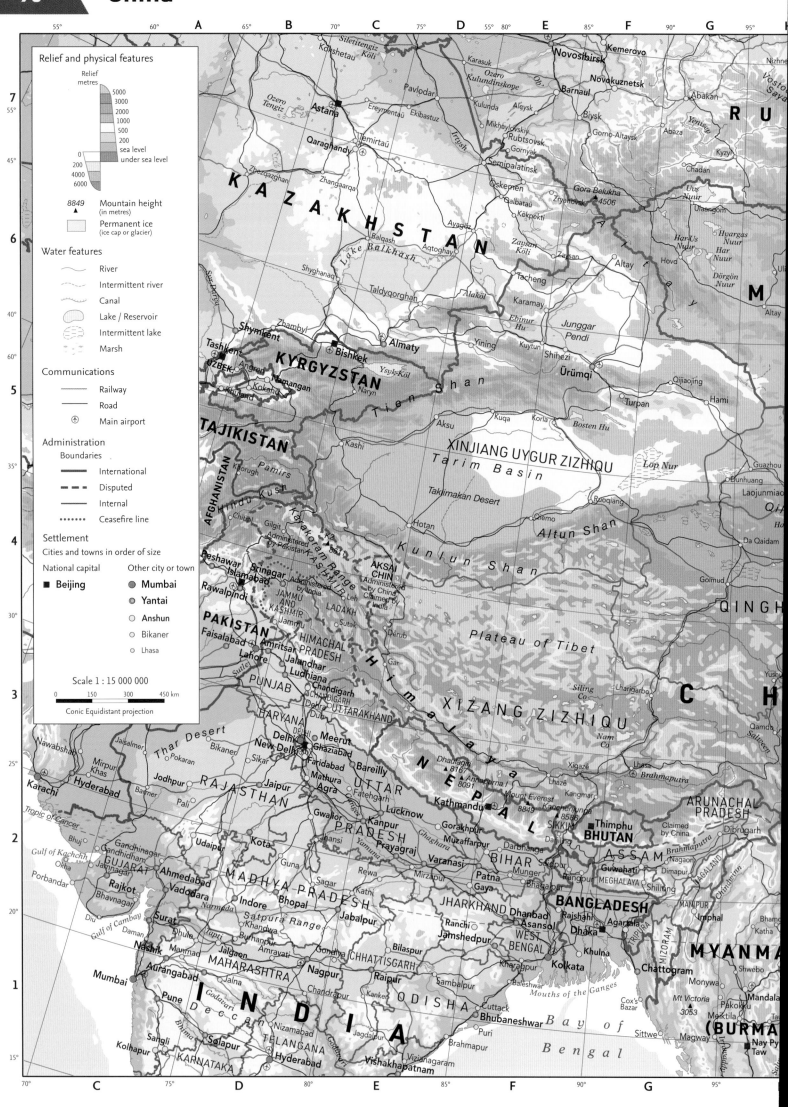

Relief and physical features

Relief
metres

5000
3000
2000
1000
500
200
sea level
0
under sea level
200
4000
6000

8849 Mountain height
(in metres)

Permanent ice
(ice cap or glacier)

Water features

River
Intermittent river
Canal
Lake / Reservoir
Intermittent lake
Marsh

Communications

Railway
Road
Main airport

Administration

Boundaries

International
Disputed
Internal
Ceasefire line

Settlement

Cities and towns in order of size

National capital | Other city or town

■ Beijing | ● Mumbai
| ● Yantai
| ○ Anshun
| ○ Bikaner
| ○ Lhasa

Scale 1 : 15 000 000

0   150   300   450 km

Conic Equidistant projection

GOLIA
MONGOLIA
Ulan Bator
Gobi
NEI MONGOL ZIZHIQU (INNER MONGOLIA)
Da Hinggan Ling
MANCHURIA
HEILONGJIANG
Harbin
JILIN
Changchun
LIAONING
Shenyang
NORTH KOREA
P'yŏngyang
SOUTH KOREA
Seoul
Incheon
Busan
Sea of Japan (East Sea)
Honshū
JAPAN
Fukuoka
Kyūshū
Beijing
HEBEI
Tianjin
Tangshan
Bo Hai
Dalian
Korea Bay
Shijiazhuang
SHANXI
Taiyuan
SHANDONG
Jinan
Qingdao
Yellow Sea
Huang He
HENAN
Zhengzhou
Luoyang
Xi'an
SHAANXI
JIANGSU
Nanjing
Shanghai
East China Sea
SICHUAN
Chengdu
Chongqing
CHONGQING
HUBEI
Wuhan
ANHUI
Hefei
ZHEJIANG
Hangzhou
Ningbo
HUNAN
Changsha
JIANGXI
Nanchang
FUJIAN
Fuzhou
TAIWAN
Taipei
Kaohsiung
PACIFIC OCEAN
Ryukyu Islands
Okinawa Jima
Naha
GUIZHOU
Guiyang
YUNNAN
Kunming
GUANGXI ZHUANGZU ZIZHIQU
Nanning
GUANGDONG
Guangzhou
Hong Kong
Macao
Shenzhen
Zhanjiang
HAINAN
Haikou
VIETNAM
Hanoi
LAOS
Gulf of Tonkin
Luzon Strait
PHILIPPINES
Luzon

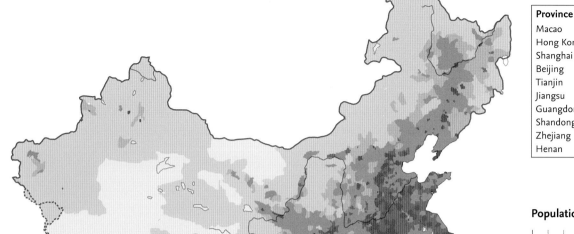

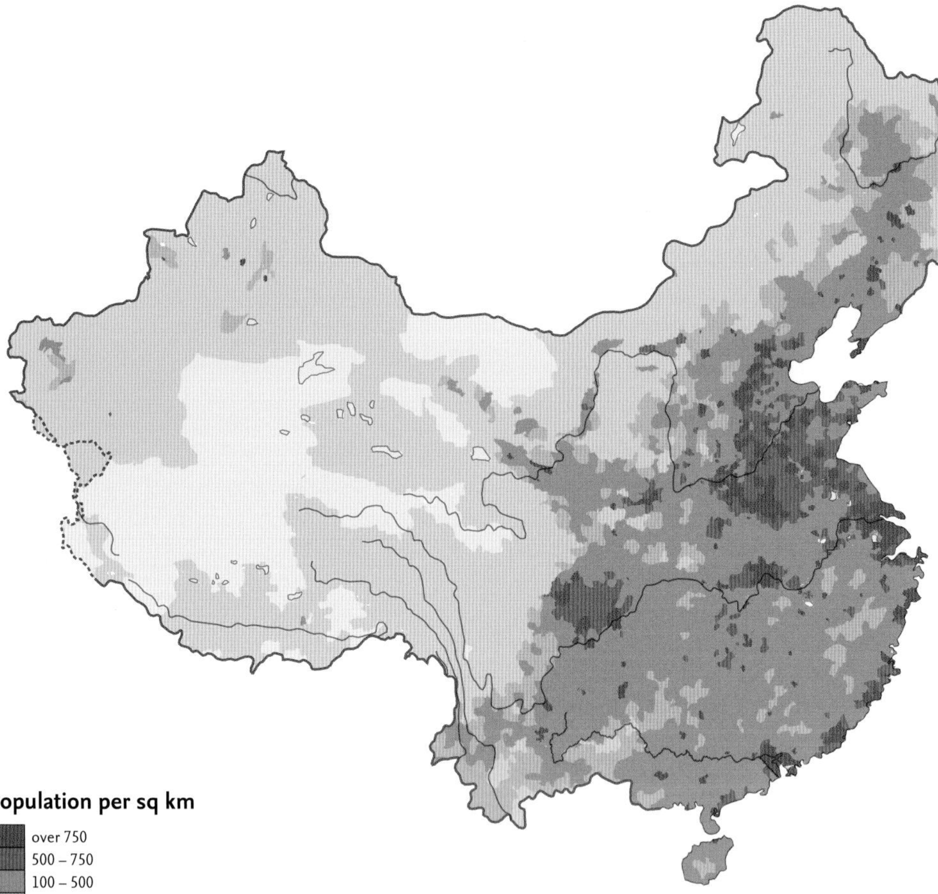

Population per sq km

■	over 750
■	500 – 750
■	100 – 500
■	50 – 100
■	1 – 50
□	less than 1

Scale 1 : 35 000 000

National Bureau of Statistics of China
www.stats.gov.cn/english

Top 10 densely populated provinces

Province	Population per sq km
Macao	22 770
Hong Kong	6727
Shanghai	3923
Beijing	1334
Tianjin	1164
Jiangsu	826
Guangdong	701
Shandong	646
Zhejiang	634
Henan	595

Population growth rates

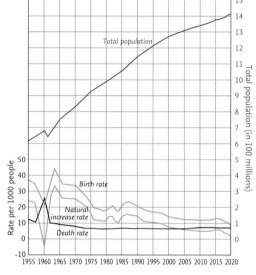

Population movement

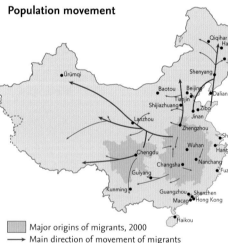

�earthtone▮	Major origins of migrants, 2000
⟶	Main direction of movement of migrants
—	Other direction of movement of migrants

Scale 1 : 70 000 000

Cities

●	over 10 000 000
●	5 000 000 – 10 000 000
○	1 000 000 – 5 000 000
○	500 000 – 1 000 000

Scale 1 : 35 000 000

Top 10 largest urban agglomerations, 2020

Urban agglomeration	Population
Shanghai	27 058 479
Beijing	20 462 610
Chongqing	15 872 179
Tianjin	13 589 078
Guangzhou	13 301 532
Shenzhen	12 356 820
Chengdu	9 135 768
Nanjing	8 847 372
Wuhan	8 364 978
Xi'an	8 000 965

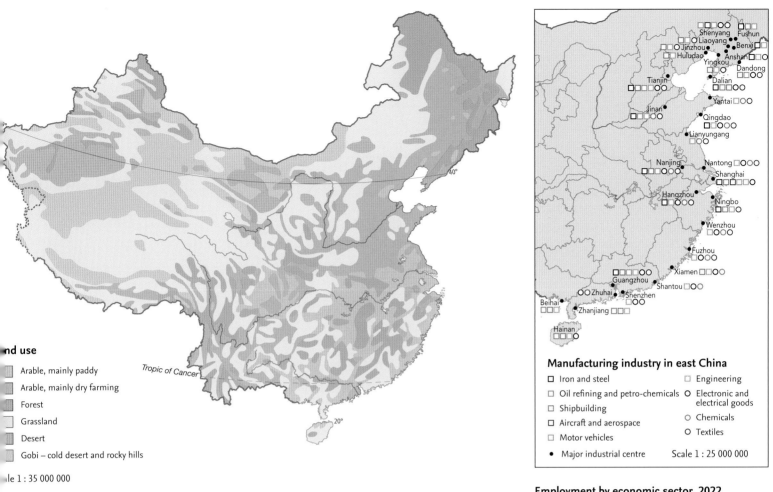

Manufacturing industry in east China

- ☐ Iron and steel
- ☐ Oil refining and petro-chemicals
- ☐ Shipbuilding
- ☐ Aircraft and aerospace
- ☐ Motor vehicles
- ☐ Engineering
- ○ Electronic and electrical goods
- ○ Chemicals
- ○ Textiles
- ● Major industrial centre

Scale 1 : 25 000 000

nd use

- Arable, mainly paddy
- Arable, mainly dry farming
- Forest
- Grassland
- Desert
- Gobi – cold desert and rocky hills

Tropic of Cancer

le 1 : 35 000 000

Employment by economic sector, 2022

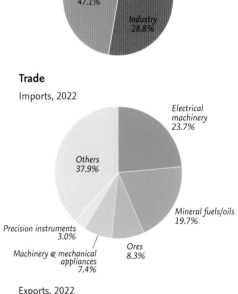

- Agriculture 24.1%
- Services 47.1%
- Industry 28.8%

ain trading partners, 2022

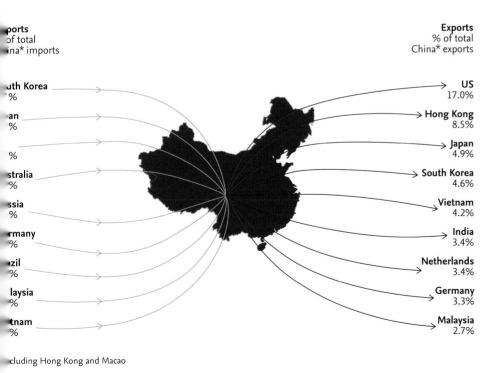

ports
of total
ina* imports

Exports
% of total
China* exports

uth Korea
%

an
%

%

stralia
%

ssia
%

rmany
%

zil
%

laysia
%

tnam
%

→ **US** 17.0%

→ **Hong Kong** 8.5%

→ **Japan** 4.9%

→ **South Korea** 4.6%

→ **Vietnam** 4.2%

→ **India** 3.4%

→ **Netherlands** 3.4%

→ **Germany** 3.3%

→ **Malaysia** 2.7%

cluding Hong Kong and Macao

Trade

Imports, 2022

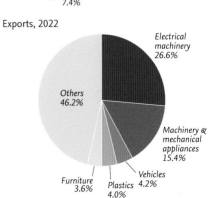

- Electrical machinery 23.7%
- Others 37.9%
- Mineral fuels/oils 19.7%
- Ores 8.3%
- Machinery & mechanical appliances 7.4%
- Precision instruments 3.0%

Exports, 2022

- Electrical machinery 26.6%
- Others 46.2%
- Machinery & mechanical appliances 15.4%
- Vehicles 4.2%
- Plastics 4.0%
- Furniture 3.6%

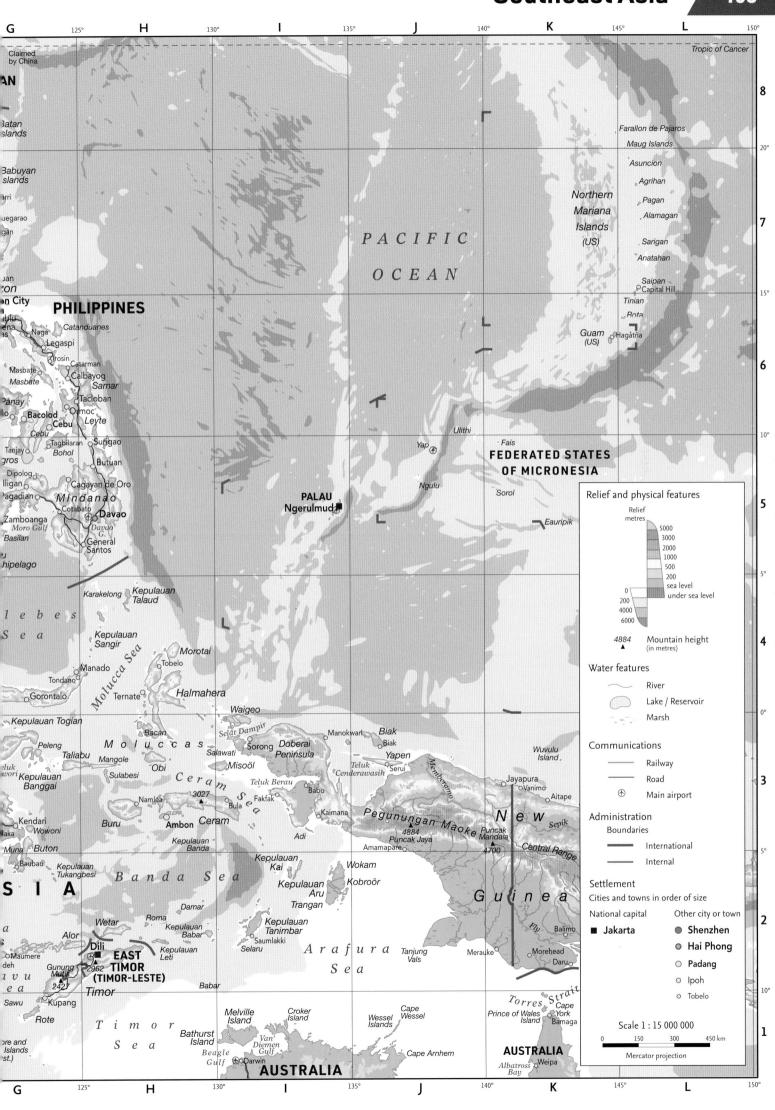

Claimed by China

Tropic of Cancer

Batan Islands

Babuyan Islands

arri

uegarao

gan

on City

PHILIPPINES

Catanduanes

ena · Naga
Legaspi
Irosin
Masbate · Catarman
Masbate · Calbayog
· Samar
· Tacloban
Ormoc · Leyte
Bacolod
Cebu
Cebu
Tanjay
gros · Tagbilaran · Surigao
Bohol · Butuan
Dipolog
lligan · Cagayan de Oro
Pagadian
Zamboanga · Cotabato
Davao
Mindanao
Moro Gulf · Davao G.
Basilan · General Santos
hipelago

PACIFIC OCEAN

Northern Mariana Islands (US)

Farallon de Pajaros

Maug Islands

Asuncion
Agrihan
Pagan
Alamagan

Sarigan

Anatahan

Saipan · Capital Hill
Tinian
Rota

Guam (US) · Hagåtña

Ulithi

Yap · Yap

Fais

FEDERATED STATES OF MICRONESIA

Ngulu

Sorol

PALAU
Ngerulmud

Eauripik

elebes Sea

Karakelong
Kepulauan Talaud

Kepulauan Sangir

Morotai
Tobelo
Manado
Tondano
Gorontalo
Ternate
Molucca Sea
Halmahera

Kepulauan Togian

Peleng
Taliabu · Bacan
Waigeo
Selat Dampir
Mangole
Kepulauan Banggai
Obi · Sulabesi
Moluccas
Salawati
Sorong
Misoöl
Doberai Peninsula
Manokwari
Biak
Biak
Yapen
Serui
Wuvulu Island

Kendari
Wowoni · Namlea
Ceram Sea
3027
Bula
Teluk Berau
Babo
Fakfak
Kaimana
Teluk Cenderawasih
Memberamo
Jayapura
Vanimo
Aitape

Kepulauan Banggai · Buru
Ambon · *Ceram*
Adi
Pegunungan Maoke
New
Sepik

Muna · Buton
Kepulauan Banda
4884
Puncak Jaya
Amamapare
Puncak Mandala
4700
Central Range

Baubau
Kepulauan Tukangbesi
Banda Sea
Kepulauan Kai
Wokam
Kobroör
Guinea

SIA

Damar
Kepulauan Aru
Trangan

Flu
Balimo

Wetar
Roma
Alor · *Kepulauan Babar*
Kepulauan Tanimbar
Saumlakki
Arafura Sea
Tanjung Vals
Merauke
Morehead
Daru

Dili
EAST TIMOR (TIMOR-LESTE)
Kepulauan Leti
Selaru

Maumere
deh
Gunung Mutis 2962
Babar
Timor
2427
Kupang
Rote

Timor Sea

Melville Island
Croker Island
Wessel Islands
Cape Wessel
Torres Strait
Prince of Wales Island
Cape York
Bamaga

Bathurst Island
Van Diemen Gulf
Cape Arnhem

Beagle Gulf · Darwin

AUSTRALIA

Albatross Bay · Weipa

Relief and physical features

Relief metres

5000
3000
2000
1000
500
200
sea level
0
under sea level
200
4000
6000

▲ 4884 Mountain height (in metres)

Water features

~ River

Lake / Reservoir

Marsh

Communications

Railway

Road

⊕ Main airport

Administration

Boundaries

International

Internal

Settlement

Cities and towns in order of size

National capital
■ **Jakarta**

Other city or town
● **Shenzhen**
● **Hai Phong**
○ Padang
○ Ipoh
○ Tobelo

Scale 1 : 15 000 000

0 150 300 450 km

Mercator projection

Land use

- Rice
- Tea
- Mulberry
- Orchards
- Upland fields
- Forest
- Built-up

Scale 1 : 15 000 000

Grassland 0.9%
Roads 3.6%
Built-up 5.1%
Others 12%
Farmland 12.1%
Forest 66.3%

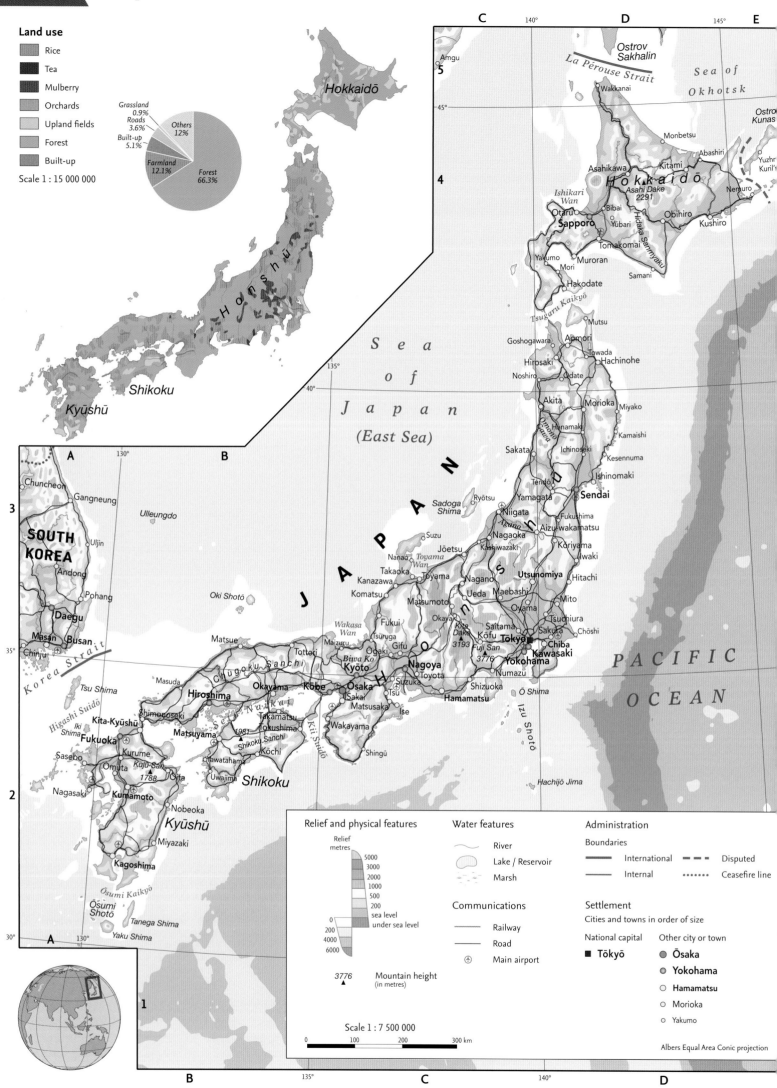

Hokkaidō

Honshū

Shikoku

Kyūshū

Ostrov Sakhalin

La Pérouse Strait

Sea of Okhotsk

Ostrov Kunas

Amgu

Wakkanai

Monbetsu

Abashiri

Yuzhr Kuril'

Asahikawa

Kitami

Nemuro

H o k k a i d ō

Asahi Dake 2291

Ishikari Wan

Otaru

Bibai

Yūbari

Hidaka Sammyaku

Obihiro

Kushiro

Sapporo

Tomakomai

Samani

Yakumo

Muroran

Mori

Hakodate

Tsugaru Kaikyō

Mutsu

Goshogawara

Aomori

Noshiro

Hirosaki

Towada

Hachinohe

Ōdate

Akita

Morioka

Miyako

Omono kawa

Hanamaki

Kamaishi

Sakata

Ichinoseki

Kesennuma

Tendō

Ishinomaki

Yamagata

Sendai

Ryōtsu

Niigata

Fukushima

Sadoga Shima

Agano

Aizu-wakamatsu

Suzu

Nagaoka

Kōriyama

Nanao

Toyama Wan

Jōetsu

Kashiwazaki

Iwaki

Takaoka

Toyama

Nagano

Utsunomiya

Hitachi

Kanazawa

Nagano

Komatsu

Ueda

Maebashi

Mito

Matsumoto

Oyama

Tsuchiura

Fukui

Okaya

Saitama

Sakura

Chōshi

Tsuruga

Gifu

Kōfu

Tōkyō

Chiba

Maizuru

Ōgaki

Kita Dake 3193

Fuji San 3776

Kawasaki

Matsue

Tottori

Biwa Ko

Kyōto

Nagoya

Yokohama

Wakasa Wan

Toyota

Numazu

Masuda

Okayama

Kōbe

Ōsaka

Suzuka

Shizuoka

Ō Shima

Hiroshima

Sakai

Tsu

Hamamatsu

Shimonoseki

Seto Naikai

Takamatsu

Matsusaka

Izu Shotō

Kita-Kyūshū

Matsuyama

1981

Tokushima

Ise

Fukuoka

Shikoku Sanchi

Kōchi

Wakayama

Kurume

Ōita

Yawatahama

Sasebo

Ōmuta

Kuju-San 1788

Uwajima

Shikoku

Shingū

Nagasaki

Kumamoto

Kii Suidō

Nobeoka

Kyūshū

Miyazaki

Kagoshima

Ōsumi Kaikyō

Ōsumi Shotō

Tanega Shima

Yaku Shima

SOUTH KOREA

Chuncheon

Gangneung

Ulleungdo

Uljin

Andong

Pohang

Daegu

Masan

Busan

Chinju

Korea Strait

Tsu Shima

Higashi Suidō

Iki Shima

S e a   o f   J a p a n   (East Sea)

P A C I F I C

O C E A N

Hachijō Jima

Relief and physical features

Relief metres
5000
3000
2000
1000
500
200
sea level
under sea level
200
4000
6000

3776 Mountain height (in metres)

Water features

~~~ River
Lake / Reservoir
Marsh

Communications

Railway
Road
⊕ Main airport

Administration

Boundaries

International
Internal
Disputed
Ceasefire line

Settlement

Cities and towns in order of size

National capital
■ Tōkyō

Other city or town
● Ōsaka
● Yokohama
◉ Hamamatsu
○ Morioka
○ Yakumo

Scale 1 : 7 500 000

0   100   200   300 km

Albers Equal Area Conic projection

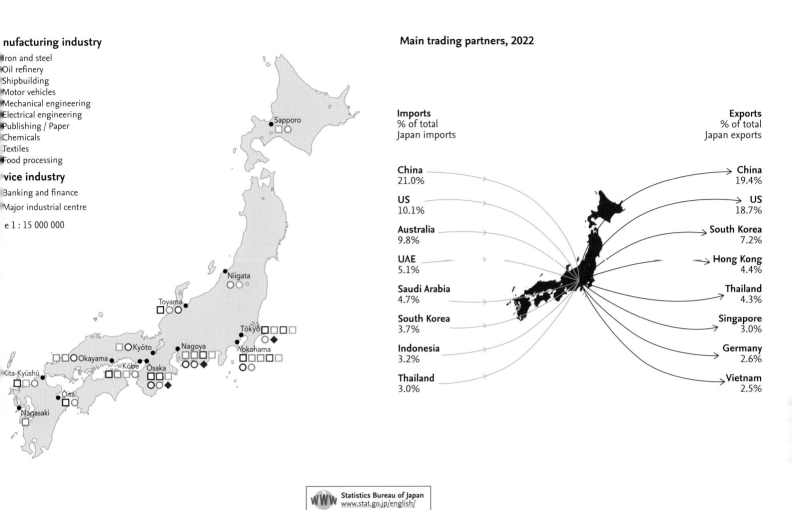

nufacturing industry

- Iron and steel
- Oil refinery
- Shipbuilding
- Motor vehicles
- Mechanical engineering
- Electrical engineering
- Publishing / Paper
- Chemicals
- Textiles
- Food processing

vice industry

- Banking and finance
- Major industrial centre

e 1 : 15 000 000

Main trading partners, 2022

Imports
% of total
Japan imports

China	21.0%
US	10.1%
Australia	9.8%
UAE	5.1%
Saudi Arabia	4.7%
South Korea	3.7%
Indonesia	3.2%
Thailand	3.0%

Exports
% of total
Japan exports

China	19.4%
US	18.7%
South Korea	7.2%
Hong Kong	4.4%
Thailand	4.3%
Singapore	3.0%
Germany	2.6%
Vietnam	2.5%

Statistics Bureau of Japan
www.stat.go.jp/english/

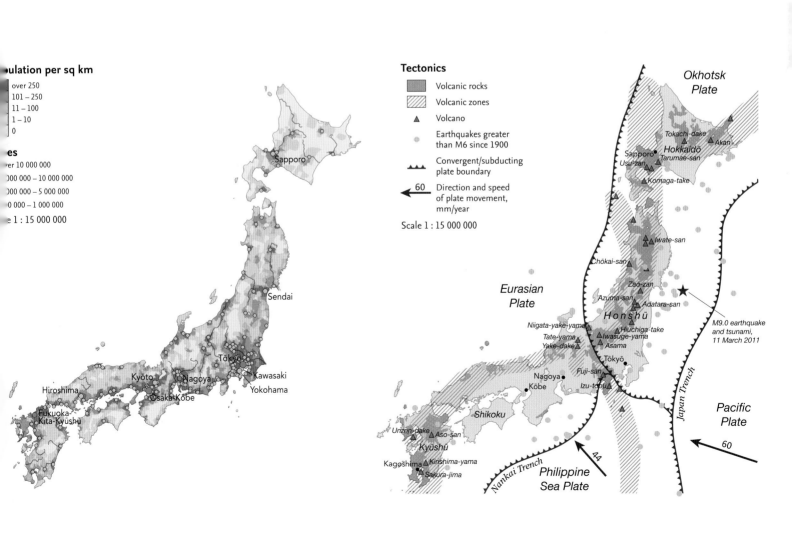

ulation per sq km

- over 250
- 101 – 250
- 11 – 100
- 1 – 10
- 0

es

- er 10 000 000
- 000 000 – 10 000 000
- 000 000 – 5 000 000
- 0 000 – 1 000 000
- 0 000 – 1 000 000

e 1 : 15 000 000

Tectonics

- Volcanic rocks
- Volcanic zones
- ▲ Volcano
- Earthquakes greater than M6 since 1900
- Convergent/subducting plate boundary
- 60 ← Direction and speed of plate movement, mm/year

Scale 1 : 15 000 000

Okhotsk Plate

Tokachi-dake ▲
Hokkaidō
Sapporo ● Tarumae-san
Usu-zan ▲ ▲ Akan
▲ Komaga-take

▲ Iwate-san

Chōkai-san ▲

Zaō-zan ▲
Azuma-san ▲ ▲ Adatara-san

Eurasian Plate

Honshū

Niigata-yake-yama ▲
Tate-yama ▲ ▲ Hiuchiga-take
Yake-dake ▲ ▲ Iwasuge-yama
▲ Asama

★ M9.0 earthquake and tsunami, 11 March 2011

Tōkyō ●

Nagoya ●
Kōbe ● Fuji-san ▲
Izu-tōbu ▲

Japan Trench

Pacific Plate

60 ←

Shikoku

Unzen-dake ▲ ▲ Aso-san
Kyūshū

Kagoshima ▲ Kirishima-yama
▲ Sakura-jima

Nankai Trench   44 ↗
Philippine Sea Plate

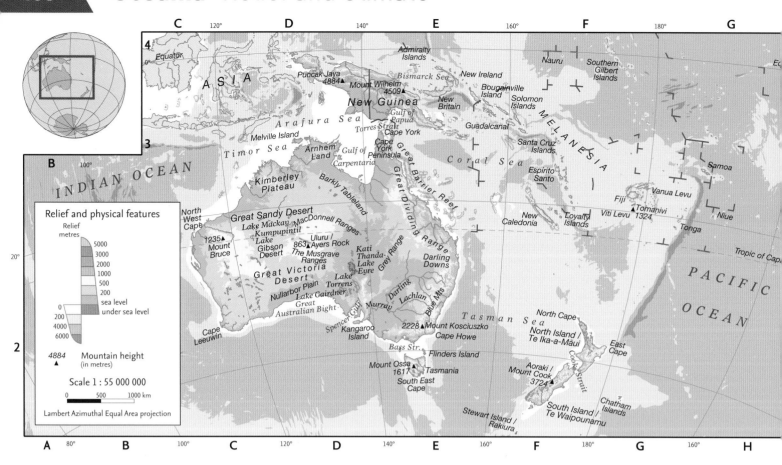

Relief and physical features

Relief metres
5000
3000
2000
1000
500
200
sea level
under sea level
200
4000
6000

4884 ▲ Mountain height (in metres)

Scale 1 : 55 000 000

0   500   1000 km

Lambert Azimuthal Equal Area projection

Australia: Cross-section

27°S

line of cross-section

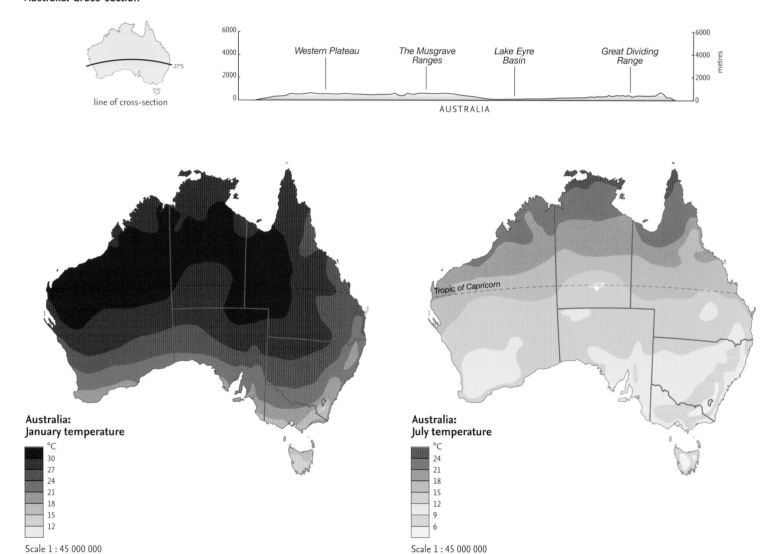

Western Plateau

The Musgrave Ranges

Lake Eyre Basin

Great Dividing Range

AUSTRALIA

Australia: January temperature

°C
30
27
24
21
18
15
12

Scale 1 : 45 000 000

Australia: July temperature

°C
24
21
18
15
12
9
6

Scale 1 : 45 000 000

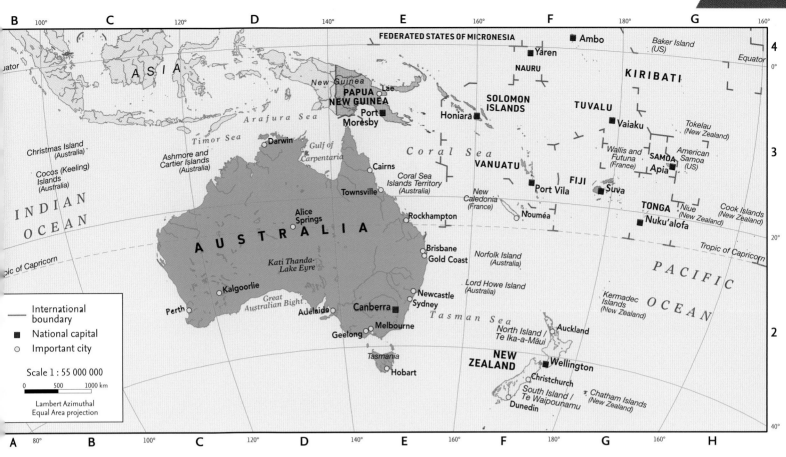

Facts about Oceania

Total land area	**8 844 516 sq km**
Highest peak	**Puncak Jaya, 4884 m**
Longest river	**Murray-Darling, 3672 km**
Largest country	**Australia, 7 692 024 sq km**
Most populous country	**Australia, 26 172 940**

Population by country, 2022
top ten countries

Samoa 222
Vanuatu 327
Solomon Islands 724
Fiji 930
Kiribati 131
F. S. Micronesia 114
Tonga 107

New Zealand 5185
Papua New Guinea 10 143
Australia 26 173

Population in thousands

GNI by country, 2022
top ten countries

Vanuatu 1163
Solomon Islands 1606
Fiji 4901
Papua New Guinea 27 700
Samoa 807
Tonga 522
F. S. Micronesia 472
Kiribati 431

New Zealand 248 333
Australia 1 569 896

Gross National Income in US $ millions

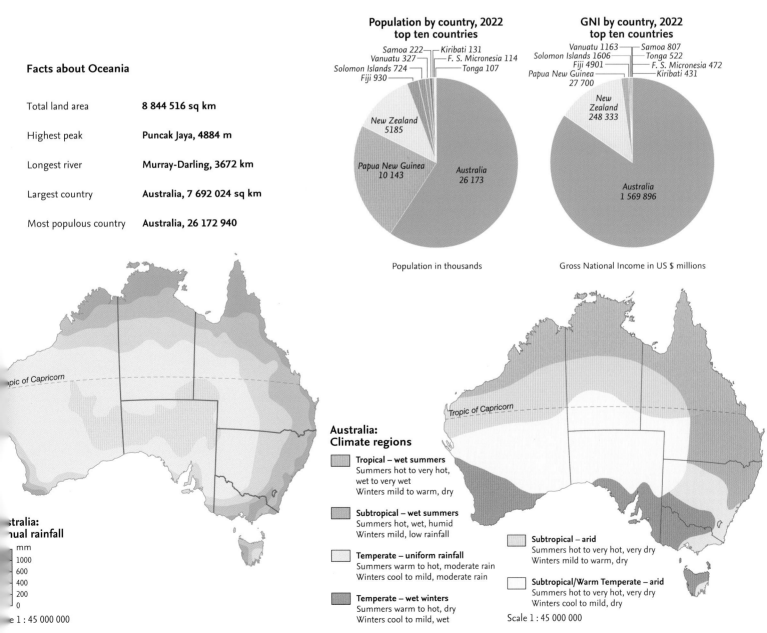

Australia:
Climate regions

Tropical – wet summers
Summers hot to very hot,
wet to very wet
Winters mild to warm, dry

Subtropical – wet summers
Summers hot, wet, humid
Winters mild, low rainfall

Temperate – uniform rainfall
Summers warm to hot, moderate rain
Winters cool to mild, moderate rain

Temperate – wet winters
Summers warm to hot, dry
Winters cool to mild, wet

Subtropical – arid
Summers hot to very hot, very dry
Winters mild to warm, dry

Subtropical/Warm Temperate – arid
Summers hot to very hot, very dry
Winters cool to mild, dry

Scale 1 : 45 000 000

Australia:
Annual rainfall

mm
1000
600
400
200
0

Scale 1 : 45 000 000

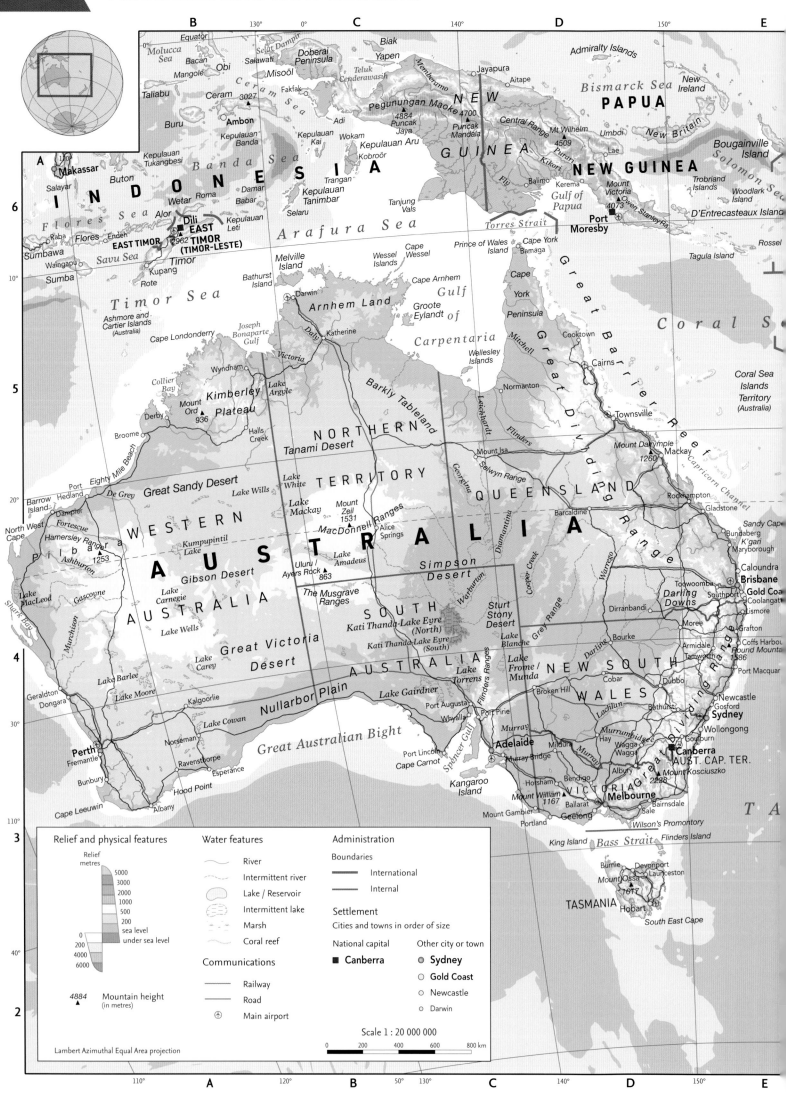

Relief and physical features

Relief metres
5000
3000
2000
1000
500
200
sea level
under sea level

▲ 4884 Mountain height (in metres)

Water features

~~~ River

Intermittent river

Lake / Reservoir

Intermittent lake

Marsh

Coral reef

Communications

Railway

Road

⊕ Main airport

Administration

Boundaries

International

Internal

Settlement

Cities and towns in order of size

National capital
■ Canberra

Other city or town
● Sydney
○ Gold Coast
○ Newcastle
○ Darwin

Scale 1 : 20 000 000

0   200   400   600   800 km

Lambert Azimuthal Equal Area projection

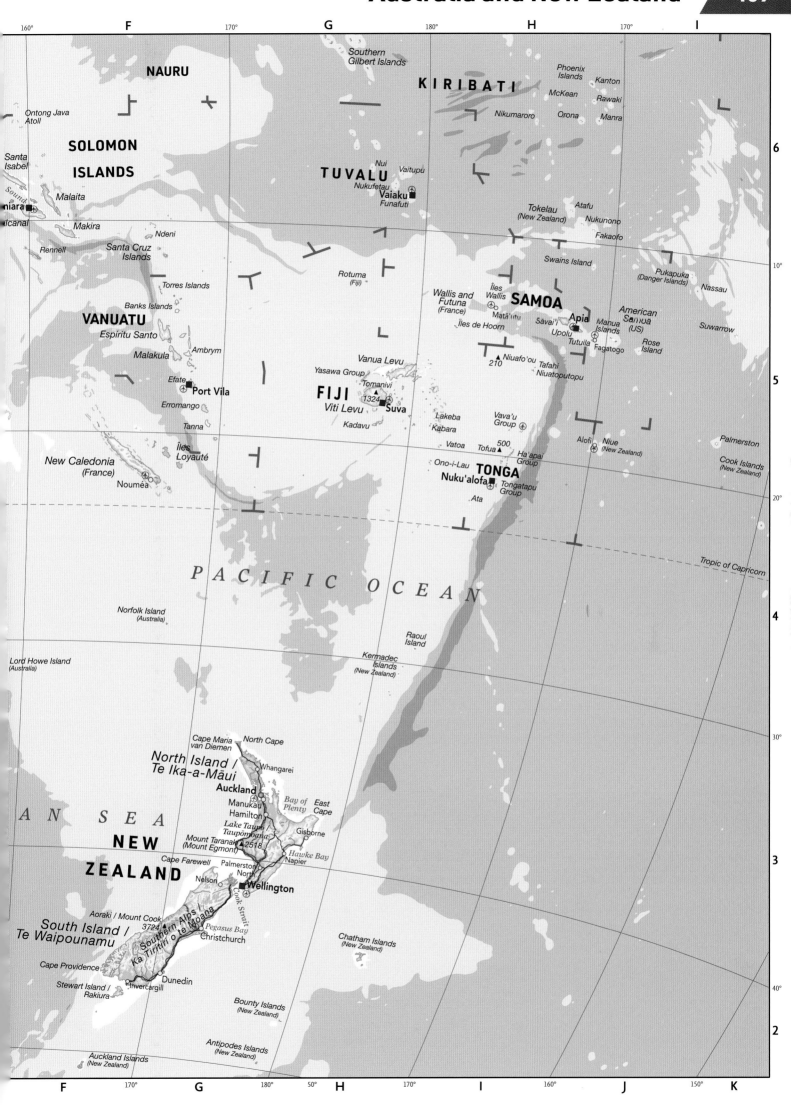

NAURU

Ontong Java
Atoll

SOLOMON

ISLANDS

Santa
Isabel

niara
lcanal

Malaita

Makira

Ndeni

Rennell

Santa Cruz
Islands

Torres Islands

Banks Islands

VANUATU

Espíritu Santo

Malakula

Ambrym

Efate
Port Vila

Erromango

Tanna

New Caledonia
(France)

Nouméa

Îles
Loyauté

Norfolk Island
(Australia)

Lord Howe Island
(Australia)

Southern
Gilbert Islands

KIRIBATI

Nui
Vaitupu

TUVALU

Nukufetau

Vaiaku
Funafuti

Phoenix
Islands

Kanton

McKean

Rawaki

Nikumaroro

Orona

Manra

Tokelau
(New Zealand)

Atafu

Nukunono

Fakaofo

Swains Island

Pukapuka
(Danger Islands)

Nassau

Rotuma
(Fiji)

Wallis and
Futuna
(France)

Îles
Wallis

SAMOA

Matā'utu

Apia

Manua
Islands

American
Samoa
(US)

Suwarrow

Îles de Hoorn

Savai'i

Upolu

Tutuila

Fagatogo

Rose
Island

Vanua Levu

Yasawa Group

Tomanivi

FIJI

1324

Viti Levu

Suva

Kadavu

Lakeba

Kabara

Niuafo'ou
210

Tafahi

Niuatoputapu

Vava'u
Group

Palmerston

Vatoa

Tofua
500

Ha'apai

Alofi

Niue
(New Zealand)

Cook Islands
(New Zealand)

Ono-i-Lau

Ata

TONGA

Nuku'alofa

Tongatapu
Group

Tropic of Capricorn

PACIFIC OCEAN

Raoul
Island

Kermadec
Islands
(New Zealand)

Cape Maria
van Diemen

North Cape

North Island /
Te Ika-a-Māui

Whangarei

Auckland

Manukau

Hamilton

Bay of
Plenty

East
Cape

Lake Taupo
Taupōmoana

Gisborne

AN SEA

NEW

ZEALAND

Mount Taranaki
(Mount Egmont)

2518

Hawke Bay

Napier

Cape Farewell

Palmerston
North

Nelson

Wellington

Aoraki / Mount Cook

3724

Cook Strait

South Island /
Te Waipounamu

Southern Alps /
Ka Tiritiri o te Moana

Pegasus
Bay

Christchurch

Cape Providence

Dunedin

Stewart Island /
Rakiura

Invercargill

Auckland Islands
(New Zealand)

Bounty Islands
(New Zealand)

Antipodes Islands
(New Zealand)

Chatham Islands
(New Zealand)

Australia Land Use, People and Natural Hazards

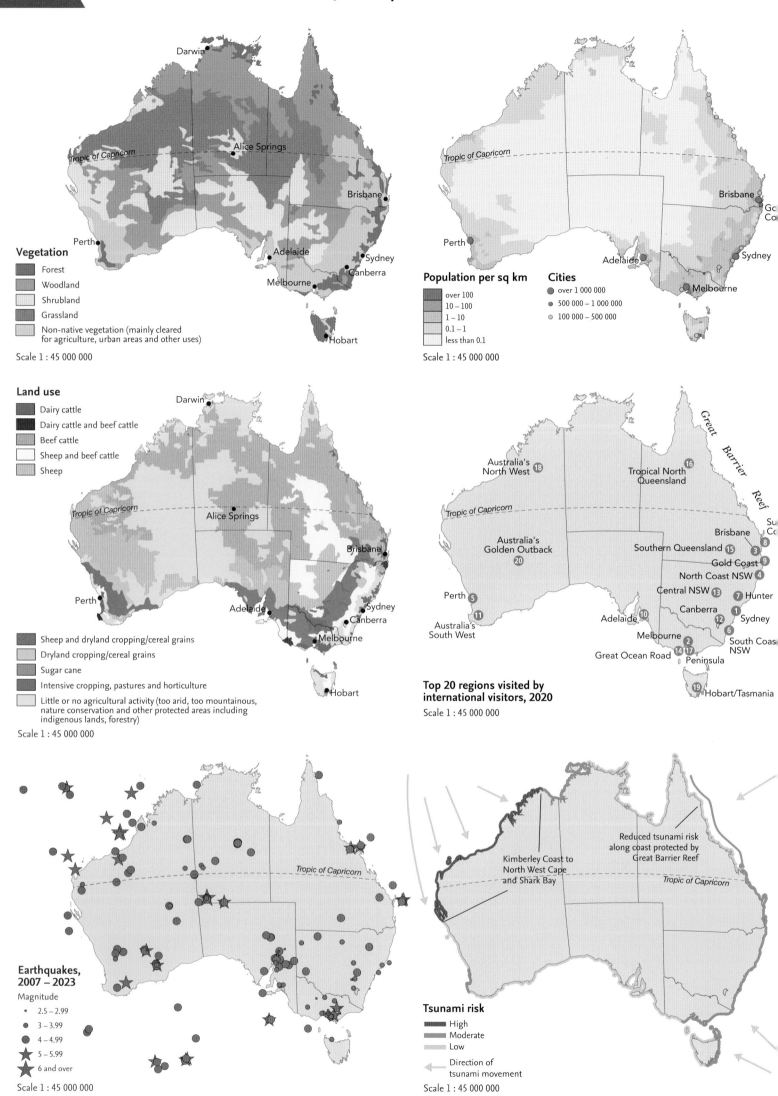

Vegetation

- Forest
- Woodland
- Shrubland
- Grassland
- Non-native vegetation (mainly cleared for agriculture, urban areas and other uses)

Scale 1 : 45 000 000

Darwin
Alice Springs
Tropic of Capricorn
Brisbane
Perth
Adelaide
Sydney
Canberra
Melbourne
Hobart

Population per sq km

- over 100
- 10 – 100
- 1 – 10
- 0.1 – 1
- less than 0.1

Cities

- over 1 000 000
- 500 000 – 1 000 000
- 100 000 – 500 000

Scale 1 : 45 000 000

Tropic of Capricorn
Brisbane
Gc
Co
Perth
Adelaide
Sydney
Melbourne

Land use

- Dairy cattle
- Dairy cattle and beef cattle
- Beef cattle
- Sheep and beef cattle
- Sheep

- Sheep and dryland cropping/cereal grains
- Dryland cropping/cereal grains
- Sugar cane
- Intensive cropping, pastures and horticulture
- Little or no agricultural activity (too arid, too mountainous, nature conservation and other protected areas including indigenous lands, forestry)

Scale 1 : 45 000 000

Darwin
Alice Springs
Tropic of Capricorn
Brisbane
Perth
Adelaide
Sydney
Canberra
Melbourne
Hobart

Top 20 regions visited by international visitors, 2020

Scale 1 : 45 000 000

Australia's North West ⑱
Tropical North Queensland ⑯
Tropic of Capricorn
Australia's Golden Outback ⑳
Brisbane
Southern Queensland ⑮
⑧
Gold Coast ③
North Coast NSW ④ ⑨
Central NSW ⑬
Perth ⑤
⑪
Australia's South West
Adelaide ⑩
Hunter ⑦
Canberra
⑫
Sydney ①
Melbourne ②
⑥
South Coast NSW
Great Ocean Road ⑭ ⑰
Peninsula
⑲ Hobart/Tasmania
Great Barrier Reef
Su Co

Earthquakes, 2007 – 2023

Magnitude
- 2.5 – 2.99
- 3 – 3.99
- 4 – 4.99
- ★ 5 – 5.99
- ★ 6 and over

Tropic of Capricorn

Scale 1 : 45 000 000

Tsunami risk

- High
- Moderate
- Low
- Direction of tsunami movement

Kimberley Coast to North West Cape and Shark Bay
Reduced tsunami risk along coast protected by Great Barrier Reef
Tropic of Capricorn

Scale 1 : 45 000 000

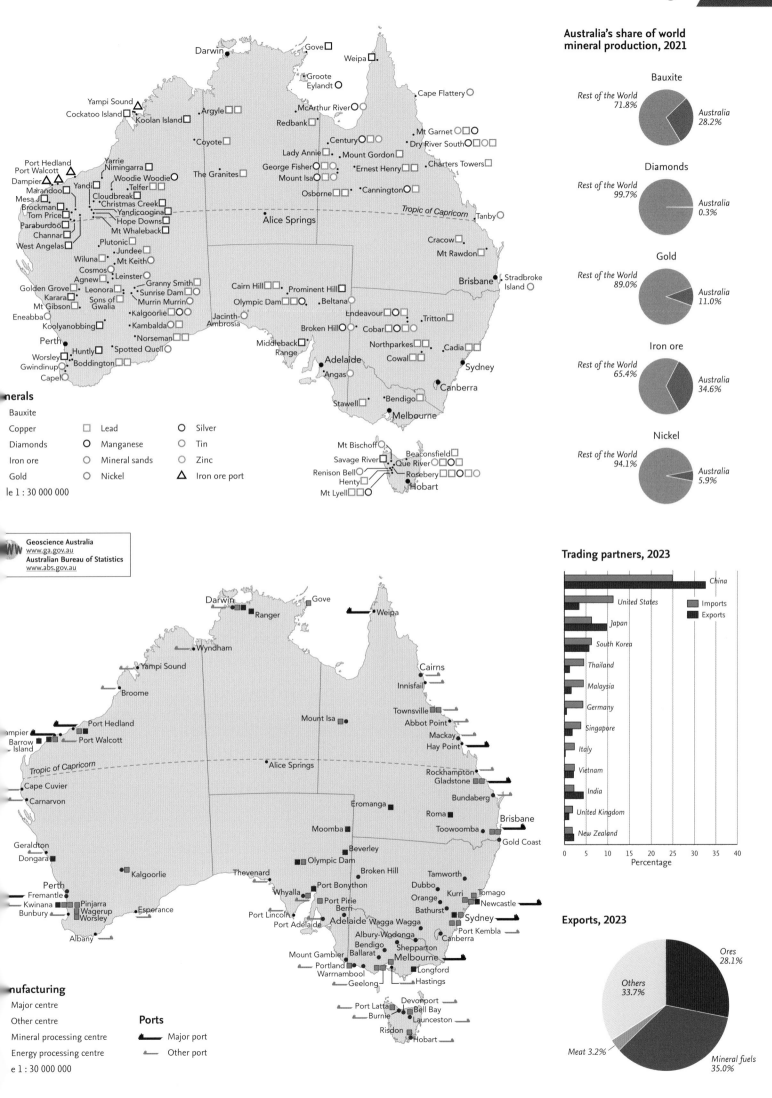

Australia's share of world mineral production, 2021

Bauxite
Rest of the World 71.8%
Australia 28.2%

Diamonds
Rest of the World 99.7%
Australia 0.3%

Gold
Rest of the World 89.0%
Australia 11.0%

Iron ore
Rest of the World 65.4%
Australia 34.6%

Nickel
Rest of the World 94.1%
Australia 5.9%

Minerals

Bauxite
Copper
Diamonds
Iron ore
Gold

☐ Lead
○ Manganese
○ Mineral sands
○ Nickel

○ Silver
○ Tin
○ Zinc
△ Iron ore port

Scale 1 : 30 000 000

Geoscience Australia
www.ga.gov.au
Australian Bureau of Statistics
www.abs.gov.au

Trading partners, 2023

China
United States
Japan
South Korea
Thailand
Malaysia
Germany
Singapore
Italy
Vietnam
India
United Kingdom
New Zealand

■ Imports
■ Exports

0 5 10 15 20 25 30 35 40
Percentage

Manufacturing

Major centre
Other centre
Mineral processing centre
Energy processing centre
Scale 1 : 30 000 000

Ports
Major port
Other port

Exports, 2023

Ores 28.1%
Others 33.7%
Meat 3.2%
Mineral fuels 35.0%

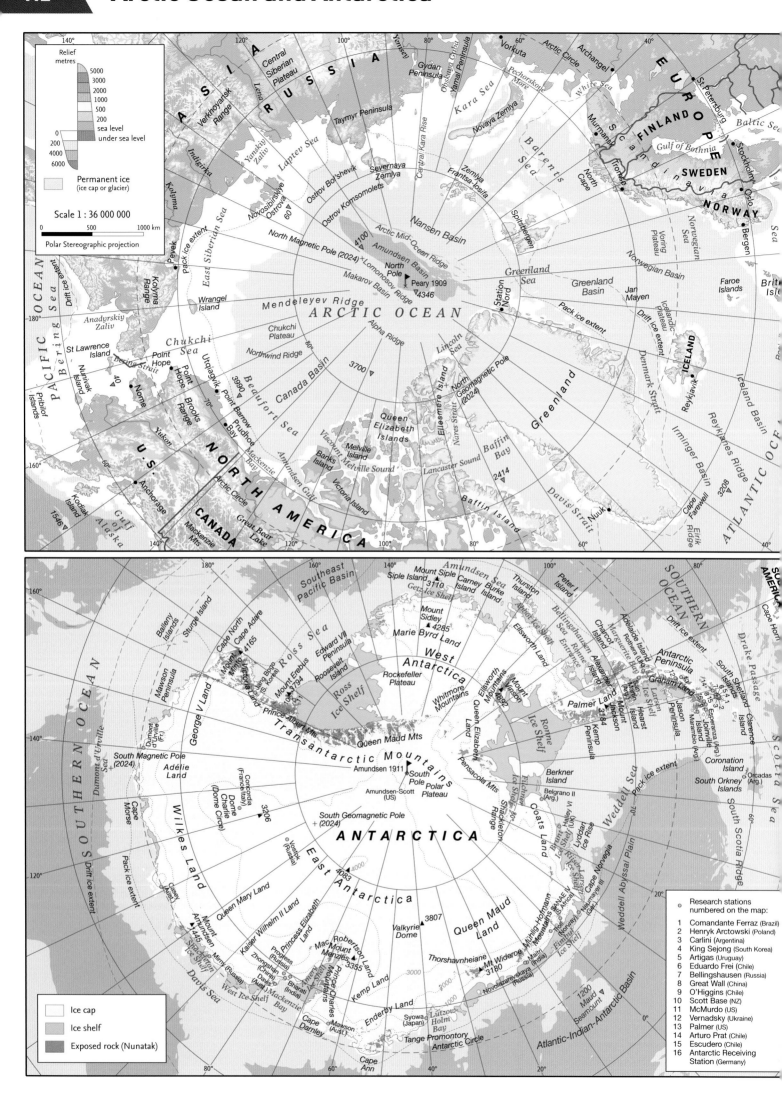

Relief metres
5000
3000
2000
1000
500
200
sea level
0
under sea level
200
4000
6000

Permanent ice (ice cap or glacier)

Scale 1 : 36 000 000

0   500   1000 km

Polar Stereographic projection

Research stations numbered on the map:

1 Comandante Ferraz (Brazil)
2 Henryk Arctowski (Poland)
3 Carlini (Argentina)
4 King Sejong (South Korea)
5 Artigas (Uruguay)
6 Eduardo Frei (Chile)
7 Bellingshausen (Russia)
8 Great Wall (China)
9 O'Higgins (Chile)
10 Scott Base (NZ)
11 McMurdo (US)
12 Vernadsky (Ukraine)
13 Palmer (US)
14 Arturo Prat (Chile)
15 Escudero (Chile)
16 Antarctic Receiving Station (Germany)

Ice cap
Ice shelf
Exposed rock (Nunatak)

United Nations factfile

Established:
4 October 1945

Headquarters:
New York, US

Purpose:
Maintain international peace and security.
Develop friendly relations among nations.
Help to solve international, economic, social
cultural and humanitarian problems.
Help promote respect for human rights.
To be a centre for harmonizing the actions
of nations in attaining these ends.

Structure:
The 6 principal organs of the UN are:
General Assembly
Security Council
Economic and Social Council
Trusteeship Council (suspended since 1994)
International Court of Justice
Secretariat

Members:
There are 193 members.
Taiwan, Vatican City and Kosovo
are the only non-member countries.

Headquarters of UN agencies

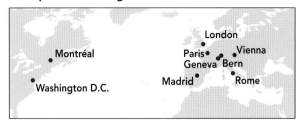

City	Organization
Rome, Italy	Food and Agricultural Organization
Washington D.C., US	The World Bank
Montréal, Canada	International Civil Aviation Organization
Rome, Italy	International Fund for Agricultural Development
Geneva, Switzerland	International Labour Organization
London, UK	International Maritime Organization
Washington D.C., US	International Monetary Fund
Geneva, Switzerland	International Telecommunication Union
Paris, France	UNESCO
Vienna, Austria	UN Industrial Development Organization
Bern, Switzerland	Universal Postal Union
Geneva, Switzerland	WHO
Geneva, Switzerland	World Intellectual Property Organization
Geneva, Switzerland	World Meteorological Organization
Madrid, Spain	World Tourism Organization

Structure of United Nations

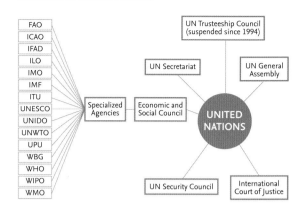

United Nations
www.un.org
Commonwealth
www.thecommonwealth.org

- Commonwealth of Nations
- NATO – North Atlantic Treaty Organization
- Pacific Islands Forum
- Arab League
- ASEAN – Association of Southeast Asian Nations

Cook Is / Fiji / French Polynesia / Kiribati / Marshall Is / Micronesia / Nauru / New Caledonia / Niue / Palau / Samoa / Solomon Is / Tonga / Tuvalu / Vanuatu

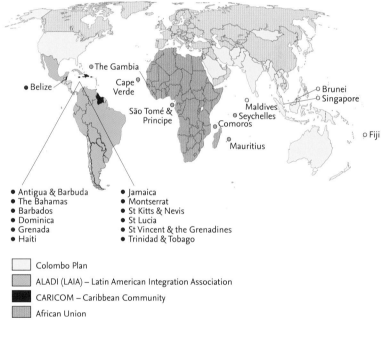

- Colombo Plan
- ALADI (LAIA) – Latin American Integration Association
- CARICOM – Caribbean Community
- African Union

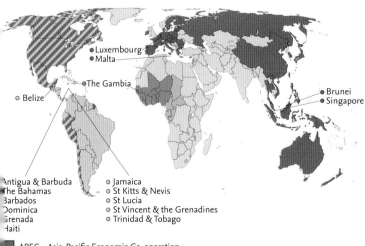

- APEC – Asia-Pacific Economic Co-operation
- OAS – Organization of American States
- EU – European Union (In 2016, the UK voted to leave the EU)
- ECOWAS – Economic Community of African States
- CEMAC – Economic and Monetary Community of Central Africa

- BRICS – a partnership of countries with emerging markets
- OECD – Organisation for Economic Co-operation and Development
- SADC – Southern African Development Community
- OPEC – Organization of Petroleum Exporting Countries

Scale 1 : 130 000 000

Countries shaded grey on all maps are not
members of the organizations listed

Settlement
■ National capital

Scale 1 : 80 000 000

0   800   1600   2400 km

Greenland
(Denmark)

RUSSIA   U.S.

Arctic Circle

CANADA

4

Nuuk
(Godthåb)   Reykjavik   ICELAN

40°

UNITED
STATES   Washington D.C.   Ral

MOR

Tropic of Cancer

Laâyóune

WESTERN
SAHARA

3   Hawai'ian
Islands
(US)   MEXICO   THE
BAHAMAS
Havana   Nassau   MAURITAN

Mexico City   CUBA
Kingston   DOMINICAN
REP.   San Juan   Nouakchott

Belmopan   BELIZE   HAITI
JAMAICA   Puerto
Rico
(US)   CAPE
VERDE   SENEGAL
Dakar   B

GUATEMALA
Guatemala City   HONDURAS   THE GAMBIA   Bissau
Guatemala City   Tegucigalpa   GUINEA-   Ouag
EL SALVADOR   NICARAGUA   BISSAU   GUINE
Managua   Caracas   TRINIDAD & TOBAGO   Conakry   Ya
COSTA RICA   Panama   Port of Spain   Freetown
San José   City   SIERRA LEONE
PANAMA   VENEZUELA   Monrovia   LIBERIA
Georgetown   Paramaribo
Bogotá   GUYANA   Cayenne
COLOMBIA   SURINAME   French
Guiana
Quito
ECUADOR

PACIFIC

Equator

Galapagos Is
(Ec)

OCEAN

KIRIBATI

Marquesas
Is
(Fr)

BRAZIL   ATLANT.

American
Samoa   French
Polynesia   PERU

Apia   Lima
SAMOA   Cook
Islands
(NZ)   Society Is
(Fr)   Tuamotu
Archipelago   La Paz   Brasília

Tahiti   BOLIVIA
Sucre

2   Nuku'alofa   PARAGUAY
TONGA   Asunción

Tropic of Capricorn   Easter I.
(Chile)   Valparaíso   URUGUAY
Santiago   Buenos   Montevideo
Aires

40°   Falkland Islands
(UK)   South Georgia and
South Sandwich Islands
(UK)

A   B   1

Antarctic Circle   SO

C   D   E

120°   80°   40°

ICELAND
Reykjavik

NORWAY   FINLAND

SWEDEN   Helsinki

Oslo   Tallinn
Stockholm   ESTONIA
Riga   LATVIA   RUSSIA

DENMARK   LITHUANIA
Copenhagen   Vilnius   Moscow

UNITED   RUSSIA
KINGDOM   Minsk
Dublin   The Hague   Amsterdam   BELARUS
IRELAND   London   NETH.   Berlin   Warsaw   Kyiv
Brussels   GERMANY   POLAND   UKRAINE
BELGIUM   Prague   CZECHIA   SLOVAKIA
Paris   LUX.   Vienna   Bratislava   MOLDOVA
FRANCE   SW.   AUSTRIA   Budapest   Chișinău
Bern   SL.   HUNGARY   ROMANIA
Ljubljana   Zagreb   Bucharest
SLOVENIA   CROATIA   B.H.   SERBIA
PORTUGAL   ANDORRA   MONACO   S.M.   Sarajevo   Belgrade   BULGARIA
Madrid   ITALY   M   Pristina   Sofia
Lisbon   V.C.   Podgorica   K   Skopje   TURKEY
SPAIN   Rome   Tirana   N.M.
ALBANIA

Athens

GREECE

MALTA

Europe

B.H.	BOSNIA AND HERZEGOVINA
K.	KOSOVO
L.	LIECHTENSTEIN
LUX.	LUXEMBOURG
M.	MONTENEGRO
NETH.	NETHERLANDS
N.M.	NORTH MACEDONIA
S.M.	SAN MARINO
SW.	SWITZERLAND
V.C.	VATICAN CITY

International boundaries in
the sea shown on this map
indicate ownership of islands
and island groups only. They
do not imply the alignment of
legal maritime boundaries.

Not all countries are named
on the map.

40°   80°   120°   160°

TIC OCEAN

Arctic Circle

R U S S I A

Moscow

Astana

KAZAKHSTAN

Ulan Bator

MONGOLIA

Beijing

4

SET BOTTOM LEFT
MORE DETAILED
AP OF EUROPE

GEORGIA Tbilisi Bishkek
Ankara ARMENIA UZBEKISTAN KYRGYZSTAN
Yerevan AZERBAIJAN Tashkent
TURKEY Baku TURKMEN- TAJIKISTAN
ISTAN Dushanbe
Ashgabat

NORTH
KOREA
P'yŏngyang
Seoul
SOUTH
KOREA

JAPAN

Tōkyō

PACIFIC

OCEAN

40°

TUNISIA
Tripoli

CYPRUS SYRIA
LEBANON Damascus
ISRAEL Baghdād
JORDAN IRAQ
Ammān
Cairo

Tehrān
Kābul AFGHAN-
ISTAN
Islamabad

CHINA

Taipei

Tunis

40°

LIBYA

EGYPT

KUWAIT Kuwait
City
BAHRAIN QATAR
Riyadh UNITED
ARAB Muscat
EMIRATES

SAUDI

ARABIA

New
Delhi
NEPAL
Kathmandu

PAKISTAN

BHUTAN
Dhaka
BANGLA-
DESH

OMAN

INDIA

TAIWAN

Tropic of Cancer

3

IGER

CHAD

N'Djaména

SUDAN

Khartoum

ERITREA YEMEN
Asmara Sanaa

DJIBOUTI
Addis
Ababa

Nay Pyi Taw

MYANMAR
(BURMA)

Vientiane

THAILAND

Bangkok

Hanoi

LAOS

VIETNAM

CAMBODIA

Phnom
Penh

PHILIPPINES

Manila

Northern
Mariana
Islands
(US)

MARSHALL
ISLANDS

Delap-
Uliga-Djarrit

GERIA

Abuja

Novo

CAMEROON

Yaoundé

IAL
EA

GABON

Brazzaville

Kinshasa

CENTRAL
AFRICAN
REPUBLIC
Bangui

SOUTH
SUDAN

Juba

ETHIOPIA

SOMALIA

SRI
LANKA

Sri Jayawardenapura Kotte

MALDIVES

Ngerulmud

PALAU

Kuala Lumpur

MALAYSIA

BRUNEI
Bandar Seri Begawan

Putrajaya

SINGAPORE

Palikir

FEDERATED STATES OF
MICRONESIA

Ambo

UGANDA

Kampala

DEMOCRATIC

REPUBLIC RWANDA
Kigali
OF THE
Gitega
CONGO BURUNDI

KENYA

Nairobi

Mogadishu

SEYCHELLES

INDONESIA

PAPUA
NEW
GUINEA

Yaren
NAURU

KIRIBATI

TUVALU

CONGO

Luanda

TANZANIA

Dodoma

INDIAN

Jakarta

Dili
EAST
TIMOR

Port
Moresby

SOLOMON
ISLANDS

Honiara

Vaiaku

0°

ANGOLA

ZAMBIA

Lusaka

COMOROS

Antananarivo

OCEAN

Harare

MALAWI

Lilongwe

ZIMBABWE

MADAGASCAR

MAURITIUS

VANUATU

Port Vila

New
Caledonia
(Fr)

FIJI

Suva

2

NAMIBIA

Windhoek

BOTS-
WANA

Gaborone

Pretoria

MOZAMBIQUE

AUSTRALIA

Tropic of Capricorn

Bloemfontein

SOUTH
AFRICA

Maputo
ESWATINI
(SWAZILAND)
LESOTHO
Máseru

Canberra

NEW
ZEALAND

Wellington

Cape Town

Îles
Kerguelen
(Fr)

1

ERN OCEAN

F   G   H

I   J

A N T A R C T I C A

40°   80°   120°

The Continents

NORTH
AMERICA

EUROPE

ASIA

SOUTH
AMERICA

AFRICA

OCEANIA

ANTARCTICA

ANTARCTICA

60°N

0° 120°W

60°W

0°

60°E

60°S

180°

0°

60°E

60°S

Country areas

	sq km
Russia	17 075 400
Canada	9 984 670
United States	9 826 635
China	9 606 802
Brazil	8 514 879
Australia	7 692 024
India	3 166 620
Argentina	2 766 889
Kazakhstan	2 717 300
Algeria	2 381 741

Relief and physical features

Relief
metres

5000
3000
2000
1000
500
200
sea level
0
200 under sea level
4000
6000

Permanent ice
(ice cap or glacier)

8849 ▲ Mountain height
(in metres)

11022 ▽ Ocean depth
(in metres)

Scale 1 : 80 000 000

0   800   1600   2400 km

Mountain heights

	metres
Mt Everest (China/Nepal)	8849
K2 (China/Pakistan)	8611
Kangchenjunga (India/Nepal)	8586
Dhaulagiri I (Nepal)	8167
Annapurna I (Nepal)	8091
Cerro Aconcagua (Argentina)	6961
Cerro Ojos del Salado (Arg./Chile)	6893
Chimborazo (Ecuador)	6263
Denali (Mt McKinley) (US)	6190
Mt Logan (Canada)	5959

Island areas

	sq km
Greenland	2 175 600
New Guinea	808 510
Borneo	745 561
Madagascar	587 040
Baffin Island	507 451
Sumatra	473 606
Honshū	227 414
Great Britain	218 476
Victoria Island	217 291
Ellesmere Island	196 236

Continents

	sq kr
Asia	45 036 49
Africa	30 343 57
North America	24 680 33
South America	17 815 42
Antarctica	12 093 00
Europe	9 908 59
Oceania	8 844 51

ceans

	sq km
cific Ocean	166 241 000
antic Ocean	86 557 000
dian Ocean	73 427 000
ctic Ocean	9 485 000

Lake areas

	sq km
Caspian Sea (Europe/Asia)	371 000
Lake Superior (N. America)	82 100
Lake Victoria (Africa)	68 870
Lake Huron (N. America)	59 600
Lake Michigan (N. America)	57 800
Lake Tanganyika (Africa)	32 600
Great Bear Lake (N. America)	31 328
Lake Baikal (Asia)	30 500
Lake Nyasa (Africa)	29 500

River lengths

	km
Nile (Africa)	6695
Amazon (S. America)	6516
Chang Jiang (Asia)	6380
Mississippi-Missouri (N. America)	5969
Ob'-Irtysh (Asia)	5568
Yenisey-Angara-Selenga (Asia)	5550
Huang He (Asia)	5464
Congo (Africa)	4667
Río de la Plata-Paraná (S. America)	4500
Irtysh (Asia)	4440

Eckert IV projection

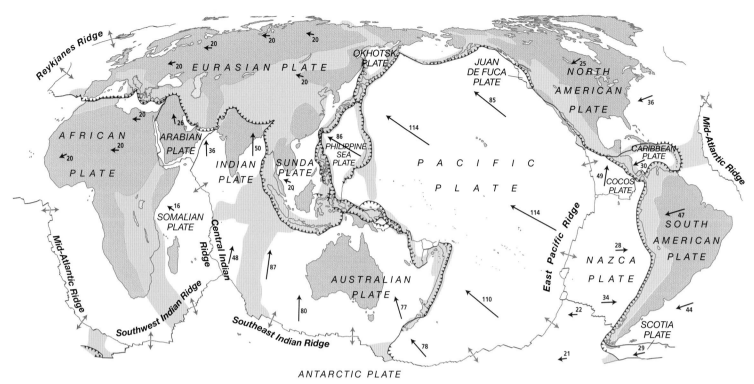

Tectonic plates

⌃⌃⌃⌃⌃⌃ Convergent plate boundary –
where plates collide and one plate
is pulled down (subducted) into
the mantle and destroyed, or
plates thicken and fracture in
complex patterns

Scale 1 : 170 000 000

——— Divergent plate boundary –
where plates move away from each
other and new crust is created as
magma reaches the surface

——— Transform plate boundary –
where plates are dragged horizontally
past each other, creating great friction
and many faults

⬛ Diffuse boundary zone –
broad zone in which plate movement
and change to the Earth's surface
occur over a wide region, often in
complex patterns with many
micro-plates

⬅44 General direction of plate
movement and approximate
speed, mm/year

↔ Movement at divergent plate
boundaries

Continental drift

200 million
years ago

150 million
years ago

100 million
years ago

50 million
years ago

Major earthquakes since 1985

Year	Location	Magnitude	Deaths	Year	Location	Magnitude	Deaths	Year	Location	Magnitude	Deaths
1985	Santiago, Chile	7.8	177	1993	Northern Japan	7.8	185	2005	Sumatra, Indonesia	8.7	1313
1985	Michoacán, Mexico	8.1	20 000	1993	Maharashtra, India	6.4	9748	2005	Muzzafarabad, Pakistan	7.6	80 361
1986	El Salvador	7.5	1000	1994	Kuril Islands, Russia	8.3	10	2008	Sichuan Province, China	8.0	87 476
1987	Ecuador	7.0	2000	1995	Kōbe, Japan	7.2	5502	2010	Léogâne, Haiti	7.0	222 570
1988	Yunnan, China	7.6	1000	1995	Sakhalin, Russia	7.6	2500	2011	Tōhoku, Japan	9.0	14 500
1988	Spitak, Armenia	6.9	25 000	1998	Papua New Guinea	7.0	2183	2015	Gorkha, Nepal	7.8	8831
1988	Nepal/India	6.9	1000	1999	İzmit, Turkey	7.4	17 118	2018	Sulawesi, Indonesia	7.5	4340
1990	Manjil, Iran	7.7	50 000	1999	Chi-Chi, Taiwan	7.7	2400	2020	Aegean Sea, Greece/Turkey	7.0	119
1990	Luzon, Philippines	7.7	1600	2001	Gujarat, India	6.9	20 085	2021	Nippes, Haiti	7.2	2248
1991	Uttar Pradesh, India	6.1	1600	2002	Hindu Kush, Afghanistan	6.0	1000	2022	Khowst, Afghanistan	6.0	1163
1992	Flores, Indonesia	7.5	2500	2003	Boumerdes, Algeria	5.8	2266	2023	Gaziantep, Turkey/Syria	7.8	57 400
1992	Erzincan, Turkey	6.8	500	2003	Bam, Iran	6.6	26 271	2023	Al Haouz, Morocco	6.8	2960
1992	Cairo, Egypt	5.9	550	2004	Sumatra, Indonesia	9.0	283 106	2023	Herāt, Afghanistan	6.3	1482

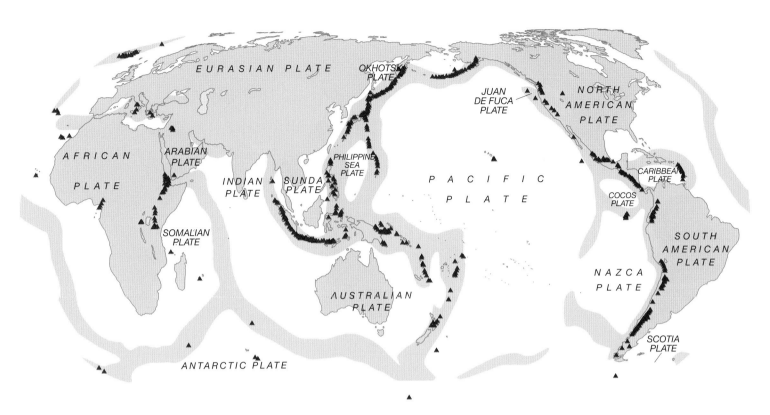

Volcanoes

Earthquake and volcano zone

▲ Major volcanoes

Scale 1 : 170 000 000

Major volcanic eruptions since 1980

Year	Location	Year	Location	Year	Location
1980	Mount St Helens, US	1991	Mount Pinatubo, Philippines	2001	Mount Etna, Italy
1982	El Chichónal, Mexico	1991	Unzen-dake, Japan	2002	Nyiragongo, Dem. Rep. of the Congo
1982	Galunggung, Indonesia	1993	Mayon, Philippines	2010	Eyjafjallajökull, Iceland
1983	Kilauea, Hawaii	1993	Volcán Galeras, Colombia	2011	Cordón de Caulle, Chile
1983	Ō-yama, Japan	1994	Volcán Llaima, Chile	2018	Anak Krakatoa, Indonesia
1985	Nevado del Ruiz, Colombia	1994	Rabaul, Papua New Guinea	2019	Mount Ulawun, Papua New Guinea
1986	Lake Nyos, Cameroon	1997	Soufrière Hills, Montserrat	2021	Fukutoku-Okanoba, Japan
1991	Hekla, Iceland	2000	Hekla, Iceland	2022	Hunga Tonga-Hunga Ha'apai, Tonga

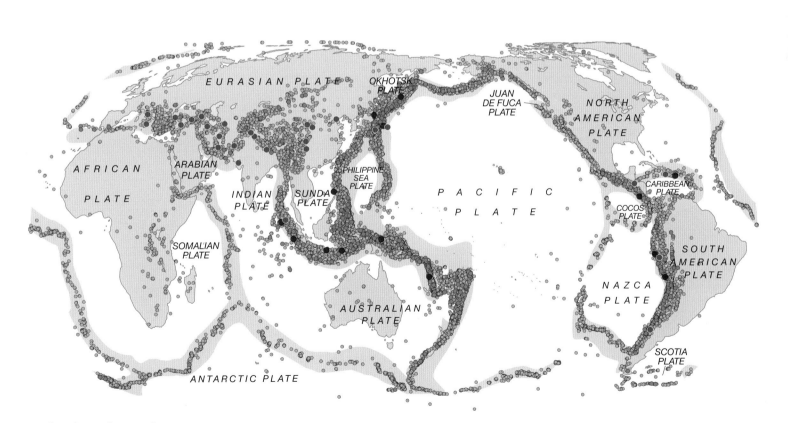

Earthquakes and tsunamis

Earthquake and volcano zone

● Major tsunamis since 1990

Scale 1 : 170 000 000

Major earthquakes since 1900

● 'Deadliest' earthquakes
● Greater than 7.5 on the moment magnitude scale
● 5.5–7.5 on the moment magnitude scale

WWW USGS Volcano Hazards Program
volcanoes.usgs.gov
USGS Earthquake Hazards Program
earthquakes.usgs.gov
British Geological Survey
www.bgs.ac.uk

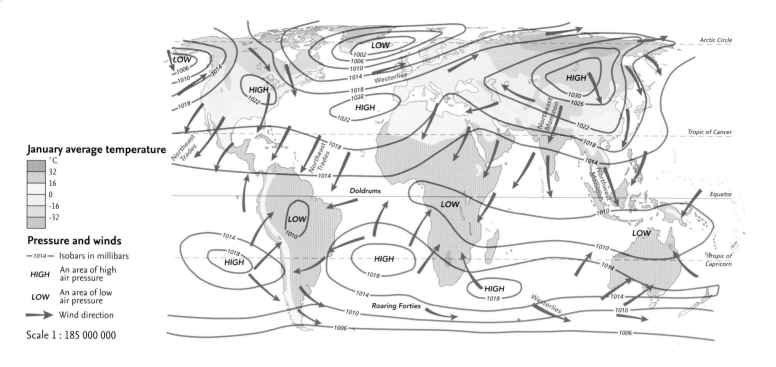

January average temperature

	°C
	32
	16
	0
	-16
	-32

Pressure and winds

— 1014 — Isobars in millibars

HIGH An area of high air pressure

LOW An area of low air pressure

→ Wind direction

Scale 1 : 185 000 000

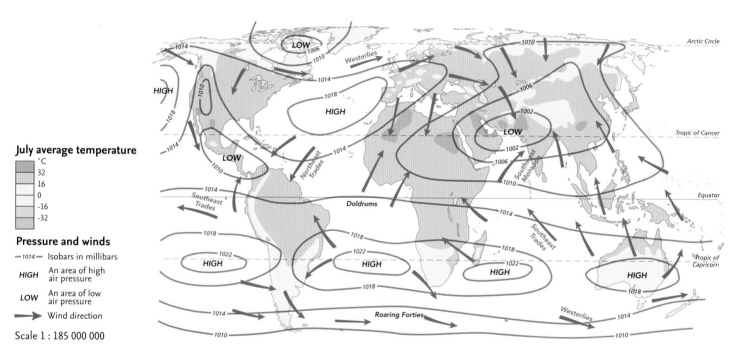

July average temperature

	°C
	32
	16
	0
	-16
	-32

Pressure and winds

— 1014 — Isobars in millibars

HIGH An area of high air pressure

LOW An area of low air pressure

→ Wind direction

Scale 1 : 185 000 000

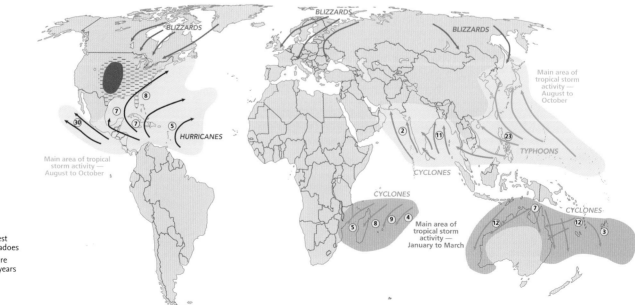

Storms

Main area of tornado activity

Tornado Alley – highest concentration of tornadoes

⑧ Likely number of severe tropical storms in 10 years

Arrows show typical storm paths

Scale 1 : 185 000 000

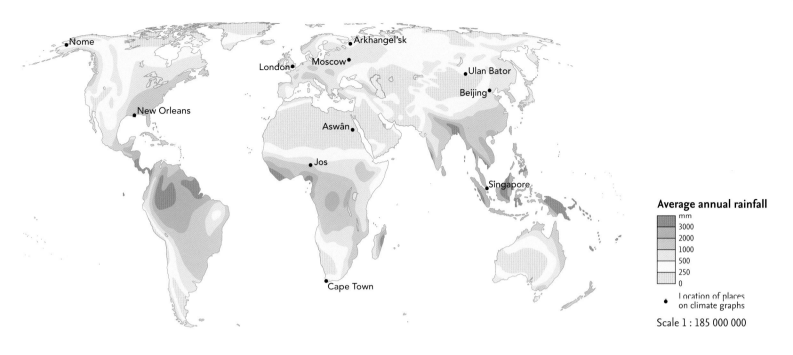

Average annual rainfall

mm
3000
2000
1000
500
250
0

• Location of places on climate graphs

Scale 1 : 185 000 000

Climate graphs

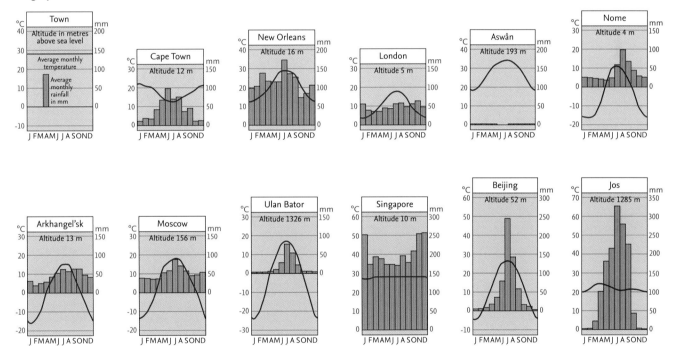

Major tropical storms since 2005

Year	Name	Location	Deaths
2005	Katrina	Southern US	1836
2006	Bilis	China	820
2007	Sidr	Bangladesh	4234
2008	Nargis	Myanmar	138 366
2009	Parma	Philippines	501
2010	Agatha	Guatemala	174
2011	Washi	Philippines	1439
2012	Sandy	Eastern US	148
2013	Haiyan	Philippines	7986
2014	Hudhud	Eastern India/Nepal	109
2016	Matthew	Caribbean	546
2017	Maria	Caribbean	3059
2019	Idai	Southeast Africa	>1300
2023	Freddy	South Indian Ocean	1434
2023	Daniel	Mediterranean	11 300

World weather extremes

Hottest place	34.4 °C (annual mean)	Dalol, Ethiopia
Driest place	0.1 mm (annual mean)	Atacama Desert, Chile
Most sunshine	90% (4000 hours) (annual mean)	Yuma, Arizona, US
Least sunshine	Nil for 182 days each year	South Pole
Coldest place	-56.6 °C (annual mean)	Plateau Station, Antarctica
Wettest place	11 873 mm (annual mean)	Meghalaya, India
Most rainy days	Up to 350 per year	Mount Waialeale, Hawaii, US
Greatest snowfall	31 102 mm (19.2.1971 – 18.2.1972)	Mount Rainier, Washington, US
Windiest place	322 km per hour in gales	Commonwealth Bay, Antarctica

World Meteorological Organization
www.wmo.int
Met Office
www.metoffice.gov.uk/weather

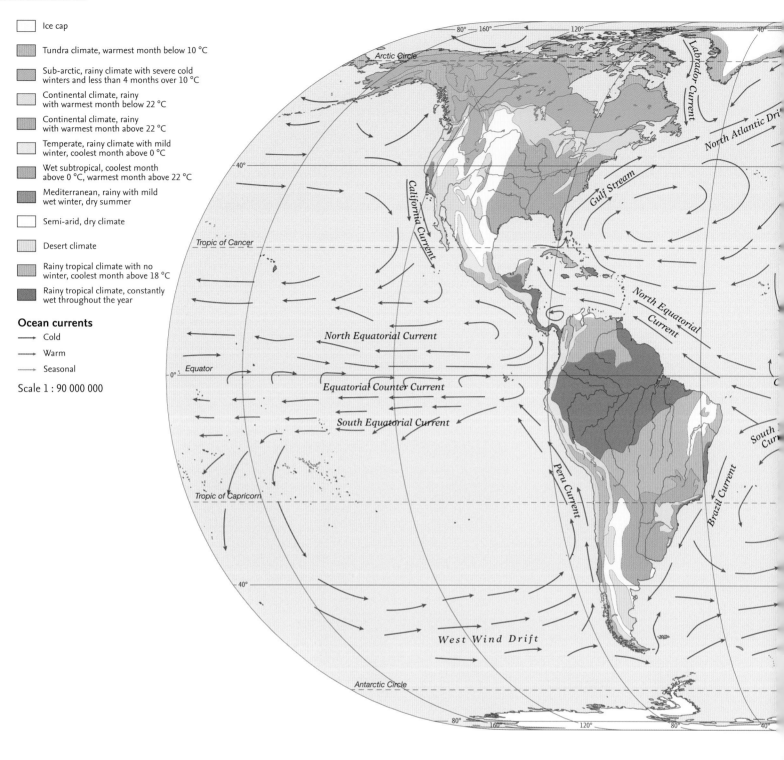

Ice cap

Tundra climate, warmest month below 10 °C

Sub-arctic, rainy climate with severe cold winters and less than 4 months over 10 °C

Continental climate, rainy with warmest month below 22 °C

Continental climate, rainy with warmest month above 22 °C

Temperate, rainy climate with mild winter, coolest month above 0 °C

Wet subtropical, coolest month above 0 °C, warmest month above 22 °C

Mediterranean, rainy with mild wet winter, dry summer

Semi-arid, dry climate

Desert climate

Rainy tropical climate with no winter, coolest month above 18 °C

Rainy tropical climate, constantly wet throughout the year

Ocean currents

⟶ Cold

⟶ Warm

⟶ Seasonal

Scale 1 : 90 000 000

The impact of oceans on climate: air

Normal circulation

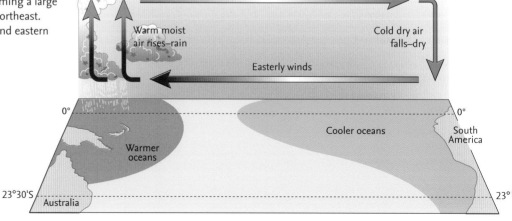

The oceans have a significant impact on climate. Under normal conditions, easterly winds push warm surface water across the Pacific Ocean to Australia, forming a large area of warmer water to the northeast. This brings rain to northern and eastern Australia.

World Meteorological Organization
www.wmo.int
Met Office
www.metoffice.gov.uk
United Nations Environment Programme
www.unep.org
World Conservation Monitoring Centre
www.unep-wcmc.org
World Resources Institute
www.wri.org

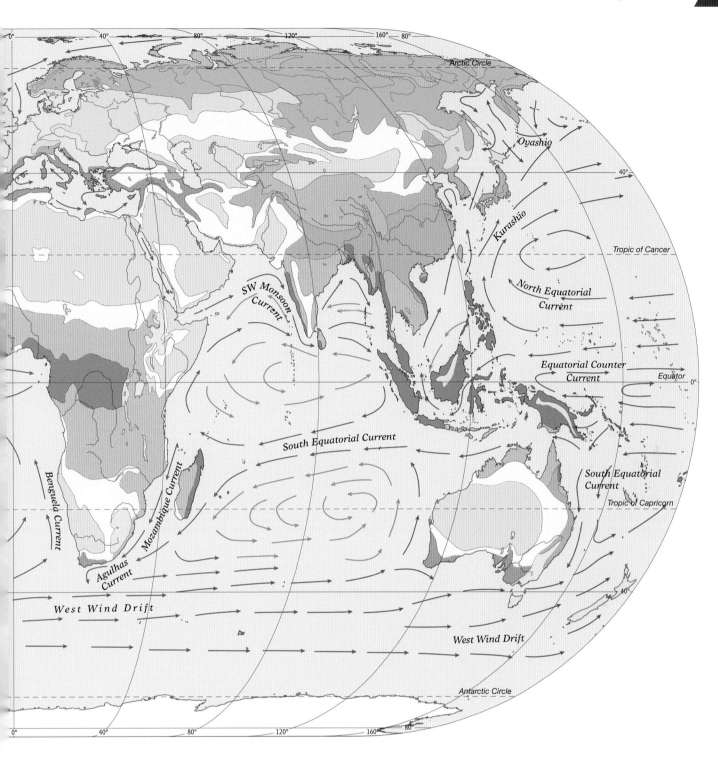

circulation in the Pacific Ocean

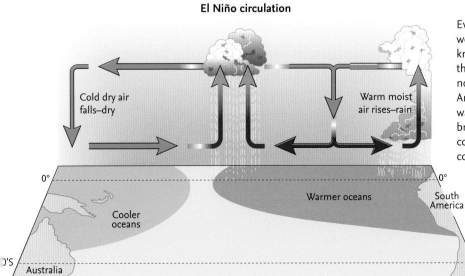

El Niño circulation

Cold dry air
falls–dry

Warm moist
air rises–rain

0°

Warmer oceans

Cooler
oceans

South
America

0°S

23°30'S

Australia

Every few years, these easterly winds weaken and reverse, which causes what is known as an El Niño event. The winds then move warm water from the northeast of Australia towards South America, forming a large area of warmer water in the eastern Pacific Ocean. This brings warmer conditions and rain to the coast of South America, and drought to countries such as Australia and Indonesia.

52.25N 4.05W

Aberystwyth	Jan	Feb	Mar	Apr	May	Jun	Jul	Aug	Sep	Oct	Nov	Dec
Temperature - max. (°C)	7	7	9	11	15	17	18	18	16	13	10	8
Temperature - min. (°C)	2	2	3	5	7	10	12	12	11	8	5	4
Rainfall - (mm)	97	72	60	56	65	76	99	93	108	118	111	96

16.55N 99.52W

Acapulco	Jan	Feb	Mar	Apr	May	Jun	Jul	Aug	Sep	Oct	Nov	Dec
Temperature - max. (°C)	31	31	31	32	32	33	32	33	32	32	32	31
Temperature - min. (°C)	22	22	22	23	25	25	25	25	24	24	23	22
Rainfall - (mm)	6	1	0	1	36	281	256	252	349	159	28	8

36.46N 3.04E

Algiers	Jan	Feb	Mar	Apr	May	Jun	Jul	Aug	Sep	Oct	Nov	Dec
Temperature - max. (°C)	15	16	17	20	23	26	28	29	27	23	19	16
Temperature - min. (°C)	9	9	11	13	15	18	21	22	21	17	13	11
Rainfall - (mm)	112	84	74	41	46	15	0	5	41	79	130	137

36.52S 174.46E

Auckland	Jan	Feb	Mar	Apr	May	Jun	Jul	Aug	Sep	Oct	Nov	Dec
Temperature - max. (°C)	23	24	22	20	17	15	15	15	16	18	20	22
Temperature - min. (°C)	15	16	15	12	12	8	7	8	9	11	12	14
Rainfall - (mm)	75	65	94	105	103	139	146	121	116	91	93	91

1.26S 48.29W

Belém	Jan	Feb	Mar	Apr	May	Jun	Jul	Aug	Sep	Oct	Nov	Dec
Temperature - max. (°C)	31	30	31	31	31	31	31	31	32	32	32	32
Temperature - min. (°C)	22	22	23	23	23	22	22	22	22	22	22	22
Rainfall - (mm)	318	358	358	320	259	170	150	112	89	84	66	155

54.36N 5.55W

Belfast	Jan	Feb	Mar	Apr	May	Jun	Jul	Aug	Sep	Oct	Nov	Dec
Temperature - max. (°C)	6	7	9	12	15	18	18	18	16	13	9	7
Temperature - min. (°C)	2	2	3	4	6	9	11	11	9	7	4	3
Rainfall - (mm)	80	52	50	48	52	68	94	77	80	83	72	90

52.29N 1.53W

Birmingham	Jan	Feb	Mar	Apr	May	Jun	Jul	Aug	Sep	Oct	Nov	Dec
Temperature - max. (°C)	5	6	9	12	16	19	20	20	17	13	9	6
Temperature - min. (°C)	2	2	3	5	7	10	12	12	10	7	5	3
Rainfall - (mm)	74	54	50	53	64	50	69	69	61	69	84	67

53.49N 3.03W

Blackpool	Jan	Feb	Mar	Apr	May	Jun	Jul	Aug	Sep	Oct	Nov	Dec
Temperature - max. (°C)	7	7	9	11	15	17	19	19	17	14	10	7
Temperature - min. (°C)	1	1	2	4	7	10	12	12	10	8	4	2
Rainfall - (mm)	78	54	64	51	53	59	61	78	86	93	89	87

30.07S 145.54E

Bourke	Jan	Feb	Mar	Apr	May	Jun	Jul	Aug	Sep	Oct	Nov	Dec
Temperature - max. (°C)	37	36	33	28	23	18	18	21	25	29	34	36
Temperature - min. (°C)	21	21	18	13	8	6	4	6	9	13	17	19
Rainfall - (mm)	36	38	28	28	25	28	23	20	20	23	31	36

44.26N 26.06E

Bucharest	Jan	Feb	Mar	Apr	May	Jun	Jul	Aug	Sep	Oct	Nov	Dec
Temperature - max. (°C)	1	4	10	18	23	27	30	30	25	18	10	4
Temperature - min. (°C)	-7	-5	-1	5	10	14	16	15	11	6	2	-3
Rainfall - (mm)	29	26	28	59	77	121	53	45	45	29	36	27

32.48N 79.58W

Charleston	Jan	Feb	Mar	Apr	May	Jun	Jul	Aug	Sep	Oct	Nov	Dec
Temperature - max. (°C)	14	15	19	23	27	30	31	31	28	24	19	15
Temperature - min. (°C)	6	7	10	14	19	23	24	24	22	16	11	7
Rainfall - (mm)	74	84	86	71	81	119	185	168	130	81	58	71

51.47N 1

Clacton-on-Sea	Jan	Feb	Mar	Apr	May	Jun	Jul	Aug	Sep	Oct	Nov	D
Temperature - max. (°C)	6	6	9	11	15	18	20	20	18	15	10	
Temperature - min. (°C)	2	2	3	5	8	11	13	14	12	9	5	
Rainfall - (mm)	49	31	43	40	40	45	43	43	48	48	55	

9.31N 13.

Conakry	Jan	Feb	Mar	Apr	May	Jun	Jul	Aug	Sep	Oct	Nov	D
Temperature - max. (°C)	31	31	32	32	32	30	28	28	29	31	31	
Temperature - min. (°C)	22	23	23	23	24	23	22	22	23	23	24	
Rainfall - (mm)	3	3	10	23	158	559	1298	1054	683	371	122	

12.27S 130

Darwin	Jan	Feb	Mar	Apr	May	Jun	Jul	Aug	Sep	Oct	Nov	D
Temperature - max. (°C)	32	32	33	33	33	31	31	32	33	34	34	
Temperature - min. (°C)	25	25	25	24	23	21	19	21	23	25	26	
Rainfall - (mm)	386	312	254	97	15	3	0	3	13	51	119	

42.19N 83.

Detroit	Jan	Feb	Mar	Apr	May	Jun	Jul	Aug	Sep	Oct	Nov	D
Temperature - max. (°C)	-1	0	6	13	19	25	28	27	23	16	8	
Temperature - min. (°C)	-7	-8	-3	3	9	14	17	17	13	7	1	
Rainfall - (mm)	53	53	64	64	84	91	84	69	71	61	61	

53.20N 6

Dublin	Jan	Feb	Mar	Apr	May	Jun	Jul	Aug	Sep	Oct	Nov	D
Temperature - max. (°C)	8	8	10	13	15	18	20	19	17	14	10	
Temperature - min. (°C)	1	2	3	4	6	9	11	11	9	6	4	
Rainfall - (mm)	67	55	51	45	60	57	70	74	72	70	67	

55.04N 3

Dumfries	Jan	Feb	Mar	Apr	May	Jun	Jul	Aug	Sep	Oct	Nov	
Temperature - max. (°C)	6	6	8	11	14	17	19	18	16	13	9	
Temperature - min. (°C)	1	1	2	3	6	9	11	10	9	6	3	
Rainfall - (mm)	110	76	81	53	72	63	71	93	104	117	100	

29.51S 3

Durban	Jan	Feb	Mar	Apr	May	Jun	Jul	Aug	Sep	Oct	Nov	
Temperature – max. (°C)	28	28	28	26	24	23	23	23	23	24	25	
Temperature – min. (°C)	21	21	20	17	14	11	10	12	15	16	18	
Rainfall (mm)	119	126	132	84	56	34	35	49	73	110	118	

55.57N 3

Edinburgh	Jan	Feb	Mar	Apr	May	Jun	Jul	Aug	Sep	Oct	Nov	
Temperature - max. (°C)	6	7	9	11	14	17	18	18	16	13	9	
Temperature - min. (°C)	1	1	2	4	6	9	11	11	9	7	3	
Rainfall - (mm)	54	40	47	39	49	50	59	63	66	63	56	

55.52N 4

Glasgow	Jan	Feb	Mar	Apr	May	Jun	Jul	Aug	Sep	Oct	Nov	
Temperature - max. (°C)	6	7	9	12	15	18	19	19	16	13	9	
Temperature - min. (°C)	0	0	2	3	6	9	10	10	9	6	2	
Rainfall - (mm)	96	63	65	50	62	58	68	83	95	98	105	

60.10N 2

Helsinki	Jan	Feb	Mar	Apr	May	Jun	Jul	Aug	Sep	Oct	Nov	
Temperature - max. (°C)	-3	-4	0	6	14	19	22	20	15	8	3	
Temperature - min. (°C)	-9	-10	-7	-1	4	9	13	12	8	3	-1	
Rainfall - (mm)	56	42	36	44	41	51	51	68	71	73	68	

6.22S 3

Iguatu	Jan	Feb	Mar	Apr	May	Jun	Jul	Aug	Sep	Oct	Nov	
Temperature - max. (°C)	34	33	32	31	31	31	32	32	35	36	36	
Temperature - min. (°C)	23	23	23	22	22	21	21	21	22	23	23	
Rainfall - (mm)	89	173	185	160	61	61	36	5	18	18	10	

Lerwick
60.09N 1.09W

	Jan	Feb	Mar	Apr	May	Jun	Jul	Aug	Sep	Oct	Nov	Dec
Temperature - max. (°C)	5	5	6	8	10	13	14	14	13	10	7	6
Temperature - min. (°C)	1	1	2	3	5	7	9	9	8	6	3	2
Rainfall - (mm)	127	93	93	72	64	64	67	78	113	119	140	147

London
51.30N 0.07W

	Jan	Feb	Mar	Apr	May	Jun	Jul	Aug	Sep	Oct	Nov	Dec
Temperature - max. (°C)	8	8	11	13	17	20	23	23	19	15	11	9
Temperature - min. (°C)	2	2	4	5	8	11	14	13	11	8	5	3
Rainfall - (mm)	52	34	42	45	47	53	38	47	57	62	52	54

Makassar
5.06S 119.27E

	Jan	Feb	Mar	Apr	May	Jun	Jul	Aug	Sep	Oct	Nov	Dec
Temperature - max. (°C)	29	29	29	30	31	30	30	31	31	31	30	29
Temperature - min. (°C)	23	24	23	23	23	22	21	21	21	22	23	23
Rainfall - (mm)	686	536	424	150	89	74	36	10	15	43	178	610

Manchester
53.29N 2.15W

	Jan	Feb	Mar	Apr	May	Jun	Jul	Aug	Sep	Oct	Nov	Dec
Temperature - max. (°C)	6	7	9	12	15	18	20	20	17	14	9	7
Temperature - min. (°C)	1	1	3	4	7	10	12	12	10	8	4	2
Rainfall - (mm)	69	50	61	51	61	67	65	79	74	77	78	78

Munich
48.08N 11.35E

	Jan	Feb	Mar	Apr	May	Jun	Jul	Aug	Sep	Oct	Nov	Dec
Temperature - max. (°C)	1	3	9	14	18	21	23	23	20	13	7	2
Temperature - min. (°C)	-5	-5	-1	3	7	11	13	12	9	4	0	-4
Rainfall - (mm)	59	53	48	62	109	125	139	107	85	66	57	47

Nairobi
1.17S 36.48E

	Jan	Feb	Mar	Apr	May	Jun	Jul	Aug	Sep	Oct	Nov	Dec
Temperature - max. (°C)	25	26	25	24	22	21	21	21	24	24	23	23
Temperature - min. (°C)	12	13	14	14	13	12	11	11	11	13	13	13
Rainfall - (mm)	38	64	125	211	158	46	15	23	31	53	109	86

Oban
56.25N 5.28W

	Jan	Feb	Mar	Apr	May	Jun	Jul	Aug	Sep	Oct	Nov	Dec
Temperature - max. (°C)	6	7	9	11	14	16	17	17	15	12	9	7
Temperature - min. (°C)	2	1	3	4	7	9	11	11	9	7	4	3
Rainfall - (mm)	146	109	83	90	72	87	120	116	141	169	146	172

Padang
0.58S 100.23E

	Jan	Feb	Mar	Apr	May	Jun	Jul	Aug	Sep	Oct	Nov	Dec
Temperature - max. (°C)	31	31	31	31	31	31	31	31	30	30	30	30
Temperature - min. (°C)	23	23	23	24	24	23	23	23	23	23	23	23
Rainfall - (mm)	351	259	307	363	315	307	277	348	152	495	518	480

Perth
31.56S 115.47E

	Jan	Feb	Mar	Apr	May	Jun	Jul	Aug	Sep	Oct	Nov	Dec
Temperature - max. (°C)	29	29	27	24	21	18	17	18	19	21	24	27
Temperature - min. (°C)	17	17	16	14	12	10	9	9	10	12	14	16
Rainfall - (mm)	8	10	20	43	130	180	170	145	86	56	20	13

Plymouth
50.22N 4.08W

	Jan	Feb	Mar	Apr	May	Jun	Jul	Aug	Sep	Oct	Nov	Dec
Temperature - max. (°C)	8	8	10	12	15	18	19	19	18	15	11	9
Temperature - min. (°C)	4	4	5	6	8	11	13	13	12	9	7	5
Rainfall - (mm)	99	74	69	53	63	53	70	77	78	91	113	110

Punta Arenas
53.09S 70.57W

	Jan	Feb	Mar	Apr	May	Jun	Jul	Aug	Sep	Oct	Nov	Dec
Temperature - max. (°C)	14	14	12	10	7	5	4	6	8	11	12	14
Temperature - min. (°C)	7	7	5	4	2	1	-1	1	2	3	4	6
Rainfall - (mm)	38	23	33	36	33	41	28	31	23	28	18	36

Quito
0.14S 78.30W

	Jan	Feb	Mar	Apr	May	Jun	Jul	Aug	Sep	Oct	Nov	Dec
Temperature - max. (°C)	22	22	22	21	21	22	22	23	23	22	22	22
Temperature - min. (°C)	8	8	8	8	8	7	7	7	7	8	7	8
Rainfall - (mm)	99	112	142	175	137	43	20	31	69	112	97	79

Riyadh
24.43N 46.41E

	Jan	Feb	Mar	Apr	May	Jun	Jul	Aug	Sep	Oct	Nov	Dec
Temperature - max. (°C)	21	23	28	32	38	42	42	42	39	34	29	21
Temperature - min. (°C)	8	9	13	18	22	25	26	24	22	16	13	9
Rainfall - (mm)	3	20	23	25	10	0	0	0	0	0	0	0

Santiago
33.28S 70.39W

	Jan	Feb	Mar	Apr	May	Jun	Jul	Aug	Sep	Oct	Nov	Dec
Temperature - max. (°C)	29	29	27	23	18	14	15	17	19	22	25	28
Temperature - min. (°C)	12	11	9	7	5	3	3	4	6	7	9	11
Rainfall - (mm)	3	3	5	13	64	84	76	56	31	15	8	5

Saskatoon
52.08N 106.39W

	Jan	Feb	Mar	Apr	May	Jun	Jul	Aug	Sep	Oct	Nov	Dec
Temperature - max. (°C)	-13	-11	-3	9	18	22	25	24	17	11	-1	-9
Temperature - min. (°C)	-24	-22	-14	-3	3	9	11	9	3	-3	-11	-19
Rainfall - (mm)	23	13	18	18	36	66	61	48	38	23	13	15

Seville
37.24N 5.58W

	Jan	Feb	Mar	Apr	May	Jun	Jul	Aug	Sep	Oct	Nov	Dec
Temperature - max. (°C)	15	17	20	24	27	32	36	36	32	26	20	16
Temperature - min. (°C)	6	7	9	11	13	17	20	20	18	14	10	7
Rainfall - (mm)	66	61	90	57	41	8	1	5	19	70	67	79

Shanghai
31.15N 121.29E

	Jan	Feb	Mar	Apr	May	Jun	Jul	Aug	Sep	Oct	Nov	Dec
Temperature - max. (°C)	8	8	13	19	25	28	32	32	28	23	17	12
Temperature - min. (°C)	1	1	4	10	15	19	23	23	19	14	7	2
Rainfall - (mm)	48	58	84	94	94	180	147	142	130	71	51	36

Timbuktu
16.46N 2.59W

	Jan	Feb	Mar	Apr	May	Jun	Jul	Aug	Sep	Oct	Nov	Dec
Temperature - max. (°C)	27	31	34	38	41	40	37	35	37	37	33	28
Temperature - min. (°C)	14	17	21	24	27	29	27	27	26	24	19	15
Rainfall - (mm)	0	0	0	0	4	19	62	79	33	3	0	0

Tomsk
56.30N 85.01E

	Jan	Feb	Mar	Apr	May	Jun	Jul	Aug	Sep	Oct	Nov	Dec
Temperature - max. (°C)	-18	-13	-6	3	12	19	23	20	14	3	-9	-16
Temperature - min. (°C)	-24	-22	-17	-7	3	9	12	10	4	-3	-14	-22
Rainfall - (mm)	28	18	20	23	41	69	66	66	41	51	46	38

Vancouver
49.16N 123.08W

	Jan	Feb	Mar	Apr	May	Jun	Jul	Aug	Sep	Oct	Nov	Dec
Temperature - max. (°C)	5	7	10	14	18	21	23	23	18	14	9	6
Temperature - min. (°C)	0	1	3	4	8	11	12	12	9	7	4	2
Rainfall - (mm)	218	147	127	84	71	64	31	43	91	147	211	224

Walvis Bay
22.58S 14.30E

	Jan	Feb	Mar	Apr	May	Jun	Jul	Aug	Sep	Oct	Nov	Dec
Temperature - max. (°C)	23	23	23	24	23	23	21	20	19	19	22	22
Temperature - min. (°C)	15	16	15	13	11	9	8	8	9	11	12	14
Rainfall - (mm)	0	5	8	3	3	0	0	3	0	0	0	0

York
53.58N 1.05W

	Jan	Feb	Mar	Apr	May	Jun	Jul	Aug	Sep	Oct	Nov	Dec
Temperature - max. (°C)	6	7	10	13	16	19	21	21	18	14	10	7
Temperature - min. (°C)	2	2	3	5	7	10	12	12	11	8	5	4
Rainfall - (mm)	59	46	37	41	50	50	62	68	55	56	65	50

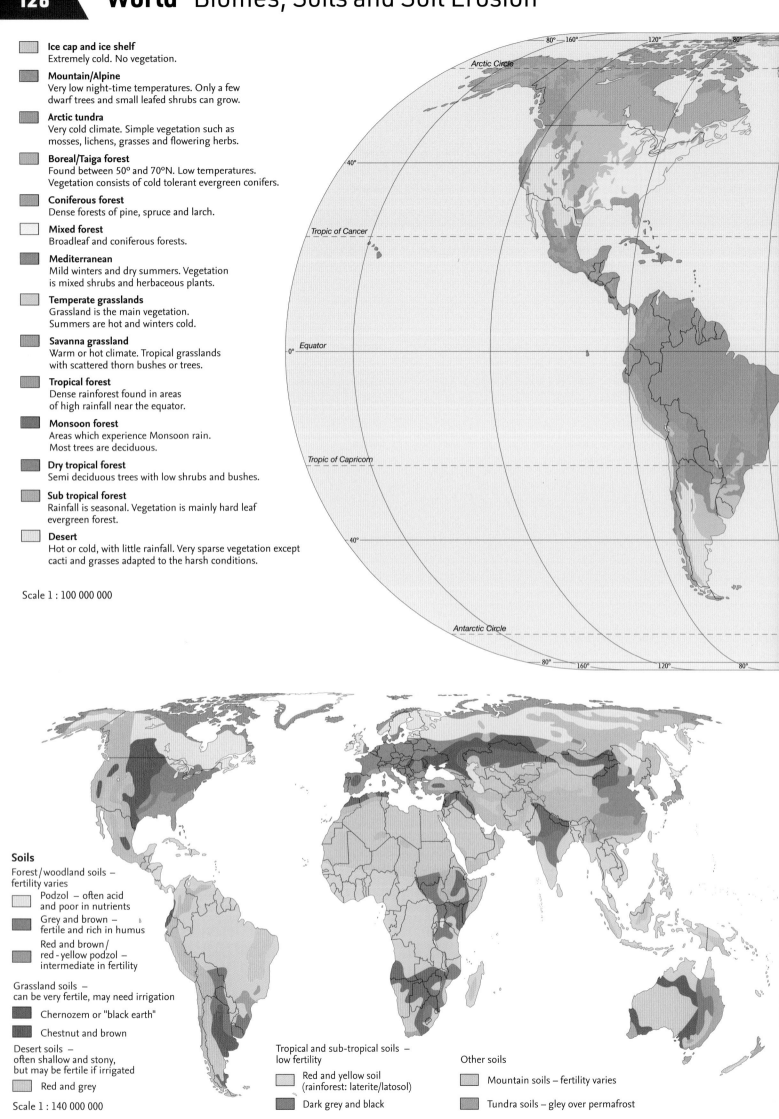

Ice cap and ice shelf
Extremely cold. No vegetation.

Mountain/Alpine
Very low night-time temperatures. Only a few dwarf trees and small leafed shrubs can grow.

Arctic tundra
Very cold climate. Simple vegetation such as mosses, lichens, grasses and flowering herbs.

Boreal/Taiga forest
Found between 50° and 70°N. Low temperatures. Vegetation consists of cold tolerant evergreen conifers.

Coniferous forest
Dense forests of pine, spruce and larch.

Mixed forest
Broadleaf and coniferous forests.

Mediterranean
Mild winters and dry summers. Vegetation is mixed shrubs and herbaceous plants.

Temperate grasslands
Grassland is the main vegetation. Summers are hot and winters cold.

Savanna grassland
Warm or hot climate. Tropical grasslands with scattered thorn bushes or trees.

Tropical forest
Dense rainforest found in areas of high rainfall near the equator.

Monsoon forest
Areas which experience Monsoon rain. Most trees are deciduous.

Dry tropical forest
Semi deciduous trees with low shrubs and bushes.

Sub tropical forest
Rainfall is seasonal. Vegetation is mainly hard leaf evergreen forest.

Desert
Hot or cold, with little rainfall. Very sparse vegetation except cacti and grasses adapted to the harsh conditions.

Scale 1 : 100 000 000

Soils

Forest/woodland soils – fertility varies

Podzol – often acid and poor in nutrients

Grey and brown – fertile and rich in humus

Red and brown/ red - yellow podzol – intermediate in fertility

Grassland soils – can be very fertile, may need irrigation

Chernozem or "black earth"

Chestnut and brown

Desert soils – often shallow and stony, but may be fertile if irrigated

Red and grey

Scale 1 : 140 000 000

Tropical and sub-tropical soils – low fertility

Red and yellow soil (rainforest: laterite/latosol)

Dark grey and black

Other soils

Mountain soils – fertility varies

Tundra soils – gley over permafrost

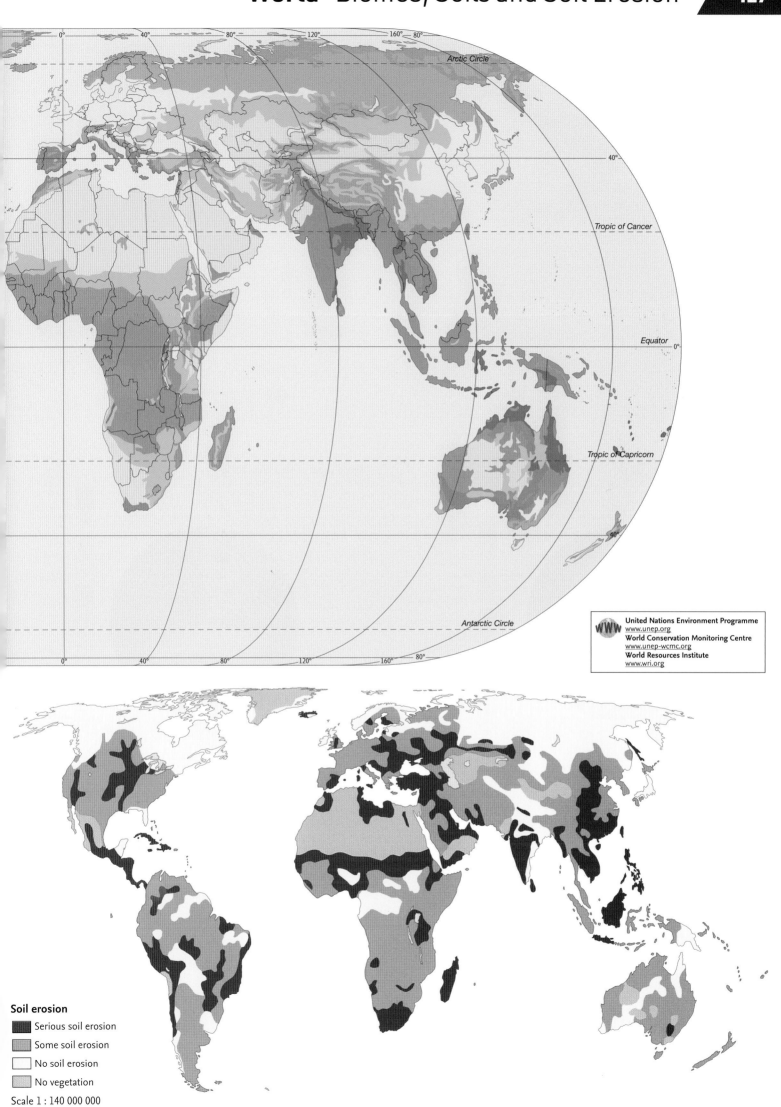

Arctic Circle

40°

Tropic of Cancer

Equator 0°

Tropic of Capricorn

Antarctic Circle

40°

United Nations Environment Programme
www.unep.org
World Conservation Monitoring Centre
www.unep-wcmc.org
World Resources Institute
www.wri.org

Soil erosion

■ Serious soil erosion

■ Some soil erosion

☐ No soil erosion

■ No vegetation

Scale 1 : 140 000 000

World Agriculture

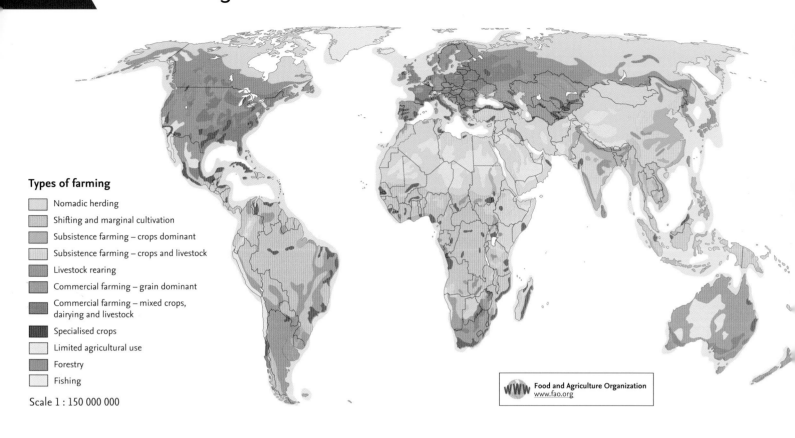

Types of farming

- Nomadic herding
- Shifting and marginal cultivation
- Subsistence farming – crops dominant
- Subsistence farming – crops and livestock
- Livestock rearing
- Commercial farming – grain dominant
- Commercial farming – mixed crops, dairying and livestock
- Specialised crops
- Limited agricultural use
- Forestry
- Fishing

Scale 1 : 150 000 000

Food and Agriculture Organization
www.fao.org

World cereal production, 2022

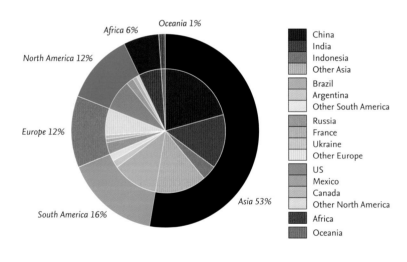

Oceania 1%
Africa 6%
North America 12%
Europe 12%
South America 16%
Asia 53%

- China
- India
- Indonesia
- Other Asia
- Brazil
- Argentina
- Other South America
- Russia
- France
- Ukraine
- Other Europe
- US
- Mexico
- Canada
- Other North America
- Africa
- Oceania

World meat production, 2022

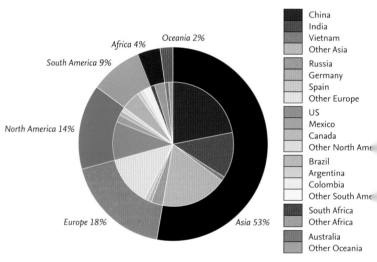

Africa 4%
Oceania 2%
South America 9%
North America 14%
Europe 18%
Asia 53%

- China
- India
- Vietnam
- Other Asia
- Russia
- Germany
- Spain
- Other Europe
- US
- Mexico
- Canada
- Other North Ame
- Brazil
- Argentina
- Colombia
- Other South Ame
- South Africa
- Other Africa
- Australia
- Other Oceania

Agicultural production, 1961 – 2021

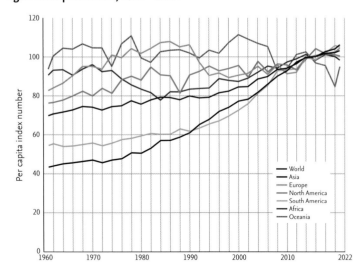

Per capita index number

- World
- Asia
- Europe
- North America
- South America
- Africa
- Oceania

Food supply, 1961 – 2018

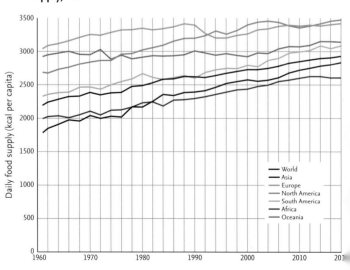

Daily food supply (kcal per capita)

- World
- Asia
- Europe
- North America
- South America
- Africa
- Oceania

MEDCs and LEDCs

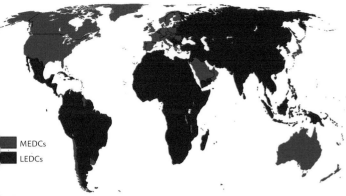

MEDCs
LEDCs

Scale 1 : 300 000 000

International organizations generally agree that countries can be categorized into more economically developed countries (MEDCs) and less economically developed countries (LEDCs). The group of MEDCs includes the following countries/regions: Canada; US; Panama; Chile; Uruguay; Europe as far east as the Baltic states, Poland, Slovakia, Romania and Croatia; Greece; Cyprus; Israel; Saudi Arabia; Kuwait; Bahrain; Qatar; UAE; Oman; Seychelles; South Korea; Japan; Brunei; Singapore; Australia; New Zealand; several small Pacific and Caribbean islands.

Level of development

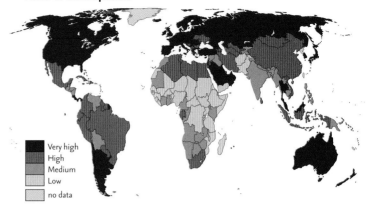

Very high
High
Medium
Low
no data

This map categorizes countries by their stage of development: Very high; High; Medium; Low. Indicators, such as life expectancy as an index of population health and longevity, education as measured by adult literacy and school enrolment, and standards of living based on the GDP per capita, are used to measure the level of development. The development of regions, cities or villages can also be assessed using these indicators.

Low development

Burundi

Health
Under-5 mortality rate (per 1000 live births)	38
Life expectancy at birth	62

Education
Adult literacy	75%
School enrolment, primary	93%

Income
GDP per capita	$836
GNI per capita	$240
Poverty line (% of population)	78%

Medium development

India

Health
Under-5 mortality rate (per 1000 live births)	26
Life expectancy at birth	67

Education
Adult literacy	74%
School enrolment, primary	90%

Income
GDP per capita	$8400
GNI per capita	$2380
Poverty line (% of population)	12%

High development

Brazil

Health
Under-5 mortality rate (per 1000 live births)	13
Life expectancy at birth	73

Education
Adult literacy	94%
School enrolment, primary	96%

Income
GDP per capita	$17 828
GNI per capita	$8140
Poverty line (% of population)	6%

Very high development

Australia

Health
Under-5 mortality rate (per 1000 live births)	3
Life expectancy at birth	83

Education
Adult literacy	>95%
School enrolment, primary	96%

Income
GDP per capita	$63 216
GNI per capita	$60 430
Poverty line (% of population)	0.5%

GDP per capita, 1990 – 2022

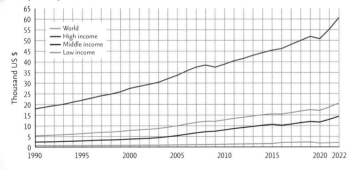

GNI per capita, 1990 – 2022

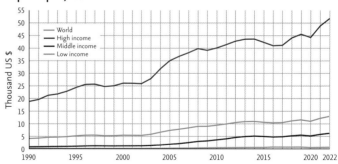

Primary school enrolment, 1990 – 2018

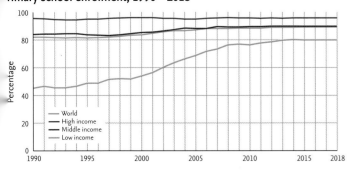

Life expectancy, 1990 – 2021

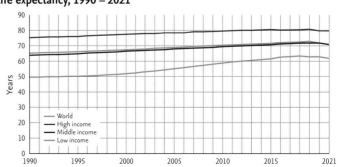

Population comparisons

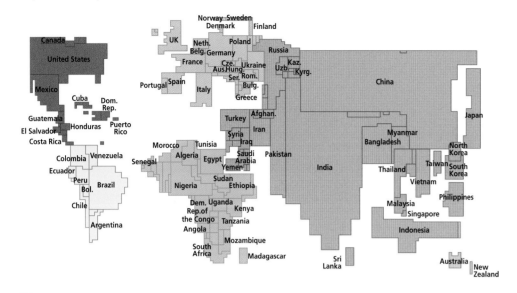

☐ 10 000 000 people

Population structure, 1950 – 2090
Each full square represents 1% of the total population

World

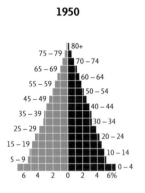

More developed regions

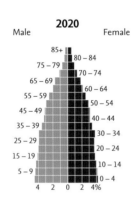

Least developed regions

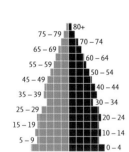

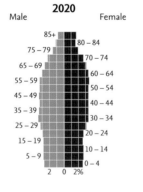

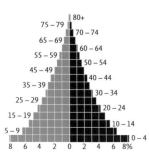

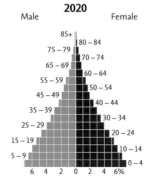

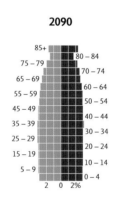

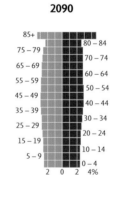

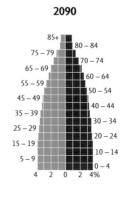

Largest countries by population, 2022

Country and continent	Population
China Asia	1 434 071 37
India Asia	1 417 173 17
United States N America	338 289 85
Indonesia Asia	275 501 33
Pakistan Asia	235 824 86
Nigeria Africa	218 541 21
Brazil S America	215 313 49
Bangladesh Asia	171 186 37
Russia Asia/Europe	144 713 31
Mexico N America	127 504 12
Japan Asia	123 951 69
Ethiopia Africa	123 379 92
Philippines Asia	115 559 00
Egypt Africa	110 990 10
Dem. Rep. of the Congo Africa	99 010 21
Vietnam Asia	98 186 85
Iran Asia	88 550 57
Turkey Asia	85 341 24
Germany Europe	83 369 84
Thailand Asia	71 697 03

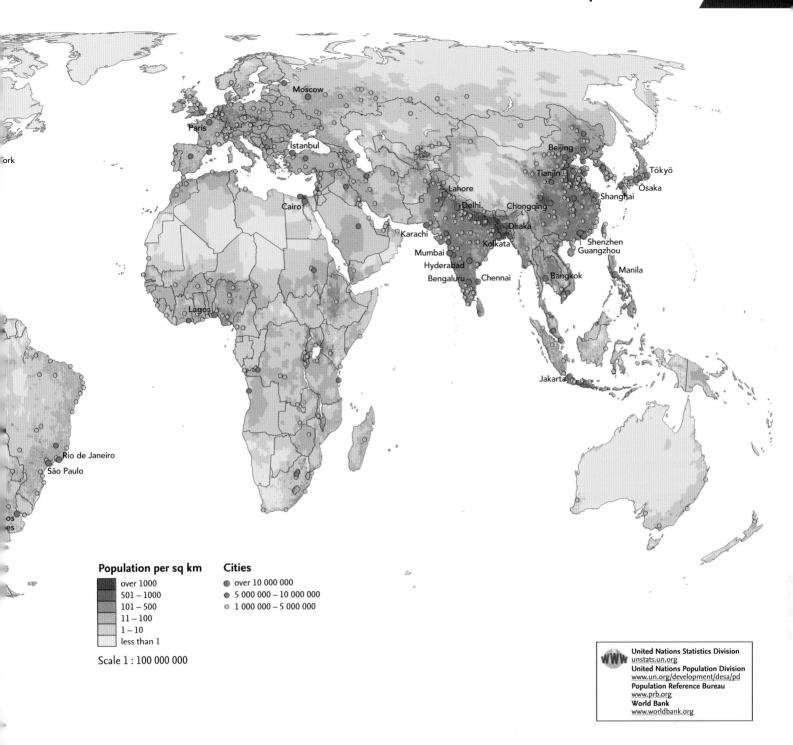

Population per sq km

▮	over 1000
▮	501 – 1000
▮	101 – 500
▮	11 – 100
▮	1 – 10
▯	less than 1

Scale 1 : 100 000 000

Cities

●	over 10 000 000
●	5 000 000 – 10 000 000
○	1 000 000 – 5 000 000

United Nations Statistics Division
unstats.un.org
United Nations Population Division
www.un.org/development/desa/pd
Population Reference Bureau
www.prb.org
World Bank
www.worldbank.org

orld population growth, 1750 – 2050

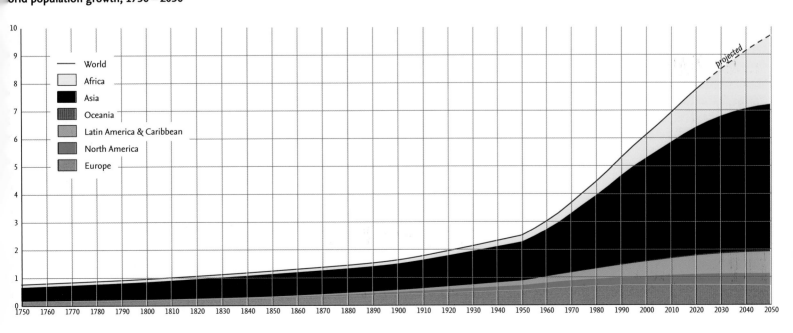

Legend:
- World
- Africa
- Asia
- Oceania
- Latin America & Caribbean
- North America
- Europe

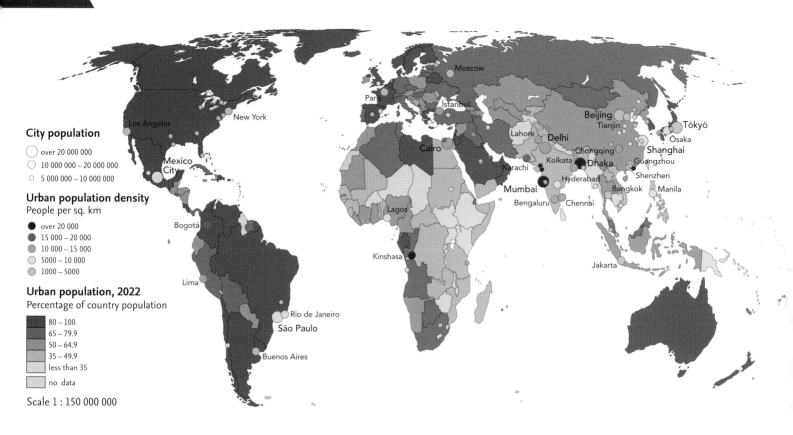

City population

- over 20 000 000
- 10 000 000 – 20 000 000
- 5 000 000 – 10 000 000

Urban population density
People per sq. km

- over 20 000
- 15 000 – 20 000
- 10 000 – 15 000
- 5000 – 10 000
- 1000 – 5000

Urban population, 2022
Percentage of country population

- 80 – 100
- 65 – 79.9
- 50 – 64.9
- 35 – 49.9
- less than 35
- no data

Scale 1 : 150 000 000

Largest urban agglomerations, 2020

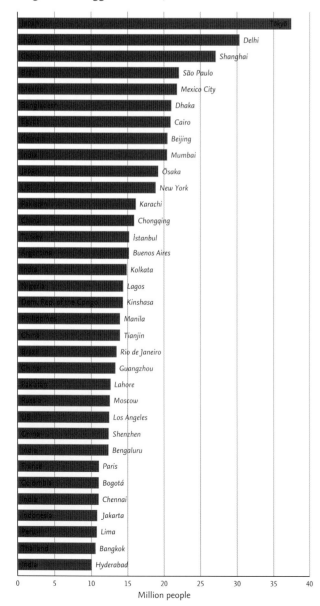

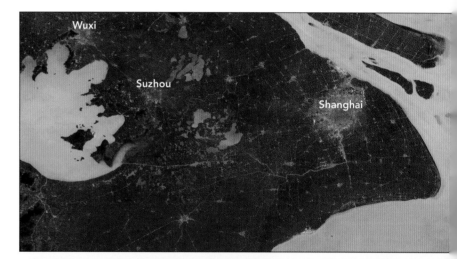

Shanghai urban growth

The images above show the city of Shanghai, located on the east coast of China. The top image is from the mid 1980s when Shanghai was a compact industrial city of about 12 million inhabitants. Since then it has grown rapidly to become one of the largest urban areas in the world with a population of over 27 million people.

The lower image is from 2017 and shows that Shanghai has merged with Suzhou and Wuxi to the west, creating one continuous metropolitan area.

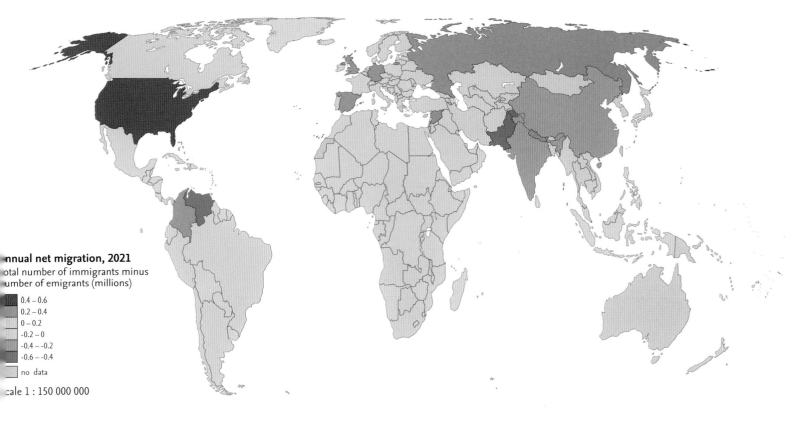

Annual net migration, 2021
Total number of immigrants minus
number of emigrants (millions)

- 0.4 – 0.6
- 0.2 – 0.4
- 0 – 0.2
- -0.2 – 0
- -0.4 – -0.2
- -0.6 – -0.4
- no data

Scale 1 : 150 000 000

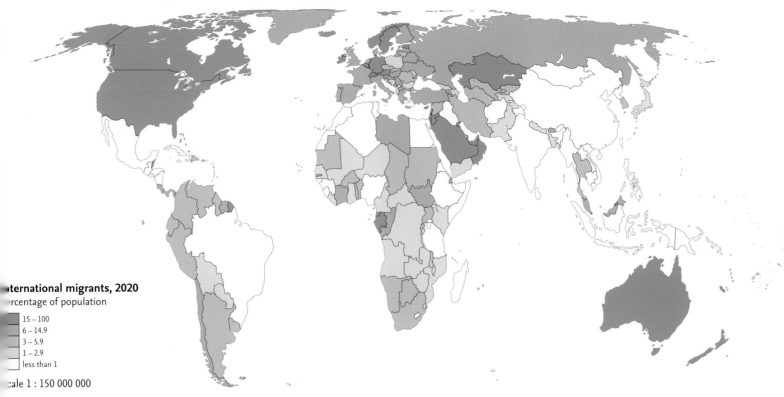

International migrants, 2020
Percentage of population

- 15 – 100
- 6 – 14.9
- 3 – 5.9
- 1 – 2.9
- less than 1

Scale 1 : 150 000 000

International migrants, 1990 – 2020

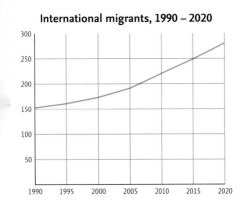

Origin of refugees, 2023

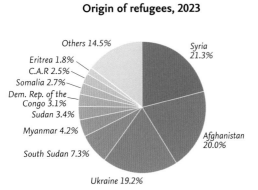

- Others 14.5%
- Syria 21.3%
- Eritrea 1.8%
- C.A.R 2.5%
- Somalia 2.7%
- Dem. Rep. of the Congo 3.1%
- Sudan 3.4%
- Myanmar 4.2%
- South Sudan 7.3%
- Afghanistan 20.0%
- Ukraine 19.2%

Destination of refugees, 2023

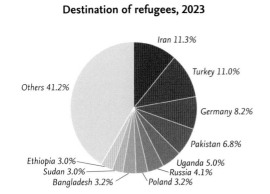

- Iran 11.3%
- Turkey 11.0%
- Germany 8.2%
- Others 41.2%
- Pakistan 6.8%
- Ethiopia 3.0%
- Uganda 5.0%
- Sudan 3.0%
- Russia 4.1%
- Bangladesh 3.2%
- Poland 3.2%

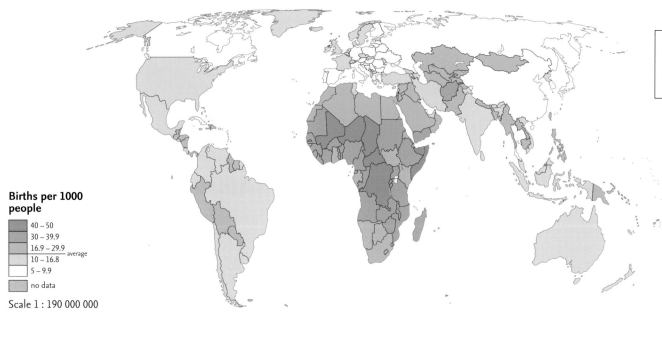

United Nations Statistics Division
unstats.un.org
United Nations Population Division
www.un.org/development/desa/pd
Population Reference Bureau
www.prb.org

Births per 1000 people

- 40 – 50
- 30 – 39.9
- 16.9 – 29.9 average
- 10 – 16.8
- 5 – 9.9
- no data

Scale 1 : 190 000 000

Birth rate
Number of births
per thousand of the
population in one yea
World average 16.9.
Statistics are for 2021

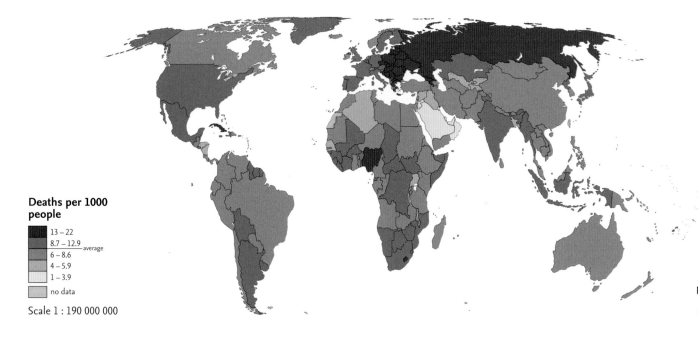

Deaths per 1000 people

- 13 – 22
- 8.7 – 12.9 average
- 6 – 8.6
- 4 – 5.9
- 1 – 3.9
- no data

Scale 1 : 190 000 000

Death rate
Number of deaths
per thousand of the
population in one yea
World average 8.7.
Statistics are for 2021

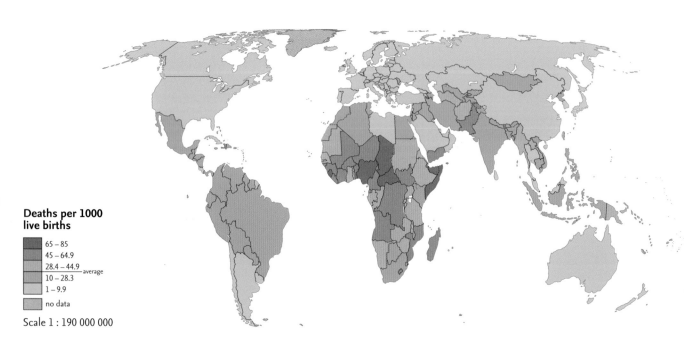

Deaths per 1000 live births

- 65 – 85
- 45 – 64.9
- 28.4 – 44.9 average
- 10 – 28.3
- 1 – 9.9
- no data

Scale 1 : 190 000 000

Infant mortality ra
Number of infants
dying before reachin
one year of age, per 1
live births in a given y
World average 28.4
Statistics are for 202

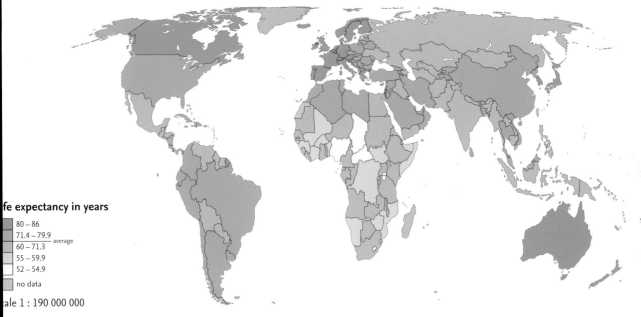

UNESCO
www.unesco.org
World Health Organization
www.who.int
World Bank
www.worldbank.org

Life expectancy in years

- 80 – 86
- 71.4 – 79.9 average
- 60 – 71.3
- 55 – 59.9
- 52 – 54.9
- no data

Scale 1 : 190 000 000

Life expectancy
Average age a newborn infant would live to if patterns of mortality prevailing for all people at the time of its birth were to stay the same throughout its life. World average 71.3. Statistics are for 2021.

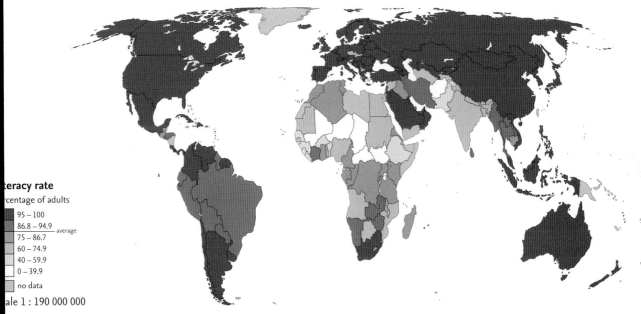

Literacy rate
Percentage of adults

- 95 – 100
- 86.8 – 94.9 average
- 75 – 86.7
- 60 – 74.9
- 40 – 59.9
- 0 – 39.9
- no data

Scale 1 : 190 000 000

Literacy
Percentage of the population over 15 years old which is literate. The definition of 'literate' may vary greatly. World average 86.8%. Statistics are for 2017 – 2021.

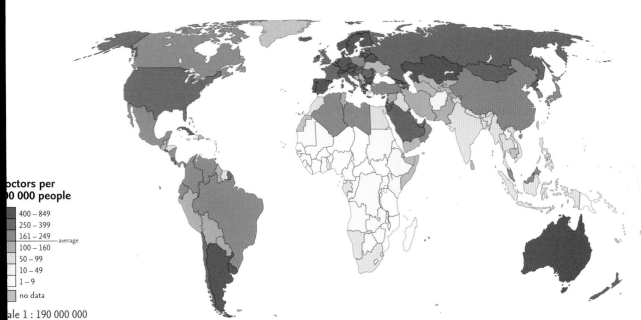

Doctors per 100 000 people

- 400 – 849
- 250 – 399
- 161 – 249 average
- 100 – 160
- 50 – 99
- 10 – 49
- 1 – 9
- no data

Scale 1 : 190 000 000

Doctors
Number of physicians per thousand of the population. World average 161. Statistics are for 2016 – 2021.

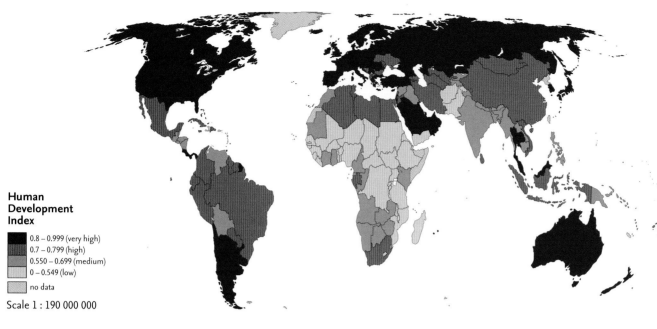

World Bank
www.worldbank.org
United Nations
Development Programm
www.undp.org
Sustainable Developmer
Goals
sdgs.un.org/goals

Human Development Index

- 0.8 – 0.999 (very high)
- 0.7 – 0.799 (high)
- 0.550 – 0.699 (medium)
- 0 – 0.549 (low)
- no data

Scale 1 : 190 000 000

HDI
Measures the achievements of a countr based on indicators of life expectancy, knowledg and standard of living. World average 0.732. Statistics are for 2021.

Percentage of population with access to safe water

- 99 – 100
- 91.2 – 98.9 — average
- 80 – 91.1
- 60 – 79.9
- 35 – 59.9
- no data

Scale 1 : 190 000 000

Access to safe water
Percentage of the population with reasonable access to an adequate amount of water from an improved source. World average 91.2%. Statistics are for 2020 – 20

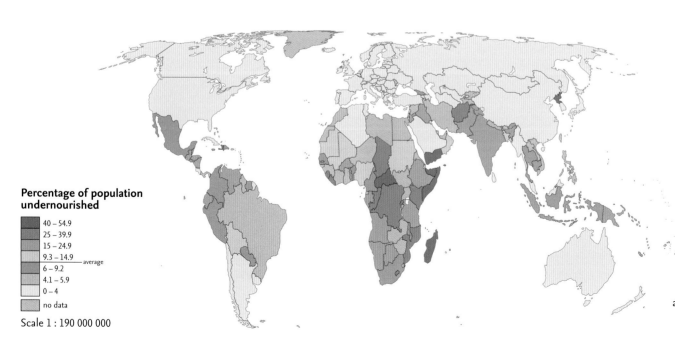

Percentage of population undernourished

- 40 – 54.9
- 25 – 39.9
- 15 – 24.9
- 9.3 – 14.9 — average
- 6 – 9.2
- 4.1 – 5.9
- 0 – 4
- no data

Scale 1 : 190 000 000

Nutrition
Percentage of the population undernourished in developing countries and countries in transitio World average 9.3%. Statistics are for 2020.

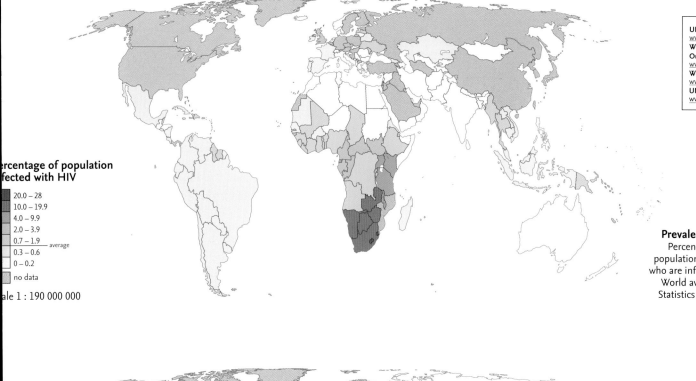

UNESCO
www.unesco.org
World Health
Organization
www.who.ch
World Bank
www.worldbank.org
UNAIDS
www.unaids.org

rcentage of population
fected with HIV

- 20.0 – 28
- 10.0 – 19.9
- 4.0 – 9.9
- 2.0 – 3.9
- 0.7 – 1.9 — average
- 0.3 – 0.6
- 0 – 0.2
- no data

ale 1 : 190 000 000

Prevalence of HIV
Percentage of the
population aged 15 – 49
who are infected with HIV.
World average 0.7%.
Statistics are for 2021.

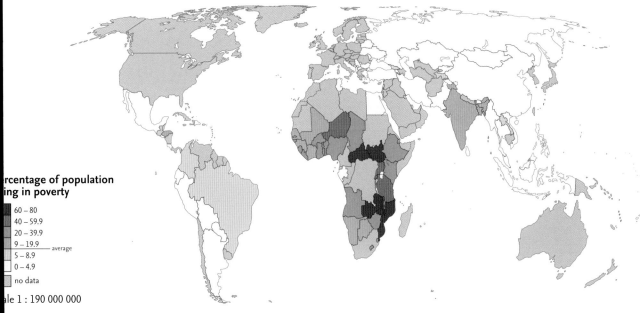

rcentage of population
ing in poverty

- 60 – 80
- 40 – 59.9
- 20 – 39.9
- 9 – 19.9 — average
- 5 – 8.9
- 0 – 4.9
- no data

ale 1 : 190 000 000

Poverty in
developing countries
Percentage of the population
of developing countries living
on less than US$ 1.90 a day.
World average 9%.
Statistics are for 2015 – 2022.

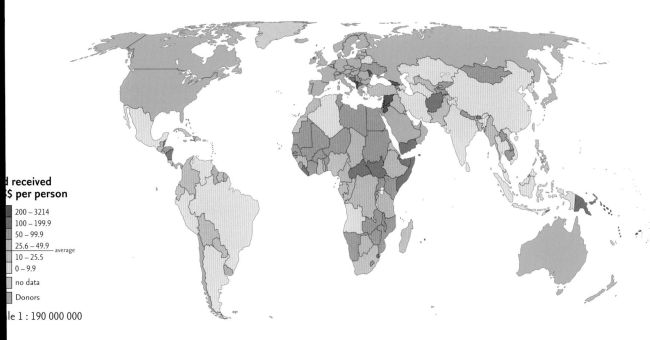

received
$ per person

- 200 – 3214
- 100 – 199.9
- 50 – 99.9
- 25.6 – 49.9 — average
- 10 – 25.5
- 0 – 9.9
- no data
- Donors

le 1 : 190 000 000

Aid received
Official development
assistance received
in US$ per person.
World average US$ 25.6.
Statistics are for 2021.

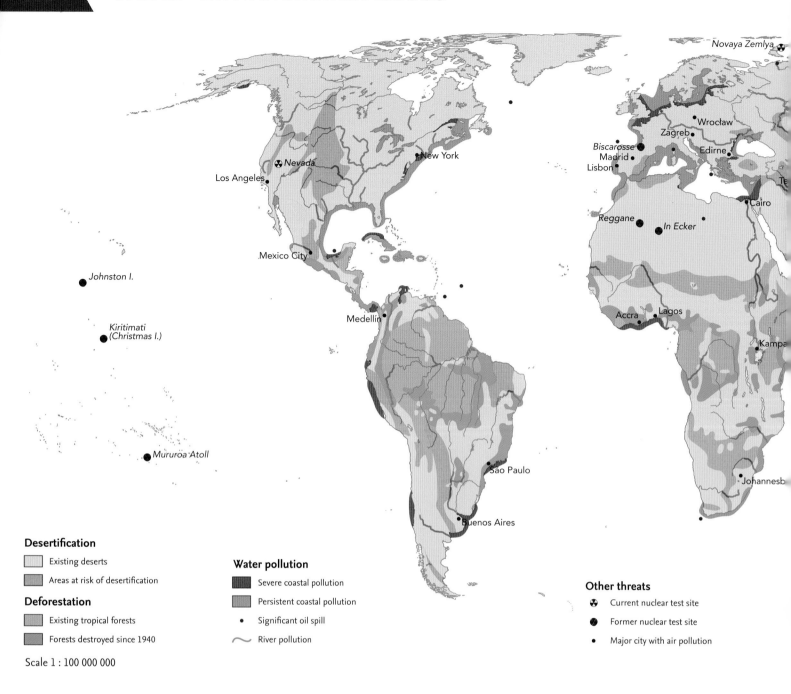

Scale 1 : 100 000 000

Desertification

- Existing deserts
- Areas at risk of desertification

Deforestation

- Existing tropical forests
- Forests destroyed since 1940

Water pollution

- Severe coastal pollution
- Persistent coastal pollution
- • Significant oil spill
- ∼ River pollution

Other threats

- ☢ Current nuclear test site
- ☢ Former nuclear test site
- • Major city with air pollution

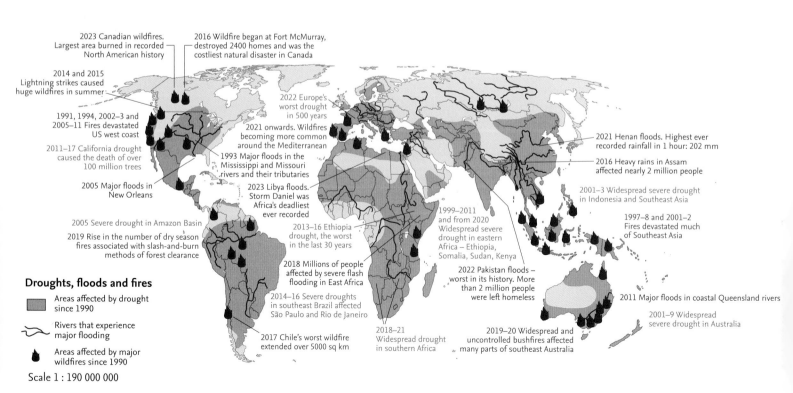

2023 Canadian wildfires. Largest area burned in recorded North American history

2016 Wildfire began at Fort McMurray, destroyed 2400 homes and was the costliest natural disaster in Canada

2014 and 2015 Lightning strikes caused huge wildfires in summer

1991, 1994, 2002–3 and 2005–11 Fires devastated US west coast

2011–17 California drought caused the death of over 100 million trees

2005 Major floods in New Orleans

2005 Severe drought in Amazon Basin

2019 Rise in the number of dry season fires associated with slash-and-burn methods of forest clearance

2022 Europe's worst drought in 500 years

2021 onwards. Wildfires becoming more common around the Mediterranean

1993 Major floods in the Mississippi and Missouri rivers and their tributaries

2023 Libya floods. Storm Daniel was Africa's deadliest ever recorded

2013–16 Ethiopia drought, the worst in the last 30 years

2018 Millions of people affected by severe flash flooding in East Africa

2014–16 Severe droughts in southeast Brazil affected São Paulo and Rio de Janeiro

2017 Chile's worst wildfire extended over 5000 sq km

2018–21 Widespread drought in southern Africa

1999–2011 and from 2020 Widespread severe drought in eastern Africa – Ethiopia, Somalia, Sudan, Kenya

2022 Pakistan floods – worst in its history. More than 2 million people were left homeless

2019–20 Widespread and uncontrolled bushfires affected many parts of southeast Australia

2021 Henan floods. Highest ever recorded rainfall in 1 hour: 202 mm

2016 Heavy rains in Assam affected nearly 2 million people

2001–3 Widespread severe drought in Indonesia and Southeast Asia

1997–8 and 2001–2 Fires devastated much of Southeast Asia

2011 Major floods in coastal Queensland rivers

2001–9 Widespread severe drought in Australia

Droughts, floods and fires

- Areas affected by drought since 1990
- ∼ Rivers that experience major flooding
- 🔥 Areas affected by major wildfires since 1990

Scale 1 : 190 000 000

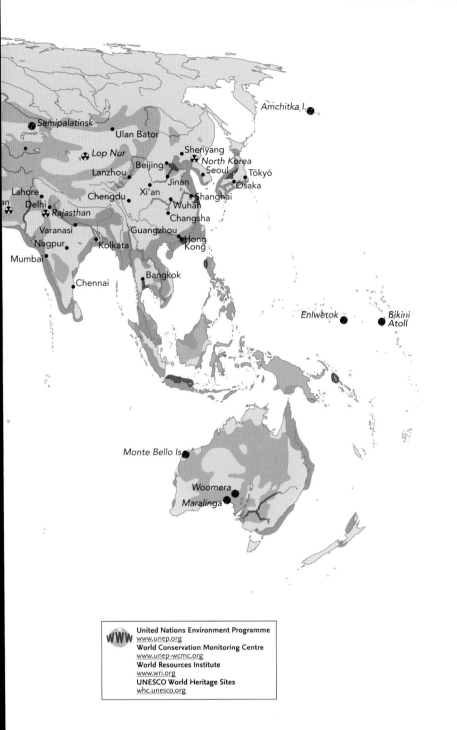

Number of threatened species, 2023

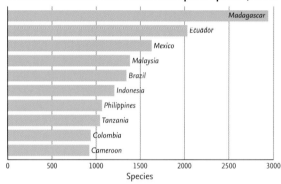

Countries with the most threatened plant species, 2023

Threats to forests (drivers of deforestation)

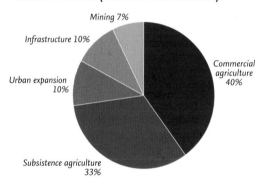

Mining 7%

Infrastructure 10%

Urban expansion 10%

Commercial agriculture 40%

Subsistence agriculture 33%

United Nations Environment Programme
www.unep.org
World Conservation Monitoring Centre
www.unep-wcmc.org
World Resources Institute
www.wri.org
UNESCO World Heritage Sites
whc.unesco.org

Forest area change, 2011 – 2016

World	**-229 470 sq km**
Africa	-195 951 sq km
Asia	54 334 sq km
Europe	17 902 sq km
North America	-1405 sq km
South America	-133 333 sq km
Oceania	28 985 sq km

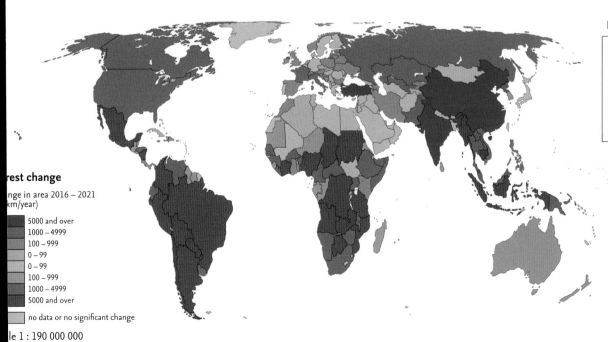

rest change

nge in area 2016 – 2021
km/year)

5000 and over
1000 – 4999
100 – 999
0 – 99
0 – 99
100 – 999
1000 – 4999
5000 and over

no data or no significant change

le 1 : 190 000 000

Global warming, 1910 – 2023

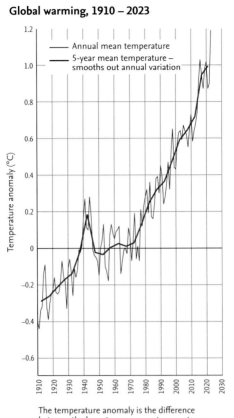

- Annual mean temperature
- 5-year mean temperature – smooths out annual variation

The temperature anomaly is the difference between the long-term average temperature and the average temperature in any given year.

World Meteorological Organization
www.wmo.int
Met Office
www.metoffice.gov.uk/weather
Intergovernmental Panel on Climate Change
www.ipcc.ch

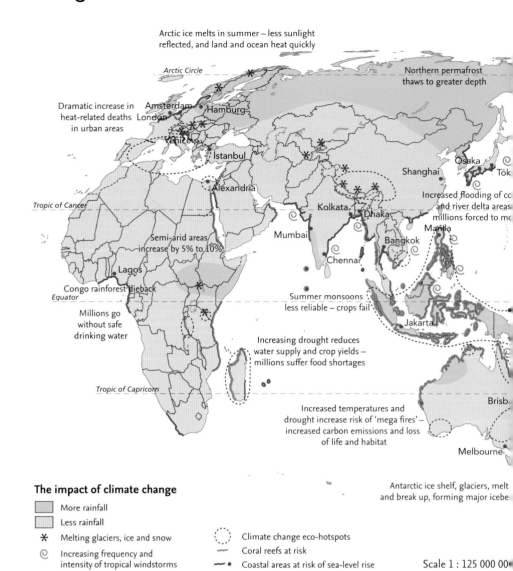

Arctic ice melts in summer – less sunlight reflected, and land and ocean heat quickly

Northern permafrost thaws to greater depth

Dramatic increase in heat-related deaths in urban areas

Semi-arid areas increase by 5% to 10%

Congo rainforest dieback

Millions go without safe drinking water

Summer monsoons less reliable – crops fail

Increasing drought reduces water supply and crop yields – millions suffer food shortages

Increased flooding of co and river delta areas millions forced to mo

Increased temperatures and drought increase risk of 'mega fires' – increased carbon emissions and loss of life and habitat

Antarctic ice shelf, glaciers, melt and break up, forming major icebe

The impact of climate change

- More rainfall
- Less rainfall
- ✳ Melting glaciers, ice and snow
- ◎ Increasing frequency and intensity of tropical windstorms
- ⟋ Climate change eco-hotspots
- ⟋ Coral reefs at risk
- ●⟋ Coastal areas at risk of sea-level rise

Scale 1 : 125 000 00

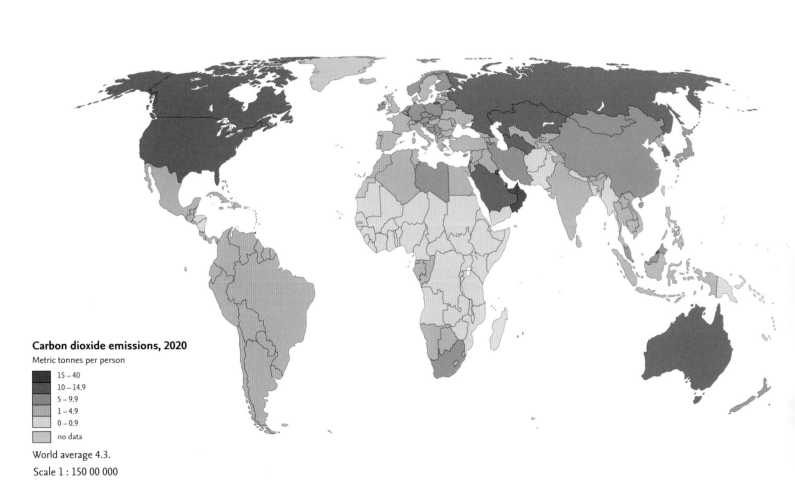

Carbon dioxide emissions, 2020

Metric tonnes per person

- 15 – 40
- 10 – 14.9
- 5 – 9.9
- 1 – 4.9
- 0 – 0.9
- no data

World average 4.3.

Scale 1 : 150 00 000

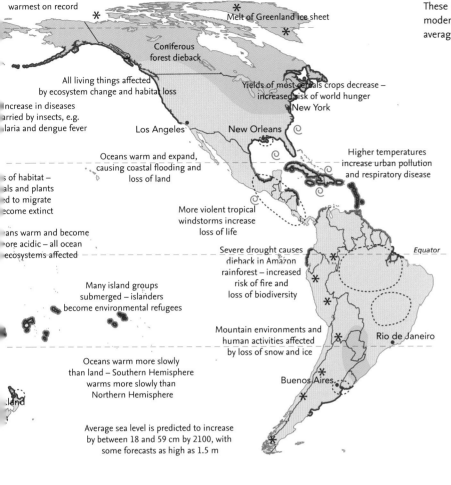

Decade 2001 – 10 warmest on record

Melt of Greenland ice sheet

Coniferous forest dieback

All living things affected by ecosystem change and habitat loss

Yields of most cereals crops decrease – increased risk of world hunger

Increase in diseases carried by insects, e.g. malaria and dengue fever

New York

Los Angeles

New Orleans

s of habitat – als and plants ed to migrate become extinct

Oceans warm and expand, causing coastal flooding and loss of land

Higher temperatures increase urban pollution and respiratory disease

ans warm and become ore acidic – all ocean ecosystems affected

More violent tropical windstorms increase loss of life

Equator

Severe drought causes dieback in Amazon rainforest – increased risk of fire and loss of biodiversity

Many island groups submerged – islanders become environmental refugees

Mountain environments and human activities affected by loss of snow and ice

Rio de Janeiro

Oceans warm more slowly than land – Southern Hemisphere warms more slowly than Northern Hemisphere

Buenos Aires

land

Average sea level is predicted to increase by between 18 and 59 cm by 2100, with some forecasts as high as 1.5 m

Projected annual mean temperature change

These maps show projected change in annual mean surface air temperature given moderate growth in CO2 emissions, for three time periods, compared with the average temperature for 1980 – 99.

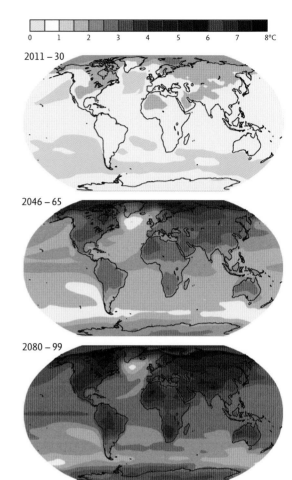

0 1 2 3 4 5 6 7 8°C

2011 – 30

2046 – 65

2080 – 99

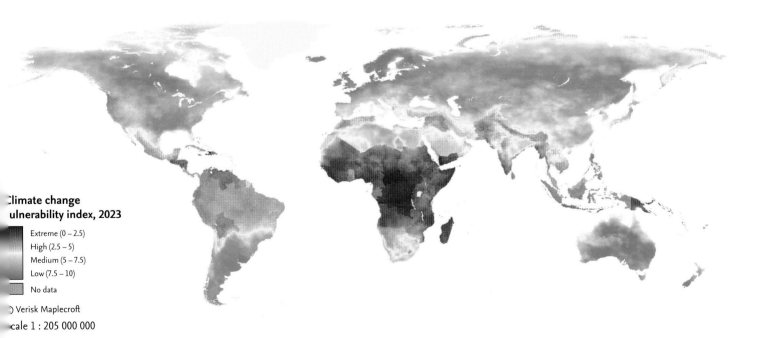

Climate change vulnerability index, 2023

Extreme (0 – 2.5)
High (2.5 – 5)
Medium (5 – 7.5)
Low (7.5 – 10)
No data

© Verisk Maplecroft

Scale 1 : 205 000 000

The climate change vulnerability index ranks how likely a country is to be harmed by changing patterns in climate, natural hazards and ecosystems caused by climate change, and how well prepared it is to combat the impacts of climate change. Denmark, with its high levels of development, is the country best equipped to deal with climate change. The highest risk country, Central African Republic, is vulnerable to climate extremes and changing weather patterns. Its population is highly sensitive to climate change given high poverty levels, limited healthcare, political violence, and pressure on natural resources.

Highest vulnerability

1 Central African Republic	5 Congo	8 Somalia
2 Haiti	6 Sierra Leone	9 Burundi
3 Dem. Rep. of the Congo	7 South Sudan	10 Madagascar
4 Liberia		

Of the 40 countries most at risk, 32 are in Africa.

Fuel production, 2022

Percentage of world production

>25%   11 – 25%   1 – 10%

○   ○   ○   Gas

●   ●   ●   Oil

●   ●   ●   Coal

Major fuel producer

Scale 1 : 190 000 000

International Energy Ag
www.iea.org
BP Statistical Review of
World Energy
www.bp.com

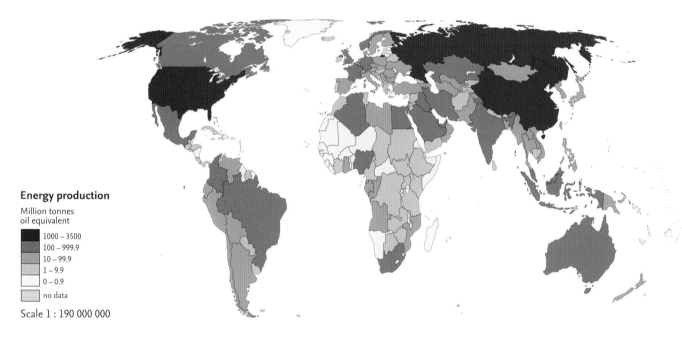

Energy production

Million tonnes
oil equivalent

	1000 – 3500
	100 – 999.9
	10 – 99.9
	1 – 9.9
	0 – 0.9
	no data

Scale 1 : 190 000 000

Energy productic
Expressed as the nun
of tonnes oil equiva
produced in one ye
Statistics are for 20.

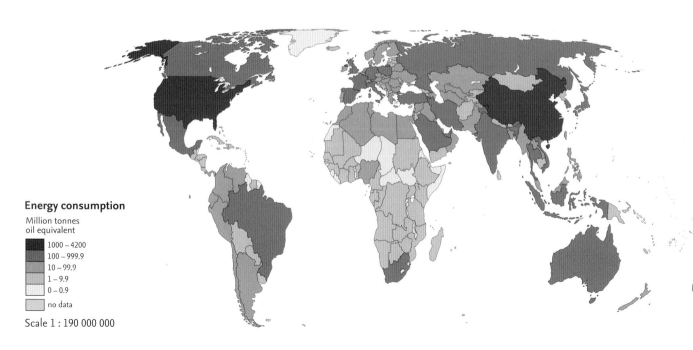

Energy consumption

Million tonnes
oil equivalent

	1000 – 4200
	100 – 999.9
	10 – 99.9
	1 – 9.9
	0 – 0.9
	no data

Scale 1 : 190 000 000

Energy consumpt
Expressed as the nun
of tonnes oil equiva
used in one year.
Statistics are for 20.

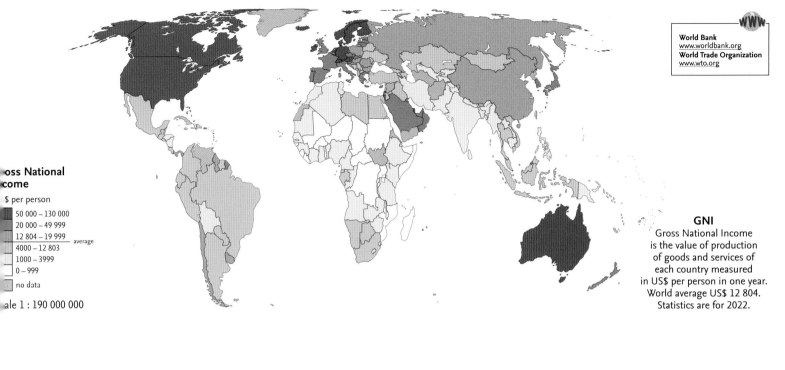

World Bank
www.worldbank.org
World Trade Organization
www.wto.org

Gross National Income

$ per person

- 50 000 – 130 000
- 20 000 – 49 999
- 12 804 – 19 999   average
- 4000 – 12 803
- 1000 – 3999
- 0 – 999
- no data

Scale 1 : 190 000 000

GNI
Gross National Income
is the value of production
of goods and services of
each country measured
in US$ per person in one year.
World average US$ 12 804.
Statistics are for 2022.

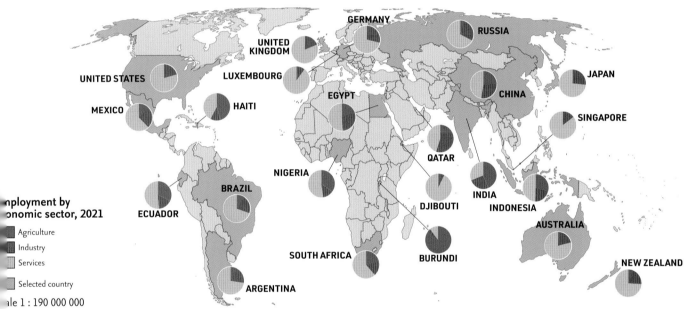

Employment by economic sector, 2021

- Agriculture
- Industry
- Services
- Selected country

Scale 1 : 190 000 000

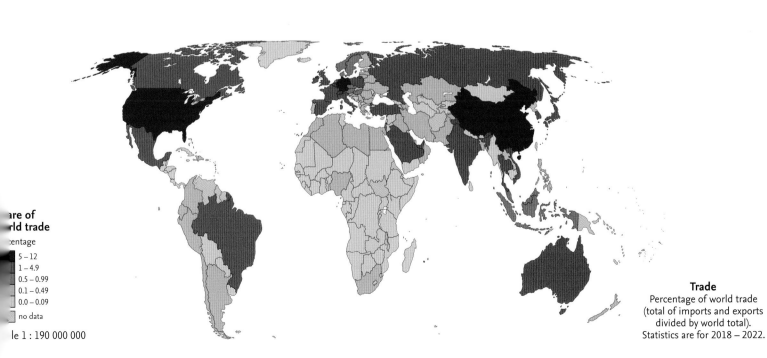

Share of world trade

percentage

- 5 – 12
- 1 – 4.9
- 0.5 – 0.99
- 0.1 – 0.49
- 0.0 – 0.09
- no data

Scale 1 : 190 000 000

Trade
Percentage of world trade
(total of imports and exports
divided by world total).
Statistics are for 2018 – 2022.

Ecological Footprint per country, per person, 2022

World average Ecological Footprint: 2.58 global hectares per person
World average biocapacity: 1.51 global hectares per person

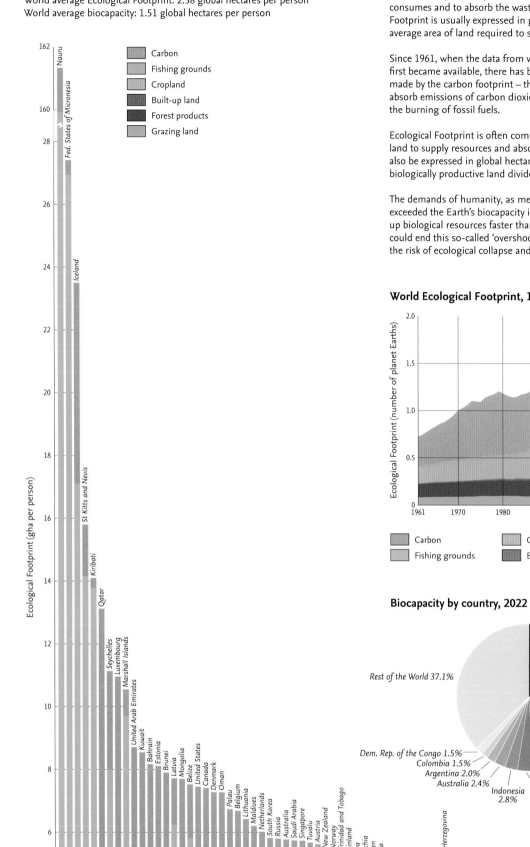

The Ecological Footprint measures the area of biologically productive land and water required to produce the resources an individual or a population consumes and to absorb the waste it generates. A country's Ecological Footprint is usually expressed in global hectares (gha) per person – the average area of land required to support each of that country's inhabitants.

Since 1961, when the data from which the Ecological Footprint is calculated first became available, there has been a marked increase in the contribution made by the carbon footprint – that is, the amount of forest land needed to absorb emissions of carbon dioxide (CO_2). Most CO_2 emissions come from the burning of fossil fuels.

Ecological Footprint is often compared with biocapacity, or the ability of the land to supply resources and absorb waste. A country's biocapacity, which can also be expressed in global hectares per person, is its total amount of biologically productive land divided by its population.

The demands of humanity, as measured by the Ecological Footprint, first exceeded the Earth's biocapacity in the 1970s. Since then, we have been using up biological resources faster than the Earth can regenerate them. Rapid steps could end this so-called 'overshoot' by the middle of the 21st century, lessen the risk of ecological collapse and create a biocapacity reserve.

World Ecological Footprint, 1961 – 2019

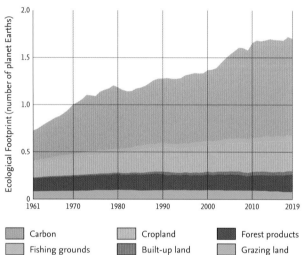

Biocapacity by country, 2022

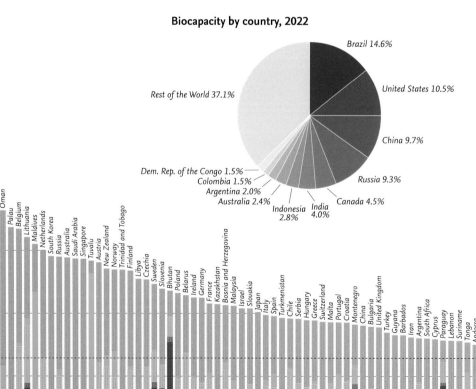

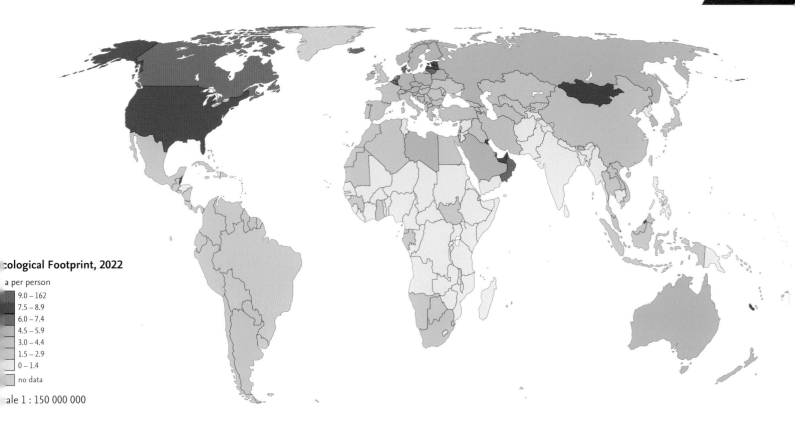

Ecological Footprint, 2022

a per person

	9.0 – 162
	7.5 – 8.9
	6.0 – 7.4
	4.5 – 5.9
	3.0 – 4.4
	1.5 – 2.9
	0 – 1.4
	no data

ale 1 : 150 000 000

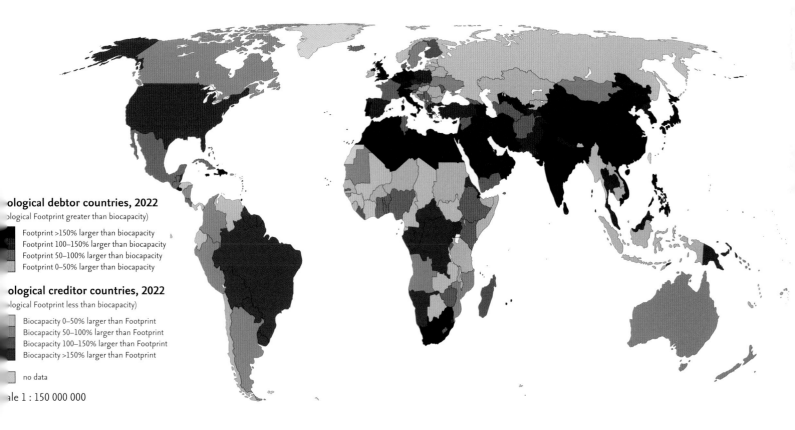

ological debtor countries, 2022
(ological Footprint greater than biocapacity)

- Footprint >150% larger than biocapacity
- Footprint 100–150% larger than biocapacity
- Footprint 50–100% larger than biocapacity
- Footprint 0–50% larger than biocapacity

ological creditor countries, 2022
(ological Footprint less than biocapacity)

- Biocapacity 0–50% larger than Footprint
- Biocapacity 50–100% larger than Footprint
- Biocapacity 100–150% larger than Footprint
- Biocapacity >150% larger than Footprint

no data

ale 1 : 150 000 000

Global Footprint Network
www.footprintnetwork.org
Footprint calculator
http://footprint.wwf.org.uk

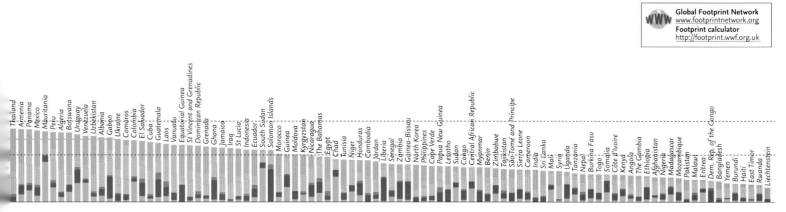

No data for: Kosovo, Monaco,
San Marino, Taiwan, Vatican City.

World Tourism Organization
unwto.org
UNESCO World Heritage Sites
whc.unesco.org

World's top tourist destinations, 2019

Tourist arrivals (million)	
France	89.4
Spain	83.7
United States	79.3
China	65.7
Italy	64.5
Turkey	51.2
Mexico	45.0
Thailand	39.8
Germany	39.6
United Kingdom	39.4

Market share	%
France	6.1
Spain	5.7
United States	5.4
China	4.5
Italy	4.4
Turkey	3.5
Mexico	3.1
Thailand	2.7
Germany	2.7
United Kingdom	2.7

Tourist locations

■ Safari / Wilderness / Trekking area
■ Beach / Leisure resort
■ City resort
■ Cultural / Historical resort

Scale 1 : 90 000 000

Earnings from tourism, 2018 – 2020

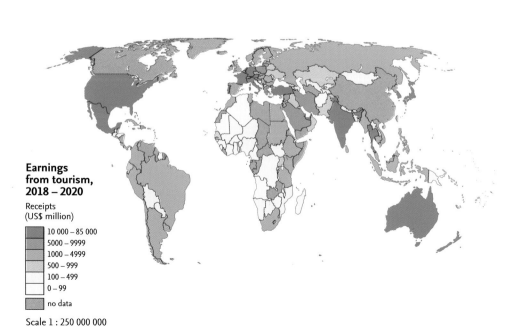

Receipts
(US$ million)

- 10 000 – 85 000
- 5000 – 9999
- 1000 – 4999
- 500 – 999
- 100 – 499
- 0 – 99
- no data

Scale 1 : 250 000 000

International tourism receipts, 2000 – 2019 (US$ billion)

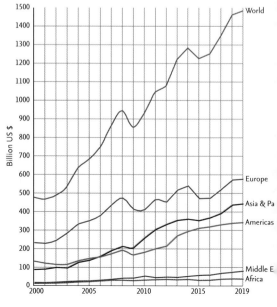

ARCTIC OCEAN

SEE PAGE 37
EUROPE TOURISM

PACIFIC OCEAN

Lake Baikal

Beijing
Great Wall
Xi'an
Kyōto Tōkyō
Shanghai

Delhi
Lhasa
Agra/ *Mt Everest*
Taj Mahal
Jaipur
Sundarbans
Hong Kong
Chiang Mai
Goa
Angkor
Bangkok
Koh Samui
Sri Lanka
Phuket
Maldives
Gunung Kinabalu
Singapore

Azores
Madeira
Fez
Marrakesh
Cyprus
Canary Islands
Petra
Cairo/Pyramids
Red Sea
Luxor
Dubai
Mecca
Gambia
Timbuktu

ATLANTIC

OCEAN

INDIAN OCEAN

Seychelles

East African National Parks
Mombasa

Comoros

Mauritius
Réunion

Lake Kariba
Victoria Falls
Chobe National Park
Hwange National Park
Fossil Hominid Sites
Kruger National Park
Durban
Cape Town
South African National Parks

Komodo National Park
Bali

Great Barrier Reef Marine Park
Fiji

Uluru / Ayers Rock
Gold Coast
Blue Mountains
Sydney
Melbourne
North Island / Te Ika-a-Māui
Auckland
South Island / Te Waipounamu

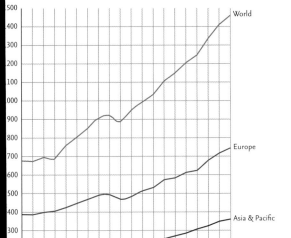

International tourist arrivals by region, 2000 – 2019

World
Europe
Asia & Pacific
Americas
Africa
Middle East

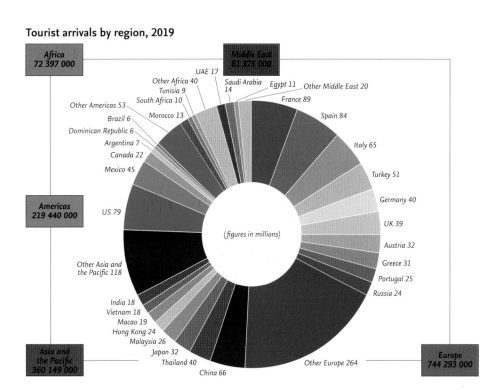

Tourist arrivals by region, 2019

Africa
72 397 000

Middle East
61 375 000

UAE 17
Other Africa 40
Tunisia 9
Saudi Arabia 14
Egypt 11
Other Middle East 20

South Africa 10
Other Americas 53
Morocco 13
France 89
Brazil 6
Spain 84
Dominican Republic 6
Argentina 7
Italy 65
Canada 22
Turkey 51
Mexico 45
Germany 40

Americas
219 440 000
US 79
UK 39
Austria 32
Greece 31
Portugal 25
Russia 24

(figures in millions)

Other Asia and the Pacific 118

India 18
Vietnam 18
Macao 19
Hong Kong 24
Malaysia 26
Japan 32
Thailand 40
China 66

Other Europe 264

Asia and the Pacific
360 149 000

Europe
744 293 000

World Communications

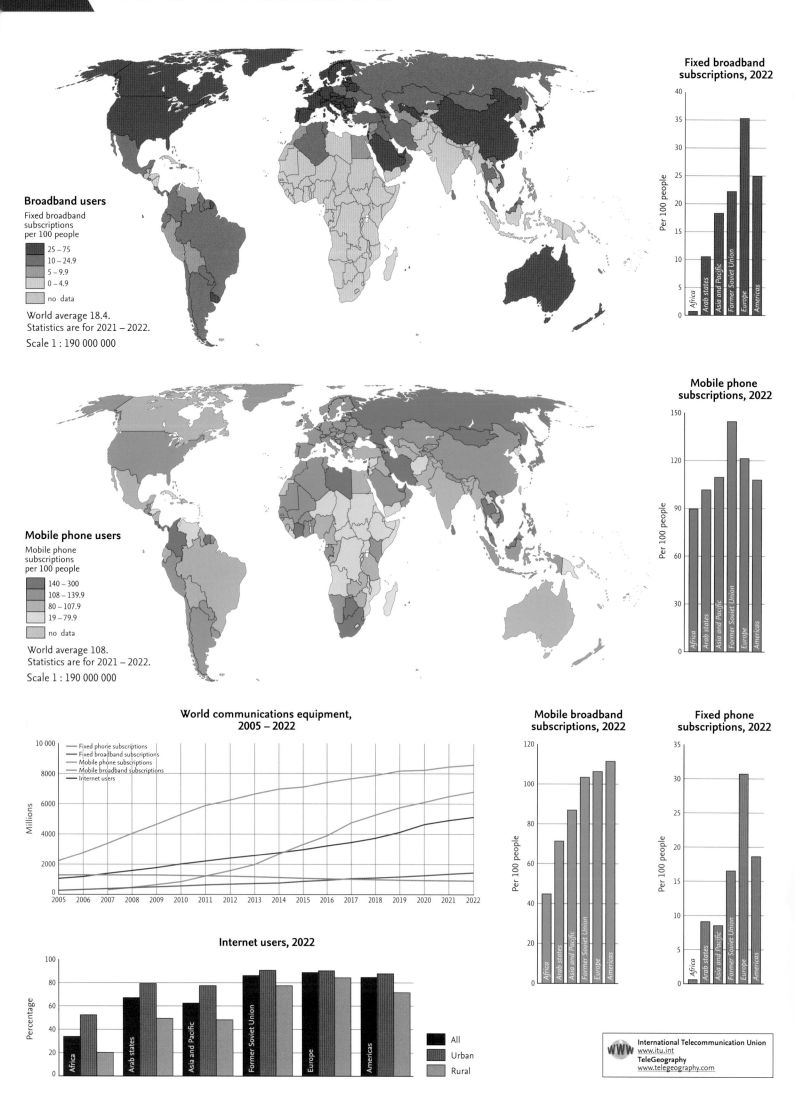

Broadband users

Fixed broadband
subscriptions
per 100 people

- 25 – 75
- 10 – 24.9
- 5 – 9.9
- 0 – 4.9
- no data

World average 18.4.
Statistics are for 2021 – 2022.

Scale 1 : 190 000 000

Fixed broadband subscriptions, 2022

Per 100 people

Africa, Arab states, Asia and Pacific, Former Soviet Union, Europe, Americas

Mobile phone users

Mobile phone
subscriptions
per 100 people

- 140 – 300
- 108 – 139.9
- 80 – 107.9
- 19 – 79.9
- no data

World average 108.
Statistics are for 2021 – 2022.

Scale 1 : 190 000 000

Mobile phone subscriptions, 2022

Per 100 people

Africa, Arab states, Asia and Pacific, Former Soviet Union, Europe, Americas

World communications equipment, 2005 – 2022

Millions

- Fixed phone subscriptions
- Fixed broadband subscriptions
- Mobile phone subscriptions
- Mobile broadband subscriptions
- Internet users

Mobile broadband subscriptions, 2022

Per 100 people

Africa, Arab states, Asia and Pacific, Former Soviet Union, Europe, Americas

Fixed phone subscriptions, 2022

Per 100 people

Africa, Arab states, Asia and Pacific, Former Soviet Union, Europe, Americas

Internet users, 2022

Percentage

Africa, Arab states, Asia and Pacific, Former Soviet Union, Europe, Americas

- All
- Urban
- Rural

International Telecommunication Union
www.itu.int
TeleGeography
www.telegeography.com

Top 20 busiest airports, 2022

	Airport	Passengers carried
1	Atlanta	93 699 630
2	Dallas/Fort Worth	73 362 946
3	Denver	69 286 461
4	Chicago	68 340 619
5	Dubai	66 069 981
6	Los Angeles	65 924 298
7	İstanbul	64 289 107
8	London Heathrow	61 614 230
9	New Delhi	59 490 074
10	Paris	57 474 033
11	New York	55 287 711
12	Las Vegas	52 694 312
13	Amsterdam	52 472 188
14	Miami	50 684 396
15	Madrid	50 602 864
16	Tōkyō Haneda	50 334 354
17	Orlando	50 178 499
18	Frankfurt	48 918 182
19	Charlotte	47 758 605
20	Mexico City	46 258 521

Air passengers carried in millions

- 100 – 666
- 25 – 99.9
- 10 – 24.9
- 1 – 9.9
- 0 – 0.9
- no data
- ● Main airport
- • Other airport
- — Main air route

Scale 1 : 140 000 000

Passengers carried
Air passengers carried include both domestic and international aircraft passengers.
Statistics are for 2018 – 2021.

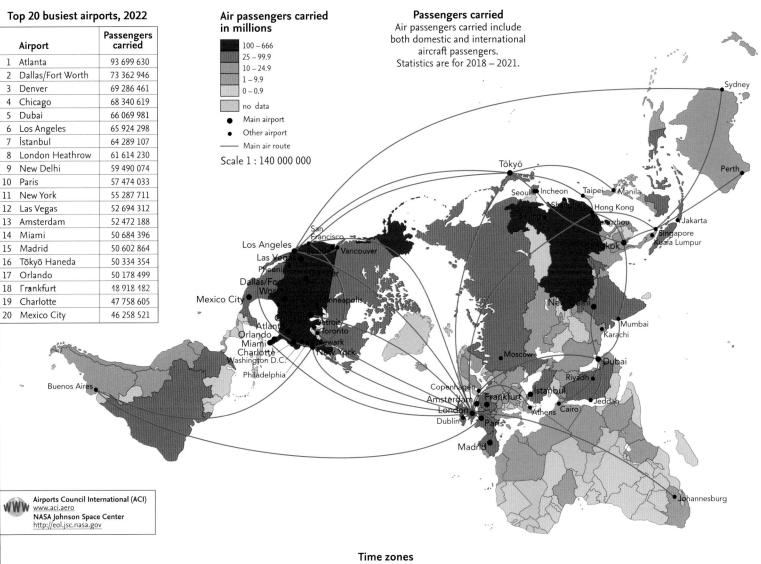

Airports Council International (ACI)
www.aci.aero
NASA Johnson Space Center
http://eol.jsc.nasa.gov

Time zones

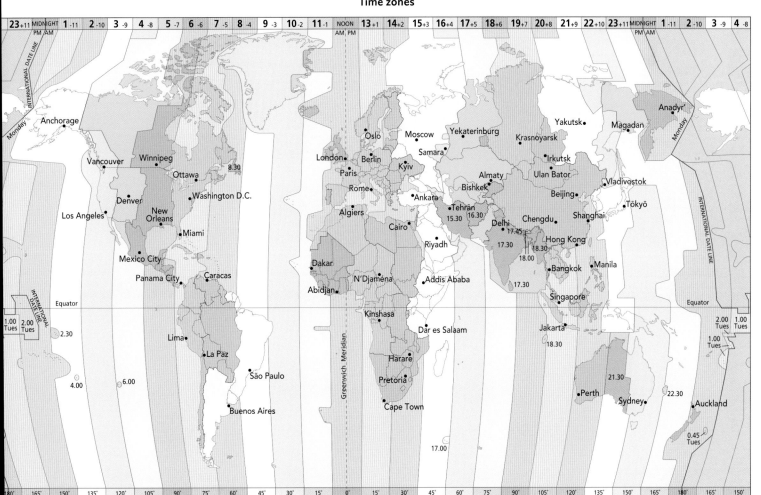

Flag	Country	Capital city	Population total 2022	Density persons per sq km 2022	Birth rate per 1000 population 2021	Death rate per 1000 population 2021	Life expectancy in years 2021	Population change % 2022	Urban populati % 2022
	Afghanistan	Kābul	41 128 771	63	36	7	62	2.5	27
	Albania	Tirana	2 842 321	99	10	11	76	-1.3	64
	Algeria	Algiers	44 903 225	19	22	5	76	1.6	75
	Andorra	Andorra la Vella	79 824	172	..	..	..	1.0	88
	Angola	Luanda	35 588 987	29	39	8	62	3.1	68
	Antigua and Barbuda	St John's	93 763	212	12	6	79	0.6	24
	Argentina	Buenos Aires	45 510 318	16	14	9	75	0.9	92
	Armenia	Yerevan	2 780 469	93	12	13	72	-0.4	64
	Australia	Canberra	26 172 940	3	12	7	83	1.1	86
	Austria	Vienna	8 939 617	107	10	10	81	1.0	59
	Azerbaijan	Baku	10 358 074	120	11	8	69	0.4	57
	Bahamas, The	Nassau	409 984	29	11	9	72	0.5	83
	Bahrain	Manama	1 472 233	2131	12	2	79	0.6	90
	Bangladesh	Dhaka	171 186 372	1189	18	6	72	1.1	40
	Barbados	Bridgetown	281 635	655	11	9	78	0.2	31
	Belarus	Minsk	9 534 954	46	9	17	72	-1.0	80
	Belgium	Brussels	11 655 930	382	10	10	82	0.7	98
	Belize	Belmopan	405 272	18	18	6	70	1.3	46
	Benin	Porto-Novo	13 352 864	119	37	9	60	2.7	50
	Bhutan	Thimphu	782 455	17	12	6	72	0.6	44
	Bolivia	La Paz/Sucre	12 224 110	11	22	10	64	1.2	71
	Bosnia and Herzegovina	Sarajevo	3 233 526	63	8	16	75	-1.2	50
	Botswana	Gaborone	2 630 296	5	24	9	61	1.6	72
	Brazil	Brasília	215 313 498	25	13	8	73	0.5	88
	Brunei	Bandar Seri Begawan	449 002	78	14	5	75	0.8	79
	Bulgaria	Sofia	6 781 953	61	9	22	72	-6.2	76
	Burkina Faso	Ouagadougou	22 673 762	83	36	9	59	2.6	32
	Burundi	Gitega	12 889 576	463	35	7	62	2.7	14
	Cambodia	Phnom Penh	16 767 842	93	19	7	70	1.1	25
	Cameroon	Yaoundé	27 914 536	59	35	9	60	2.6	59
	Canada	Ottawa	38 454 327	4	10	8	83	1.8	82
	Cape Verde	Praia	593 149	147	17	6	74	0.9	68
	Central African Republic	Bangui	5 579 144	9	43	11	54	2.2	43
	Chad	N'Djaména	17 723 315	14	43	13	53	3.1	24
	Chile	Santiago/Valparaíso	19 603 733	26	12	7	79	0.6	88
	China	Beijing	1 434 071 370	149	8	7	78	0.0	64
	Colombia	Bogotá	51 874 024	45	14	8	73	0.7	82
	Comoros	Moroni	836 774	449	29	9	63	1.8	30
	Congo	Brazzaville	5 970 424	17	31	7	64	2.3	69
	Congo, Dem. Rep. of the	Kinshasa	99 010 212	42	42	10	59	3.2	47
	Costa Rica	San José	5 180 829	101	12	7	77	0.5	82
	Côte d'Ivoire	Yamoussoukro	28 160 542	87	34	9	59	2.5	53
	Croatia	Zagreb	4 030 358	71	9	16	76	-0.7	58
	Cuba	Havana	11 212 191	101	9	15	74	-0.4	77
	Cyprus	Nicosia	1 251 488	135	10	7	81	0.6	67
	Czechia	Prague	10 493 986	133	11	13	77	0.2	74
	Denmark	Copenhagen	5 882 261	137	11	10	81	0.8	88
	Djibouti	Djibouti	1 120 849	48	22	9	62	1.4	78
	Dominica	Roseau	72 737	97	13	9	73	0.5	72

Land		Education and Health			Development			Communications		Country	Time Zones
Area sq km	Forest thousand sq km 2021	Adult literacy % 2021	Doctors per 100 000 population 2020	Nutrition population under-nourished % 2020	Energy consumption million tonnes oil equivalent 2021	GNI per capita US$ 2022	HDI index 2021	Mobile phones subs per 100 population 2022	Broadband users subs per 100 population 2022		+ or - GMT
652 225	12	37.3	25	29.8	2.3	..	0.478	56.5	<0.1	Afghanistan	+4½
28 748	8	98.5	188	3.9	3.5	6 770	0.796	97.9	20.5	Albania	+1
381 741	20	81.4	172	2.5	65.0	3 900	0.745	109.2	10.5	Algeria	+1
465	<1	..	..	..	..	..	0.858	142.2	51.1	Andorra	+1
246 700	661	72.3	21	20.8	8.3	1 900	0.586	67.4	0.4	Angola	+1
442	<1	..	277	..	0.2	18 280	0.788	197.4	8.6	Antigua and Barbuda	-4
766 889	285	99.0	406	3.7	89.3	11 620	0.842	132.4	24.6	Argentina	-3
29 800	3	99.8	..	3.5	4.2	5 960	0.759	135.3	18.4	Armenia	+4
692 024	1 340	99.9	413	2.5	149.2	60 430	0.951	107.0	35.2	Australia	+8 to +10½
83 855	39	99.9	529	2.5	36.3	56 140	0.916	123.4	29.3	Austria	+1
86 600	11	99.8	317	2.5	16.7	5 630	0.745	106.8	20.2	Azerbaijan	+4
13 939	5	..	194	..	1.2	31 530	0.812	98.5	20.5	Bahamas, The	-5
691	<1	..	..	..	20.3	27 180	0.875	145.4	11.7	Bahrain	+3
143 998	19	74.9	67	11.4	43.1	2 820	0.661	105.3	6.9	Bangladesh	+6
430	<1	..	249	3.4	0.6	19 350	0.790	114.9	37.6	Barbados	-4
207 600	88	99.9	454	2.5	25.6	7 240	0.808	123.5	32.8	Belarus	+3
30 520	7	99.9	315	2.5	68.4	48 700	0.937	101.9	43.5	Belgium	+1
22 965	13	..	108	7.4	0.3	6 800	0.683	66.0	9.0	Belize	-6
112 620	31	45.8	6	7.4	2.8	1 400	0.525	109.0	0.2	Benin	+1
46 620	27	71.0	50	..	1.9	..	0.666	94.9	0.6	Bhutan	+6
1 098 581	506	93.8	103	13.9	7.3	3 450	0.692	99.6	9.3	Bolivia	-4
51 130	22	98.1	..	2.5	6.5	7 660	0.780	117.9	27.1	Bosnia and Herzegovina	+1
581 370	151	..	38	21.9	2.1	7 350	0.693	165.3	4.2	Botswana	+2
8 514 879	4 954	94.3	231	4.1	304.6	8 140	0.754	98.9	21.0	Brazil	-2 to -5
5 765	4	97.6	161	5.9	4.0	31 410	0.829	117.8	20.1	Brunei	+8
110 994	39	98.4	421	3.0	18.8	13 250	0.795	117.4	35.1	Bulgaria	+2
274 200	62	46.0	9	18.0	1.7	840	0.449	111.7	<0.1	Burkina Faso	0
27 835	3	74.7	7	..	0.3	240	0.426	58.0	<0.1	Burundi	+2
181 035	79	83.9	..	6.3	5.8	1 700	0.593	116.3	3.0	Cambodia	+7
475 442	203	78.2	13	6.7	3.7	1 660	0.576	82.8	2.2	Cameroon	+1
9 984 670	3 469	99.9	244	2.5	357.1	52 960	0.936	91.2	43.1	Canada	-3½ to -8
4 033	<1	90.8	83	17.7	0.4	4 140	0.662	99.2	5.8	Cape Verde	-1
622 436	223	37.5	7	52.2	0.1	480	0.404	33.5	<0.1	Central African Republic	+1
284 000	42	26.8	6	32.7	0.5	690	0.394	68.2	<0.1	Chad	+1
756 945	183	97.0	284	2.6	40.5	15 360	0.855	134.8	22.7	Chile	-3, -4 & -6
9 606 802	2 219	97.2	223	2.5	4161.9	12 850	0.768	124.9	41.4	China	+8
141 748	589	95.6	233	8.2	40.8	6 510	0.752	155.8	17.0	Colombia	-5
1 862	<1	62.0	26	..	0.1	1 610	0.558	100.2	0.2	Comoros	+3
342 000	219	80.6	10	31.6	1.2	2 060	0.571	96.8	0.3	Congo	+1
345 410	1 251	80.0	38	39.8	3.4	590	0.479	50.3	<0.1	Congo, Dem. Rep. of the	+1 & +2
51 100	31	98.0	330	3.4	5.3	12 670	0.809	152.0	21.3	Costa Rica	-6
322 463	27	89.9	16	4.4	5.6	2 620	0.550	174.0	1.4	Côte d'Ivoire	0
56 538	19	99.5	347	2.5	9.2	19 470	0.858	111.2	27.0	Croatia	+1
110 860	32	99.7	842	2.5	8.9	..	0.764	67.8	3.3	Cuba	-5
9 251	2	99.4	314	2.5	3.0	30 540	0.896	148.7	38.4	Cyprus	+2
78 864	27	..	415	2.5	42.4	26 590	0.889	128.4	38.1	Czechia	+1
43 075	6	99.9	422	2.5	16.1	73 200	0.948	126.5	44.8	Denmark	+1
23 200	<1	..	..	13.5	0.3	3 180	0.509	46.3	1.4	Djibouti	+3
750	<1	..	110	6.9	<0.1	8 460	0.720	85.9	19.4	Dominica	-4

.. data available

	Key Information		Population						
Flag	Country	Capital city	Population total 2022	Density persons per sq km 2022	Birth rate per 1000 population 2021	Death rate per 1000 population 2021	Life expectancy in years 2021	Population change % 2022	Urban populati % 2022
	Dominican Republic	Santo Domingo	11 228 821	232	18	7	73	1.0	84
	East Timor	Dili	1 341 296	90	25	7	68	1.5	32
	Ecuador	Quito	18 001 000	66	17	7	74	1.1	65
	Egypt	Cairo	110 990 103	111	23	6	70	1.6	43
	El Salvador	San Salvador	6 336 392	301	16	9	71	0.4	75
	Equatorial Guinea	Malabo	1 674 908	60	31	9	61	2.4	74
	Eritrea	Asmara	3 684 032	31	29	7	67	1.7	43
	Estonia	Tallinn	1 326 062	29	10	14	77	1.0	70
	Eswatini (Swaziland)	Lobamba/Mbabane	1 201 670	69	24	11	57	0.8	25
	Ethiopia	Addis Ababa	123 379 924	109	32	7	65	2.5	23
	Fiji	Suva	929 766	51	19	9	67	0.6	58
	Finland	Helsinki	5 540 745	16	9	10	82	0.3	86
	France	Paris	64 626 628	119	11	10	82	0.3	82
	Gabon	Libreville	2 388 992	9	27	7	66	2.0	91
	Gambia, The	Banjul	2 705 992	240	33	8	62	2.5	64
	Georgia	Tbilisi	3 744 385	54	13	15	72	0.1	60
	Germany	Berlin	83 369 843	234	10	12	81	1.1	78
	Ghana	Accra	33 475 870	140	28	8	64	1.9	59
	Greece	Athens	10 384 971	79	8	14	80	-0.7	80
	Grenada	St George's	125 438	332	16	8	75	0.7	37
	Guatemala	Guatemala City	17 843 908	164	21	7	69	1.4	53
	Guinea	Conakry	13 859 341	56	34	10	59	2.4	38
	Guinea-Bissau	Bissau	2 105 566	58	31	9	60	2.2	45
	Guyana	Georgetown	808 726	4	20	10	66	0.5	27
	Haiti	Port–au–Prince	11 584 996	417	24	9	63	1.2	59
	Honduras	Tegucigalpa	10 432 860	93	21	6	70	1.5	60
	Hungary	Budapest	9 967 308	107	10	16	74	-0.3	73
	Iceland	Reykjavík	372 899	4	13	6	83	2.5	94
	India	New Delhi	1 417 173 173	448	16	9	67	0.7	36
	Indonesia	Jakarta	275 501 339	144	16	10	68	0.6	58
	Iran	Tehrān	88 550 570	54	14	6	74	0.7	77
	Iraq	Baghdād	44 496 122	102	27	5	70	2.2	71
	Ireland	Dublin	5 023 109	71	12	7	82	1.1	64
	Israel	Jerusalem [disputed]	9 038 309	409	20	5	83	2.0	93
	Italy	Rome	59 037 474	196	7	12	83	-0.4	72
	Jamaica	Kingston	2 827 377	257	12	9	71	0.0	57
	Japan	Tōkyō	123 951 692	328	7	12	84	-0.4	92
	Jordan	ʻAmmān	11 285 869	127	22	4	74	1.2	92
	Kazakhstan	Astana	19 397 998	7	24	10	70	3.2	58
	Kenya	Nairobi	54 027 487	93	28	8	61	1.9	29
	Kiribati	Ambo	131 232	183	27	6	67	1.8	57
	Kosovo	Pristina	1 659 714	152	11	7	77	-1.4	..
	Kuwait	Kuwait City	4 268 873	240	10	3	79	0.4	100
	Kyrgyzstan	Bishkek	6 630 623	33	22	6	72	1.7	37
	Laos	Vientiane	7 529 475	32	22	7	68	1.4	38
	Latvia	Rīga	1 850 651	29	9	18	73	-0.1	69
	Lebanon	Beirut	5 489 739	525	15	8	75	-1.9	89
	Lesotho	Maseru	2 305 825	76	26	14	53	1.1	30
	Liberia	Monrovia	5 302 681	48	31	9	61	2.1	53

Land		Education and Health			Development			Communications		Country	Time Zones
Area sq km	Forest thousand sq km 2021	Adult literacy % 2021	Doctors per 100 000 population 2020	Nutrition population under-nourished % 2020	Energy consumption million tonnes oil equivalent 2021	GNI per capita US$ 2022	HDI index 2021	Mobile phones subs per 100 population 2022	Broadband users subs per 100 population 2022		+ or - GMT
48 442	22	95.2	145	6.7	9.5	9 050	0.767	90.4	10.7	Dominican Republic	-4
14 874	9	69.9	76	26.2	0.2	1 970	0.607	110.4	<0.1	East Timor	+9
272 045	124	94.5	222	15.4	16.3	6 310	0.740	97.2	14.9	Ecuador	-5
1 001 450	<1	73.1	75	5.1	96.0	4 100	0.731	93.2	9.8	Egypt	+2
21 041	6	90.0	287	7.7	3.8	4 720	0.675	181.6	10.6	El Salvador	-6
28 051	24	..	40	..	1.7	5 320	0.596	53.3	0.1	Equatorial Guinea	+1
117 400	11	76.6	8	..	0.3	..	0.492	49.8	0.1	Eritrea	+3
45 200	24	99.9	347	2.5	2.9	27 640	0.890	155.0	40.4	Estonia	+2
17 364	5	89.3	14	11.0	0.6	3 800	0.597	122.2	2.3	Eswatini (Swaziland)	+2
1 133 880	170	51.8	11	24.9	9.0	1 020	0.498	56.0	0.5	Ethiopia	+3
18 330	11	..	..	5.7	0.7	5 270	0.730	107.2	2.5	Fiji	+12
338 145	224	99.9	464	2.5	29.1	54 360	0.940	128.7	33.9	Finland	+2
543 965	173	99.9	327	2.5	245.3	45 860	0.903	118.8	49.4	France	+1
267 667	235	85.5	65	17.2	1.6	7 540	0.706	125.4	3.4	Gabon	+1
11 295	2	58.1	8	21.6	0.2	810	0.500	101.4	0.2	Gambia, The	0
69 700	28	99.6	511	7.6	6.7	5 620	0.802	156.1	28.7	Georgia	+4
357 022	114	99.9	443	2.5	315.0	53 390	0.942	125.2	45.0	Germany	+1
238 537	80	80.4	17	4.1	9.8	2 350	0.632	119.6	0.6	Ghana	0
131 957	39	97.9	631	2.5	26.7	21 740	0.887	109.1	42.8	Greece	+2
378	<1	..	144	..	0.1	9 340	0.795	81.1	24.5	Grenada	-4
108 890	35	83.3	124	16.0	8.6	5 350	0.627	115.2	..	Guatemala	-6
245 857	61	45.3	22	..	1.5	1 180	0.465	101.9	<0.1	Guinea	0
36 125	20	52.9	20	..	0.1	820	0.483	125.9	0.2	Guinea-Bissau	0
214 969	184	88.8	142	4.9	0.9	15 050	0.714	106.4	11.8	Guyana	-4
27 750	3	..	23	47.2	1.0	1 610	0.535	63.9	0.3	Haiti	-5
112 088	63	88.5	50	15.3	4.5	2 740	0.621	76.1	4.6	Honduras	-6
93 030	21	99.1	352	2.5	27.3	19 010	0.846	104.1	35.5	Hungary	+1
102 820	<1	99.9	414	2.5	5.1	68 220	0.959	122.5	38.2	Iceland	0
3 166 620	724	74.4	74	16.3	805.4	2 380	0.633	80.7	2.4	India	+5½
1 919 445	915	96.0	62	6.5	205.2	4 580	0.705	114.9	4.9	Indonesia	+7 to +9
1 648 000	108	88.7	158	4.1	303.7	3 900	0.774	164.5	12.3	Iran	+3½
438 317	8	85.6	97	15.9	52.6	5 270	0.686	98.2	14.4	Iraq	+3
70 282	8	99.9	349	2.5	15.7	81 070	0.945	113.3	32.1	Ireland	0
22 072	1	..	363	2.5	26.0	54 650	0.919	152.2	29.4	Israel	+2
301 245	96	99.3	395	2.5	165.6	37 700	0.895	133.0	33.9	Italy	+1
10 991	6	..	53	6.9	3.0	5 670	0.709	106.2	15.0	Jamaica	-5
377 727	249	99.9	248	3.2	456.7	42 440	0.925	167.5	36.0	Japan	+9
89 206	<1	98.4	266	16.9	8.8	4 260	0.720	67.6	7.1	Jordan	+3
2 717 300	35	99.8	407	2.5	85.9	9 470	0.811	130.4	15.4	Kazakhstan	+5
582 646	36	82.6	16	26.9	8.9	2 170	0.575	121.7	1.5	Kenya	+3
717	<1	..	..	4.2	<0.1	3 280	0.624	48.8	0.3	Kiribati	+12 to +14
10 908	..	..	..	..	..	5 590	..	..	..	Kosovo	+1
17 818	<1	96.5	234	2.7	40.9	39 570	0.831	181.0	1.5	Kuwait	+3
198 500	13	99.6	..	5.3	5.2	1 410	0.692	130.4	4.4	Kyrgyzstan	+6
236 800	166	87.1	35	5.1	12.0	2 360	0.607	65.0	2.0	Laos	+7
64 589	34	99.9	340	2.5	4.0	21 500	0.863	117.1	26.4	Latvia	+2
10 452	1	95.3	221	10.9	9.1	..	0.706	76.7	7.7	Lebanon	+2
30 355	<1	81.0	47	34.7	0.4	1 260	0.514	67.5	0.4	Lesotho	+2
111 369	76	48.3	5	38.3	0.5	680	0.481	31.8	0.3	Liberia	0

.. data available

Flag	Key Information			Population						
	Country	Capital city	Population total 2022	Density persons per sq km 2022	Birth rate per 1000 population 2021	Death rate per 1000 population 2021	Life expectancy in years 2021	Population change % 2022	Urban populati % 2022
	Libya	Tripoli	6 812 341	4	18	6	72	1.1	81
	Liechtenstein	Vaduz	39 327	246	10	7	84	0.7	15
	Lithuania	Vilnius	2 750 055	42	8	17	74	1.1	68
	Luxembourg	Luxembourg	647 599	250	11	7	83	1.7	92
	Madagascar	Antananarivo	29 611 714	50	31	7	64	2.4	40
	Malawi	Lilongwe	20 405 317	172	33	7	63	2.6	18
	Malaysia	Kuala Lumpur/Putrajaya	33 938 221	102	15	6	75	1.1	78
	Maldives	Male'	523 787	1758	14	3	80	0.5	42
	Mali	Bamako	22 593 590	18	42	9	59	3.1	45
	Malta	Valletta	533 286	1688	9	8	83	0.9	95
	Marshall Islands	Delap-Uliga-Djarrit	41 569	230	19	8	65	-1.2	79
	Mauritania	Nouakchott	4 736 139	5	33	7	64	2.6	57
	Mauritius	Port Louis	1 299 469	637	10	11	74	-0.3	41
	Mexico	Mexico City	127 504 125	65	15	9	70	0.6	81
	Micronesia, Fed. States of	Palikir	114 164	163	21	6	71	0.9	23
	Moldova	Chişinău	3 272 996	97	12	16	69	-0.9	43
	Monaco	Monaco-Ville	36 469	18235	..	..	..	-0.6	100
	Mongolia	Ulan Bator	3 398 366	2	21	6	71	1.5	69
	Montenegro	Podgorica	627 082	45	11	15	74	-0.5	68
	Morocco	Rabat	37 457 971	84	18	6	74	1.0	65
	Mozambique	Maputo	32 969 518	41	37	9	59	2.7	38
	Myanmar (Burma)	Nay Pyi Taw	54 179 306	80	17	10	66	0.7	32
	Namibia	Windhoek	2 567 012	3	27	11	59	1.5	54
	Nauru	Yaren	12 668	603	28	7	64	1.3	100
	Nepal	Kathmandu	30 547 580	208	20	8	68	1.7	21
	Netherlands	Amsterdam/The Hague	17 564 014	423	10	10	81	1.0	93
	New Zealand	Wellington	5 185 288	19	11	7	82	0.3	87
	Nicaragua	Managua	6 948 392	53	21	5	74	1.4	60
	Niger	Niamey	26 207 977	21	45	8	62	3.7	17
	Nigeria	Abuja	218 541 212	237	37	13	53	2.4	54
	North Korea	P'yŏngyang	26 069 416	216	13	9	73	0.4	63
	North Macedonia	Skopje	2 093 599	81	10	16	75	-0.4	59
	Norway	Oslo	5 436 823	17	10	8	83	0.9	84
	Oman	Muscat	4 576 298	15	18	4	73	1.2	88
	Pakistan	Islamabad	235 824 862	267	28	7	66	1.9	38
	Palau	Ngerulmud	18 055	36	13	10	..	0.2	82
	Panama	Panama City	4 408 581	57	18	6	76	1.3	69
	Papua New Guinea	Port Moresby	10 142 619	22	26	7	65	1.9	14
	Paraguay	Asunción	6 780 744	17	21	8	70	1.1	63
	Peru	Lima	34 049 588	26	18	8	72	1.0	79
	Philippines	Manila	115 559 009	385	22	7	69	1.5	48
	Poland	Warsaw	39 857 145	127	9	14	76	-0.5	60
	Portugal	Lisbon	10 270 865	115	8	12	81	0.5	67
	Qatar	Doha	2 695 122	236	10	1	79	0.3	99
	Romania	Bucharest	19 659 267	83	9	18	73	-0.9	54
	Russia	Moscow	144 713 314	8	10	17	69	0.1	75
	Rwanda	Kigali	13 776 698	523	30	6	66	2.3	18
	St Kitts and Nevis	Basseterre	47 657	183	12	10	72	0.1	31
	St Lucia	Castries	179 857	292	11	10	71	0.1	19

| Land | | Education and Health | | | Development | | | Communications | | Country | Time Zones |
Area sq km	Forest thousand sq km 2021	Adult literacy % 2021	Doctors per 100 000 population 2020	Nutrition population under-nourished % 2020	Energy consumption million tonnes oil equivalent 2021	GNI per capita US$ 2022	HDI index 2021	Mobile phones subs per 100 population 2022	Broadband users subs per 100 population 2022		+ or − GMT
1 759 540	2	..	209	..	16.4	7 260	0.718	204.6	4.8	Libya	+2
160	<1	..	..	..	..	..	0.935	126.3	48.8	Liechtenstein	+1
65 200	22	99.8	463	2.5	7.1	23 690	0.875	139.1	29.4	Lithuania	+2
2 586	<1	99.9	301	2.5	4.4	91 200	0.930	137.1	38.7	Luxembourg	+1
587 041	124	77.3	20	48.5	1.3	510	0.501	70.2	0.1	Madagascar	+3
118 484	22	67.3	5	17.8	0.8	640	0.512	60.1	<0.1	Malawi	+2
332 965	191	95.0	229	2.5	92.6	11 780	0.803	141.3	12.4	Malaysia	+8
298	<1	97.9	205	..	0.8	11 030	0.747	136.5	17.4	Maldives	+5
1 240 140	133	30.8	13	9.8	2.2	850	0.428	114.5	0.8	Mali	0
316	<1	94.9	..	2.5	3.4	33 550	0.918	131.6	43.0	Malta	+1
181	<1	..	..	..	..	7 920	0.639	38.0	..	Marshall Islands	+12
1 030 700	3	67.0	19	10.1	1.6	2 160	0.556	113.1	0.3	Mauritania	0
2 040	<1	92.2	271	7.8	2.2	10 760	0.802	161.4	25.7	Mauritius	+4
1 972 545	656	95.3	243	6.1	177.6	10 410	0.758	100.3	19.5	Mexico	−5 to −8
701	<1	..	94	..	<0.1	4 130	0.628	19.4	5.3	Micronesia, F.S. of	+10 & +11
33 700	4	99.6	310	..	4.2	5 340	0.767	127.4	24.4	Moldova	+2
2	<1	..	..	..	..	..	..	106.8	59.0	Monaco	+1
1 565 000	142	99.2	385	3.6	6.5	4 210	0.739	142.3	12.9	Mongolia	+7 & +8
13 812	8	99.0	274	2.5	1.0	10 400	0.832	203.2	31.3	Montenegro	+1
446 550	58	75.9	73	5.6	23.9	3 710	0.683	137.5	6.1	Morocco	+1
799 380	365	63.4	9	32.7	6.2	500	0.446	42.1	0.2	Mozambique	+2
676 577	283	89.1	74	3.1	14.2	1 210	0.585	106.7	2.1	Myanmar (Burma)	+6½
824 292	66	92.3	59	18.0	1.9	4 880	0.615	113.2	3.8	Namibia	+2
21	<1	..	..	..	<0.1	17 870	..	79.9	..	Nauru	+12
147 181	60	71.2	85	5.5	4.2	1 340	0.602	127.2	4.2	Nepal	+5¾
41 526	4	99.9	408	2.5	92.9	57 430	0.941	118.1	44.5	Netherlands	+1
270 534	99	99.9	362	2.5	20.8	48 460	0.937	114.7	35.9	New Zealand	+12 & +12¾
130 000	33	..	166	18.6	2.5	2 090	0.667	97.1	4.9	Nicaragua	−6
267 000	11	37.3	3	..	0.9	610	0.400	56.4	<0.1	Niger	+1
923 768	215	62.0	38	12.7	46.8	2 140	0.535	101.7	<0.1	Nigeria	+1
120 538	60	99.9	368	41.6	8.6	..	..	23.1	..	North Korea	+9
25 713	10	..	..	3.3	2.8	6 640	0.770	97.8	24.2	North Macedonia	+1
323 878	122	99.9	505	2.5	50.1	95 510	0.961	110.7	45.8	Norway	+1
309 500	<1	95.7	177	9.8	32.9	20 150	0.816	135.1	11.6	Oman	+4
881 888	37	58.0	112	16.9	84.4	1 580	0.544	81.8	1.3	Pakistan	+5
497	<1	..	177	..	..	..	0.767	132.9	..	Palau	+9
77 082	42	95.7	163	5.8	10.1	16 750	0.805	156.3	15.5	Panama	−5
462 840	358	..	7	21.6	1.8	2 730	0.558	48.4	0.2	Papua New Guinea	+10 & +11
406 752	158	94.5	105	8.7	9.1	5 920	0.717	127.7	10.9	Paraguay	−4
285 216	722	94.5	137	8.3	26.7	6 770	0.762	122.0	9.3	Peru	−5
300 000	72	96.3	77	5.2	40.5	3 950	0.699	144.0	7.6	Philippines	+8
312 683	95	99.8	238	2.5	107.1	18 350	0.876	131.9	23.0	Poland	+1
88 940	33	96.8	548	2.5	23.6	25 800	0.866	124.5	43.5	Portugal	0
11 437	<1	93.5	249	..	52.9	70 500	0.855	174.1	13.6	Qatar	+3
237 500	69	98.9	298	2.5	34.9	15 660	0.821	118.1	32.4	Romania	+2
17 075 400	8 153	99.7	382	2.5	862.1	12 830	0.822	169.0	23.7	Russia	+2 to +12
26 338	3	75.9	12	35.8	0.5	930	0.534	79.9	0.4	Rwanda	+2
261	<1	..	277	..	<0.1	19 730	0.777	119.1	42.3	St Kitts and Nevis	−4
616	<1	..	64	..	0.2	11 160	0.715	95.6	21.2	St Lucia	−4

.. no data available

Flag	Country	Capital city	Population total 2022	Density persons per sq km 2022	Birth rate per 1000 population 2021	Death rate per 1000 population 2021	Life expectancy in years 2021	Population change % 2022	Urban population % 2022
	St Vincent and the Grenadines	Kingstown	103 948	267	13	13	70	-0.4	54
	Samoa	Apia	222 382	79	27	5	73	1.6	18
	San Marino	San Marino	33 660	552	6	9	..	-0.3	98
	São Tomé and Príncipe	São Tomé	227 380	236	28	6	68	1.9	76
	Saudi Arabia	Riyadh	36 408 820	17	17	3	77	1.3	85
	Senegal	Dakar	17 316 449	88	33	6	67	2.6	49
	Serbia	Belgrade	7 221 365	93	9	20	73	-1.1	57
	Seychelles	Victoria	107 118	235	17	9	73	0.8	58
	Sierra Leone	Freetown	8 605 718	120	31	9	60	2.2	44
	Singapore	Singapore	5 975 689	9352	9	6	83	3.3	100
	Slovakia	Bratislava	5 643 453	115	10	14	75	-0.3	54
	Slovenia	Ljubljana	2 119 844	105	9	11	81	0.0	56
	Solomon Islands	Honiara	724 273	26	30	5	70	2.3	26
	Somalia	Mogadishu	17 597 511	28	44	12	55	3.1	47
	South Africa	Bloemfontein/Cape Town/Pretoria	59 893 885	49	20	11	62	0.8	68
	South Korea	Seoul	51 815 810	522	5	6	84	-0.2	81
	South Sudan	Juba	10 913 164	17	29	11	55	1.5	21
	Spain	Madrid	45 132 019	89	7	10	83	0.4	81
	Sri Lanka	Sri Jayawardenapura Kotte	21 832 143	333	14	7	76	0.1	19
	Sudan	Khartoum	46 874 204	25	34	7	65	2.6	36
	Suriname	Paramaribo	618 040	4	18	9	70	0.8	66
	Sweden	Stockholm	10 549 347	23	11	9	83	0.7	88
	Switzerland	Bern	8 740 472	212	10	8	84	0.8	74
	Syria	Damascus	22 125 249	120	20	5	72	3.7	57
	Taiwan	Taipei	23 893 394	660	..	..	..	..	..
	Tajikistan	Dushanbe	9 952 787	70	27	5	72	2.1	28
	Tanzania	Dodoma	65 497 748	69	36	6	66	3.0	37
	Thailand	Bangkok	71 697 030	140	9	8	79	0.1	53
	Togo	Lomé	8 848 699	156	32	8	62	2.3	44
	Tonga	Nuku'alofa	106 858	143	23	7	71	0.8	23
	Trinidad and Tobago	Port of Spain	1 531 044	298	12	9	73	0.4	53
	Tunisia	Tunis	12 356 117	75	16	8	74	0.8	70
	Turkey	Ankara	85 341 241	109	15	6	76	0.7	77
	Turkmenistan	Ashgabat	6 430 770	13	22	7	69	1.4	53
	Tuvalu	Vaiaku	11 312	452	23	10	65	1.0	66
	Uganda	Kampala	47 249 585	196	37	6	63	3.0	26
	Ukraine	Kyiv	39 701 739	66	7	19	70	-14.2	70
	United Arab Emirates	Abu Dhabi	9 441 129	122	10	2	79	0.8	88
	United Kingdom	London	67 026 292	277	10	10	81	-0.1	84
	United States	Washington D.C.	338 289 857	34	11	10	76	0.4	83
	Uruguay	Montevideo	3 422 794	19	10	12	75	-0.1	96
	Uzbekistan	Tashkent	34 627 652	77	26	5	71	2.1	50
	Vanuatu	Port Vila	326 740	27	29	5	70	2.4	26
	Vatican City	Vatican City	510	1020	..	..	..	..	..
	Venezuela	Caracas	28 301 696	31	16	8	71	0.4	88
	Vietnam	Hanoi	98 186 856	298	15	7	74	0.7	39
	Yemen	Sanaa	33 696 614	64	31	7	64	2.1	39
	Zambia	Lusaka	20 017 675	27	35	7	61	2.8	46
	Zimbabwe	Harare	16 320 537	42	31	9	59	2.0	32

Land		Education and Health			Development			Communications				
Area sq km	Forest thousand sq km 2021	Adult literacy % 2021	Doctors per 100 000 population 2020	Nutrition population under-nourished % 2020	Energy consumption million tonnes oil equivalent 2021	GNI per capita US$ 2022	HDI index 2021	Mobile phones subs per 100 population 2022	Broadband users subs per 100 population 2022	Country		Time Zones + or - GMT
389	<1	..	..	7.6	<0.1	9 110	0.751	100.5	28.5	St Vincent and the Grenadines		-4
2 831	2	99.1	60	4.4	0.1	3 630	0.707	60.4	0.8	Samoa		+13
61	<1	..	..	..	..	..	0.853	121.8	36.2	San Marino		+1
964	<1	93.8	49	13.5	<0.1	2 410	0.618	86.8	2.0	São Tomé and Príncipe		0
2 200 000	10	97.6	274	3.7	231.2	27 590	0.875	132.4	37.0	Saudi Arabia		+3
196 720	80	56.3	9	7.5	3.6	1 640	0.511	120.4	1.4	Senegal		0
77 453	27	99.5	..	3.3	17.3	9 140	0.802	123.7	26.2	Serbia		+1
455	<1	96.2	225	..	0.4	14 340	0.785	191.5	35.0	Seychelles		+4
71 740	25	47.7	7	27.4	0.4	510	0.477	97.7	<0.1	Sierra Leone		0
639	<1	97.1	246	..	84.6	67 200	0.939	156.5	37.4	Singapore		+8
49 035	19	..	356	3.8	18.7	22 060	0.848	131.9	33.0	Slovakia		+1
20 251	12	..	328	2.5	6.8	30 600	0.918	126.2	32.2	Slovenia		+1
28 370	25	..	19	18.1	0.1	2 220	0.564	67.0	0.1	Solomon Islands		+11
637 657	59	..	..	53.1	0.3	470	..	50.3	0.7	Somalia		+3
219 090	170	95.0	79	6.9	136.6	6 780	0.713	167.4	3.3	South Africa		+2
99 274	63	98.8	248	2.5	320.4	35 990	0.925	148.6	45.4	South Korea		+9
644 329	72	34.5	4	..	0.7	..	0.385	30.0	<0.1	South Sudan		+2
504 782	186	98.6	444	2.5	136.8	31 680	0.905	124.1	35.6	Spain		+1
65 610	21	92.4	123	3.4	8.7	3 610	0.782	143.1	10.1	Sri Lanka		+5½
1 861 484	182	60.7	26	12.8	9.1	760	0.508	74.0	<0.1	Sudan		+2
163 820	152	95.0	82	8.2	1.1	4 880	0.730	150.3	20.2	Suriname		-3
449 964	280	99.9	441	2.5	54.4	62 990	0.947	125.1	40.4	Sweden		+1
41 293	13	99.9	438	2.5	27.4	89 450	0.962	119.6	49.5	Switzerland		+1
184 026	5	..	129	..	10.1	..	0.577	79.7	7.4	Syria		+3
36 179	..	..	..	..	99.0	..	..	..	..	Taiwan		+8
143 100	4	..	..	..	6.4	1 210	0.685	118.8	<0.1	Tajikistan		+5
945 087	453	81.8	5	22.6	5.0	1 200	0.549	91.9	2.1	Tanzania		+3
513 115	198	94.1	95	8.8	132.1	7 230	0.800	176.3	18.4	Thailand		+7
56 785	12	66.5	8	18.8	0.8	990	0.539	74.2	1.1	Togo		0
748	<1	99.4	95	..	<0.1	..	0.745	60.7	6.4	Tonga		+13
5 130	2	..	448	7.5	16.8	16 330	0.810	130.6	24.4	Trinidad and Tobago		-4
164 150	7	82.7	130	3.1	10.0	3 840	0.731	129.3	13.7	Tunisia		+1
779 452	224	96.7	193	2.5	171.7	10 590	0.838	105.8	22.3	Turkey		+3
488 100	41	..	..	3.5	47.8	..	0.745	98.6	5.9	Turkmenistan		+5
25	<1	..	119	..	<0.1	7 210	0.641	80.3	4.0	Tuvalu		+12
241 038	23	79.0	15	..	3.0	930	0.525	70.0	<0.1	Uganda		+3
603 700	97	99.9	..	2.8	89.3	4 270	0.773	135.0	18.3	Ukraine	+2 & +4 (Crimea)	
77 700	3	98.1	260	5.6	117.0	48 950	0.911	212.2	39.9	United Arab Emirates		+4
243 609	32	99.9	300	2.5	179.8	48 890	0.929	120.8	41.5	United Kingdom		0
9 826 635	3 098	99.9	261	2.5	2467.2	76 370	0.921	110.0	37.6	United States		-5 to -10
176 215	21	98.8	494	2.5	5.4	18 030	0.809	138.5	33.2	Uruguay		-3
447 400	37	99.9	..	2.5	48.5	2 190	0.727	103.1	26.0	Uzbekistan		+5
12 190	4	89.1	17	11.9	<0.1	3 560	0.607	78.2	1.1	Vanuatu		+11
1	..	..	..	..	..	..	..	..	..	Vatican City		+1
912 050	462	97.5	173	22.9	45.7	..	0.691	63.4	8.9	Venezuela		-4
329 565	147	95.8	83	5.7	107.5	4 010	0.703	139.9	21.6	Vietnam		+7
527 968	5	..	..	41.4	3.1	..	0.455	46.0	1.2	Yemen		+3
752 614	446	87.5	12	..	5.7	1 170	0.565	99.1	0.4	Zambia		+2
390 759	174	89.7	20	..	3.6	1 500	0.593	87.6	1.3	Zimbabwe		+2

data available

Pages 158 – 163 show a variety of demographic and economic indicators by the world's seven regional groupings (defined by the World Bank), as shown on the right.

The colours on the maps below show the average figures for each region. The highest and lowest countries for most indicators are also named.

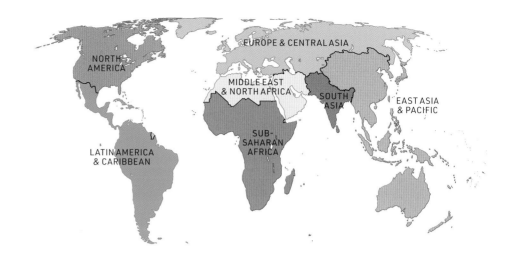

NORTH AMERICA

EUROPE & CENTRAL ASIA

MIDDLE EAST & NORTH AFRICA

SOUTH ASIA

EAST ASIA & PACIFIC

LATIN AMERICA & CARIBBEAN

SUB-SAHARAN AFRICA

Scale 1 : 250 000 000

Birth rate

Number of births per 1000 people

	25 – 35
	20 – 24.9
	15 – 19.9
	10 – 14.9
	no data

World average 16.9
Statistics are for 2021

Scale 1 : 250 000 000

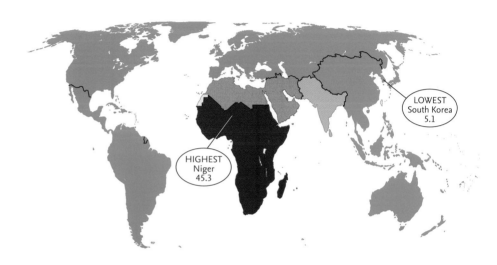

LOWEST
South Korea
5.1

HIGHEST
Niger
45.3

Death rate

Number of deaths per 1000 people

	10 – 11.8
	8 – 9.9
	7 – 7.9
	4.9 – 6.9
	no data

World average 8.7
Statistics are for 2021

Scale 1 : 250 000 000

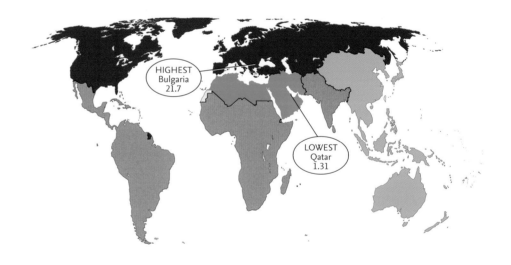

HIGHEST
Bulgaria
21.7

LOWEST
Qatar
1.31

Infant mortality rate

Number of infants dying before reaching one year of age, per 1000 live births

	20 – 50
	15 – 19.9
	10 – 14.9
	5 – 9.9
	no data

World average 28.4
Statistics are for 2021

Scale 1 : 250 000 000

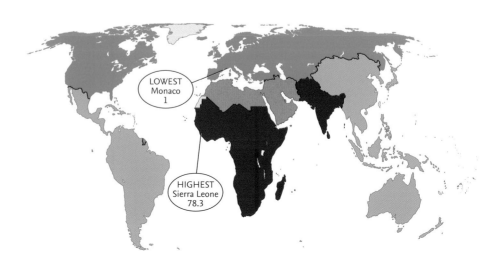

LOWEST
Monaco
1

HIGHEST
Sierra Leone
78.3

Life expectancy

Years

- 75 – 77
- 70 – 74.9
- 65 – 69.9
- 61 – 64.9
- no data

World average 71.3
Statistics are for 2021

Scale 1 : 250 000 000

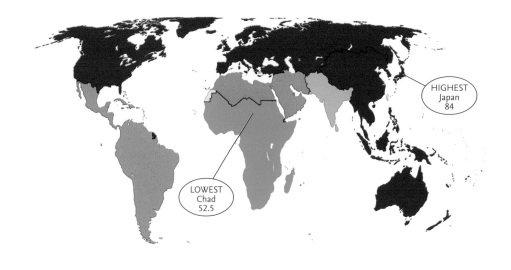

HIGHEST
Japan
84

LOWEST
Chad
52.5

Population growth

Annual average growth, percentage

- 1.6 – 2.6
- 0.9 – 1.6
- 0 – 0.8
- -0.3 – 0
- no data

World average 0.8
Statistics are for 2022

Scale 1 : 250 000 000

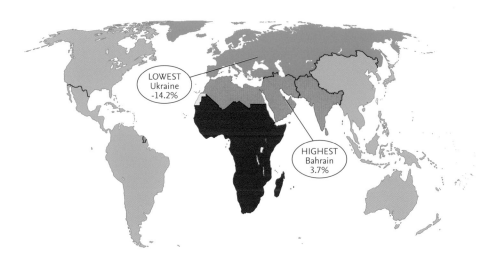

LOWEST
Ukraine
-14.2%

HIGHEST
Bahrain
3.7%

Migration

Annual net migration, millions

- 0.5 – 1.3
- 0 – 0.5
- -0.5 – 0
- -1 – -0.5
- no data

Statistics are for 2021

Scale 1 : 250 000 000

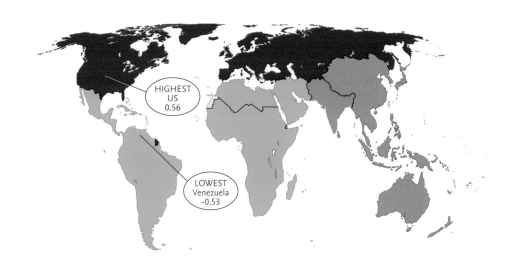

HIGHEST
US
0.56

LOWEST
Venezuela
-0.53

Urbanization

Urban population, percentage

- 80 – 83
- 65 – 79.9
- 50 – 64.9
- 35 – 49.9
- no data

World average 56.9
Statistics are for 2022

Scale 1 : 250 000 000

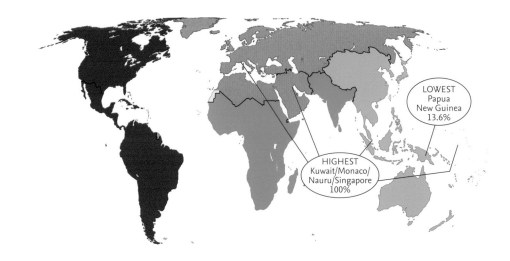

LOWEST
Papua
New Guinea
13.6%

HIGHEST
Kuwait/Monaco/
Nauru/Singapore
100%

Human Development Index

HDI is based on life expectancy, knowledge and standard of living

- 0.800 –0.999 (very high)
- 0.700 – 0.799 (high)
- 0.550 – 0.699 (medium)
- 0 – 0.549 (low)
- no data

World average 0.732
Statistics are for 2021

Scale 1 : 250 000 000

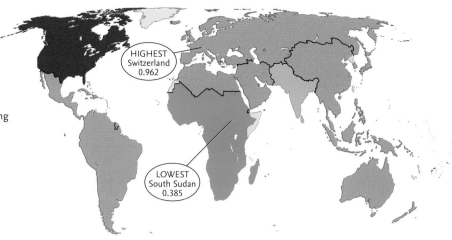

Literacy rate

Percentage of adults

- 95 – 100
- 90 – 94.9
- 75 – 89.9
- 65 – 74.9
- no data

World average 86.8
Statistics are for 2021

Scale 1 : 250 000 000

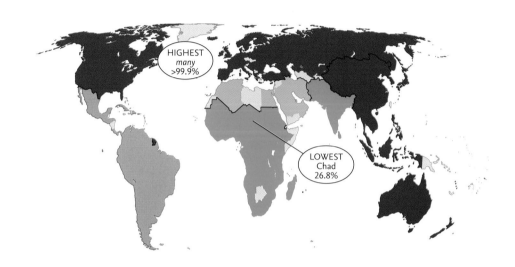

Nutrition

Percentage of population undernourished

- 17.5 – 21
- 12.5 – 17.4
- 7.5 – 12.4
- 2.5 – 7.4
- no data

World average 9.3
Statistics are for 2020

Scale 1 : 250 000 000

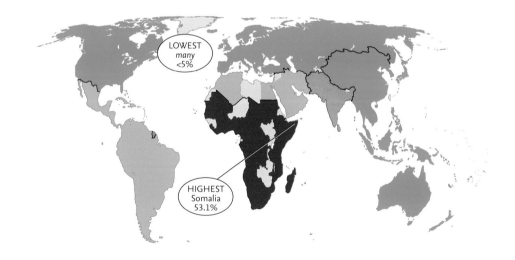

Access to safe water

Percentage of population with access
to water from an improved source

- 98 – 100
- 94 – 97.9
- 90 – 93.9
- 65 – 89.9
- no data

World average 91.2
Statistics are for 2022

Scale 1 : 250 000 000

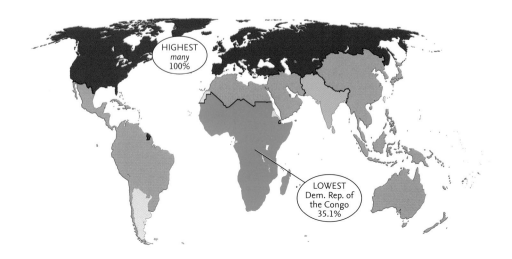

Doctors

Number of physicians per 100 000 people

- 300 – 399
- 200 – 299
- 100 – 199
- 0 – 99
- no data

World average 161
Statistics are for 2018

Scale 1 : 250 000 000

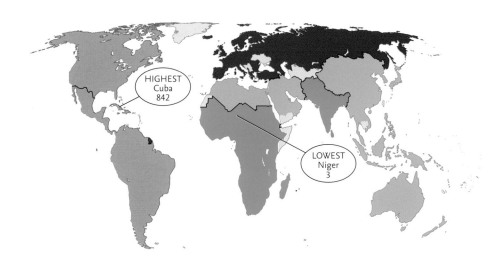

HIGHEST
Cuba
842

LOWEST
Niger
3

HIV

Percentage of population aged 15 – 49 infected with HIV

- 0.6 – 4
- 0.4 – 0.5
- 0.1 – 0.3
- no data

World average 0.7
Statistics are for 2021

Scale 1 : 250 000 000

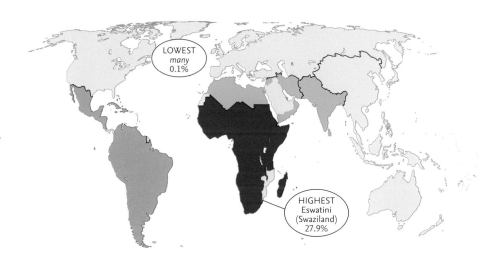

LOWEST
many
0.1%

HIGHEST
Eswatini
(Swaziland)
27.9%

Poverty

Percentage of population living on less than US$ 2.15 a day

- 20 – 35.4
- 10 – 19.9
- 5 – 9.9
- 1 – 4.9
- no data

World average 9.0
Statistics are for 2018 – 2021

Scale 1 : 250 000 000

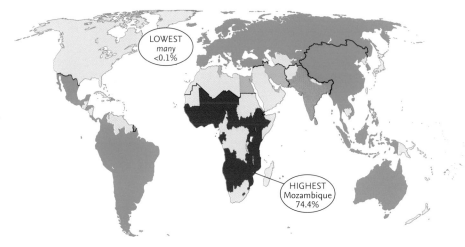

LOWEST
many
<0.1%

HIGHEST
Mozambique
74.4%

Aid

Official development assistance received, US$ per person

- 20 – 71.8
- 10 – 19.9
- 5 – 9.9
- 0 – 4.9
- no data
- Donors

World average 25.6
Statistics are for 2021

Scale 1 : 250 000 000

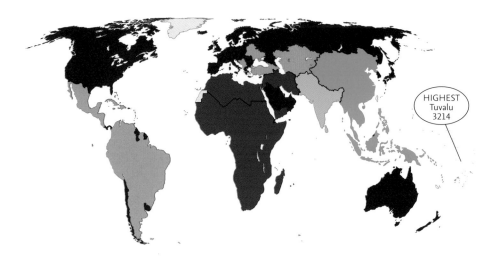

HIGHEST
Tuvalu
3214

Regional Indicators

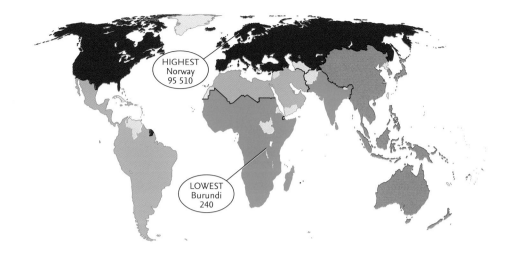

Gross National Income

GNI is the value of production of goods
and services of each country, US$ per person

- 25 000 – 74 000
- 10 000 – 24 999
- 5000 – 9999
- 1000 – 4999
- no data

World average 12 804
Statistics are for 2022

Scale 1 : 250 000 000

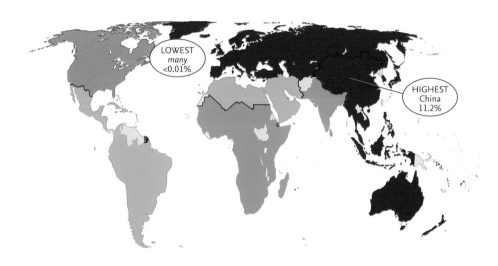

Trade

Percentage of world trade

- 30.1 – 40.1
- 10.1 – 30
- 5.1 – 10
- 1 – 5
- no data

Statistics are for 2020 – 2022

Scale 1 : 250 000 000

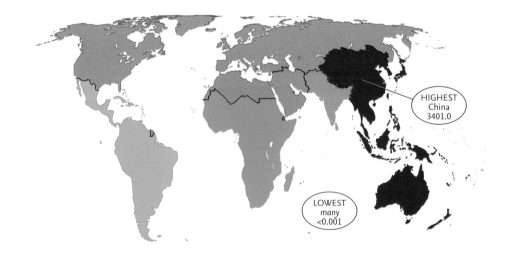

Energy production

Million tonnes oil equivalent

- 3500 – 4800
- 2000 – 3499
- 750 – 1999
- 0 – 749
- no data

Statistics are for 2021

Scale 1 : 250 000 000

Energy consumption

Million tonnes oil equivalent

- 3500 – 6000
- 2000 – 3499
- 750 – 1999
- 0 – 749
- no data

Statistics are for 2021

Scale 1 : 250 000 000

Carbon dioxide emissions

Metric tonnes per person

- 10 – 13.1
- 5 – 9.9
- 0 – 4.9
- no data

World average 4.3
Statistics are for 2020

Scale 1 : 250 000 000

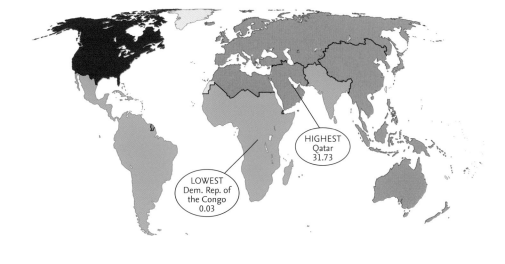

HIGHEST
Qatar
31.73

LOWEST
Dem. Rep. of
the Congo
0.03

Mobile phones

Subscriptions per 100 people

- 125 – 130
- 110 – 124.9
- 95 – 109.9
- 80 – 94.9
- no data

World average 108.0
Statistics are for 2022

Scale 1 : 250 000 000

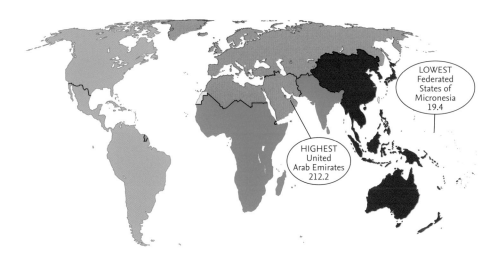

LOWEST
Federated
States of
Micronesia
19.4

HIGHEST
United
Arab Emirates
212.2

Air passengers

Millions carried

- 600 – 700
- 300 – 599
- 100 – 299
- 0 – 99
- no data

Statistics are for 2021

Scale 1 : 250 000 000

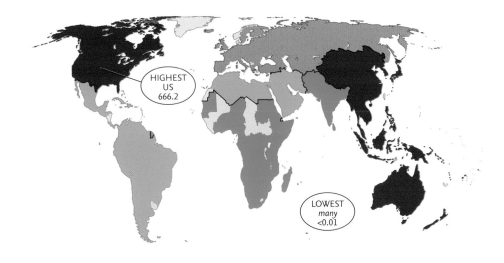

HIGHEST
US
666.2

LOWEST
many
<0.01

Tourism

Earnings from international tourism, US$ billion

- 500 – 600
- 300 – 499
- 100 – 299
- 0 – 99
- no data

Statistics are for 2021

Scale 1 : 250 000 000

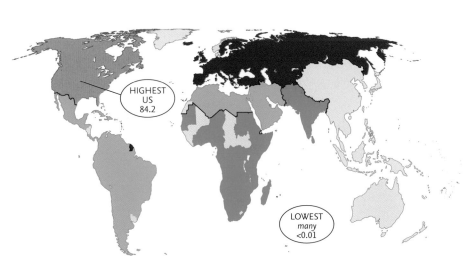

HIGHEST
US
84.2

LOWEST
many
<0.01

How to use the Index

All the names on the maps in this atlas, except some of those on the special topic maps, are included in the index.

The names are arranged in **alphabetical order.** Where the name has more than one word the separate words are considered as one to decide the position of the name in the index:

Thetford
The Trossachs
The Wash
The Weald
Thiers
Thiès

Where there is more than one place with the same name, the country name is used to decide the order:

London Canada
London England

If both places are in the same country, the county or state name is also used:

Avon *r.* Brist. England
Avon *r.* Dor. England

Each entry in the index starts with the name of the place or feature, followed by the name of the country or region in which it is located. This is followed by the number of the most appropriate page on which the name appears, usually the largest scale map. Next comes the alphanumeric reference followed by the latitude and longitude.

Names of physical features such as rivers, capes, mountains etc are followed by a description. The descriptions are usually shortened to one or two letters – these abbreviations are keyed below. Town names are followed by a description only when the name may be confused with that of a physical feature:

Big Trout Lake *town*

To help to distinguish the different parts of each entry, different styles of type are used:

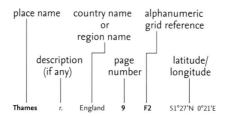

place name	country name or region name	alphanumeric grid reference
description (if any)	page number	latitude/ longitude
Thames	*r.* England **9** **F2**	51°27′N 0°21′E

To use the **alphanumeric grid reference** to find a feature on the map, first find the correct page and then look at the letters and numbers printed outside the frame along the top, bottom and sides of the map.

When you have found the correct letter and number follow the grid boxes up and along until you find the correct grid box in which the feature appears. You must then search the grid box until you find the name of the feature.

The **latitude and longitude reference** gives a more exact description of the position of the feature.

Page 1 of the atlas describes lines of latitude and lines of longitude, and explains how they are numbered and divided into degrees and minutes. Each name in the index has a different latitude and longitude reference, so the feature can be located accurately. The lines of latitude and lines of longitude shown on each map are numbered in degrees. These numbers are printed in black along the top, bottom and sides of the map frame.

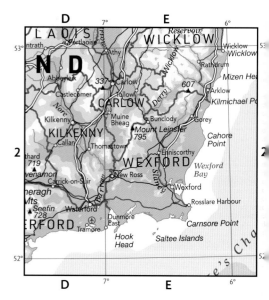

The drawing above shows part of the map on page 18 and the lines of latitude and lines of longitude.

The index entry for Wexford is given as follows:

Wexford Ireland **18 E2** .... 52°20′N 6°28′W

To locate Wexford, first find latitude 52°N and estimate 20 minutes north from 52 degrees to find 52°20′N, then find longitude 6°W and estimate 28 minutes west from 6 degrees to find 6°28′W. The symbol for the town of Wexford is where latitude 52°20′N and longitude 6°28′W meet.

On maps at a smaller scale than the map of Ireland, it is not possible to show every line of latitude and longitude. Only every 5 or 10 degrees of latitude and longitude may be shown. On these maps you must estimate the degrees and minutes to find the exact location of a feature.

Abbreviations

A. and B.	Argyll and Bute	*i.*	island	Oreg.	Oregon
Afgh.	Afghanistan	Ill.	Illinois	Orkn.	Orkney
Ala.	Alabama	I. o. W.	Isle of Wight	Oxon.	Oxfordshire
Ang.	Angus	*is*	islands	Pacific Oc.	Pacific Ocean
b.	bay	*l.*	lake	P. and K.	Perth and Kinross
Baja Calif.	Baja California	La.	Louisiana	P'boro.	Peterborough
Bangl.	Bangladesh	Lancs.	Lancashire	Pem.	Pembrokeshire
Bos. and Herz.	Bosnia and Herzegovina	Leics.	Leicestershire	*pen.*	peninsula
Brist.	Bristol	Lincs.	Lincolnshire	Phil.	Philippines
c.	cape	Lux.	Luxembourg	P.N.G.	Papua New Guinea
Cambs.	Cambridgeshire	Man.	Manitoba	*pt*	point
C.A.R.	Central African Republic	Mass.	Massachusetts	*r.*	river
Colo.	Colorado	Me.	Maine	*r. mouth*	river mouth
Corn.	Cornwall	Mich.	Michigan	*resr*	reservoir
Cumb.	Cumbria	Minn.	Minnesota	S. Africa	South Africa
d.	internal division e.g. county, state	Miss.	Mississippi	S. America	South America
		Mo.	Missouri	S. Atlantic Oc.	South Atlantic Ocean
Del.	Delaware	Mor.	Moray	S. C.	South Carolina
Dem. Rep. Congo	Democratic Republic of the Congo	*mt.*	mountain	S. China Sea	South China Sea
		mts	mountains	Shetl.	Shetland
Derbys.	Derbyshire	N. Africa	North Africa	S. Korea	South Korea
des.	desert	Na h-E. S.	Na h-Eileanan Siar	Som.	Somerset
Dev.	Devon	N. America	North America	S. Pacific Oc.	South Pacific Ocean
Dom. Rep.	Dominican Republic	N. Atlantic Oc.	North Atlantic Ocean	*str.*	strait
Don.	Donegal	*nature res.*	nature reserve	Suff.	Suffolk
Dor.	Dorset	N. C.	North Carolina	Switz.	Switzerland
Dur.	Durham	Neth.	Netherlands	T. and W.	Tyne and Wear
Equat. Guinea	Equatorial Guinea	Neth. Antilles	Netherlands Antilles	Tel. Wre.	Telford and Wrekin
Ess.	Essex	Nev.	Nevada	Tex.	Texas
est.	estuary	New.	Newport	Tipp.	Tipperary
E. Sussex	East Sussex	Nfld. and Lab.	Newfoundland and Labrador	U.A.E.	United Arab Emirates
E. Yorks.	East Riding of Yorkshire	N. Korea	North Korea	U.K.	United Kingdom
f.	physical feature, e.g. valley, plain, geographic area	N. M.	New Mexico	U.S.	United States
		N. Mariana Is	Northern Marianas Islands	Va.	Virginia
Falk.	Falkirk	Norf.	Norfolk	*vol.*	volcano
g.	gulf	Northum.	Northumberland	Vt.	Vermont
Ga.	Georgia	Notts.	Nottinghamshire	Water.	Waterford
Glos.	Gloucestershire	N. Pacific Oc.	North Pacific Ocean	Warwicks.	Warwickshire
Hants.	Hampshire	N. Y.	New York	Wick.	Wicklow
High.	Highland	Oc.	Ocean	W. Va.	West Virginia
hd	headland	Oh.	Ohio	Wyo.	Wyoming

Aa r. France 9 H2.....51°00'N 2°07'E
Aabenraa Denmark 43 B1.....55°02'N 9°25'E
Aachen Germany 46 B4.....50°46'N 6°05'E
Aalen Germany 46 D3.....48°50'N 10°06'E
Aalst Belgium 42 D3.....50°56'N 4°03'E
Aarhus Denmark 43 B2.....56°09'N 10°12'E
Ābādān Iran 95 G6.....30°20'N 48°15'E
Ābādeh Iran 95 H6.....31°08'N 52°36'E
Abadla Algeria 84 D5.....31°00'N 2°43'W
Abakan Russia 55 K3.....53°42'N 91°25'E
Abarqū Iran 95 H6.....31°06'N 53°13'E
Abashiri Japan 104 D4.....44°01'N 144°15'E
Abaya, Lake Ethiopia 85 H2.....6°19'N 37°53'E
Abaza Russia 98 G8.....51°33'N 90°06'E
Abbeville France 44 D7.....50°06'N 1°50'E
Abbeyfeale Ireland 18 B2.....52°23'N 9°18'W
Abbey Head Scotland 15 F2.....54°46'N 3°58'W
Abbeyleix Ireland 18 D2.....52°55'N 7°21'W
Abbottabad Pakistan 95 L6.....34°13'N 73°17'E
Abéché Chad 85 G3.....13°50'N 20°49'E
Abeokuta Nigeria 84 E2.....7°07'N 3°18'E
Aberaeron Wales 10 C4.....52°15'N 4°15'W
Aberchirder Scotland 17 G2.....57°34'N 2°38'W
Aberdare Wales 10 D3.....51°43'N 3°27'W
Aberdaron Wales 10 C4.....52°48'N 4°43'W
Aberdeen Scotland 17 G2.....57°09'N 2°06'W
Aberdeen d. Scotland 20 D5.....57°10'N 2°11'W
Aberdeen U.S. 62 G6.....45°28'N 98°31'W
Aberdeenshire d. Scotland 20 D5.....57°21'N 2°32'W
Aberfeldy Scotland 17 F1.....56°37'N 3°52'W
Aberford England 13 F2.....53°50'N 1°21'W
Aberfoyle Scotland 14 E4.....56°11'N 4°23'W
Abergavenny Wales 10 D3.....51°49'N 3°01'W
Abergele Wales 10 D5.....53°17'N 3°35'W
Aberlour Scotland 17 F2.....57°29'N 3°13'W
Aberporth Wales 10 C4.....52°08'N 4°33'W
Abersoch Wales 10 C4.....52°50'N 4°30'W
Abertillery Wales 10 D3.....51°44'N 3°08'W
Aberystwyth Wales 10 C4.....52°25'N 4°05'W
Abhā Saudi Arabia 94 F3.....18°14'N 42°27'E
Abidjan Côte d'Ivoire 84 D2.....5°21'N 4°02'W
Abilene U.S. 62 G3.....32°26'N 99°45'W
Abingdon England 8 D2.....51°40'N 1°17'W
Abington Scotland 15 F3.....55°30'N 3°41'W
Abitibi, Lake Canada 63 J6.....48°55'N 80°01'W
Abkhazia d. Georgia 53 E2.....43°15'N 40°45'E
Aboyne Scotland 15 F2.....55°20'N 2°47'W
Abqaiq Saudi Arabia 95 G5.....25°56'N 49°42'E
Abū 'Arīsh Saudi Arabia 94 F3.....16°59'N 42°45'E
Abu Dhabi U.A.E. 95 H4.....24°28'N 54°20'E
Abu Hamed Sudan 85 H3.....19°30'N 33°24'E
Abuja Nigeria 84 E2.....9°06'N 7°19'E
Abū Kamāl Syria 94 F6.....34°26'N 40°56'E
Abū Nujaym Libya 49 G3.....30°28'N 15°27'E
Abū Sunbul Egypt 94 D4.....22°26'N 31°39'E
Abyad Sudan 94 C2.....13°46'N 26°26'E
A Cañiza Spain 45 A5.....42°13'N 8°16'W
Acaponeta Mexico 66 C5.....22°30'N 105°25'W
Acapulco Mexico 66 E4.....16°55'N 99°52'W
Acarigua Venezuela 72 C7.....9°33'N 69°11'W
Accra Ghana 84 D2.....5°35'N 0°14'W
Accrington England 13 E2.....53°45'N 2°22'W
Acheloos r. Greece 50 D4.....38°20'N 21°06'E
Achill Island Ireland 18 A3.....53°56'N 10°00'W
Achinsk Russia 55 K3.....56°17'N 90°34'E
A' Chràileag mt. Scotland 16 D2.....57°11'N 5°09'W
Acle England 9 G3.....52°38'N 1°33'E
Aconcagua, Cerro mt. Argentina 73 B3.....32°38'S 70°01'W
A Coruña Spain 45 A5.....43°22'N 8°23'W
Adaja r. Spain 45 C4.....41°33'N 4°51'W
Adam's Peak Sri Lanka 96 F2.....6°49'N 80°28'E
Adana Turkey 51 K3.....36°59'N 35°19'E
Adapazarı Turkey 51 I5.....40°47'N 30°23'E
Ad Dabbah Sudan 85 H3.....18°00'N 30°55'E
Ad Dahnā' des. Saudi Arabia 95 G4.....20°40'N 46°52'E
Adderbury England 8 D3.....52°01'N 1°19'W
Ad Dir'īyah Saudi Arabia 95 G4.....24°45'N 46°34'E
Addis Ababa Ethiopia 85 H2.....9°01'N 38°45'E
Ad Dīwānīyah Iraq 94 F6.....31°59'N 44°57'E
Adelaide Australia 108 C3.....34°56'S 138°40'E
Aden Yemen 94 F2.....12°49'N 44°59'E
Aden, Gulf of Somalia/Yemen 85 I3.....11°44'N 45°16'E
Adi i. Indonesia 103 I3.....4°15'S 133°27'E
Ādī Ārk'ay Ethiopia 94 E2.....13°24'N 38°03'E
Adigrat Ethiopia 94 E2.....14°16'N 39°29'E
Adıyaman Turkey 51 M3.....37°46'N 38°17'E
Admiralty Islands P.N.G. 108 D6.....1°44'S 146°17'E
Adour r. France 44 C3.....43°32'N 1°31'W
Adriatic Sea Europe 48 F5.....44°19'N 13°24'E
Adwa Ethiopia 85 H3.....14°09'N 38°52'E
Adwick le Street England 13 F2.....53°34'N 1°12'W
Adycha r. Russia 55 O4.....66°42'N 136°32'E
Aegean Sea Greece/Turkey 50 F4.....39°00'N 24°51'E
Afghanistan Asia 95 K6.....33°53'N 65°52'E
Africa 78
Afyonkarahisar Turkey 51 I4.....38°46'N 30°33'E
Agadez Niger 84 E3.....16°57'N 7°59'E
Agadir Morocco 84 D5.....30°27'N 9°37'W
Agano r. Japan 104 C3.....37°58'N 139°02'E
Agartala India 97 H5.....23°50'N 91°16'E
Agde France 44 E3.....43°18'N 3°28'E
Agen France 44 D4.....44°12'N 0°38'E
Agios Dimitrios Greece 50 E3.....37°49'N 23°51'E
Agios Efstratios i. Greece 50 F4.....39°30'N 25°01'E
Agios Konstantinos Greece 50 E4.....38°45'N 22°51'E
Agios Nikolaos Greece 50 F2.....35°12'N 25°43'E
Agra India 96 E6.....27°09'N 78°02'E
Ağrı Turkey 94 F7.....39°43'N 43°04'E
Agrigento Italy 48 F4.....37°18'N 13°35'E
Agrihan i. N. Mariana Is 103 L7.....18°46'N 145°42'E
Agrwat Hills Sudan 94 E3.....16°26'N 35°03'E
Aguadulce Panama 67 H2.....8°12'N 80°33'W
Aguascalientes Mexico 66 D5.....21°51'N 102°18'W
Aguascalientes d. Mexico 66 D5.....21°57'N 102°11'W
Aguilar de Campóo Spain 45 C5.....42°47'N 4°14'W
Águilas Spain 45 E2.....37°25'N 1°35'W
Agulhas, Cape S. Africa 83 B1.....34°50'S 20°03'E
Ahaggar f. Algeria 84 E4.....24°00'N 5°50'E
Ahar Iran 95 G7.....38°27'N 47°02'E
Ahaus Germany 42 G5.....52°05'N 10°51'E
Ahmadpur East Pakistan 96 D6.....29°10'N 71°22'E
Ahmedabad India 96 D5.....23°03'N 72°37'E

Ahvāz Iran 95 G6.....31°15'N 48°40'E
Aigialousa Cyprus 51 K2.....35°31'N 34°11'E
Aigina i. Greece 50 E3.....37°41'N 23°31'E
Ailsa Craig i. Scotland 14 D3.....55°15'N 5°06'W
Aïn Beïda Algeria 48 E4.....35°47'N 7°25'E
'Aïn Ben Tili Mauritania 84 D4.....25°58'N 9°31'W
Aïn Sefra Algeria 84 D5.....32°42'N 0°35'W
Aïr, Massif de l' mts Niger 84 E3.....18°46'N 8°15'E
Airdrie Canada 60 G3.....51°17'N 114°01'W
Airdrie Scotland 15 F3.....55°52'N 3°58'W
Aisne r. France 44 E6.....49°26'N 2°51'E
Aitape P.N.G. 103 K3.....3°09'S 142°22'E
Aix-en-Provence France 44 F3.....43°32'N 5°27'E
Aizkraukle Latvia 47 K7.....56°36'N 25°15'E
Aizu-wakamatsu Japan 104 C3.....37°29'N 139°56'E
Ajaccio France 44 H2.....41°55'N 8°44'E
Ajdābiyā Libya 85 G5.....30°45'N 20°13'E
Akbulak Russia 53 F3.....50°59'N 55°36'E
Akçakale Turkey 51 M3.....36°43'N 38°57'E
Akdağmadeni Turkey 51 K4.....39°39'N 35°54'E
Akhalkalaki Georgia 53 E2.....41°25'N 43°29'E
Akhḑar, Al Jabal al mts Libya 49 H3.....31°46'N 20°46'E
Akhḑar, Al Jabal al mts Oman 95 I4.....23°22'N 57°00'E
Akhisar Turkey 51 G4.....38°55'N 27°50'E
Akhtubinsk Russia 53 E2.....48°20'N 46°05'E
Akimiski Island Canada 61 J3.....53°08'N 81°17'W
Akita Japan 104 D3.....39°43'N 140°07'E
Akkajaure l. Sweden 43 D4.....67°41'N 17°29'E
Aknoul Morocco 45 D1.....34°38'N 3°51'W
Akordat Eritrea 85 H3.....15°31'N 37°54'E
Akpatok Island Canada 61 L4.....60°24'N 67°45'W
Akranes Iceland 43 X2.....64°19'N 22°05'W
Akron U.S. 63 J5.....41°07'N 81°33'W
Aksai Chin China 96 E8.....35°08'N 79°11'E
Aksaray Turkey 51 K4.....38°23'N 34°02'E
Aksarka Russia 52 G4.....66°31'N 67°51'E
Akşehir Turkey 51 I4.....38°21'N 31°24'E
Aksu China 98 E6.....41°06'N 80°21'E
Āksum Ethiopia 94 E2.....14°07'N 38°46'E
Akureyri Iceland 43 Y2.....65°41'N 18°07'W
Alabama d. U.S. 63 I3.....32°41'N 86°42'W
Alabama r. U.S. 63 I3.....31°09'N 87°57'W
Alagoinhas Brazil 72 F5.....12°07'S 38°17'W
Al Aḥmadī Kuwait 95 G5.....29°04'N 48°02'E
Alaköl l. Kazakhstan 98 E7.....46°03'N 81°30'E
Alakurtti Russia 43 G4.....66°58'N 30°20'E
Alamagan i. N. Mariana Is 103 L7.....17°35'N 145°52'E
Åland Islands Finland 43 D3.....60°28'N 19°53'E
Alanya Turkey 51 J3.....36°33'N 32°00'E
Alappuzha India 96 E2.....9°30'N 76°21'E
Al 'Aqabah Jordan 94 E5.....29°31'N 35°01'E
Al Arţāwīyah Saudi Arabia 95 G5.....26°30'N 45°21'E
Alaşehir Turkey 51 H4.....38°21'N 28°30'E
Alaska d. U.S. 60 D4.....63°41'N 143°45'W
Alaska, Gulf of U.S. 60 D3.....58°10'N 147°57'W
Alaska Peninsula U.S. 60 C3.....55°18'N 162°25'W
Alaska Range mts U.S. 60 D4.....63°19'N 148°01'W
Alausí Ecuador 72 B6.....2°10'S 78°52'W
Alavus Finland 43 E3.....62°35'N 23°37'E
Alaw, Llyn resr Wales 10 C5.....53°21'N 4°25'W
Albacete Spain 45 E3.....39°00'N 1°50'W
Alba Iulia Romania 50 E8.....46°05'N 23°36'E
Albania Europe 50 C5.....41°56'N 19°34'E
Albany Australia 108 A3.....34°58'S 117°54'E
Albany r. Canada 61 J3.....52°08'N 81°59'W
Albany U.S. 63 L5.....42°40'N 73°46'W
Albatross Bay Australia 103 K1.....12°41'S 141°44'E
Al Bawītī Egypt 85 G4.....28°21'N 28°50'E
Al Bayḑā' Libya 85 G5.....32°44'N 21°44'E
Alberche r. Spain 45 C3.....39°58'N 4°46'W
Albert France 42 B2.....49°59'N 2°39'E
Albert, Lake Dem. Rep. Congo/Uganda 83 C5.....1°43'N 30°52'E
Alberta d. Canada 60 G3.....52°45'N 113°59'W
Albert Lea U.S. 63 H5.....43°39'N 93°22'W
Albert Nile r. South Sudan/Uganda 85 H2.....3°36'N 32°02'E
Albi France 44 E3.....43°56'N 2°08'E
Al Biyāḑh f. Saudi Arabia 95 G4.....20°57'N 46°14'E
Alborán, Isla de i. Spain 45 D1.....35°57'N 3°02'W
Alboran Sea Europe 45 C1.....36°00'N 4°00'W
Alborz Mountains Iran 95 H7.....36°52'N 49°43'E
Albuquerque U.S. 62 E4.....35°07'N 106°38'W
Albury Australia 108 D3.....36°03'S 146°54'E
Alcalá de Henares Spain 45 D4.....40°29'N 3°21'W
Alcalá la Real Spain 45 D2.....37°28'N 3°55'W
Alcañiz Spain 45 E4.....41°03'N 0°07'W
Alcázar de San Juan Spain 45 D3.....39°23'N 3°11'W
Alcester England 8 D3.....52°13'N 1°52'W
Alcoi/Alcoy Spain 45 E3.....38°42'N 0°27'W
Alcúdia Spain 45 G3.....39°52'N 3°08'E
Aldabra Islands Seychelles 85 I1.....9°16'S 46°30'E
Aldan Russia 55 N3.....58°36'N 125°25'E
Aldan r. Russia 55 N4.....63°32'N 128°46'E
Aldbrough England 13 G2.....53°50'N 0°07'W
Aldeburgh England 9 G3.....52°09'N 1°36'E
Alderley Edge England 13 E2.....53°18'N 2°14'W
Alderney i. Channel Is 11 Z9.....49°42'N 2°15'W
Aldershot England 8 E2.....51°15'N 0°45'W
Aldingham England 12 D3.....54°08'N 3°06'W
Aldridge England 8 D3.....52°36'N 1°55'W
Aleksandrovsk-Sakhalinskiy Russia 55 P3.....51°08'N 142°21'E
Aleksin Russia 47 Q6.....54°31'N 37°05'E
Alençon France 44 D6.....48°26'N 0°06'E
Aleppo Syria 94 E7.....36°12'N 37°09'E
Alès France 44 F4.....44°08'N 4°05'E
Alessandria Italy 46 C1.....44°55'N 8°38'E
Ålesund Norway 43 A3.....62°28'N 6°12'E
Aleutian Islands U.S. 60 A3.....53°03'N 176°15'W
Aleutian Range mts U.S. 60 C3.....56°10'N 159°17'W
Alexander Archipelago is U.S. 60 E3.....57°59'N 137°33'W
Alexandra, Cape S. Atlantic Oc. 73 F1.....54°05'S 37°56'W
Alexandria Egypt 85 G5.....31°13'N 29°56'E
Alexandria Romania 50 F6.....43°58'N 25°20'E
Alexandria Scotland 14 E3.....55°59'N 4°35'W
Alexandria La. U.S. 63 H3.....31°17'N 92°28'W
Alexandria Va. U.S. 63 K4.....38°48'N 77°05'W
Alexandroupoli Greece 50 F5.....40°51'N 25°53'E
Alford England 13 H2.....53°16'N 0°11'E
Alford Scotland 17 G2.....57°14'N 2°42'W
Alfreton England 13 F2.....53°06'N 1°23'W
Algarve f. Portugal 45 A2.....37°16'N 8°07'W
Algeciras Spain 45 C2.....36°07'N 5°27'W
Algeria Africa 84 E4.....28°15'N 3°31'E
Al Ghaydah Yemen 95 H3.....16°14'N 52°13'E
Al Ghurdaqah Egypt 49 J2.....27°12'N 33°48'E

Al Ghwaybiyah Saudi Arabia 95 G5.....25°14'N 49°43'E
Algiers Algeria 84 E5.....36°46'N 3°04'E
Algorta Spain 45 D5.....43°21'N 2°59'W
Al Ḥasakah Syria 94 F7.....36°30'N 40°44'E
Al Ḥibāk des. Saudi Arabia 95 H3.....19°30'N 52°27'E
Al Hoceïma Morocco 48 C4.....35°15'N 3°56'W
Al Ḥufūf Saudi Arabia 95 G5.....25°22'N 49°35'E
Aliağa Turkey 50 G4.....38°47'N 26°58'E
'Ali 'Addé Djibouti 85 I3.....11°08'N 42°53'E
Aliakmonas r. Greece 50 E5.....40°28'N 22°38'E
Äli Bayramlı Azerbaijan 95 G7.....39°56'N 48°56'E
Alicante Spain 45 E3.....38°21'N 0°28'W
Alice Springs town Australia 108 C4.....23°42'S 133°52'E
Alingsås Sweden 43 C2.....57°56'N 12°33'E
Al Ismā'īlīyah Egypt 49 J3.....30°35'N 32°17'E
Al Jaghbūb Libya 85 G4.....29°43'N 24°31'E
Al Jahrā' Kuwait 95 G5.....29°20'N 47°41'E
Al Jawf Libya 85 G4.....24°14'N 23°24'E
Al Jawf Saudi Arabia 94 E5.....29°47'N 39°55'E
Al Jawsh Libya 48 F3.....32°01'N 11°42'E
Al Jubayl Saudi Arabia 95 G5.....27°02'N 49°38'E
Aljustrel Portugal 45 A2.....37°53'N 8°10'W
Al Karak Jordan 94 E6.....31°10'N 35°42'E
Al Khābūrah Oman 95 I4.....23°58'N 57°06'E
Al Khārijah Egypt 85 H4.....25°26'N 30°33'E
Al Khaşab Oman 95 I5.....26°11'N 56°14'E
Al Khums Libya 48 F3.....32°35'N 14°22'E
Alkmaar Neth. 42 D5.....52°38'N 4°45'E
Al Kūt Iraq 95 G6.....32°31'N 45°47'E
Allakh-Yun' Russia 55 O4.....61°05'N 138°03'E
Allegheny r. U.S. 63 K5.....40°27'N 79°59'W
Allegheny Mountains U.S. 63 J4.....36°46'N 82°22'W
Allen, Lough l. Ireland 18 C4.....54°09'N 8°03'W
Allendale Town England 13 E3.....54°54'N 2°15'W
Allentown U.S. 63 K5.....40°37'N 75°30'W
Aller r. Germany 46 C5.....52°57'N 9°11'E
Al Līth Saudi Arabia 94 F4.....20°10'N 40°16'E
Alloa Scotland 15 F4.....56°07'N 3°47'W
Almansa Spain 45 E3.....38°52'N 1°05'W
Al Manşūrah Egypt 49 J3.....31°02'N 31°23'E
Almanzor mt. Spain 45 C4.....40°15'N 5°18'W
Al Marj Libya 49 H3.....32°29'N 20°50'E
Almaty Kazakhstan 54 I2.....43°16'N 77°01'E
Almelo Neth. 42 F5.....52°21'N 6°40'E
Almendra, Embalse de resr Spain 45 B4.....41°17'N 6°14'W
Almería Spain 45 D2.....36°50'N 2°27'W
Al'met'yevsk Russia 53 F3.....54°51'N 52°23'E
Almina, Punta pt Spain 45 C1.....35°54'N 5°16'W
Al Minyā Egypt 85 H4.....28°05'N 30°45'E
Almodôvar Portugal 45 A2.....37°31'N 8°04'W
Almond r. Scotland 15 F4.....56°25'N 3°28'W
Al Mudawwara Jordan 94 E5.....29°19'N 36°02'E
Almuñécar Spain 45 D2.....36°44'N 3°41'W
Alnwick England 13 F4.....55°25'N 1°42'W
Alofi Niue 109 I5.....19°03'S 169°54'W
Alor i. Indonesia 103 G2.....8°17'S 124°45'E
Alor Setar Malaysia 102 C5.....6°08'N 100°22'E
Alpena U.S. 63 J6.....45°03'N 83°27'W
Alpine U.S. 62 F3.....30°18'N 103°35'W
Alps mts Europe 48 F6.....46°00'N 7°30'E
Al Qa'āmīyāt f. Saudi Arabia 95 G3.....17°59'N 47°47'E
Al Qaddāḩīyah Libya 48 G3.....30°11'N 15°12'E
Al Qāmishlī Syria 94 F7.....37°03'N 41°13'E
Al Qaryatayn Syria 51 L2.....34°13'N 37°14'E
Al Qunfidhah Saudi Arabia 94 F3.....19°09'N 41°04'E
Al Quşayr Egypt 85 H4.....26°05'N 34°13'E
Alsager England 13 E2.....53°06'N 2°18'W
Alston England 13 E3.....54°49'N 2°26'W
Altaelva r. Norway 43 E5.....69°57'N 23°20'E
Altai mts Asia 98 F7.....48°55'N 87°16'E
Altamira Brazil 72 D6.....3°14'S 52°14'W
Altay China 98 F7.....47°48'N 88°10'E
Altay Mongolia 98 H7.....46°18'N 96°15'E
Altiplano f. Bolivia 72 C5.....16°24'S 69°39'W
Altiplano Mexicano mts N. America 56 E3.....24°00'N 105°00'W
Alton England 8 E2.....51°09'N 0°58'W
Altoona U.S. 63 K5.....40°30'N 78°24'W
Altötting Germany 46 E3.....48°14'N 12°41'E
Altrincham England 13 E2.....53°23'N 2°21'W
Altun Shan mts China 98 F5.....37°45'N 86°38'E
Alturas U.S. 62 B5.....41°30'N 120°31'W
Al 'Uqaylah Libya 49 G3.....30°13'N 19°12'E
Al 'Uwaynāt Libya 94 B4.....21°48'N 24°58'E
Älvdalen Sweden 43 C3.....61°13'N 14°04'E
Alveley England 8 C3.....52°27'N 2°21'W
Älvsbyn Sweden 43 E4.....65°40'N 20°59'E
Al Wajh Saudi Arabia 94 E5.....26°17'N 36°25'E
Alwen Reservoir Wales 10 D5.....53°05'N 3°35'W
Al Widyān f. Iraq/Saudi Arabia 94 F6.....32°09'N 40°22'E
Alyth Scotland 17 F1.....56°38'N 3°14'W
Alytus Lithuania 47 K6.....54°23'N 24°03'E
Amadeus, Lake Australia 108 C4.....24°50'S 131°09'E
Amadjuak Lake Canada 61 K4.....64°57'N 71°09'W
Amadora Portugal 45 A3.....38°46'N 9°14'W
Åmål Sweden 43 C2.....59°03'N 12°44'E
Amamapare Indonesia 103 J3.....4°54'S 136°58'E
Amapá Brazil 72 D7.....2°02'S 50°50'W
Amaravati India 96 F4.....16°34'N 80°21'W
Amarillo U.S. 62 F4.....35°15'N 101°50'W
Amasya Turkey 51 K5.....40°39'N 35°50'E
Amazon r. Brazil 72 D7.....0°01'N 50°37'W
Amazon, Mouths of the Brazil 72 E7.....0°41'N 49°28'W
Ambarchik Russia 55 R4.....69°35'N 162°13'E
Ambergate England 13 F2.....53°04'N 1°29'W
Ambergris Cay i. Belize 66 G4.....18°08'N 87°52'W
Amble England 13 F4.....55°20'N 1°34'W
Ambleside England 12 E3.....54°26'N 2°58'W
Ambo Kiribati 107 F4.....1°21'N 172°57'E
Ambon Indonesia 103 H3.....3°43'S 128°11'E
Ambrym i. Vanuatu 109 F5.....16°12'S 168°13'E
Ameland i. Neth. 42 E6.....53°28'N 5°48'E
American Samoa is S. Pacific Oc. 109 I5.....12°00'S 170°00'W
Amersfoort Neth. 42 E5.....52°09'N 5°23'E
Amersham England 8 E2.....51°40'N 0°37'W
Amesbury England 8 D2.....51°10'N 1°47'W
Amfissa Greece 50 E4.....38°32'N 22°22'E
Amga r. Russia 55 O3.....62°38'N 134°45'E
Amgun' r. Russia 55 O3.....52°01'N 139°38'E
Amiens France 44 E6.....49°54'N 2°18'E
Amlwch Wales 10 C5.....53°25'N 4°21'W
'Ammān Jordan 94 E6.....31°57'N 35°56'E
Ammanford Wales 10 D3.....51°48'N 3°59'W
Amol Iran 95 H7.....36°32'N 52°20'E
Amorgos i. Greece 50 F3.....36°49'N 25°54'E
Amos Canada 61 K2.....48°34'N 78°08'W
Ampthill England 9 E3.....52°02'N 0°30'W
Amravati India 96 E5.....20°56'N 77°51'E

Amritsar India 96 D7.....31°34'N 74°56'E
Amstelveen Neth. 42 D5.....52°19'N 4°52'E
Amsterdam Neth. 42 D5.....52°23'N 4°54'E
Amstetten Austria 46 F3.....48°08'N 14°52'E
Amu Darya r. Asia 54 H2.....43°50'N 59°00'E
Amund Ringnes Island Canada 61 I5.....78°17'N 96°35'W
Amundsen Gulf Canada 60 F5.....70°25'N 121°26'W
Amuntai Indonesia 102 F3.....2°25'S 115°13'E
Amur r. Russia 55 P3.....53°17'N 140°37'E
Anabar r. Russia 55 M5.....73°13'N 113°31'E
Anadyr' Russia 55 S4.....64°44'N 177°20'E
Anadyrskiy Zaliv b. Russia 55 T4.....63°56'N 177°42'W
Anambas, Kepulauan is Indonesia 102 D4.....3°17'N 105°55'E
Anamur Turkey 51 J3.....36°06'N 32°50'E
Anapa Russia 51 L4.....44°54'N 37°20'E
Anápolis Brazil 72 E5.....16°20'S 48°55'W
Anatahan i. N. Mariana Is 103 L7.....16°21'N 145°42'E
Anatolia f. Turkey 51 J4.....38°58'N 33°19'E
Anchorage U.S. 60 D4.....61°12'N 149°52'W
Ancona Italy 46 E5.....43°37'N 13°31'E
Åndalsnes Norway 43 A3.....62°34'N 7°42'E
Andalusia f. Spain 45 C2.....37°35'N 4°10'W
Andaman Islands India 97 H3.....12°46'N 93°17'E
Andaman Sea Indian Oc. 97 I3.....11°33'N 95°19'E
Anderlecht Belgium 42 D3.....50°49'N 4°18'E
Andermatt Switz. 46 C2.....46°38'N 8°36'E
Anderson r. Canada 60 F4.....69°41'N 128°56'W
Anderson U.S. 60 D4.....64°22'N 149°12'E
Andes mts S. America 73 B6.....9°10'S 77°03'W
Andfjorden str. Norway 43 D5.....68°53'N 16°04'E
Andhra Pradesh d. India 96 E4.....16°03'N 79°11'E
Andkhvoy Afgh. 95 K7.....36°59'N 65°08'E
Andong S. Korea 104 A3.....36°33'N 128°43'E
Andorra Europe 45 F5.....42°32'N 1°35'E
Andorra la Vella Andorra 45 F5.....42°31'N 1°32'E
Andover England 8 D2.....51°12'N 1°29'W
Andøya i. Norway 43 C5.....69°11'N 15°48'E
Andreas Isle of Man 12 C3.....54°22'N 4°27'W
Andria Italy 49 G5.....41°14'N 16°18'E
Andros i. Bahamas 67 I5.....24°25'N 78°09'W
Andros i. Greece 50 F3.....37°53'N 24°57'E
Andújar Spain 45 C3.....38°02'N 4°03'W
Anéfis Mali 84 E3.....18°02'N 0°32'E
Anegada i. Virgin Is (U.K.) 67 L4.....18°44'N 64°19'W
Aneto mt. Spain 45 F5.....42°38'N 0°39'E
Angara r. Russia 55 K3.....58°05'N 92°59'E
Angarsk Russia 99 I8.....52°24'N 103°45'E
Ånge Sweden 43 C3.....62°32'N 15°40'E
Ángel de la Guarda, Isla i. Mexico 66 B6.....29°25'N 113°24'W
Ängelholm Sweden 43 C2.....56°15'N 12°52'E
Angers France 44 C5.....47°28'N 0°33'W
Anglesey i. Wales 10 C5.....53°18'N 4°23'W
Angola Africa 83 A3.....11°40'S 17°34'E
Angola Basin f. Atlantic Oc. 117 F2.....15°00'S 0°00'E
Angoulême France 44 D4.....45°39'N 0°10'E
Angren Uzbekistan 98 C4.....41°02'N 70°07'E
Anguilla i. Central America 67 L4.....18°14'N 63°02'W
Angus d. Scotland 20 D5.....56°43'N 2°55'W
Anhui d. China 99 L4.....32°10'N 117°07'E
Ankara Turkey 51 J4.....39°56'N 32°50'E
Anlaby England 13 G2.....53°45'N 0°26'W
Annaba Algeria 84 E5.....36°54'N 7°46'E
An Nabk Syria 51 L2.....34°01'N 36°44'E
An Nafūd des. Saudi Arabia 94 F5.....28°28'N 41°17'E
'Annah Iraq 94 F6.....34°25'N 41°57'E
An Najaf Iraq 94 F6.....31°59'N 44°20'E
Annalee r. Ireland 18 D4.....54°02'N 7°23'W
Annalong Northern Ireland 14 D2.....54°06'N 5°54'W
Annan Scotland 15 F2.....54°59'N 3°15'W
Annan r. Scotland 15 F2.....54°59'N 3°15'W
Annapolis U.S. 63 K4.....38°58'N 76°30'W
Annapurna mt. Nepal 96 F6.....28°34'N 83°49'E
Ann Arbor U.S. 63 J5.....42°17'N 83°45'W
An Nāşirīyah Iraq 94 G6.....31°01'N 46°14'E
An Nawfalīyah Libya 49 G3.....30°51'N 17°52'E
Annecy France 44 G4.....45°54'N 6°08'E
Anniston U.S. 63 I3.....33°39'N 85°43'W
An Nu'ayriyah Saudi Arabia 95 G5.....27°29'N 48°26'E
An Nuşayrīyah, Jabal mts Syria 51 L2.....35°15'N 36°05'E
Ansbach Germany 46 D3.....49°18'N 10°36'E
Anshan China 99 M6.....41°06'N 123°02'E
Anshun China 99 J3.....26°15'N 105°57'E
Anstruther Scotland 15 G4.....56°13'N 2°42'W
Antakya Turkey 51 L3.....36°11'N 36°07'E
Antalya Turkey 51 I3.....36°53'N 30°41'E
Antalya Körfezi g. Turkey 51 I3.....36°40'N 30°58'E
Antananarivo Madagascar 83 D3.....18°54'S 47°33'E
Antarctica 112
Antarctic Peninsula f. Antarctica 116 D1.....65°00'S 64°00'W
An Teallach mt. Scotland 16 D2.....57°48'N 5°16'W
Antequera Spain 45 C2.....37°02'N 4°33'W
Antibes France 44 G3.....43°35'N 7°07'E
Anticosti, Île d' i. Canada 61 L2.....49°27'N 62°59'W
Antigua i. Antigua 67 L4.....17°02'N 61°43'W
Antigua and Barbuda Central America 67 L4.....17°20'N 61°20'W
Antikythira i. Greece 50 E2.....35°52'N 23°20'E
Antofagasta Chile 73 B4.....23°37'S 70°22'W
Antrim Northern Ireland 14 C2.....54°43'N 6°12'W
Antrim f. Northern Ireland 14 C2.....54°57'N 6°11'W
Antrim and Newtownabbey d. Northern Ireland 21 B4.....54°43'N 6°16'W
Antrim Hills Northern Ireland 14 C3.....55°05'N 6°16'W
Antsirabe Madagascar 83 D3.....19°53'S 47°03'E
Antsiranana Madagascar 83 D3.....12°19'S 49°17'E
Antsohihy Madagascar 83 D3.....14°53'S 47°59'E
Antwerp Belgium 42 D4.....51°12'N 4°26'E
Antwerpen d. Belgium 42 D4.....51°17'N 4°46'E
Anyang China 99 K5.....36°04'N 114°22'E
Anzhero-Sudzhensk Russia 54 J3.....56°08'N 86°01'E
Aomori Japan 104 D4.....40°49'N 140°45'E
Aoraki / Mount Cook mt. New Zealand 109 G2.....43°37'S 170°08'E
Apalachee Bay U.S. 63 J2.....29°55'N 84°06'W
Aparri Phil. 103 G7.....18°21'N 121°40'E
Apatity Russia 43 H4.....67°34'N 33°23'E
Apeldoorn Neth. 42 E5.....52°12'N 5°58'E
Apennines mts Italy 48 F5.....44°37'N 9°22'E
Apia Samoa 109 H5.....13°50'S 171°44'W
Apostolos Andreas, Cape Cyprus 51 K2.....35°41'N 34°35'E
Appalachian Mountains U.S. 63 J4.....39°30'N 78°00'W
Appleby-in-Westmorland England 13 E3.....54°35'N 2°29'W
Appledore England 11 C3.....51°03'N 4°12'W
Aqaba, Gulf of Asia 94 D5.....29°19'N 34°54'E
Aqtau Kazakhstan 53 F2.....43°39'N 51°12'E

Aqtöbe Kazakhstan 53 F3.....50°13'N 57°10'E
Aqtoghay Kazakhstan 54 I2.....47°06'N 79°42'E
Arabian Peninsula Asia 85 I4.....24°00'N 45°00'E
Arabian Sea Indian Oc. 86 E2.....18°08'N 66°38'E
Aracaju Brazil 72 F5.....10°52'S 37°03'W
Araçatuba Brazil 73 D4.....21°12'S 50°22'W
Aracena, Sierra de hills Spain 45 B2.....37°51'N 7°07'W
Arad Romania 50 D8.....46°11'N 21°21'E
Arafura Sea Australia/Indonesia 108 C6.....9°04'S 132°58'E
Aragon f. Spain 45 E4.....41°20'N 0°50'W
Aragón r. Spain 45 E5.....42°13'N 1°45'W
Araguaia r. Brazil 72 E6.....5°24'S 48°41'W
Araguaína Brazil 72 E6.....7°20'S 48°15'W
Arak Algeria 84 E4.....25°18'N 3°39'E
Ārāk Iran 95 G6.....34°05'N 49°42'E
Arakan Yoma mts Myanmar 97 H5.....20°18'N 94°07'E
Aral Kazakhstan 54 H2.....46°46'N 61°43'E
Aral Sea Kazakhstan/Uzbekistan 54 H2.....45°07'N 60°05'E
Aranda de Duero Spain 45 D4.....41°41'N 3°40'W
Aran Island Ireland 18 C4.....54°59'N 8°35'W
Aran Islands Ireland 18 B3.....53°07'N 9°44'W
Aranjuez Spain 45 D4.....40°02'N 3°36'W
Arapgir Turkey 51 M4.....39°02'N 38°29'E
Arapis, Akra pt Greece 50 F5.....40°27'N 24°00'E
'Ar'ar Saudi Arabia 94 F6.....30°58'N 40°58'E
Araraquara Brazil 73 E4.....21°47'S 48°06'W
Ararat, Mount Turkey 53 E1.....39°45'N 44°15'E
Arbīl/Hewlêr Iraq 94 F7.....36°11'N 44°01'E
Arboga Sweden 43 C2.....59°23'N 15°51'E
Arbroath Scotland 15 G4.....56°34'N 2°35'W
Arbu Lut, Dasht-e des. Afgh. 95 J5.....32°57'N 63°56'E
Arcachon France 44 C4.....44°40'N 1°10'W
Arctic Bay town Canada 61 J5.....72°55'N 85°10'W
Arctic Ocean 112
Arctic Red r. Canada 60 E4.....67°27'N 133°44'W
Ardabīl Iran 95 G7.....38°14'N 48°15'E
Ardas r. Greece 50 G5.....41°40'N 26°30'E
Ardèche r. France 44 F4.....44°16'N 4°39'E
Ardennes f. Belgium 42 D2.....49°56'N 4°52'E
Ardestān Iran 95 H6.....33°20'N 52°21'E
Ardglass Northern Ireland 14 D2.....54°15'N 5°36'W
Ardila r. Portugal 45 B3.....38°10'N 7°28'W
Ardnamurchan, Point of Scotland 16 C1.....56°43'N 6°13'W
Ardrishaig Scotland 14 D4.....56°01'N 5°27'W
Ardrossan Scotland 14 E3.....55°39'N 4°49'W
Ards and North Down d. Northern Ireland 21 C4.....54°28'N 5°37'W
Ards Peninsula Northern Ireland 14 D2.....54°30'N 5°25'W
Ardvasar Scotland 16 D2.....57°03'N 5°55'W
Arena, Point U.S. 62 B4.....38°57'N 123°44'W
Arendal Norway 43 B2.....58°27'N 8°46'E
Arenig Fawr hill Wales 10 D4.....52°55'N 3°45'W
Arequipa Peru 72 B5.....16°23'S 71°32'W
Arganda Spain 45 D4.....40°18'N 3°25'W
Argentan France 44 C6.....48°45'N 0°01'W
Argentina S. America 73 C3.....35°00'S 68°00'W
Argentino, Lago l. Argentina 73 B1.....50°20'S 72°51'W
Argenton-sur-Creuse France 44 D5.....46°36'N 1°31'E
Argeş r. Romania 50 G7.....44°04'N 26°37'E
Argun' r. China/Russia 99 M8.....53°18'N 121°20'E
Argyle, Lake Australia 108 B5.....16°37'S 128°41'E
Argyll f. Scotland 14 D4.....56°08'N 5°19'W
Argyll and Bute d. Scotland 20 C4.....55°46'N 5°25'W
Arica Chile 72 B5.....18°29'S 70°20'W
Arienas, Loch l. Scotland 14 D4.....56°35'N 5°46'W
Arinos r. Brazil 72 D5.....10°25'S 58°13'W
Ariquemes Brazil 72 C5.....9°59'S 63°05'W
Arisaig Scotland 16 D1.....56°55'N 5°50'W
Arisaig, Sound of str. Scotland 16 D1.....56°51'N 5°56'W
Arizona d. U.S. 62 D3.....34°11'N 111°37'W
Arkadelphia U.S. 63 H3.....34°09'N 93°03'W
Arkaig, Loch l. Scotland 16 D1.....56°58'N 5°13'W
Arkansas d. U.S. 63 H4.....35°49'N 92°00'W
Arkansas r. U.S. 63 H3.....33°49'N 91°08'W
Arkansas City U.S. 62 G4.....37°04'N 97°03'W
Arkhangel'sk Russia 52 E4.....64°33'N 40°33'E
Arklow Ireland 18 E2.....52°48'N 6°10'W
Arkona, Kap c. Germany 46 E6.....54°41'N 13°27'E
Arles France 44 F3.....43°41'N 4°38'E
Arlit Niger 84 E3.....18°42'N 7°21'E
Arlon Belgium 42 E2.....49°41'N 5°49'E
Armagh Northern Ireland 14 C2.....54°20'N 6°39'W
Armagh f. Northern Ireland 18 E4.....54°18'N 6°39'W
Armagh City, Banbridge and Craigavon d. Northern Ireland 21 B4.....54°21'N 6°39'W
Armant Egypt 49 J2.....25°37'N 32°32'E
Armavir Russia 53 E2.....45°01'N 41°06'E
Armenia Asia 53 E2.....40°26'N 44°30'E
Armenia Colombia 72 B7.....4°30'N 75°39'W
Armiansk Ukraine 51 J8.....46°07'N 33°41'E
Armidale Australia 108 E3.....30°32'S 151°41'E
Arnauti, Cape Cyprus 51 J2.....35°06'N 32°16'E
Arnhem Neth. 42 E4.....51°59'N 5°55'E
Arnhem, Cape Australia 108 C5.....12°19'S 136°58'E
Arnhem Land f. Australia 108 C5.....13°26'S 133°57'E
Arnsberg Germany 46 C4.....51°23'N 8°04'E
Ar Ramādī Iraq 94 F6.....33°23'N 43°16'E
Arran i. Scotland 14 D3.....55°35'N 5°20'W
Ar Raqqah Syria 94 E7.....35°57'N 39°01'E
Arras France 44 E7.....50°17'N 2°46'E
Arrecife Canary Islands 45 Z2.....28°57'N 13°33'W
Arriaga Mexico 66 F4.....16°16'N 93°52'W
Arrieta Canary Islands 45 Z2.....29°08'N 13°28'W
Ar Rimāl f. Saudi Arabia 95 H4.....21°43'N 52°53'E
Arrochar Scotland 14 E4.....56°12'N 4°44'W
Ar Ruţbah Iraq 94 F6.....33°01'N 40°11'E
Arta Greece 50 D4.....39°10'N 20°59'E
Artesia U.S. 62 F3.....32°52'N 104°25'W
Artois f. France 42 A3.....50°40'N 1°55'E
Artois, Collines de l' hills France 9 G1.....50°33'N 1°54'E
Artsyz Ukraine 51 H7.....45°59'N 29°27'E
Aru, Kepulauan is Indonesia 103 I2.....6°09'S 134°05'E
Aruba i. Central America 67 K3.....12°30'N 69°56'W
Arunachal Pradesh d. India 97 H6.....27°28'N 92°48'E
Arundel England 9 E1.....50°51'N 0°33'W
Arusha Tanzania 83 C4.....3°22'S 36°37'E
Aruwimi r. Dem. Rep. Congo 83 B5.....1°14'N 23°38'E
Arvayheer Mongolia 99 I7.....46°08'N 102°47'E
Arviat Canada 61 I4.....61°12'N 94°09'W
Arvidsjaur Sweden 43 D4.....65°35'N 19°12'E
Arvika Sweden 43 C2.....59°39'N 12°37'E
Arzamas Russia 52 E3.....55°23'N 43°49'E
Asad, Buḩayrat al resr Syria 51 M3.....36°05'N 38°03'E
Asahi Dake vol. Japan 104 D4.....43°41'N 142°54'E
Asahikawa Japan 104 D4.....43°46'N 142°22'E
Asansol India 96 G5.....23°41'N 87°01'E
Ascension Island Atlantic Oc. 78 B2.....8°00'S 14°00'W

Åsele Sweden 43 D4.....64°10'N 17°22'E
Asenovgrad Bulgaria 50 F6.....42°00'N 24°52'E
Asfordby England 8 E3.....52°46'N 0°57'W
Ashbourne England 13 F2.....53°01'N 1°44'W
Ashbourne Ireland 18 E3.....53°31'N 6°23'W
Ashburton watercourse Australia 108 A4.....21°43'S 114°54'E
Ashburton England 11 D2.....50°31'N 3°45'W
Ashby de la Zouch England 8 D3.....52°45'N 1°28'W
Ashford England 9 F2.....51°09'N 0°53'E
Ashgabat Turkmenistan 54 G1.....37°53'N 58°21'E
Ashington England 13 F4.....55°11'N 1°34'W
Ashland U.S. 63 H6.....46°35'N 90°53'W
Ashmore and Cartier Islands Australia 108 B5.....12°38'S 122°40'E
Ash Shiḩr Yemen 95 G2.....14°49'N 49°45'E
Ash Shurayk Sudan 94 D3.....18°42'N 33°40'E
Ashton-under-Lyne England 13 E2.....53°30'N 2°06'W
Asia 86
Asipovichy Belarus 47 M5.....53°18'N 28°38'E
'Asīr, Jibāl al f. Saudi Arabia 94 F4.....20°53'N 40°14'E
Askern England 13 F2.....53°37'N 1°09'W
Askim Norway 43 B2.....59°35'N 11°10'E
Asmara Eritrea 85 H3.....15°20'N 38°56'E
Åsnen l. Sweden 43 C2.....56°37'N 14°50'E
Aspang-Markt Austria 46 G2.....47°33'N 16°05'E
Aspatria England 12 D3.....54°46'N 3°20'W
Aspen U.S. 62 E4.....39°11'N 106°49'W
Assab Eritrea 85 I3.....12°59'N 42°43'E
Assam d. India 97 H6.....26°14'N 91°22'E
As Samāwah Iraq 94 G6.....31°15'N 45°19'E
As Sarīr f. Libya 49 H2.....27°00'N 21°36'E
Assen Neth. 42 F6.....53°00'N 6°33'E
As Sidrah Libya 49 G3.....30°38'N 18°18'E
Assiah Morocco 45 B1.....35°28'N 6°02'W
Assiniboine, Mount Canada 60 G3.....50°57'N 115°34'W
As Sulaymānīyah/Slêmanî Iraq 95 G7.....35°32'N 45°27'E
Assumption i. Seychelles 83 D4.....9°30'S 47°20'E
As Sūq Saudi Arabia 94 F4.....21°57'N 41°59'E
Assynt, Loch l. Scotland 16 D3.....58°11'N 5°05'W
Astana Kazakhstan 54 I3.....51°09'N 71°27'E
Āstārā Iran 95 G7.....38°27'N 48°52'E
Asti Italy 46 C1.....44°54'N 8°13'E
Astorga Spain 45 B5.....42°28'N 6°03'W
Astoria U.S. 62 B6.....46°08'N 123°46'W
Astove i. Seychelles 83 D4.....10°05'S 47°40'E
Astrakhan' Russia 53 E2.....46°20'N 48°03'E
Asunción i. N. Mariana Is 103 L7.....19°40'N 145°25'E
Asunción Paraguay 73 D4.....25°16'S 57°39'W
Aswad, Ras el c. Morocco 45 C1.....35°41'N 5°17'W
Aswān Egypt 85 H4.....24°02'N 32°56'E
Asyūţ Egypt 85 H4.....27°07'N 31°08'E
Atacama Desert Chile 73 C4.....26°13'S 69°39'W
Atafu i. Tokelau 109 H6.....8°33'S 172°30'W
Atamyrat Turkmenistan 95 K7.....37°51'N 65°13'E
Atār Mauritania 84 C4.....20°32'N 13°03'W
Atatürk Baraji resr Turkey 51 M3.....37°28'N 38°26'E
Atbara Sudan 85 H3.....17°43'N 33°55'E
Atbara r. Sudan 85 H3.....17°40'N 33°58'E
Ath Belgium 42 C3.....50°38'N 3°47'E
Athabasca r. Canada 60 G3.....58°28'N 111°09'W
Athabasca, Lake Canada 60 H3.....59°17'N 109°24'W
Athboy Ireland 18 E3.....53°37'N 6°55'W
Athenry Ireland 18 C3.....53°18'N 8°45'W
Athens Greece 50 E3.....37°59'N 23°43'E
Atherstone England 8 D3.....52°35'N 1°33'W
Athlone Ireland 18 D3.....53°25'N 7°57'W
Atholl, Forest of Scotland 17 E1.....56°51'N 4°10'W
Athos mt. Greece 50 F5.....40°10'N 24°19'E
Ath Thawrah Syria 51 M2.....35°51'N 38°33'E
Athy Ireland 18 E2.....52°59'N 6°59'W
Ati Chad 85 F3.....13°14'N 18°20'E
Atikokan Canada 63 H6.....48°45'N 91°37'W
Atlanta U.S. 63 J3.....33°46'N 84°22'W
Atlantic City U.S. 63 L4.....39°21'N 74°26'W
Atlantic Ocean 116 D3
Atlas Mountains Africa 84 D5.....30°13'N 7°41'W
Atlas Saharien mts Algeria 84 E5.....32°41'N 0°20'E
Aţ Ţā'if Saudi Arabia 94 F4.....21°15'N 40°20'E
Attleborough England 9 G3.....52°31'N 1°01'E
Atyraū Kazakhstan 53 F2.....47°08'N 51°56'E
Aube r. France 44 E6.....48°34'N 3°43'E
Auchterarder Scotland 15 F4.....56°18'N 3°42'W
Auchtermuchty Scotland 15 F4.....56°18'N 3°14'W
Auckland New Zealand 109 G3.....36°52'S 174°46'E
Auckland Islands New Zealand 109 F1.....50°43'S 166°12'E
Auderville France 11 Z9.....49°43'N 1°55'W
Audlem England 8 C3.....52°59'N 2°31'W
Audruicq France 9 H1.....50°52'N 2°05'E
Augher Northern Ireland 14 B2.....54°25'N 7°08'W
Aughton England 12 D2.....53°22'N 1°19'W
Augsburg Germany 46 D3.....48°22'N 10°52'E
Augusta Ga. U.S. 63 J3.....33°28'N 82°02'W
Augusta Me. U.S. 63 M5.....44°19'N 69°46'W
Aulnoye-Aymeries France 42 C3.....50°12'N 3°51'E
Aurangabad India 96 E4.....19°53'N 75°24'E
Aurich Germany 42 G6.....53°28'N 7°30'E
Aurora U.S. 62 F4.....39°43'N 104°53'W
Auskerry i. Scotland 17 G4.....59°02'N 2°33'W
Austin U.S. 62 G3.....30°16'N 97°42'W
Australia Oceania 108 B4.....25°27'S 129°18'E
Australian Capital Territory d. Australia 108 D3.....35°27'S 148°52'E
Austria Europe 46 E2.....47°12'N 13°26'E
Authie r. France 9 G1.....50°22'N 1°37'E
Auvergne, Monts d' mts France 44 E4.....45°55'N 2°59'E
Auxerre France 44 E5.....47°48'N 3°35'E
Avallon France 44 E5.....47°29'N 3°54'E
Avanos Turkey 51 K4.....38°43'N 34°51'E
Aveiro Portugal 45 A4.....40°39'N 8°38'W
Avesta Sweden 43 D3.....60°09'N 16°10'E
Aveyron r. France 44 D4.....44°05'N 1°16'E
Aviemore Scotland 17 F2.....57°12'N 3°49'W
Avignon France 44 F3.....43°57'N 4°49'E
Ávila Spain 45 C4.....40°40'N 4°41'W
Avilés Spain 45 C5.....43°33'N 5°54'W
Avon r. Brist. England 8 C2.....51°29'N 2°40'W
Avon r. Dor. England 8 D1.....50°44'N 1°46'W
Avon r. Glos. England 8 C3.....52°00'N 2°10'W
Avon r. Scotland 17 F2.....57°25'N 3°22'W
Avonmore r. Ireland 10 A4.....52°48'N 6°08'W
Avonmouth England 8 C2.....51°30'N 2°42'W
Åwash Ethiopia 85 I2.....8°59'N 40°10'E
Awbārī Libya 84 F4.....26°34'N 12°46'E
Awbārī, Idhān des. Libya 48 F2.....27°23'N 11°08'E
Awe, Loch l. Scotland 14 D4.....56°16'N 5°14'W
Axe r. England 11 D2.....50°42'N 3°04'W
Axel Heiberg Island Canada 61 I5.....79°47'N 91°00'W

Axminster England 8 C1.....50°47'N 2°59'W
Ayacucho Peru 72 B5.....13°10'S 74°13'W
Ayagöz Kazakhstan 54 J2.....47°56'N 80°23'E
Ayan Russia 55 O3.....56°26'N 138°12'E
Aydarko'l ko'li l. Uzbekistan 54 H2.....41°02'N 66°33'E
Aydın Turkey 51 G3.....37°50'N 27°49'E
Ayers Rock hill Australia 108 C4.....25°20'S 131°05'E
Aylesbury England 8 E2.....51°49'N 0°48'W
Aylesham England 9 G2.....51°14'N 1°12'E
Aylsham England 9 G3.....52°48'N 1°15'E
Ayr Scotland 14 E3.....55°28'N 4°38'W
Ayr r. Scotland 14 E3.....55°28'N 4°38'W
Ayr, Point of Wales 10 D5.....53°21'N 3°18'W
Ayre, Point of Isle of Man 12 C3.....54°25'N 4°22'W
Ayvalık Turkey 50 G4.....39°17'N 26°41'E
Azawad f. Mali 84 D4.....20°20'N 3°00'W
Azerbaijan Asia 53 E2.....40°23'N 48°09'E
Azopol'ye Russia 52 E4.....65°18'N 45°11'E
Azores is Portugal 116 E3.....37°45'N 25°40'W
Azrou Morocco 84 D5.....33°26'N 5°11'W
Azuero, Península de pen. Panama 67 H2.....7°39'N 80°41'W
Azul, Cordillera mts Peru 72 B6.....8°31'S 75°56'W
Az Zaqāzīq Egypt 49 J3.....30°35'N 31°30'E
Az Zarqā' Jordan 94 E6.....32°04'N 36°05'E

B

Baardheere Somalia 85 I2.....2°19'N 42°18'E
Bābā, Kūh-e mts Afgh. 95 K6.....34°48'N 68°27'E
Babadag Romania 51 H7.....44°54'N 28°42'E
Babaeski Turkey 50 G5.....41°26'N 27°06'E
Babar i. Indonesia 103 H2.....7°57'S 129°51'E
Babbacombe Bay England 11 D2.....50°31'N 3°28'W
Babo Indonesia 103 I3.....2°35'S 133°21'E
Babruysk Belarus 47 M5.....53°09'N 29°14'E
Bab-Termas hill Morocco 45 D1.....34°29'N 3°33'W
Babuyan Islands Phil. 103 G7.....19°13'N 121°59'E
Bacabal Brazil 72 E6.....4°16'S 44°47'W
Bacan i. Indonesia 103 H3.....0°44'S 127°35'E
Bacău Romania 47 L2.....46°34'N 26°55'E
Back r. Canada 62 I4.....66°32'N 95°51'W
Backwater Reservoir Scotland 17 F1.....56°44'N 3°13'W
Bacolod Phil. 103 G6.....10°37'N 122°57'E
Bac Lieu Vietnam 102 D5.....9°15'N 105°45'E
Badajoz Spain 45 B3.....38°53'N 6°57'W
Baden Austria 46 G3.....48°00'N 16°15'E
Baden-Baden Germany 46 C3.....48°45'N 8°15'E
Bad Neuenahr-Ahrweiler Germany 42 G3.....50°33'N 7°07'E
Badulla Sri Lanka 96 F2.....6°58'N 81°01'E
Baffin Bay sea Canada/Greenland 61 L5.....72°51'N 66°20'W
Baffin Island Canada 61 L4.....67°54'N 68°47'W
Bafoussam Cameroon 84 F2.....5°28'N 10°26'E
Bafq Iran 95 I6.....31°34'N 55°21'E
Bafra Turkey 51 K5.....41°34'N 35°55'E
Bāft Iran 95 I5.....29°14'N 56°36'E
Bagé Brazil 73 D3.....31°20'S 54°06'W
Baggy Point England 11 C3.....51°08'N 4°16'W
Baghdad Iraq 94 F6.....33°18'N 44°22'E
Baghlān Afgh. 95 K7.....36°11'N 68°47'E
Bago Myanmar 97 I4.....17°18'N 96°28'E
Bahariya Oasis Egypt 94 C5.....27°56'N 28°51'E
Bahawalpur Pakistan 96 D6.....29°23'N 71°45'E
Bāherden Turkmenistan 95 I7.....38°27'N 57°24'E
Bahía, Islas de la is Honduras 67 G4.....16°13'N 86°56'W
Bahía Blanca Argentina 73 C3.....38°43'S 62°18'W
Bahrain Asia 95 H5.....26°05'N 50°51'E
Baia Mare Romania 47 J2.....47°39'N 23°35'E
Baicheng China 99 M7.....45°29'N 122°50'E
Baie-Comeau Canada 61 L2.....49°13'N 68°10'W
Baikal, Lake Russia 55 L3.....52°37'N 107°12'E
Baile Átha Cliath Ireland 18 E3.....53°20'N 6°16'W
Bailieborough Ireland 18 E3.....53°55'N 6°58'W
Bain r. England 13 G2.....53°05'N 0°12'W
Bainbridge U.S. 63 J3.....30°54'N 84°40'W
Bairnsdale Australia 108 D3.....37°51'S 147°37'E
Baise China 99 J2.....23°54'N 106°37'E
Baiyuda Desert Sudan 94 D3.....18°03'N 32°59'E
Baja Hungary 46 H2.....46°12'N 18°57'E
Baja California d. Mexico 66 A6.....29°49'N 115°07'W
Baja California pen. Mexico 66 B6.....30°40'N 115°41'W
Baja California Sur d. Mexico 66 B6.....25°19'N 112°09'W
Baker, Mount vol. U.S. 62 B6.....48°46'N 121°47'W
Baker Lake Canada 61 I4.....64°09'N 95°23'W
Bakersfield U.S. 62 C4.....35°22'N 118°59'W
Bakhtegan, Daryācheh-ye l. Iran 95 H5.....29°18'N 53°52'E
Bakırköy Turkey 51 H5.....40°58'N 28°51'E
Baku Azerbaijan 53 E2.....40°22'N 49°50'E
Bala Wales 10 D4.....52°55'N 3°36'W
Bala, Cerros de mts Bolivia 72 C5.....13°49'S 68°25'W
Balabac Strait Malaysia/Phil. 102 F5.....7°36'N 116°45'E
Balakovo Russia 53 E3.....52°00'N 47°47'E
Bala Lake Wales 10 D4.....52°53'N 3°37'W
Balashikha Russia 47 Q6.....55°49'N 37°57'E
Balashov Russia 53 E3.....51°32'N 43°09'E
Balaton, Lake Hungary 46 G2.....46°46'N 17°32'E
Balbina, Represa de resr Brazil 72 D6.....1°34'S 59°27'W
Balbriggan Ireland 18 E3.....53°36'N 6°11'W
Baldock England 9 E2.....51°59'N 0°11'W
Baldy, Mount U.S. 62 E3.....33°54'N 109°34'W
Balearic Islands Spain 45 F3.....39°28'N 1°30'E
Balearic Sea Europe 45 F3.....40°30'N 2°00'E
Baleine, Rivière à la r. Canada 61 L3.....57°67'N 67°37'W
Baleshwar India 96 G5.....21°30'N 86°56'E
Bali i. Indonesia 102 E2.....8°41'S 114°55'E
Balige Indonesia 102 B4.....2°20'N 99°03'E
Balıkesir Turkey 51 G4.....39°38'N 27°52'E
Balīkh r. Syria/Turkey 51 M2.....35°56'N 39°03'E
Balikpapan Indonesia 102 F3.....1°12'S 116°49'E
Balimo P.N.G. 103 K2.....7°59'S 143°01'E
Balintore Scotland 17 F2.....57°45'N 3°54'W
Bali Sea Indonesia 102 E2.....7°31'S 114°31'E
Balivanich Scotland 16 B2.....57°28'N 7°23'W
Balkanabat Turkmenistan 95 H7.....39°27'N 54°17'E
Balkan Mountains Bulgaria/Serbia 50 E6.....43°23'N 22°47'E
Balkhash, Lake Kazakhstan 54 I2.....45°30'N 73°51'E
Ballachulish Scotland 14 D4.....56°40'N 5°08'W
Ballantrae Scotland 14 D3.....55°06'N 5°00'W
Ballarat Australia 108 D3.....37°35'S 143°52'E
Ballary India 96 E4.....15°09'N 76°56'E
Ballater Scotland 17 F2.....57°03'N 3°02'W
Ballencleuch Law hill Scotland 15 F3.....55°20'N 3°41'W

Ballenita, Punta pt Chile 73 B4.....25°47'S 70°47'W
Ballina Ireland 18 B4.....54°07'N 9°10'W
Ballinasloe Ireland 18 C3.....53°20'N 8°13'W
Ballybay Ireland 14 C2.....54°07'N 6°54'W
Ballybunion Ireland 18 B2.....52°31'N 9°40'W
Ballycastle Northern Ireland 14 C3.....55°12'N 6°14'W
Ballyclare Northern Ireland 14 D2.....54°45'N 5°59'W
Ballygawley Northern Ireland 14 B2.....54°27'N 7°02'W
Ballyhaunis Ireland 18 C3.....53°46'N 8°46'W
Ballymena Northern Ireland 14 C2.....54°52'N 6°16'W
Ballymoney Northern Ireland 14 C3.....55°04'N 6°31'W
Ballynahinch Northern Ireland 14 D2.....54°24'N 5°53'W
Ballyquintin Point Northern Ireland 14 D2.....54°19'N 5°29'W
Ballyshannon Ireland 14 C3.....54°30'N 8°12'W
Balochistan f. Pakistan 96 B6.....27°30'N 63°31'E
Balqash Kazakhstan 54 I2.....46°50'N 74°59'E
Balsas r. Mexico 66 D4.....17°57'N 102°09'W
Balta Ukraine 47 M2.....47°56'N 29°37'E
Baltasound Scotland 17 I5.....60°46'N 0°52'W
Baltic Sea g. Europe 43 D1.....55°28'N 16°46'E
Baltimore U.S. 63 K4.....39°17'N 76°37'W
Baltiysk Russia 46 H6.....54°39'N 19°55'E
Balyqshy Kazakhstan 53 F2.....47°03'N 51°53'E
Bam Iran 95 I5.....29°07'N 58°22'E
Bamaga Australia 108 D5.....10°53'S 142°23'E
Bamako Mali 84 D3.....12°38'N 7°59'W
Bamberg Germany 46 D3.....49°54'N 10°53'E
Bambili Dem. Rep. Congo 83 B5.....3°38'N 26°07'E
Bambouti C.A.R. 85 G2.....5°22'N 27°12'E
Bāmīān Afgh. 95 K6.....34°52'N 67°49'E
Bampton Dev. England 11 D2.....50°59'N 3°29'W
Bampton Oxon. England 8 D2.....51°43'N 1°33'W
Bañados del Izozog f. Bolivia 72 C5.....18°20'S 61°45'W
Banagher Ireland 18 D3.....53°11'N 7°59'W
Banaz Turkey 51 H4.....38°44'N 29°44'E
Banbridge Northern Ireland 14 C2.....54°21'N 6°16'W
Banbury England 8 D3.....52°04'N 1°20'W
Banchory Scotland 17 G2.....57°03'N 2°29'W
Banda, Kepulauan is Indonesia 103 H3.....4°33'S 129°53'E
Banda Aceh Indonesia 102 B5.....5°30'N 95°18'E
Bandar-e 'Abbās Iran 95 I5.....27°11'N 56°18'E
Bandar-e Anzalī Iran 95 G7.....37°26'N 49°26'E
Bandar-e Büshehr Iran 95 H5.....28°58'N 50°51'E
Bandar-e Jāsk Iran 95 I5.....25°40'N 57°48'E
Bandar-e Kangān Iran 95 H5.....27°50'N 52°05'E
Bandar-e Lengeh Iran 95 H5.....26°34'N 54°53'E
Bandar-e Torkeman Iran 95 H7.....36°54'N 53°59'E
Bandar Lampung Indonesia 102 D2.....5°27'S 105°17'E
Bandar Seri Begawan Brunei 102 E4.....4°57'N 114°58'E
Banda Sea Indonesia 103 I2.....5°40'S 130°07'E
Bandırma Turkey 51 G5.....40°21'N 27°57'E
Bandon Ireland 18 C1.....51°45'N 8°44'W
Bandon r. Ireland 18 C1.....51°45'N 8°38'W
Bandundu Dem. Rep. Congo 83 A4.....3°17'S 17°22'E
Bandung Indonesia 102 D2.....6°56'S 107°35'E
Banff Canada 60 G3.....51°11'N 115°35'W
Banff Scotland 17 G2.....57°40'N 2°31'W
Bangassou C.A.R. 83 B5.....4°44'N 22°50'E
Banggai, Kepulauan is Indonesia 103 G3.....1°59'S 123°22'E
Bangka i. Indonesia 102 D3.....2°07'S 106°17'E
Bangkok Thailand 102 C6.....13°44'N 100°33'E
Bangladesh Asia 97 H5.....23°47'N 89°49'E
Bangor Northern Ireland 14 D2.....54°39'N 5°40'W
Bangor U.S. 63 M5.....44°48'N 68°47'W
Bangor Wales 10 C5.....53°14'N 4°08'W
Bangui C.A.R. 82 F2.....4°20'N 18°33'E
Bangweulu, Lake Zambia 83 B3.....11°13'S 29°39'E
Bani r. Mali 84 D3.....14°30'N 4°13'W
Banī Mazār Egypt 49 J2.....28°29'N 30°48'E
Banī Suwayf Egypt 49 J2.....29°05'N 31°06'E
Banī Walīd Libya 48 F3.....31°47'N 14°00'E
Bāniyās Syria 51 K2.....35°11'N 35°57'E
Banja Luka Bos. and Herz. 50 B7.....44°46'N 17°12'E
Banjarmasin Indonesia 102 E3.....3°23'S 114°33'E
Banjul Gambia 84 C3.....13°27'N 16°36'W
Banks Canada 60 F5.....73°06'N 121°26'W
Banks Islands Vanuatu 109 F5.....13°55'S 167°13'E
Banmi Pakistan 95 L6.....33°00'N 70°40'E
Bann r. Ireland 10 A4.....52°33'N 6°23'W
Bann r. Northern Ireland 14 C3.....55°09'N 6°42'W
Ban Tha Song Yang Thailand 102 B7.....17°34'N 97°56'E
Bantry Ireland 18 B1.....51°41'N 9°27'W
Bantry Bay Ireland 18 B1.....51°34'N 9°53'W
Baoding China 99 L5.....38°46'N 115°29'E
Baoshan China 99 H3.....25°07'N 99°09'E
Baotou China 99 K6.....40°31'N 110°04'E
Ba'qūbah Iraq 94 F6.....33°42'N 44°37'E
Bar Montenegro 50 C6.....42°05'N 19°05'E
Bara Sudan 94 D2.....13°40'N 30°22'E
Baracoa Cuba 67 J5.....20°21'N 74°29'W
Baranavichy Belarus 47 L5.....53°08'N 26°01'E
Baranīs Egypt 49 K1.....23°53'N 35°2'E
Barbacena Brazil 73 E4.....21°13'S 43°45'W
Barbados Central America 67 M3.....13°09'N 59°25'W
Barbuda i. Antigua 67 L4.....17°39'N 61°47'W
Barcaldine Australia 108 D4.....23°32'S 145°16'E
Barcelona Spain 45 G4.....41°25'N 2°11'E
Barcelona Venezuela 72 C8.....10°06'N 64°41'W
Bárðarbunga mt. Iceland 43 Y2.....64°38'N 17°32'W
Bardney England 13 G2.....53°13'N 0°19'W
Bardsey Island Wales 10 C4.....52°45'N 4°46'W
Bardsey Sound str. Wales 10 C4.....52°47'N 4°48'W
Bareilly India 96 E6.....28°22'N 79°22'E
Barentsburg Arctic Oc. 54 C5.....77°49'N 14°23'E
Barents Sea Arctic Oc. 54 F5.....75°18'N 42°11'E
Barham England 9 G2.....51°12'N 1°1'E
Bari Italy 49 G5.....41°07'N 16°52'E
Barinas Venezuela 72 B7.....8°34'N 70°11'W
Barisan, Pegunungan mts Indonesia 102 C3.....1°12'S 100°30'E
Barkly Tableland f. Australia 108 C5.....18°06'S 135°2'E
Bârlad Romania 50 G8.....46°13'N 27°3'E
Barlee, Lake Australia 108 A4.....28°58'S 119°4'E
Barmer India 96 D6.....25°44'N 71°2'E
Barmouth Wales 10 C4.....52°43'N 4°03'W
Barmouth Bay Wales 10 C4.....52°43'N 4°1'W
Barnard Castle England 13 F3.....54°33'N 1°55'W
Barnaul Russia 54 J3.....53°22'N 83°4'E
Barnet England 9 E2.....51°39'N 0°12'W
Barnoldswick England 13 E2.....53°55'N 2°11'W
Barnsley England 13 F2.....53°33'N 1°29'W
Barnstaple England 11 C3.....51°05'N 4°03'W
Barnstaple or Bideford Bay England 11 C3.....51°05'N 4°23'W
Barquisimeto Venezuela 72 C8.....10°03'N 69°15'W
Barra i. Scotland 16 B1.....56°59'N 7°30'W

arra, Sound of str. Scotland 16 B2............57°04'N 7°27'W
arranquilla Colombia 72 B8............10°59'N 74°51'W
arretos Brazil 73 E4............20°35'S 48°34'W
arrhead Scotland 14 E3............55°48'N 4°24'W
arrow r. Ireland 18 E2............52°23'N 6°57'W
arrow, Point U.S. 60 C5............71°23'N 156°22'W
arrow-in-Furness England 12 D3............54°07'N 3°13'W
arrow Island Australia 108 A4............20°49'S 115°22'E
arry Wales 11 D3............51°24'N 3°17'W
arstow U.S. 62 C3............34°54'N 117°01'W
artin Turkey 51 J5............41°38'N 32°21'E
arton-upon-Humber England 13 G2............53°41'N 0°27'W
artoszyce Poland 46 I6............54°15'N 20°49'E
aruun-Urt Mongolia 99 K7............46°31'N 113°22'E
arysaw Belarus 47 M6............54°14'N 28°31'E
aschurch England 8 C3............52°47'N 2°51'W
asel Switz. 46 B2............47°33'N 7°35'E
asilan i. Phil. 103 G5............6°32'N 121°52'E
asildon England 9 F2............51°35'N 0°29'E
asingstoke England 8 D2............51°16'N 1°06'W
asra Iraq 95 G6............30°29'N 47°48'E
assenthwaite Lake England 12 D3............54°40'N 3°14'W
asse-Terre Guadeloupe 67 L4............16°01'N 61°44'W
ass Rock i. Scotland 15 G4............56°05'N 2°38'W
ass Strait Australia 108 D3............39°43'S 146°11'E
astak Iran 95 H5............27°12'N 54°21'E
astia France 44 H3............42°42'N 9°27'E
astogne Belgium 42 E3............50°00'N 5°43'E
ata Equat. Guinea 84 E2............1°50'N 9°48'E
atabanó, Golfo de b. Cuba 67 H5............22°16'N 82°38'W
atam Indonesia 102 C4............1°09'N 104°01'E
atang China 99 H4............30°01'N 99°08'E
atang Indonesia 97 I6............6°57'S 109°43'E
atangas Phil. 103 G6............13°46'N 121°01'E
atan Islands Phil. 103 C8............20°46'N 122°05'E
ath England 8 C2............51°23'N 2°22'W
ath and North East Somerset d. England 21 D2
............51°21'N 2°28'W
athgate Scotland 15 F3............55°54'N 3°39'W
athurst Australia 108 D3............33°25'S 149°34'E
athurst Canada 61 L2............47°36'N 65°39'W
athurst Australia 108 C5............11°29'S 130°11'E
athurst Island England 13 F2............53°43'N 1°38'W
atley England 13 F2............53°43'N 1°38'W
atna Algeria 84 E5............35°32'N 6°13'E
aton Rouge U.S. 63 H3............30°27'N 91°11'W
attambang Cambodia 102 C6............13°06'N 103°14'E
atticaloa Sri Lanka 96 F2............7°42'N 81°39'E
attle England 9 F1............50°55'N 0°29'E
atu, Pulau-pulau is Indonesia 102 B3............0°14'S 98°16'E
atumi Georgia 53 E2............41°39'N 41°38'E
aubau Indonesia 103 G2............5°29'S 122°37'E
auchi Nigeria 84 E3............10°19'N 9°50'E
auru Brazil 73 E4............22°20'S 49°05'W
auska Latvia 47 K7............56°25'N 24°13'E
autzen Germany 46 F4............51°11'N 14°26'E
awean i. Indonesia 102 E2............5°48'S 112°34'E
ayamo Cuba 67 I5............20°22'N 76°38'W
ayanhongor Mongolia 99 I7............46°09'N 100°41'E
ayan-Uul Mongolia 99 K7............48°55'N 112°44'E
ayburt Turkey 51 N5............40°15'N 40°14'E
ay City Mich. U.S. 63 J5............43°35'N 83°53'W
ay City Tex. U.S. 63 G2............28°59'N 96°02'W
aydaratskaya Guba Russia 52 G4............69°29'N 66°01'E
aymak Russia 53 F3............52°31'N 58°15'E
ayonne France 44 C3............43°29'N 1°29'W
ayreuth Germany 46 E4............49°56'N 11°36'E

ay al Kabīr, Wādī watercourse Libya 48 G3
............31°11'N 15°53'E
azardyuzyu, Gora mt. Azerbaijan 53 E2............41°12'N 47°52'E
eachy Head England 9 F1............50°44'N 0°15'E
eaconsfield England 9 E2............51°36'N 0°39'W
eagle Gulf Australia 103 H1............12°04'S 129°55'E
eaminster England 8 C1............50°49'N 2°45'W
eardmore Canada 63 I6............49°36'N 87°58'W
eata, Cabo c. Dom. Rep. 67 J4............17°38'N 71°23'W
eata, Isla i. Dom. Rep. 67 J4............17°36'N 71°30'W
eaufort Sea Canada/U.S. 60 F5............73°19'N 129°52'W
eaufort West S. Africa 83 B1............32°20'S 22°36'E
eauly Scotland 17 E2............57°29'N 4°28'W
eauly r. Scotland 17 E2............57°29'N 4°27'W
eauly Firth est. Scotland 17 E2............57°29'N 4°23'W
eaumaris Wales 10 C5............53°16'N 4°05'W
eaumont France 11 D3............49°40'N 1°50'W
eaumont U.S. 63 H3............30°05'N 94°09'W
eaune France 44 E5............47°01'N 4°50'E
eauvais France 44 E6............49°26'N 2°05'E
eaver r. Canada 60 H3............55°22'N 107°45'W
eaver Creek town Canada 60 D4............62°23'N 140°49'W
ebington England 12 D2............53°21'N 3°00'W
eccles England 9 G3............52°28'N 1°34'E
echerreá Spain 45 B5............42°51'N 7°09'W
echar Algeria 84 D5............31°36'N 2°13'W
eckingham England 13 G2............53°24'N 0°49'W
eckley U.S. 63 J4............37°47'N 81°11'W
edale England 13 F3............54°17'N 1°35'W
edele Ethiopia 85 H2............8°28'N 36°21'E
edford England 9 E2............52°08'N 0°28'W
edford d. England 21 E3............52°10'N 0°28'W
edlington England 13 F4............55°08'N 1°36'W
edworth England 8 D3............52°29'N 1°28'W
eersheba Israel 49 J3............31°15'N 34°48'E
eeville U.S. 62 G2............28°25'N 97°45'W
eg, Lough l. Northern Ireland 14 C2............54°47'N 6°27'W
ei'an China 99 N7............48°11'N 126°31'E
eihai China 99 J2............21°27'N 109°08'E
eijing China 99 L5............39°52'N 116°27'E
einn an Oir hill Scotland 14 D3............55°54'N 5°59'W
einn Dearg hill Scotland 16 E2............57°47'N 4°56'W
einn Dearg mt. H. and K. Scotland 17 F1............56°53'N 3°53'W
inn Heasgarnich mt. Scotland 14 E4............56°31'N 4°35'W
eira Mozambique 83 C3............19°50'S 34°52'E
eirut Lebanon 49 K3............33°52'N 35°30'E
eith Scotland 14 E3............55°45'N 4°38'W
eius Romania 47 J2............46°40'N 22°23'E
eja Portugal 45 B3............38°01'N 7°52'W
ejaïa Algeria 84 E5............36°44'N 5°03'E
ejar Spain 45 C4............40°24'N 5°46'W
ékéscsaba Hungary 46 I2............46°41'N 21°05'E
ela Pakistan 96 C6............26°12'N 66°21'E
elarus Europe 47 L5............54°01'N 28°39'E
elchatów Poland 46 H4............51°22'N 19°22'E
elcher Islands Canada 61 K3............56°10'N 78°47'W
eleb Russia 53 F3............50°26'N 54°08'E
ebey Russia 53 F3............54°03'N 54°08'E
edweyne Somalia 85 I2............4°44'N 45°13'E

Belém Brazil 72 E6............1°26'S 48°29'W
Belev Russia 47 Q5............53°48'N 36°10'E
Belfast Northern Ireland 14 D2............54°36'N 5°55'W
Belfast City d. Northern Ireland 21 C4............54°36'N 5°55'W
Belfast Lough inlet Northern Ireland 14 D2
............54°40'N 5°52'W
Belford England 13 F4............55°36'N 1°50'W
Belgium Europe 42 D3............50°55'N 4°14'E
Belgorod Russia 53 D3............50°35'N 36°37'E
Belgrade Serbia 50 D7............44°48'N 20°29'E
Belitung i. Indonesia 102 D3............2°47'S 108°14'E
Belize town Belize 66 G4............17°31'N 88°14'W
Belize Central America 66 G4............17°10'N 88°18'W
Bellac France 44 D5............46°08'N 1°03'E
Belle-Île i. France 44 B5............47°19'N 3°15'W
Belle Isle, Strait of Canada 61 M3............51°16'N 56°57'W
Bellingham England 13 E4............55°09'N 2°15'W
Bellingham U.S. 62 B6............48°45'N 122°28'W
Bellinzona Switz. 46 C2............46°12'N 9°01'E
Belluno Italy 46 E2............46°08'N 12°13'E
Belmopan Belize 66 G4............17°14'N 88°46'W
Belmullet Ireland 18 B4............54°14'N 9°59'W
Belo Horizonte Brazil 73 E5............19°55'S 43°56'W
Beloretsk Russia 53 F3............53°55'N 58°24'E
Beloye, Ozero l. Russia 52 D4............60°10'N 38°00'E
Belozersk Russia 52 D3............60°02'N 37°47'E
Belper England 13 F2............53°02'N 1°29'W
Belukha, Gora mt. Kazakhstan/Russia 54 J2
............49°50'N 86°41'E
Belush'ye Russia 52 E4............66°55'N 47°36'E
Belyy Russia 47 O6............55°50'N 32°57'E
Bembridge England 8 D1............50°41'N 1°05'W
Bemidji U.S. 63 H6............47°27'N 94°52'W
Ben Alder mt. Scotland 17 E1............56°49'N 4°28'W
Bonavente Spain 45 C5............42°00'N 5°40'W
Benbane Head Northern Ireland 14 C3............55°15'N 6°30'W
Benbecula i. Scotland 16 B2............57°27'N 7°23'W
Ben Cleuch hill Scotland 15 F4............56°11'N 3°46'W
Ben Cruachan mt. Scotland 14 D4............56°25'N 5°08'W
Bend U.S. 62 B5............44°04'N 121°17'W
Bender Moldova 49 I6............46°49'N 29°29'E
Bendigo Australia 108 D3............36°46'S 144°18'E
Benešov Czechia 46 F3............49°47'N 14°42'E
Bengal, Bay of sea Indian Oc. 96 G4............17°51'N 88°40'E
Bengaluru India 96 E3............12°57'N 77°34'E
Bengbu China 99 L4............32°54'N 117°23'E
Benghazi Libya 85 G5............32°06'N 20°04'E
Bengkulu Indonesia 102 C3............3°45'S 102°18'E
Benguela Angola 83 A3............12°36'S 13°21'E
Ben Hope hill Scotland 17 E3............58°25'N 4°36'W
Beni r. Bolivia 72 C5............11°01'S 66°07'W
Benidorm Spain 45 E3............38°32'N 0°08'W
Béni Mellal Morocco 84 D5............32°17'N 6°25'W
Benin Africa 84 E2............8°26'N 2°11'E
Benin, Bight of g. Africa 84 E2............5°17'N 3°27'E
Benin City Nigeria 84 E2............6°19'N 5°36'E
Beni-Saf Algeria 48 C4............35°20'N 1°21'W
Benjamin Constant Brazil 72 C6............4°23'S 69°58'W
Ben Klibreck hill Scotland 17 E3............58°15'N 4°24'W
Ben Lawers mt. Scotland 14 E4............56°33'N 4°13'W
Ben Lomond hill Scotland 14 E4............56°11'N 4°38'W
Ben Loyal hill Scotland 17 E3............58°24'N 4°27'W
Ben Lui mt. Scotland 14 E4............56°24'N 4°49'W
Ben Macdui mt. Scotland 17 F2............57°05'N 3°40'W
Ben More mt. Scotland 14 D4............56°26'N 6°00'W
Ben More mt. Scotland 14 E4............56°23'N 4°32'W
Ben More Assynt hill Scotland 16 E3............58°08'N 4°51'W
Ben Nevis mt. Scotland 16 D1............56°48'N 5°00'W
Bentley England 13 F2............53°33'N 1°09'W
Benue r. Nigeria 84 E2............7°49'N 6°48'E
Ben Vorlich hill Scotland 14 E4............56°21'N 4°13'W
Ben Wyvis mt. Scotland 17 E2............57°41'N 4°35'W
Benxi China 99 M6............41°16'N 123°45'E
Beoraid, Loch l. Scotland 16 D1............56°58'N 5°41'W
Berat Albania 50 C5............40°42'N 19°58'E
Berau, Teluk b. Indonesia 103 I3............2°28'S 132°36'E
Berber Sudan 94 D3............18°00'N 34°02'E
Berbera Somalia 85 I3............10°24'N 45°02'E
Berbérati C.A.R. 84 F2............4°14'N 15°47'E
Berck France 9 G1............50°25'N 1°35'E
Berdiansk Ukraine 49 K6............46°46'N 36°48'E
Berdychiv Ukraine 47 M3............49°53'N 28°36'E
Berens River town Canada 60 I3............52°21'N 97°01'W
Berezivka Ukraine 47 N2............47°12'N 30°55'E
Berezniki Russia 52 F3............59°25'N 56°48'E
Berezovo Russia 52 G4............63°54'N 65°07'E
Bergama Turkey 50 G4............39°07'N 27°11'E
Bergamo Italy 46 C1............45°42'N 9°41'E
Bergen Norway 43 A3............60°23'N 5°22'E
Bergerac France 44 D4............44°51'N 0°29'E
Bergisch Gladbach Germany 46 B4............50°58'N 7°08'E
Bering Sea N. Pacific Oc. 56 B5............60°00'N 170°00'E
Bering Strait Russia/U.S. 55 U4............66°18'N 168°40'W
Berkel r. Neth. 42 F5............52°08'N 6°11'E
Berkeley England 8 C2............51°41'N 2°27'W
Berkshire Downs hills England 8 D2............51°30'N 1°20'W
Berlin Germany 46 E5............52°31'N 13°23'E
Bermuda i. N. Atlantic Oc. 67 L7............32°24'N 64°56'W
Bern Switz. 46 B2............46°57'N 7°27'E
Berneray i. Na h-E. S. Scotland 16 B1............56°47'N 7°38'W
Berneray i. Na h-E. S. Scotland 16 B2............57°44'N 7°18'W
Berry Head England 11 D2............50°24'N 3°29'W
Bertoua Cameroon 84 F2............4°35'N 13°41'E
Berwick-upon-Tweed England 13 E4............55°46'N 2°00'W
Besançon France 44 G5............47°15'N 6°01'E
Bessbrook Northern Ireland 14 C2............54°12'N 6°23'W
Betanzos Spain 45 A5............43°17'N 8°12'W
Beth, Oued r. Morocco 45 B1............34°06'N 6°26'W
Bethesda Wales 10 C5............53°11'N 4°03'W
Béthune France 42 B3............50°31'N 2°38'E
Betsiboka r. Madagascar 83 D3............15°58'S 46°27'E
Bettystown Ireland 10 A5............53°42'N 6°15'W
Betws-y-Coed Wales 10 D5............53°05'N 3°48'W
Beult r. England 9 F2............51°13'N 0°25'E
Beverley England 13 G2............53°51'N 0°26'W
Bewdley England 8 C3............52°23'N 2°19'W
Bewl Water resr England 9 F2............51°04'N 0°23'E
Bexhill England 9 F1............50°50'N 0°29'E
Beykoz Turkey 51 H5............41°07'N 29°05'E
Beyla Guinea 84 D2............8°41'N 8°41'W
Beyneū Kazakhstan 53 F2............45°18'N 55°11'E
Beypazarı Turkey 51 I5............40°10'N 31°56'E
Beyşehir Turkey 51 I3............37°41'N 31°43'E
Beyşehir Gölü l. Turkey 51 I3............37°42'N 31°33'E
Béziers France 44 E3............43°21'N 3°13'E
Bhagalpur India 96 G6............25°15'N 86°56'E
Bhamo Myanmar 97 I5............24°18'N 97°17'E

Bhavnagar India 96 D5............21°46'N 72°14'E
Bhima r. India 96 E4............16°26'N 77°13'E
Bhisho S. Africa 83 B1............32°51'S 27°24'E
Bhopal India 96 E5............23°15'N 77°23'E
Bhubaneshwar India 96 G5............20°13'N 85°53'E
Bhuj India 96 C5............23°11'N 69°44'E
Bhutan Asia 97 H6............27°38'N 90°33'E
Biak Indonesia 103 J3............1°12'S 136°05'E
Biak i. Indonesia 103 J3............0°59'S 135°59'E
Biała Podlaska Poland 47 J5............52°02'N 23°07'E
Białystok Poland 47 J5............53°08'N 23°10'E
Biarritz France 44 C3............43°29'N 1°33'W
Bibai Japan 104 D4............43°18'N 141°52'E
Biberach an der Riß Germany 46 C3............48°06'N 9°47'E
Bicester England 8 D2............51°54'N 1°09'W
Bidar India 96 E4............17°54'N 77°34'E
Biddulph England 13 E2............53°07'N 2°10'W
Bidean nam Bian mt. Scotland 16 D1............56°39'N 5°02'W
Bideford England 11 C3............51°01'N 4°12'W
Biel/Bienne Switz. 46 B2............47°09'N 7°15'E
Bielefeld Germany 46 C5............52°01'N 8°32'E
Biella Italy 46 C1............45°34'N 8°04'E
Bielsko-Biała Poland 46 H3............49°49'N 19°03'E
Bié Plateau f. Angola 78 C2............13°00'S 17°00'E
Bifoun Gabon 84 F1............0°15'S 10°25'E
Biga Turkey 51 G5............40°13'N 27°13'E
Bigbury Bay England 11 D2............50°15'N 3°54'W
Biggar Scotland 15 F3............55°37'N 3°31'W
Biggleswade England 9 E3............52°05'N 0°16'W
Bighorn r. U.S. 62 E6............46°10'N 107°30'W
Bighorn Mountains U.S. 62 E5............44°06'N 106°55'W
Big Spring U.S. 62 F3............32°16'N 101°24'W
Big Trout Lake town Canada 61 J3............53°49'N 89°50'W
Bihać Bos. and Herz. 50 A7............44°49'N 15°53'E
Bihar d. India 96 G5............24°13'N 85°37'F
Bihor, Vârful mt. Romania 47 J2............46°27'N 22°44'E
Bijeljina Bos. and Herz. 50 C7............44°46'N 19°14'E
Bijelo Polje Montenegro 50 C6............43°02'N 19°45'E
Bikaner India 96 D6............28°00'N 73°23'E
Bilaspur India 98 E2............22°05'N 82°09'E
Bila Tserkva Ukraine 47 N3............49°48'N 30°07'E
Bilbao Spain 45 D5............43°15'N 2°54'W
Bilecik Turkey 51 H5............40°09'N 29°57'E
Bilhorod-Dnistrovskyi Ukraine 49 J6............46°11'N 30°20'E
Billericay England 9 F2............51°38'N 0°25'E
Billingham England 13 F3............54°37'N 1°17'W
Billinghay England 13 G2............53°05'N 0°17'W
Billings U.S. 62 E6............45°48'N 108°27'W
Billingshurst England 9 E2............51°01'N 0°27'W
Bill of Portland hd England 8 C1............50°30'N 2°30'W
Bilopillia Ukraine 47 P4............51°09'N 34°20'E
Biloxi U.S. 63 I3............30°24'N 88°57'W
Bilston Scotland 15 F3............55°52'N 3°11'W
Bilton England 13 G2............53°47'N 0°15'W
Bimini Islands Bahamas 67 I6............25°46'N 79°14'W
Bindura Zimbabwe 83 C3............17°18'S 31°19'E
Bingham England 8 E3............52°57'N 0°57'W
Binghamton U.S. 63 K5............42°06'N 75°55'W
Bingley England 13 F2............53°51'N 1°50'W
Bintulu Malaysia 102 E4............3°12'N 113°03'E
Bioko i. Equat. Guinea 84 E2............3°16'N 8°31'E
Birāk Libya 48 F2............27°33'N 14°16'E
Birao C.A.R. 94 B2............10°15'N 22°48'E
Birecik Turkey 51 L3............37°01'N 37°59'E
Birhan mt. Ethiopia 85 H3............10°43'N 37°52'E
Bīrjand Iran 95 I6............32°56'N 59°11'E
Birkenhead England 12 D2............53°23'N 3°01'W
Bir Lahlou Western Sahara 84 D4............26°19'N 9°33'W
Birmingham England 8 D3............52°29'N 1°53'W
Birmingham U.S. 63 I3............33°32'N 86°47'W
Birnin Konni Niger 84 E3............13°48'N 5°14'E
Birobidzhan Russia 99 O7............48°45'N 132°52'E
Birr Ireland 18 D3............53°06'N 7°55'W
Birsay Scotland 17 F4............59°08'N 3°18'W
Birstall England 8 D3............52°41'N 1°07'W
Biržai Lithuania 47 K7............56°12'N 24°45'E
Biscay, Bay of sea France/Spain 45 C6............45°40'N 5°07'W
Bischofshofen Austria 46 E2............47°25'N 13°13'E
Bishkek Kyrgyzstan 98 C6............42°54'N 74°32'E
Bishop Auckland England 13 F3............54°40'N 1°41'W
Bishops Lydeard England 11 D3............51°04'N 3°11'W
Bishop's Stortford England 9 F2............51°52'N 0°10'E
Bishop's Waltham England 8 D1............50°57'N 1°13'W
Biskra Algeria 84 E5............34°49'N 5°44'E
Bismarck U.S. 62 F6............46°50'N 100°46'W
Bismarck Sea P.N.G. 108 D6............4°01'S 149°01'E
Bissau Guinea-Bissau 84 C3............11°53'N 15°38'W
Bistrița Romania 47 K2............47°08'N 24°30'E
Bistrița r. Romania 47 K2............46°30'N 26°58'E
Bitburg Germany 42 F2............49°58'N 6°32'E
Bitola North Macedonia 50 D5............41°01'N 21°20'E
Bitterroot Range mts U.S. 62 D6............47°16'N 115°41'W
Biwa Ko l. Japan 104 C3............35°09'N 135°59'E
Biysk Russia 54 J3............52°31'N 85°17'E
Bizerte Tunisia 48 F4............37°16'N 9°52'E
Bjørnøya i. Arctic Oc. 54 C5............74°24'N 19°07'E
Blackburn England 13 E2............53°45'N 2°29'W
Blackburn with Darwen d. England 21 D3............53°44'N 2°27'W
Black Combe hill England 12 D3............54°15'N 3°20'W
Blackfield England 8 D1............50°49'N 1°22'W
Black Forest mts Germany 46 C2............47°56'N 8°08'E
Black Head England 11 B2............50°00'N 5°07'W
Black Hill hill England 13 E2............53°32'N 1°53'W
Black Isle pen. Scotland 17 E2............57°35'N 4°19'W
Black Mountains hills Wales 10 D3............51°58'N 3°08'W
Blackpool England 13 D2............53°49'N 3°03'W
Blackpool d. England 21 D3............53°50'N 3°01'W
Black Sea Asia/Europe 51 M6............42°31'N 38°22'E
Blacksod Bay Ireland 18 A4............54°03'N 10°03'W
Black Volta r. Africa 84 D2............8°29'N 0°51'W
Blackwater r. England 9 F2............51°44'N 0°41'E
Blackwater r. Meath Ireland 18 E3............53°39'N 6°41'W
Blackwater r. Water. Ireland 18 D2............52°08'N 7°51'W
Blackwater r. Northern Ireland 14 C2............54°31'N 6°34'W
Blackwood Wales 10 D3............51°40'N 3°12'W
Blaenau Ffestiniog Wales 10 D4............52°59'N 3°56'W
Blaenau Gwent d. Wales 21 D2............51°46'N 3°12'W
Blaenavon Wales 10 D3............51°46'N 3°06'W
Blagdon England 8 C2............51°20'N 2°43'W
Blagoevgrad Bulgaria 50 E6............42°01'N 23°06'E
Blagoveshchensk Russia 55 N3............50°17'N 127°29'E
Blair Atholl Scotland 17 F1............56°46'N 3°51'W
Blairgowrie Scotland 17 F1............56°35'N 3°21'W
Blanc, Cap c. Mauritania 84 C4............20°51'N 17°04'W
Blanc, Mont mt. France/Italy 44 G4............45°50'N 6°51'E

Blanca, Bahía b. Argentina 73 C3............39°08'S 61°47'W
Blanche, Lake Australia 108 C4............29°15'S 139°42'E
Blanc Nez, Cap c. France 9 G1............50°56'N 1°44'E
Blanco, Cape U.S. 62 B5............42°51'N 124°34'W
Blandford Forum England 8 C1............50°51'N 2°10'W
Blanquilla, Isla i. Venezuela 67 L3............11°51'N 64°35'W
Blantyre Malawi 83 C3............15°47'S 35°02'E
Blarney Ireland 18 C1............51°56'N 8°34'W
Bletchley England 8 E2............51°59'N 0°45'W
Blida Algeria 84 E5............36°33'N 2°55'E
Bloemfontein S. Africa 83 B2............29°07'S 26°13'E
Blois France 44 D5............47°35'N 1°20'E
Bloody Foreland pt Ireland 18 C5............55°10'N 8°18'W
Bloomington U.S. 63 I5............40°29'N 88°59'W
Blue Mountains U.S. 62 C6............45°27'N 118°38'W
Blue Nile r. Sudan 85 H3............15°38'N 32°30'E
Blue Stack hill Ireland 14 A2............54°45'N 8°05'W
Blue Stack Mountains hills Ireland 18 C4............54°42'N 8°14'W
Blyth Northum. England 13 F4............55°08'N 1°30'W
Blyth Notts. England 13 F2............53°22'N 1°04'W
Blyth r. Iraq 14............35°56'N 89°52'W
Blytheville U.S. 63 I4............35°56'N 89°52'W
Bo Sierra Leone 84 C2............7°55'N 11°45'W
Boa Vista Brazil 72 C7............2°51'N 60°43'W
Boa Vista i. Cape Verde 84 B3............16°05'N 22°40'W
Bobaomby, Tanjona c. Madagascar 83 D3............11°57'S 49°15'E
Bobo-Dioulasso Burkina Faso 84 D3............11°11'N 4°18'W
Bobotov Kuk mt. Montenegro 50 C6............43°07'N 19°03'E
Bóbr r. Poland 46 F4............52°03'N 15°04'E
Boby mt. Madagascar 83 D2............22°13'S 46°54'E
Bocholt Germany 46 B4............51°50'N 6°36'E
Boddam Scotland 17 H2............57°28'N 1°47'W
Bodélé f. Chad 85 F3............16°12'N 16°17'E
Boden Sweden 43 E4............65°49'N 21°41'E
Bodenham England 8 C3............52°09'N 2°41'W
Bodmin England 11 C2............50°28'N 4°43'W
Bodmin Moor f. England 11 C2............50°34'N 4°36'W
Bodø Norway 43 C4............67°17'N 14°23'E
Bodrum Turkey 50 G3............37°02'N 27°25'E
Boğazliyan Turkey 51 K4............39°11'N 35°15'E
Boggeragh Mountains hills Ireland 18 B2............52°01'N 9°01'E
Bogie r. Scotland 17 G2............57°27'N 2°46'W
Bognor Regis England 8 E1............50°47'N 0°40'W
Bogor Indonesia 102 D2............6°35'S 106°45'E
Bogotá Colombia 72 B7............4°35'N 74°04'W
Bo Hai g. China 99 L5............38°32'N 119°14'E
Bohain-en-Vermandois France 42 C2............49°59'N 3°28'E
Bohemian Forest mts Germany 46 E3............49°42'N 12°27'E
Bohol i. Phil. 103 G5............9°55'N 124°16'E
Boise U.S. 62 C5............43°38'N 116°11'W
Bojnürd Iran 95 I7............37°27'N 57°19'E
Bolhrad Ukraine 49 I6............45°41'N 28°37'E
Bolívar, Pico mt. Venezuela 67 J2............8°33'N 70°59'W
Bolivia S. America 72 C5............16°23'S 64°00'W
Bollnäs Sweden 43 D3............61°21'N 16°24'E
Bolmen l. Sweden 43 C2............56°52'N 13°43'E
Bologna Italy 46 D1............44°29'N 11°22'E
Bol'shevik, Ostrov i. Russia 55 L5............78°39'N 102°16'E
Bol'shezemel'skaya Tundra f. Russia 52 F4
............67°00'N 58°00'E
Bol'shoy Aluy r. Russia 55 Q4............66°29'N 159°26'E
Bol'shoy Lyakhovskiy, Ostrov i. Russia 55 P5
............73°26'N 142°14'E
Bolsover England 13 F2............53°14'N 1°17'W
Bolt Head England 11 D2............50°12'N 3°47'W
Bolton England 13 E2............53°35'N 2°26'W
Bolu Turkey 51 I5............40°44'N 31°36'E
Bolus Head Ireland 18 A1............51°47'N 10°20'W
Bolzano Italy 46 D2............46°29'N 11°21'E
Boma Dem. Rep. Congo 83 A4............5°48'S 13°03'E
Bømlo i. Norway 43 A2............59°45'N 5°13'E
Bon, Cap c. Tunisia 48 F4............37°04'N 11°04'E
Bonaire i. Neth. Antilles 67 K3............12°02'N 68°12'W
Bonar Bridge Scotland 17 E2............57°54'N 4°21'W
Bonavista Canada 61 M2............48°33'N 52°43'W
Bondoukou Côte d'Ivoire 84 D2............8°03'N 2°48'W
Bo'ness Scotland 15 F4............56°01'N 3°36'W
Bonifacio France 44 H2............41°23'N 9°10'E
Bonifacio, Strait of France/Italy 44 H2............41°15'N 8°45'E
Bonn Germany 46 B4............50°44'N 7°04'E
Bonnyrigg Scotland 15 F3............55°52'N 3°06'W
Bontosunggu Indonesia 102 F2............5°41'S 119°43'E
Boothia, Gulf of Canada 61 J4............68°48'N 86°41'W
Boothia Peninsula Canada 61 I5............70°40'N 94°39'W
Bootle England 12 D2............53°27'N 2°59'W
Bor Turkey 51 K3............37°54'N 34°33'E
Borås Sweden 43 C2............57°44'N 12°57'E
Borāzjān Iran 95 H5............29°16'N 51°12'E
Bordeaux France 44 C4............44°51'N 0°34'W
Borden Island Canada 60 G5............78°31'N 111°01'W
Borden Peninsula Canada 61 J5............72°45'N 82°32'W
Boreray i. Scotland 16 B2............57°42'N 7°16'W
Borisoglebsk Russia 53 E3............51°23'N 42°05'E
Borken Germany 42 F4............51°50'N 6°51'E
Borkum i. Germany 42 F6............53°37'N 6°44'E
Borlänge Sweden 43 C3............60°29'N 15°26'E
Borneo i. Asia 102 E4............0°08'N 113°25'E
Bornholm i. Denmark 43 C1............55°09'N 14°38'E
Bornova Turkey 50 G4............38°27'N 27°11'E
Borodianka Ukraine 47 M4............50°39'N 29°56'E
Boroughbridge England 13 F3............54°06'N 1°24'W
Borovichi Russia 52 D3............58°23'N 33°55'E
Borovskoy Kazakhstan 53 G2............53°47'N 64°12'E
Borūjerd Iran 95 G6............33°53'N 48°43'E
Boryspil Ukraine 47 N4............50°21'N 30°59'E
Borzna Ukraine 47 O4............51°15'N 32°26'E
Borzya Russia 55 M3............50°11'N 116°31'E
Bosna r. Bos. and Herz. 50 C7............45°04'N 18°29'E
Bosnia and Herzegovina Europe 50 B7............44°23'N 17°40'E
Bosobolo Dem. Rep. Congo 83 A5............4°10'N 19°52'E
Bosporus str. Turkey 51 H5............41°07'N 29°06'E
Bossembélé C.A.R. 85 F2............5°15'N 17°38'E
Bosten Hu l. China 98 F6............41°53'N 87°24'E
Boston England 9 E3............52°58'N 0°01'W
Boston U.S. 63 L5............42°23'N 71°06'W
Boston Spa England 13 F2............53°54'N 1°20'W
Botevgrad Bulgaria 50 E6............42°54'N 23°47'E
Bothnia, Gulf of Finland/Sweden 43 D3............61°00'N 19°15'E
Botoşani Romania 47 L2............47°45'N 26°39'E
Botswana Africa 83 B2............24°56'S 22°47'E
Bottesford England 13 G2............53°33'N 0°40'W
Bouaké Côte d'Ivoire 84 D2............7°42'N 5°03'W
Bouar C.A.R. 84 F2............5°58'N 15°36'E
Bouârfa Morocco 84 D5............32°34'N 1°56'W
Bougainville Island P.N.G. 108 E6............6°04'S 154°55'E

Bouillon Belgium 42 E2 ....49°48'N 5°06'E
Boujdour Western Sahara 84 C4 ....26°08'N 14°28'W
Boulder U.S. 62 E5 ....40°02'N 105°16'W
Boulogne-Billancourt France 44 E6 ....48°50'N 2°15'E
Boulogne-sur-Mer France 44 D7 ....50°43'N 1°37'E
Bounty Islands New Zealand 109 G2 ....47°40'S 179°02'E
Bourg-en-Bresse France 44 F5 ....46°12'N 5°14'E
Bourges France 44 E5 ....47°05'N 2°24'E
Bourke Australia 108 D3 ....30°07'S 145°54'E
Bourne England 9 E3 ....52°46'N 0°23'W
Bournemouth England 8 D1 ....50°43'N 1°53'W
Bournemouth, Christchurch and Poole d. England 21 E2
....50°45'N 1°50'W
Bou Saâda Algeria 48 D4 ....35°13'N 4°11'E
Bow r. Canada 62 D6 ....49°58'N 111°41'W
Bowes England 13 E3 ....54°31'N 2°00'W
Bowland, Forest of England 12 E2 ....53°59'N 2°33'W
Boxtel Neth. 42 E4 ....51°35'N 5°20'E
Boyabat Turkey 51 K5 ....41°28'N 34°46'E
Boyle Ireland 18 C3 ....53°58'N 8°18'W
Boyne r. Ireland 18 E3 ....53°43'N 6°14'W
Bozeman U.S. 62 D6 ....45°42'N 111°02'W
Bozüyük Turkey 51 I4 ....39°55'N 30°01'E
Braan r. Scotland 15 F4 ....56°34'N 3°36'W
Brabant Wallon d. Belgium 42 D3 ....50°39'N 4°35'E
Brač i. Croatia 50 B6 ....43°17'N 16°31'E
Bracadale, Loch i. Scotland 16 C2 ....57°21'N 6°33'W
Bräcke Sweden 43 C3 ....62°46'N 15°26'E
Brackley England 8 D3 ....52°02'N 1°08'W
Bracknell England 8 E2 ....51°25'N 0°45'W
Bracknell Forest d. England 21 E2 ....51°24'N 0°45'W
Brad Romania 50 E8 ....46°07'N 22°48'E
Bradford England 13 F2 ....53°48'N 1°45'W
Bradford-on-Avon England 8 C2 ....51°21'N 2°15'W
Braemar Scotland 17 F2 ....57°00'N 3°24'W
Braga Portugal 45 A4 ....41°33'N 8°26'W
Bragança Brazil 72 E6 ....1°00'S 46°49'W
Bragança Portugal 45 B4 ....41°49'N 6°45'W
Brahmapur India 96 F4 ....19°21'N 84°52'E
Brahmaputra r. China/India 98 G2 ....23°36'N 90°31'E
Brăila Romania 51 G7 ....45°17'N 27°58'E
Braintree England 9 F2 ....51°53'N 0°33'E
Brämön i. Sweden 43 D3 ....62°13'N 17°45'E
Brampton England 12 E3 ....54°57'N 2°44'W
Branco r. Brazil 72 C7 ....1°18'S 61°52'W
Brandenburg an der Havel Germany 46 E5 52°25'N 12°34'E
Brandesburton England 13 G2 ....53°55'N 0°18'W
Brandon Canada 60 I2 ....49°51'N 99°57'W
Brandon England 9 F3 ....52°27'N 0°37'E
Brandon Head Ireland 18 A2 ....52°17'N 10°13'W
Brandon Mountain hill Ireland 18 A2 ....52°14'N 10°15'W
Bransgore England 8 D1 ....50°47'N 1°44'W
Brasília Brazil 72 E5 ....15°49'S 47°55'W
Brașov Romania 50 F7 ....45°40'N 25°36'E
Bratislava Slovakia 46 G3 ....48°09'N 17°06'E
Bratsk Russia 55 L3 ....56°16'N 101°41'E
Braunau am Inn Austria 46 E3 ....48°16'N 13°02'E
Braunschweig Germany 46 D5 ....52°17'N 10°32'E
Braunton England 11 C3 ....51°06'N 4°10'W
Brawley U.S. 62 D6 ....32°58'N 115°32'W
Bray Ireland 18 E3 ....53°12'N 6°07'W
Bray Head Ireland 18 A1 ....51°52'N 10°25'W
Brazil S. America 73 D6 ....29°58'S 54°33'W
Brazil Basin f. Atlantic Oc. 116 E2 ....15°00'S 30°00'W
Brazilian Highlands mts Brazil 72 E5 ....17°00'S 48°00'W
Brazos r. U.S. 62 G2 ....28°52'N 95°25'W
Brazzaville Congo 84 F1 ....4°17'S 15°11'E
Breamish r. England 13 E4 ....55°41'N 2°13'W
Brechin Scotland 17 G1 ....56°44'N 2°39'W
Breckland f. England 9 F3 ....52°28'N 0°39'E
Břeclav Czechia 46 G3 ....48°46'N 16°53'E
Brecon Wales 10 D3 ....51°57'N 3°24'W
Brecon Beacons f. Wales 10 D3 ....51°53'N 3°26'W
Breda Neth. 42 D4 ....51°35'N 4°46'E
Breiðafjörður b. Iceland 43 W2 ....65°03'N 24°07'W
Breiðdalsvík Iceland 43 Z2 ....64°48'N 14°02'W
Bremen Germany 46 C5 ....53°05'N 8°51'E
Bremerhaven Germany 46 C5 ....53°33'N 8°35'E
Brenner Pass Austria/Italy 46 D2 ....46°59'N 11°32'E
Brentwood England 9 F2 ....51°37'N 0°19'E
Brescia Italy 46 D1 ....45°32'N 10°13'E
Bressanone Italy 46 D2 ....46°43'N 11°40'E
Bressay i. Scotland 17 H5 ....60°16'N 1°18'W
Bressuire France 44 C5 ....46°50'N 0°30'W
Brest Belarus 47 J5 ....52°05'N 23°40'E
Brest France 44 A6 ....48°24'N 4°29'W
Bretton England 10 E5 ....53°10'N 2°58'W
Bria C.A.R. 85 G2 ....6°32'N 21°59'E
Briançon France 44 G4 ....44°54'N 6°38'E
Brianne, Llyn resr Wales 10 D4 ....52°08'N 3°45'W
Bride r. Ireland 18 D2 ....52°04'N 7°52'W
Bridgend Wales 10 D3 ....51°30'N 3°35'W
Bridgend d. Wales 21 D2 ....51°34'N 3°33'W
Bridgeport U.S. 63 L5 ....41°12'N 73°12'W
Bridgetown Barbados 67 M3 ....13°05'N 59°36'W
Bridgnorth England 8 C3 ....52°32'N 2°25'W
Bridgwater England 11 D3 ....51°08'N 3°00'W
Bridgwater Bay England 11 D3 ....51°16'N 3°19'W
Bridlington England 13 G3 ....54°05'N 0°12'W
Bridlington Bay England 13 G3 ....54°03'N 0°07'W
Bridport England 8 C1 ....50°44'N 2°45'W
Brig Switz. 46 B2 ....46°19'N 7°59'E
Brigg England 13 G2 ....53°33'N 0°29'W
Brighstone England 8 D1 ....50°39'N 1°23'W
Brightlingsea England 9 G2 ....51°49'N 1°01'E
Brighton England 9 E1 ....50°49'N 0°08'W
Brighton and Hove d. England 21 E2 ....50°51'N 0°08'W
Brindisi Italy 49 G5 ....40°38'N 17°56'E
Brisbane Australia 108 E4 ....27°33'S 153°03'E
Bristol England 8 C2 ....51°27'N 2°35'W
Bristol d. England 21 D2 ....51°28'N 2°36'W
Bristol U.S. 63 J4 ....36°36'N 82°10'W
Bristol Bay U.S. 60 B3 ....57°22'N 161°29'W
Bristol Channel est. England 8 B2 ....51°20'N 4°16'W
British Columbia d. Canada 60 F3 ....54°12'N 125°48'W
British Empire Range mts Canada 61 J6 ....82°22'N 80°08'W
British Indian Ocean Territory Indian Oc. 87 E1
....6°34'S 72°51'E
British Isles Europe 116 E4 ....54°00'N 5°00'W
Briton Ferry Wales 10 D3 ....51°38'N 3°49'W
Britstown S. Africa 83 B1 ....30°35'S 23°30'E
Brittany f. France 44 B6 ....48°10'N 3°22'W
Brittas Bay Ireland 18 A4 ....52°52'N 6°03'W
Brive-la-Gaillarde France 44 D4 ....45°10'N 1°32'E
Brixham England 11 D2 ....50°24'N 3°31'W
Brno Czechia 46 G3 ....49°11'N 16°37'E
Broad r. U.S. 63 J3 ....34°00'N 81°04'W

Broadback r. Canada 63 K7 ....51°21'N 78°50'W
Broad Bay Scotland 16 C3 ....58°15'N 6°15'W
Broad Law hill Scotland 15 F3 ....55°30'N 3°21'W
Broadstairs England 9 G2 ....51°22'N 1°26'E
Broadway England 8 D3 ....52°02'N 1°51'W
Broadwey England 8 C1 ....50°39'N 2°28'W
Broadwindsor England 8 C1 ....50°49'N 2°48'W
Brockenhurst England 8 D1 ....50°49'N 1°34'W
Brock Island Canada 60 G5 ....77°53'N 114°21'W
Brodeur Peninsula Canada 61 J5 ....71°50'N 88°32'W
Brodick Scotland 14 D3 ....55°35'N 5°09'W
Brody Ukraine 47 K4 ....50°05'N 25°09'E
Broken Hill town Australia 108 D3 ....31°55'S 141°27'E
Bromley England 9 F2 ....51°24'N 0°01'E
Bromsgrove England 8 C3 ....52°20'N 2°04'W
Bromyard England 8 C3 ....52°11'N 2°30'W
Brønderslev Denmark 43 B2 ....57°17'N 9°58'E
Brønnøysund Norway 43 C4 ....65°28'N 12°12'E
Brooke England 9 G3 ....52°33'N 1°23'E
Brooke's Point town Phil. 102 F5 ....8°50'N 117°51'E
Brookings U.S. 62 G5 ....44°19'N 96°44'W
Brooks Canada 62 D7 ....50°35'N 111°54'W
Brooks Range mts U.S. 60 D4 ....69°18'N 144°41'W
Broom, Loch inlet Scotland 16 D2 ....57°56'N 5°19'W
Broome Australia 108 B5 ....17°57'S 122°14'E
Brora Scotland 17 F3 ....58°01'N 3°51'W
Brora r. Scotland 17 F3 ....58°01'N 3°50'W
Brosna r. Ireland 18 D3 ....53°13'N 7°57'W
Brotton England 13 G3 ....54°34'N 0°56'W
Brough Cumb. England 13 E3 ....54°32'N 2°19'W
Brough E. Yorks. England 13 G2 ....53°44'N 0°34'W
Brough Head Scotland 17 F4 ....59°08'N 3°21'W
Brough Ness pt Scotland 17 G3 ....58°44'N 2°58'W
Broughshane Northern Ireland 14 C2 ......54°54'N 6°12'W
Brownhills England 8 D3 ....52°39'N 1°56'W
Broxburn Scotland 15 F3 ....55°56'N 3°28'W
Bruay-la-Buissière France 42 B3 ....50°29'N 2°33'E
Brue r. England 8 C2 ....51°13'N 2°59'W
Brugge Belgium 42 C4 ....51°12'N 3°15'E
Brunei Asia 102 E4 ....5°06'N 114°18'E
Brunflo Sweden 43 C3 ....63°05'N 14°51'E
Brunswick U.S. 63 J3 ....31°09'N 81°30'W
Brussels Belgium 42 D3 ....50°50'N 4°21'E
Bruton England 8 C2 ....51°07'N 2°27'W
Bryansk Russia 53 D3 ....53°15'N 34°23'E
Bryher i. England 11 A1 ....49°57'N 6°23'W
Bryn-mawr Wales 10 D3 ....51°48'N 3°10'W
Brynamman Wales 10 D3 ....51°49'N 3°52'W
Buca Turkey 50 G4 ....38°22'N 27°11'E
Bucaramanga Colombia 72 B7 ....7°05'N 73°09'W
Bucharest Romania 50 G7 ....44°26'N 26°06'E
Buckhaven Scotland 15 F4 ....56°11'N 3°02'W
Buckie Scotland 17 G2 ....57°41'N 2°58'W
Buckingham England 8 E2 ....51°59'N 0°59'W
Buckinghamshire d. England 21 E2 ....51°47'N 0°56'W
Buckley Wales 10 D5 ....53°10'N 3°05'W
Budapest Hungary 46 H2 ....47°30'N 19°04'E
Buddon Ness pt Scotland 15 G4 ....56°28'N 2°43'W
Bude England 11 C2 ....50°50'N 4°32'W
Bude Bay England 11 C2 ....50°50'N 4°38'W
Budennovsk Russia 53 E2 ....44°45'N 44°06'E
Buenaventura Colombia 72 B7 ....3°52'N 77°00'W
Buenos Aires Argentina 73 D3 ....34°36'S 58°24'W
Buenos Aires, Lago l. Argentina/Chile 73 B2
....46°31'S 72°13'W
Buffalo N. Y. U.S. 63 K5 ....42°53'N 78°52'W
Buffalo Wyo. U.S. 62 E5 ....44°20'N 106°41'W
Bug r. Poland 47 J5 ....51°30'N 23°39'E
Buguruslan Russia 53 F3 ....53°35'N 52°23'E
Builth Wells Wales 10 D4 ....52°09'N 3°24'W
Bujumbura Burundi 85 G1 ....3°24'S 29°22'E
Bukavu Dem. Rep. Congo 83 B4 ....2°30'S 28°49'E
Bukittinggi Indonesia 102 C3 ....0°15'S 100°20'E
Bukoba Tanzania 83 C4 ....1°18'S 31°48'E
Bula Indonesia 103 I3 ....3°06'S 130°28'E
Bulawayo Zimbabwe 83 B2 ....20°09'S 28°36'E
Bulgan Mongolia 99 I7 ....48°48'N 103°28'E
Bulgaria Europe 50 F6 ....42°51'N 25°15'E
Bulun Russia 55 N5 ....70°59'N 127°16'E
Bunbury Australia 108 A3 ....33°20'S 115°36'E
Bunclody Ireland 18 E2 ....52°39'N 6°39'W
Buncrana Ireland 14 D5 ....55°09'N 7°27'W
Bundaberg Australia 108 E4 ....24°52'S 152°22'E
Bundoran Ireland 18 C4 ....54°28'N 8°18'W
Bungay England 9 G3 ....52°27'N 1°26'E
Buon Ma Thuot Vietnam 102 D6 ....12°38'N 108°05'E
Buraydah Saudi Arabia 94 F5 ....26°20'N 43°57'E
Burbage England 8 D2 ....51°21'N 1°40'W
Burdur Turkey 51 I3 ....37°43'N 30°17'E
Bure r. England 9 G3 ....52°37'N 1°43'E
Burē Ethiopia 85 H3 ....10°50'N 36°57'E
Burford England 8 D2 ....51°48'N 1°38'W
Burgas Bulgaria 50 G6 ....42°30'N 27°28'E
Burgess Hill town England 9 E1 ....50°57'N 0°08'W
Burghausen Germany 46 E3 ....48°10'N 12°50'E
Burghead Scotland 17 F2 ....57°42'N 3°29'W
Burgh le Marsh England 13 H2 ....53°10'N 0°14'E
Burgos Spain 45 D5 ....42°21'N 3°41'W
Burhanpur India 96 E5 ....21°18'N 76°14'E
Burkina Faso Africa 84 D3 ....12°15'N 1°18'W
Burlington Colo. U.S. 62 F4 ....39°19'N 102°17'W
Burlington Iowa U.S. 63 H5 ....40°49'N 91°06'W
Burlington Vt. U.S. 63 L5 ....44°28'N 73°13'W
Burma Asia 97 I5 ....22°37'N 95°02'E
Burnham England 8 E2 ....51°32'N 0°39'W
Burnham Market England 9 F3 ....52°57'N 0°44'E
Burnham-on-Crouch England 9 F2 ....51°38'N 0°49'E
Burnham-on-Sea England 8 C2 ....51°14'N 2°59'W
Burnie Australia 108 D2 ....41°03'S 145°57'E
Burniston England 13 G3 ....54°19'N 0°27'W
Burnley England 13 E2 ....53°47'N 2°15'W
Burns U.S. 62 C5 ....43°36'N 119°01'W
Burns Lake town Canada 60 F3 ....54°15'N 125°46'W
Burntisland Scotland 15 F4 ....56°04'N 3°14'W
Burntwood Green England 8 D3 ....52°41'N 1°54'W
Burra i. Scotland 17 H5 ....60°05'N 1°12'W
Burray i. Scotland 17 G3 ....58°51'N 2°53'W
Burro, Serranías del mts Mexico 66 D6 ...29°02'N 102°00'W
Burrow Head Scotland 14 E2 ....54°41'N 4°23'W
Burry Inlet Wales 10 C3 ....51°38'N 4°18'W
Burry Port Wales 10 C3 ....51°41'N 4°16'W
Bursa Turkey 51 H5 ....40°14'N 29°03'E
Bûr Safâjah Egypt 49 J2 ....26°45'N 33°55'E
Burscough Bridge England 12 E2 ....53°36'N 2°51'W
Burton-in-Kendal England 12 E3 ....54°11'N 2°43'W
Burton Latimer England 8 E3 ....52°22'N 0°41'W
Burton upon Trent England 8 D3 ....52°48'N 1°39'W

Buru i. Indonesia 103 H3 ....3°24'S 126°35'E
Burundi Africa 85 H1 ....3°36'S 30°03'E
Burwash Landing Canada 60 E4 ....61°21'N 138°58'W
Burwell England 9 F3 ....52°16'N 0°20'E
Burwick Scotland 17 G3 ....58°45'N 2°58'W
Bury England 13 E2 ....53°36'N 2°18'W
Bury St Edmunds England 9 F3 ....52°15'N 0°44'E
Busan S. Korea 99 N5 ....35°09'N 129°03'E
Bush r. Northern Ireland 14 C3 ....55°13'N 6°31'W
Bushmills Northern Ireland 14 C3 ....55°12'N 6°31'W
Buta Dem. Rep. Congo 83 B5 ....2°49'N 24°45'E
Bute i. Scotland 14 D3 ....55°49'N 5°06'W
Bute, Sound of str. Scotland 14 D3 ....55°44'N 5°19'W
Buton i. Indonesia 103 G3 ....4°57'S 123°00'E
Butte U.S. 62 D6 ....46°01'N 112°32'W
Butterworth Malaysia 102 C5 ....5°22'N 100°22'E
Buttevant Ireland 18 C2 ....52°14'N 8°40'W
Butt of Lewis hd Scotland 16 C3 ....58°32'N 6°17'W
Butuan Phil. 103 H5 ....8°56'N 125°32'E
Buxoro Uzbekistan 54 H1 ....39°46'N 64°25'E
Buxton England 13 F2 ....53°16'N 1°55'W
Buy Russia 52 E3 ....58°29'N 41°32'E
Buyr Nuur l. Mongolia 99 L7 ....47°47'N 117°53'E
Büyükmenderes r. Turkey 51 G3 ....37°28'N 27°11'E
Buzău Romania 50 G7 ....45°09'N 26°48'E
Buzuluk Russia 53 F3 ....52°45'N 52°09'E
Byarezina r. Belarus 47 K5 ....53°48'N 25°58'E
Byaroza Belarus 47 K5 ....52°32'N 24°59'E
Bydgoszcz Poland 46 H5 ....53°08'N 18°02'E
Byfield England 8 D3 ....52°11'N 1°14'W
Bylot Island Canada 61 K5 ....73°07'N 79°01'W
Byrranga, Gory mts Russia 55 K5 ....74°25'N 99°53'E
Bytom Poland 46 H4 ....50°21'N 18°55'E

C

Cabanatuan Phil. 103 G7 ....15°31'N 120°58'E
Caban Coch Reservoir Wales 10 D4 ....52°15'N 3°35'W
Cabimas Venezuela 72 B8 ....10°23'N 71°26'W
Cabinda Angola 84 F1 ....5°33'S 12°15'E
Cabo Frio Brazil 73 E4 ....22°51'S 42°02'W
Cabonga, Réservoir Canada 63 K6 ....47°21'N 76°32'W
Cabora Bassa, Lake resr Mozambique 83 C3
....15°46'S 31°11'E
Caborca Mexico 66 B7 ....30°44'N 112°09'W
Cabot Strait Canada 61 L2 ....47°39'N 60°16'W
Cabrera, Sierra de la mts Spain 45 B5 .....42°13'N 6°51'W
Cabriel r. Spain 45 E4 ....39°16'N 1°04'W
Cachimbo, Serra do hills Brazil 72 D6 .....9°18'S 54°11'W
Cachoeiro de Itapemirim Brazil 73 E4 .....20°51'S 41°08'W
Cadillac U.S. 63 I5 ....44°14'N 85°23'W
Cádiz Spain 45 B2 ....36°32'N 6°17'W
Cádiz, Golfo de g. Spain 45 B2 ....36°44'N 7°14'W
Caen France 44 C6 ....49°11'N 0°21'W
Caer-went Wales 10 E3 ....51°37'N 2°46'W
Caerleon Wales 10 E3 ....51°37'N 2°57'W
Caernarfon Wales 10 C5 ....53°08'N 4°16'W
Caernarfon Bay Wales 10 C5 ....53°06'N 4°34'W
Caerphilly Wales 10 D3 ....51°35'N 3°13'W
Caerphilly d. Wales 21 D2 ....51°38'N 3°11'W
Cagayan de Oro Phil. 103 G5 ....8°29'N 124°39'E
Cagliari Italy 48 E4 ....39°13'N 9°08'E
Caha Mountains hills Ireland 18 B1 ....51°41'N 9°44'W
Cahersiveen Ireland 18 A1 ....51°57'N 10°13'W
Cahore Point Ireland 18 E2 ....52°33'N 6°11'W
Cahors France 44 D4 ....44°28'N 1°26'E
Cahul Moldova 51 H7 ....45°54'N 28°12'E
Caia Mozambique 83 C3 ....17°50'S 35°19'E
Caiabis, Serra dos hills Brazil 72 D5 ....12°46'S 56°21'W
Caicos Islands Turks and Caicos Is 67 J5 .21°45'N 71°53'W
Caimodorro mt. Spain 45 E4 ....40°32'N 1°40'W
Cairn Gorm mt. Scotland 17 F2 ....57°07'N 3°39'W
Cairngorm Mountains Scotland 17 F2 .....57°08'N 3°45'W
Cairnryan Scotland 14 D2 ....54°59'N 5°02'W
Cairns Australia 108 D5 ....16°54'S 145°45'E
Cairn Toul mt. Scotland 17 F2 ....57°04'N 3°43'W
Cairo Egypt 85 H5 ....30°01'N 31°15'E
Caister-on-Sea England 9 G3 ....52°39'N 1°44'E
Caistor England 13 G2 ....53°30'N 0°19'W
Caithness f. Scotland 17 F3 ....58°24'N 3°22'W
Cajamarca Peru 72 B6 ....7°11'S 78°31'W
Calabar Nigeria 84 E2 ....4°59'N 8°19'E
Calafat Romania 50 E6 ....43°59'N 22°57'E
Calais France 44 D7 ....50°57'N 1°51'E
Calais U.S. 63 M6 ....45°10'N 67°18'W
Calama Chile 73 C4 ....22°29'S 68°56'W
Calamian Group is Phil. 102 F6 ....11°59'N 119°58'E
Calamocha Spain 45 E4 ....40°56'N 1°17'W
Calanscio Sand Sea des. Libya 49 H3 .....30°11'N 22°22'E
Calapan Phil. 103 G6 ....13°24'N 121°11'E
Călărași Romania 50 G7 ....44°12'N 27°19'E
Calatayud Spain 45 E4 ....41°22'N 1°37'W
Calbayog Phil. 103 G6 ....12°05'N 124°37'E
Caldas da Rainha Portugal 45 A3 ....39°24'N 9°08'W
Caldey Island Wales 10 C3 ....51°38'N 4°40'W
Calf of Man i. Isle of Man 12 C3 ....54°04'N 4°48'W
Calgary Canada 60 G3 ....51°02'N 114°04'W
Cali Colombia 72 B7 ....3°25'N 76°28'W
Caliente U.S. 62 D4 ....37°37'N 114°31'W
California d. U.S. 62 B5 ....41°35'N 122°50'W
California, Gulf of Mexico 66 B7 ....30°51'N 113°58'W
Callan Ireland 18 D2 ....52°32'N 7°24'W
Callander Scotland 14 E4 ....56°15'N 4°13'W
Callanish Scotland 16 C3 ....58°12'N 6°45'W
Callao Peru 72 B5 ....12°04'S 77°08'W
Callington England 11 C2 ....50°30'N 4°19'W
Calne England 8 C2 ....51°26'N 2°00'W
Caltagirone Italy 48 F4 ....37°14'N 14°32'E
Caltanissetta Italy 48 F4 ....37°30'N 14°03'E
Calvi France 44 H3 ....42°34'N 8°45'E
Camaçari Brazil 73 F5 ....12°42'S 38°20'W
Camagüey Cuba 67 I5 ....21°23'N 77°54'W
Camagüey, Archipiélago de is Cuba 67 I5 22°44'N 78°34'W
Ca Mau, Mui c. Vietnam 102 C5 ....8°35'N 104°45'E
Camberley England 8 E2 ....51°20'N 0°44'W
Cambodia Asia 102 C6 ....13°05'N 105°10'E
Camborne England 11 B2 ....50°13'N 5°18'W
Cambrai France 42 C3 ....50°10'N 3°14'E
Cambrian Mountains Wales 10 D4 ....52°37'N 3°40'W
Cambridge England 9 F3 ....52°12'N 0°08'E
Cambridge Bay town Canada 60 H4 ....69°02'N 105°14'W
Cambridgeshire d. England 21 F3 ....52°25'N 0°02'E
Camden England 11 C2 ....52°00'N 0°27'W
Cameroon Africa 84 F2 ....5°45'N 12°41'E

Cameroon Highlands f. Cameroon/Nigeria 84 E2
....5°59'N 10°49'E
Cameroun, Mont vol. Cameroon 84 E2 ...4°12'N 9°12'E
Cametá Brazil 72 E6 ....2°13'S 49°30'W
Campbell River town Canada 60 F3 ....50°01'N 125°14'W
Campbeltown Scotland 14 D3 ....55°25'N 5°36'W
Campeche Mexico 66 F4 ....19°51'N 90°30'W
Campeche d. Mexico 66 F4 ....18°53'N 90°28'W
Campeche, Bahía de g. Mexico 66 F4 ....19°30'N 93°30'W
Campina Grande Brazil 72 F6 ....7°14'S 35°49'W
Campinas Brazil 73 E4 ....22°55'S 47°04'W
Campo Grande Brazil 73 D4 ....20°24'S 54°34'W
Campos dos Goytacazes Brazil 73 E4 .....21°45'S 41°20'W
Câmpulung Moldovenesc Romania 47 K2 47°32'N 25°30'E
Camrose Canada 62 D7 ....53°00'N 112°50'W
Çan Turkey 50 G5 ....40°02'N 27°02'E
Canada N. America 60 F4 ....46°44'N 81°59'W
Canadian r. U.S. 62 G4 ....35°11'N 95°52'W
Canadian Shield f. N. America 56 F4 ....50°00'N 80°00'W
Çanakkale Turkey 50 G5 ....40°08'N 26°23'E
Canarreos, Archipiélago de los is Cuba 67 H4
....21°44'N 82°12'W
Canary Islands N. Atlantic Oc. 45 X2 ....30°08'N 18°27'W
Canaveral, Cape U.S. 63 J2 ....28°26'N 80°36'W
Canberra Australia 108 D3 ....35°19'S 149°09'E
Cancún Mexico 66 G5 ....21°10'N 86°50'W
Caniapiscau r. Canada 61 L3 ....57°39'N 69°25'W
Caniapiscau, Lac l. Canada 61 K3 ....54°21'N 70°31'W
Canisp hill Scotland 16 D3 ....58°07'N 5°03'W
Çankaya Turkey 51 J4 ....39°53'N 32°45'E
Çankırı Turkey 51 J5 ....40°36'N 33°36'E
Canna i. Scotland 16 C2 ....57°04'N 6°34'W
Cannes France 44 G3 ....43°33'N 7°01'E
Cannock England 8 C3 ....52°41'N 2°02'W
Canora Canada 62 F7 ....51°39'N 102°26'W
Cantabrian Mountains Spain 45 C5 ....43°07'N 4°13'W
Canterbury England 9 G2 ....51°17'N 1°05'E
Can Tho Vietnam 102 D6 ....10°01'N 105°46'E
Canvey Island England 9 F2 ....51°31'N 0°35'E
Cao Bang Vietnam 102 D8 ....22°41'N 106°12'E
Capbreton France 44 C3 ....43°39'N 1°26'W
Cape Breton Island Canada 61 L2 ....46°45'N 60°24'W
Capel St Mary England 9 G3 ....52°00'N 1°03'E
Cape Town S. Africa 83 A1 ....33°57'S 18°28'E
Cape Verde N. Atlantic Oc. 84 B3 ....15°47'N 24°31'W
Cape York Peninsula Australia 108 D5 .....12°33'S 142°33'E
Cap-Haïtien Haiti 67 J4 ....19°42'N 72°15'W
Capital Hill town N. Mariana Is 103 L7 ....15°12'N 145°44'E
Capraia, Isola di i. Italy 48 D5 ....43°03'N 9°49'E
Capricorn Channel Australia 108 E4 ....22°20'S 151°46'E
Caprivi Strip f. Namibia 83 B3 ....18°11'S 21°44'E
Caquetá r. Colombia 72 C6 ....1°27'S 69°25'W
Caracal Romania 50 F7 ....44°07'N 24°22'E
Caracas Venezuela 72 C8 ....10°28'N 66°59'W
Caransebeș Romania 50 E7 ....45°25'N 22°14'E
Caratasca, Laguna de lagoon Honduras 67 H4
....15°20'N 83°57'W
Caratinga Brazil 73 E5 ....19°45'S 42°04'W
Caravaca de la Cruz Spain 45 E3 ....38°07'N 1°51'W
Carbonara, Capo c. Italy 48 E4 ....39°06'N 9°31'E
Carcassonne France 44 E3 ....43°13'N 2°21'E
Cardiff Wales 11 D3 ....51°29'N 3°11'W
Cardiff d. Wales 21 D2 ....51°30'N 3°12'W
Cardigan Wales 10 C4 ....52°05'N 4°40'W
Cardigan Bay Wales 10 C4 ....52°33'N 4°32'W
Carei Romania 47 J2 ....47°41'N 22°28'E
Carey, Lake Australia 108 B4 ....28°57'S 122°22'E
Caribbean Sea N. Atlantic Oc. 67 H4 ....19°03'N 83°05'W
Caribou Mountains Canada 60 G3 ....59°02'N 115°22'W
Cark Mountain hill Ireland 14 B2 ....54°53'N 7°52'W
Carletonville S. Africa 83 B2 ....26°21'S 27°22'E
Carlingford Lough inlet Ireland/U.K. 18 E4 54°05'N 6°14'W
Carlisle England 12 E3 ....54°54'N 2°56'W
Carlow Ireland 18 E2 ....52°50'N 6°56'W
Carlow d. Ireland 18 E2 ....52°43'N 6°52'W
Carluke Scotland 15 F3 ....55°44'N 3°50'W
Carmacks Canada 60 E4 ....62°05'N 136°17'W
Carmarthen Wales 10 C3 ....51°51'N 4°19'W
Carmarthen Bay Wales 10 C3 ....51°38'N 4°32'W
Carmarthenshire d. Wales 21 C2 ....51°57'N 4°19'W
Carmel Head Wales 10 C5 ....53°25'N 4°34'W
Carmen, Isla del i. Mexico 66 B6 ....25°59'N 111°09'W
Carnac France 44 B5 ....47°35'N 3°04'W
Càrn Dearg hill Scotland 17 F2 ....57°06'N 4°16'W
Carndonagh Ireland 14 D3 ....55°15'N 7°15'W
Carnedd Llywelyn mt. Wales 10 D5 ....53°10'N 3°58'W
Carnedd y Filiast England 10 D4 ....53°10'N 3°45'W
Carnegie, Lake Australia 108 B4 ....26°10'S 122°5'E
Carn Eighe mt. Scotland 16 D2 ....57°17'N 5°07'W
Carnforth England 12 E3 ....54°08'N 2°46'W
Carnic Alps mts Italy 46 E2 ....46°40'N 12°4'E
Car Nicobar Island i. India 97 H2 ....9°10'N 92°4'E
Carnlough Northern Ireland 14 D2 ....54°59'N 5°59'W
Càrn Mòr hill Scotland 17 F2 ....57°15'N 3°13'W
Carn nan Gabhar mt. Scotland 17 F1 ......56°58'N 3°42'W
Carnot, Cape Australia 108 C3 ....34°55'S 135°33'E
Carnoustie Scotland 15 G4 ....56°30'N 2°42'W
Carnsore Point Ireland 18 E2 ....52°10'N 6°22'W
Caroline Islands N. Pacific Oc. 117 I3 ......6°35'N 144°2'E
Carpathian Mountains Europe 47 J3 ....48°45'N 23°4'E
Carpentaria, Gulf of Australia 108 C5 ......14°06'S 139°0'E
Carpentras France 44 F4 ....44°04'N 5°0'E
Carra, Lough l. Ireland 18 B4 ....53°41'N 9°4'W
Carrauntoohil mt. Ireland 18 B1 ....51°59'N 9°44'W
Carrara Italy 46 D1 ....44°04'N 10°0'E
Carrickfergus Northern Ireland 14 D2 .....54°43'N 5°48'W
Carrickmacross Ireland 18 E3 ....53°59'N 6°43'W
Carrick-on-Shannon Ireland 18 C3 ....53°57'N 8°05'W
Carrick-on-Suir Ireland 18 D2 ....52°21'N 7°25'W
Carron r. Falk. Scotland 15 F4 ....56°02'N 3°44'W
Carron r. High. Scotland 16 E2 ....57°53'N 4°22'W
Carson City U.S. 62 C4 ....39°10'N 119°46'W
Carrowmore Lake Ireland 18 B4 ....54°11'N 9°47'W
Carson City U.S. 62 C4 ....39°10'N 119°46'W
Carspairn Scotland 14 E3 ....55°13'N 4°16'W
Cartagena Colombia 72 B8 ....10°23'N 75°33'W
Cartagena Spain 45 E2 ....37°36'N 0°59'W
Carteret France 11 Z9 ....49°23'N 1°47'W
Carteret, Cap de c. France 11 Z9 ....49°22'N 1°48'W
Carterton England 8 D2 ....51°46'N 1°36'W
Cartmel England 12 E3 ....54°12'N 2°57'W
Caruaru Brazil 72 F6 ....8°13'S 35°52'W
Carvin France 42 B3 ....50°29'N 2°5'E
Casablanca Morocco 84 D5 ....33°33'N 7°34'W
Casa Grande U.S. 62 D3 ....32°53'N 111°45'W
Cascade Range mts Canada/U.S. 60 F2
....41°49'N 122°2'W
Cascavel Brazil 73 D4 ....24°55'S 53°28'W

shel Ireland 18 D2 ...... 52°31'N 7°53'W
sper U.S. 62 E5 ...... 42°52'N 106°20'W
spian Depression f. Kazakhstan/Russia 53 E2
　　44°15'N 45°47'E
spian Sea l. Asia/Europe 53 F2 ...... 42°00'N 51°00'E
ssiar Mountains Canada 60 E3 ...... 59°40'N 130°31'W
ssley r. Scotland 16 E2 ...... 57°58'N 4°34'W
stanhal Brazil 72 E6 ...... 1°18'S 47°54'W
stelló de la Plana Spain 45 E3 ...... 39°59'N 0°02'W
stlebar Ireland 18 B3 ...... 53°51'N 9°17'W
stlebay Scotland 16 B1 ...... 56°57'N 7°29'W
stleblayney Ireland 18 E4 ...... 54°07'N 6°43'W
stle Cary England 8 C2 ...... 51°05'N 2°31'W
stlecomer Ireland 18 D2 ...... 52°48'N 7°13'W
stleconnell Ireland 18 C2 ...... 52°43'N 8°30'W
stlederg Northern Ireland 14 B2 ...... 54°42'N 7°35'W
stle Donington England 8 D3 ...... 52°50'N 1°20'W
stle Douglas Scotland 15 F2 ...... 54°56'N 3°56'W
stleford England 13 F2 ...... 53°43'N 1°21'W
stleisland Ireland 18 B2 ...... 52°14'N 9°27'W
stletown Isle of Man 12 C3 ...... 54°05'N 4°39'W
stres France 44 E3 ...... 43°36'N 2°14'E
stries St Lucia 67 L3 ...... 14°00'N 60°59'W
stro Verde Portugal 45 A2 ...... 37°42'N 8°05'W
talonia f. Spain 45 F4 ...... 41°50'N 1°30'E
tamarca Argentina 73 C4 ...... 28°26'S 65°45'W
tanduanes i. Phil. 103 G6 ...... 13°46'N 124°14'E
tania Italy 48 G4 ...... 37°30'N 15°05'E
tanzaro Italy 49 G4 ...... 38°55'N 16°36'E
tarman Phil. 103 G6 ...... 12°29'N 124°38'E
terham England 9 E2 ...... 51°17'N 0°05'W
t Island Bahamas 67 I5 ...... 24°28'N 75°30'W
toche, Cabo c. Mexico 66 G5 ...... 21°37'N 87°06'W
tterick England 13 F3 ...... 54°23'N 1°38'W
uca r. Colombia 67 I2 ...... 8°54'N 74°29'W
ucaia Brazil 72 F6 ...... 3°42'S 38°42'W
ucasus mts Asia/Europe 53 E2 ...... 43°53'N 40°00'E
udry France 42 C3 ...... 50°07'N 3°25'E
useway Coast and Glens d. Northern Ireland 20 B4
　　54°58'N 6°28'W
van Ireland 18 D3 ...... 53°59'N 7°22'W
van d. Ireland 18 D3 ...... 53°57'N 7°15'W
wston England 9 G3 ...... 52°46'N 1°10'E
xias Brazil 72 E6 ...... 4°54'S 43°19'W
xias do Sul Brazil 73 D4 ...... 29°13'S 51°11'W
yenne French Guiana 72 D7 ...... 4°53'N 52°21'W
yman Brac i. Cayman Is 67 I4 ...... 19°43'N 79°48'W
yman Islands Central America 67 H4 ...... 19°31'N 81°15'W
ou Phil. 103 G6 ...... 10°17'N 123°55'E
ou i. Phil. 103 G6 ...... 10°26'N 123°53'E
dar i. 63 J5 ...... 43°40'N 84°23'W
dar City U.S. 62 D4 ...... 37°41'N 113°04'W
dar Rapids town U.S. 63 H5 ...... 41°59'N 91°40'W
dros, Isla i. Mexico 66 A6 ...... 28°11'N 115°20'W
gléd Hungary 46 H2 ...... 47°10'N 19°48'E
lebes i. Indonesia 102 D3 ...... 2°01'S 120°28'E
lebes Sea Indonesia/Phil. 102 G4 ...... 3°03'N 121°10'E
je Slovenia 46 F2 ...... 46°14'N 15°15'E
le Germany 46 F5 ...... 52°38'N 10°05'E
tic Sea Ireland/U.K. 11 A2 ...... 50°54'N 6°33'W
lyn, Llyn l. Wales 10 D4 ...... 52°57'N 3°43'W
nderawasih, Teluk b. Indonesia 103 J3 ...... 2°05'S 135°33'E
ntral, Cordillera mts Colombia 72 B7 ...... 1°38'N 76°51'W
ntral, Cordillera mts Peru 72 B6 ...... 10°02'S 76°25'W
ntral African Republic Africa 85 G2 ...... 6°25'N 20°12'E
ntral Bedfordshire d. England 21 E3 ...... 51°59'N 0°30'W
ntral Range mts P.N.G. 103 K3 ...... 4°57'S 142°36'E
ntral Russian Upland Russia 53 D3 ...... 53°00'N 38°00'E
ntral Siberian Plateau f. Russia 55 M4 ...... 67°03'N 110°35'E
phalonia i. Greece 50 D4 ...... 38°14'N 20°21'E
ram i. Indonesia 103 H3 ...... 3°03'S 129°24'E
ram Sea Indonesia 103 I3 ...... 2°33'S 130°11'E
redigion d. Wales 21 D3 ...... 52°19'N 3°58'W
rnavodă Romania 51 H7 ...... 44°21'N 28°02'E
rro de Pasco Peru 72 B6 ...... 10°42'S 76°14'W
rvo Spain 45 B5 ...... 43°41'N 7°26'W
ské Budějovice Czechia 46 F3 ...... 48°59'N 14°29'E
tinje Montenegro 50 C6 ...... 42°23'N 18°55'E
uta N. Africa 48 B4 ...... 35°53'N 5°20'W
vennes mts France 44 E3 ...... 43°50'N 3°17'E
yhan Turkey 51 K3 ...... 37°01'N 35°47'E
yhan r. Turkey 51 K3 ...... 36°42'N 35°37'E
abāhār Iran 95 J5 ...... 25°18'N 60°38'E
ad Africa 85 F3 ...... 15°07'N 18°13'E
ad, Lake Africa 84 F3 ...... 13°27'N 14°24'E
adan Russia 98 G8 ...... 51°18'N 91°31'E
adron U.S. 62 F5 ...... 42°50'N 102°57'W
agai Hills Afgh./Pakistan 96 B6 ...... 29°17'N 63°23'E
agos Archipelago is Indian Oc. 117 G2 ...... 6°00'S 72°00'E
ale England 8 D1 ...... 50°36'N 1°19'W
alkida Greece 50 E4 ...... 38°27'N 23°37'E
allenger Deep N. Pacific Oc. 117 I3 ...... 11°17'N 142°30'E
alons-en-Champagne France 44 F6 ...... 48°58'N 4°22'E
alon-sur-Saône France 44 F5 ...... 46°48'N 4°51'E
alus Iran 95 H7 ...... 36°37'N 51°26'E
aman Pakistan 96 C7 ...... 30°55'N 66°28'E
ambéry France 44 F4 ...... 45°34'N 5°55'E
amonix-Mont-Blanc France 44 G4 ...... 45°55'N 6°52'E
ampaign U.S. 63 I5 ...... 40°06'N 88°17'W
amplain, Lake Canada/U.S. 63 L5 ...... 44°36'N 73°21'W
andalar r. U.S. 60 D4 ...... 66°36'N 145°51'W
andigarh India 96 E7 ...... 30°42'N 76°48'E
andigarh d. India 98 D4 ...... 30°43'N 76°52'E
andrapur India 96 E4 ...... 19°57'N 79°21'E
angchun China 99 N6 ...... 43°53'N 125°20'E
ngde China 99 K3 ...... 29°03'N 111°42'E
ng Jiang r. China 99 M4 ...... 31°24'N 121°48'E
ngsha China 99 K3 ...... 28°10'N 112°59'E
ngzhi China 99 K5 ...... 36°06'N 113°09'E
ngzhou China 99 L4 ...... 31°47'N 119°59'E
nia Greece 50 F2 ...... 35°30'N 24°02'E
nnel Islands English Channel 11 Z9 ...... 49°20'N 2°20'W
nnel Islands U.S. 62 D3 ...... 33°41'N 119°26'W
nnel-Port-aux-Basques Canada 61 M2
　　47°33'N 59°01'W
nnel Tunnel France/U.K. 9 G2 ...... 51°04'N 1°24'E
nthaburi Thailand 102 C6 ...... 12°37'N 100°58'E
o Phraya r. Thailand 102 C6 ...... 13°40'N 100°36'E
paev Kazakhstan 53 F3 ...... 50°12'N 51°10'E
pala, Laguna de l. Mexico 66 D5 ...... 20°15'N 103°04'W
pel-en-le-Frith England 13 F2 ...... 53°20'N 1°54'W
apeltown England 13 F2 ...... 53°28'N 1°28'W
pleau Canada 61 J2 ...... 47°51'N 83°24'W
rd England 8 C1 ...... 50°52'N 2°58'W
rikār Afgh. 96 D7 ...... 35°02'N 69°15'E
rkayovm Russia 52 F4 ...... 65°49'N 54°51'E
rlbury England 8 D2 ...... 51°52'N 1°29'W

Charleroi Belgium 42 D3 ...... 50°25'N 4°27'E
Charles, Cape U.S. 63 K4 ...... 37°10'N 75°58'W
Charleston S. C. U.S. 63 K3 ...... 32°48'N 79°58'W
Charleston W. Va. U.S. 63 J4 ...... 38°21'N 81°39'W
Charlestown Ireland 18 C3 ...... 53°57'N 8°47'W
Charleville-Mézières France 44 F6 ...... 49°46'N 4°44'E
Charlotte U.S. 63 J4 ...... 35°14'N 80°50'W
Charlottesville U.S. 63 K4 ...... 38°02'N 78°30'W
Charlottetown Canada 61 L2 ...... 46°16'N 63°09'W
Chartres France 44 D6 ...... 48°27'N 1°30'E
Chassiron, Pointe de pt France 44 C5 ...... 46°03'N 1°24'W
Châteaubriant France 44 C5 ...... 47°43'N 1°22'W
Châteaudun France 44 D6 ...... 48°04'N 1°20'E
Châteauroux France 44 D5 ...... 46°48'N 1°41'E
Château-Thierry France 44 E6 ...... 49°03'N 3°25'E
Châtellerault France 44 D5 ...... 46°49'N 0°33'E
Chatham England 9 F2 ...... 51°23'N 0°31'E
Chatham Islands New Zealand 109 H2 ...... 43°24'S 176°32'W
Chattahoochee r. U.S. 63 J3 ...... 30°55'N 84°58'W
Chattanooga U.S. 63 I4 ...... 35°02'N 85°21'W
Chatteris England 9 F3 ...... 52°27'N 0°03'E
Chattogram Bangl. 97 H5 ...... 22°20'N 91°49'E
Chaumont France 44 F6 ...... 48°07'N 5°08'E
Cheadle England 8 D3 ...... 52°59'N 1°59'W
Cheb Czechia 46 E4 ...... 50°05'N 12°23'E
Cheboksary Russia 52 E3 ...... 56°09'N 47°13'E
Cheboygan U.S. 63 J6 ...... 45°39'N 84°28'W
Cheddar England 8 C2 ...... 51°17'N 2°47'W
Chefchaouen Morocco 48 B4 ...... 35°11'N 5°16'W
Chekhov Russia 47 Q6 ...... 55°09'N 37°28'E
Chełm Poland 47 J4 ...... 51°08'N 23°29'E
Chelmer r. England 9 F2 ...... 51°45'N 0°40'E
Chelmsford England 9 F2 ...... 51°44'N 0°29'E
Cheltenham England 8 C2 ...... 51°54'N 2°04'W
Chelyabinsk Russia 52 G3 ...... 55°11'N 61°24'E
Chemnitz Germany 46 E4 ...... 50°50'N 12°56'E
Chencang China 99 J4 ...... 34°21'N 107°09'E
Chengde China 99 L6 ...... 40°52'N 117°58'E
Chengdu China 99 I4 ...... 30°43'N 104°04'E
Chennai India 96 F3 ...... 13°06'N 80°16'E
Chenzhou China 99 K3 ...... 25°44'N 113°00'E
Chepstow Wales 10 E3 ...... 51°38'N 2°40'W
Cher r. France 44 D5 ...... 47°20'N 0°29'E
Cherbourg-Octeville France 44 C6 ...... 49°38'N 1°37'W
Cherepovets Russia 52 D3 ...... 59°08'N 37°55'E
Chergui, Chott ech l. Algeria 48 D3 ...... 34°03'N 0°16'W
Cherkasy Ukraine 47 O3 ...... 49°26'N 32°05'E
Cherkessk Russia 53 E2 ...... 44°13'N 42°03'E
Chernihiv Ukraine 47 N4 ...... 51°29'N 31°19'E
Chernivtsi Ukraine 47 K3 ...... 48°19'N 25°56'E
Chernyakhovsk Russia 47 I6 ...... 54°38'N 21°49'E
Chernyshevskiy Russia 55 M4 ...... 62°56'N 112°36'E
Cherskogo, Khrebet mts Russia 55 P4 ...... 63°42'N 146°57'E
Chervonohrad Ukraine 47 K4 ...... 50°23'N 24°14'E
Cherwell r. England 8 D2 ...... 51°44'N 1°15'W
Chesapeake Bay U.S. 63 K4 ...... 38°05'N 76°14'W
Chesham England 9 E2 ...... 51°43'N 0°37'W
Cheshire East d. England 21 D3 ...... 53°09'N 2°18'W
Cheshire West and Chester d. England 21 D3
　　53°11'N 2°46'W
Cheshskaya Guba b. Russia 52 E4 ...... 67°20'N 46°30'E
Cheshunt England 9 E2 ...... 51°42'N 0°02'W
Chesil Beach f. England 8 C1 ...... 50°38'N 2°36'W
Chester England 12 E2 ...... 53°12'N 2°54'W
Chesterfield England 13 F2 ...... 53°14'N 1°25'W
Chester-le-Street England 13 F3 ...... 54°52'N 1°34'W
Chetumal Mexico 66 G4 ...... 18°30'N 88°18'W
Cheviot Hills England 13 E4 ...... 55°12'N 2°39'W
Chew Magna England 8 C2 ...... 51°22'N 2°37'W
Chew Valley Lake resr England 8 C2 ...... 51°20'N 2°38'W
Cheyenne U.S. 62 F5 ...... 41°09'N 104°49'W
Cheyenne r. U.S. 62 F5 ...... 44°44'N 101°09'W
Chhattisgarh d. India 96 F5 ...... 21°29'N 81°46'E
Chiang Mai Thailand 102 B7 ...... 18°47'N 98°59'E
Chiang Rai Thailand 102 B7 ...... 19°55'N 99°53'E
Chiapas d. Mexico 66 F4 ...... 16°23'N 92°17'W
Chiba Japan 104 D3 ...... 35°37'N 140°07'E
Chibougamau Canada 61 K2 ...... 49°55'N 74°22'W
Chicago U.S. 63 I5 ...... 41°55'N 87°38'W
Chichester England 8 E1 ...... 50°50'N 0°46'W
Chiclayo Peru 72 B6 ...... 6°44'S 79°51'W
Chicoutimi Canada 61 K2 ...... 48°26'N 71°03'W
Chidley, Cape Canada 61 L4 ...... 60°26'N 64°20'W
Chiemsee l. Germany 46 E2 ...... 47°52'N 12°28'E
Chifeng China 99 L6 ...... 42°11'N 119°02'E
Chihuahua Mexico 66 C6 ...... 28°38'N 106°07'W
Chihuahua d. Mexico 66 C6 ...... 29°10'N 106°11'W
Chile S. America 73 B3 ...... 34°06'S 71°23'W
Chilham England 9 F2 ...... 51°15'N 0°58'E
Chillán Chile 73 B3 ...... 36°37'S 72°07'W
Chiloé, Isla Grande de i. Chile 73 B2 ...... 42°26'S 74°29'W
Chilpancingo Mexico 66 E4 ...... 17°33'N 99°30'W
Chiltern Hills England 8 E2 ...... 51°39'N 0°50'W
Chimborazo mt. Ecuador 72 B6 ...... 1°27'S 78°50'W
Chimbote Peru 72 B6 ...... 9°03'S 78°35'W
Chimboy Uzbekistan 53 F2 ...... 42°56'N 59°47'E
Chimoio Mozambique 83 C3 ...... 19°07'S 33°28'E
China Asia 98 H3 ...... 38°39'N 78°40'E
Chindwinn r. Myanmar 97 H5 ...... 21°27'N 95°15'E
Chingola Zambia 83 B3 ...... 12°33'S 27°54'E
Chinhoyi Zimbabwe 83 C3 ...... 17°21'S 30°11'E
Chinju S. Korea 104 A3 ...... 35°10'N 128°05'E
Chioggia Italy 46 E1 ...... 45°12'N 12°16'E
Chios Greece 50 G4 ...... 38°22'N 26°08'E
Chios i. Greece 50 F4 ...... 38°24'N 25°58'E
Chipata Zambia 83 C3 ...... 13°37'S 32°38'E
Chippenham England 8 C2 ...... 51°27'N 2°07'W
Chipping Campden England 8 D3 ...... 52°03'N 1°47'W
Chipping Norton England 8 D2 ...... 51°57'N 1°32'W
Chipping Ongar England 9 F2 ...... 51°42'N 0°15'E
Chipping Sodbury England 8 C2 ...... 51°32'N 2°23'W
Chiriquí, Golfo de b. Panama 67 H2 ...... 8°02'N 82°04'W
Chirk Wales 10 D4 ...... 52°56'N 3°03'W
Chirnside Scotland 15 G3 ...... 55°48'N 2°12'W
Chirripó, Cerro mt. Costa Rica 67 H2 ...... 9°30'N 83°30'W
Chisasibi Canada 61 K3 ...... 53°49'N 78°59'W
Chișinău Moldova 49 I6 ...... 47°02'N 28°50'E
Chistopol' Russia 52 F3 ...... 55°21'N 50°36'E
Chita Russia 55 M3 ...... 51°54'N 113°27'E
Chitambo Zambia 83 C3 ...... 12°54'S 30°37'E
Chitradurga India 96 E3 ...... 14°14'N 76°22'E
Chitral Pakistan 96 D8 ...... 35°53'N 71°47'E
Chittoor India 96 E3 ...... 13°12'N 79°05'E
Chitungwiza Zimbabwe 83 C3 ...... 18°01'S 31°04'E
Chlef Algeria 84 E5 ...... 36°09'N 1°20'E
Chojnice Poland 46 G5 ...... 53°42'N 17°34'E
Cholet France 44 C5 ...... 47°04'N 0°53'W

Chomutov Czechia 46 E4 ...... 50°28'N 13°24'E
Chon Buri Thailand 102 C6 ...... 13°22'N 101°02'E
Ch'ŏngjin N. Korea 99 N6 ...... 41°46'N 129°45'E
Chongqing China 99 J3 ...... 29°34'N 106°32'E
Chongqing d. China 99 J3 ...... 30°04'N 107°39'E
Chonos, Archipiélago de los is Chile 73 B2
　　44°59'S 75°31'W
Chorley England 12 E2 ...... 53°39'N 2°38'W
Chornobyl (abandoned) Ukraine 47 N4 ...... 51°16'N 30°14'E
Chornomorske Ukraine 51 J7 ...... 45°30'N 32°43'E
Chortkiv Ukraine 47 K3 ...... 49°01'N 25°47'E
Chōshi Japan 104 D3 ...... 35°44'N 140°49'E
Choûm Mauritania 84 C4 ...... 21°20'N 12°59'W
Choybalsan Mongolia 99 K7 ...... 47°57'N 114°34'E
Christchurch England 8 D1 ...... 50°44'N 1°47'W
Christchurch New Zealand 109 G2 ...... 43°31'S 172°37'E
Christmas Island Indian Oc. 102 D1 ...... 10°30'S 105°44'E
Chūgoku-sanchi mts Japan 104 B2 ...... 34°45'N 132°19'E
Chukchi Sea Russia/U.S. 55 T4 ...... 69°12'N 171°31'W
Chukotskiy Poluostrov pen. Russia 55 T4
　　65°58'N 175°16'W
Chulmleigh England 11 D2 ...... 50°55'N 3°52'W
Chumphon Thailand 102 B6 ...... 10°31'N 99°23'E
Chuncheon S. Korea 99 N5 ...... 37°52'N 127°46'E
Chunya r. Russia 55 K4 ...... 61°36'N 96°31'E
Chur Switz. 46 C2 ...... 46°51'N 9°32'E
Churchill Canada 61 I3 ...... 58°44'N 94°05'W
Churchill r. Man. Canada 61 I3 ...... 58°11'N 94°23'W
Churchill r. Nfld. and Lab. Canada 61 L3
　　53°16'N 60°14'W
Churchill, Cape Canada 61 I3 ...... 58°45'N 93°16'W
Church Stretton England 8 C3 ...... 52°32'N 2°48'W
Chusovoy Russia 52 F3 ...... 58°18'N 57°48'E
Chuxiong China 99 I3 ...... 25°02'N 101°32'E
Ciechanów Poland 46 I5 ...... 52°53'N 20°38'E
Ciego de Avila Cuba 67 I5 ...... 21°50'N 78°45'W
Cienfuegos Cuba 67 H5 ...... 22°10'N 80°25'W
Cigüela r. Spain 45 D3 ...... 39°08'N 3°43'W
Cihanbeyli Turkey 51 J4 ...... 38°40'N 32°56'E
Cilacap Indonesia 102 D2 ...... 7°41'S 109°00'E
Cimone, Monte mt. Italy 46 D1 ...... 44°11'N 10°42'E
Cinca r. Spain 45 F4 ...... 41°26'N 0°21'E
Cincinnati U.S. 63 J4 ...... 39°06'N 84°32'W
Cinderford England 8 C2 ...... 51°49'N 2°30'W
Ciney Belgium 42 E3 ...... 50°18'N 5°06'E
Cinto, Monte mt. France 44 H3 ...... 42°23'N 8°56'E
Cirebon Indonesia 102 D2 ...... 6°45'S 108°34'E
Cirencester England 8 D2 ...... 51°43'N 1°58'W
City of Edinburgh d. Scotland 20 D4 ...... 55°56'N 3°17'W
City of Kingston upon Hull d. England 21 E3
　　53°46'N 0°19'W
Ciudad Bolívar Venezuela 72 C7 ...... 8°01'N 63°35'W
Ciudad de la Paz Equat. Guinea 84 F2 ...... 1°37'N 10°50'E
Ciudad del Carmen Mexico 66 F4 ...... 18°39'N 91°51'W
Ciudad Guayana Venezuela 72 C7 ...... 8°20'N 62°37'W
Ciudad Insurgentes Mexico 66 B6 ...... 25°16'N 111°47'W
Ciudad Ixtepec Mexico 66 E4 ...... 16°35'N 95°06'W
Ciudad Juárez Mexico 66 C7 ...... 31°44'N 106°28'W
Ciudad Madero Mexico 66 E5 ...... 22°19'N 97°51'W
Ciudad Obregón Mexico 66 C6 ...... 27°28'N 109°57'W
Ciudad Real Spain 45 D3 ...... 38°59'N 3°54'W
Ciudad Rodrigo Spain 45 B4 ...... 40°36'N 6°31'W
Ciudad Valles Mexico 66 E5 ...... 21°59'N 99°00'W
Ciudad Victoria Mexico 66 E5 ...... 23°45'N 99°08'W
Ciutadella de Menorca Spain 45 G4 ...... 40°00'N 3°52'E
Civitavecchia Italy 48 F5 ...... 42°05'N 11°48'E
Çivril Turkey 51 H4 ...... 38°18'N 29°43'E
Cixi China 99 M4 ...... 30°10'N 121°14'E
Clackmannanshire d. Scotland 20 D5 ...... 56°09'N 3°45'W
Clacton-on-Sea England 9 G2 ...... 51°47'N 1°09'E
Claonaig Scotland 14 D3 ...... 55°45'N 5°24'W
Clara Ireland 18 D3 ...... 53°20'N 7°37'W
Clare d. Ireland 18 C2 ...... 52°50'N 8°50'W
Clare r. Ireland 18 B3 ...... 53°19'N 9°03'W
Clare Island Ireland 18 A3 ...... 53°49'N 10°01'W
Claremorris Ireland 18 C3 ...... 53°43'N 8°59'W
Clarksville U.S. 63 I4 ...... 36°32'N 87°20'W
Clay Cross England 13 F2 ...... 53°10'N 1°25'W
Claydon England 9 G3 ...... 52°06'N 1°07'E
Clay Head Isle of Man 12 C3 ...... 54°12'N 4°23'W
Clayton U.S. 62 F4 ...... 36°28'N 103°12'W
Clear, Cape Ireland 18 B1 ...... 51°25'N 9°31'W
Clear Island Ireland 18 B1 ...... 51°26'N 9°28'W
Cleator Moor England 12 D3 ...... 54°31'N 3°31'W
Cleethorpes England 13 G2 ...... 53°33'N 0°02'W
Cleobury Mortimer England 8 C3 ...... 52°23'N 2°29'W
Clermont-Ferrand France 44 E4 ...... 45°46'N 3°05'E
Clevedon England 8 C2 ...... 51°26'N 2°51'W
Cleveland U.S. 63 J5 ...... 41°30'N 81°41'W
Cleveland Hills England 13 F3 ...... 54°22'N 1°13'W
Cleveleys England 12 D2 ...... 53°53'N 3°02'W
Clew Bay Ireland 18 B3 ...... 53°48'N 9°47'W
Cliffe England 9 F2 ...... 51°28'N 0°30'E
Clinton U.S. 63 G4 ...... 35°32'N 98°58'W
Clipperton, Île N. Pacific Oc. 56 E2 ...... 10°21'N 109°19'W
Clisham hill Scotland 16 C2 ...... 57°58'N 6°49'W
Clitheroe England 12 E2 ...... 53°52'N 2°23'W
Clogher Head Ireland 18 E3 ...... 53°48'N 6°13'W
Clonakilty Ireland 18 C1 ...... 51°37'N 8°53'W
Clones Ireland 18 D4 ...... 54°10'N 7°13'W
Clonmel Ireland 18 D2 ...... 52°21'N 7°43'W
Cloud Peak U.S. 62 E5 ...... 44°24'N 107°01'W
Clovis U.S. 62 F3 ...... 34°27'N 103°12'W
Cluanie, Loch l. Scotland 16 D2 ...... 57°09'N 5°07'W
Cluj-Napoca Romania 47 J2 ...... 46°46'N 23°36'E
Clun England 8 B3 ...... 52°25'N 3°02'W
Clydach Wales 10 D3 ...... 51°42'N 3°54'W
Clyde r. Scotland 15 F3 ...... 55°55'N 4°29'W
Clyde, Firth of est. Scotland 14 E3 ...... 55°25'N 4°59'W
Clydebank Scotland 14 E3 ...... 55°54'N 4°24'W
Clyde River town Canada 61 L5 ...... 70°23'N 68°31'W
Coahuila de Zaragoza d. Mexico 66 D6 ...... 27°30'N 102°24'W
Coalville England 8 D3 ...... 52°43'N 1°22'W
Coast Mountains Canada 60 F3 ...... 54°20'N 127°43'W
Coast Ranges mts U.S. 62 B5 ...... 40°40'N 123°39'W
Coatbridge Scotland 15 E3 ...... 55°52'N 4°01'W
Coats Island Canada 61 J4 ...... 62°41'N 82°53'W
Coatzacoalcos Mexico 66 F4 ...... 18°08'N 94°26'W
Cobar Australia 108 D3 ...... 31°31'S 145°49'E
Cobh Ireland 18 C1 ...... 51°51'N 8°18'W
Cochabamba Bolivia 72 C5 ...... 17°25'S 66°11'W
Cochrane Canada 61 J2 ...... 49°04'N 81°02'W
Cockburnspath Scotland 15 G3 ...... 55°56'N 2°22'W
Cockburn Town Turks and Caicos Is 67 J5
　　21°28'N 71°08'W
Cockermouth England 12 D3 ...... 54°40'N 3°22'W

Coco r. Honduras/Nicaragua 67 H3 ...... 14°59'N 83°15'W
Coco, Isla del i. N. Pacific Oc. 68 B4 ...... 5°32'N 87°04'W
Cocos Islands Indian Oc. 102 B1 ...... 11°56'S 96°56'E
Cocuy, Sierra Nevada del mt. Colombia 67 J2
　　6°28'N 72°19'W
Cod, Cape U.S. 63 L5 ...... 41°58'N 70°01'W
Coddington England 13 G2 ...... 53°05'N 0°45'W
Codó Brazil 72 E6 ...... 4°28'S 43°50'W
Codsall England 8 C3 ...... 52°38'N 2°11'W
Coeur d'Alene U.S. 62 C6 ...... 47°41'N 116°47'W
Coffs Harbour Australia 108 E3 ...... 30°19'S 153°06'E
Coggeshall England 9 F2 ...... 51°52'N 0°42'E
Coiba, Isla de i. Panama 67 H2 ...... 7°27'N 81°51'W
Coigeach, Rubha pt Scotland 16 D3 ...... 58°06'N 5°28'W
Coimbatore India 96 E3 ...... 10°59'N 76°57'E
Coimbra Portugal 45 A4 ...... 40°13'N 8°25'W
Colchester England 9 F2 ...... 51°53'N 0°54'E
Coldstream Scotland 15 G3 ...... 55°39'N 2°15'W
Coleford England 8 C2 ...... 51°48'N 2°37'W
Coleraine Northern Ireland 14 C3 ...... 55°08'N 6°40'W
Colima Mexico 66 D4 ...... 19°14'N 103°42'W
Colima d. Mexico 66 D4 ...... 19°03'N 103°59'W
Colima, Nevado de vol. Mexico 66 D4 ...... 19°33'N 103°37'W
Coll i. Scotland 16 C1 ...... 56°36'N 6°36'W
Collier Bay Australia 108 B5 ...... 16°15'S 124°15'E
Colmar France 44 G6 ...... 48°05'N 7°21'E
Colne England 13 E2 ...... 53°51'N 2°11'W
Colne r. England 9 F2 ...... 51°51'N 0°57'E
Cologne Germany 46 B4 ...... 50°56'N 6°57'E
Colombia S. America 72 B7 ...... 3°45'N 72°22'W
Colombo Sri Lanka 96 E2 ...... 6°56'N 79°50'E
Colón Panama 67 I2 ...... 9°22'N 79°55'W
Colonsay i. Scotland 14 C4 ...... 56°05'N 6°15'W
Colorado r. Argentina 73 C3 ...... 39°42'S 62°07'W
Colorado r. Mexico/U.S. 62 C3 ...... 31°56'N 115°01'W
Colorado d. U.S. 62 E4 ...... 39°02'N 105°31'W
Colorado r. U.S. 62 G2 ...... 28°40'N 96°01'W
Colorado Plateau f. U.S. 62 E4 ...... 37°27'N 109°04'W
Colorado Springs town U.S. 62 F4 ...... 38°52'N 104°47'W
Coltishall England 9 G3 ...... 52°44'N 1°22'E
Columbia U.S. 63 J3 ...... 33°59'N 81°01'W
Columbia r. U.S. 62 B6 ...... 46°11'N 123°23'W
Columbia, Mount Canada 60 G3 ...... 52°08'N 117°25'W
Columbus Ga. U.S. 63 J3 ...... 32°32'N 84°59'W
Columbus Miss. U.S. 63 I3 ...... 33°33'N 88°25'W
Columbus Oh. U.S. 63 J4 ...... 39°58'N 83°00'W
Colville r. U.S. 60 C5 ...... 70°20'N 150°32'W
Colwyn Bay Wales 10 D5 ...... 53°18'N 3°43'W
Comacchio Italy 46 E1 ...... 44°41'N 12°11'E
Combe Martin England 11 C3 ...... 51°12'N 4°01'W
Comber Northern Ireland 14 D2 ...... 54°33'N 5°44'W
Comeragh Mountains Ireland 18 D2 ...... 52°18'N 7°39'W
Como Italy 46 C1 ...... 45°48'N 9°05'E
Como, Lake Italy 46 C1 ...... 45°57'N 9°11'E
Comodoro Rivadavia Argentina 73 C2 ...... 45°56'S 67°30'W
Comorin, Cape India 86 E2 ...... 8°04'N 77°35'E
Comoros Africa 83 D3 ...... 11°50'S 44°17'E
Comrat Moldova 51 H8 ...... 46°18'N 28°40'E
Comrie Scotland 15 F4 ...... 56°23'N 3°59'W
Conakry Guinea 84 C2 ...... 9°31'N 13°42'W
Concarneau France 44 B5 ...... 47°53'N 3°55'W
Concepción Chile 73 B3 ...... 36°50'S 73°04'W
Conception, Point U.S. 62 B3 ...... 34°27'N 120°26'W
Conchos r. Mexico 66 D6 ...... 29°35'N 104°29'W
Concord U.S. 63 L5 ...... 43°12'N 71°33'W
Concordia Argentina 73 D3 ...... 31°23'S 57°59'W
Congleton England 8 C2 ...... 53°10'N 2°13'W
Congo Africa 84 F1 ...... 2°24'S 15°10'E
Congo r. Congo/Dem. Rep. Congo 83 A4 ...... 6°05'S 12°26'E
Congo, Democratic Republic of the Africa 83 B4
　　3°43'S 22°17'E
Congo Basin f. Africa 85 G2 ...... 1°00'S 20°00'E
Coningsby England 13 G2 ...... 53°06'N 0°10'W
Coniston England 12 D3 ...... 54°22'N 3°05'W
Coniston Water l. England 12 D3 ...... 54°19'N 3°04'W
Conn, Lough l. Ireland 18 B4 ...... 54°01'N 9°16'W
Connah's Quay Wales 10 D5 ...... 53°13'N 3°04'W
Connecticut d. U.S. 63 L5 ...... 41°41'N 72°36'W
Connecticut r. U.S. 63 L5 ...... 41°16'N 72°22'W
Connemara f. Ireland 18 B3 ...... 53°28'N 9°52'W
Conon Bridge Scotland 17 E2 ...... 57°34'N 4°26'W
Consett England 13 F3 ...... 54°51'N 1°50'W
Con Son i. Vietnam 102 D5 ...... 8°42'N 106°40'E
Constance, Lake Germany/Switz. 46 C2 ...... 47°40'N 9°17'E
Constanța Romania 51 H7 ...... 44°11'N 28°37'E
Constantine Algeria 84 E5 ...... 36°23'N 6°38'E
Conwy Wales 10 D5 ...... 53°17'N 3°50'W
Conwy r. Wales 10 D5 ...... 53°10'N 3°37'W
Conwy r. Wales 10 D5 ...... 53°14'N 3°48'W
Conwy Bay Wales 10 C5 ...... 53°16'N 4°02'W
Cook, Mount mt. New Zealand 109 G2 ...... 43°37'S 170°08'E
Cook Islands S. Pacific Oc. 109 I5 ...... 20°05'S 160°06'W
Cookstown Northern Ireland 14 C2 ...... 54°38'N 6°44'W
Cook Strait New Zealand 109 G2 ...... 40°32'S 174°01'E
Cooktown Australia 108 D5 ...... 15°28'S 145°17'E
Coolangatta Australia 108 E4 ...... 28°10'S 153°31'E
Cooper Creek watercourse Australia 108 C4
　　28°29'S 137°43'E
Coos Bay town U.S. 62 B5 ...... 43°21'N 124°12'W
Copenhagen Denmark 43 C1 ...... 55°40'N 12°34'E
Copiapó Chile 73 B4 ...... 27°18'S 70°23'W
Copinsay i. Scotland 17 G3 ...... 58°54'N 2°40'W
Corabia Romania 50 F6 ...... 43°47'N 24°29'E
Coral Harbour Canada 61 J4 ...... 64°12'N 83°19'W
Coral Sea S. Pacific Oc. 108 E5 ...... 13°25'S 151°06'E
Coral Sea Islands Territory Australia 108 E5
　　15°01'S 150°43'E
Corbie France 42 B2 ...... 49°55'N 2°31'E
Corbridge England 13 E3 ...... 54°58'N 2°01'W
Corby England 8 E3 ...... 52°29'N 0°41'W
Corcaigh Ireland 18 C1 ...... 51°54'N 8°28'W
Córdoba Argentina 73 C3 ...... 31°24'S 64°11'W
Córdoba Mexico 66 E4 ...... 18°55'N 96°53'W
Córdoba Spain 45 C2 ...... 37°53'N 4°46'W
Córdoba, Sierras de mts Argentina 73 C3 ...... 32°55'S 64°22'W
Corfe Castle England 8 C1 ...... 50°38'N 2°03'W
Corfu i. Greece 50 C4 ...... 39°36'N 19°47'E
Corinth Greece 50 E3 ...... 37°56'N 22°55'E
Corixa Grande r. Bolivia/Brazil 72 D5 ...... 17°30'S 57°56'W
Cork Ireland 18 C1 ...... 51°54'N 8°28'W
Cork d. Ireland 18 C2 ...... 52°01'N 8°39'W
Cork City d. Ireland 18 C2 ...... 51°54'N 8°28'W
Çorlu Turkey 51 G5 ...... 41°09'N 27°48'E
Corner Brook Canada 61 M2 ...... 48°54'N 57°47'W
Cornwall d. England 11 C2 ...... 50°32'N 4°33'W
Cornwall, Cape England 11 B2 ...... 50°08'N 5°47'W
Cornwallis Island Canada 61 I5 ...... 75°08'N 94°56'W

Coro Venezuela 72 C8 .... 11°23'N 69°40'W
Coronado, Bahía de b. Costa Rica 67 H2... 8°55'N 83°48'W
Coronation Gulf Canada 60 G4 .... 68°08'N 112°32'W
Corpus Christi U.S. 62 G2 .... 27°44'N 97°27'W
Corral de Cantos mt. Spain 45 C3 .... 39°34'N 4°27'W
Corrib, Lough l. Ireland 18 B3 .... 53°27'N 9°19'W
Corrientes Argentina 73 D4 .... 27°27'S 58°46'W
Corrientes, Cabo c. Mexico 66 C5 .... 20°26'N 105°42'W
Corse, Cap c. France 44 H3 .... 43°02'N 9°22'E
Corserine hill Scotland 14 E3 .... 55°09'N 4°21'W
Corsham England 8 C2 .... 51°26'N 2°11'W
Corsica i. France 44 H3 .... 42°20'N 8°29'E
Corte France 44 H3 .... 42°18'N 9°09'E
Cortegana Spain 45 B2 .... 37°55'N 6°49'W
Cortina d'Ampezzo Italy 46 E2 .... 46°32'N 12°09'E
Corton England 9 G3 .... 52°31'N 1°45'E
Çorum Turkey 51 K5 .... 40°33'N 34°57'E
Corumbá Brazil 72 D5 .... 19°00'S 57°37'W
Corwen Wales 10 D4 .... 52°59'N 3°22'W
Cosenza Italy 49 G4 .... 39°18'N 16°15'E
Cosmoledo Islands Seychelles 83 D4 .... 9°30'S 49°00'E
Cosne-Cours-sur-Loire France 44 E5 .... 47°25'N 2°56'E
Costa Blanca f. Spain 45 E3 .... 38°03'N 0°20'W
Costa Brava f. Spain 45 G4 .... 41°28'N 3°05'E
Costa del Sol f. Spain 45 C2 .... 36°25'N 5°06'W
Costa de Mosquitos f. Nicaragua 67 H3 ... 12°08'N 83°52'W
Costa Rica Central America 67 H3 .... 10°08'N 84°19'W
Cotabato Phil. 103 G5 .... 7°13'N 124°14'E
Côte d'Azur f. France 44 G3 .... 43°33'N 7°13'E
Côte d'Ivoire Africa 84 D2 .... 7°35'N 4°22'W
Cothi r. Wales 10 C3 .... 51°52'N 4°10'W
Cotonou Benin 84 E2 .... 6°21'N 2°27'E
Cotopaxi, Volcán vol. Ecuador 72 B6 .... 0°39'S 78°26'W
Cotswold Hills England 8 C2 .... 51°36'N 2°15'W
Cottbus Germany 46 F4 .... 51°45'N 14°21'E
Cottenham England 9 F3 .... 52°17'N 0°08'E
Cottesmore England 8 E3 .... 52°43'N 0°40'W
Coulogne France 42 A3 .... 50°55'N 1°53'E
Coupar Angus Scotland 15 F4 .... 56°33'N 3°16'W
Coutances France 44 C6 .... 49°03'N 1°27'W
Coventry England 8 D3 .... 52°24'N 1°31'W
Covilhã Portugal 45 B4 .... 40°17'N 7°29'W
Cowan, Lake Australia 108 B3 .... 31°45'S 121°59'E
Cowbridge Wales 11 D3 .... 51°28'N 3°27'W
Cowdenbeath Scotland 15 F4 .... 56°07'N 3°20'W
Cowes England 8 D1 .... 50°46'N 1°18'W
Cowfold England 9 E1 .... 50°59'N 0°16'W
Cow Green Reservoir England 13 E3 .... 54°40'N 2°20'W
Cox's Bazar Bangl. 97 H5 .... 21°27'N 91°59'E
Coyhaique Chile 73 B2 .... 45°36'S 72°05'W
Cozumel, Isla i. Mexico 66 G5 .... 20°22'N 86°53'W
Craig U.S. 62 E5 .... 40°31'N 107°32'W
Craigavon Northern Ireland 14 C2 .... 54°26'N 6°21'W
Craig Goch Reservoir Wales 10 D4 .... 52°19'N 3°37'W
Craignure Scotland 14 D4 .... 56°28'N 5°43'W
Crail Scotland 15 G4 .... 56°16'N 2°38'W
Craiova Romania 50 E7 .... 44°19'N 23°48'E
Cramlington England 13 F4 .... 55°05'N 1°35'W
Cranbrook Canada 60 G2 .... 49°32'N 115°45'W
Cranleigh England 9 E2 .... 51°09'N 0°29'W
Crawley England 9 E2 .... 51°07'N 0°11'W
Creag Mèagaidh mt. Scotland 17 E1 .... 56°57'N 4°36'W
Credenhill England 8 C3 .... 52°05'N 2°48'W
Crediton England 11 D2 .... 50°47'N 3°39'W
Cree Lake Canada 60 H3 .... 57°31'N 106°29'W
Cremona Italy 46 D1 .... 45°08'N 10°01'E
Cres i. Croatia 50 A7 .... 44°51'N 14°28'E
Crescent City U.S. 62 B5 .... 41°47'N 124°09'W
Creston U.S. 63 H5 .... 41°03'N 94°22'W
Crete i. Greece 50 F2 .... 35°28'N 24°41'E
Creuse r. France 44 D5 .... 47°00'N 0°34'E
Crewe England 13 E2 .... 53°06'N 2°26'W
Crewkerne England 8 C1 .... 50°53'N 2°48'W
Crianlarich Scotland 14 E4 .... 56°24'N 4°37'W
Criccieth Wales 10 C4 .... 52°55'N 4°14'W
Criciúma Brazil 73 E4 .... 28°45'S 49°25'W
Crickhowell Wales 10 D3 .... 51°51'N 3°08'W
Crieff Scotland 15 F4 .... 56°23'N 3°50'W
Criffel hill Scotland 15 F2 .... 54°57'N 3°38'W
Crimea pen. Ukraine 49 J6 .... 45°20'N 34°05'E
Crimond Scotland 17 H2 .... 57°36'N 1°55'W
Croatia Europe 50 B7 .... 45°02'N 15°14'E
Croisilles France 9 H1 .... 50°12'N 2°53'E
Croker Island Australia 103 I1 .... 11°04'S 132°38'E
Cromarty Scotland 17 E2 .... 57°41'N 4°02'W
Cromarty Firth est. Scotland 17 E2 .... 57°38'N 4°19'W
Cromdale, Hills of Scotland 17 F2 .... 57°19'N 3°31'W
Cromer England 9 G3 .... 52°56'N 1°18'E
Cronamuck Mountain hill Ireland 14 B2 .... 54°54'N 7°51'W
Crook England 13 F3 .... 54°43'N 1°45'W
Crooked Island Bahamas 67 J5 .... 22°48'N 74°14'W
Crooked Island Passage str. Bahamas 67 J5 .... 22°29'N 74°55'W
Croom Ireland 18 C2 .... 52°31'N 8°43'W
Crosby England 12 D2 .... 53°29'N 3°02'W
Cross Fell hill England 13 E3 .... 54°42'N 2°29'W
Crossgar Northern Ireland 14 D2 .... 54°24'N 5°45'W
Crossmaglen Northern Ireland 14 C2 .... 54°04'N 6°36'W
Crotone Italy 49 G4 .... 39°05'N 17°08'E
Crouch r. England 9 F2 .... 51°38'N 0°36'E
Crowborough England 9 F2 .... 51°04'N 0°10'E
Crowland England 9 E3 .... 52°41'N 0°10'W
Crowle England 13 G2 .... 53°37'N 0°50'W
Crowthorne England 8 E2 .... 51°22'N 0°48'W
Croyde England 11 C3 .... 51°08'N 4°13'W
Croydon England 9 E2 .... 51°23'N 0°06'W
Crozet Islands Indian Oc. 117 G1 .... 47°00'S 52°00'E
Cruden Bay town Scotland 17 H2 .... 57°25'N 1°51'W
Crumlin Northern Ireland 14 C2 .... 54°38'N 6°13'W
Cruz, Cabo c. Cuba 67 I4 .... 19°51'N 77°43'W
Cruzeiro do Sul Brazil 72 B6 .... 7°41'S 72°40'W
Cuando r. Angola/Zambia 83 B3 .... 17°39'S 23°24'E
Cuanza r. Angola 83 A4 .... 9°21'S 13°08'E
Cuauhtémoc Mexico 66 C6 .... 28°24'N 106°53'W
Cuba Central America 67 H5 .... 22°18'N 80°06'W
Cubango r. Angola/Namibia 83 B3 .... 18°01'S 21°26'E
Cuckfield England 9 E2 .... 51°00'N 0°09'W
Cúcuta Colombia 72 B7 .... 7°53'N 72°31'W
Cuddalore India 96 E3 .... 11°42'N 79°43'E
Cuenca Ecuador 72 B6 .... 2°53'S 79°00'W
Cuenca Spain 45 D4 .... 40°04'N 2°08'W
Cuenca, Serranía de mts Spain 45 D4 .... 40°38'N 2°08'W
Cuernavaca Mexico 66 E4 .... 18°56'N 99°11'W
Cuiabá Brazil 72 D5 .... 15°33'S 56°04'W
Cuilcagh hill Ireland/U.K. 14 B2 .... 54°12'N 7°49'W
Cuillin Sound str. Scotland 16 C2 .... 57°08'N 6°21'W

Cuito Angola 83 A3 .... 12°23'S 16°57'E
Culiacán Mexico 66 C5 .... 24°47'N 107°27'W
Cullen Scotland 17 G2 .... 57°41'N 2°49'W
Cullera Spain 45 E3 .... 39°10'N 0°13'W
Cullompton England 11 D2 .... 50°51'N 3°23'W
Cullybackey Northern Ireland 14 C2 .... 54°53'N 6°21'W
Cul Mòr hill Scotland 16 D3 .... 58°03'N 5°07'W
Culuene r. Brazil 72 D5 .... 11°11'S 53°09'W
Culzean Bay Scotland 14 E3 .... 55°22'N 4°49'W
Cumaná Venezuela 72 C8 .... 10°24'N 64°09'W
Cumberland r. U.S. 63 I4 .... 36°30'N 87°49'W
Cumberland Sound str. Canada 61 L4 ... 64°08'N 63°14'W
Cumbernauld Scotland 15 F3 .... 55°57'N 3°59'W
Cumbria d. England 21 D4 .... 54°42'N 3°17'W
Cumnock Scotland 14 E3 .... 55°27'N 4°16'W
Cunene r. Angola 83 A3 .... 17°15'S 11°46'E
Cuneo Italy 48 E5 .... 44°24'N 7°33'E
Cupar Scotland 15 F4 .... 56°19'N 3°01'W
Cupica, Golfo de b. Colombia 67 I2 .... 6°25'N 77°46'W
Curaçao i. Neth. Antilles 67 K3 .... 12°12'N 69°04'W
Curitiba Brazil 73 E4 .... 25°28'S 49°17'W
Curonian Lagoon b. Lithuania/Russia 43 E1
.... 55°16'N 21°06'E
Cusco Peru 72 B5 .... 13°31'S 71°59'W
Cushendall Northern Ireland 14 C3 .... 55°05'N 6°04'W
Cuttack India 96 G5 .... 20°27'N 85°55'E
Cuxhaven Germany 46 C5 .... 53°52'N 8°42'E
Cuyo Islands Phil. 103 G6 .... 11°11'N 121°10'E
Cwmbrân Wales 10 D3 .... 51°39'N 3°02'W
Cyclades is Greece 50 F3 .... 37°14'N 24°37'E
Cyprus Asia 51 J2 .... 35°38'N 33°17'E
Cyrenaica f. Libya 49 H2 .... 26°00'N 22°24'E
Czechia Europe 46 F3 .... 49°38'N 15°37'E
Częstochowa Poland 46 H4 .... 50°48'N 19°07'E

D

Dąbrowa Górnicza Poland 46 H4 .... 50°21'N 19°15'E
Dachau Germany 46 D3 .... 48°15'N 11°27'E
Dadaab Kenya 85 I2 .... 0°07'N 40°19'E
Daegu S. Korea 99 N5 .... 35°52'N 128°35'E
Daejeon S. Korea 99 N5 .... 36°22'N 127°24'E
Dagupan Phil. 102 G7 .... 16°04'N 120°21'E
Da Hinggan Ling mts China 99 L6 .... 43°33'N 117°52'E
Dahlak Archipelago is Eritrea 94 F4 .... 15°58'N 40°04'E
Dahm, Ramlat des. Saudi Arabia/Yemen 94 G3
.... 15°59'N 45°00'E
Dailly Scotland 14 E3 .... 55°17'N 4°43'W
Dakar Senegal 84 C3 .... 14°43'N 17°28'W
Dakhla Western Sahara 84 C4 .... 23°42'N 15°56'W
Dakhla Oasis Egypt 94 C5 .... 25°25'N 28°53'E
Dakol'ka r. Belarus 47 M5 .... 52°08'N 28°52'E
Dalaman Turkey 51 H3 .... 36°47'N 28°48'E
Da Lat Vietnam 102 D6 .... 11°56'N 108°26'E
Dalbandin Pakistan 95 J5 .... 28°56'N 64°30'E
Dalbeattie Scotland 15 F2 .... 54°56'N 3°49'W
Dali China 99 I3 .... 25°33'N 100°13'E
Dalian China 99 M5 .... 38°51'N 121°37'E
Dalkeith Scotland 15 F3 .... 55°54'N 3°04'W
Dallas U.S. 62 G3 .... 32°46'N 96°48'W
Dalmally Scotland 14 E4 .... 56°24'N 4°58'W
Dalmatia f. Bos. and Herz./Croatia 50 A7 ... 44°01'N 15°30'E
Dalmellington Scotland 14 E3 .... 55°19'N 4°24'W
Daloa Côte d'Ivoire 84 D2 .... 6°54'N 6°28'W
Dalry Scotland 14 E3 .... 55°43'N 4°43'W
Dalrymple Scotland 14 E3 .... 55°24'N 4°35'W
Dalrymple, Mount Australia 108 D4 .... 20°59'S 148°37'E
Dalton U.S. 63 I3 .... 34°49'N 84°56'W
Dalton-in-Furness England 12 D3 .... 54°09'N 3°11'W
Daly r. Australia 108 C5 .... 13°31'S 130°28'E
Daman India 96 D5 .... 20°24'N 72°58'E
Damanhûr Egypt 49 J3 .... 31°02'N 30°28'E
Damar i. Indonesia 103 H2 .... 7°08'S 128°32'E
Damaraland f. Namibia 83 A2 .... 21°58'S 17°06'E
Damascus Syria 94 E6 .... 33°30'N 36°20'E
Damävand, Qolleh-ye mt. Iran 95 H7 .... 35°58'N 52°07'E
Damghan Iran 95 H7 .... 36°09'N 54°19'E
Dammam Saudi Arabia 95 H5 .... 26°24'N 50°10'E
Dampier Australia 108 A4 .... 20°41'S 116°47'E
Dampir, Selat str. Indonesia 103 I3 .... 0°40'S 130°43'E
Da Nang Vietnam 102 D7 .... 16°01'N 108°12'E
Dandong China 99 M6 .... 40°06'N 124°22'E
Dane r. England 13 E2 .... 53°15'N 2°31'W
Danube r. Bulgaria/Croatia/Serbia 49 I6 ... 45°26'N 29°38'E
Danube Delta Romania/Ukraine 51 H7 ... 45°11'N 29°13'E
Danville U.S. 63 K4 .... 36°35'N 79°24'W
Dapaong Togo 84 E3 .... 10°53'N 0°15'E
Da Qaidam China 98 H5 .... 37°49'N 95°18'E
Daqing China 99 N7 .... 46°28'N 125°01'E
Dar'ā Syria 94 E6 .... 32°38'N 36°07'E
Dārāb Iran 95 H5 .... 28°45'N 54°32'E
Darabani Romania 47 L3 .... 48°11'N 26°36'E
Darbhanga India 96 G6 .... 26°10'N 85°57'E
Dardanelles str. Turkey 50 G5 .... 40°12'N 26°25'E
Dar es Salaam Tanzania 83 C4 .... 6°48'S 39°16'E
Darhan Mongolia 99 J7 .... 49°23'N 105°49'E
Darién, Golfo del g. Colombia 72 B7 .... 8°56'N 77°01'W
Darjiling India 96 G6 .... 27°02'N 88°19'E
Darling r. Australia 108 D3 .... 34°05'S 141°56'E
Darling Downs hills Australia 108 D4 .... 27°58'S 149°54'E
Darlington England 13 F3 .... 54°31'N 1°33'W
Darlington d. England 21 E4 .... 54°33'N 1°34'W
Darmstadt Germany 44 H6 .... 49°52'N 8°38'E
Darnah Libya 85 G5 .... 32°42'N 22°40'E
Dart r. England 11 D2 .... 50°25'N 3°39'W
Dartford England 9 F2 .... 51°27'N 0°13'E
Dartmoor hills England 11 C2 .... 50°36'N 4°01'W
Dartmouth Canada 63 N5 .... 44°41'N 63°35'W
Dartmouth England 11 D2 .... 50°21'N 3°35'W
Darton England 13 F2 .... 53°35'N 1°31'W
Daru P.N.G. 103 K2 .... 9°03'S 143°12'E
Darvel Scotland 14 E3 .... 55°37'N 4°17'W
Darwen England 13 E2 .... 53°42'N 2°28'W
Darwin Australia 108 C5 .... 12°25'S 130°51'E
Datong China 99 K6 .... 40°03'N 113°20'E
Daud Khel Pakistan 95 L6 .... 32°51'N 71°37'E
Daugava r. Latvia 43 F1 .... 57°03'N 24°04'E
Daugavpils Latvia 43 F1 .... 55°53'N 26°31'E
Dauphin Canada 60 H3 .... 51°09'N 100°02'W
Dauphiné f. France 44 F4 .... 45°02'N 5°07'E
Davangere India 96 E3 .... 14°27'N 75°51'E
Davao Phil. 103 H5 .... 7°05'N 125°34'E
Davao Gulf Phil. 103 H5 .... 6°22'N 125°49'E
Davenport U.S. 63 H5 .... 41°32'N 90°33'W
Daventry England 8 D3 .... 52°15'N 1°10'W
David Panama 67 H2 .... 8°27'N 82°25'W

Davis Strait Canada/Greenland 61 M4 .... 63°48'N 56°19'W
Davos Switz. 46 C2 .... 46°48'N 9°49'E
Dawei Myanmar 97 I3 .... 14°06'N 98°13'E
Dawlish England 11 D2 .... 50°35'N 3°28'W
Dawqah Oman 95 H3 .... 18°37'N 54°04'E
Dawson Canada 60 E4 .... 64°04'N 139°24'W
Dawson Creek town Canada 60 F3 .... 55°46'N 120°17'W
Daxian China 99 J4 .... 31°05'N 107°26'E
Dayr az Zawr Syria 94 F7 .... 35°19'N 40°06'E
Dayton U.S. 63 J4 .... 39°45'N 84°11'W
Daytona Beach U.S. 63 J2 .... 29°08'N 81°05'W
Dazhou China 99 J4 .... 31°12'N 107°28'E
Dead Sea l. Asia 94 E6 .... 31°08'N 35°27'E
Deal England 9 G2 .... 51°13'N 1°24'E
Dean, Forest of England 8 C2 .... 51°48'N 2°32'W
Dearne r. England 13 F2 .... 53°29'N 1°14'W
Death Valley f. U.S. 62 C4 .... 36°34'N 117°01'W
Debak Malaysia 102 E4 .... 1°31'N 111°29'E
Debar North Macedonia 50 D5 .... 41°31'N 20°31'E
Debenham England 9 G3 .... 52°14'N 1°11'E
Debrecen Hungary 47 I2 .... 47°32'N 21°37'E
Debre Zeyit Ethiopia 83 C5 .... 8°45'N 38°57'E
Decatur U.S. 63 I3 .... 34°37'N 86°59'W
Deccan f. India 96 E4 .... 18°40'N 77°05'E
Děčín Czechia 46 F4 .... 50°47'N 14°13'E
Dee r. Scotland 17 G2 .... 57°09'N 2°05'W
Dee est. Wales 10 D5 .... 53°18'N 3°09'W
Dee r. Wales 10 D5 .... 53°13'N 3°01'W
Deele r. Ireland 14 B2 .... 54°51'N 7°28'W
De Grey r. Australia 108 A4 .... 20°19'S 119°14'E
Dehra Dun India 96 E7 .... 30°20'N 78°05'E
Dej Romania 47 J2 .... 47°09'N 23°53'E
Delano Peak U.S. 62 D4 .... 38°23'N 112°21'W
Delap-Uliga-Djarrit Marshall Is. 115 J3 ... 7°07'N 171°22'E
Delārām Afgh. 95 J6 .... 32°11'N 63°28'E
Delaware d. U.S. 63 K4 .... 38°58'N 75°28'W
Delft Neth. 42 D5 .... 52°01'N 4°21'E
Delfzijl Neth. 42 F6 .... 53°20'N 6°55'E
Delgado, Cabo c. Mozambique 83 D3 ... 10°41'S 40°36'E
Delhi India 96 E6 .... 28°38'N 77°17'E
Delhi d. India 98 D5 .... 28°38'N 77°08'E
Delice r. Turkey 51 K5 .... 40°31'N 34°13'E
Delicias Mexico 66 C6 .... 28°10'N 105°30'W
Del Rio U.S. 62 F2 .... 29°21'N 100°54'W
Demanda, Sierra de la mts Spain 45 D5 ... 42°13'N 3°27'W
Deming U.S. 62 E3 .... 32°16'N 107°45'W
Demirci Turkey 51 H4 .... 39°02'N 28°39'E
Demirkazık Tepe mt. Turkey 51 K3 .... 37°48'N 35°09'E
Dempo, Gunung vol. Indonesia 102 C3 ... 4°02'S 103°06'E
Denakil f. Africa 85 I3 .... 12°40'N 40°44'E
Denali mt. U.S. 60 C4 .... 63°05'N 150°20'W
Denbigh Wales 10 D5 .... 53°11'N 3°25'W
Denbighshire d. Wales 21 D3 .... 53°06'N 3°20'W
Den Burg Neth. 42 D6 .... 53°03'N 4°49'E
Den Helder Neth. 42 D5 .... 52°58'N 4°46'E
Denizli Turkey 51 H3 .... 37°45'N 29°05'E
Denmark Europe 43 B2 .... 56°13'N 10°09'E
Denmark Strait Greenland/Iceland 61 P4 ... 66°11'N 28°09'W
Denny Scotland 15 F4 .... 56°01'N 3°54'W
Denpasar Indonesia 102 F2 .... 8°41'S 115°10'E
Denton U.S. 62 G3 .... 33°15'N 97°08'W
D'Entrecasteaux Islands P.N.G. 108 E6 ... 9°38'S 151°02'E
Denver U.S. 62 E4 .... 39°45'N 105°02'W
Dêqên China 99 H3 .... 28°26'N 98°50'E
Dera Ghazi Khan Pakistan 96 D7 .... 30°05'N 70°44'E
Dera Ismail Khan Pakistan 96 D7 .... 31°51'N 70°56'E
Derbent Russia 53 E2 .... 42°04'N 48°17'E
Derby Australia 108 B5 .... 17°19'S 123°38'E
Derby England 8 D3 .... 52°55'N 1°28'W
Derby d. England 21 E3 .... 52°55'N 1°28'W
Derbyshire d. England 21 E3 .... 53°11'N 1°36'W
Dereham England 9 F3 .... 52°41'N 0°56'E
Derg r. Ireland/U.K. 14 B2 .... 54°44'N 7°26'W
Derg, Lough l. Don. Ireland 18 D4 .... 54°37'N 7°51'W
Derg, Lough l. Tipp. Ireland 18 C3 .... 52°54'N 8°28'W
Derry r. Ireland 18 E2 .... 52°41'N 6°40'W
Derry Northern Ireland 14 B2 .... 54°59'N 7°20'W
Derry and Strabane d. Northern Ireland 20 B4
.... 54°56'N 7°10'W
Derryveagh Mountains Ireland 18 C4 .... 54°56'N 8°14'W
Dersingham England 9 F3 .... 52°51'N 0°31'E
Derudeb Sudan 94 E3 .... 17°38'N 36°05'E
Derwent r. England 13 F2 .... 53°45'N 0°58'W
Derwent Reservoir Derbys. England 13 F2 ... 53°25'N 1°44'W
Derwent Reservoir Dur. England 13 F3 ... 54°52'N 1°58'W
Derwent Water l. England 12 D3 .... 54°34'N 3°10'W
Desaguadero r. Argentina 73 C3 .... 34°03'S 66°43'W
Desë Ethiopia 85 H3 .... 11°07'N 39°38'E
Des Moines U.S. 63 H5 .... 41°36'N 93°37'W
Des Moines r. U.S. 63 H5 .... 40°23'N 91°28'W
Desna r. Russia 47 P5 .... 50°32'N 30°33'E
Desna r. Russia/Ukraine 47 N4 .... 50°32'N 30°33'E
Dessau-Roßlau Germany 46 E4 .... 51°50'N 12°15'E
Desventuradas, Islas is Chile 68 B2 .... 28°54'S 80°00'W
Detroit U.S. 63 J5 .... 42°19'N 83°04'W
Deva Romania 50 E7 .... 45°54'N 22°55'E
Deventer Neth. 42 F5 .... 52°15'N 6°10'E
Deveron r. Scotland 17 G2 .... 57°40'N 2°31'W
Devil's Bit Mountain hill Ireland 18 D2 ... 52°50'N 7°55'W
Devil's Bridge Wales 10 D4 .... 52°23'N 3°51'W
Devil's Lake town U.S. 62 G6 .... 48°02'N 98°46'W
Devizes England 8 D2 .... 51°21'N 1°59'W
Devon d. England 21 D2 .... 50°50'N 3°51'W
Devon r. Scotland 15 F4 .... 56°07'N 3°51'W
Devon Island Canada 61 I5 .... 75°20'N 91°06'W
Devonport Australia 108 D2 .... 41°11'S 146°20'E
Devrez r. Turkey 51 K5 .... 41°07'N 35°01'E
Dewsbury England 13 F2 .... 53°41'N 1°38'W
Dezfūl Iran 95 G6 .... 32°22'N 48°24'E
Dezhou China 99 L5 .... 37°25'N 116°19'E
Dhahran Saudi Arabia 95 H5 .... 26°19'N 50°07'E
Dhaka Bangl. 97 H5 .... 23°42'N 90°22'E
Dhamär Yemen 94 G2 .... 14°34'N 44°26'E
Dhanbad India 96 G5 .... 23°47'N 86°25'E
Dharwad India 96 E4 .... 15°27'N 75°04'E
Dhaulagiri mt. Nepal 96 F6 .... 28°40'N 83°28'E
Dhule India 96 D5 .... 20°54'N 74°52'E
Diablo, Picacho del mt. Mexico 66 A7 ... 30°59'N 115°24'W
Diamantina watercourse Australia 108 C4 ... 26°30'S 139°22'E
Diamantina, Chapada f. Brazil 72 E5 ... 14°21'S 43°09'W
Dibrugarh India 97 H6 .... 27°27'N 94°55'E
Dickinson U.S. 62 F6 .... 46°53'N 102°48'W
Didcot England 8 D2 .... 51°36'N 1°15'W
Dieppe France 44 D6 .... 49°55'N 1°05'E

Diest Belgium 42 E3 .... 50°59'N 5°03'E
Digne-les-Bains France 44 G4 .... 44°06'N 6°15'E
Dijon France 44 F5 .... 47°20'N 5°03'E
Diksmuide Belgium 42 B4 .... 51°02'N 2°52'E
Dili East Timor 103 H2 .... 8°35'S 125°36'E
Dillon U.S. 62 D6 .... 45°13'N 112°37'W
Dimapur India 97 H6 .... 25°54'N 93°47'E
Dimitrovgrad Bulgaria 50 F6 .... 42°03'N 25°35'E
Dimitrovgrad Russia 53 E3 .... 54°13'N 49°35'E
Dinan France 44 B6 .... 48°27'N 2°03'W
Dinant Belgium 42 D3 .... 50°16'N 4°56'E
Dinar Turkey 51 I4 .... 38°04'N 30°10'E
Dīnār, Kūh-e mt. Iran 95 H6 .... 30°49'N 51°32'E
Dinard France 44 B6 .... 48°38'N 2°04'W
Dinaric Alps mts Bos. and Herz./Croatia 50 B7
.... 44°13'N 16°16'E
Dindigul India 96 E3 .... 10°22'N 77°59'E
Dingle Ireland 18 A2 .... 52°08'N 10°16'W
Dingle Bay Ireland 18 A2 .... 52°00'N 10°22'W
Dingwall Scotland 17 E2 .... 57°36'N 3°32'W
Dipolog Phil. 103 G5 .... 8°39'N 123°20'E
Dir Pakistan 95 L7 .... 35°12'N 71°52'E
Dirē Dawa Ethiopia 85 I2 .... 9°34'N 41°53'E
Dirj Libya 84 F5 .... 30°10'N 10°29'E
Dirranbandi Australia 108 D4 .... 28°35'S 148°14'E
Disappointment, Cape S. Atlantic Oc. 73 F1
.... 54°51'S 36°07'W
Disko I. Greenland 61 M4 .... 69°44'N 53°33'W
Diss England 9 G3 .... 52°23'N 1°07'E
Distington England 12 D3 .... 54°36'N 3°32'W
Diu India 96 D5 .... 20°40'N 71°03'E
Divinópolis Brazil 73 D4 .... 20°09'S 44°53'W
Divnoye Russia 49 L6 .... 45°55'N 43°20'E
Divriği Turkey 51 M4 .... 39°22'N 38°06'E
Dixon Entrance str. Canada/U.S. 60 E3
.... 54°18'N 133°32'W
Diyarbakır Turkey 49 L4 .... 37°55'N 40°14'E
Djado, Plateau du f. Niger 84 F4 .... 21°30'N 12°53'E
Djelfa Algeria 84 E5 .... 34°38'N 3°16'E
Djibouti Africa 85 I3 .... 11°34'N 42°25'E
Djibouti town Djibouti 85 I3 .... 11°32'N 43°00'E
Djouce Mountain hill Ireland 10 A5 .... 53°08'N 6°15'W
Dnieper r. Belarus 47 N4 .... 51°16'N 30°3
Dnieper r. Ukraine 47 O2 .... 46°30'N 32°1
Dniester r. Moldova 47 N2 .... 46°25'N 30°1
Dniester r. Ukraine 47 M3 .... 48°06'N 28°30
Dnipro Ukraine 47 P3 .... 48°29'N 35°0
Dniprorudne Ukraine 47 P2 .... 47°23'N 34°5
Doba Chad 85 F2 .... 8°40'N 16°5
Doberai Peninsula Indonesia 103 I3 .... 1°19'S 132°2
Doboj Bos. and Herz. 50 C7 .... 44°45'N 18°0
Dobrich Bulgaria 50 G6 .... 43°33'N 27°4
Dochart r. Scotland 14 E4 .... 56°28'N 4°18
Docking England 9 F3 .... 52°54'N 0°3
Dodecanese is Greece 50 G2 .... 35°57'N 27°4
Dodge City U.S. 62 F4 .... 37°46'N 100°0
Dodman Point England 11 C2 .... 50°13'N 4°48
Dodoma Tanzania 83 C4 .... 6°10'S 35°4
Doetinchem Neth. 42 F4 .... 51°58'N 6°1
Doha Qatar 95 H5 .... 25°17'N 51°3
Dokkum Neth. 42 E6 .... 53°19'N 5°5
Dolbenmaen Wales 10 C4 .... 52°58'N 4°14
Dole France 44 F5 .... 47°06'N 5°3
Dolgellau Wales 10 D4 .... 52°45'N 3°53
Dolomites mts Italy 46 D1 .... 45°42'N 11°3
Dolo Odo Ethiopia 85 I2 .... 4°09'N 42°0
Dolyna Ukraine 47 J3 .... 48°58'N 23°5
Dolynska Ukraine 47 O3 .... 48°07'N 32°4
Dominica Central America 67 L4 .... 15°18'N 61°1
Dominican Republic Central America 67 J4
.... 18°57'N 70°2
Don r. Russia 54 F2 .... 47°06'N 39°1
Don r. Scotland 17 G2 .... 57°10'N 2°05
Donaghadee Northern Ireland 14 D2 .... 54°38'N 5°3
Donbas f. Ukraine 53 D2 .... 48°18'N 38°1
Don Benito Spain 45 C3 .... 38°58'N 5°5
Doncaster England 13 F2 .... 53°31'N 1°08
Dondo Angola 83 A4 .... 9°41'S 14°2
Donegal Ireland 18 C4 .... 54°39'N 8°07
Donegal d. Ireland 18 C4 .... 54°56'N 8°0
Donegal Bay Ireland 18 C4 .... 54°31'N 8°2
Donegal Point Ireland 18 B2 .... 52°43'N 9°3
Donetsk Ukraine 49 K6 .... 47°59'N 37°4
Dongara Australia 108 A4 .... 29°17'S 114°5
Dongfang China 99 J1 .... 19°03'N 108°3
Dong Hoi Vietnam 102 D7 .... 17°26'N 106°3
Dongting Hu l. China 99 K3 .... 29°20'N 112°5
Dongying China 99 L5 .... 37°25'N 118°4
Donostia/San Sebastián Spain 45 D5 ... 43°19'N 1°59
Doon r. Scotland 14 E3 .... 55°26'N 4°39
Doon, Loch l. Scotland 14 E3 .... 55°15'N 4°2
Dorchester England 8 C1 .... 50°43'N 2°2
Dordogne r. France 44 C4 .... 45°01'N 0°0
Dordrecht Neth. 42 D4 .... 51°48'N 4°4
Dörgön Nuur l. Mongolia 98 G7 .... 47°33'N 93°2
Dorking England 9 E2 .... 51°14'N 0°2
Dornbirn Austria 46 C2 .... 47°26'N 9°4
Dornoch Scotland 17 E2 .... 57°52'N 4°02
Dornoch Firth est. Scotland 17 E2 .... 57°51'N 4°04
Dorset d. England 21 D2 .... 50°55'N 2°1
Dortmund Germany 46 B4 .... 51°30'N 7°2
Dos Bahías, Cabo c. Argentina 73 C2 ... 44°56'S 65°3
Dōshī Afgh. 95 K7 .... 35°38'N 68°4
Dosso Niger 84 E3 .... 13°03'N 3°1
Dothan U.S. 63 I3 .... 31°14'N 85°2
Douai France 44 E7 .... 50°22'N 3°0
Douala Cameroon 84 E2 .... 4°03'N 9°4
Douglas Isle of Man 12 C3 .... 54°09'N 4°2
Douglas Scotland 15 F3 .... 55°33'N 3°5
Douglas U.S. 62 E3 .... 31°20'N 109°3
Doullens France 44 E7 .... 50°09'N 2°2
Doune Scotland 15 E4 .... 56°11'N 4°0
Dounreay Scotland 17 F3 .... 58°35'N 3°4
Dourados Brazil 73 D4 .... 22°13'S 54°4
Douro r. Portugal 45 A4 .... 41°09'N 8°3
Dove r. Derbys. England 8 D4 .... 53°11'N 1°4
Dove r. Suff. England 9 G3 .... 52°21'N 1°1
Dover England 9 G2 .... 51°08'N 1°1
Dover U.S. 63 K4 .... 39°09'N 75°3
Dover, Strait of France/U.K. 9 G1 .... 50°53'N 1°1
Down d. Northern Ireland 18 F4 .... 54°20'N 5°5
Downham Market England 9 F3 .... 52°36'N 0°2
Downpatrick Northern Ireland 14 D2 .... 54°19'N 5°4
Downpatrick Head Ireland 18 B4 .... 54°20'N 9°2
Downton England 8 D1 .... 50°59'N 1°4
Drachten Neth. 42 F6 .... 53°06'N 6°0
Draguignan France 44 G3 .... 43°32'N 6°
Drahichyn Belarus 47 K5 .... 52°11'N 25°

akensberg *mts* Lesotho/S. Africa 83 B2......29°59'S 28°56'E
ama Greece 50 F5..........................41°09'N 24°08'E
ammen Norway 43 B2.......................59°45'N 10°12'E
aperstown Northern Ireland 14 C2.....54°48'N 6°46'W
au *r.* Austria 46 E2...........................46°38'N 14°57'E
ava *r.* Europe 50 C7........................45°33'N 18°56'E
enthe *d.* Neth. 42 F5.........................52°53'N 6°43'E
esden Germany 46 E4.........................51°03'N 13°45'E
eux France 44 D6.............................48°44'N 1°23'E
iffield England 13 G2........................54°00'N 0°27'W
ina *r.* Bos. and Herz./Serbia 50 C7....44°55'N 19°22'E
ogheda Ireland 18 E3........................53°43'N 6°21'W
ohobych Ukraine 47 J3......................49°22'N 23°32'E
oitwich Spa England 8 C3..................52°16'N 2°09'W
omore Northern Ireland 14 C2...........54°25'N 6°08'W
onfield England 13 F2.......................53°18'N 1°28'W
osh Pakistan 95 L7..........................35°33'N 71°50'E
umheller Canada 60 G3....................51°27'N 112°42'W
ummore Scotland 14 E2....................54°41'N 4°54'W
uskininkai Lithuania 47 K5................53°59'N 24°01'E
uts' *r.* Belarus 47 N5........................53°03'N 30°03'E
ygarn Fawr *hill* Wales 10 D4.............52°13'N 3°40'W
ymen Scotland 14 E4.......................56°04'N 4°27'W
arte, Pico *mt.* Dom. Rep. 67 J4.........19°03'N 70°59'W
abā Saudi Arabia 94 E5.....................27°20'N 35°45'E
bai U.A.E. 95 I5..............................25°14'N 55°17'E
bawnt Lake Canada 60 H4...............63°05'N 107°42'W
bbo Australia 108 D3.......................32°16'S 148°39'E
blin Ireland 18 E3............................53°20'N 6°16'W
blin Bay Ireland 18 E3......................53°21'N 6°10'W
blin City *d.* Ireland 18 E3..................53°24'N 6°18'W
bno Ukraine 47 L4...........................50°25'N 25°43'E
brovnik Croatia 50 C6.......................42°39'N 18°06'E
brovytsia Ukraine 47 L4...................51°34'N 26°34'E
dinka Russia 55 J4...........................69°22'N 86°11'E
dley England 8 C3............................52°31'N 2°05'W
ero *r.* Spain 45 B4............................41°02'N 6°56'W
fftown Scotland 17 F2.......................57°27'N 3°08'W
fourspitze *mt.* Italy/Switz. 46 B1........45°57'N 7°53'E
gi Otok *i.* Croatia 50 A7....................44°01'N 15°01'E
isburg Germany 46 B4......................51°28'N 6°47'E
khān Qatar 95 H5.............................25°25'N 50°47'E
luth U.S. 63 H6...............................46°45'N 92°07'W
lverton England 11 D3.......................51°02'N 3°33'W
mas U.S. 62 F4................................35°53'N 101°59'W
mbarton Scotland 14 E3....................55°57'N 4°34'W
mfries Scotland 15 F3........................55°04'N 3°36'W
mfries and Galloway *d.* Scotland 20 D4...55°09'N 3°46'W
myât Egypt 49 J3.............................31°25'N 31°49'E
naff Head Ireland 14 B3....................55°18'N 7°31'W
nany Point Ireland 18 E3...................53°52'N 6°14'W
naújváros Hungary 46 H2..................46°59'N 18°56'E
nbar Scotland 15 G4.........................56°00'N 2°31'W
nblane Scotland 15 F4.......................56°11'N 3°58'W
ncansby Head Scotland 17 F3............58°39'N 3°01'W
nchurch England 8 D3......................52°00'N 1°17'W
ndalk Ireland 18 E4..........................54°00'N 6°24'W
ndalk Bay Ireland 18 E3...................53°57'N 6°13'W
ndee Scotland 15 G4........................56°28'N 2°58'W
ndee *d.* Scotland 20 D5....................56°29'N 2°59'W
ndonald Northern Ireland 14 D2........54°36'N 5°48'W
nedin New Zealand 109 G2...............45°53'S 170°30'E
nfermline Scotland 15 F4..................56°04'N 3°27'W
ngannon Northern Ireland 14 C2........54°30'N 6°46'W
ngarvan Ireland 18 D2.....................52°05'N 7°38'W
ngeness *hd* England 9 F1..................50°55'N 0°59'E
ngiven Northern Ireland 14 C2...........54°55'N 6°55'W
ngun Malaysia 102 C4.......................4°46'N 103°23'E
ngunab Sudan 94 E4........................21°04'N 37°04'E
nholme England 13 G2.....................53°18'N 0°28'W
nhuang China 98 G6.........................40°07'N 94°40'E
nkerque France 44 E7......................51°02'N 2°22'E
nkery Beacon *hill* England 11 D3........51°10'N 3°35'W
nkirk France 44 E7...........................51°02'N 2°22'E
n Laoghaire Ireland 18 E3.................53°17'N 6°08'W
n Laoghaire-Rathdown *d.* Ireland 18 E3...53°15'N 6°12'W
nleer Ireland 18 E3..........................53°50'N 6°23'W
nloy Northern Ireland 14 C3.............55°00'N 6°24'W
nmore East Ireland 18 E2.................52°09'N 6°59'W
nmurry Northern Ireland 14 D2.........54°33'N 5°59'W
nnet Bay Scotland 17 F3..................58°37'N 3°24'W
nnet Head Scotland 17 F3................58°41'N 3°23'W
noon Scotland 14 E3.......................55°57'N 4°56'W
ns Scotland 15 G3...........................55°47'N 2°21'W
nstable England 9 E2.......................51°53'N 0°31'W
nvegan, Loch *b.* Scotland 16 C2.........57°31'N 6°41'W
rance *r.* France 44 F3.......................43°55'N 4°45'E
rango Mexico 66 D5........................24°02'N 104°43'W
rango *d.* Mexico 66 D5.....................24°44'N 104°59'W
rango U.S. 62 E4.............................37°16'N 107°52'W
rban S. Africa 83 C2.........................29°51'S 31°02'E
ren Germany 42 F3..........................50°48'N 6°29'E
rham England 13 F3.........................54°47'N 1°35'W
rham *d.* England 21 D4....................54°42'N 2°09'W
rham U.S. 63 K4.............................35°59'N 78°54'W
rness Scotland 16 E3........................58°34'N 4°45'W
rness, Kyle of *inlet* Scotland 16 E3....58°34'N 4°44'W
rrës Albania 50 C5...........................41°19'N 19°27'E
rsey Head Ireland 18 A1....................51°34'N 10°13'W
rsley England 13 G2.........................53°25'N 1°21'W
shanbe Tajikistan 96 C8...................38°38'N 68°51'E
sseldorf Germany 46 B4....................51°13'N 6°47'E
tce Turkey 51 I5..............................40°50'N 31°09'E
st'kovo Russia 47 P5........................53°36'N 34°21'E
e *r.* Wales 10 D4.............................52°33'N 3°56'W
nchurch England 9 F2.......................51°01'N 0°59'E
nock England 8 C2..........................52°44'N 2°06'W
rzhinsk Russia 52 E3.........................56°14'N 43°28'E
ankoi Ukraine 49 J6.........................45°43'N 34°24'E
ugdzhur, Khrebet *mts* Russia 55 O3...55°53'N 135°07'E
sna *r.* Belarus 47 M6.......................53°33'N 28°13'E

ng England 9 E2.............................51°31'N 0°18'W
ston England 15 G3.........................55°38'N 2°41'W
n *r.* Scotland 15 F4..........................56°20'N 3°20'W
n, Loch *l.* Scotland 14 E4..................56°23'N 4°15'W
ington England 13 F3......................54°47'N 1°21'W
ngwold England 13 F3.....................54°07'N 1°11'W

East Anglian Heights *hills* England 9 F3........52°03'N 0°15'E
East Ayrshire *d.* Scotland 20 C4..........55°29'N 4°15'W
Eastbourne England 9 F1...................50°46'N 0°18'E
East Cape New Zealand 109 G3..........37°40'S 178°33'E
East China Sea N. Pacific Oc. 99 N4.....31°00'N 127°22'E
East Dunbartonshire *d.* Scotland 20 C4...55°58'N 4°12'W
Easter Island S. Pacific Oc. 116 C2........27°05'S 109°17'W
Eastern Desert Egypt 49 J2................26°39'N 32°50'E
Eastern Ghats *mts* India 96 E3............11°54'N 77°22'E
Easter Ross *f.* Scotland 16 E2..............57°49'N 4°24'W
East Falkland *i.* Falkland Is 73 D1.........52°11'S 57°55'W
East Fen *f.* England 13 H2...................53°05'N 0°04'E
Eastfield England 13 G3.....................54°15'N 0°24'W
East Frisian Islands Germany 46 B5.....53°45'N 7°00'E
East Grinstead England 9 E2..............51°08'N 0°01'W
East Kilbride Scotland 14 E3...............55°46'N 4°10'W
Eastleigh England 8 D1.....................50°58'N 1°22'W
East Linton Scotland 15 G3...............55°59'N 2°39'W
East London S. Africa 83 B1...............33°01'S 27°56'E
East Looe England 11 C2..................50°21'N 4°27'W
East Lothian *d.* Scotland 20 D4...........55°57'N 2°45'W
Eastmain Canada 61 K3...................52°14'N 78°30'W
Eastmain *r.* Canada 61 K3................52°14'N 78°24'W
Easton England 8 C1.......................50°33'N 2°26'W
East Renfrewshire *d.* Scotland 20 C4...55°46'N 4°21'W
East Riding of Yorkshire *d.* England 21 E3...53°55'N 0°19'W
Eastry England 9 G2........................51°15'N 1°18'E
East Sea N. Pacific Oc. 104 B3...........39°13'N 133°37'E
East Siberian Sea Russia 55 P5..........72°59'N 148°21'E
East Sussex *d.* England 21 F2............50°53'N 0°17'E
East Timor Asia 103 H2.....................8°57'S 125°59'E
Eastwood England 13 F2..................53°01'N 1°18'W
Eaton Socon England 9 E3...............52°13'N 0°17'W
Eau Claire U.S. 63 H5......................44°49'N 91°30'W
Eau Claire, Lac à l' *l.* Canada 61 K3.....56°13'N 74°07'W
Eauripik *atoll* Micronesia 103 K5..........6°43'N 143°04'E
Ebbw Vale Wales 10 D3....................51°47'N 3°12'W
Eberswalde Germany 46 E5................52°50'N 13°49'E
Ebinur Hu *f.* China 98 E6...................44°46'N 82°51'E
Ebro *r.* Spain 45 F4...........................40°43'N 0°51'E
Ecclefechan Scotland 15 F3...............55°04'N 3°16'W
Eccleshall England 8 C3....................52°52'N 2°15'W
Écija Spain 45 C2.............................37°33'N 5°04'W
Eck, Loch *l.* Scotland 14 E4...............56°04'N 4°59'W
Eckington England 8 C3....................52°04'N 2°07'W
Ecuador S. America 72 B6..................1°08'S 78°05'W
Eday *i.* Scotland 17 G4......................59°11'N 2°50'W
Ed Da'ein Sudan 94 F2.....................11°27'N 26°09'E
Ed Damazin Sudan 85 H3..................11°47'N 34°20'E
Ed Damer Sudan 85 H3....................17°26'N 33°58'E
Ed Dueim Sudan 94 D2....................13°57'N 32°17'E
Eden *r.* England 12 D3.....................54°57'N 3°01'W
Edessa Greece 50 E5........................40°48'N 22°04'E
Edgeøya *i.* Arctic Oc. 54 D5..............77°32'N 22°45'E
Edinburgh Scotland 15 F3.................55°57'N 3°11'W
Edirne Turkey 51 G4.........................41°39'N 26°34'E
Edmonton Canada 60 G3..................53°33'N 113°33'W
Edmundston Canada 61 L2................47°23'N 68°20'W
Edremit Turkey 50 G4......................39°35'N 27°00'E
Edson Canada 60 G3.......................53°35'N 116°25'W
Edward, Lake Dem. Rep. Congo/Uganda 83 B4
....0°17'S 29°40'E
Edwards Plateau *f.* U.S. 62 F3...........30°28'N 100°22'W
Efate *i.* Vanuatu 109 F5...................17°38'S 168°30'E
Effingham U.S. 63 I4........................39°07'N 88°33'W
Eger Hungary 46 I2..........................47°54'N 20°22'E
Egilsay *i.* Scotland 17 G4..................59°09'N 2°55'W
Egilsstaðir Iceland 43 Z2..................65°16'N 14°25'W
Eğirdir Turkey 51 I3.........................37°51'N 30°51'E
Eğirdir Gölü *l.* Turkey 51 I3...............37°59'N 30°53'E
Eglinton Northern Ireland 14 B3.........55°02'N 7°11'W
Egremont England 12 D3..................54°29'N 3°32'W
Egvekinot Russia 55 T4....................66°20'N 179°17'W
Egypt Africa 85 G4...........................29°53'N 31°16'E
Eifel *hills* Germany 46 B4..................50°10'N 6°39'E
Eigg *i.* Scotland 16 C1......................56°54'N 6°10'W
Eighty Mile Beach *f.* Australia 108 B5...19°54'S 120°10'E
Eilat Israel 49 J2.............................29°33'N 34°56'E
Eilean Siar *d.* Scotland 20 B6............58°15'N 6°33'W
Eindhoven Neth. 42 E4.....................51°26'N 5°29'E
Eisenhüttenstadt Germany 46 F5.......52°09'N 14°38'E
Eishort, Loch *inlet* Scotland 16 D2.......57°09'N 5°59'W
Ekibastuz Kazakhstan 98 D8.............51°46'N 75°27'E
Ekostrovskaya Imandra, Ozero *l.* Russia 43 H4
....67°29'N 32°23'E
Eksjö Sweden 43 C2.........................57°40'N 14°59'E
Elazığ Turkey 51 M4........................38°39'N 39°15'E
Elba, Isola d' *i.* Italy 48 F5................42°50'N 10°16'E
El'ban Russia 99 P8.........................50°03'N 136°26'E
Elbasan Albania 50 D5.....................41°07'N 20°05'E
El Bayadh Algeria 48 D3...................33°41'N 0°56'E
Elbe *r.* Germany 46 C5......................53°53'N 9°05'E
Elbert, Mount U.S. 62 E4.................39°05'N 106°25'W
Elbistan Turkey 51 L4......................38°12'N 37°11'E
Elbląg Poland 46 H6........................54°10'N 19°24'E
El'brus *mt.* Russia 53 E2...................43°22'N 42°25'E
Elda Spain 45 E3.............................38°29'N 0°47'W
El Dorado U.S. 63 H3.......................33°13'N 92°36'W
Eldoret Kenya 85 H2.........................0°31'N 35°15'E
El Eulma Algeria 48 E4.....................36°07'N 5°48'E
Eleuthera *i.* Bahamas 67 I6...............25°21'N 76°22'W
El Fasher Sudan 85 G3.....................13°36'N 25°20'E
El Geneina Sudan 85 G3...................13°26'N 22°26'E
Elgin Scotland 17 F2........................57°39'N 3°19'W
El'ginskiy Russia 55 P4.....................64°32'N 141°40'E
Elgon, Mount Kenya/Uganda 85 H2...1°08'N 34°34'E
El Hierro *i.* Canary Islands 45 X1.........27°40'N 17°56'W
Elhovo Bulgaria 50 G6......................42°11'N 26°34'E
Elista Russia 53 E2..........................46°19'N 44°16'E
El Jadida Morocco 84 D5...................33°12'N 8°27'W
Ełk Poland 47 J5.............................53°50'N 22°22'E
Elko U.S. 62 D5..............................40°51'N 115°46'W
Ellef Ringnes Island Canada 61 H5.....78°38'N 101°56'W
Ellensburg U.S. 62 B6......................46°59'N 120°32'W
Ellesmere England 8 C3...................52°54'N 2°54'W
Ellesmere Island Canada 61 J5...........77°10'N 83°03'W
Ellesmere Port England 12 E2............53°17'N 2°54'W
Ellice *r.* Canada 60 H4......................67°56'N 103°59'W
Ellon Scotland 17 G2.......................57°22'N 2°04'W
Elmalı Turkey 51 H3.........................36°44'N 29°55'E
El Meghaïer Algeria 48 E3.................33°56'N 5°56'E
El Meniaa Algeria 84 E5....................30°34'N 2°58'E
El Muglad Sudan 85 G3....................11°01'N 27°44'E
El Obeid Sudan 85 H3......................13°10'N 30°11'E
El Oued Algeria 48 E3.......................33°21'N 6°54'E
El Paso U.S. 62 E3...........................31°46'N 106°29'W

El Puerto de Santa María Spain 45 B2..........36°36'N 6°13'W
El Salvador Central America 66 G3........13°22'N 88°59'W
El Tigre Venezuela 67 L2....................8°52'N 64°16'W
Eluru India 96 F4.............................16°44'N 81°09'E
Elvas Portugal 45 B3........................38°53'N 7°10'W
Elverum Norway 43 B3......................60°53'N 11°33'E
Elx/Elche Spain 45 E3.......................38°16'N 0°41'W
Ely England 9 F3.............................52°24'N 0°15'E
Ely U.S. 62 D4................................39°15'N 114°53'W
Ely, Isle of *f.* England 9 F3.................52°27'N 0°14'E
Embi Kazakhstan 53 F2.....................48°47'N 58°07'E
Emden Germany 46 B5.....................53°22'N 7°13'E
Emerson Canada 62 G6....................49°02'N 97°11'W
Emi Koussi *mt.* Chad 85 F3.................19°46'N 18°34'E
Emirdağ Turkey 51 I4......................39°01'N 31°09'E
Emmeloord Neth. 42 E5....................52°43'N 5°45'E
Emmen Neth. 42 F5.........................52°47'N 6°54'E
Emory Peak U.S. 62 F2.....................29°15'N 103°18'W
Endeh Indonesia 103 G2....................8°47'S 121°38'E
Endicott Mountains U.S. 60 C4...........67°50'N 152°33'W
Enfield England 9 E2........................51°39'N 0°05'W
Engel's Russia 53 E3.........................51°29'N 46°06'E
Enggano *i.* Indonesia 102 C2...............5°25'S 102°20'E
England U.K. 21 E3...........................52°48'N 1°24'W
English Channel France/U.K. 9 E1.........49°59'N 1°24'W
Enköping Sweden 43 D2....................59°38'N 17°06'E
En Nahud Sudan 85 G3.....................12°42'N 28°25'E
Ennedi, Massif *mts* Chad 94 B3..........16°59'N 22°58'E
Ennerdale Water *l.* England 12 D3.......54°30'N 3°22'W
Ennis Ireland 18 C2..........................52°51'N 8°59'W
Enniscorthy Ireland 18 E2..................52°30'N 6°34'W
Enniskerry Ireland 10 A5....................53°11'N 6°10'W
Enniskillen Northern Ireland 14 B2.......54°20'N 7°37'W
Ennistymon Ireland 18 B2.................52°56'N 9°17'W
Enns *r.* Austria 46 F3........................48°14'N 14°31'E
Enschede Neth. 42 F5.......................52°13'N 6°54'E
Ensenada Mexico 66 A7....................31°52'N 116°37'W
Enshi China 99 J4............................30°13'N 109°28'E
Enugu Nigeria 84 E2..........................6°24'N 7°31'E
Envira *r.* Brazil 72 B6.........................7°31'S 70°14'W
Épinal France 44 G6.........................48°11'N 6°27'E
Epping England 9 F2........................51°42'N 0°07'E
Epsom England 9 E2........................51°20'N 0°16'W
Epworth England 13 G2....................53°32'N 0°49'W
Epynt, Mynydd *hills* Wales 10 D4........52°05'N 3°28'W
Eqlid Iran 95 H6..............................30°53'N 52°42'E
Equatorial Guinea Africa 84 E2............1°08'N 8°36'E
Équeurdreville-Hainneville France 11 Z9...49°39'N 1°39'W
Erbeskopf *hill* Germany 42 G2............49°43'N 7°04'E
Erciyes Dağı *mt.* Turkey 51 K4...........38°32'N 35°27'E
Erdemli Turkey 51 K3.......................36°36'N 34°19'E
Erdi *f.* Chad 94 B3...........................19°02'N 21°36'E
Ereğli Konya Turkey 51 K3.................37°30'N 34°03'E
Ereğli Zonguldak Turkey 51 I5............41°17'N 31°25'E
Ereymentaū Kazakhstan 98 C8..........51°36'N 73°08'E
Erfurt Germany 46 D4.......................50°59'N 11°02'E
Ergani Turkey 51 M4.........................38°15'N 39°46'E
Ergene *r.* Turkey 50 G5......................40°59'N 26°22'E
Ericht *r.* Scotland 15 F4.....................56°34'N 3°15'W
Ericht, Loch *l.* Scotland 17 E1............56°48'N 4°25'W
Erie U.S. 63 J5................................42°07'N 80°06'W
Erie, Lake Canada/U.S. 61 J2............42°14'N 80°53'W
Eriskay *i.* Scotland 16 B2...................57°04'N 7°16'W
Eritrea Africa 85 H3..........................15°57'N 37°33'E
Erlangen Germany 46 D3...................49°35'N 11°01'E
Ermenek Turkey 51 J3......................36°37'N 32°54'E
Ermoupoli Greece 50 F3....................37°26'N 24°56'E
Erode India 96 E3............................11°21'N 77°43'E
Errachidia Morocco 84 D5..................31°54'N 4°29'W
Er Rahad Sudan 85 H3......................12°44'N 30°38'E
Errigal *hill* Ireland 18 C5....................55°02'N 8°07'W
Erris Head Ireland 18 A4...................54°19'N 10°01'W
Errochty, Loch *l.* Scotland 17 E1.........56°45'N 4°11'W
Erromango *i.* Vanuatu 109 F5............18°49'S 168°58'E
Erzincan Turkey 94 F7.......................39°45'N 39°29'E
Erzurum Turkey 94 F7.......................39°53'N 41°17'E
Esbjerg Denmark 43 B1....................55°28'N 8°27'E
Escanaba U.S. 63 I6.........................45°45'N 87°03'W
Escárcega Mexico 66 F4....................18°39'N 90°43'W
Esch-sur-Alzette Lux. 42 E2...............49°30'N 5°59'E
Eschweiler Germany 42 F3.................50°49'N 6°18'E
Eşfahān Iran 95 H6..........................32°41'N 51°39'E
Esha Ness *hd* Scotland 17 H5.............60°30'N 1°37'W
Esk *r.* Scotland 15 F3........................55°56'N 3°04'W
Eske, Lough *l.* Ireland 14 A2..............54°42'N 8°04'W
Eski Gediz Turkey 51 H4...................39°03'N 29°25'E
Eskilstuna Sweden 43 D2..................59°22'N 16°32'E
Eskişehir Turkey 51 I4.......................39°47'N 30°31'E
Esla *r.* Spain 45 B4..........................41°30'N 6°01'W
Eslāmābād-e Gharb Iran 95 G6..........34°06'N 46°31'E
Esperance Australia 108 B3................33°49'S 121°52'E
Espigüete *mt.* Spain 45 C5................42°57'N 4°47'W
Espíritu Santo *i.* Vanuatu 109 F5.........15°16'S 166°35'E
Espoo Finland 43 F3.........................60°12'N 24°40'E
Esquel Argentina 73 B2.....................42°55'S 71°20'W
Essen Germany 46 B4.......................51°28'N 7°03'E
Essequibo *r.* Guyana 72 D7.................6°23'N 58°36'W
Essex *d.* England 21 F2......................51°51'N 0°42'E
Estados, Isla de los *i.* Argentina 73 C1...54°44'S 64°16'W
Estats, Pique d' *mt.* France/Spain 45 F5...42°40'N 1°24'E
Estevan Canada 60 H2......................49°08'N 102°59'W
Estonia Europe 43 F2........................58°44'N 25°26'E
Estrela, Serra da *mts* Portugal 45 B4....40°11'N 7°57'W
Estremoz Portugal 45 B3...................38°24'N 3°36'W
Eswatini Africa 83 C2.......................26°29'S 31°30'E
Étaples France 44 D7........................50°31'N 1°39'E
Ethiopia Africa 85 H2.........................6°30'N 39°41'E
Ethiopian Highlands *f.* Ethiopia 85 H2...8°49'N 36°39'E
Etimesğut Turkey 51 J4.....................39°56'N 32°39'E
Etive, Loch *inlet* Scotland 14 D4.........56°27'N 5°12'W
Etna, Mount *vol.* Italy 48 G4..............37°46'N 15°00'E
Etosha Pan *f.* Namibia 83 A3..............18°52'S 16°19'E
Ettelbruck Lux. 42 F2.......................49°51'N 6°06'E
Ettrick Forest Scotland 15 F3..............55°31'N 3°05'W
Ettrick Water *r.* Scotland 15 G3...........55°34'N 2°49'W
Etwall England 8 D3........................52°53'N 1°36'W
Eugene U.S. 62 B5..........................44°04'N 123°05'W
Eugenia, Punta *pt* Mexico 66 A6.........27°51'N 115°04'W
Euphrates *r.* Asia 94 F6....................30°48'N 47°24'E
Eureka U.S. 62 B5...........................40°48'N 124°09'W
Europa, Picos de *mts* Spain 45 C5.......43°07'N 5°01'W
Europe 34
Evans, Lac *l.* Canada 61 K3................50°49'N 77°00'W
Evanston U.S. 62 E5.........................41°17'N 110°58'W
Evansville U.S. 63 I4........................37°59'N 87°32'W
Evaton S. Africa 83 B2......................26°32'S 27°49'E

Everest, Mount China/Nepal 98 F3.............27°59'N 86°55'E
Everglades *f.* U.S. 63 J2.....................26°15'N 81°02'W
Evesham England 8 D3.....................52°06'N 1°57'W
Evesham, Vale of *f.* England 8 D3........52°05'N 1°57'W
Évora Portugal 45 B3........................38°34'N 7°54'W
Évreux France 44 D6........................49°01'N 1°09'E
Evvoia *i.* Greece 50 F4......................38°12'N 24°14'E
Ewe, Loch *b.* Scotland 16 D2.............57°50'N 5°40'W
Exe *r.* England 11 D2........................50°41'N 3°29'W
Exeter England 11 D2......................50°43'N 3°32'W
Exminster England 11 D2..................50°41'N 3°30'W
Exmoor *hills* England 11 D3...............51°10'N 3°46'W
Exmouth England 11 D2...................50°37'N 3°25'W
Exuma Cays *is* Bahamas 67 I5...........24°35'N 76°34'W
Exuma Sound *str.* Bahamas 67 I5........24°17'N 75°59'W
Eyasi, Lake Tanzania 83 C4.................3°38'S 35°05'E
Eye P'boro. England 9 E3..................52°37'N 0°11'W
Eye Suff. England 9 G3.....................52°19'N 1°09'E
Eyemouth Scotland 15 G3.................55°52'N 2°05'W
Eye Peninsula *f.* Scotland 16 C3...........58°14'N 6°14'W
Ezhva Russia 52 E4..........................61°48'N 50°45'E
Ezine Turkey 50 G4.........................39°46'N 26°19'E

F

Faenza Italy 46 D1...........................44°17'N 11°53'E
Făgăraş Romania 50 F7.....................45°51'N 24°59'E
Fagatogo American Samoa 109 H5......14°17'S 170°41'W
Fagersta Sweden 43 C2.....................59°59'N 15°49'E
Fairbanks U.S. 60 D4.......................64°50'N 147°47'W
Fair Head Northern Ireland 14 C3.......55°14'N 6°08'W
Fair Isle *i.* Scotland 17 H4.................59°34'N 1°38'W
Fairmont U.S. 63 H5........................43°39'N 94°28'W
Fairweather, Mount Canada/U.S. 60 E3
....58°54'N 137°29'W
Fais *i.* Micronesia 103 K5....................9°45'N 140°33'E
Faisalabad Pakistan 96 D7.................31°24'N 73°09'E
Fakaofo *atoll* Tokelau 109 H6...............9°23'S 171°08'W
Fakenham England 9 F3....................52°50'N 0°51'E
Fakfak Indonesia 103 J3......................2°55'S 132°17'E
Fal *r.* England 11 C2.........................50°14'N 4°58'W
Falcon Lake Mexico/U.S. 66 E6..........26°53'N 99°20'W
Falkenberg Sweden 43 C2.................56°55'N 12°31'E
Falkirk Scotland 15 F4......................56°00'N 3°47'W
Falkirk *d.* Scotland 20 D4..................55°59'N 3°48'W
Falkland Islands S. Atlantic Oc. 73 D1...50°55'S 59°36'W
Falköping Sweden 43 C2...................58°10'N 13°33'E
Falmouth England 11 B2...................50°09'N 5°04'W
Falmouth Bay England 11 B2.............50°08'N 5°04'W
Falso, Cabo *c.* Mexico 66 C5.............22°53'N 109°59'W
Falster *i.* Denmark 43 B1...................54°49'N 11°58'E
Falun Sweden 43 C3........................60°36'N 15°38'E
Famagusta Cyprus 51 J2..................35°06'N 33°57'E
Fanad Head Ireland 14 B3.................55°17'N 7°38'W
Fane *r.* Ireland 18 E3.......................53°57'N 6°22'W
Fannich, Loch *l.* Scotland 16 D2.........57°39'N 5°03'W
Farafra Oasis Egypt 94 C5................26°43'N 28°09'E
Farāh Afgh. 95 J6............................32°23'N 62°07'E
Farallon de Pajaros *vol.* N. Mariana Is 103 K8
....20°32'N 144°55'E
Farasān, Jazā'ir *is* Saudi Arabia 94 F3....16°48'N 41°41'E
Fareham England 8 D1.....................50°51'N 1°11'W
Farewell, Cape New Zealand 109 G2...40°29'S 172°40'E
Fargo U.S. 62 G6............................46°52'N 96°49'W
Faridabad India 96 E6......................28°25'N 77°19'E
Farnborough England 8 E2................51°17'N 0°45'W
Farndon England 12 E2....................53°05'N 2°53'W
Farne Islands England 13 F4.............55°38'N 1°37'W
Farnham England 8 E2.....................51°13'N 0°48'W
Faro Portugal 45 B2.........................37°01'N 7°56'W
Fårö *i.* Sweden 43 D2.......................57°58'N 19°22'E
Faroe Islands Europe 34 D5...............62°00'N 7°00'W
Farrāshband Iran 95 H5....................28°52'N 52°05'E
Fasā Iran 95 H5..............................28°56'N 53°38'E
Fastiv Ukraine 47 M4........................50°04'N 29°55'E
Fatehgarh India 96 E6......................27°22'N 79°36'E
Faulquemont France 42 F2................49°03'N 6°36'E
Faversham England 9 F2...................51°19'N 0°53'E
Faxaflói *b.* Iceland 43 X2..................64°27'N 22°58'W
Fayetteville U.S. 63 K4....................35°02'N 78°53'W
Fayrōz Köh Afgh. 95 K6...................34°28'N 65°03'E
Fdérik Mauritania 84 C4...................22°42'N 12°44'W
Feale *r.* Ireland 18 B2.......................52°28'N 9°38'W
Fear, Cape U.S. 63 K3.....................33°51'N 77°58'W
Fehmarn *i.* Germany 46 D6................54°29'N 11°07'E
Feira de Santana Brazil 72 F5............12°12'S 38°57'W
Feldkirch Austria 46 C2....................47°15'N 9°36'E
Felixstowe England 9 G2..................51°58'N 1°21'E
Femunden *l.* Norway 43 B3...............62°05'N 11°48'E
Feniton England 11 D2.....................50°47'N 3°16'W
Feodosiia Ukraine 49 K6..................45°02'N 35°22'E
Ferdows Iran 95 I6...........................33°59'N 58°10'E
Fergus Falls *town* U.S. 62 G6............46°17'N 96°07'W
Ferkessédougou Côte d'Ivoire 84 D2.....9°35'N 5°13'W
Fermanagh *f.* Northern Ireland 14 B2...54°17'N 7°35'W
Fermanagh and Omagh *d.* Northern Ireland 21 B4
....54°27'N 7°45'W
Fermoy Ireland 18 C2.......................52°08'N 8°17'W
Ferndown England 8 D1...................50°48'N 1°54'W
Ferrara Italy 46 D1...........................44°50'N 11°38'E
Ferrol Spain 45 A5...........................43°29'N 8°13'W
Ferryhill England 13 F3.....................54°41'N 1°33'W
Fès Morocco 84 D5..........................34°04'N 4°57'W
Fethaland, Point of Scotland 17 H5.....60°39'N 1°18'W
Fethard Ireland 18 D2......................52°28'N 7°42'E
Fethiye Turkey 51 H3.......................36°37'N 29°06'E
Fetlar *i.* Scotland 17 I5.....................60°38'N 0°49'W
Feuilles, Rivière aux *r.* Canada 61 K3...58°46'N 70°13'W
Feyzābād Afgh. 95 L7.......................37°05'N 70°41'E
Fez Morocco 84 D5..........................34°04'N 4°57'W
Fezzan *f.* Libya 84 F4.......................25°00'N 14°00'E
Ffestiniog Wales 10 D4.....................52°58'N 3°56'W
Fianarantsoa Madagascar 83 D2.........21°27'S 47°07'E
Fife *d.* Scotland 20 D4......................56°16'N 2°58'W
Fife Ness *pt* Scotland 15 G4..............56°16'N 2°35'W
Figeac France 44 E4.........................44°37'N 2°01'E
Figueira da Foz Portugal 45 A4...........40°10'N 8°51'W
Figueres Spain 45 G5.......................42°16'N 2°56'E
Figuig Morocco 48 C3......................32°09'N 1°17'W
Fiji S. Pacific Oc. 109 G5...................17°51'S 177°08'E
Filadelfia Paraguay 73 C4..................22°22'S 60°08'W
Filey England 13 G3.........................54°13'N 0°18'W
Filton England 8 C2.........................51°30'N 2°34'W
Findhorn *r.* Scotland 17 F2................57°38'N 3°38'W
Fingal *d.* Ireland 18 E3......................53°30'N 6°15'W

Finisterre, Cape Spain 45 A5 ....42°53'N 9°15'W
Finland Europe 43 F3 ....63°43'N 26°54'E
Finland, Gulf of Europe 43 E2 ....59°31'N 22°42'E
Finlay r. Canada 60 F3 ....56°41'N 124°49'W
Finn r. Ireland 18 D4 ....54°50'N 7°28'W
Finspång Sweden 43 C2 ....58°42'N 15°46'E
Finstown Scotland 17 F4 ....59°00'N 3°07'W
Fintona Northern Ireland 14 B2 ....54°29'N 7°19'W
Fionn Loch l. Scotland 16 D2 ....57°46'N 5°28'W
Fionnphort Scotland 14 C4 ....56°19'N 6°22'W
Fisher Strait Canada 61 J4 ....63°14'N 83°06'W
Fishguard Wales 10 C3 ....51°59'N 4°58'W
Fishguard Bay Wales 10 C4 ....52°01'N 4°58'W
Five Barrows Hill England 11 D3 ....51°07'N 3°49'W
Flagstaff U.S. 62 D4 ....35°12'N 111°39'W
Flamborough England 13 G3 ....54°07'N 0°07'W
Flamborough Head England 13 G3 ....54°07'N 0°03'W
Flannan Isles Scotland 16 B3 ....58°18'N 7°39'W
Flåsjön l. Sweden 43 C4 ....64°06'N 15°53'E
Flathead Lake U.S. 62 D6 ....47°52'N 114°03'W
Flat Holm i. Wales 11 D3 ....51°23'N 3°07'W
Fleet England 8 E2 ....51°17'N 0°50'W
Fleetwood England 12 D2 ....53°55'N 3°02'W
Flensburg Germany 46 C6 ....54°47'N 9°25'E
Flevoland d. Neth. 42 E5 ....52°17'N 5°07'E
Flinders r. Australia 108 D5 ....17°37'S 140°35'E
Flinders Island Australia 108 D3 ....39°56'S 148°04'E
Flinders Ranges mts Australia 108 C3 ..32°24'S 137°57'E
Flin Flon Canada 60 H3 ....54°46'N 101°51'W
Flint U.S. 63 J5 ....43°01'N 83°42'W
Flint Wales 10 D5 ....53°15'N 3°08'W
Flintshire d. Wales 21 D3 ....53°11'N 3°07'W
Florence Italy 48 F5 ....43°46'N 11°16'E
Florence U.S. 63 K3 ....34°11'N 79°45'W
Florencia Colombia 72 B7 ....1°36'N 75°36'W
Flores i. Indonesia 103 G2 ....8°29'S 121°14'E
Flores Sea Indonesia 102 F2 ....7°41'S 119°59'E
Florianópolis Brazil 73 E4 ....27°32'S 48°32'W
Florida d. U.S. 63 J3 ....30°12'N 83°39'W
Florida, Straits of Bahamas/U.S. 67 H5 ..23°59'N 81°35'W
Florida Keys i. U.S. 63 J1 ....24°41'N 81°38'W
Florina Greece 50 D5 ....40°46'N 21°24'E
Florø Norway 43 A3 ....61°36'N 5°01'E
Flotta i. Scotland 17 F3 ....58°50'N 3°55'W
Fly r. P.N.G. 103 K2 ....8°18'S 142°36'E
Foča Bos. and Herz. 50 C6 ....43°29'N 18°45'E
Fochabers Scotland 17 F2 ....57°37'N 3°06'W
Focşani Romania 50 G7 ....45°42'N 27°11'E
Foggia Italy 49 G5 ....41°28'N 15°33'E
Fogo i. Cape Verde 84 B3 ....14°59'N 24°18'W
Foinaven hill Scotland 16 E3 ....58°25'N 4°53'W
Foix France 44 D3 ....42°58'N 1°36'E
Folkestone England 9 G2 ....51°05'N 1°10'E
Fonseca, Golfo de b. Central America 66 G3
....13°03'N 88°12'W
Fontainebleau France 44 E6 ....48°25'N 2°43'E
Fontur pt Iceland 43 Z2 ....66°23'N 14°32'W
Førde Norway 43 A3 ....61°27'N 5°52'E
Fordingbridge England 8 D1 ....50°56'N 1°47'W
Foreland hd England 8 D1 ....50°41'N 1°04'W
Foreland Point England 11 D3 ....51°15'N 3°47'W
Forfar Scotland 17 G1 ....56°39'N 2°53'W
Forlì Italy 46 E1 ....44°14'N 12°02'E
Formby England 12 D2 ....53°34'N 3°04'W
Formentera i. Spain 45 E3 ....38°40'N 1°24'E
Formosa Argentina 73 D4 ....26°07'S 58°12'W
Forres Scotland 17 F2 ....57°37'N 3°37'W
Forssa Finland 43 E3 ....60°49'N 23°39'E
Fort Albany Canada 61 J3 ....52°13'N 81°41'W
Fortaleza Brazil 72 F6 ....3°43'S 38°32'W
Fort Augustus Scotland 16 E2 ....57°09'N 4°41'W
Fort Chipewyan Canada 60 G3 ....58°42'N 111°07'W
Fort Collins U.S. 62 E5 ....40°35'N 105°05'W
Fort-de-France Martinique 67 L3 ......14°37'N 61°05'W
Fortescue r. Australia 108 A4 ....21°02'S 116°06'E
Fort Frances Canada 61 I2 ....48°37'N 93°24'W
Fort Good Hope Canada 60 F4 ....66°16'N 128°39'W
Forth r. Scotland 14 F4 ....56°10'N 3°52'W
Forth, Firth of est. Scotland 15 F4 ....56°01'N 3°13'W
Fort Lauderdale U.S. 63 J2 ....26°04'N 80°11'W
Fort Liard Canada 60 F4 ....60°14'N 123°24'W
Fort McMurray Canada 60 G3 ....56°43'N 111°21'W
Fort McPherson Canada 60 E4 ....67°33'N 134°44'W
Fort Nelson Canada 60 F3 ....58°45'N 122°39'W
Fort Peck Reservoir U.S. 62 E6 ....47°47'N 106°55'W
Fort Pierce U.S. 63 J2 ....27°18'N 80°24'W
Fortrose Scotland 17 E2 ....57°35'N 4°08'W
Fort St John Canada 60 F3 ....56°15'N 120°49'W
Fort Severn Canada 61 J3 ....56°00'N 87°39'W
Fort-Shevchenko Kazakhstan 53 F2 ..44°29'N 50°17'E
Fort Simpson Canada 60 F4 ....61°52'N 121°22'W
Fort Smith Canada 60 G4 ....60°00'N 112°13'W
Fort Smith U.S. 63 H4 ....35°26'N 94°24'W
Fortuneswell England 8 C1 ....50°34'N 2°27'W
Fort Wayne U.S. 63 I5 ....41°04'N 85°08'W
Fort William Scotland 16 D1 ....56°49'N 5°06'W
Fort Worth U.S. 62 G4 ....32°46'N 97°19'W
Fort Yukon U.S. 60 D4 ....66°35'N 145°13'W
Foshan China 99 K2 ....23°03'N 113°06'E
Fossano Italy 46 B1 ....44°33'N 7°43'E
Fougères France 44 C6 ....48°21'N 1°12'W
Foula i. Scotland 17 G5 ....60°10'N 2°10'W
Foulness Point England 9 F2 ....51°37'N 0°57'E
Fouta Djallon f. Guinea 84 C3 ....11°26'N 12°34'W
Fowey r. England 11 C2 ....50°20'N 4°38'W
Foxe Basin g. Canada 61 K4 ....66°53'N 78°58'W
Foxe Channel Canada 61 K4 ....64°56'N 81°03'W
Foxe Peninsula Canada 61 K4 ....64°48'N 77°03'W
Foxford Ireland 18 B3 ....53°58'N 9°07'W
Fox Islands U.S. 60 B3 ....52°45'N 168°53'W
Foyle r. Ireland/U.K. 18 D4 ....54°53'N 7°26'W
Foyle, Lough inlet Ireland/U.K. 18 D5 ..55°07'N 7°07'W
Foz do Iguaçu Brazil 73 D4 ....25°30'S 54°32'W
Framlingham England 9 G3 ....52°13'N 1°21'E
France Europe 44 E5 ....46°57'N 1°17'E
Franceville Gabon 84 F1 ....1°37'S 13°37'E
Francistown Botswana 83 B2 ....21°10'S 27°29'E
Frankfort U.S. 63 J4 ....38°12'N 84°53'W
Frankfurt am Main Germany 46 C4 ..50°07'N 8°41'E
Frankfurt (Oder) Germany 46 F5 ......52°21'N 14°33'E
Franklin D. Roosevelt Lake resr U.S. 62 C6
....48°16'N 118°09'W
Frantsa-Iosifa, Zemlya is Russia 54 G5 ..79°40'N 58°29'E
Fraser r. Canada 60 F2 ....49°19'N 121°38'W
Fraserburgh Scotland 17 G2 ....57°42'N 2°01'W
Freckleton England 12 E2 ....53°45'N 2°52'W
Fredericia Denmark 43 B1 ....55°34'N 9°45'E

Fredericton Canada 61 L2 ....45°57'N 66°39'W
Frederikshavn Denmark 43 B2 ....57°27'N 10°32'E
Fredrikstad Norway 43 B2 ....59°13'N 10°56'E
Freeport Bahamas 67 I6 ....26°30'N 78°45'W
Freetown Sierra Leone 84 C2 ....8°28'N 13°12'W
Freiburg im Breisgau Germany 46 B3 ..48°00'N 7°50'E
Fréjus France 44 G3 ....43°26'N 6°45'E
Fremantle Australia 108 A3 ....32°05'S 115°42'E
French Guiana S. America 72 D7 ....3°56'N 53°03'W
French Polynesia is S. Pacific Oc. 114 B2
....18°43'S 147°32'W
Freshwater England 8 D1 ....50°41'N 1°31'W
Fresno U.S. 62 C4 ....36°46'N 119°46'W
Frévent France 9 H1 ....50°16'N 2°17'E
Freyming-Merlebach France 42 F2 ..49°09'N 6°48'E
Fria Guinea 84 C3 ....10°24'N 13°35'W
Friedrichshafen Germany 46 C2 ......47°39'N 9°31'E
Friesland d. Neth. 42 E6 ....53°08'N 5°48'E
Frinton-on-Sea England 9 G2 ....51°50'N 1°15'E
Frisa, Loch l. Scotland 14 C4 ....56°34'N 6°06'W
Frisian Islands Europe 34 E4 ....54°00'N 7°00'E
Frizington England 12 D3 ....54°32'N 3°30'W
Frobisher Bay Canada 61 L4 ....63°18'N 67°31'W
Frodsham England 12 E2 ....53°18'N 2°44'W
Frohavet b. Norway 43 B3 ....63°52'N 9°12'E
Frome England 8 C2 ....51°14'N 2°19'W
Frome r. England 8 C1 ....50°41'N 2°05'W
Frøya i. Norway 43 B3 ....63°41'N 8°39'E
Fruges France 9 H1 ....50°31'N 2°08'E
Frýdek-Místek Czechia 46 H3 ....49°41'N 18°21'E
Fuenlabrada Spain 45 D4 ....40°17'N 3°47'W
Fuerteventura i. Canary Islands 45 Y2 ..28°36'N 14°04'W
Fujairah U.A.E. 95 I5 ....25°06'N 56°21'E
Fuji San vol. Japan 104 C3 ....35°22'N 138°43'E
Fujian d. China 99 L3 ....25°52'N 117°59'E
Fukui Japan 104 C3 ....36°04'N 136°13'E
Fukuoka Japan 104 B2 ....33°35'N 130°24'E
Fukushima Japan 104 D3 ....37°45'N 140°28'E
Fulda Germany 46 C4 ....50°33'N 9°41'E
Fulford England 13 F2 ....53°56'N 1°04'W
Fulham England 9 E2 ....51°29'N 0°13'W
Fumay France 42 D2 ....49°59'N 4°42'E
Funafuti atoll Tuvalu 109 G6 ....8°25'S 179°13'E
Funchal Atlantic Oc. 84 C5 ....32°39'N 16°54'W
Fundy, Bay of Canada 61 L2 ....44°06'N 67°03'W
Fürth Germany 46 D3 ....49°29'N 10°57'E
Fushun China 99 M6 ....41°51'N 123°50'E
Fuxin China 99 M6 ....42°02'N 121°41'E
Fuyang China 99 L4 ....32°51'N 115°52'E
Fuyu China 99 M7 ....47°44'N 124°28'E
Fuzhou Fujian China 99 L3 ....26°07'N 119°21'E
Fuzhou Jiangxi China 99 L3 ....27°58'N 116°17'E
Fyn i. Denmark 43 B1 ....55°38'N 10°17'E

G

Gaalkacyo Somalia 85 I2 ....6°46'N 47°25'E
Gabès Tunisia 48 F3 ....33°53'N 10°07'E
Gabès, Golfe de g. Tunisia 48 F3 ......34°08'N 10°40'E
Gabon Africa 84 F1 ....0°56'S 11°32'E
Gaborone Botswana 83 B2 ....24°38'S 25°56'E
Gabrovo Bulgaria 50 F6 ....42°53'N 25°20'E
Gadsden U.S. 63 I3 ....34°03'N 86°04'W
Gaer Wales 10 D3 ....51°53'N 3°12'W
Gafsa Tunisia 48 E3 ....34°26'N 8°51'E
Gagarin Russia 47 P6 ....55°33'N 35°01'E
Gagnon Canada 61 L3 ....51°52'N 68°07'W
Gagra Georgia 51 N6 ....43°18'N 40°16'E
Gainesville U.S. 63 J2 ....29°36'N 82°20'W
Gainsborough England 13 G2 ....53°24'N 0°46'W
Gairdner, Lake Australia 108 C3 ......31°17'S 135°38'E
Gairloch Scotland 16 D2 ....57°44'N 5°42'W
Gairloch, Loch b. Scotland 16 D2 ....57°43'N 5°44'W
Galapagos Islands Ecuador 68 B3 ..0°03'S 89°05'W
Galashiels Scotland 15 G3 ....55°37'N 2°49'W
Galaţi Romania 51 H7 ....45°27'N 28°03'E
Gala Water r. Scotland 15 G3 ....55°36'N 2°47'W
Galdhøpiggen mt. Norway 43 B3 ......61°38'N 8°19'E
Galich Russia 52 E3 ....58°22'N 42°20'E
Galilee, Sea of l. Israel 49 K3 ....32°49'N 35°37'E
Gallabat Sudan 94 F2 ....12°57'N 36°06'E
Galle Sri Lanka 96 F2 ....6°04'N 80°09'E
Galley Head Ireland 18 C1 ....51°32'N 8°57'W
Gallinas, Punta pt Colombia 67 J3 ..12°27'N 71°42'W
Gallipoli Italy 49 G5 ....40°03'N 18°00'E
Gallipoli Turkey 50 G5 ....40°25'N 26°39'E
Gällivare Sweden 43 E4 ....67°08'N 20°40'E
Gallup U.S. 62 E4 ....35°32'N 108°45'W
Galston Scotland 14 E3 ....55°36'N 4°23'W
Galtat Zemmour Western Sahara 84 C4 ..25°08'N 12°24'W
Galtee Mountains hills Ireland 18 C2 ..52°19'N 8°16'W
Galveston U.S. 63 H2 ....29°15'N 94°54'W
Galveston Bay U.S. 63 H2 ....29°19'N 94°46'W
Galway Ireland 18 B3 ....53°16'N 9°03'W
Galway d. Ireland 18 B3 ....53°22'N 9°16'W
Galway Bay Ireland 18 B3 ....53°12'N 9°16'W
Galway City d. Ireland 18 B3 ....53°16'N 9°03'W
Gambia r. Bangl./India 96 H5 ....28°18'N 16°35'W
Gäncä Azerbaijan 53 E2 ....40°41'N 46°22'E
Gandadiwata, Bukit mt. Indonesia 102 F3 ..2°43'S 119°25'E
Gander Canada 61 M2 ....48°54'N 54°17'W
Gandhidham India 96 D5 ....23°06'N 70°08'E
Gandhinagar India 96 D5 ....23°14'N 72°44'E
Gandía Spain 45 E3 ....38°58'N 0°10'W
Ganges r. Bangl./India 96 H5 ....23°32'N 90°08'E
Ganges, Mouths of the Bangl./India 96 G5
....21°17'N 88°23'E
Gangneung S. Korea 104 A3 ....37°46'N 128°52'E
Gansu d. China 98 H6 ....40°17'N 97°56'E
Ganzhou China 99 K3 ....25°50'N 114°53'E
Gao Mali 84 D3 ....16°16'N 0°02'W
Gap France 44 G4 ....44°34'N 6°05'E
Gar China 98 E4 ....32°33'N 80°05'E
Gara, Lough l. Ireland 18 C3 ....53°57'N 8°28'W
Garabogaz Turkmenistan 53 F2 ......41°33'N 52°34'E
Garabogaz Köli b. Turkmenistan 53 F2
....41°24'N 53°32'E
Garabogazköl Turkmenistan 53 F2 ..41°04'N 52°56'E
Garanhuns Brazil 72 F6 ....8°52'S 36°22'W
Garcia Sola, Embalse de resr Spain 45 C3
....39°14'N 5°02'W
Gard r. France 44 F3 ....43°51'N 4°37'E
Garda, Lake Italy 46 D1 ....45°28'N 10°33'E
Garden City U.S. 62 F4 ....37°59'N 100°53'W

Gardëz Afgh. 95 K6 ....33°38'N 69°09'E
Garelochhead Scotland 14 E4 ....56°05'N 4°50'W
Garforth England 13 F2 ....53°48'N 1°23'W
Gargždai Lithuania 43 E1 ....55°43'N 21°24'E
Garissa Kenya 85 H1 ....0°25'S 39°40'E
Garmisch-Partenkirchen Germany 46 D2 ..47°30'N 11°06'E
Garonne r. France 44 C4 ....44°53'N 0°32'W
Garoowe Somalia 85 I2 ....8°23'N 48°28'E
Garoua Cameroon 84 F2 ....9°19'N 13°23'E
Garron Point Northern Ireland 14 D3 ..55°03'N 5°57'W
Garry r. Scotland 16 D2 ....57°04'N 4°46'W
Garry, Loch l. Scotland 17 E1 ....56°48'N 4°15'W
Garstang England 12 E2 ....53°54'N 2°46'W
Garvagh Northern Ireland 14 C2 ......54°59'N 6°41'W
Gary U.S. 63 I5 ....41°35'N 87°20'W
Gascony, Gulf of France 44 B3 ....43°43'N 2°00'W
Gascoyne r. Australia 108 A4 ....24°44'S 114°03'E
Gashua Nigeria 84 F3 ....12°51'N 11°04'E
Gaspé Canada 61 L2 ....48°48'N 64°32'W
Gaspé, Péninsule de pen. Canada 61 L2 ..48°35'N 65°31'W
Gastonia U.S. 63 J4 ....35°17'N 81°13'W
Gata, Cabo de c. Spain 45 D2 ....36°43'N 2°11'W
Gatehouse of Fleet Scotland 14 E2 ..54°53'N 4°11'W
Gateshead England 13 F3 ....54°57'N 1°36'W
Gatineau r. Canada 63 K6 ....45°27'N 75°42'W
Gävle Sweden 43 D3 ....60°41'N 17°08'E
Gaya India 96 G5 ....24°48'N 85°00'E
Gaya Niger 84 E3 ....11°54'N 3°27'E
Gaza Asia 49 J3 ....31°22'N 34°19'E
Gaza town Gaza 94 D6 ....31°31'N 34°26'E
Gaziantep Turkey 51 L3 ....37°03'N 37°21'E
Gdańsk Poland 46 H6 ....54°21'N 18°39'E
Gdansk, Gulf of Poland/Russia 46 H6 ..54°32'N 19°12'E
Gdynia Poland 46 H6 ....54°31'N 18°33'E
Geal Charn hill Scotland 17 F2 ....57°12'N 3°30'W
Gedaref Sudan 85 H3 ....14°02'N 35°23'E
Gediz r. Turkey 51 G4 ....38°35'N 26°48'E
Geel Belgium 42 E4 ....51°09'N 5°00'E
Geelong Australia 108 D3 ....38°08'S 144°21'E
Gejiu China 99 I2 ....23°22'N 103°09'E
Gela Italy 48 F4 ....37°04'N 14°15'E
Gelderland d. Neth. 42 F5 ....52°04'N 6°08'E
Gelincik Dağı mt. Turkey 51 I4 ....38°03'N 30°42'E
Gelli-gaer Wales 10 D3 ....51°40'N 3°15'W
Gelsenkirchen Germany 46 B4 ....51°33'N 7°06'E
Gemlik Turkey 51 H5 ....40°25'N 29°09'E
General Santos Phil. 103 H5 ....6°08'N 125°15'E
Geneva Switz. 48 E6 ....46°13'N 6°09'E
Geneva, Lake France/Switz. 44 G5 ..46°22'N 6°16'E
Genil r. Spain 45 C2 ....37°42'N 5°18'W
Genk Belgium 42 E3 ....50°57'N 5°31'E
Genoa Italy 46 C1 ....44°25'N 8°56'E
Genoa, Gulf of Italy 48 E5 ....44°08'N 8°57'E
George r. Canada 61 L3 ....58°19'N 65°55'W
George Town Malaysia 102 C5 ....5°26'N 100°17'E
Georgetown Guyana 72 D7 ....6°49'N 58°09'W
Georgia Asia 53 E2 ....41°49'N 43°59'E
Georgia d. U.S. 63 J3 ....32°35'N 83°28'W
Georgian Bay Canada 61 J2 ....45°17'N 80°51'W
Georgina watercourse Australia 108 C4 ..24°54'S 139°35'E
Georgiyevsk Russia 53 E2 ....44°09'N 43°29'E
Gera Germany 46 E4 ....50°53'N 12°06'E
Geraldton Australia 108 A4 ....28°46'S 114°37'E
Gerede Turkey 51 J5 ....40°48'N 32°12'E
Gereshk Afgh. 95 J6 ....31°51'N 64°37'E
Gerlachovský štít mt. Slovakia 46 I3 ..49°10'N 20°07'E
Germany Europe 46 D4 ....51°18'N 10°22'E
Gevgelija North Macedonia 50 E5 ..41°09'N 22°30'E
Geyik Dağı mt. Turkey 51 J3 ....36°52'N 32°11'E
Geyve Turkey 51 I5 ....40°30'N 30°15'E
Ghadāmis Libya 84 E5 ....30°05'N 9°34'E
Ghaem Shahr Iran 95 H7 ....36°32'N 52°39'E
Ghaghara r. India 96 F6 ....25°42'N 84°51'E
Ghana Africa 84 D2 ....8°23'N 0°47'W
Ghardaïa Algeria 84 E5 ....32°20'N 3°49'E
Gharyān Libya 48 F3 ....32°11'N 13°01'E
Ghazaouet Algeria 48 C4 ....35°06'N 1°51'W
Ghaziabad India 96 E6 ....28°40'N 77°25'E
Ghazni Afgh. 95 K6 ....33°33'N 68°27'E
Ghent Belgium 42 C4 ....51°03'N 3°43'E
Giant's Causeway f. Northern Ireland 14 C3
....55°14'N 6°31'W
Gibraltar Gibraltar 45 C2 ....36°08'N 5°21'W
Gibraltar, Strait of Morocco/Spain 45 B1 ..35°50'N 6°05'W
Gibson Desert Australia 108 B4 ......24°46'S 123°25'E
Gien France 44 E5 ....47°41'N 2°38'E
Gießen Germany 46 C4 ....50°35'N 8°41'E
Gifu Japan 104 C3 ....35°25'N 136°46'E
Gigha i. Scotland 14 D3 ....55°41'N 5°46'W
Gijón/Xixón Spain 45 C5 ....43°32'N 5°39'W
Gila r. U.S. 62 D3 ....32°45'N 114°31'W
Gilgit Pakistan 96 D8 ....35°54'N 74°21'E
Gill, Lough l. Ireland 18 C4 ....54°15'N 8°25'W
Gillette U.S. 62 E5 ....44°18'N 105°29'W
Gillingham Dor. England 8 C2 ....51°02'N 2°17'W
Gillingham Medway England 9 F2 ....51°23'N 0°33'E
Gilwern Wales 10 D3 ....51°49'N 3°06'W
Gimbala, Jebel mt. Sudan 94 B2 ......13°00'N 24°20'E
Giresun Turkey 51 M5 ....40°55'N 38°23'E
Girona Spain 45 G4 ....41°58'N 2°49'E
Gironde est. France 44 C4 ....45°31'N 0°59'W
Girvan Scotland 14 E3 ....55°15'N 4°51'W
Gisborne New Zealand 109 G3 ....38°39'S 178°01'E
Gitega Burundi 85 G1 ....3°27'S 29°56'E
Giurgiu Romania 50 F6 ....43°54'N 25°57'E
Giza Egypt 85 H4 ....29°59'N 31°12'E
Gizhiga Russia 55 R4 ....62°01'N 160°28'E
Gjirokastër Albania 50 D5 ....40°04'N 20°09'E
Gjøvik Norway 43 B3 ....60°48'N 10°42'E
Gladstone Australia 108 E4 ....23°51'S 151°18'E
Glan r. Germany 42 G2 ....49°47'N 7°42'E
Glanton England 13 F4 ....55°26'N 1°54'W
Glasgow Scotland 14 E3 ....55°52'N 4°15'W
Glasgow d. Scotland 20 C4 ....55°52'N 4°15'W
Glasgow U.S. 62 E6 ....48°10'N 106°34'W
Glass, Loch l. Scotland 17 E2 ....57°44'N 4°31'W
Glastonbury England 8 C2 ....51°09'N 2°43'W
Glazov Russia 52 F3 ....58°09'N 52°41'E
Glenarm Northern Ireland 14 D2 ......54°58'N 5°56'W
Glen Coe f. Scotland 16 D1 ....56°41'N 5°05'W
Glendale U.S. 62 D3 ....33°32'N 112°12'W
Glengad Head Ireland 18 D5 ....55°20'N 7°10'W
Glen Garry f. Scotland 16 D2 ....57°03'N 5°05'W
Glenluce Scotland 14 E2 ....54°53'N 4°49'W
Glen Moriston f. Scotland 16 E2 ......57°09'N 4°52'W
Glennallen U.S. 60 D4 ....62°09'N 145°32'W

Glenrothes Scotland 15 F4 ....56°12'N 3°10'W
Glen Shee f. Scotland 17 F1 ....56°48'N 3°29'W
Glinton England 9 E3 ....52°38'N 0°18'W
Gliwice Poland 46 H4 ....50°18'N 18°40'E
Głogów Poland 46 G4 ....51°40'N 16°05'E
Glomfjord Norway 43 C4 ....66°49'N 13°57'E
Glorieuses, Îles is Indian Oc. 83 D3 ..11°34'S 47°18'E
Glossop England 13 F2 ....53°27'N 1°57'W
Gloucester England 8 C2 ....51°52'N 2°14'W
Gloucestershire d. England 21 D2 ....51°49'N 2°11'W
Glusburn England 13 F2 ....53°54'N 1°59'W
Glyder Fawr hill Wales 10 C5 ....53°06'N 4°02'W
Glynneath Wales 10 D3 ....51°45'N 3°37'W
Gmünd Austria 46 F3 ....48°47'N 14°59'E
Gniezno Poland 46 G5 ....52°32'N 17°36'E
Goa India 96 D4 ....15°24'N 74°11'E
Goat Fell hill Scotland 14 D3 ....55°37'N 5°11'W
Gobabis Namibia 83 A2 ....22°27'S 18°58'E
Gobi des. China/Mongolia 99 J6 ......44°59'N 107°15'E
Gobowen England 8 B3 ....52°54'N 3°02'W
Goch Germany 42 F4 ....51°40'N 6°09'E
Godalming England 9 E2 ....51°11'N 0°37'W
Godavari r. India 96 F4 ....16°57'N 81°49'E
Godmanchester England 9 E3 ....52°19'N 0°10'W
Goes Neth. 42 C4 ....51°30'N 3°54'E
Goiânia Brazil 72 E5 ....16°41'S 49°16'W
Gökçeada i. Turkey 50 F5 ....40°12'N 25°48'E
Göksun Turkey 51 L4 ....38°02'N 36°30'E
Gölcük Turkey 51 H5 ....40°43'N 29°49'E
Gold Coast town Australia 108 E4 ....28°03'S 153°26'E
Golmud China 98 G5 ....36°21'N 94°50'E
Golpāyegān Iran 95 H6 ....33°23'N 50°15'E
Golspie Scotland 17 F2 ....57°58'N 3°59'W
Gómez Palacio Mexico 66 D6 ....25°35'N 103°32'W
Gonaïves Haiti 67 J4 ....19°27'N 72°42'W
Gonbad-e Kavus Iran 95 I7 ....37°14'N 55°07'E
Gonder Ethiopia 85 H3 ....12°39'N 37°29'E
Gondiya India 96 F5 ....21°28'N 80°12'E
Gongga Shan mt. China 99 I3 ....29°57'N 101°55'E
Good Hope, Cape of S. Africa 83 A1 ..34°22'S 18°29'E
Goodwick Wales 10 C4 ....52°00'N 4°59'W
Goole England 13 G2 ....53°42'N 0°53'W
Göppingen Germany 46 C3 ....48°43'N 9°39'E
Gorakhpur India 96 F6 ....26°45'N 83°25'E
Gorebridge Scotland 15 F3 ....55°50'N 3°03'W
Gorey Ireland 18 E2 ....52°40'N 6°18'W
Gorgān Iran 95 H7 ....36°50'N 54°24'E
Gori Georgia 53 E2 ....41°59'N 44°07'E
Goris Armenia 95 G7 ....39°30'N 46°20'E
Gorizia Italy 46 E1 ....45°57'N 13°38'E
Görlitz Germany 46 F4 ....51°09'N 14°59'E
Gornji Vakuf Bos. and Herz. 50 B6 ..43°55'N 17°34'E
Gorno-Altaysk Russia 98 F8 ....51°59'N 85°52'E
Gornyak Russia 98 E8 ....50°59'N 81°22'E
Gorontalo Indonesia 103 G4 ....0°34'N 123°01'E
Gort Ireland 18 C3 ....53°04'N 8°49'W
Gorzów Wielkopolski Poland 46 F5 ..52°44'N 15°14'E
Gosberton England 9 E3 ....52°52'N 0°10'W
Gosford Australia 108 E3 ....33°25'S 151°20'E
Gosforth Cumb. England 12 D3 ......54°25'N 3°27'W
Gosforth T. and W. England 13 F4 ..55°00'N 1°37'W
Goshogawara Japan 104 D4 ....40°48'N 140°26'E
Gospić Croatia 50 A7 ....44°33'N 15°23'E
Gosport England 8 D1 ....50°48'N 1°08'W
Gostivar North Macedonia 50 D5 ....41°47'N 20°55'E
Gotha Germany 46 D4 ....50°57'N 10°42'E
Gothenburg Sweden 43 B2 ....57°43'N 11°59'E
Gotland i. Sweden 43 D2 ....57°36'N 18°52'E
Göttingen Germany 46 C4 ....51°32'N 9°55'E
Gouda Neth. 42 D5 ....52°00'N 4°42'E
Gouin, Réservoir resr Canada 61 K2 ..48°39'N 74°39'W
Goulburn Australia 108 D3 ....34°47'S 149°44'E
Gourdon France 44 D4 ....44°45'N 1°22'E
Governador Valadares Brazil 72 E5 ..18°49'S 41°57'W
Gower pen. Wales 10 C3 ....51°36'N 4°15'W
Gowna, Lough l. Ireland 18 D3 ....53°53'N 7°35'W
Goyang S. Korea 99 N5 ....37°38'N 126°49'E
Göynük Turkey 51 I5 ....40°24'N 30°46'E
Gqeberha S. Africa 83 B1 ....33°57'S 25°36'E
Grafham Water resr England 9 E3 ....52°18'N 0°19'W
Grafton Australia 108 E4 ....29°41'S 152°56'E
Grafton U.S. 62 G6 ....48°24'N 97°26'W
Grain England 9 F2 ....51°27'N 0°43'E
Grampian Mountains Scotland 17 E1 ..56°54'N 4°37'W
Granada Spain 45 D2 ....37°11'N 3°36'W
Gran Canaria i. Canary Islands 45 Y1 ..27°47'N 15°23'W
Gran Chaco f. Argentina/Paraguay 73 C4 ..27°08'S 62°24'W
Grand Bahama i. Bahamas 67 I6 ......26°34'N 78°25'W
Grand Canyon U.S. 62 D4 ....36°03'N 112°09'W
Grand Canyon town U.S. 62 D4 ....36°03'N 112°09'W
Grand Cayman i. Cayman Is 67 H4 ..19°23'N 81°06'W
Grande, Bahía b. Argentina 73 C1 ..50°40'S 68°13'W
Grande Prairie Canada 60 G3 ....55°11'N 118°42'W
Grandes, Salinas f. Argentina 73 C3 ..30°24'S 65°32'W
Grand Est d. France 42 E2 ....49°10'N 5°35'E
Grand Falls - Windsor Canada 61 M2 ..48°53'N 55°25'W
Grand Forks U.S. 62 G6 ....47°55'N 97°00'W
Grand Island U.S. 62 G5 ....40°56'N 98°23'W
Grand Junction U.S. 62 E4 ....39°04'N 108°33'W
Grândola Portugal 45 B3 ....38°11'N 8°34'W
Grand Rapids town U.S. 63 I5 ....42°57'N 85°40'W
Grangemouth Scotland 15 F4 ....56°01'N 3°42'W
Grange-over-Sands England 12 E3 ..54°11'N 2°55'W
Gran Tarajal Canary Islands 45 Y2 ..28°12'N 14°01'W
Grantham England 13 G2 ....52°55'N 0°39'W
Grantown-on-Spey Scotland 17 F2 ..57°20'N 3°37'W
Grants Pass U.S. 62 B5 ....42°29'N 123°19'W
Grasse France 44 G3 ....43°39'N 6°55'E
Grassington England 13 F3 ....54°04'N 1°59'W
Grave, Pointe de pt France 44 C4 ....45°35'N 1°04'W
Gravelines France 9 H1 ....50°59'N 2°07'E
Gravesend England 9 F2 ....51°28'N 0°22'E
Grays England 9 F2 ....51°28'N 0°20'E
Graz Austria 46 F2 ....47°04'N 15°25'E
Great Abaco i. Bahamas 67 I6 ....26°30'N 77°11'W
Great Australian Bight g. Australia 108 B3
....33°06'S 129°56'E
Great Baddow England 9 F2 ....51°43'N 0°29'E
Great Barrier Reef Australia 108 D5 ..11°25'S 144°00'E
Great Basin U.S. 62 C5 ....39°25'N 116°20'W
Great Bear Lake Canada 60 G4 ....66°03'N 119°05'W
Great Belt str. Denmark 46 D6 ....55°34'N 10°51'E
Great Bend U.S. 62 G4 ....38°23'N 98°47'W
Great Bernera i. Scotland 16 C3 ......58°14'N 6°52'W
Great Blasket Island Ireland 18 A2 ..52°06'N 10°32'W
Great Clifton England 12 D3 ....54°39'N 3°29'W
Great Cumbrae i. Scotland 14 E3 ....55°47'N 4°57'W

reat Dividing Range mts Australia 108 D3 ..... 37°30'S 144°27'E
reat Dunmow England 9 F2 ..... 51°52'N 0°22'E
reater Antilles is Caribbean Sea 67 H5 ..... 21°05'N 81°40'W
reater London d. England 21 E2 ..... 51°30'N 0°11'W
reater Manchester d. England 21 D3 ..... 53°31'N 2°22'W
reat Exuma i. Bahamas 67 I5 ..... 23°35'N 75°54'W
reat Falls town U.S. 62 D6 ..... 47°30'N 111°17'W
reat Glen, The f. Scotland 17 E2 ..... 57°09'N 4°44'W
reat Gonerby England 8 E3 ..... 52°56'N 0°40'W
reatham England 13 F3 ..... 54°38'N 1°14'W
reat Harwood England 13 E2 ..... 53°47'N 2°24'W
reat Inagua i. Bahamas 67 J5 ..... 21°13'N 73°26'W
reat Karoo f. S. Africa 83 B1 ..... 32°29'S 23°21'E
reat Linford England 8 E3 ..... 52°04'N 0°46'W
reat Malvern England 8 C3 ..... 52°07'N 2°19'W
reat Namaqualand f. Namibia 83 A2 ..... 26°29'S 16°25'E
reat Nicobar i. India 97 H1 ..... 7°06'N 94°08'E
reat Ormes Head Wales 10 D5 ..... 53°21'N 3°52'W
reat Ouse r. England 9 F3 ..... 52°46'N 0°23'E
reat Plains f. N. America 56 E4 ..... 45°00'N 100°00'W
reat Rhos hill Wales 10 D4 ..... 52°16'N 3°12'W
reat Rift Valley f. Africa 83 C4 ..... 7°00'S 33°00'E
reat Salt Lake U.S. 62 D5 ..... 40°58'N 112°26'W
reat Sand Sea des. Egypt/Libya 49 H2 ..... 28°55'N 24°22'E
reat Sandy Desert Australia 108 B4 ..... 20°35'S 123°36'E
reat Shelford England 9 F3 ..... 52°09'N 0°08'E
reat Slave Lake Canada 60 G4 ..... 61°26'N 114°35'W
reat Stour r. England 9 G2 ..... 51°20'N 1°14'E
reat Torrington England 11 C2 ..... 50°57'N 4°08'W
reat Victoria Desert Australia 108 B4 ..... 28°43'S 128°38'E
reat Whernside hill England 13 F3 ..... 54°10'N 1°59'W
reat Yarmouth England 9 G3 ..... 52°36'N 1°44'E
redos, Sierra de mts Spain 45 C4 ..... 40°08'N 5°43'W
reece Europe 50 D4 ..... 39°03'N 21°56'E
reeley U.S. 62 F5 ..... 40°25'N 104°41'W
reen r. U.S. 62 E4 ..... 38°12'N 109°53'W
reen Bay town U.S. 63 I5 ..... 44°30'N 88°02'W
reenland i. N. America 61 N5 ..... 72°21'N 41°01'W
reenlaw Scotland 15 G3 ..... 55°42'N 2°28'W
reenock Scotland 14 E3 ..... 55°57'N 4°46'W
reenore Point Ireland 10 A4 ..... 52°14'N 6°18'W
reen River town U.S. 62 E5 ..... 41°36'N 109°29'W
reensboro U.S. 63 K4 ..... 36°04'N 79°48'W
reenstone Point Scotland 16 D2 ..... 57°56'N 5°40'W
reenville Liberia 84 D2 ..... 5°01'N 9°02'W
reenville Miss. U.S. 63 H3 ..... 33°22'N 91°01'W
reenville S. C. U.S. 63 J3 ..... 34°50'N 82°27'W
reenwich England 9 E2 ..... 51°29'N 0°00'W
reifswald Germany 46 E6 ..... 54°05'N 13°24'E
renaa Denmark 43 B2 ..... 56°24'N 10°54'E
renada Central America 67 L3 ..... 12°03'N 61°38'W
renade France 44 D3 ..... 43°46'N 1°18'E
renoble France 44 F4 ..... 45°11'N 5°44'E
reta r. England 13 E3 ..... 54°09'N 2°37'W
retna Scotland 15 F2 ..... 54°59'N 3°04'W
revena Greece 50 D5 ..... 40°05'N 21°25'E
rey Range hills Australia 108 D4 ..... 28°13'S 142°35'E
rimsby England 13 G2 ..... 53°34'N 0°04'W
rímsey i. Iceland 43 Y2 ..... 66°32'N 17°59'W
ris Nez, Cap c. France 9 G1 ..... 50°52'N 1°36'E
ritley Scotland 17 G3 ..... 58°56'N 2°45'W
rodzisk Wielkopolski Poland 46 G5 ..... 52°13'N 16°22'E
roningen Neth. 42 F6 ..... 53°13'N 6°34'E
roningen d. Neth. 42 F6 ..... 53°16'N 6°40'E
roote Eylandt i. Australia 108 C5 ..... 13°58'S 137°09'E
rosser Speikkogel mt. Austria 46 F2 ..... 46°48'N 14°58'E
roßglockner mt. Austria 46 E2 ..... 47°05'N 12°41'E
roundhog r. Canada 61 J2 ..... 49°40'N 81°56'W
roznyy Russia 53 E2 ..... 43°19'N 45°42'E
rudziądz Poland 46 H5 ..... 53°30'N 18°46'E
uinard Bay Scotland 16 D2 ..... 57°53'N 5°32'W
uacanayabo, Golfo de b. Cuba 67 I5 ..... 20°31'N 77°38'W
uadajoz r. Spain 45 C2 ..... 37°51'N 4°51'W
uadalajara Mexico 66 D5 ..... 20°40'N 103°24'W
uadalajara Spain 45 D4 ..... 40°38'N 3°09'W
uadalcanal i. Solomon Is 109 F6 ..... 9°38'S 160°05'E
uadalete r. Spain 45 B2 ..... 36°32'N 6°14'W
uadalope r. Spain 45 E4 ..... 41°15'N 0°02'W
uadalquivir r. Spain 45 C2 ..... 36°48'N 6°21'W
uadalupe, Isla i. Mexico 62 C2 ..... 29°09'N 118°23'W
uadarrama, Sierra de mts Spain 45 C3 ..... 39°20'N 5°49'W
uadeloupe i. Central America 67 L4 ..... 16°30'N 61°29'W
uadiana r. Portugal 45 B2 ..... 37°11'N 7°24'W
uadix Spain 45 D2 ..... 37°18'N 3°07'W
uajira, Península de la pen. Colombia 72 B8 ..... 11°59'N 71°45'W
uam i. N. Pacific Oc. 103 K6 ..... 13°29'N 144°58'E
uanajuato Mexico 66 D5 ..... 21°01'N 101°15'W
uanajuato d. Mexico 66 D5 ..... 21°16'N 100°47'W
uanare Venezuela 67 K2 ..... 9°03'N 69°44'W
uane Cuba 67 H5 ..... 22°13'N 84°05'W
uangdong d. China 99 K2 ..... 23°49'N 114°45'E
uangxi Zhuangzu Zizhiqu d. China 99 J2 ..... 23°52'N 108°27'E
uangyuan China 99 J4 ..... 32°24'N 105°51'E
uangzhou China 99 K2 ..... 23°09'N 113°21'E
uanipa r. Venezuela 67 L2 ..... 9°53'N 62°26'W
uantánamo Cuba 67 I5 ..... 20°07'N 75°13'W
uaporé r. Bolivia/Brazil 72 C5 ..... 11°57'S 65°04'W
uara, Sierra de mts Spain 45 E5 ..... 42°15'N 0°20'W
uarda Portugal 45 B4 ..... 40°33'N 7°16'W
uasave Mexico 66 C6 ..... 25°33'N 108°30'W
uatemala Central America 66 F4 ..... 15°43'N 90°16'W
uatemala City Guatemala 66 F3 ..... 14°37'N 90°31'W
uaviare r. Colombia 72 C7 ..... 4°02'N 67°45'W
uayaquil Ecuador 72 B6 ..... 2°10'S 79°56'W
uayaquil, Golfo de g. Ecuador 68 B3 ..... 3°10'S 80°53'W
uaymas Mexico 66 B6 ..... 27°57'N 110°53'W
uazhou China 98 H6 ..... 40°27'N 95°48'E
uba Ethiopia 85 H3 ..... 11°16'N 35°17'E
uba Dolgaya Russia 52 F5 ..... 70°18'N 58°37'E
udbrandsdalen f. Norway 43 B3 ..... 61°58'N 9°20'E
uéckédou Guinea 84 C4 ..... 8°33'N 10°11'W
uelma Algeria 48 E4 ..... 36°27'N 7°29'E
uelmim Morocco 84 C4 ..... 28°59'N 10°02'W
uéret France 44 D5 ..... 46°10'N 1°53'E
uernsey i. Channel Is 11 Y9 ..... 49°27'N 2°35'W
uerrero d. Mexico 66 D4 ..... 17°41'N 100°48'W
uiana Highlands mts Guyana/Venezuela 72 C7 ..... 6°18'N 63°41'W
uildford England 9 E2 ..... 51°14'N 0°34'W
uilin China 99 K3 ..... 25°17'N 110°19'E
uinea Africa 84 C3 ..... 10°50'N 11°28'W
uinea, Gulf of Africa 84 E2 ..... 2°31'N 4°26'E

Guinea-Bissau Africa 84 C3 ..... 11°54'N 14°45'W
Guînes France 42 A3 ..... 50°52'N 1°52'E
Güiria Venezuela 67 L3 ..... 10°33'N 62°19'W
Guisborough England 13 F3 ..... 54°32'N 1°03'W
Guise France 42 C2 ..... 49°54'N 3°38'E
Guiyang China 99 J3 ..... 26°33'N 106°39'E
Guizhou d. China 99 J3 ..... 26°59'N 106°45'E
Gujarat d. India 96 D5 ..... 22°51'N 72°32'E
Gujranwala Pakistan 96 D7 ..... 32°07'N 74°13'E
Gullane Scotland 15 G4 ..... 56°02'N 2°50'W
Gulu Uganda 85 H2 ..... 2°44'N 32°17'E
Gumdag Turkmenistan 95 H7 ..... 39°11'N 54°29'E
Gümüşhane Turkey 51 M5 ..... 40°29'N 39°28'E
Guna India 96 E5 ..... 24°39'N 77°19'E
Guntur India 96 F4 ..... 16°19'N 80°26'E
Guri, Embalse de resr Venezuela 67 L2 ..... 7°38'N 62°47'W
Gusau Nigeria 84 E3 ..... 12°15'N 6°37'E
Güstrow Germany 46 E5 ..... 53°48'N 12°11'E
Guwahati India 97 H6 ..... 26°09'N 91°46'E
Guyana S. America 72 D7 ..... 5°59'N 59°59'W
Gwadar Pakistan 96 B6 ..... 25°09'N 62°20'E
Gwalior India 96 E6 ..... 26°15'N 78°10'E
Gwangju S. Korea 99 N5 ..... 35°09'N 126°54'E
Gwardafuy, Gees c. Somalia 85 J3 ..... 11°49'N 51°16'E
Gweebarra Bay Ireland 18 C4 ..... 54°53'N 8°30'W
Gweru Zimbabwe 83 B3 ..... 19°27'S 29°50'E
Gwynedd d. Wales 21 C3 ..... 53°00'N 4°02'W
Gydan Peninsula Russia 54 I5 ..... 70°08'N 77°30'E
Gyöngyös Hungary 46 H2 ..... 47°46'N 19°56'E
Győr Hungary 46 G2 ..... 47°41'N 17°39'E
Gypsumville Canada 60 I3 ..... 51°47'N 98°37'W
Gyumri Armenia 94 F8 ..... 40°47'N 43°51'E

H

Haapajärvi Finland 43 F3 ..... 63°45'N 25°20'E
Haapsalu Estonia 43 E2 ..... 58°56'N 23°33'E
Haarlem Neth. 42 D5 ..... 52°22'N 4°38'E
Habbān Yemen 95 G2 ..... 14°20'N 47°05'E
Hachijō Jima i. Japan 104 C2 ..... 33°07'N 139°50'E
Hachinohe Japan 104 D4 ..... 40°32'N 141°31'E
Hadd, Ra's al pt Oman 95 I4 ..... 22°30'N 59°50'E
Haddington Scotland 15 G3 ..... 55°58'N 2°46'W
Haderslev Denmark 43 B1 ..... 55°15'N 9°29'E
Hadiach Ukraine 47 O4 ..... 50°22'N 33°59'E
Hadjer Hadid Chad 85 G3 ..... 13°23'N 21°20'E
Had Kourt Morocco 45 C1 ..... 34°31'N 5°48'W
Hadleigh England 9 F3 ..... 52°03'N 0°57'E
Ḩaḑramawt f. Yemen 95 G3 ..... 15°07'N 47°48'E
Haeju N. Korea 99 N5 ..... 38°02'N 125°45'E
Hagar Nish Plateau f. Eritrea 94 E3 ..... 17°03'N 37°58'E
Hagåtña Guam 103 K6 ..... 13°29'N 144°45'E
Hagen Germany 46 B4 ..... 51°22'N 7°28'E
Hag's Head Ireland 18 B2 ..... 52°56'N 9°29'W
Hague, Cap de la c. France 11 Z9 ..... 49°44'N 1°55'W
Haida Gwaii is Canada 60 E3 ..... 53°59'N 133°20'W
Haifa Israel 49 J3 ..... 32°50'N 34°58'E
Haikou China 99 K2 ..... 20°01'N 110°18'E
Ḩāʾil Saudi Arabia 94 F5 ..... 27°33'N 41°41'E
Hailsham England 9 F1 ..... 50°52'N 0°15'E
Hainan d. China 99 J1 ..... 19°09'N 109°33'E
Hainan i. China 99 J1 ..... 18°51'N 110°29'E
Hainaut d. Belgium 42 D3 ..... 50°29'N 4°00'E
Haines U.S. 60 E3 ..... 59°13'N 135°25'W
Hai Phong Vietnam 102 D8 ..... 20°48'N 106°43'E
Haiti Central America 67 J4 ..... 19°19'N 73°30'W
Haiya Sudan 85 H3 ..... 18°20'N 36°23'E
Hakodate Japan 104 D4 ..... 41°47'N 140°44'E
Ḩalabjah/Ḩełebce Iraq 95 G6 ..... 35°11'N 45°56'E
Halden Norway 43 B2 ..... 59°07'N 11°25'E
Halesowen England 8 C3 ..... 52°27'N 2°03'W
Halesworth England 9 G3 ..... 52°21'N 1°30'E
Halifax Canada 61 L2 ..... 44°39'N 63°36'W
Halifax England 13 F2 ..... 53°44'N 1°51'W
Halkirk Scotland 17 F3 ..... 58°31'N 3°29'W
Halladale r. Scotland 17 F3 ..... 58°33'N 3°54'W
Halle Belgium 42 D3 ..... 50°44'N 4°14'E
Halle Germany 46 D4 ..... 51°29'N 11°59'E
Halls Creek town Australia 108 B5 ..... 18°17'S 127°40'E
Halmahera i. Indonesia 103 H4 ..... 1°06'N 128°32'E
Halmstad Sweden 43 C2 ..... 56°40'N 12°52'E
Halstead England 9 F2 ..... 51°57'N 0°39'E
Halton d. England 21 D3 ..... 53°20'N 2°43'W
Haltwhistle England 13 E3 ..... 54°58'N 2°27'W
Ḩalwān Egypt 49 J2 ..... 29°55'N 31°18'E
Hamadān Iran 95 G6 ..... 34°46'N 48°30'E
Ḩamāh Syria 94 E7 ..... 35°08'N 36°45'E
Hamamatsu Japan 104 C2 ..... 34°42'N 137°44'E
Hamar Norway 43 B3 ..... 60°48'N 11°05'E
Hambleton Hills England 13 F3 ..... 54°16'N 1°14'W
Hamburg Germany 46 C5 ..... 53°34'N 9°59'E
Hämeenlinna Finland 43 F3 ..... 60°59'N 24°27'E
Hamersley Range mts Australia 108 A4 ..... 22°11'S 116°31'E
Hamhŭng N. Korea 99 N5 ..... 39°55'N 127°33'E
Hami China 98 H6 ..... 42°48'N 93°27'E
Hamilton Bermuda 67 L7 ..... 32°18'N 64°46'W
Hamilton Canada 61 K2 ..... 43°15'N 79°51'W
Hamilton New Zealand 109 G3 ..... 37°48'S 175°16'E
Hamilton Scotland 15 E3 ..... 55°47'N 4°03'W
Ḩamīm, Wādī al watercourse Libya 49 H3 ..... 30°04'N 21°35'E
Hamina Finland 43 F3 ..... 60°34'N 27°12'E
Hamm Germany 46 B4 ..... 51°41'N 7°49'E
Hammamet, Golfe de g. Tunisia 48 F4 ..... 36°09'N 10°50'E
Hammerdal Sweden 43 C3 ..... 63°35'N 15°21'E
Hammerfest Norway 43 E5 ..... 70°39'N 23°41'E
Hampshire d. England 21 E2 ..... 51°10'N 1°13'W
Hampshire Downs hills England 8 D2 ..... 51°20'N 1°35'W
Ḩamrāʾ, Al Ḩamādah al f. Libya 48 F2 ..... 29°40'N 11°48'E
Hamstreet England 9 F2 ..... 51°04'N 0°52'E
Hanamaki Japan 104 D3 ..... 39°23'N 141°07'E
Hancock U.S. 63 I6 ..... 47°08'N 88°36'W
Handa Island Scotland 16 D3 ..... 58°23'N 5°13'W
Handan China 99 K5 ..... 36°35'N 114°32'E
Hangzhou China 99 M4 ..... 30°15'N 120°10'E
Hanna Canada 60 G3 ..... 51°38'N 111°56'W
Hannover Germany 46 C5 ..... 52°23'N 9°44'E
Hanöbukten b. Sweden 46 F6 ..... 55°48'N 14°37'E
Hanoi Vietnam 102 D8 ..... 21°01'N 105°51'E
Hantsavichy Belarus 47 L5 ..... 52°46'N 26°27'E
Hanzhong China 99 J4 ..... 33°04'N 107°03'E
Haparanda Sweden 43 F4 ..... 65°50'N 24°08'E
Happy Valley-Goose Bay town Canada 61 L3 ..... 53°19'N 60°07'W
Harare Zimbabwe 83 C3 ..... 17°49'S 31°04'E
Ḩarāsīs, Jiddat al des. Oman 95 I3 ..... 18°55'N 55°33'E

Harderwijk Neth. 42 E5 ..... 52°21'N 5°38'E
Haren Germany 42 G5 ..... 52°48'N 7°15'E
Hargeysa Somalia 85 I2 ..... 9°32'N 44°05'E
Har Hu l. China 98 H5 ..... 38°18'N 97°23'E
Hari Rūd r. Afgh./Iran 95 J7 ..... 30°50'N 60°58'E
Harlech Wales 10 C4 ..... 52°52'N 4°06'W
Harleston England 9 G3 ..... 52°24'N 1°18'E
Harlingen Neth. 42 E6 ..... 53°10'N 5°25'E
Harlow England 9 F2 ..... 51°46'N 0°05'E
Harney Basin U.S. 62 C5 ..... 43°23'N 119°55'W
Härnösand Sweden 43 D3 ..... 62°38'N 17°56'E
Har Nuur l. Mongolia 98 G7 ..... 48°02'N 93°23'E
Harpenden England 9 E2 ..... 51°49'N 0°21'W
Harray, Loch of l. Scotland 17 F4 ..... 59°01'N 3°13'W
Harricanaw r. Canada 61 K3 ..... 50°58'N 79°33'W
Harris, Sound of str. Scotland 16 B2 ..... 57°46'N 7°10'W
Harrisburg U.S. 63 K5 ..... 40°17'N 76°54'W
Harrison, Cape Canada 61 M3 ..... 54°56'N 57°42'W
Harrogate England 13 F2 ..... 53°59'N 1°32'W
Hârşova Romania 51 G7 ..... 44°41'N 27°57'E
Harstad Norway 43 D5 ..... 68°47'N 16°32'E
Harteigan mt. Norway 43 A3 ..... 60°12'N 7°05'E
Harter Fell hill England 12 E3 ..... 54°29'N 2°52'W
Hart Fell hill Scotland 15 F3 ..... 55°24'N 3°24'W
Hartford U.S. 63 L5 ..... 41°46'N 72°42'W
Hartland England 11 C2 ..... 50°59'N 4°29'W
Hartland Point England 11 C3 ..... 51°01'N 4°33'W
Hartlepool England 13 F3 ..... 54°41'N 1°13'W
Hartlepool d. England 21 E4 ..... 54°40'N 1°15'W
Har-Us Nuur l. Mongolia 98 G7 ..... 47°53'N 92°19'E
Harwich England 9 G2 ..... 51°56'N 1°16'E
Haryana d. India 96 E6 ..... 29°11'N 76°12'E
Haskovo Bulgaria 50 F5 ..... 41°56'N 25°32'E
Haslemere England 8 E2 ..... 51°05'N 0°43'W
Hasselt Belgium 42 E3 ..... 50°56'N 5°20'E
Hassi Messaoud Algeria 84 E5 ..... 31°41'N 6°10'E
Hässleholm Sweden 43 C2 ..... 56°10'N 13°46'E
Hastings England 9 F1 ..... 50°51'N 0°35'E
Hatfield England 9 E2 ..... 51°46'N 0°13'W
Ha Tinh Vietnam 102 D7 ..... 18°18'N 105°55'E
Hatteras, Cape U.S. 63 K4 ..... 35°14'N 75°34'W
Hattiesburg U.S. 63 I3 ..... 31°23'N 89°19'W
Hat Yai Thailand 102 C5 ..... 7°01'N 100°26'E
Haud f. Ethiopia 85 I2 ..... 8°37'N 44°15'E
Haugesund Norway 43 A2 ..... 59°24'N 5°18'E
Haukivesi l. Finland 43 G3 ..... 62°06'N 28°28'E
Haut Atlas mts Morocco 84 D5 ..... 30°51'N 8°03'W
Haut-Folin hill France 44 F5 ..... 46°59'N 4°01'E
Hauts-de-France d. France 42 B3 ..... 50°14'N 2°43'E
Hauts Plateaux f. Algeria 48 C3 ..... 33°42'N 0°42'W
Havana Cuba 67 H5 ..... 23°07'N 82°22'W
Havant England 8 E1 ..... 50°52'N 0°59'W
Haverfordwest Wales 10 C3 ..... 51°48'N 4°58'W
Haverhill England 9 F3 ..... 52°05'N 0°26'E
Havre U.S. 62 E6 ..... 48°32'N 109°41'W
Havre-St-Pierre Canada 61 L3 ..... 50°14'N 63°28'W
Hawaii i. U.S. 116 A3 ..... 20°02'N 155°17'W
Hawaiian Islands N. Pacific Oc. 116 A3 ..... 28°26'N 174°25'W
Hawarden Wales 10 D5 ..... 53°11'N 3°02'W
Hawes England 13 E3 ..... 54°18'N 2°12'W
Haweswater Reservoir England 12 E3 ..... 54°30'N 2°48'W
Hawick Scotland 15 G3 ..... 55°26'N 2°47'W
Hawke Bay New Zealand 109 G3 ..... 39°24'S 177°23'E
Hawkhurst England 9 F2 ..... 51°03'N 0°31'E
Haxby England 13 F3 ..... 54°01'N 1°04'W
Hay r. Canada 60 G4 ..... 60°48'N 115°47'W
Hay r. Australia 108 C4 ..... 24°31'S 144°48'E
Haydarābād Iran 94 G7 ..... 37°04'N 45°05'E
Haydon Bridge England 13 E3 ..... 54°59'N 2°15'W
Hayle England 11 B2 ..... 50°11'N 5°25'W
Haymā' Oman 95 I3 ..... 19°54'N 56°13'E
Hay-on-Wye Wales 10 D4 ..... 52°05'N 3°07'W
Hay River town Canada 60 G4 ..... 60°51'N 115°40'W
Hayshah, Sabkhal al f. Libya 49 G3 ..... 31°55'N 15°19'E
Haywards Heath England 9 E1 ..... 50°59'N 0°06'W
Hazar Turkmenistan 95 H7 ..... 39°25'N 53°01'E
Hazarajat f. Afgh. 95 K6 ..... 32°29'N 65°07'E
Hazebrouck France 42 B3 ..... 50°43'N 2°32'E
Heacham England 9 F3 ..... 52°54'N 0°30'E
Headcorn England 9 F2 ..... 51°10'N 0°38'E
Heanor England 13 F2 ..... 53°01'N 1°21'W
Hearst Canada 63 J6 ..... 49°41'N 83°41'W
Heathfield England 9 F1 ..... 50°58'N 0°16'E
Hebei d. China 99 L5 ..... 38°33'N 115°49'E
Hebron West Bank 49 J3 ..... 31°53'N 34°49'E
Hecate Strait Canada 60 E3 ..... 52°36'N 130°22'W
Hechi China 99 J2 ..... 24°38'N 108°04'E
Heckington England 9 E3 ..... 52°59'N 0°18'W
Hede Sweden 43 C3 ..... 62°25'N 13°32'E
Heerenveen Neth. 42 E5 ..... 52°58'N 5°56'E
Heerlen Neth. 42 E3 ..... 50°53'N 5°59'E
Hefei China 99 L4 ..... 31°51'N 117°19'E
Hegang China 99 O7 ..... 47°13'N 130°13'E
Heidelberg Germany 46 C3 ..... 49°24'N 8°41'E
Heighington England 13 G2 ..... 53°13'N 0°27'W
Heilbronn Germany 46 C3 ..... 49°08'N 9°12'E
Heilen, Loch l. Scotland 17 F3 ..... 58°36'N 3°17'W
Heilongjiang d. China 99 N7 ..... 46°55'N 128°30'E
Heilong Jiang r. China 99 O7 ..... 48°25'N 134°59'E
Heinola Finland 43 F3 ..... 61°12'N 26°02'E
Hekla vol. Iceland 43 Y1 ..... 63°59'N 19°41'W
Helena U.S. 62 D6 ..... 46°36'N 112°01'W
Helensburgh Scotland 14 E4 ..... 56°00'N 4°44'W
Helgoländer Bucht g. Germany 46 C6 ..... 54°10'N 8°14'E
Hellín Spain 45 E3 ..... 38°31'N 1°41'W
Helmand r. Afgh. 95 J6 ..... 31°13'N 61°35'E
Helmond Neth. 42 E4 ..... 51°28'N 5°40'E
Helmsdale Scotland 17 F3 ..... 58°07'N 3°39'W
Helmsdale r. Scotland 17 F3 ..... 58°07'N 3°38'W
Helmsley England 13 F3 ..... 54°15'N 1°04'W
Helsingborg Sweden 43 C2 ..... 56°03'N 12°42'E
Helsingør Denmark 46 E7 ..... 56°03'N 12°37'E
Helsinki Finland 43 F3 ..... 60°10'N 24°57'E
Helston England 11 B2 ..... 50°06'N 5°16'W
Helvellyn hill England 12 D3 ..... 54°32'N 3°01'W
Hemel Hempstead England 9 E2 ..... 51°45'N 0°27'W
Henan d. China 99 K4 ..... 33°59'N 112°54'E
Henares r. Spain 45 D4 ..... 40°25'N 3°29'W
Hendon England 9 E2 ..... 51°35'N 0°13'W
Henfield England 9 E1 ..... 50°56'N 0°16'W
Hengelo Neth. 42 F5 ..... 52°16'N 6°48'E
Hengoed Wales 10 D3 ..... 51°39'N 3°13'W
Hengyang China 99 K3 ..... 26°53'N 112°32'E
Henichesk Ukraine 49 J6 ..... 46°10'N 34°48'E
Henley-on-Thames England 8 E2 ..... 51°32'N 0°54'W
Hennef Germany 42 G3 ..... 50°47'N 7°18'E
Henrietta Maria, Cape Canada 61 J3 ..... 55°21'N 82°13'W

Henzada Myanmar 97 I4 ..... 17°36'N 95°26'E
Herāt Afgh. 95 J6 ..... 34°22'N 62°11'E
Hereford England 8 C3 ..... 52°03'N 2°43'W
Herefordshire d. England 21 D3 ..... 52°07'N 2°40'W
Herm i. Channel Is 11 Y9 ..... 49°28'N 2°26'W
Herma Ness hd Scotland 17 I5 ..... 60°51'N 0°54'W
Hermosillo Mexico 66 B6 ..... 29°04'N 110°58'W
Herne Germany 42 G4 ..... 51°32'N 7°13'E
Herne Bay town England 9 G2 ..... 51°22'N 1°08'E
Herning Denmark 43 B2 ..... 56°08'N 8°58'E
Hertford England 9 E2 ..... 51°48'N 0°05'W
Hertfordshire d. England 21 F2 ..... 51°55'N 0°09'E
Hesdin France 9 H1 ..... 50°22'N 2°03'E
Heswall England 12 D2 ..... 53°20'N 3°06'W
Hetton England 13 E3 ..... 54°01'N 2°03'W
Hexham England 13 E3 ..... 54°58'N 2°07'W
Heysham England 12 E3 ..... 54°02'N 2°54'W
Heywood England 12 E2 ..... 53°36'N 2°13'W
Heze China 99 L5 ..... 35°17'N 115°32'E
Hidaka Sanmyaku mts Japan 104 D4 ..... 42°49'N 142°38'E
Hidalgo d. Mexico 66 E5 ..... 20°35'N 99°07'W
Hidalgo del Parral Mexico 66 C6 ..... 26°56'N 105°41'W
Higashi Suidō str. Japan 104 A2 ..... 33°55'N 129°23'E
Higham Ferrers England 9 E3 ..... 52°18'N 0°36'W
Highbridge England 8 C2 ..... 51°13'N 2°59'W
Highclere England 8 D2 ..... 51°20'N 1°22'W
Highland d. Scotland 20 C5 ..... 57°38'N 4°59'W
High Peak hills England 13 F2 ..... 53°23'N 1°54'W
High Seat hill England 13 E3 ..... 54°24'N 2°18'W
Highworth England 8 D2 ..... 51°38'N 1°43'W
High Wycombe England 8 E2 ..... 51°38'N 0°45'W
Hiiumaa i. Estonia 43 E2 ..... 58°50'N 22°24'E
Hijaz f. Saudi Arabia 94 E5 ..... 26°08'N 37°01'E
Hilāl, Ra's al pt Libya 49 H3 ..... 32°54'N 22°09'E
Hildesheim Germany 46 C5 ..... 52°09'N 9°57'E
Hillah Iraq 94 F6 ..... 32°27'N 44°24'E
Hillerød Denmark 43 C1 ..... 55°56'N 12°18'E
Hillside Scotland 17 G1 ..... 56°45'N 2°29'W
Hillswick Scotland 17 H5 ..... 60°29'N 1°29'W
Hilpsford Point England 12 D3 ..... 54°02'N 3°12'W
Hilversum Neth. 42 E5 ..... 52°13'N 5°11'E
Himachal Pradesh d. India 96 E7 ..... 31°59'N 77°23'E
Himalaya mts Asia 96 E7 ..... 33°06'N 76°46'E
Hinckley England 8 D3 ..... 52°33'N 1°23'W
Hinderwell England 13 G3 ..... 54°32'N 0°46'W
Hindhead England 8 E2 ..... 51°07'N 0°44'W
Hindley England 12 E2 ..... 53°32'N 2°35'W
Hindu Kush mts Afgh./Pakistan 95 K6 ..... 34°58'N 67°52'E
Hinnøya i. Norway 43 C5 ..... 68°37'N 15°58'E
Hirosaki Japan 104 D4 ..... 40°36'N 140°28'E
Hiroshima Japan 104 B2 ..... 34°22'N 132°27'E
Hirson France 42 D2 ..... 49°55'N 4°05'E
Hirwaun Wales 10 D3 ..... 51°44'N 3°31'W
Hispaniola i. Caribbean Sea 67 J5 ..... 20°18'N 72°57'W
Hitachi Japan 104 D3 ..... 36°35'N 140°39'E
Hitchin England 9 E2 ..... 51°57'N 0°17'W
Hitra i. Norway 43 B3 ..... 63°31'N 8°49'E
Hjälmaren l. Sweden 43 C2 ..... 59°14'N 15°51'E
Hjørring Denmark 43 B2 ..... 57°28'N 10°01'E
Hlybokaye Belarus 47 L6 ..... 55°08'N 27°40'E
Hobart Australia 108 D2 ..... 42°52'S 147°19'E
Hobro Denmark 43 B2 ..... 56°38'N 9°48'E
Ho Chi Minh City Vietnam 102 D6 ..... 10°45'N 106°42'E
Hochschwab mt. Austria 46 F2 ..... 47°38'N 15°09'E
Hoddesdon England 9 E2 ..... 51°46'N 0°01'W
Hodeidah Yemen 94 F2 ..... 14°50'N 42°54'E
Hódmezővásárhely Hungary 46 I2 ..... 46°25'N 20°21'E
Hodna, Chott el f. Algeria 48 D4 ..... 35°27'N 4°55'E
Hodnet England 8 C3 ..... 52°51'N 2°35'W
Hoek van Holland Neth. 42 D4 ..... 51°58'N 4°08'E
Hof Germany 46 D4 ..... 50°19'N 11°55'E
Höfn Iceland 43 Z2 ..... 64°16'N 15°13'W
Hofsjökull ice cap Iceland 43 Y2 ..... 64°49'N 18°52'W
Hohhot China 99 K6 ..... 40°43'N 111°44'E
Hokkaido i. Japan 104 D4 ..... 43°33'N 143°27'E
Holbæk Denmark 43 B1 ..... 55°43'N 11°44'E
Holbeach England 9 F3 ..... 52°48'N 0°01'E
Holbeach Marsh England 9 F3 ..... 52°51'N 0°02'E
Holderness pen. England 13 G2 ..... 53°52'N 0°08'W
Holguín Cuba 67 I5 ..... 20°54'N 76°14'W
Hollabrunn Austria 46 G3 ..... 48°34'N 16°05'E
Holland Fen f. England 9 E3 ..... 52°59'N 0°11'W
Hollesley Bay England 9 G3 ..... 52°02'N 1°28'E
Hollington England 9 F1 ..... 50°53'N 0°33'E
Hollingworth England 13 F2 ..... 53°28'N 1°59'W
Holme-on-Spalding-Moor England 13 G2 ..... 53°50'N 0°47'W
Holmfirth England 13 F2 ..... 53°34'N 1°47'W
Holstebro Denmark 43 B2 ..... 56°21'N 8°37'E
Holsworthy England 11 C2 ..... 50°49'N 4°21'W
Holt England 9 G3 ..... 52°55'N 1°05'E
Holyhead Wales 10 C5 ..... 53°19'N 4°38'W
Holyhead Bay Wales 10 C5 ..... 53°22'N 4°40'W
Holy Island England 13 F4 ..... 55°41'N 1°47'W
Holy Island Wales 10 C5 ..... 53°15'N 4°41'W
Holywell Wales 10 D5 ..... 53°17'N 3°13'W
Homāyunshahr Iran 95 H6 ..... 32°59'N 50°23'E
Homburg Germany 42 G2 ..... 49°19'N 7°20'E
Home Bay Canada 61 L4 ..... 68°52'N 67°27'W
Homs Syria 94 E6 ..... 34°44'N 36°44'E
Homyel'/Gomel' Belarus 47 N5 ..... 52°25'N 31°01'E
Honduras Central America 66 G3 ..... 14°47'N 86°43'W
Honduras, Gulf of Belize/Honduras 66 G4 ..... 16°20'N 87°30'W
Hønefoss Norway 43 B3 ..... 60°10'N 10°14'E
Hong Kong China 99 K2 ..... 22°16'N 114°11'E
Hong Kong d. China 99 K2 ..... 22°21'N 114°19'E
Honiara Solomon Is 109 E6 ..... 9°26'S 159°57'E
Honiton England 11 D2 ..... 50°48'N 3°11'W
Honley England 13 F2 ..... 53°36'N 1°48'W
Honshū i. Japan 104 D3 ..... 36°33'N 133°20'E
Hood, Mount vol. U.S. 62 B6 ..... 45°23'N 121°42'W
Hood Point Australia 108 A3 ..... 34°19'S 119°33'E
Hoogeveen Neth. 42 F5 ..... 52°44'N 6°30'E
Hook England 8 E2 ..... 51°17'N 0°58'W
Hook Head Ireland 18 E2 ..... 52°07'N 6°56'W
Hoorn Neth. 42 E5 ..... 52°39'N 5°04'E
Hope, Loch l. Scotland 17 E3 ..... 58°27'N 4°39'W
Hope, Point U.S. 60 B4 ..... 68°21'N 166°49'W
Hopedale Canada 61 L3 ..... 55°27'N 60°00'W
Hörby Sweden 46 E6 ..... 55°51'N 13°40'E
Horley England 9 E2 ..... 51°10'N 0°10'W
Hormuz, Strait of Iran/Oman 95 I5 ..... 26°35'N 56°59'E
Horn c. Iceland 43 X2 ..... 66°28'N 22°29'W
Horn, Cape Chile 73 C1 ..... 56°04'S 67°17'W
Hornavan l. Sweden 43 D4 ..... 66°11'N 17°44'E
Horncastle England 13 G2 ..... 53°12'N 0°07'W
Hornepayne Canada 63 J6 ..... 49°13'N 84°47'W

Hornsea England 13 G2.....................53°55'N 0°10'W
Horodnia Ukraine 47 N4.................51°53'N 31°36'E
Horodok Ukraine 47 J3....................49°47'N 23°39'E
Horrabridge England 11 C2..............50°31'N 4°06'W
Horsens Denmark 43 B1...................55°52'N 9°51'E
Horsham Australia 108 D3...........36°43'S 142°13'E
Horsham England 9 E2.....................51°04'N 0°19'W
Horten Norway 43 B2.....................59°25'N 10°28'E
Horwich England 12 E2...................53°36'N 2°33'W
Hotan China 98 E5..........................37°07'N 80°02'E
Houffalize Belgium 42 E3................50°08'N 5°48'E
Houghton le Spring England 13 F3.....54°50'N 1°28'W
Houghton Regis England 9 E2.........51°54'N 0°31'W
Hourn, Loch inlet Scotland 16 D2.....57°08'N 5°42'W
Houston U.S. 63 G2......................29°43'N 95°19'W
Hovd Mongolia 98 G7...................47°59'N 91°41'E
Hove England 9 E1..........................50°50'N 0°10'W
Hoveton England 9 G3....................52°43'N 1°25'E
Hövsgöl Nuur l. Mongolia 99 I8.......50°59'N 100°42'E
Howden England 13 G2..................53°45'N 0°52'W
Hoy i. Scotland 17 F3.....................58°50'N 3°16'W
Høyanger Norway 43 A3................61°13'N 6°04'E
Hoyerswerda Germany 46 F4.........51°27'N 14°16'E
Höytiäinen l. Finland 43 G3............62°46'N 29°43'E
Hradec Králové Czechia 46 F4.........50°13'N 15°50'E
Hrebinka Ukraine 47 O4.................50°06'N 32°26'E
Hrodna Belarus 47 J5......................53°41'N 23°49'E
Hsinchu Taiwan 99 M2.................24°48'N 120°58'E
Huai'an China 99 L4.......................33°33'N 119°02'E
Huaibei China 99 L4.......................33°57'N 116°51'E
Huainan China 99 L4......................32°36'N 117°00'E
Huambo Angola 83 A3..................12°46'S 15°44'E
Huancayo Peru 72 B5....................12°03'S 75°11'W
Huang He r. China 99 L5...............37°46'N 118°57'E
Huangshi China 99 L4....................30°10'N 115°08'E
Huascarán, Nevado de mt. Peru 72 B6......9°09'S 77°36'W
Hubballi India 96 E4......................15°18'N 75°15'E
Hubei d. China 99 K4.....................31°09'N 113°06'E
Hucknall England 13 F2.................53°02'N 1°12'W
Huddersfield England 13 F2.............53°39'N 1°47'W
Hudiksvall Sweden 43 D3...............61°44'N 17°06'E
Hudson r. U.S. 63 L5.....................40°54'N 73°56'W
Hudson Bay sea Canada 61 J3........59°05'N 86°00'W
Hudson Strait Canada 61 K4...........63°31'N 74°25'W
Hue Vietnam 102 D7...................16°26'N 107°33'E
Huelva Spain 45 B2........................37°16'N 6°55'W
Huércal-Overa Spain 45 E2............37°23'N 1°55'W
Huesca Spain 45 E5........................42°09'N 0°25'W
Huizhou China 99 K2.....................23°05'N 114°25'E
Hull Canada 63 K6.........................45°27'N 75°45'W
Hulun Buir China 99 L7.................49°04'N 119°46'E
Hulun Nur l. China 99 L7...............48°32'N 117°11'E
Humber, Mouth of the England 13 H2......53°33'N 0°06'E
Humboldt r. U.S. 62 C5.................40°04'N 118°36'W
Humphreys Peak U.S. 62 D4..........35°21'N 111°40'W
Húnaflói b. Iceland 43 X2..............65°46'N 20°50'W
Hunan d. China 99 K3....................27°26'N 111°22'E
Hungarian Plain f. Hungary 49 G6....46°30'N 19°00'E
Hungary Europe 46 H2..................47°01'N 18°59'E
Hungerford England 8 D2..............51°25'N 1°31'W
Hunish, Rubha pt Scotland 16 C2.....57°42'N 6°24'W
Hunmanby England 13 G3.............54°11'N 0°19'W
Hunsrück hills Germany 46 B3.........49°47'N 7°00'E
Hunstanton England 9 F3..............52°56'N 0°30'E
Huntingdon England 9 E3.............52°20'N 0°11'W
Huntington U.S. 63 J4..................38°25'N 82°18'W
Huntly Scotland 17 G2..................57°27'N 2°47'W
Huntsville Ala. U.S. 63 I3..............34°46'N 86°34'W
Huntsville Tex. U.S. 63 G3.............30°42'N 95°34'W
Hurghada Egypt 49 J2...................27°12'N 33°48'E
Huron U.S. 62 G5.........................44°23'N 98°13'W
Huron, Lake Canada/U.S. 61 J2......44°39'N 82°23'W
Hurstpierpoint England 9 E1..........50°56'N 0°11'W
Husum Germany 46 C6..................54°29'N 9°04'E
Hutton Rudby England 13 F3..........54°27'N 1°17'W
Huzhou China 99 M4.....................30°50'N 120°08'E
Hvannadalshnúkur vol. Iceland 43 Y2....64°01'N 16°41'W
Hvar i. Croatia 50 B6.....................43°08'N 16°33'E
Hyargas Nuur l. Mongolia 98 G7.....49°02'N 93°18'E
Hyderabad India 96 E4..................17°21'N 78°25'E
Hyderabad Pakistan 96 C6.............25°21'N 68°23'E
Hyères France 44 G3.....................43°07'N 6°08'E
Hyrynsalmi Finland 43 G4.............64°40'N 28°29'E
Hythe Hants. England 8 D1.............50°52'N 1°24'W
Hythe Kent England 9 G2...............51°04'N 1°05'E
Hyvinkää Finland 43 F3.................60°38'N 24°51'E

I

Ialomiţa r. Romania 50 G7..............44°43'N 27°51'E
Iar Connaught f. Ireland 18 B3.........53°21'N 9°19'W
Iaşi Romania 49 I6.........................47°10'N 27°35'E
Ibadan Nigeria 84 E2.....................7°24'N 3°55'E
Ibagué Colombia 72 B7..................4°24'N 75°13'W
Ibar r. Kosovo/Serbia 50 D6...........43°43'N 20°45'E
Ibb Yemen 94 F2...........................14°03'N 44°09'E
Ibiza Spain 45 F3...........................38°54'N 1°27'E
Ibiza i. Spain 45 F3........................39°10'N 1°39'E
Ibra' Oman 95 I4...........................22°41'N 58°33'E
Ibstock England 8 D3.....................52°42'N 1°24'W
Ica Peru 72 B5...............................14°04'S 75°43'W
Iceland Europe 43 X2.....................64°42'N 18°19'W
Ichinoseki Japan 104 D3................38°55'N 141°07'E
Icklesham England 9 F1..................50°55'N 0°40'E
Idaho d. U.S. 62 D5.......................44°08'N 114°08'W
Idaho Falls town U.S. 62 D5...........43°32'N 112°01'W
Idar-Oberstein Germany 42 G2.......49°42'N 7°18'E
Idfū Egypt 49 J1............................24°55'N 32°49'E
Idi mt. Greece 50 F2.......................35°13'N 24°47'E
Idlib Syria 51 L2............................35°56'N 36°38'E
Ieper Belgium 42 B3......................50°51'N 2°53'E
Iešjávri l. Norway 43 F5..................69°39'N 24°28'E
Igan Malaysia 102 E4....................2°51'N 111°44'E
Iggesund Sweden 43 D3................61°39'N 17°05'E
Iglesias Italy 48 C3.......................39°19'N 8°32'E
Iguaçu r. Brazil 73 E3....................25°36'S 54°35'W
Iisalmi Finland 43 F3.....................63°34'N 27°11'E
IJmuiden Neth. 42 D5....................52°27'N 4°37'E
IJssel r. Neth. 42 E5.......................52°35'N 5°50'E
IJsselmeer l. Neth. 42 E5...............52°45'N 5°20'E
IJzer r. Belgium 9 H2.....................51°09'N 2°44'E
Ikaahuk Canada 60 F5...................71°55'N 125°05'W
Ikaria i. Greece 50 G3...................37°39'N 26°13'E
Iki Shima i. Japan 104 A2..............33°45'N 129°39'E

Ilagan Phil. 103 G7........................17°06'N 121°53'E
Ilchester England 8 C2...................51°00'N 2°41'W
Ilebo Dem. Rep. Congo 83 B4.........4°21'S 20°36'E
Île-de-France d. France 42 B1..........48°39'N 2°36'E
Ilford England 9 F2........................51°33'N 0°05'E
Ilfracombe England 11 C3..............51°12'N 4°07'W
Ilhéus Brazil 72 F5.........................14°46'S 39°02'W
Iligan Phil. 103 G5.........................8°13'N 124°15'E
Ilkeston England 8 D3...................52°58'N 1°18'W
Ilkley England 13 F2......................53°56'N 1°49'W
Illinois d. U.S. 63 I4.......................39°52'N 89°07'W
Illinois r. U.S. 63 H4......................38°56'N 90°30'W
Illizi Algeria 84 E4........................26°29'N 8°30'E
Ilminster England 8 C1..................50°56'N 2°54'W
Iloilo Phil. 103 G6.........................10°41'N 122°32'E
Ilorin Nigeria 84 E2......................8°30'N 4°34'E
Ilovlya Russia 53 E2.......................49°19'N 43°59'E
Imatra Finland 43 G3.....................61°11'N 28°47'E
Immingham England 13 G2...........53°37'N 0°13'W
Imola Italy 46 D1..........................44°21'N 11°42'E
Imperatriz Brazil 72 E6..................5°33'S 47°26'W
Imphal India 97 H5.......................24°46'N 93°56'E
İmroz Turkey 50 F5.......................40°10'N 25°55'E
Inarijärvi l. Finland 43 F5...............68°57'N 27°37'E
Inchard, Loch b. Scotland 16 D3.....58°27'N 5°04'W
Incheon S. Korea 99 N5.................37°28'N 126°39'E
Inchkeith i. Scotland 15 F4.............56°02'N 3°08'W
Indalsälven r. Sweden 43 D3...........62°32'N 17°24'E
Independence U.S. 63 H4..............39°07'N 94°26'W
İnderbor Kazakhstan 53 F2.............48°33'N 51°44'E
India Asia 96 E5............................22°00'N 79°00'E
Indiana d. U.S. 63 I5......................40°09'N 86°01'W
Indianapolis U.S. 63 I4..................39°46'N 86°10'W
Indian Ocean 117 G2
Indigirka r. Russia 55 P5................71°28'N 149°53'E
Indonesia Asia 102 E2...................4°12'S 112°02'E
Indore India 96 E5.........................22°40'N 75°53'E
Indre r. France 44 D5.....................47°14'N 0°12'E
Indus r. China/Pakistan 96 C5.........23°56'N 67°38'E
Indus, Mouths of the Pakistan 96 C5......24°36'N 66°36'E
İnebolu Turkey 51 J5.....................41°58'N 33°45'E
İnegöl Turkey 51 H5......................40°04'N 29°30'E
Infiernillo, Presa resr Mexico 66 D4......18°41'N 101°57'W
Infiesto Spain 45 C5.......................43°21'N 5°20'W
Ingatestone England 9 F2...............51°40'N 0°23'E
Ingleborough hill England 13 E3......54°10'N 2°24'W
Ingleton England 13 E3..................54°09'N 2°28'W
Ingoldmells England 13 H2............53°12'N 0°20'E
Ingolstadt Germany 46 D3.............48°46'N 11°27'E
Inhambane Mozambique 83 C2......23°47'S 35°31'E
Inhul r. Ukraine 47 N2...................46°58'N 31°58'E
Inhulets r. Ukraine 47 O2...............46°41'N 32°49'E
Inishbofin i. Ireland 18 A3.............53°38'N 10°14'W
Inisheer i. Ireland 18 B3.................53°04'N 9°30'W
Inishmaan i. Ireland 18 B3.............53°05'N 9°33'W
Inishmore i. Ireland 18 B3...............53°09'N 9°47'W
Inishmurray i. Ireland 18 C4...........54°26'N 8°40'W
Inishowen pen. Ireland 18 D5..........55°13'N 7°17'W
Inishowen Head Ireland 14 C3.........55°14'N 6°55'W
Inishtrahull i. Ireland 18 D5............55°28'N 7°13'W
Inishtrahull Sound str. Ireland 14 B3......55°27'N 7°28'W
Inishturk i. Ireland 18 A3...............53°42'N 10°08'W
Inn r. Europe 46 D2.......................46°55'N 10°29'E
Inner Mongolia d. China 99 I6........40°12'N 103°26'E
Inner Sound str. Scotland 16 D2......57°21'N 5°57'W
Innsbruck Austria 46 D2................47°16'N 11°24'E
Inny r. Ireland 18 D3.....................53°33'N 7°50'W
Inowrocław Poland 46 H5...............52°48'N 18°16'E
In Salah Algeria 84 E4...................27°13'N 2°25'E
Insch Scotland 17 G2.....................57°20'N 2°37'W
Inta Russia 52 F4...........................65°59'N 60°00'E
International Falls town U.S. 63 H6......48°36'N 93°25'W
Inukjuak Canada 61 K3.................58°28'N 78°04'W
Inuvialuit f. Canada 60 F4..............69°10'N 128°00'W
Inuvik Canada 60 E4.....................68°24'N 133°43'W
Inveraray Scotland 14 D4...............56°14'N 5°04'W
Inverbervie Scotland 17 G1.............56°51'N 2°17'W
Invercargill New Zealand 109 F2......46°25'S 168°22'E
Inverclyde d. Scotland 20 C4...........55°54'N 4°44'W
Invergordon Scotland 17 E2...........57°42'N 4°10'W
Inverkeithing Scotland 15 F4...........56°02'N 3°24'W
Inverness Scotland 17 E2...............57°29'N 4°13'W
Inverurie Scotland 17 G2................57°17'N 2°22'W
Ioannina Greece 50 D4..................39°40'N 20°51'E
Iona i. Scotland 14 C4....................56°19'N 6°25'W
Ionian Islands Greece 50 C4............39°26'N 19°33'E
Ionian Sea Greece/Italy 50 C4.........38°11'N 18°29'E
Ios i. Greece 50 F3........................36°44'N 25°22'E
Iowa d. U.S. 63 H5........................42°12'N 92°47'W
Iowa City U.S. 63 H5.....................41°40'N 91°32'W
Ipoh Malaysia 102 C4...................4°40'N 101°04'E
Ipswich England 9 G3...................52°03'N 1°09'E
Iput' r. Russia 47 N5......................52°30'N 31°03'E
Iputs' r. Belarus 47 N5..................52°30'N 31°04'E
Iqaluit Canada 61 L4.....................63°45'N 68°36'W
Iquique Chile 73 B4.......................20°14'S 70°07'W
Iquitos Peru 72 B6........................3°50'S 73°13'W
Iraklion Greece 50 F2....................35°19'N 25°08'E
Iran Asia 95 H6............................31°28'N 55°05'E
Iran, Pegunungan mts Indonesia 102 E4......1°47'N 114°46'E
Iranian Plateau f. Iran 86 D7..........32°00'N 51°00'E
Īrānshahr Iran 95 J5.....................27°13'N 60°42'E
Irapuato Mexico 66 D5.................20°41'N 101°23'W
Iraq Asia 94 F6.............................32°50'N 42°21'E
Irbid Jordan 94 E6........................32°34'N 35°51'E
Ireland Europe 18 D3....................53°33'N 7°43'W
Ireland's Eye i. Ireland 18 E3...........53°24'N 6°03'W
Iringa Tanzania 83 C4...................7°48'S 35°43'E
Iriri r. Brazil 72 D6.......................3°52'S 52°37'W
Irish Sea Ireland/U.K. 18 F3............53°40'N 5°11'W
Irkutsk Russia 55 L3......................52°11'N 104°09'E
Iron Mountain U.S. 63 I6................45°49'N 88°04'W
Ironwood U.S. 63 H6....................46°28'N 90°09'W
Irosin Phil. 103 G6........................12°42'N 124°00'E
Irrawaddy r. Myanmar 97 H4..........15°48'N 95°05'E
Irrawaddy, Mouths of the Myanmar 97 H4......15°35'N 94°02'E
Irsha r. Ukraine 47 M4..................50°46'N 29°35'E
Irthing r. England 12 E3.................54°55'N 2°49'W
Irtysh r. Kazakhstan/Russia 54 H4......61°01'N 68°50'E
Irún Spain 45 E5...........................43°20'N 1°48'W
Irvine Scotland 14 E3.....................55°37'N 4°40'W
Irvinestown Northern Ireland 14 B2......54°28'N 7°39'W
Isabela Phil. 103 G5.......................6°40'N 121°59'E
Isabelia, Cordillera mts Nicaragua 67 G3......13°18'N 85°59'W
Ísafjörður Iceland 43 X2.................66°05'N 23°10'W
Isar r. Germany 46 E3....................48°49'N 12°59'E

Isbister Scotland 17 H5..................60°36'N 1°19'W
Ise Japan 104 C2...........................34°29'N 136°43'E
Isère, Pointe pt French Guiana 72 D7......5°47'N 53°57'W
Ishikari Wan b. Japan 104 D4.........43°17'N 140°58'E
Ishim r. Kazakhstan/Russia 54 I3......57°43'N 71°13'E
Ishinomaki Japan 104 D3..............38°25'N 141°17'E
Isiro Dem. Rep. Congo 83 B5...........2°46'N 27°36'E
İskenderun Turkey 51 L3...............36°34'N 36°08'E
İskenderun Körfezi b. Turkey 51 K3......36°38'N 35°54'E
Iskŭr r. Bulgaria 50 F6...................43°44'N 24°27'E
Isla r. Ang. Scotland 17 F1..............56°32'N 3°22'W
Isla r. Mor. Scotland 17 G2.............57°31'N 2°47'W
Islamabad Pakistan 96 D7.............33°42'N 73°08'E
Islandmagee pen. Northern Ireland 14 D2......54°50'N 5°41'W
Islas Malvinas is S. Atlantic Oc. 73 D1......50°55'S 59°36'W
Islay i. Scotland 14 C3...................55°48'N 6°20'W
Isle of Anglesey d. Wales 21 D5......53°18'N 4°23'W
Isle of Wight d. England 21 E2.......50°41'N 1°18'W
Isles of Scilly d. England 21 B1.......49°55'N 6°17'W
Isna Egypt 49 J2...........................25°16'N 32°30'E
Isparta Turkey 51 I3......................37°46'N 30°32'E
Israel Asia 49 J3...........................32°12'N 34°48'E
İstanbul Turkey 51 H5...................41°07'N 28°58'E
Istria pen. Croatia 46 E1.................45°12'N 13°53'E
Itabuna Brazil 72 F5......................14°47'S 39°17'W
Itaituba Brazil 72 D6.....................4°16'S 56°00'W
Itajaí Brazil 73 E4.........................26°52'S 48°41'W
Italy Europe 48 F5........................41°46'N 14°35'E
Itambé, Pico de mt. Brazil 72 E5......18°23'S 43°20'W
Itapetininga Brazil 73 E4...............23°36'S 48°03'W
Itiquira r. Brazil 72 D5...................17°18'S 56°20'W
Iul'tin Russia 55 T4.......................67°51'N 178°47'W
Ivalo Finland 43 F5.......................68°39'N 27°32'E
Ivano-Frankivsk Ukraine 47 K3......48°55'N 24°43'E
Ivanovo Russia 52 E3.....................56°59'N 40°59'E
Ivatsevichy Belarus 47 K5...............52°43'N 25°21'E
Ivdel' Russia 52 G4.......................60°39'N 60°26'E
Ivittuut Greenland 61 N4...............61°13'N 48°10'W
Ivory Coast Africa 84 D2................7°35'N 4°22'W
Ivybridge England 11 D2...............50°23'N 3°55'W
Iwaki Japan 104 D3.......................37°03'N 140°53'E
Iwo Nigeria 84 E2.........................7°38'N 4°10'E
Ixworth England 9 F3....................52°18'N 0°50'E
Izabal, Lago de l. Guatemala 66 G4......15°36'N 89°08'W
Izhevsk Russia 52 F3......................56°48'N 53°10'E
Izhma Russia 52 F4.......................65°01'N 53°56'E
Izium Ukraine 53 D2.....................49°13'N 37°16'E
Izmail Ukraine 49 I6......................45°21'N 28°51'E
İzmir Turkey 50 G4........................38°24'N 27°10'E
İzmir Körfezi g. Turkey 50 G4.........38°30'N 26°44'E
İzmit Turkey 51 H5........................40°46'N 29°55'E
Izu Shotō is Japan 104 C2..............34°24'N 139°14'E

J

Jabalón r. Spain 45 C3...................38°53'N 4°05'W
Jabalpur India 96 E5......................23°10'N 79°57'E
Jablah Syria 51 K2........................35°21'N 35°56'E
Jaca Spain 45 E5...........................42°34'N 0°34'W
Jackson U.S. 63 H3........................32°19'N 90°12'W
Jacksonville U.S. 63 J3..................30°18'N 81°42'W
Jacmel Haiti 67 J4........................18°16'N 72°32'W
Jacobabad Pakistan 96 C6.............28°15'N 68°29'E
Jacques Cousteau, Isla i. Mexico 66 C5......24°10'N 109°48'W
Jādū Libya 48 F3..........................31°58'N 12°04'E
Jaén Spain 45 D2..........................37°46'N 3°47'W
Jaffna Sri Lanka 96 E2...................9°41'N 79°59'E
Jagdalpur India 96 F4....................19°04'N 82°07'E
Jahrom Iran 95 H5........................28°31'N 53°33'E
Jaipur India 96 E6.........................26°51'N 75°50'E
Jaisalmer India 96 D6....................26°52'N 70°56'E
Jajce Bos. and Herz. 50 B7.............44°21'N 17°16'E
Jakarta Indonesia 102 D2...............6°07'S 106°48'E
Jakobstad Finland 43 E3................63°40'N 22°42'E
Jalālābād Afgh. 95 L6....................34°26'N 70°28'E
Jalandhar India 96 E7....................31°18'N 75°40'E
Jalgaon India 96 E5.......................21°01'N 75°41'E
Jalisco d. Mexico 66 D4................19°59'N 104°18'W
Jalna India 96 E4..........................19°49'N 75°57'E
Jalón r. Spain 45 E4.......................41°47'N 1°02'W
Jālū Libya 85 G4..........................29°03'N 21°33'E
Jamaica Central America 67 I4.........17°30'N 77°19'W
Jamaica Channel Haiti/Jamaica 67 I4......18°29'N 75°24'W
Jambi Indonesia 102 C3.................1°37'S 103°37'E
James r. U.S. 62 G5.......................42°53'N 97°17'W
James Bay Canada 61 J3.................53°23'N 80°25'W
James Shoal S. China Sea 102 E4......3°58'N 112°21'E
Jamestown U.S. 62 G6...................46°53'N 98°43'W
Jammu India 96 D7.......................32°42'N 74°56'E
Jammu and Kashmir d. India 96 E7......33°33'N 75°10'E
Jamnagar India 96 D5...................22°26'N 70°06'E
Jampur Pakistan 96 D6..................29°37'N 70°41'E
Jämsänkoski Finland 43 F3.............61°56'N 25°11'E
Jamshedpur India 96 G5...............22°46'N 86°12'E
Jandía hill Canary Islands 45 Y2......28°06'N 14°21'W
Jan Mayen i. Arctic Oc. 34 D6........72°00'N 8°00'W
Japan Asia 104 C3........................34°40'N 138°17'E
Japan, Sea of N. Pacific Oc. 104 B3......39°13'N 133°37'E
Japurá r. Brazil 72 C6....................3°05'S 64°45'W
Jardines de la Reina, Archipiélago de los is Cuba 67 I5......20°46'N 79°01'W
Järpen Sweden 43 C3.....................63°22'N 13°28'E
Järvenpää Finland 43 F3.................60°29'N 25°06'E
Jasper Canada 60 G3.....................52°53'N 118°05'W
Jastrzębie-Zdrój Poland 46 H3........49°57'N 18°35'E
Java i. Indonesia 102 D2................8°12'S 107°16'E
Java Sea Indonesia 102 D3.............4°56'S 110°49'E
Jawhar Somalia 85 I2.....................2°43'N 45°27'E
Jaya, Puncak mt. Indonesia 103 J3......4°03'S 137°12'E
Jayapura Indonesia 103 K3............2°34'S 140°42'E
Jaz Mūrīān, Hāmūn-e l. Iran 95 I5......27°32'N 58°47'E
Jāzān Saudi Arabia 94 F3..............16°56'N 42°30'E
Jebel Abyad Plateau f. Sudan 94 C3......19°25'N 28°59'E
Jedburgh Scotland 15 G3..............55°29'N 2°33'W
Jeddah Saudi Arabia 94 E4.............21°30'N 39°08'E
Jefferson City U.S. 63 H4..............38°37'N 92°11'W
Jelenia Góra Poland 46 F4.............50°55'N 15°44'E
Jelgava Latvia 43 E2.....................56°39'N 23°44'E
Jejudo i. S. Korea 99 N4................33°34'N 126°43'E
Jember Indonesia 102 E2...............8°05'S 113°45'E
Jena Germany 46 D4.....................50°56'N 11°36'E
Jendouba Tunisia 48 E4.................36°28'N 8°47'E
Jeonju S. Korea 99 N5..................35°51'N 127°09'E
Jequié Brazil 72 E5.......................13°48'S 40°00'W

Jequitinhonha r. Brazil 72 E5.........15°51'S 38°52'W
Jérémie Haiti 67 J4........................18°38'N 74°09'W
Jerez de la Frontera Spain 45 B2......36°41'N 6°08'W
Jerid, Chott el f. Tunisia 48 E3........33°38'N 8°28'E
Jersey i. Channel Is 11 Z8..............49°16'N 2°10'W
Jerusalem Israel/West Bank 49 K3......31°47'N 35°13'E
Jesup U.S. 63 J3............................31°34'N 81°59'W
Jhang Pakistan 95 L6....................31°17'N 72°23'E
Jhansi India 96 E6.........................25°27'N 78°37'E
Jharkhand d. India 96 G5..............23°36'N 85°06'E
Jiamusi China 99 O7.....................46°47'N 130°21'E
Ji'an China 99 K3.........................27°09'N 114°56'E
Jiangmen China 99 K2..................22°35'N 113°06'E
Jiangsu d. China 99 L4.................33°10'N 119°42'E
Jiangxi d. China 99 L3..................27°21'N 115°22'E
Jiaozuo China 99 K5.....................35°12'N 113°15'E
Jiaxing China 99 M4.....................30°46'N 120°49'E
Jiayi Taiwan 99 M2......................23°29'N 120°27'E
Jiehkkevárri mt. Norway 43 D5......69°28'N 19°51'E
Jieyang China 99 L2......................23°34'N 116°19'E
Jihlava Czechia 46 F3...................49°24'N 15°36'E
Jilf al Kabīr, Hadabat al f. Egypt 94 C4......23°12'N 25°56'E
Jilib Somalia 85 I2........................0°30'N 42°47'E
Jilin China 99 N6..........................43°53'N 126°33'E
Jilin d. China 99 N6......................43°33'N 125°10'E
Jīma Ethiopia 85 H2.....................7°40'N 36°49'E
Jiménez Mexico 66 D6..................27°08'N 104°57'W
Jinan China 99 L5.........................36°38'N 117°01'E
Jingdezhen China 99 L3................29°21'N 117°06'E
Jinghong China 99 I2....................21°57'N 100°52'E
Jingmen China 99 K4....................30°58'N 112°10'E
Jingzhou China 99 K4...................30°17'N 112°17'E
Jinhua China 99 L3.......................29°10'N 119°41'E
Jining Nei Mongol China 99 K6......40°54'N 113°06'E
Jining Shandong China 99 L5..........35°22'N 116°29'E
Jinja Uganda 85 H2......................0°28'N 33°14'E
Jinjiang China 99 L2.....................24°49'N 118°38'E
Jinzhou China 99 M6...................41°02'N 121°10'E
Jiparaná r. Brazil 72 C5.................8°09'S 62°50'W
Jiu r. Romania 50 E6....................43°47'N 23°48'E
Jiujiang China 99 L3.....................29°43'N 116°00'E
Jiwani Pakistan 95 J5....................25°07'N 61°48'E
Jixi China 99 O7...........................45°13'N 130°53'E
João Pessoa Brazil 72 F6...............7°05'S 34°50'W
Jodhpur India 96 D6....................26°16'N 73°07'E
Joensuu Finland 43 G3..................62°36'N 29°46'E
Jōetsu Japan 104 C3.....................37°10'N 138°14'E
Johannesburg S. Africa 83 B2.........26°09'S 27°59'E
John o'Groats Scotland 17 F3.........58°38'N 3°04'W
Johnston Wales 10 C3..................51°45'N 4°59'W
Johnstone Scotland 14 E3.............55°50'N 4°31'W
Johor Bahru Malaysia 102 C4.........1°29'N 103°46'E
Jokkmokk Sweden 43 D4..............66°37'N 19°49'E
Jolo i. Phil. 103 G5.......................5°57'N 121°06'E
Jones Sound str. Canada 61 J5........75°58'N 88°58'W
Jönköping Sweden 43 C2...............57°46'N 14°08'E
Jonquière Canada 61 K2................48°25'N 71°14'W
Joplin U.S. 63 H4.........................37°12'N 94°31'W
Jordan Asia 94 E6.........................31°17'N 36°26'E
Jörn Sweden 43 E4.......................65°03'N 20°03'E
Jos Nigeria 84 E2..........................9°55'N 8°53'E
Joseph Bonaparte Gulf Australia 108 B5......14°08'S 128°39'E
Juan Fernández, Archipiélago is S. Pacific Oc. 68 B2......33°24'S 80°00'W
Juàzeiro do Norte Brazil 72 F6........7°11'S 39°14'W
Juba South Sudan 85 H2................4°53'N 31°38'E
Jubaland Somalia 85 I2.................0°45'N 39°45'E
Jubba, Webi r. Somalia 85 I2..........0°15'S 42°37'E
Júcar r. Spain 45 E3......................39°09'N 0°13'W
Juchitán Mexico 66 E4..................16°29'N 95°02'W
Judenburg Austria 46 F2...............47°11'N 14°41'E
Juist i. Germany 42 G6.................53°40'N 7°03'E
Juliaca Peru 72 B5........................15°28'S 70°11'W
Junction City U.S. 62 G4...............39°03'N 96°50'W
Juneau U.S. 60 E3........................58°19'N 134°23'W
Jungfrau mt. Switz. 46 B2..............46°33'N 7°58'E
Junggar Pendi basin China 98 F7......45°02'N 87°38'E
Jura mts France/Switz. 44 F4..........45°38'N 5°26'E
Jura i. Scotland 14 D4...................56°02'N 5°56'W
Jura, Sound of str. Scotland 14 D3......55°51'N 5°49'W
Jurbarkas Lithuania 47 J6..............55°05'N 22°46'E
Jūrmala Latvia 47 J7....................56°57'N 23°40'E
Juruá r. Brazil 72 C6.....................2°39'S 65°48'W
Juruena r. Brazil 72 D5..................7°21'S 58°08'W
Jutaí r. Brazil 72 C6.....................2°45'S 66°58'W
Jutland pen. Denmark 43 B2..........56°13'N 9°08'E
Juventud, Isla de la i. Cuba 67 H5......21°27'N 82°50'W
Jyväskylä Finland 43 F3.................62°14'N 25°44'E

K

K2 mt. China/Pakistan 98 D5..........35°52'N 76°3'E
Kabaena i. Indonesia 103 G2..........5°15'S 121°5'E
Kabalo Dem. Rep. Congo 83 B4......6°02'S 26°5'E
Kābul Afgh. 95 K6........................34°30'N 69°1'E
Kabwe Zambia 83 B3....................14°27'S 28°2'E
Kachchh, Gulf of India 96 C5.........22°35'N 68°5'E
Kachug Russia 55 L3.....................53°54'N 105°4'E
Kadapa India 96 E3......................14°29'N 78°45'E
Kadavu i. Fiji 109 G5...................19°00'S 178°1'E
Kadıköy Turkey 51 H5..................40°59'N 29°0'E
Kadirli Turkey 51 L3.....................37°22'N 36°0'E
Kaduglı Sudan 85 B3.....................11°01'N 29°4'E
Kaduna Nigeria 84 E3....................10°30'N 7°2'E
Kadzherom Russia 52 F4...............64°42'N 55°5'E
Kaesŏng N. Korea 99 N5...............37°58'N 126°3'E
Kafireas, Akra pt Greece 50 F4........38°10'N 24°3'E
Kaga Bandoro C.A.R. 82 F2...........6°57'N 19°1'E
Kagoshima Japan 104 B2...............31°34'N 130°3'E
Kahramanmaraş Turkey 51 L3........37°35'N 36°5'E
Kai, Kepulauan is Indonesia 103 I2......5°26'S 132°5'E
Kaifeng China 99 K4.....................34°43'N 114°2'E
Kaimana Indonesia 103 I3.............3°42'S 133°4'E
Kairouan Tunisia 48 F4.................35°41'N 10°0'E
Kaiserslautern Germany 46 B3........49°27'N 7°4'E
Kaiyuan China 99 I1.....................23°40'N 103°1'E
Kajaani Finland 43 F4....................64°13'N 27°4'E
Kakhovske Vodoskhovyshche resr Ukraine 47 P2......47°00'N 33°4'E
Kakinada India 96 F4...................16°57'N 82°8'E
Kaktovik U.S. 60 D5....................70°04'N 143°4'W
Kakuma Kenya 85 H2...................3°40'N 34°5'E
Kalaburagi India 96 E4.................17°20'N 76°4'E
Kalach-na-Donu Russia 53 E2........48°42'N 43°3'E
Kalahari Desert Africa 83 B2.........23°28'S 22°5'E

alajoki Finland 43 E4 ...64°15'N 23°57'E
alamaria Greece 50 E5 ...40°36'N 22°57'E
alamata Greece 50 E3 ...37°02'N 22°07'E
alät Afgh. 95 K6 ...32°05'N 66°58'E
alecik Turkey 51 J5 ...40°05'N 33°26'E
alemie Dem. Rep. Congo 83 B4 ...5°56'S 29°08'E
algoorlie Australia 108 B3 ...30°50'S 121°30'E
aliakra, Nos pt Bulgaria 51 H6 ...43°22'N 28°28'E
alimantan f. Indonesia 102 E3 ...2°10'S 111°35'E
aliningrad Russia 46 I6 ...54°42'N 20°31'E
alinkavichy Belarus 47 M5 ...52°08'N 29°15'E
alispell U.S. 62 D6 ...48°11'N 114°19'W
alisz Poland 46 H4 ...51°46'N 18°05'E
alixälven r. Sweden 43 E4 ...65°51'N 23°08'E
allavesi l. Finland 43 F3 ...62°47'N 27°47'E
allsjön l. Sweden 43 C3 ...63°37'N 13°00'E
almar Sweden 43 D2 ...56°40'N 16°22'E
altag U.S. 60 C4 ...64°20'N 158°52'W
aluga Russia 53 D3 ...54°31'N 36°16'E
alundborg Denmark 43 B1 ...55°41'N 11°06'E
alush Ukraine 47 K3 ...49°02'N 24°22'E
ama r. Russia 52 F3 ...56°01'N 53°46'E
amaishi Japan 104 D3 ...39°16'N 141°53'E
aman Turkey 51 J4 ...39°22'N 33°43'E
amchatka Peninsula Russia 55 Q3 ...56°10'N 159°12'E
amen', Gora mt. Russia 55 K4 ...69°06'N 95°00'E
amenskoye Russia 55 R4 ...62°33'N 166°10'E
amensk-Ural'skiy Russia 52 G3 ...56°28'N 61°48'E
amianets-Podilskyi Ukraine 47 L3 ...48°41'N 26°35'E
amianske Ukraine 47 P3 ...48°30'N 34°39'E
amin-Kashyrskyi Ukraine 47 K4 ...51°37'N 24°58'E
amina Dem. Rep. Congo 83 B4 ...8°44'S 24°57'E
amloops Canada 60 F3 ...50°41'N 120°21'W
ampala Uganda 85 H2 ...0°20'N 32°34'E
ampen Neth. 42 E5,, ...52°33'N 5°55'E
ampong Cham Cambodia 102 D6 ...11°59'N 105°26'E
ampot Cambodia 102 C6 ...10°36'N 104°12'E
amyshin Russia 53 E3 ...50°06'N 45°25'E
ananga Dem. Rep. Congo 83 B4 ...5°51'S 22°22'E
anash Russia 52 E3 ...55°30'N 47°28'E
anazawa Japan 104 C3 ...36°34'N 136°39'E
anchenjunga mt. India/Nepal 96 G6 ...27°41'N 88°12'E
anchipuram India 96 E3 ...12°51'N 79°43'E
andahār Afgh. 95 K6 ...31°37'N 65°47'E
andalaksha Russia 43 H4 ...67°10'N 32°23'E
andalakshskiy Zaliv g. Russia 43 H4 ...66°38'N 33°25'E
andıra Turkey 51 I5 ...41°04'N 30°08'E
andy Sri Lanka 96 F2 ...7°19'N 80°34'E
angal Turkey 51 L4 ...39°14'N 37°23'E
angaroo Island Australia 108 C3 ...35°48'S 137°11'E
angävar Iran 95 G6 ...34°29'N 47°51'E
angding China 97 J7 ...30°03'N 101°56'E
angean, Kepulauan is Indonesia 102 F2...6°56'S 115°13'E
angertittivaq str. Greenland 61 P5 ...70°31'N 24°44'W
angiqsualujjuaq Canada 61 L3 ...58°35'N 65°45'W
angiqsujuaq Canada 61 K4 ...61°34'N 71°56'W
angmar China 98 F3 ...28°30'N 89°33'E
anin, Poluostrov pen. Russia 52 E4 ...66°50'N 44°50'E
anin Nos, Mys c. Russia 52 E4 ...68°00'N 43°00'E
ankaanpää Finland 43 E3 ...61°49'N 22°25'E
ankakee U.S. 63 I5 ...41°07'N 87°51'W
ankan Guinea 84 D3 ...10°23'N 9°19'W
anker India 96 F5 ...20°16'N 81°32'E
ano Nigeria 84 E3 ...12°01'N 8°31'E
anpur India 96 F6 ...26°27'N 80°24'E
ansas d. U.S. 62 G4 ...38°35'N 98°34'W
ansas r. U.S. 62 H4 ...39°07'N 94°40'W
ansas City U.S. 63 H4 ...39°11'N 94°45'W
ansk Russia 55 K3 ...56°10'N 95°43'E
antchari Burkina Faso 84 E3 ...12°29'N 1°30'E
anton atoll Kiribati 109 H6 ...2°44'S 171°42'W
anye Botswana 83 B2 ...24°58'S 25°21'E
aohsiung Taiwan 99 M2 ...22°39'N 120°20'E
aokoveld f. Namibia 83 A3 ...17°41'S 12°33'E
aolack Senegal 84 C3 ...14°09'N 16°04'W
aposvár Hungary 46 G2 ...46°22'N 17°48'E
apuskasing Canada 61 J2 ...49°26'N 82°26'W
arabük Turkey 51 J5 ...41°11'N 32°38'E
arachi Pakistan 96 C5 ...24°51'N 67°03'E
araginskiy Zaliv b. Russia 55 R3 ...59°32'N 164°48'E
araj Iran 95 H7 ...35°45'N 50°54'E
arakelong i. Indonesia 103 H4 ...4°22'N 126°43'E
arakoram Range mts Asia 96 D8 ...36°18'N 74°54'E
arakum Desert Turkmenistan 54 G2 ...38°58'N 60°05'E
araman Turkey 51 K5 ...37°11'N 33°13'E
aramay China 98 E7 ...45°31'N 84°54'E
arand Iran 95 G6 ...34°14'N 46°16'E
arapınar Turkey 51 J3 ...37°43'N 33°33'E
arasburg Namibia 83 A2 ...28°01'S 18°45'E
ara Sea Russia 54 I5 ...74°13'N 71°44'E
arasuk Russia 54 I3 ...53°43'N 78°03'E
arbala' Iraq 94 F6 ...32°36'N 44°01'E
arcag Hungary 46 I2 ...47°19'N 20°55'E
arditsa Greece 50 D4 ...39°21'N 21°55'E
ardla Estonia 43 E2 ...58°59'N 22°45'E
areima Sudan 85 H3 ...18°31'N 31°49'E
ariba, Lake resr Zambia/Zimbabwe 83 B3 ...17°37'S 27°17'E
imata, Selat str. Indonesia 102 D3 ...1°50'S 108°08'E
kinitska Zatoka g. Ukraine 49 J6 ...45°27'N 32°11'E
rlovac Croatia 50 A7 ...45°29'N 15°33'E
rlovo Bulgaria 50 F6 ...42°39'N 24°48'E
rlovy Vary Czechia 46 E4 ...50°14'N 12°53'E
rlshamn Sweden 43 C2 ...56°11'N 14°52'E
rlskoga Sweden 43 C2 ...59°20'N 14°33'E
rlskrona Sweden 43 C2 ...56°12'N 15°38'E
rlsruhe Germany 46 C3 ...49°01'N 8°24'E
rlstad Sweden 43 C2 ...59°23'N 13°31'E
rmøy i. Norway 43 A2 ...59°11'N 5°15'E
rnataka d. India 96 E4 ...15°37'N 75°29'E
rnobat Bulgaria 50 G6 ...42°38'N 26°59'E
rora Eritrea 85 H4 ...17°41'N 38°23'E
rpathos i. Greece 50 G2 ...35°36'N 27°10'E
rpenisi Greece 50 D4 ...38°55'N 21°48'E
rpogory Russia 52 E4 ...64°01'N 44°25'E
rsava Latvia 47 L7 ...56°47'N 27°41'E
rşıyaka Turkey 50 G4 ...38°27'N 27°06'E
rstula Finland 43 F3 ...62°53'N 24°48'E
rtal Turkey 51 H5 ...40°54'N 29°11'E
rtaly Iraq 94 F6 ...35°37'N 44°20'E
rymskoye Russia 55 M3 ...51°30'N 114°25'E
s Turkey 51 H3 ...36°12'N 29°37'E
saï r. Dem. Rep. Congo 83 A4 ...3°02'S 16°58'E
sama Zambia 83 C3 ...10°12'S 31°12'E
sese Uganda 85 H2 ...0°10'N 30°05'E
shān Iran 95 H6 ...33°58'N 51°30'E
shi China 98 D5 ...39°29'N 76°03'E

Kashiwazaki Japan 104 C3 ...37°22'N 138°34'E
Käshmar Iran 95 I7 ...35°10'N 58°22'E
Kashmir Asia 96 E8 ...35°00'N 77°00'E
Kasos i. Greece 50 G2 ...35°23'N 26°52'E
Kassala Sudan 85 H3 ...15°24'N 36°20'E
Kassel Germany 46 C4 ...51°19'N 9°30'E
Kasserine Tunisia 48 E4 ...35°11'N 8°50'E
Kastamonu Turkey 51 J5 ...41°22'N 33°46'E
Kastelli Greece 50 E2 ...35°30'N 23°38'E
Kastoria Greece 50 D5 ...40°31'N 21°16'E
Kastsyukovichy Belarus 47 O5 ...53°21'N 32°09'E
Katerini Greece 50 E5 ...40°16'N 22°31'E
Kates Needle mt. Canada/U.S. 60 E3 ...57°02'N 132°02'W
Katha Myanmar 97 I5 ...24°11'N 96°20'E
Katherine Australia 108 C5 ...14°28'S 132°18'E
Katima Mulilo Namibia 83 B3 ...17°32'S 24°15'E
Kati Thanda-Lake Eyre (North) Australia 108 C4 ...28°24'S 137°16'E
Katni India 96 F5 ...23°50'N 80°23'E
Kati Thanda-Lake Eyre (South) Australia 108 C4 ...28°30'S 137°25'E
Katowice Poland 46 H4 ...50°16'N 19°01'E
Kātrīnā, Jabal mt. Egypt 49 J2 ...28°31'N 33°58'E
Katrine, Loch l. Scotland 14 E4 ...56°15'N 4°34'W
Katrineholm Sweden 43 D2 ...58°59'N 16°14'E
Katsina Nigeria 84 E3 ...12°59'N 7°36'E
Kattegat str. Denmark/Sweden 43 B2 ...56°49'N 11°21'E
Kauhajoki Finland 43 E3 ...62°25'N 22°11'E
Kaunas Lithuania 43 E1 ...54°54'N 23°55'E
Kaura-Namoda Nigeria 84 E3 ...12°37'N 6°35'E
Kavala Greece 50 F5 ...40°56'N 24°23'E
Kavarna Bulgaria 51 H6 ...43°26'N 28°19'E
Kavīr, Dasht-e des. Iran 95 H6 ...34°36'N 54°41'E
Kawasaki Japan 104 C3 ...35°32'N 139°43'E
Kawm Umbū Egypt 49 J1 ...24°28'N 32°55'E
Kayes Mali 84 C3 ...14°26'N 11°27'W
Kayseri Turkey 51 K4 ...38°43'N 35°29'E
Kazach'ye Russia 55 O5 ...70°45'N 136°09'E
Kazakhstan Asia 54 H2 ...49°18'N 82°53'E
Kazan' Russia 52 E3 ...55°47'N 49°07'E
Kazanlak Bulgaria 50 F6 ...42°37'N 25°23'E
Käzerūn Iran 95 H5 ...29°37'N 51°39'E
Kazym-Mys Russia 52 G4 ...64°43'N 65°36'E
Keady Northern Ireland 14 C2 ...54°15'N 6°42'W
Kearney U.S. 62 G5 ...40°43'N 99°05'W
Keban Barajı resr Turkey 51 M4 ...38°53'N 38°55'E
Kebkabiya Sudan 94 B2 ...13°37'N 24°06'E
Kebnekaise mt. Sweden 43 D4 ...67°55'N 18°31'E
Kebock Head Scotland 16 C3 ...58°03'N 6°21'W
Keçiören Turkey 51 J5 ...40°00'N 32°50'E
Kecskemét Hungary 46 H2 ...46°55'N 19°42'E
Kėdainiai Lithuania 43 E1 ...55°17'N 23°59'E
Keelung Taiwan 99 M3 ...25°07'N 121°43'E
Keen, Mount hill Scotland 17 G1 ...56°58'N 2°59'W
Keetmanshoop Namibia 83 A2 ...26°35'S 18°09'E
Keewatin Canada 63 H6 ...49°46'N 94°34'W
Keflavík Iceland 43 X2 ...64°00'N 22°34'W
Kegworth England 8 D3 ...52°50'N 1°17'W
Keighley England 13 F2 ...53°52'N 1°55'W
Keitele l. Finland 43 F3 ...62°52'N 26°00'E
Keith Scotland 17 G2 ...57°33'N 2°57'W
Kelifskiy Uzboy f. Turkmenistan 95 J7 ...38°07'N 63°33'E
Kelkit r. Turkey 51 L5 ...40°51'N 36°26'E
Kellett, Cape Canada 60 F5 ...71°59'N 125°59'W
Kells Ireland 18 E3 ...53°44'N 6°52'W
Kelmė Lithuania 47 J6 ...55°38'N 22°56'E
Kélo Chad 84 F2 ...9°18'N 15°49'E
Kelowna Canada 60 G2 ...49°53'N 119°29'W
Kelso Scotland 15 G3 ...55°36'N 2°26'W
Kelvedon England 9 F2 ...51°50'N 0°42'E
Kem' Russia 52 D4 ...64°57'N 34°34'E
Kemerovo Russia 54 J3 ...55°23'N 86°01'E
Kemi Finland 43 F4 ...65°46'N 24°33'E
Kemijärvi Finland 43 F4 ...66°43'N 27°23'E
Kemijärvi l. Finland 43 F4 ...66°35'N 27°25'E
Kemijoki r. Finland 43 F4 ...65°47'N 24°32'E
Kemnay Scotland 17 G2 ...57°14'N 2°27'W
Kempston England 9 E3 ...52°07'N 0°30'W
Kempten Germany 46 D2 ...47°43'N 10°18'E
Kenai U.S. 60 C4 ...60°33'N 151°16'W
Kendal England 12 E3 ...54°20'N 2°45'W
Kendari Indonesia 103 G3 ...3°59'S 122°35'E
Kendawangan Indonesia 102 E3 ...2°30'S 110°14'E
Kengtung Myanmar 97 I5 ...21°18'N 99°38'E
Kenilworth England 8 D3 ...52°21'N 1°35'W
Kénitra Morocco 84 D5 ...34°16'N 6°33'W
Kenmare Ireland 18 B1 ...51°53'N 9°35'W
Kenmare River inlet Ireland 18 A1 ...51°43'N 10°03'W
Kennet r. England 8 E2 ...51°27'N 0°57'W
Kenora Canada 61 I2 ...49°47'N 94°30'W
Kent d. England 21 F2 ...51°12'N 0°37'E
Kent r. England 12 E3 ...54°15'N 2°48'W
Kentucky d. U.S. 63 J4 ...37°24'N 84°54'W
Kentucky r. U.S. 63 I4 ...38°41'N 85°10'W
Kenya Africa 85 H2 ...0°59'N 37°32'E
Kenya, Mount Kenya 85 H1 ...0°08'S 37°18'E
Kerala d. India 96 E3 ...11°31'N 75°51'E
Kerch Ukraine 49 K6 ...45°22'N 36°29'E
Kerema P.N.G. 108 D6 ...7°56'S 145°48'E
Keren Eritrea 85 H3 ...15°46'N 38°28'E
Kerinci, Gunung vol. Indonesia 102 C3 ...1°42'S 101°15'E
Kerkyra Greece 50 C4 ...39°37'N 19°55'E
Kerma Sudan 94 D3 ...19°37'N 30°26'E
Kermadec Islands S. Pacific Oc. 109 H3 ...30°19'S 178°19'W
Kermān Iran 95 I6 ...30°17'N 57°04'E
Kermān Desert Iran 95 I5 ...28°27'N 59°19'E
Kermānshāh Iran 95 G6 ...34°19'N 47°02'E
Kerry d. Ireland 18 B2 ...52°09'N 9°28'W
Kerry Head Ireland 18 B2 ...52°25'N 9°57'W
Keşan Turkey 50 G5 ...40°51'N 26°37'E
Kesennuma Japan 104 D3 ...38°54'N 141°33'E
Kessingland England 9 G3 ...52°25'N 1°43'E
Keswick England 12 D3 ...54°36'N 3°07'W
Ketapang Indonesia 102 E3 ...1°50'S 109°59'E
Ketchikan U.S. 60 E3 ...55°20'N 131°38'W
Kettering England 8 E3 ...52°24'N 0°44'W
Keweenaw Bay U.S. 63 I6 ...46°52'N 88°26'W
Key, Lough l. Ireland 18 C4 ...54°01'N 8°15'W
Keynsham England 8 C2 ...51°25'N 2°30'W
K'gari Australia 108 E4 ...25°12'S 153°11'E
Khabarovsk Russia 55 O2 ...48°30'N 135°08'E
Khadyzhensk Russia 53 M7 ...44°25'N 39°31'E
Khairpur Pakistan 96 C6 ...27°31'N 68°45'E
Khambhat, Gulf of India 96 D4 ...20°53'N 71°29'E
Khānābād Afgh. 95 K7 ...36°42'N 69°09'E
Khandwa India 96 E5 ...21°49'N 76°21'E

Khanewal Pakistan 95 L6 ...30°19'N 71°59'E
Khanka, Lake China/Russia 99 O6 ...44°54'N 132°45'E
Khanpur Pakistan 96 D6 ...28°37'N 70°41'E
Khantayskoye, Ozero l. Russia 55 K4 ...68°25'N 91°57'E
Khanty-Mansiysk Russia 52 G4 ...61°05'N 69°01'E
Kharagpur India 96 G5 ...22°20'N 87°20'E
Kharkiv Ukraine 47 Q3 ...49°59'N 36°16'E
Khartoum Sudan 85 H3 ...15°32'N 32°32'E
Khasavyurt Russia 53 E2 ...43°14'N 46°35'E
Khāsh Iran 95 J5 ...28°13'N 61°11'E
Khashm el Girba Sudan 85 H3 ...14°56'N 35°51'E
Khatanga Russia 55 L5 ...71°57'N 102°24'E
Khatangskiy Zaliv b. Russia 55 L5 ...73°19'N 107°17'E
Khayelitsha S. Africa 83 A1 ...34°05'S 18°39'E
Khenchela Algeria 48 E4 ...35°26'N 7°10'E
Khenifra Morocco 48 B3 ...32°58'N 5°37'W
Kherson Ukraine 49 J6 ...46°39'N 32°37'E
Kheta r. Russia 55 L5 ...71°55'N 102°04'E
Khimki Russia 47 Q6 ...55°53'N 37°26'E
Khmelnytskyi Ukraine 47 L3 ...49°26'N 26°59'E
Khon Kaen Thailand 102 C7 ...16°27'N 102°52'E
Khorinsk Russia 99 J8 ...52°09'N 109°48'E
Khorramābād Iran 95 G6 ...33°27'N 48°19'E
Khorugh Tajikistan 95 L7 ...37°29'N 71°35'E
Khoshgort Russia 52 G4 ...65°22'N 65°43'E
Khouribga Morocco 48 B3 ...32°53'N 6°55'W
Khowst Afgh. 95 K6 ...33°21'N 69°59'E
Khromtaū Kazakhstan 53 F3 ...50°10'N 58°22'E
Khrustalnyi Ukraine 53 D2 ...48°08'N 38°55'E
Khujand Tajikistan 98 B6 ...40°15'N 69°38'E
Khulna Bangl. 97 G5 ...22°50'N 89°33'E
Khunsar Iran 95 H6 ...33°10'N 50°17'E
Khurīyā Murīyā, Jazā'ir is Oman 95 I3 ...17°30'N 56°11'E
Khust Ukraine 47 J3 ...48°10'N 23°18'E
Khvoy Iran 94 F7 ...38°33'N 44°58'E
Khyber Pass Afgh./Pakistan 95 L6 ...34°08'N 71°12'E
Kiantajärvi l. Finland 43 G4 ...64°58'N 29°06'E
Kičevo North Macedonia 50 D5 ...41°30'N 20°58'E
Kidderminster England 8 C3 ...52°23'N 2°15'W
Kidsgrove England 13 E2 ...53°05'N 2°14'W
Kidwelly Wales 10 C3 ...51°44'N 4°18'W
Kiel Germany 46 D6 ...54°19'N 10°08'E
Kiel Canal Germany 43 B1 ...54°10'N 9°27'E
Kielce Poland 46 I4 ...50°51'N 20°37'E
Kielder Water resr England 13 E4 ...55°12'N 2°34'W
Kieler Bucht b. Germany 46 D6 ...54°27'N 10°41'E
Kigali Rwanda 85 H1 ...1°59'S 30°05'E
Kigoma Tanzania 83 B4 ...4°51'S 29°40'E
Kii Suidō str. Japan 104 B2 ...33°57'N 134°49'E
Kikinda Serbia 50 D7 ...45°50'N 20°28'E
Kikori r. P.N.G. 108 D6 ...7°22'S 144°14'E
Kikwit Dem. Rep. Congo 83 A4 ...5°03'S 18°50'E
Kilbrannan Sound str. Scotland 14 D3 ...55°25'N 5°27'W
Kilcoole Ireland 10 A5 ...53°06'N 6°03'W
Kilcormac Ireland 18 D3 ...53°10'N 7°44'W
Kilcullen Ireland 18 E3 ...53°08'N 6°45'W
Kildare Ireland 18 E3 ...53°09'N 6°55'W
Kildare d. Ireland 18 E3 ...53°17'N 6°47'W
Kilimanjaro vol. Tanzania 83 C4 ...3°03'S 37°21'E
Kilis Turkey 51 L3 ...36°43'N 37°07'E
Kilkee Ireland 18 B2 ...52°41'N 9°38'W
Kilkeel Northern Ireland 14 D2 ...54°04'N 5°59'W
Kilkenny Ireland 18 D2 ...52°39'N 7°15'W
Kilkenny d. Ireland 18 D2 ...52°35'N 7°15'W
Kilkis Greece 50 E5 ...40°59'N 22°52'E
Killala Bay Ireland 18 B4 ...54°16'N 9°08'W
Killarney Ireland 18 B2 ...52°03'N 9°30'W
Killeen U.S. 62 G3 ...31°08'N 97°44'W
Killin Scotland 14 E4 ...56°28'N 4°19'W
Killorglin Ireland 18 B2 ...52°06'N 9°47'W
Killybegs Ireland 18 C4 ...54°38'N 8°27'W
Kilmallock Ireland 18 C2 ...52°24'N 8°35'W
Kilmarnock Scotland 14 E3 ...55°37'N 4°30'W
Kilmelford Scotland 14 D4 ...56°16'N 5°28'W
Kilmichael Point Ireland 18 E2 ...52°44'N 6°08'W
Kilrea Northern Ireland 14 C2 ...54°57'N 6°33'W
Kilrush Ireland 18 B2 ...52°38'N 9°29'W
Kilsyth Scotland 15 E3 ...55°59'N 4°03'W
Kilwinning Scotland 14 E3 ...55°39'N 4°42'W
Kimberley S. Africa 83 B2 ...28°44'S 24°46'E
Kimberley Plateau f. Australia 108 B5 ...17°26'S 127°05'E
Kimch'aek N. Korea 99 N6 ...40°41'N 129°12'E
Kinabalu, Gunung mt. Malaysia 102 F5...6°04'N 116°33'E
Kinder Scout hill England 13 F2 ...53°23'N 1°52'W
Kindersley Canada 62 E7 ...51°28'N 109°10'W
Kindu Dem. Rep. Congo 83 B4 ...2°57'S 25°53'E
Kineshma Russia 52 E3 ...57°27'N 42°07'E
King Abdullah Economic City Saudi Arabia 94 E4 ...22°24'N 39°05'E
King Island Australia 108 D3 ...39°50'S 143°58'E
Kingman U.S. 62 D4 ...35°14'N 114°02'W
Kingsbridge England 11 D2 ...50°17'N 3°47'W
Kingsclere England 8 D2 ...51°19'N 1°14'W
Kingscourt Ireland 18 E3 ...53°54'N 6°48'W
King's Lynn England 9 F3 ...52°45'N 0°24'E
Kingsnorth England 9 F2 ...51°07'N 0°52'E
Kings Peak U.S. 62 D5 ...40°45'N 110°23'W
Kingston Canada 61 K2 ...44°14'N 76°30'W
Kingston Jamaica 67 I4 ...18°00'N 76°47'W
Kingston upon Hull England 13 G2 ...53°45'N 0°20'W
Kingston upon Thames England 9 E2 ...51°25'N 0°18'W
Kingstown St Vincent 67 L3 ...13°10'N 61°15'W
Kingsville U.S. 62 G2 ...27°27'N 97°48'W
Kingswood England 8 C2 ...51°28'N 2°30'W
Kings Worthy England 8 D2 ...51°06'N 1°18'W
Kington England 8 B3 ...52°12'N 3°02'W
Kingussie Scotland 17 E2 ...57°05'N 4°04'W
King William Island Canada 61 I4 ...69°10'N 97°45'W
Kinlochbervie Scotland 16 D3 ...58°28'N 5°03'W
Kinlochleven Scotland 16 E1 ...56°43'N 4°58'W
Kinloss Scotland 17 F2 ...57°38'N 3°34'W
Kinna Sweden 43 C2 ...57°31'N 12°40'E
Kinnegad Ireland 18 D3 ...53°27'N 7°06'W
Kinross Scotland 15 F4 ...56°12'N 3°25'W
Kinsale Ireland 18 C1 ...51°42'N 8°31'W
Kinshasa Dem. Rep. Congo 83 A4 ...4°22'S 15°23'E
Kintore Scotland 17 G2 ...57°14'N 2°21'W
Kintyre pen. Scotland 14 D3 ...55°32'N 5°35'W
Kircubbin Northern Ireland 14 D2 ...54°29'N 5°31'W
Kiribati Pacific Oc. 109 H6 ...3°26'N 172°45'E
Kırıkhan Turkey 51 L3 ...36°29'N 36°22'E
Kırıkkale Turkey 51 J4 ...39°50'N 33°30'E
Kirkbean Scotland 15 F2 ...54°55'N 3°36'W
Kirkby England 12 E2 ...53°29'N 2°54'W
Kirkby in Ashfield England 13 F2 ...53°06'N 1°16'W
Kirkby Lonsdale England 12 E3 ...54°12'N 2°36'W
Kirkbymoorside England 13 G3 ...54°16'N 0°56'W

Kirkby Stephen England 13 E3 ...54°29'N 2°21'W
Kirkcaldy Scotland 15 F4 ...56°07'N 3°09'W
Kirkcolm Scotland 14 D2 ...54°58'N 5°05'W
Kirkconnel Scotland 15 E3 ...55°23'N 4°00'W
Kirkcudbright Scotland 15 E2 ...54°50'N 4°03'W
Kirkenes Norway 43 G5 ...69°43'N 30°01'E
Kirkham England 12 E2 ...53°47'N 2°52'W
Kirkintilloch Scotland 14 E3 ...55°56'N 4°09'W
Kirkland Lake town Canada 61 J2 ...48°10'N 80°02'W
Kırklareli Turkey 50 G5 ...41°44'N 27°13'E
Kirk Michael Isle of Man 12 C3 ...54°17'N 4°35'W
Kirkük Iraq 94 F7 ...35°24'N 44°24'E
Kirkwall Scotland 17 G3 ...58°59'N 2°58'W
Kirov Russia 47 P6 ...54°04'N 34°20'E
Kirovsk Russia 43 G2 ...59°52'N 30°59'E
Kirovsk Russia 43 H4 ...67°37'N 33°40'E
Kirriemuir Scotland 17 F1 ...56°41'N 3°00'W
Kirs Russia 52 F3 ...59°20'N 52°13'E
Kırşehir Turkey 51 K4 ...39°09'N 34°09'E
Kirtlington England 8 D2 ...51°52'N 1°16'W
Kirton in Lindsey England 13 G2 ...53°29'N 0°35'W
Kiruna Sweden 43 E4 ...67°51'N 20°14'E
Kisangani Dem. Rep. Congo 83 B5 ...0°34'N 25°11'E
Kislovodsk Russia 49 L5 ...43°55'N 42°44'E
Kismaayo Somalia 85 I1 ...0°19'S 42°31'E
Kisoro Uganda 85 G1 ...1°17'S 29°45'E
Kisumu Kenya 85 H2 ...0°04'S 34°47'E
Kita Dake mt. Japan 104 C3 ...35°40'N 138°13'E
Kita-Kyūshū Japan 104 B2 ...33°52'N 130°50'E
Kitami Japan 104 D4 ...43°49'N 143°53'E
Kitimat Canada 60 F3 ...54°03'N 128°39'W
Kittilä Finland 43 F4 ...67°38'N 24°54'E
Kitwe Zambia 83 B3 ...12°48'S 28°12'E
Kiuruvesi Finland 43 F3 ...63°39'N 26°38'E
Kivu, Lake Dem. Rep. Congo/Rwanda 83 B4 ...1°55'S 29°09'E
Kizel Russia 52 F3 ...59°03'N 57°39'E
Kızıl Dağı mt. Turkey 51 M4 ...39°57'N 38°12'E
Kızılırmak r. Turkey 51 K5 ...41°49'N 35°54'E
Kladno Czechia 46 F4 ...50°09'N 14°08'E
Klagenfurt am Wörthersee Austria 46 F2 ...46°38'N 14°19'E
Klaipėda Lithuania 43 E1 ...55°43'N 21°09'E
Klamath r. U.S. 62 B5 ...41°27'N 124°02'W
Klamath Falls town U.S. 62 B5 ...42°15'N 121°46'W
Klang Malaysia 102 C4 ...3°02'N 101°25'E
Klazienaveen Neth. 42 F5 ...52°44'N 6°59'E
Kleve Germany 42 F4 ...51°47'N 6°08'E
Klimovo Russia 47 O5 ...52°23'N 32°12'E
Klin Russia 52 D3 ...56°20'N 36°43'E
Klintsy Russia 47 O5 ...52°45'N 32°15'E
Kłodzko Poland 46 G4 ...50°26'N 16°39'E
Kluang Malaysia 102 C4 ...1°59'N 103°19'E
Klyuchevskaya, Sopka vol. Russia 55 R3 ...56°01'N 160°41'E
Knaresborough England 13 F3 ...54°01'N 1°28'W
Knighton Wales 10 D4 ...52°20'N 3°03'W
Knin Croatia 50 B7 ...44°03'N 16°12'E
Knockaboy hill Ireland 18 B1 ...51°48'N 9°26'W
Knockadoon Head Ireland 18 D1 ...51°53'N 7°52'W
Knockalongy hill Ireland 18 C4 ...54°12'N 8°46'W
Knock Hill Scotland 17 G2 ...57°35'N 2°46'W
Knocklayd hill Northern Ireland 14 C3 ...55°10'N 6°15'W
Knockmealdown Mountains hills Ireland 18 C2 ...52°14'N 8°04'W
Knottingley England 13 F2 ...53°42'N 1°15'W
Knowle England 8 D3 ...52°23'N 1°44'W
Knoxville U.S. 63 J4 ...35°59'N 83°56'W
Knutsford England 13 E2 ...53°18'N 2°22'W
Kōbe Japan 104 C2 ...34°41'N 135°11'E
Koblenz Germany 46 B4 ...50°21'N 7°35'E
Kobroör i. Indonesia 103 I2 ...6°07'S 134°30'E
Kobryn Belarus 47 K5 ...52°12'N 24°23'E
Kočani North Macedonia 50 E5 ...41°55'N 22°23'E
Kochi India 96 E2 ...9°55'N 76°14'E
Kōchi Japan 104 B2 ...33°33'N 133°32'E
Kochubey Russia 53 E2 ...44°29'N 46°38'E
Kodiak U.S. 60 C3 ...57°46'N 152°30'W
Kodiak Island U.S. 60 C3 ...57°26'N 153°20'W
Kōfu Japan 104 C3 ...35°39'N 138°34'E
Køge Denmark 43 C1 ...55°27'N 12°11'E
Kohat Pakistan 95 L6 ...33°37'N 71°30'E
Kokand Uzbekistan 98 C6 ...40°31'N 70°57'E
Kokkola Finland 43 E3 ...63°51'N 23°08'E
Kökpekti Kazakhstan 98 E7 ...48°46'N 82°21'E
Kökshetaü Kazakhstan 54 H3 ...53°17'N 69°23'E
Kola Russia 43 H5 ...68°52'N 33°03'E
Kolaka Indonesia 103 G3 ...4°03'S 121°38'E
Kola Peninsula Russia 52 D4 ...67°29'N 34°49'E
Kolding Denmark 43 B1 ...55°30'N 9°28'E
Kolguyev, Ostrov i. Russia 52 E4 ...69°07'N 49°03'E
Kolhapur India 96 D4 ...16°40'N 74°19'E
Kolkata India 96 G5 ...22°32'N 88°21'E
Kollam India 96 E2 ...8°53'N 76°36'E
Kołobrzeg Poland 46 F6 ...54°11'N 15°35'E
Kolomna Russia 53 D3 ...55°05'N 38°47'E
Kolomyia Ukraine 47 K3 ...48°32'N 25°02'E
Koluli Eritrea 94 F2 ...14°24'N 40°20'E
Kolvitskoye, Ozero l. Russia 43 H4 ...67°04'N 33°36'E
Kolwezi Dem. Rep. Congo 83 B3 ...10°42'S 25°28'E
Kolyma r. Russia 55 R4 ...69°22'N 161°24'E
Kolymskiy, Khrebet mts Russia 55 R4 ...66°50'N 167°12'E
Komatsu Japan 104 C3 ...36°23'N 136°28'E
Komotini Greece 50 F5 ...41°07'N 25°24'E
Komsomolets, Ostrov i. Russia 55 K6 ...80°42'N 94°20'E
Komsomol's'k Ukraine 47 O3 ...49°01'N 33°39'E
Komsomol'sk-na-Amure Russia 55 O3 ...50°36'N 136°55'E
Kong Christian IX Land f. Greenland 61 O4 ...66°49'N 37°44'W
Kongsberg Norway 43 B2 ...59°40'N 9°39'E
Kongsvinger Norway 43 C3 ...60°12'N 12°01'E
Konin Poland 46 H5 ...52°14'N 18°15'E
Konosha Russia 52 E4 ...60°58'N 40°16'E
Konotop Ukraine 47 O4 ...51°14'N 33°12'E
Konstanz Germany 46 C2 ...47°40'N 9°10'E
Konya Turkey 51 J3 ...37°52'N 32°29'E
Konzhakovskiy Kamen', Gora mt. Russia 52 F3 ...59°37'N 59°08'E
Köping Sweden 43 D2 ...59°31'N 16°00'E
Koprivnica Croatia 46 G2 ...46°10'N 16°50'E
Korçë Albania 50 D5 ...40°37'N 20°47'E
Korčula i. Croatia 50 B6 ...42°54'N 16°56'E
Korea Bay China/N. Korea 99 M5 ...39°05'N 124°20'E
Korea Strait Japan/S. Korea 104 A2 ...34°12'N 128°36'E
Körfez Turkey 51 H5 ...40°47'N 29°42'E
Korinthiakos Kolpos str. Greece 50 E4 ...38°16'N 22°11'E
Kōriyama Japan 104 D3 ...37°24'N 140°22'E
Korkuteli Turkey 51 I3 ...37°04'N 30°11'E

Korla China 98 F6..............................41°39'N 86°08'E
Köroğlu Tepesi mt. Turkey 51 J5............40°30'N 32°01'E
Korosten Ukraine 47 M4........................50°57'N 28°39'E
Koro Toro Chad 85 F3.........................16°05'N 18°30'E
Korsakov Russia 55 P2........................46°38'N 142°45'E
Kortrijk Belgium 42 C3.........................50°50'N 3°16'E
Koryakskiy Khrebet mts Russia 55 S4.....62°59'N 177°49'E
Koryazhma Russia 52 E4......................61°19'N 47°12'E
Kos i. Greece 50 G3.............................36°46'N 27°07'E
Kościerzyna Poland 46 G6....................54°07'N 17°59'E
Kosciuszko, Mount Australia 108 D3......36°28'S 148°15'E
Košice Slovakia 46 I3...........................48°43'N 21°16'E
Kosovo Europe 50 D6...........................42°35'N 21°00'E
Kosti Sudan 85 H3...............................13°09'N 32°38'E
Kostomuksha Russia 52 D4...................64°34'N 30°33'E
Kostroma Russia 52 E3.........................57°46'N 40°58'E
Kostrzyn nad Odrą Poland 46 F5............52°35'N 14°39'E
Koszalin Poland 46 G6.........................54°11'N 16°11'E
Kota India 96 E6.................................25°10'N 75°57'E
Kota Bharu Malaysia 102 C5.................6°08'N 102°16'E
Kotabumi Indonesia 102 C3..................4°51'S 104°55'E
Kota Kinabalu Malaysia 102 C5.............5°58'N 116°05'E
Kotel'nich Russia 52 E3.........................58°18'N 48°20'E
Kotel'nyy Russia 55 O5.........................76°00'N 137°59'E
Kotel'nyy, Ostrov i. Russia 55 O5...........75°07'N 139°31'E
Kotlas Russia 52 E4.............................61°16'N 46°38'E
Kötlutangi pt Iceland 43 Y1....................63°24'N 18°45'W
Kotuy r. Russia 55 L5...........................71°55'N 102°06'E
Kotzebue U.S. 60 B4............................66°53'N 162°32'W
Kotzebue Sound str. U.S. 60 B4.............66°33'N 163°11'W
Koundâra Guinea 84 C3.......................12°30'N 13°18'W
Kouvola Finland 43 F3..........................60°52'N 26°42'E
Kovel Ukraine 47 K4............................51°13'N 24°43'E
Kovrov Russia 52 E3............................56°22'N 41°19'E
Kowloon China 102 E8.........................22°20'N 114°13'E
Kozan Turkey 51 K3.............................37°28'N 35°48'E
Kozani Greece 50 D5............................40°18'N 21°48'E
Kozarska Dubica Bos. and Herz. 50 B7...45°11'N 16°48'E
Kozelets Ukraine 47 N4.........................50°55'N 31°07'E
Kozhikode India 96 E3..........................11°15'N 75°45'E
Koziatyn Ukraine 47 M3........................49°42'N 28°49'E
Krabi Thailand 102 B5..........................8°05'N 98°56'E
Kragujevac Serbia 50 D7.......................44°01'N 20°55'E
Kraków Poland 46 H4...........................50°03'N 19°56'E
Kraljevo Serbia 49 H5...........................43°43'N 20°41'E
Kramfors Sweden 43 D3........................62°56'N 17°46'E
Kranj Slovenia 46 F2............................46°15'N 14°21'E
Krasino (abandoned) Russia 52 F5.........70°44'N 54°28'E
Krasnoborsk Russia 52 E4.....................61°33'N 45°56'E
Krasnodar Russia 53 D2........................45°02'N 38°59'E
Krasnohrad Ukraine 47 P3.....................49°22'N 35°28'E
Krasnokamsk Russia 52 F3....................58°05'N 55°45'E
Krasnotur'insk Russia 52 G3...................59°47'N 60°13'E
Krasnoufimsk Russia 52 F3....................56°36'N 57°46'E
Krasnoyarsk Russia 55 K3......................56°03'N 92°50'E
Kratie Cambodia 102 D6........................12°27'N 106°03'E
Krefeld Germany 46 B4..........................51°20'N 6°33'E
Kremenchuk Ukraine 47 O3....................49°04'N 33°25'E
Kremenchutske Vodoskhovyshche resr Ukraine 47 O3
                                                            49°18'N 32°42'E
Kretinga Lithuania 46 I6........................55°53'N 21°14'E
Krishna r. India 96 F4............................16°01'N 80°53'E
Kristiansand Norway 43 A2.....................58°08'N 7°59'E
Kristianstad Sweden 43 C2.....................56°02'N 14°10'E
Kristiansund Norway 43 A3.....................63°07'N 7°45'E
Kristinehamn Sweden 43 C2...................59°19'N 14°07'E
Kritiko Pelagos sea Greece 50 F2............36°11'N 25°24'E
Krk i. Croatia 50 A7..............................45°02'N 14°47'E
Kropotkin Russia 53 E2..........................45°26'N 40°34'E
Kropyvnytskyi Ukraine 47 O3..................48°30'N 32°16'E
Krosno Poland 47 I3..............................49°41'N 21°46'E
Kruševac Serbia 50 D6..........................43°35'N 21°19'E
Krychaw Belarus 47 N5..........................53°44'N 31°43'E
Krymsk Russia 51 L7.............................44°55'N 37°59'E
Kryvyi Rih Ukraine 47 O2........................47°54'N 33°21'E
Ksabi Algeria 84 D4..............................28°54'N 0°47'W
Ksar el Boukhari Algeria 48 D4...............35°52'N 2°45'E
Ksar el Kebir Morocco 48 B4..................35°01'N 5°54'W
Kuala Lumpur Malaysia 102 C4..............3°06'N 101°42'E
Kuala Terengganu Malaysia 102 C5.........5°19'N 103°07'E
Kuantan Malaysia 102 C4......................3°50'N 103°21'E
Kuban' r. Russia 51 L7...........................45°19'N 37°22'E
Kuching Malaysia 102 C4.......................1°32'N 110°20'E
Kugluktuk Canada 60 H4.......................67°46'N 115°07'W
Kuhmo Finland 43 G4............................64°07'N 29°30'E
Kujū San vol. Japan 104 B2.....................33°05'N 131°16'E
Kūl r. Iran 95 I5....................................27°04'N 55°44'E
Kuldīga Latvia 43 E2.............................56°58'N 21°59'E
Külob Tajikistan 95 K7............................37°54'N 69°51'E
Kulunda Russia 98 D8...........................53°08'N 78°56'E
Kulundinskoye, Ozero l. Russia 98 D8.....53°08'N 79°46'E
Kumamoto Japan 104 B2........................32°47'N 130°43'E
Kumanovo North Macedonia 50 D6.........42°08'N 21°43'E
Kumasi Ghana 84 D2............................6°42'N 1°38'W
Kumbakonam India 96 E3......................10°58'N 79°23'E
Kumertau Russia 53 F3..........................52°44'N 55°46'E
Kumla Sweden 43 C2.............................59°07'N 15°10'E
Kumo Nigeria 84 F3..............................10°06'N 11°11'E
Kumpupintil Lake Australia 108 B4...........23°30'S 122°40'E
Kunashir, Ostrov i. Russia 104 E4............44°13'N 146°23'E
Kungur Russia 52 F3.............................57°24'N 56°56'E
Kunlun Shan mts China 98 D5................36°11'N 78°10'E
Kunming China 99 I3.............................25°02'N 102°44'E
Kuohijärvi l. Finland 43 F3......................61°12'N 24°59'E
Kuopio Finland 43 F3.............................62°53'N 27°41'E
Kupa r. Croatia/Slovenia 50 B7...............45°28'N 16°25'E
Kupang Indonesia 103 G1......................10°12'S 123°35'E
Kupiansk Ukraine 53 D2........................49°42'N 37°37'E
Kupiškis Lithuania 43 F1........................55°49'N 24°59'E
Kuqa China 98 E6................................41°38'N 83°01'E
Kurdistan f. Asia 94 F7...........................37°00'N 42°00'E
Kuressaare Estonia 43 E2......................58°16'N 22°29'E
Kurgan Russia 54 H3.............................55°28'N 65°23'E
Kurikka Finland 43 E3............................62°37'N 22°25'E
Kuril Islands Russia 55 P2......................46°04'N 148°33'E
Kuril'sk Russia 55 P2.............................45°13'N 147°57'E
Kuril-Kamchatka Trench f. N. Pacific Oc. 117 I4
                                                            41°44'N 146°31'E
Kurmuk Sudan 85 H3.............................10°31'N 34°16'E
Kurnool India 96 E4...............................15°49'N 77°59'E
Kursk Russia 53 D3...............................51°45'N 36°12'E
Kuršumlija Serbia 50 D6.........................43°08'N 21°17'E
Kurume Japan 104 B2............................33°18'N 130°31'E
Kurunegala Sri Lanka 96 F2....................7°30'N 80°19'E
Kuşadası Turkey 50 G3..........................37°52'N 27°15'E
Kushiro Japan 104 D4............................42°59'N 144°23'E
Kuskokwim Mountains U.S. 60 C4...........64°24'N 155°17'W

Kütahya Turkey 51 H4............................39°25'N 29°59'E
Kutaisi Georgia 53 E2............................42°16'N 42°43'E
Kutno Poland 46 H5..............................52°14'N 19°22'E
Kuujjuaq Canada 61 L3..........................58°10'N 68°13'W
Kuusamo Finland 43 G4.........................65°58'N 29°09'E
Kuwait Asia 95 G5.................................29°22'N 47°08'E
Kuwait City Kuwait 95 G5.......................29°18'N 47°55'E
Kuybyshevskoye Vodokhranilische resr Russia 53 E3
                                                            54°55'N 49°00'E
Kuytun China 98 E6...............................44°20'N 84°55'E
Kuznetsk Russia 53 E3...........................53°07'N 46°37'E
Kvaløya i. Norway 43 D5.........................69°38'N 18°30'E
KwaMashu S. Africa 83 C2......................29°44'S 30°59'E
KwaNobuhle S. Africa 83 B1...................33°48'S 25°24'E
Kwilu r. Angola/Dem. Rep. Congo 83 A4...3°23'S 17°22'E
Kyakhta Russia 55 L3............................50°21'N 106°30'E
Kyangwali Uganda 85 H2........................1°15'N 30°45'E
Kyiv Ukraine 47 N4................................50°26'N 30°34'E
Kyle of Lochalsh Scotland 16 D2..............57°17'N 5°43'W
Kyle of Tongue inlet Scotland 17 E3..........58°28'N 4°27'W
Kyllini mt. Greece 50 E3.........................37°56'N 22°24'E
Kyoga, Lake Uganda 85 H2.....................1°28'N 32°53'E
Kyōto Japan 104 C2..............................34°59'N 135°46'E
Kyparissia Greece 50 D3........................37°15'N 21°41'E
Kyrenia Cyprus 51 J2.............................35°20'N 33°19'E
Kyrgyzstan Asia 98 C6...........................41°47'N 74°37'E
Kyrta Russia 52 F4................................64°04'N 57°40'E
Kythira i. Greece 50 E3...........................36°16'N 22°55'E
Kythnos i. Greece 50 F3..........................37°26'N 24°27'E
Kyūshū i. Japan 104 B2..........................31°30'N 131°45'E
Kyustendil Bulgaria 50 E6.......................42°17'N 22°41'E
Kyivske Vodoskhovyshche resr Ukraine 47 N4
                                                            50°54'N 30°30'E
Kyzyl Russia 55 K3................................51°43'N 94°24'E

L

Laâyoune Western Sahara 84 C4.............27°09'N 13°12'W
Labé Guinea 84 C3...............................11°20'N 12°18'W
Labrador f. Canada 61 L3.......................54°04'N 62°29'W
Labrador City Canada 61 L3....................52°59'N 66°54'W
Labrador Sea Canada/Greenland 61 M4...60°07'N 56°06'W
Labytnangi Russia 52 G4........................66°42'N 66°18'E
Laccadive Sea Asia 96 D2.......................10°00'N 73°00'E
Laceby England 13 G2...........................53°32'N 0°10'W
Lachlan r. Australia 108 D3......................34°21'S 143°57'E
La Crosse U.S. 63 H5............................43°48'N 91°12'W
Ladakh d. India 96 E7............................34°05'N 77°10'E
Ladhar Bheinn mt. Scotland 16 D2............57°05'N 5°36'W
Lādīz Iran 95 J5...................................28°55'N 61°18'E
Ladoga, Lake Russia 54 E4......................60°48'N 31°37'E
Ladybank Scotland 15 F4........................56°17'N 3°08'W
Ladybower Reservoir England 13 F2.........53°23'N 1°45'W
Ladysmith S. Africa 83 B2.......................28°34'S 29°47'E
Lae P.N.G. 108 D6................................6°43'S 147°00'E
Læsø i. Denmark 43 B2...........................57°15'N 11°05'E
Lafayette U.S. 63 H3..............................30°14'N 92°03'W
Lagan r. Northern Ireland 14 D2...............54°37'N 5°54'W
Lagan' Russia 53 E2.............................45°25'N 47°18'E
Laggan, Loch l. Scotland 17 E1...............56°56'N 4°31'W
Laghouat Algeria 84 E5..........................33°42'N 2°53'E
La Gomera i. Canary Islands 45 X2...........28°14'N 17°18'W
Lagos Nigeria 84 E2..............................6°26'N 3°20'E
Lagos Portugal 45 A2.............................37°06'N 8°41'W
La Grande U.S. 62 D6............................45°19'N 118°02'W
La Grande 3, Réservoir Canada 61 K3......53°36'N 75°18'W
La Grande 4, Réservoir Canada 61 K3......54°13'N 73°17'W
La Gran Sabana f. Venezuela 67 L2..........5°13'N 61°40'W
Lahad Datu Malaysia 102 F5...................5°02'N 118°20'E
Lahat Indonesia 102 C3.........................3°46'S 103°34'E
Laḥij Yemen 94 F2................................13°02'N 44°50'E
Lāhījān Iran 95 G7................................37°11'N 49°56'E
Lahore Pakistan 96 D7...........................31°33'N 74°23'E
Lahti Finland 43 F3...............................60°59'N 25°41'E
Laidon, Loch l. Scotland 17 E1................56°39'N 4°39'W
Laihia Fin. 43 E3...................................62°58'N 22°01'E
Lainioälven r. Sweden 43 E4...................67°22'N 22°39'E
Lairg Scotland 17 E3.............................58°01'N 4°24'W
Lake City U.S. 63 J3..............................30°10'N 82°39'W
Lake District f. England 12 D3..................54°30'N 3°10'W
Lake Frome / Munda Australia 108 C3......30°43'S 139°48'E
Lakeland U.S. 63 J2..............................28°03'N 81°58'W
Lake Taupō / Taupōmoana New Zealand 109 G3
                                                            38°48'S 175°55'E
Lakki Pakistan 95 L6.............................32°35'N 70°58'E
Lakonikos Kolpos b. Greece 50 E3...........36°32'N 22°42'E
Laksefjorden str. Norway 43 F5...............70°52'N 27°00'E
Lakshadweep d. India 96 D3...................10°35'N 73°13'E
Lakshadweep is India 96 D3...................10°59'N 72°11'E
La Línea de la Concepción Spain 45 C2....36°10'N 5°21'W
La Louvière Belgium 42 D3.....................50°28'N 4°11'E
La Mancha f. Spain 45 D3......................39°15'N 2°58'W
Lamar U.S. 62 F4.................................38°06'N 102°38'W
La Martre, Lac l. Canada 60 G4...............63°19'N 118°02'W
Lambay Island Ireland 18 F3...................53°29'N 5°59'W
Lambourn England 8 D2........................51°30'N 1°32'W
Lambourn Downs hills England 8 D2.........51°32'N 1°32'W
Lamego Portugal 45 B4..........................41°06'N 7°48'W
Lāmerd Iran 95 H5................................27°22'N 53°08'E
Lamia Greece 50 E4..............................38°54'N 22°25'E
Lamlash Scotland 14 D3.........................55°32'N 5°08'W
Lammermuir Hills Scotland 15 G3.............55°49'N 2°50'W
Lampang Thailand 102 B7.......................18°16'N 99°32'E
Lampeter Wales 10 C4...........................52°07'N 4°05'W
Lanark Scotland 15 F3............................55°40'N 3°47'W
Lancashire d. England 21 D3...................53°57'N 2°51'W
Lancaster England 12 E3........................54°03'N 2°48'W
Lancaster Canal England 12 E3...............53°59'N 2°31'W
Lancaster Sound str. Canada 61 J5...........74°15'N 89°18'W
Landeck Austria 46 D2...........................47°08'N 10°34'E
Lander U.S. 62 E5................................42°50'N 108°42'W
Landes f. France 44 C4...........................44°48'N 0°55'W
Landguard Point England 9 G2................51°56'N 1°19'E
Land's End pt England 11 B2...................50°03'N 5°46'W
Landshut Germany 46 E3........................48°33'N 12°10'E
Landskrona Sweden 46 B4......................55°52'N 12°50'E
Lanesborough Ireland 18 D3...................53°40'N 7°59'W
Langabhat, Loch l. Na h-E. S. Scotland 16 C2
                                                            57°48'N 6°59'W
Langabhat, Loch l. Na h-E. S. Scotland 16 C3
                                                            58°02'N 6°49'W
Langeland i. Denmark 43 B1....................55°02'N 10°55'E
Langeoog i. Germany 42 G6....................53°46'N 7°36'E
Langholm Scotland 15 G3.......................55°09'N 2°59'W
Langøya i. Norway 43 C5........................68°44'N 14°27'E

Langport England 8 C2...........................51°02'N 2°50'W
Langres France 44 F5.............................47°52'N 5°20'E
Langsa Indonesia 102 B4.......................4°25'N 97°57'E
Langstrothdale Chase hills England 13 E3...54°13'N 2°18'W
Languedoc f. France 44 D3.....................43°10'N 1°57'E
Lanivet England 11 C2...........................50°26'N 4°46'W
Lannion France 44 B6............................48°44'N 3°27'W
Lansing U.S. 63 J5...............................42°44'N 84°33'W
Lanzarote i. Canary Islands 45 Z2............29°09'N 13°35'W
Lanzhou China 99 I5..............................36°04'N 103°43'E
Laoag Phil. 102 G7...............................18°14'N 120°36'E
Lao Cai Vietnam 102 C8.........................22°26'N 103°59'E
Laois d. Ireland 18 D2............................52°57'N 7°23'W
Laojunmiao China 98 H5.......................39°46'N 97°33'E
Laon France 44 E6................................49°34'N 3°38'E
Laos Asia 102 C7................................19°30'N 103°01'E
La Palma i. Canary Islands 45 X2.............28°33'N 17°44'W
La Palma Panama 67 I2.........................8°21'N 78°11'W
La Palma del Condado Spain 45 B2.........37°23'N 6°33'W
La Paragua Venezuela 67 L2...................6°50'N 63°19'W
La Paz Bolivia 72 C5.............................16°30'S 68°10'W
La Paz Mexico 66 B5............................24°08'N 110°17'W
La Pérouse Strait Japan/Russia 104 D5....45°35'N 141°33'E
La Plata Argentina 73 D3.......................34°55'S 57°58'W
La Plata, Río de str. Argentina/Uruguay 73 D3
                                                            34°39'S 57°53'W
Lappajärvi l. Finland 43 E3......................63°07'N 23°41'E
Lappeenranta Finland 43 G3...................61°03'N 28°11'E
Laptev Sea Russia 55 N5........................76°05'N 125°40'E
Lapua Finland 43 E3.............................62°58'N 23°00'E
Larache Morocco 48 B4.........................35°12'N 6°09'W
Laramie U.S. 62 E5..............................41°20'N 105°36'W
Laredo U.S. 62 G2...............................27°30'N 99°30'W
Largs Scotland 14 E3............................55°48'N 4°52'W
La Rioja Argentina 73 C4........................29°25'S 66°51'W
Larisa Greece 50 E4.............................39°38'N 22°25'E
Larkana Pakistan 96 C6.........................27°31'N 68°15'E
Larnaca Cyprus 51 J2............................34°55'N 33°38'E
Larne Northern Ireland 14 D2...................54°51'N 5°49'W
Larne Lough inlet Northern Ireland 14 D2...54°49'N 5°47'W
La Rochelle France 44 C5.......................46°10'N 1°09'W
La Roche-sur-Yon France 44 C5..............46°40'N 1°25'W
La Ronge Canada 60 H3.........................55°06'N 105°17'W
Larvik Norway 43 B2.............................59°03'N 10°05'E
La Sagra f. Spain 45 D2.........................37°57'N 2°34'W
La Sarre Canada 61 K2..........................48°48'N 79°12'W
Las Cruces U.S. 62 E3..........................32°19'N 106°47'W
La Serena Chile 73 B4...........................29°53'S 71°16'W
Lashio Myanmar 97 I5............................22°57'N 97°44'E
Las Marismas marsh Spain 45 B2.............37°00'N 6°35'W
Las Palmas de Gran Canaria Canary Islands 45 Y2
                                                            28°06'N 15°26'W
Las Tunas Cuba 67 I5............................20°57'N 76°57'W
Las Vegas U.S. 62 C4............................36°10'N 115°09'W
Las Villuercas mt. Spain 45 C3................39°29'N 5°23'W
Latakia Syria 94 E7...............................35°31'N 35°47'E
Latheron Scotland 17 F3........................58°17'N 3°22'W
Latina Italy 48 E5.................................41°28'N 12°54'E
La Tortuga, Isla i. Venezuela 67 K3...........10°58'N 65°17'W
La Tuque Canada 63 L6.........................47°27'N 72°47'W
Latvia Europe 43 E2.............................56°47'N 23°49'E
Lauchhammer Germany 46 E4................51°30'N 13°46'E
Launceston Australia 108 D2..................41°27'S 147°09'E
Launceston England 11 C2....................50°38'N 4°21'W
Laurencekirk Scotland 17 G1..................56°50'N 2°28'W
Lausanne Switz. 48 E6...........................46°32'N 6°39'E
Laut i. Indonesia 102 F3..........................3°09'S 116°18'E
Laval France 44 C6...............................48°04'N 0°46'W
Lavenham England 9 F3.........................52°06'N 0°48'E
Lawton U.S. 62 G3...............................34°37'N 98°24'W
Lawz, Jabal al mt. Saudi Arabia 49 K2.......28°39'N 35°18'E
Laxey Isle of Man 12 C3.........................54°14'N 4°24'W
Laxford, Loch inlet Scotland 16 D3............58°25'N 5°06'W
Lázaro Cárdenas Baja Calif. Mexico 66 A7
                                                            30°30'N 115°56'W
Lázaro Cárdenas Michoacán Mexico 66 D4
                                                            17°57'N 102°12'W
Leader Water r. Scotland 15 G3...............55°36'N 2°40'W
Leane, Lough l. Ireland 18 B2..................52°02'N 9°34'W
Leatherhead England 9 E2......................51°17'N 0°19'W
Lebanon Asia 49 K3..............................33°17'N 35°20'E
Lębork Poland 46 G6.............................54°32'N 17°45'E
Lecce Italy 49 G5.................................40°20'N 18°11'E
Lech r. Austria/Germany 46 D2.................47°32'N 10°40'E
Lechlade-on-Thames England 8 D2..........51°42'N 1°41'W
Le Crotoy France 9 G1...........................50°13'N 1°38'E
Ledbury England 8 C2...........................52°02'N 2°25'W
Lee r. Ireland 18 C1..............................51°54'N 8°25'W
Leeds England 13 F2............................53°48'N 1°33'W
Leek England 13 E2..............................53°07'N 2°01'W
Leeming England 13 F3.........................54°18'N 1°33'W
Lee Moor England 11 C2.......................50°26'N 4°01'W
Leer Germany 42 G6.............................53°15'N 7°28'E
Leeuwarden Neth. 42 E6........................53°12'N 5°48'E
Leeuwin, Cape Australia 108 A3..............34°23'S 115°09'E
Leeward Islands Caribbean Sea 67 L4......18°59'N 64°04'W
Lefkada i. Greece 50 D4.........................38°45'N 20°35'E
Legaspi Phil. 103 G6.............................13°08'N 123°44'E
Legnica Poland 46 G4...........................51°13'N 16°10'E
Leh India 96 E7....................................34°09'N 77°36'E
Le Havre France 44 D6..........................49°30'N 0°08'E
Leiah Pakistan 95 L6.............................30°58'N 70°58'E
Leicester England 8 D3..........................52°38'N 1°08'W
Leicester d. England 21 E3......................52°39'N 1°07'W
Leicestershire d. England 21 E3................52°38'N 1°09'W
Leichhardt r. Australia 108 C5..................17°35'S 139°44'E
Leiden Neth. 42 D5...............................52°10'N 4°30'E
Leigh England 13 E2.............................53°30'N 2°31'W
Leighton Buzzard England 8 E2...............51°55'N 0°40'W
Leine r. Germany 42 H5..........................52°43'N 9°36'E
Leinster, Mount hill Ireland 18 E2..............52°37'N 6°47'W
Leipzig Germany 46 E4..........................51°21'N 12°23'E
Leiston England 9 G3............................52°13'N 1°35'E
Leith Scotland 15 F3.............................55°59'N 3°10'W
Leith Hill England 9 E2...........................51°11'N 0°22'W
Leitrim d. Ireland 18 C4..........................54°08'N 8°00'W
Leixlip Ireland 18 E3..............................53°22'N 6°29'W
Leizhou Bandao pen. China 99 J2.............21°03'N 109°41'E
Lek r. Neth. 42 D4................................51°54'N 4°34'E
Leka Norway 43 B4...............................65°05'N 11°44'E
Leksozero, Ozero l. Russia 43 G3.............63°51'N 30°48'E
Lelystad Neth. 42 E5.............................52°32'N 5°29'E
Le Mans France 44 D6...........................48°00'N 0°12'E
Lena r. Russia 55 N5.............................72°25'N 126°23'E
Lens France 44 E7...............................50°26'N 2°50'E
Lensk Russia 55 M4..............................60°44'N 114°53'E

Leoben Austria 46 F2............................47°23'N 15°06'E
Leominster England 8 C3........................52°14'N 2°44'W
León Mexico 66 D5...............................21°07'N 101°44'W
León Spain 45 C5.................................42°36'N 5°34'W
Le Puy-en-Velay France 44 E4.................45°03'N 3°53'E
Lerum Sweden 43 C2............................57°46'N 12°17'E
Lerwick Scotland 17 H5..........................60°09'N 1°09'W
Lesbos i. Greece 50 F4...........................39°08'N 25°56'E
Les Cayes Haiti 67 J4............................18°14'N 73°47'W
Leshan China 99 I3...............................29°37'N 103°44'E
Leskovac Serbia 50 D6...........................42°59'N 21°56'E
Lesosibirsk Russia 55 K3........................58°17'N 92°24'E
Lesotho Africa 83 B2.............................29°38'S 28°02'E
Les Pieux France 11 Z9..........................49°31'N 1°48'W
Les Sables-d'Olonne France 44 C5..........46°30'N 1°46'W
Lesser Antilles is Caribbean Sea 67 K3.....12°28'N 65°56'W
Lesser Slave Lake Canada 60 G3.............55°28'N 115°29'W
Lestijärvi l. Finland 43 F3........................63°30'N 24°47'E
Leszno Poland 46 G4.............................51°51'N 16°35'E
Letchworth Garden City England 9 E2........51°59'N 0°13'W
Lethbridge Canada 60 G2.......................49°41'N 112°49'W
Leti, Kepulauan is Indonesia 103 H2..........8°18'S 127°58'E
Letterkenny Ireland 18 D4.......................54°57'N 7°43'W
Leuchars Scotland 15 G4........................56°23'N 2°53'W
Leuser, Gunung mt. Indonesia 102 B4.......3°46'N 97°11'E
Leuven Belgium 42 D3...........................50°52'N 4°43'E
Levadeia Greece 50 E4..........................38°26'N 22°53'E
Leven England 13 G2............................53°54'N 0°18'W
Leven Scotland 15 G4............................56°12'N 2°59'W
Leven, Loch inlet Scotland 16 D1..............56°41'N 5°06'W
Leven, Loch l. Scotland 15 F4.................56°12'N 3°23'W
Levens England 12 E3...........................54°16'N 2°47'W
Leverkusen Germany 46 B4.....................51°03'N 6°59'E
Lewes England 9 F1..............................50°52'N 0°01'E
Lewis, Isle of i. Scotland 16 C3................58°09'N 6°59'W
Lexington U.S. 63 J4.............................38°02'N 84°31'W
Leyburn England 13 F3..........................54°19'N 1°50'W
Leyland England 12 E2..........................53°42'N 2°42'W
Leyte i. Phil. 103 G6.............................11°05'N 124°31'E
Lezhë Albania 50 C5.............................41°46'N 19°39'E
L'gov Russia 47 P4...............................51°39'N 35°16'E
Lharigarbo China 98 E4..........................32°15'N 91°43'E
Lhasa China 98 G3..............................29°39'N 91°05'E
Lhazê China 98 F3................................29°08'N 87°36'E
Lhokseumawe Indonesia 102 B5.............5°09'N 97°08'E
L'Hospitalet de Llobregat Spain 45 G4.......41°22'N 2°10'E
Lianshan China 99 M6...........................40°41'N 120°55'E
Lianyungang China 99 L4.......................34°37'N 119°11'E
Liaoning d. China 99 M6........................41°30'N 122°45'E
Liaoyuan China 99 N6...........................42°54'N 125°08'E
Liard r. Canada 60 F4............................61°51'N 121°17'W
Libenge Dem. Rep. Congo 83 A5............3°37'N 18°42'E
Liberal U.S. 62 F4................................37°03'N 100°57'W
Liberec Czechia 46 F4...........................50°45'N 15°03'E
Liberia Africa 84 D2..............................6°52'N 9°55'W
Libin Belgium 42 E2..............................49°59'N 5°16'E
Libourne France 44 C4...........................44°55'N 0°14'W
Libreville Gabon 84 E2...........................0°28'N 9°27'E
Libya Africa 84 F4.................................26°07'N 17°09'E
Libyan Desert Egypt/Libya 85 G4.............24°51'N 25°00'E
Libyan Plateau f. Egypt/Libya 49 I3...........30°59'N 25°49'E
Lichfield England 8 D3...........................52°41'N 1°50'W
Lichinga Mozambique 83 C3...................13°17'S 35°14'E
Lida Belarus 47 K5................................53°53'N 25°19'E
Liddel r. Scotland 15 G3.........................55°04'N 2°57'W
Lidköping Sweden 43 C2........................58°30'N 13°11'E
Liechtenstein Europe 44 H5....................47°07'N 9°36'E
Liège Belgium 42 E3.............................50°38'N 5°35'E
Liège d. Belgium 42 E3..........................50°29'N 5°42'E
Lieksa Finland 43 G3............................63°19'N 30°02'E
Lienz Austria 46 E2..............................46°50'N 12°46'E
Liepāja Latvia 43 E2.............................56°31'N 21°01'E
Liévin France 42 B3..............................50°25'N 2°47'E
Liffey r. Ireland 18 E3............................53°21'N 6°14'W
Lifford Ireland 18 D4.............................54°50'N 7°29'W
Ligurian Sea France/Italy 44 H3...............43°30'N 8°50'E
Likasi Dem. Rep. Congo 83 B3................10°58'S 26°47'E
Lilla Edet Sweden 43 C2........................58°08'N 12°08'E
Lille Belgium 42 D4...............................51°14'N 4°50'E
Lille France 44 E7................................50°38'N 3°04'E
Lillehammer Norway 43 B3......................61°06'N 10°29'E
Lilleshall England 8 C3...........................52°44'N 2°24'W
Lillestrøm Norway 43 B2.........................59°59'N 11°02'E
Lilongwe Malawi 83 C3..........................13°57'S 33°47'E
Lima Peru 72 B5..................................12°04'S 77°03'W
Limassol Cyprus 51 J2..........................34°41'N 33°02'E
Limavady Northern Ireland 14 C3.............55°03'N 6°57'W
Limburg f. Belgium 42 E4........................51°04'N 5°27'E
Limburg d. Neth. 42 E4..........................51°15'N 5°54'E
Limerick Ireland 18 C2...........................52°40'N 8°37'W
Limerick d. Ireland 18 C2.......................52°29'N 8°50'W
Limingen l. Norway 43 C4.......................64°48'N 13°33'E
Limnos i. Greece 50 F4..........................39°51'N 25°22'E
Limoges France 44 D4...........................45°50'N 1°16'E
Limousin f. France 44 D4........................45°34'N 1°11'E
Limoux France 44 E3.............................43°04'N 2°14'E
Limpopo r. S. Africa/Zimbabwe 83 C2.......25°13'S 33°32'E
Linares Spain 45 D3.............................38°06'N 3°37'W
Lincoln England 13 G2..........................53°14'N 0°32'W
Lincoln U.S. 62 G5...............................40°51'N 96°40'W
Lincolnshire d. England 21 E3..................53°07'N 0°14'W
Lincolnshire Wolds hills England 13 G2.....53°20'N 0°09'W
Lindesnes c. Norway 43 A2.....................58°00'N 7°06'E
Lindfield England 9 E2...........................51°01'N 0°05'W
Lindi Tanzania 83 C4.............................9°59'S 39°42'E
Lindos Greece 51 H3............................36°05'N 28°05'E
Line Islands Kiribati 116 B3.....................5°19'N 161°36'W
Linfen China 99 K5...............................36°05'N 111°33'E
Lingen Germany 46 B5...........................52°32'N 7°19'E
Lingfield England 9 E2...........................51°11'N 0°01'W
Lingga, Kepulauan is Indonesia 102 D3......0°02'S 105°01'E
Linhares Brazil 73 E5.............................19°27'S 40°04'W
Linköping Sweden 43 C2........................58°25'N 15°37'E
Linlithgow Scotland 15 F3......................55°58'N 3°36'W
Linney Head Wales 10 B3.......................51°37'N 5°05'W
Linnhe, Loch inlet Scotland 14 D4............56°31'N 5°35'W
Linqing China 99 L5.............................36°49'N 115°42'E
Linxia China 99 I5................................35°31'N 103°07'E
Linz Austria 46 F3...............................48°19'N 14°17'E
Lions, Gulf of France 44 E3....................43°00'N 3°32'E
Lipari, Isole is Italy 48 F4.......................38°39'N 14°45'E
Lipetsk Russia 53 D3............................52°37'N 39°36'E
Liphook England 8 E2...........................51°04'N 0°48'W
Lippe r. Germany 46 B4..........................51°39'N 6°53'E
Lisakov Kazakhstan 53 G3......................52°28'N 62°23'E
Lisala Dem. Rep. Congo 83 B5................2°10'N 21°31'E

isbon Portugal 45 A3 ....38°44'N 9°08'W
isburn Northern Ireland 14 C2 ....54°31'N 6°02'W
isburn and Castlereagh d. Northern Ireland 21 B4
....54°31'N 6°04'W
iscannor Bay Ireland 18 B2 ....52°55'N 9°26'W
iskeard England 11 C2 ....50°27'N 4°28'W
ismore Australia 108 E4 ....28°47'S 153°19'E
ismore Ireland 18 D2 ....52°08'N 7°56'W
isnaskea Northern Ireland 14 B2 .....54°15'N 7°26'W
iss England 8 E2 ....51°03'N 0°53'W
istowel Ireland 18 B2 ....52°26'N 9°29'W
ithuania Europe 47 J6 ....55°29'N 23°45'E
ittle Abaco i. Bahamas 67 I6 ....26°54'N 77°50'W
ittle Andaman i. India 97 H3 ....10°38'N 92°31'E
ittle Belt str. Denmark 43 B1 ....55°15'N 9°47'E
ittleborough England 13 E2 ....53°39'N 2°06'W
ittle Cayman i. Cayman Is 67 H4 ...19°42'N 80°04'W
ittlehampton England 9 E1 ....50°49'N 0°32'W
ittle Inagua Island Bahamas 67 J5 ...21°31'N 72°59'W
ittle Karoo f. S. Africa 83 B1 ....33°43'S 20°46'E
ittle Minch str. Scotland 16 B2 ......57°32'N 7°00'W
ittle Ouse r. England 9 F3 ....52°30'N 0°22'E
ittleport England 9 F3 ....52°27'N 0°19'E
ittle Rock town U.S. 63 H3 ....34°46'N 92°18'W
iupanshui China 99 I3 ....26°40'N 104°48'E
iuzhou China 99 J2 ....24°21'N 109°22'E
iverpool Canada 63 N5 ....44°02'N 64°43'W
iverpool England 12 E2 ....53°25'N 2°59'W
ivingston Scotland 15 F3 ....55°54'N 3°31'W
ivingstone Zambia 83 B3 ....17°52'S 25°52'E
ivorno Italy 48 F5 ....43°32'N 10°19'E
izard England 11 B1 ....49°58'N 5°12'W
izard Point England 11 B1 ....49°57'N 5°17'W
ubljana Slovenia 46 F2 ....46°03'N 14°30'E
ungan r. Sweden 43 D3 ....62°18'N 17°23'E
ungby Sweden 43 C2 ....56°51'N 13°59'E
usdal Sweden 43 D3 ....61°50'N 16°06'E
anarth Wales 10 C4 ....52°12'N 4°18'W
anbadarn Fawr Wales 10 C4 ....52°24'N 4°04'W
anberis Wales 10 C5 ....53°07'N 4°08'W
andeilo Wales 10 D3 ....51°53'N 3°59'W
andovery Wales 10 D3 ....51°59'N 3°48'W
andrindod Wells Wales 10 D4 ....52°14'N 3°23'W
andudno Wales 10 C5 ....53°19'N 3°50'W
andwrog Wales 10 C5 ....53°05'N 4°19'W
andysul Wales 10 C4 ....52°03'N 4°18'W
anegwad Wales 10 C3 ....51°52'N 4°09'W
anelli Wales 10 C3 ....51°41'N 4°10'W
anes Spain 45 C5 ....43°25'N 4°44'W
anfairfechan Wales 10 D5 ....53°15'N 3°58'W
anfair Pwllgwyngyll Wales 10 C5 ...53°13'N 4°12'W
anfair-yn-Neubwll Wales 10 C5 ....53°16'N 4°33'W
anfyllin Wales 10 D4 ....52°46'N 3°16'W
angadog Wales 10 D3 ....51°56'N 3°53'W
angefni Wales 10 C5 ....53°15'N 4°19'W
angeler Wales 10 C4 ....52°02'N 4°22'W
angelynin Wales 10 C4 ....52°39'N 4°07'W
angoed Wales 10 C5 ....53°18'N 4°05'W
angollen Wales 10 D4 ....52°58'N 3°10'W
angurig Wales 10 D4 ....52°24'N 3°36'W
anidloes Wales 10 D4 ....52°27'N 3°32'W
anllwchaiarn Wales 10 D4 ....52°32'N 3°17'W
anllyfni Wales 10 C5 ....53°03'N 4°17'W
anos f. Col./Venez. 72 C7 ....5°54'N 69°50'W
anrumney Wales 11 D3 ....51°31'N 3°07'W
anrwst Wales 10 D5 ....53°08'N 3°48'W
ansannan Wales 10 D5 ....53°11'N 3°36'W
antrisant Wales 10 D3 ....51°33'N 3°22'W
antwit Major Wales 11 D3 ....51°25'N 3°29'W
anwnda Wales 10 C5 ....53°05'N 4°17'W
anwnog Wales 10 D4 ....52°32'N 3°27'W
anybydder Wales 10 C4 ....52°04'N 4°09'W
ay Wales 10 D5 ....53°06'N 3°00'W
eida Spain 45 F4 ....41°36'N 0°38'E
erena Spain 45 B3 ....38°15'N 6°01'W
eyn Peninsula Wales 10 C4 ....52°51'N 4°34'W
oyd George, Mount Canada 60 F3 ...57°50'N 124°57'W
oydminster Canada 60 G3 ....53°17'N 110°00'W
uarca Spain 45 B5 ....43°32'N 6°31'W
ullaillaco, Volcán vol. Chile 73 C4 ...24°42'S 68°33'W
bamba Swaziland 83 C2 ....26°26'S 31°12'E
bito Angola 83 A3 ....12°24'S 13°32'E
chaline Scotland 14 D4 ....56°32'N 5°47'W
chboisdale Scotland 16 B2 ....57°09'N 7°19'W
chgelly Scotland 15 F4 ....56°08'N 3°18'W
chinver Scotland 16 D3 ....58°09'N 5°14'W
chmaben Scotland 15 F3 ....55°08'N 3°26'W
chmaddy Scotland 16 B2 ....57°36'N 7°10'W
chnagar mt. Scotland 17 F1 ....56°58'N 3°15'W
chranza Scotland 14 D3 ....55°42'N 5°17'W
chy, Loch l. Scotland 16 E1 ....56°56'N 4°58'W
ckerbie Scotland 15 F3 ....55°07'N 3°21'W
ddon England 8 D3 ....52°32'N 1°29'E
deynoye Pole Russia 52 D4 ....60°44'N 33°34'E
dwar Kenya 85 H2 ....3°06'N 35°34'E
dź Poland 46 H4 ....51°46'N 19°27'E
foten is Norway 43 C5 ....68°06'N 12°44'E
gan, Mount Canada 60 D4 ....60°40'N 140°02'W
ggerheads England 8 C3 ....52°55'N 2°23'W
groño Spain 45 D5 ....42°28'N 2°26'W
re r. France 44 B5 ....47°17'N 2°07'W
ia Ecuador 72 B6 ....4°00'S 79°14'W
ia Spain 45 C2 ....37°10'N 4°09'W
kan tekojärvi resr Finland 43 F4 ...67°56'N 27°35'E
keren Belgium 42 D4 ....51°06'N 4°00'E
kken Norway 43 B3 ....63°07'N 9°42'E
koja Nigeria 84 E2 ....7°49'N 6°44'E
lland i. Denmark 43 B1 ....54°47'N 11°21'E
m Bulgaria 50 E6 ....43°49'N 23°14'E
mami r. Dem. Rep. Congo 83 B5 ...0°47'N 24°17'E
mbok i. Indonesia 102 F2 ....9°07'S 116°13'E
mé Togo 84 E2 ....6°09'N 1°13'E
mmel Belgium 42 E4 ....51°14'N 5°19'E
mond, Loch l. Scotland 14 E4 ....56°04'N 4°37'W
mża Poland 47 J5 ....53°11'N 22°05'E
ndon Canada 61 J2 ....42°59'N 81°14'W
ndon England 9 F2 ....51°30'N 0°07'W
ndonderry Northern Ireland 14 B2 ...54°59'N 7°20'W
ndonderry, Cape Australia 108 B5 ...13°47'S 126°53'E
ng, Loch inlet Scotland 14 E4 ....56°06'N 4°51'W
nga, Proliv str. Russia 55 S5 ....70°10'N 178°12'E
ng Ashton England 8 C2 ....51°26'N 2°39'W
ng Beach town U.S. 62 C3 ....33°47'N 118°20'W
ng Bennington England 8 E3 ....52°59'N 0°46'W
ng Eaton England 8 D3 ....52°54'N 1°16'W

Longford Ireland 18 D3 ....53°44'N 7°48'W
Longford d. Ireland 18 D3 ....53°45'N 7°41'W
Longhorsley England 13 F4 ....55°15'N 1°46'W
Longhoughton England 13 F4 ....55°26'N 1°37'W
Long Island Bahamas 67 I5 ....23°18'N 75°06'W
Long Island U.S. 63 L5 ....40°49'N 72°36'W
Longlac Canada 61 J2 ....49°47'N 86°33'W
Longridge England 12 E2 ....53°50'N 2°36'W
Long Stratton England 9 G3 ....52°29'N 1°14'E
Longton England 12 E2 ....53°44'N 2°48'W
Longtown England 12 E4 ....55°00'N 2°58'W
Longuyon France 42 E2 ....49°27'N 5°37'E
Longview U.S. 63 H3 ....32°32'N 94°44'W
Long Xuyen Vietnam 102 D6 ....10°20'N 105°25'E
Longyearbyen Arctic Oc. 54 C5 ......77°59'N 15°44'E
Lons-le-Saunier France 44 F5 ....46°41'N 5°33'E
Lookout, Cape U.S. 63 K3 ....34°37'N 76°33'W
Loop Head Ireland 18 B2 ....52°33'N 9°56'W
Lop Nur l. China 98 G6 ....40°28'N 90°20'E
Lopphavet b. Norway 43 E5 ....70°21'N 21°03'E
Loralai Pakistan 95 K6 ....30°21'N 68°43'E
Lorca Spain 45 E2 ....37°41'N 1°41'W
Lord Howe Island Australia 109 E3 ...31°26'S 158°57'E
Lorient France 44 B4 ....47°45'N 3°22'W
Lorn, Firth of est. Scotland 14 D4 ...56°15'N 5°54'W
Los Ángeles Chile 73 B3 ....37°28'S 72°21'W
Los Angeles U.S. 63 C3 ....34°01'N 118°15'W
Los Mochis Mexico 66 C6 ....25°48'N 108°59'W
Los Roques, Islas is Venezuela 67 K3 ...11°55'N 66°39'W
Lossie r. Scotland 17 F2 ....57°43'N 3°17'W
Lossiemouth Scotland 17 F2 ....57°43'N 3°17'W
Lostwithiel England 11 C2 ....50°24'N 4°40'W
Lot r. France 44 D4 ....44°19'N 0°20'E
Loth Scotland 17 E3 ....59°12'N 2°41'W
Lotta r. Finland/Russia 43 G5 ....68°40'N 30°14'E
Louangnamtha Laos 102 C8 ....21°03'N 101°29'E
Louangphabang Laos 102 C7 ....19°54'N 102°10'E
Loughborough England 8 D3 ....52°46'N 1°12'W
Loughor r. Wales 10 C3 ....51°42'N 4°03'W
Loughrea Ireland 18 C3 ....53°12'N 8°35'W
Loughton England 9 F2 ....51°39'N 0°04'E
Louisiana d. U.S. 63 H3 ....30°40'N 91°56'W
Louisville U.S. 63 I4 ....38°15'N 85°46'W
Loukhi Russia 43 H4 ....66°04'N 33°03'E
Lourdes France 44 C3 ....43°06'N 0°02'W
Louth England 13 G2 ....53°22'N 0°01'W
Louth d. Ireland 18 E3 ....53°53'N 6°31'W
Lovech Bulgaria 50 F6 ....43°09'N 24°42'E
Lovozero Russia 52 D4 ....68°01'N 34°59'E
Lowell U.S. 63 L5 ....42°39'N 71°19'W
Lower Lough Erne l. Northern Ireland 14 B2
....54°29'N 7°51'W
Lowestoft England 9 G3 ....52°29'N 1°45'E
Loyal, Loch l. Scotland 17 E3 ....58°25'N 4°22'W
Loyauté, Îles is New Caledonia 109 F4 ...20°23'S 167°17'E
Loyne, Loch l. Scotland 16 D2 ....57°06'N 5°05'W
Loznica Serbia 50 C7 ....44°33'N 19°15'E
Lozova Ukraine 53 D2 ....49°26'N 35°56'E
Lu'an China 99 L4 ....31°45'N 116°32'E
Luanda Angola 83 A4 ....8°50'S 13°14'E
Luau Angola 83 B3 ....10°42'S 22°15'E
Lubango Angola 83 B3 ....14°55'S 13°30'E
Lubartów Poland 47 J4 ....51°28'N 22°37'E
Lubbock U.S. 62 F3 ....33°38'N 101°51'W
Lübeck Germany 46 D5 ....53°52'N 10°42'E
Lübecker Bucht b. Germany 46 D6 ...54°03'N 10°47'E
Lubin Poland 46 G4 ....51°24'N 16°13'E
Lublin Poland 47 J4 ....51°14'N 22°35'E
Lubnaig, Loch l. Scotland 14 E4 ....56°18'N 4°19'W
Lubny Ukraine 47 O4 ....50°01'N 33°00'E
Lubuklinggau Indonesia 102 C3 ......3°23'S 102°56'E
Lubumbashi Dem. Rep. Congo 83 B3 ...11°40'S 27°29'E
Lubutu Dem. Rep. Congo 83 B4 ......0°44'S 26°35'E
Lucan Ireland 10 A5 ....53°21'N 6°27'W
Luce Bay Scotland 14 E2 ....54°47'N 4°52'W
Lucena Phil. 103 G6 ....13°56'N 121°36'E
Lucena Spain 45 C2 ....37°25'N 4°29'W
Lučenec Slovakia 46 H3 ....48°21'N 19°41'E
Lucerne Switz. 46 C2 ....47°03'N 8°18'E
Lucknow India 96 F6 ....26°51'N 80°58'E
Lüderitz Namibia 83 A2 ....26°40'S 15°09'E
Ludgershall England 8 D2 ....51°15'N 1°37'W
Ludhiana India 96 E7 ....30°54'N 75°53'E
Ludlow England 8 C3 ....52°22'N 2°43'W
Ludvika Sweden 43 D3 ....60°09'N 15°12'E
Ludwigsburg Germany 46 C3 ....48°54'N 9°12'E
Ludwigshafen am Rhein Germany 46 C3
....49°28'N 8°26'E
Ludwigslust Germany 46 D5 ....53°20'N 11°30'E
Luena r. Colombia 72 C8 ....11°47'S 19°54'E
Lufeng China 99 L2 ....22°58'N 115°41'E
Lufkin U.S. 63 H3 ....31°21'N 94°44'W
Luga Russia 43 G2 ....58°43'N 29°51'E
Luga r. Russia 43 G2 ....59°40'N 28°18'E
Lugano Switz. 46 C2 ....46°01'N 8°57'E
Lugg r. Wales 10 E4 ....52°02'N 2°38'W
Lugo Spain 45 B5 ....43°01'N 7°33'W
Lugoj Romania 50 D7 ....45°42'N 21°55'E
Luhansk Ukraine 53 D2 ....48°33'N 39°19'E
Luichart, Loch l. Scotland 16 E2 ....57°37'N 4°48'W
Luing i. Scotland 14 D4 ....56°14'N 5°39'W
Łuków Poland 47 J4 ....51°56'N 22°24'E
Luleå Sweden 43 E4 ....65°35'N 22°10'E
Luleälven r. Sweden 43 E4 ....65°35'N 22°03'E
Lüleburgaz Turkey 50 G5 ....41°25'N 27°21'E
Lumberton U.S. 63 K3 ....34°36'N 79°05'W
Lunan Bay Scotland 17 G1 ....56°39'N 2°30'W
Lund Sweden 43 C1 ....55°42'N 13°12'E
Lundy i. England 11 C3 ....51°11'N 4°39'W
Lune r. England 12 E3 ....54°03'N 2°49'W
Lüneburg Germany 46 D5 ....53°15'N 10°25'E
Lunéville France 44 G6 ....48°36'N 6°30'E
Luninyets Belarus 47 L5 ....52°14'N 26°48'E
Luoyang China 99 K4 ....34°38'N 112°27'E
Lure France 44 G5 ....47°41'N 6°30'E
Lurgainn, Loch l. Scotland 16 D3 ....58°02'N 5°14'W
Lurgan Northern Ireland 14 C2 ....54°27'N 6°19'W
Lusaka Zambia 83 B3 ....15°23'S 28°16'E
Lushnjë Albania 50 C5 ....40°57'N 19°42'E
Lut, Dasht-e des. Iran 95 I6 ....30°47'N 58°45'E
Lutherstadt Wittenberg Germany 46 E4 ...51°52'N 12°39'E
Luton England 9 E2 ....51°53'N 0°25'W
Luton d. England 21 E2 ....51°54'N 0°25'W
Lutsk Ukraine 47 K4 ....50°45'N 25°21'E
Lutterworth England 8 D3 ....52°27'N 1°12'W
Luxembourg Europe 42 F2 ....49°49'N 6°01'E
Luxembourg town Lux. 42 F2 ....49°36'N 6°08'E

Luxor Egypt 85 H4 ....25°43'N 32°39'E
Luza Russia 52 E4 ....60°38'N 47°16'E
Luziânia Brazil 72 E5 ....16°17'S 47°53'W
Luzon i. Phil. 103 G7 ....15°24'N 122°02'E
Luzon Strait Phil. 102 G8 ....20°19'N 121°07'E
Lviv Ukraine 47 K3 ....49°50'N 24°02'E
Lyckele Sweden 43 D4 ....64°36'N 18°41'E
Lydd England 9 F1 ....50°57'N 0°55'E
Lydford England 11 C2 ....50°39'N 4°06'W
Lydney England 8 C2 ....51°44'N 2°32'W
Lyepyel' Belarus 47 M6 ....54°53'N 28°42'E
Lyme Bay England 8 C1 ....50°39'N 2°59'W
Lyme Regis England 8 C1 ....50°43'N 2°56'W
Lymington England 8 D1 ....50°45'N 1°33'W
Lynchburg U.S. 63 K4 ....37°24'N 79°09'W
Lyndhurst England 8 D1 ....50°52'N 1°35'W
Lynmouth England 11 D3 ....51°14'N 3°50'W
Lynn Lake town Canada 60 H3 ......56°51'N 101°03'W
Lynton England 11 D3 ....51°14'N 3°50'W
Lyon France 44 F4 ....45°45'N 4°52'E
Lyon r. Scotland 17 F1 ....56°36'N 3°58'W
Lys'va Russia 52 F3 ....58°08'N 57°48'E
Lysychansk Ukraine 53 D2 ....48°55'N 38°26'E
Lysyye Gory Russia 53 E3 ....51°31'N 44°49'E
Lytchett Minster England 8 C1 ......50°44'N 2°03'W
Lytham St Anne's England 12 D2 ...53°45'N 3°02'W

M

Ma'ān Jordan 94 E6 ....30°12'N 35°43'E
Ma'arrat an Nu'mān Syria 51 L2 ....35°39'N 36°40'E
Maas r. Neth. 42 D4 ....51°43'N 4°53'E
Maaseik Belgium 42 E4 ....51°05'N 5°40'E
Maastricht Neth. 42 E3 ....50°51'N 5°42'E
Mabalane Mozambique 83 C2 ....23°50'S 32°37'E
Mablethorpe England 13 H2 ....53°20'N 0°16'E
Macao China 99 K2 ....22°15'N 113°34'E
Macapá Brazil 72 D7 ....0°03'N 51°02'W
Macassar Strait Indonesia 102 F3 ....3°55'S 117°24'E
Macclesfield England 12 E2 ....53°16'N 2°08'W
MacDonnell Ranges mts Australia 108 C4 ...23°33'S 131°18'E
Macduff Scotland 17 G2 ....57°40'N 2°30'W
Macedo de Cavaleiros Portugal 45 B4 ...41°32'N 6°57'W
Maceió Brazil 72 F6 ....9°36'S 35°40'W
Macgillycuddy's Reeks mts Ireland 18 B1 ...51°57'N 9°52'W
Mach Pakistan 96 C6 ....29°52'N 67°20'E
Machala Ecuador 72 B6 ....3°17'S 79°57'W
Machilipatnam India 96 F4 ....16°11'N 81°10'E
Machrihanish Scotland 14 D3 ....55°25'N 5°44'W
Machynlleth Wales 10 C4 ....52°35'N 3°51'W
Mackay Australia 108 D4 ....21°10'S 149°11'E
Mackay, Lake Australia 108 B4 .....22°36'S 128°28'E
Mackenzie r. Canada 60 F4 ....69°15'N 134°11'W
Mackenzie King Island Canada 60 G5 ...77°42'N 111°56'W
Mackenzie Mountains Canada 60 E4 ...65°04'N 133°04'W
MacLeod, Lake Australia 108 A4 ....24°08'S 113°43'E
Mâcon France 44 F5 ....46°19'N 4°50'E
Macon U.S. 63 J3 ....32°53'N 83°37'W
Macroom Ireland 18 C1 ....51°54'N 8°58'W
Madadeni S. Africa 83 C2 ....27°45'S 30°02'E
Madagascar Africa 83 D3 ....19°57'S 46°27'E
Madeira r. Brazil 72 C6 ....3°23'S 58°47'W
Madeira is N. Atlantic Oc. 84 C5 ...32°35'N 16°57'W
Madeley England 8 C3 ....52°38'N 2°26'W
Madera Mexico 66 C6 ....29°11'N 108°11'W
Madhya Pradesh d. India 96 E5 .....23°32'N 78°56'E
Madison U.S. 63 I5 ....43°04'N 89°23'W
Madona Latvia 47 L7 ....56°51'N 26°13'E
Madrakah, Ra's c. Oman 95 I3 ....19°01'N 57°51'E
Madre, Laguna lagoon Mexico 66 E6 ...25°00'N 97°37'W
Madre, Sierra mts C. America 56 F2 ...15°00'N 90°00'W
Madre de Dios r. Peru 72 C5 ....10°59'S 66°07'W
Madre del Sur, Sierra mts Mexico 66 D4
....18°07'N 101°24'W
Madre Occidental, Sierra mts Mexico 66 C6
....28°46'N 108°51'W
Madre Oriental, Sierra mts Mexico 66 D6
....26°41'N 101°44'W
Madrid Spain 45 D4 ....40°26'N 3°40'W
Madura i. Indonesia 102 E2 ....7°02'S 113°11'E
Madurai India 96 E2 ....9°55'N 78°07'E
Maebashi Japan 104 C3 ....36°23'N 139°04'E
Maesteg Wales 10 D3 ....51°36'N 3°39'W
Maestra, Sierra mts Cuba 67 I4 ....19°54'N 77°33'W
Mafia Island Tanzania 83 C4 ....7°48'S 39°52'E
Mafraq Jordan 94 E6 ....32°20'N 36°13'E
Magadan Russia 55 Q3 ....59°38'N 151°00'E
Magdalena r. Colombia 72 C8 ....11°06'N 74°52'W
Magdalena Mexico 66 B7 ....30°38'N 110°59'W
Magdeburg Germany 46 D5 ....52°07'N 11°38'E
Magellan, Strait of Chile 73 B1 .....53°45'S 71°59'W
Magerøya i. Norway 43 F5 ....70°59'N 25°40'E
Maggiorasca, Monte mt. Italy 46 C1 ...44°33'N 9°30'E
Maggiore, Lake Italy 46 C1 ....45°56'N 8°36'E
Maghera Northern Ireland 14 C2 ...54°50'N 6°40'W
Magherafelt Northern Ireland 14 C2 ...54°45'N 6°36'W
Maghull England 12 E2 ....53°31'N 2°57'W
Magilligan Point Northern Ireland 14 C3 ...55°12'N 6°56'W
Magnitogorsk Russia 53 F3 ....53°24'N 59°08'E
Magway Myanmar 97 H5 ....20°09'N 94°56'E
Mahābād Iran 95 G7 ....36°44'N 45°41'E
Mahagi Dem. Rep. Congo 85 H5 ....2°16'N 30°55'E
Mahajanga Madagascar 83 D3 .....15°41'S 46°21'E
Mahalevona Madagascar 83 D3 ....15°24'S 49°53'E
Maharashtra d. India 96 E4 ....19°24'N 75°18'E
Mahé i. Seychelles 85 J1 ....4°36'S 55°24'E
Mahilyow/Mogilëv Belarus 47 N5 ...53°55'N 30°20'E
Mahrāt, Jabal mt. Yemen 95 H3 .....17°07'N 51°07'E
Maicao Colombia 67 J3 ....11°25'N 72°23'W
Maidenhead England 8 E2 ....51°31'N 0°43'W
Maidstone England 9 F2 ....51°16'N 0°31'E
Maiduguri Nigeria 84 F3 ....11°50'N 13°08'E
Main r. Northern Ireland 14 C2 ....54°43'N 6°18'W
Mai-Ndombe, Lac l. Dem. Rep. Congo 83 A4
....2°15'S 18°22'E
Maine d. U.S. 63 M6 ....45°20'N 69°21'W
Mainland i. Orkn. Scotland 17 F4 ...59°04'N 3°15'W
Mainland i. Shetl. Scotland 17 H5 ...60°21'N 1°17'W
Mainz Germany 46 C4 ....50°00'N 8°16'E
Maiquetía Venezuela 67 K3 ....10°32'N 66°56'W
Maíz, Islas del is Nicaragua 67 H3 ...12°10'N 83°02'W
Maizuru Japan 104 C3 ....35°28'N 135°24'E
Maja Jezercë mt. Albania 50 C6 ....42°26'N 19°50'E
Majene Indonesia 102 F3 ....3°30'S 118°54'E
Major, Puig mt. Spain 45 G3 ....39°48'N 2°49'E

Majorca i. Spain 45 G3 ....39°57'N 2°43'E
Makale Indonesia 102 F3 ....3°06'S 119°52'E
Makarska Croatia 50 B6 ....43°18'N 17°02'E
Makassar Indonesia 102 F2 ....5°06'S 119°27'E
Makgadikgadi Pans f. Botswana 83 B2 ...20°45'S 25°35'E
Makhachkala Russia 53 E2 ....42°59'N 47°30'E
Makhanda S. Africa 83 B1 ....33°19'S 26°32'E
Makira i. Solomon Is 109 F5 ....10°38'S 161°38'E
Makran f. Iran/Pakistan 95 J5 ....26°29'N 60°27'E
Makurdi Nigeria 84 E2 ....7°43'N 8°33'E
Mala, Punta pt Panama 67 H2 ....7°27'N 80°00'W
Malabar Coast f. India 96 D3 ....12°16'N 74°30'E
Malabo Equat. Guinea 84 E2 ....3°45'N 8°46'E
Malacca, Strait of Indonesia/Malaysia 102 B5
....5°41'N 98°38'E
Maladzyechna Belarus 47 L6 ....54°18'N 26°52'E
Málaga Spain 45 C2 ....36°43'N 4°25'W
Malahide Ireland 18 E3 ....53°27'N 6°09'W
Malaita i. Solomon Is 109 F6 ....8°58'S 161°00'E
Malakal South Sudan 85 H2 ....9°30'N 31°40'E
Malakula i. Vanuatu 109 F5 ....16°16'S 167°19'E
Malang Indonesia 102 E2 ....7°56'S 112°46'E
Malanje Angola 83 A4 ....9°33'S 16°23'E
Mälaren l. Sweden 43 D2 ....59°27'N 17°13'E
Malatya Turkey 51 M4 ....38°20'N 38°20'E
Malawi Africa 83 C3 ....11°32'S 33°43'E
Maläyer Iran 95 G6 ....34°17'N 48°48'E
Malaysia Asia 102 C4/E4 ....3°39'N 108°45'E
Malbork Poland 46 H6 ....54°02'N 19°02'E
Maldives Indian Oc. 96 C1 ....6°09'N 72°23'E
Maldon England 9 F2 ....51°44'N 0°40'E
Male' Maldives 96 D1 ....4°18'N 73°29'E
Maleas, Akra pt Greece 50 E3 ....36°26'N 23°12'E
Malgomaj l. Sweden 43 D4 ....64°44'N 16°15'E
Mali Africa 84 D3 ....13°54'N 5°34'W
Malili Indonesia 103 G3 ....2°37'S 121°07'E
Malin Head Ireland 18 D5 ....55°23'N 7°24'W
Mallaig Scotland 16 D2 ....57°00'N 5°50'W
Mallawī Egypt 49 J2 ....27°43'N 30°50'E
Mallow Ireland 18 C2 ....52°08'N 8°39'W
Malmedy Belgium 42 F3 ....50°26'N 6°02'E
Malmesbury England 8 C2 ....51°35'N 2°06'W
Malmö Sweden 43 C1 ....55°36'N 13°01'E
Måløy Norway 43 A3 ....61°56'N 5°07'E
Malozemel'skaya Tundra f. Russia 52 F4 ...67°50'N 50°00'E
Malpas England 12 E2 ....53°01'N 2°46'W
Malpaso mt. Canary Islands 45 W1 ...27°44'N 18°01'W
Malpelo, Isla de i. N. Pacific Oc. 68 B4 ...3°59'N 81°34'W
Malta Europe 48 F4 ....35°49'N 14°18'E
Maltby England 13 F2 ....53°25'N 1°12'W
Malton England 13 G3 ....54°08'N 0°48'W
Malvern Hills England 8 C3 ....52°04'N 2°20'W
Malyy Anyuy r. Russia 55 R3 ....68°27'N 161°01'E
Mama r. Russia 55 P4 ....66°28'N 143°13'E
Mamelodi S. Africa 83 B2 ....25°42'S 28°23'E
Mamuju Indonesia 102 F3 ....2°40'S 118°51'E
Man, Isle of i. Irish Sea 14 E2 ....54°16'N 4°41'W
Manacor Spain 45 G3 ....39°34'N 3°14'E
Manado Indonesia 103 G4 ....1°33'N 124°52'E
Managua Nicaragua 67 G3 ....12°07'N 86°17'W
Manama Bahrain 95 H5 ....26°12'N 50°35'E
Mananjary Madagascar 83 D2 ....21°14'S 48°20'E
Manaus Brazil 72 C6 ....3°04'S 60°00'W
Manavgat Turkey 51 I3 ....36°48'N 31°26'E
Manchester England 12 E2 ....53°29'N 2°15'W
Manchuria f. China 99 M7 ....46°27'N 123°48'E
Mand r. Iran 95 H5 ....28°11'N 51°21'E
Mandala, Puncak mt. Indonesia 103 K3 ...4°43'S 140°21'E
Mandalay Myanmar 97 I5 ....21°59'N 96°06'E
Mandalgovĭ Mongolia 99 J7 ....45°42'N 106°19'E
Mangalia Romania 51 H6 ....43°49'N 28°34'E
Mangaluru India 96 D3 ....12°53'N 74°51'E
Mangaung S. Africa 83 B2 ....29°09'S 26°16'E
Mangokv r. Madagascar 83 D2 .....23°25'S 45°25'E
Mangole i. Indonesia 103 H3 ....1°51'S 125°49'E
Mangotsfield England 8 C2 ....51°29'N 2°31'W
Manicouagan, Réservoir Canada 63 L3 ...51°18'N 68°18'W
Maniitsoq Greenland 61 M4 ....65°26'N 52°55'W
Manila Phil. 103 G6 ....14°34'N 120°59'E
Manipur d. India 97 H5 ....24°53'N 93°56'E
Manisa Turkey 50 G4 ....38°36'N 27°25'E
Manitoba d. Canada 60 I3 ....53°40'N 98°06'W
Manitoba, Lake Canada 60 I3 ....51°34'N 99°04'W
Manizales Colombia 72 B7 ....5°00'N 75°30'W
Mannad India 96 D5 ....20°15'N 74°30'E
Mannheim Germany 46 C4 ....49°29'N 8°28'E
Manningtree England 9 G2 ....51°57'N 1°04'E
Manokwari Indonesia 103 I3 ....0°52'S 134°06'E
Manorbier Wales 10 C3 ....51°39'N 4°48'W
Manorhamilton Ireland 18 C4 ....54°18'N 8°11'W
Manra i. Kiribati 109 H6 ....4°26'S 171°13'W
Manresa Spain 45 F4 ....41°43'N 1°50'E
Mansa Zambia 83 B3 ....11°11'S 28°53'E
Mansel Island Canada 61 K4 ....62°05'N 79°35'W
Mansfield England 13 F2 ....53°09'N 1°12'W
Mansfield U.S. 63 J5 ....40°45'N 82°32'W
Manston England 8 C1 ....50°56'N 2°16'W
Mantua Italy 46 D1 ....45°09'N 10°47'E
Manukau New Zealand 109 G3 .....36°58'S 174°50'E
Manzanares Spain 45 D3 ....39°00'N 3°21'W
Manzhouli China 99 L7 ....49°20'N 117°29'E
Maó Spain 45 H3 ....39°53'N 4°17'E
Maoke, Pegunungan mts Indonesia 103 J3 ...3°14'S 138°02'E
Mapinhane Mozambique 83 C2 ....22°17'S 35°06'E
Maputo Mozambique 83 C2 ....25°56'S 32°34'E
Maqat Kazakhstan 53 F2 ....47°37'N 53°14'E
Marabá Brazil 72 E6 ....5°23'S 49°08'W
Maracaibo Venezuela 72 B8 ....9°45'N 71°36'W
Maracaibo, Lake inlet Venezuela 72 B7 ...9°45'N 71°36'W
Maracaju, Serra de hills Brazil 73 D4 ...21°59'S 55°53'W
Maracay Venezuela 72 C8 ....10°16'N 67°35'W
Marādah Libya 85 G4 ....29°12'N 19°12'E
Maradi Niger 84 E3 ....13°31'N 7°07'E
Marāgheh Iran 95 G7 ....37°23'N 46°14'E
Marajó, Ilha de i. Brazil 72 E6 ....0°45'S 50°38'W
Marand Iran 95 G7 ....38°26'N 45°46'E
Marañón r. Peru 72 B6 ....4°27'S 73°30'W
Marathon Canada 63 I6 ....48°43'N 86°23'W
Marathonas Greece 50 E4 ....38°09'N 23°58'E
Marazion England 11 B2 ....50°07'N 5°28'W
Marbella Spain 45 C2 ....36°31'N 4°53'W
Marburg Germany 46 C4 ....50°48'N 8°46'E
March S. Africa 83 C1 ....33°35'S 30°26'E
March England 9 F3 ....52°33'N 0°05'E
Marche-en-Famenne Belgium 42 E3 ...50°14'N 5°21'E
Marchtrenk Austria 46 F3 ....48°12'N 14°07'E
Mardan Pakistan 95 L6 ....34°14'N 72°04'E

Mar del Plata Argentina 73 D3 .....37°59'S 57°35'W
Mardin Turkey 94 F7 .....37°18'N 40°46'E
Maree, Loch l. Scotland 16 D2 .....57°38'N 5°21'W
Maresfield England 9 F1 .....51°00'N 0°05'E
Margarita, Isla de i. Venezuela 72 C8 .....11°06'N 63°53'W
Margate England 9 G2 .....51°23'N 1°23'E
Margery Hill England 13 F2 .....53°28'N 1°43'W
Märgow, Dasht-e des. Afgh. 95 J6 .....30°27'N 62°22'E
Marhanets Ukraine 47 P2 .....47°40'N 34°37'E
Marías, Islas is Mexico 66 C5 .....21°25'N 106°33'W
Maria van Diemen, Cape New Zealand 109 G3 .....34°29'S 172°38'E
Ma'rib Yemen 95 G3 .....15°32'N 45°26'E
Maribor Slovenia 46 F2 .....46°32'N 15°40'E
Marie-Galante i. Guadeloupe 67 L4 .....15°56'N 61°14'W
Mariehamn Finland 43 D3 .....60°06'N 19°57'E
Mariental Namibia 83 A2 .....24°39'S 17°58'E
Mariestad Sweden 43 C2 .....58°43'N 13°50'E
Marijampolè Lithuania 47 J6 .....54°33'N 23°22'E
Marília Brazil 73 E4 .....22°13'S 49°57'W
Mar'ina Horka Belarus 47 M5 .....53°31'N 28°08'E
Maringá Brazil 73 E4 .....23°27'S 51°59'W
Maritime Alps mts France/Italy 44 G4 .....44°16'N 6°56'E
Maritsa r. Bulgaria 50 G5 .....41°43'N 26°20'E
Mariupol Ukraine 49 K6 .....47°06'N 37°33'E
Marka Somalia 85 I2 .....1°43'N 44°44'E
Markermeer l. Neth. 42 E5 .....52°34'N 5°14'E
Market Deeping England 9 E3 .....52°41'N 0°19'W
Market Drayton England 8 C3 .....52°54'N 2°29'W
Market Harborough England 8 E3 .....52°29'N 0°55'W
Markethill Northern Ireland 14 C2 .....54°17'N 6°31'W
Market Rasen England 13 G2 .....53°23'N 0°20'W
Market Warsop England 13 F2 .....53°12'N 1°09'W
Market Weighton England 13 G2 .....53°52'N 0°40'W
Markha r. Russia 55 M4 .....63°29'N 118°52'E
Marlborough England 8 D2 .....51°25'N 1°44'W
Marlborough Downs hills England 8 D2 .....51°29'N 1°48'W
Marlow England 8 E2 .....51°34'N 0°46'W
Marmande France 44 D4 .....44°31'N 0°10'E
Marmara, Sea of g. Turkey 51 H5 .....40°43'N 28°26'E
Marmaris Turkey 51 H3 .....36°50'N 28°15'E
Marne r. France 44 E6 .....48°49'N 2°25'E
Marne-la-Vallée France 44 E6 .....48°51'N 2°36'E
Maromokotro mt. Madagascar 83 D3 .....14°01'S 48°58'E
Marondera Zimbabwe 83 C3 .....18°13'S 31°34'E
Maroni r. French Guiana 72 D7 .....5°44'N 54°01'W
Maroua Cameroon 84 F3 .....10°37'N 14°19'E
Marple England 13 E2 .....53°24'N 2°04'W
Marquesas Islands French Polynesia 114 B2 .....8°39'S 139°15'W
Marquette U.S. 63 I6 .....46°32'N 87°25'W
Marra, Jebel mt. Sudan 85 G3 .....12°54'N 24°11'E
Marrakesh Morocco 84 D5 .....31°39'N 7°58'W
Marra Plateau f. Sudan 94 B2 .....13°24'N 24°25'E
Marsá 'Alam Egypt 49 J2 .....25°04'N 34°50'E
Marsa al Burayqah Libya 85 F5 .....30°22'N 19°35'E
Marsabit Kenya 85 H2 .....2°20'N 37°59'E
Marsala Italy 48 F4 .....37°48'N 12°26'E
Marsá Maţrūḩ Egypt 85 G5 .....31°20'N 27°16'E
Marseille France 44 F3 .....43°18'N 5°23'E
Marsfjället mt. Sweden 43 C4 .....65°06'N 15°23'E
Märsta Sweden 43 D2 .....59°37'N 17°53'E
Martaban Myanmar 97 I4 .....16°34'N 97°34'E
Martaban, Gulf of Myanmar 97 I4 .....16°20'N 96°57'E
Martapura Indonesia 102 C3 .....4°20'S 104°21'E
Martin Slovakia 46 H3 .....49°04'N 18°55'E
Martinique i. Central America 67 L3 .....14°36'N 60°56'W
Martin Vaz, Islas is S. Atlantic Ocean 68 E2 .....20°30'S 28°51'W
Martock England 8 C1 .....50°58'N 2°46'W
Märtök Kazakhstan 53 F3 .....50°43'N 56°28'E
Mary Turkmenistan 95 J7 .....37°34'N 61°52'E
Maryborough Australia 108 E4 .....25°32'S 152°41'E
Maryland d. U.S. 63 K4 .....38°39'N 76°30'W
Maryport England 12 D3 .....54°43'N 3°30'W
Masan S. Korea 99 N5 .....35°14'N 128°36'E
Masbate Phil. 103 G6 .....12°20'N 123°37'E
Masbate i. Phil. 103 G6 .....12°20'N 123°36'E
Maseru Lesotho 83 B2 .....29°19'S 27°29'E
Mashhad Iran 95 I7 .....36°18'N 59°35'E
Mashkel, Hamun-i- f. Pakistan 96 B6 .....28°15'N 63°02'E
Maşīrah, Jazīrat i. Oman 95 I4 .....20°16'N 58°58'E
Maşīrah, Khalīj b. Oman 95 I3 .....19°47'N 58°22'E
Masjed Soleymān Iran 95 G6 .....31°57'N 49°17'E
Mask, Lough l. Ireland 18 B3 .....53°37'N 9°21'W
Mason City U.S. 63 H5 .....43°09'N 93°12'W
Massachusetts d. U.S. 63 L5 .....42°23'N 72°18'W
Massachusetts Bay U.S. 63 L5 .....42°25'N 70°51'W
Massakory Chad 84 F3 .....12°59'N 15°43'E
Massif Central mts France 44 E4 .....45°16'N 3°25'E
Mastung Pakistan 95 K5 .....29°45'N 66°56'E
Masuda Japan 104 B2 .....34°40'N 131°50'E
Masvingo Zimbabwe 83 C2 .....20°04'S 30°48'E
Matadi Dem. Rep. Congo 83 A4 .....5°49'S 13°29'E
Matagami Canada 63 K6 .....49°46'N 77°38'W
Matam Senegal 84 C3 .....15°40'N 13°16'W
Matamoros Mexico 66 E6 .....25°53'N 97°34'W
Matanzas Cuba 67 H5 .....23°04'N 81°34'W
Matara Sri Lanka 96 F2 .....5°58'N 80°29'E
Mataram Indonesia 102 F2 .....8°35'S 116°10'E
Mataró Spain 45 G4 .....41°33'N 2°26'E
Matā'utu Wallis and Futuna Is 109 H5 .....13°17'S 176°07'W
Matehuala Mexico 62 F1 .....23°40'N 100°38'W
Mathura India 96 E6 .....27°26'N 77°43'E
Matlock England 13 F2 .....53°08'N 1°33'W
Maţraḩ Oman 95 I4 .....23°37'N 58°32'E
Matsue Japan 104 B2 .....35°28'N 133°03'E
Matsumoto Japan 104 C3 .....36°15'N 137°58'E
Matsusaka Japan 104 C2 .....34°34'N 136°33'E
Matsuyama Japan 104 B2 .....33°49'N 132°46'E
Matterhorn mt. Italy/Switz. 46 B1 .....45°59'N 7°40'E
Maturín Venezuela 72 C7 .....9°44'N 63°09'W
Maubeuge France 42 C3 .....50°17'N 3°58'E
Mauchline Scotland 14 E3 .....55°31'N 4°23'W
Maughold Head Isle of Man 12 C3 .....54°18'N 4°18'W
Maug Islands N. Mariana Is 103 L8 .....20°02'N 145°16'E
Maun Botswana 83 B3 .....19°57'S 23°25'E
Mauritania Africa 84 C3 .....19°51'N 11°35'W
Mauritius country Indian Oc. 79 E1 .....20°10'S 58°00'E
May, Isle of i. Scotland 15 G4 .....56°11'N 2°33'W
Maya r. Russia 55 O4 .....60°26'N 134°33'E
Mayaguana i. Bahamas 67 J5 .....22°23'N 72°56'W
Mayagüez Puerto Rico 67 K4 .....18°12'N 67°08'W
Mayamey Iran 95 I7 .....36°27'N 55°40'E
Mayar hill Scotland 17 F1 .....56°51'N 3°15'W
Maybole Scotland 14 E3 .....55°21'N 4°41'W

Mayen Germany 42 G3 .....50°19'N 7°13'E
Mayenne r. France 44 C5 .....47°30'N 0°32'W
Maykop Russia 53 E2 .....44°36'N 40°07'E
Mayo Canada 60 E4 .....63°37'N 135°54'W
Mayo d. Ireland 18 B3 .....53°46'N 9°13'W
Mayotte i. Africa 83 D3 .....12°59'S 45°09'E
Mazar-e Sharīf Afgh. 95 K7 .....36°43'N 67°07'E
Mazatlán Mexico 66 C5 .....23°14'N 106°27'W
Mažeikiai Lithuania 43 E2 .....56°18'N 22°22'E
Mazyr Belarus 47 M5 .....52°03'N 29°15'E
Mbabane Swaziland 83 C2 .....26°20'S 31°09'E
Mbandaka Dem. Rep. Congo 83 A4 .....0°00'S 18°17'E
Mbanza Kongo Angola 83 A4 .....6°14'S 14°15'E
Mbarara Uganda 85 H1 .....0°35'S 30°37'E
Mbeya Tanzania 83 C4 .....8°53'S 33°26'E
Mbuji-Mayi Dem. Rep. Congo 83 B4 .....6°06'S 23°36'E
McClure Strait Canada 60 G5 .....74°09'N 114°57'W
McCook U.S. 62 F5 .....40°14'N 100°39'W
M'Clintock Channel Canada 60 H5 .....71°10'N 101°39'W
McGrath U.S. 60 C4 .....62°52'N 155°37'W
McKinley, Mount U.S. 60 C4 .....63°05'N 150°30'W
Mdantsane S. Africa 83 B1 .....32°58'S 27°48'E
Mead, Lake resr U.S. 62 D4 .....36°12'N 114°24'W
Mealasta Island i. Scotland 16 B3 .....58°05'N 7°10'W
Meall a' Bhùiridh mt. Scotland 16 E1 .....56°37'N 4°51'W
Meath d. Ireland 18 E3 .....53°41'N 6°35'W
Meaux France 44 E6 .....48°58'N 2°53'E
Mecca Saudi Arabia 94 E4 .....21°25'N 39°47'E
Mechelen Belgium 42 D4 .....51°01'N 4°29'E
Mecheria Algeria 48 C3 .....33°33'N 0°19'W
Meckenheim Germany 42 G3 .....50°37'N 7°02'E
Medan Indonesia 102 B4 .....3°38'N 98°40'E
Medellín Colombia 72 B7 .....6°13'N 75°35'W
Meden r. England 13 G2 .....53°25'N 0°59'W
Medenine Tunisia 48 F3 .....33°21'N 10°31'E
Medetsiz Tepe mt. Turkey 51 K3 .....37°24'N 34°37'E
Mediaş Romania 50 F8 .....46°10'N 24°22'E
Medicine Hat Canada 60 G3 .....50°03'N 110°41'W
Medina Saudi Arabia 94 E4 .....24°31'N 39°32'E
Medina del Campo Spain 45 C4 .....41°19'N 4°54'W
Mediterranean Sea World 48 D4 .....33°25'N 32°44'E
Mednogorsk Russia 53 F3 .....51°19'N 57°35'E
Medvezh'yegorsk Russia 52 E4 .....62°55'N 34°29'E
Medway d. England 21 F2 .....51°22'N 0°34'E
Medway r. England 9 F2 .....51°20'N 0°27'E
Meerut India 96 E6 .....29°02'N 77°45'E
Megara Greece 50 E4 .....38°00'N 23°21'E
Meghalaya d. India 97 H6 .....25°36'N 91°22'E
Mehrestān Iran 95 J6 .....30°59'N 61°31'E
Meiktila Myanmar 97 I5 .....20°50'N 95°53'E
Meiningen Germany 46 D4 .....50°34'N 10°25'E
Meißen Germany 46 E4 .....51°10'N 13°28'E
Meizhou China 99 L2 .....24°17'N 116°09'E
Mek'elē Ethiopia 85 H3 .....13°31'N 39°28'E
Meknès Morocco 84 D5 .....33°53'N 5°30'W
Mekong r. Asia 97 K3 .....10°53'N 105°14'E
Mekong, Mouths of the Vietnam 102 D5 .....9°03'N 106°31'E
Melaka Malaysia 102 C4 .....2°09'N 102°17'E
Melanesia is Pacific Oc. 106 F3 .....10°00'S 165°00'E
Melbourn England 9 F3 .....52°05'N 0°02'E
Melbourne Australia 108 D3 .....37°49'S 144°59'E
Melbourne U.S. 63 J2 .....28°01'N 80°43'W
Melby Scotland 17 H5 .....60°18'N 1°40'W
Melilla N. Africa 48 C4 .....35°18'N 2°57'W
Melitopol Ukraine 47 P2 .....46°51'N 35°22'E
Melksham England 8 C2 .....51°22'N 2°08'W
Melrhir, Chott f. Algeria 84 E5 .....34°15'N 6°23'E
Melrose Scotland 15 G3 .....55°36'N 2°43'W
Meltham England 13 F2 .....53°36'N 1°51'W
Melton Mowbray England 8 E3 .....52°46'N 0°53'W
Melun France 44 E6 .....48°32'N 2°39'E
Melvich Scotland 17 F3 .....58°33'N 3°55'W
Melville Canada 60 H3 .....50°56'N 102°49'W
Melville Bay Greenland 61 L4 .....76°00'N 64°00'W
Melville Island Australia 108 C5 .....11°37'S 130°55'E
Melville Island Canada 60 H5 .....75°14'N 109°26'W
Melville Peninsula Canada 61 J4 .....68°09'N 84°12'W
Melvin, Lough l. Ireland/U.K. 18 C4 .....54°25'N 8°09'W
Memberamo r. Indonesia 103 J3 .....1°32'S 137°52'E
Memmingen Germany 46 D2 .....47°59'N 10°11'E
Memphis U.S. 63 H4 .....35°09'N 90°04'W
Mena Ukraine 47 O4 .....51°31'N 32°14'E
Menai Bridge Wales 10 C5 .....53°13'N 4°10'W
Menai Strait Wales 10 C5 .....53°09'N 4°17'W
Mende France 44 E4 .....44°31'N 3°30'E
Mendī Ethiopia 85 H2 .....9°49'N 35°03'E
Mendip Hills England 8 C2 .....51°19'N 2°46'W
Mendoza Argentina 73 C3 .....32°53'S 68°50'W
Mendefera Eritrea 94 E2 .....14°52'N 38°48'E
Menongue Angola 83 A3 .....14°38'S 17°41'E
Mentawai, Kepulauan is Indonesia 102 B3 .....3°17'S 99°55'E
Mentok Indonesia 102 D3 .....2°01'S 105°12'E
Menzel Bourguiba Tunisia 48 E4 .....37°09'N 9°46'E
Meppel Neth. 42 F5 .....52°42'N 6°11'E
Meppen Germany 42 G5 .....52°41'N 7°18'E
Merano Italy 46 D2 .....46°41'N 11°10'E
Merauke Indonesia 103 K2 .....8°31'S 140°25'E
Mere England 8 C2 .....51°05'N 2°16'W
Merefa Ukraine 47 Q3 .....49°49'N 36°04'E
Mergui Myanmar 97 I3 .....12°27'N 98°37'E
Mergui Archipelago is Myanmar 97 I3 .....11°38'N 97°41'E
Mérida Mexico 66 G5 .....20°59'N 89°37'W
Mérida Spain 45 B3 .....38°56'N 6°20'W
Mérida Venezuela 72 B7 .....8°36'N 71°07'W
Mérida, Cordillera de mts Venezuela 67 J2 .....7°59'N 71°35'W
Meridian U.S. 63 I3 .....32°23'N 88°40'W
Merowe Sudan 85 H3 .....18°27'N 31°51'E
Merowe Dam resr. Sudan D3 .....18°30'N 31°55'E
Merrick hill Scotland 14 E3 .....55°08'N 4°28'W
Mersch Lux. 42 F2 .....49°45'N 6°07'E
Mersey r. England 12 E2 .....53°21'N 2°56'W
Merseyside d. England 21 D3 .....53°23'N 3°06'W
Mersin Turkey 51 K3 .....36°49'N 34°37'E
Merthyr Tydfil Wales 10 D3 .....51°45'N 3°23'W
Merthyr Tydfil d. Wales 21 D2 .....51°44'N 3°20'W
Mértola Portugal 45 B2 .....37°38'N 7°39'W
Merzifon Turkey 51 K5 .....40°52'N 35°27'E
Merzig Germany 42 F2 .....49°27'N 6°39'E
Mesolongi Greece 50 D4 .....38°22'N 21°26'E
Mesopotamia f. Iraq 85 I5 .....35°00'N 42°19'E
Messina Italy 48 G4 .....38°11'N 15°33'E
Messiniakos Kolpos b. Greece 50 E3 .....36°51'N 22°03'E
Mesta r. Bulgaria 50 F5 .....41°26'N 24°02'E
Meta r. Col./Venez. 72 C7 .....6°10'N 67°24'W
Metheringham England 13 G2 .....53°08'N 0°24'W
Methwold England 9 F3 .....52°31'N 0°33'E

Metković Croatia 50 B6 .....43°03'N 17°40'E
Metlika Slovenia 46 F1 .....45°39'N 15°19'E
Metz France 44 G6 .....49°07'N 6°11'E
Meuse r. Belgium/France 42 E4 .....51°08'N 5°51'E
Mevagissey England 11 C2 .....50°16'N 4°47'W
Mexborough England 13 F2 .....53°30'N 1°17'W
Mexicali Mexico 66 A7 .....32°39'N 115°28'W
México Central America 66 C5 .....31°47'N 114°01'W
México d. Mexico 66 E4 .....19°38'N 99°46'W
México, Ciudad de d. Mexico 66 E4 .....19°15'N 99°08'W
Mexico, Gulf of Mexico/U.S. 66 F5 .....22°09'N 95°51'W
Mexico City Mexico 66 E4 .....19°24'N 99°12'W
Meymaneh Afgh. 95 J7 .....35°56'N 64°45'E
Mezen' Russia 52 E4 .....65°50'N 44°18'E
Mezen' r. Russia 52 E4 .....65°50'N 44°18'E
Mezha r. Russia 47 N6 .....55°43'N 31°30'E
Miami U.S. 63 J2 .....25°41'N 80°18'W
Mīāndoāb Iran 95 G7 .....36°58'N 46°07'E
Miandrivazo Madagascar 83 D3 .....19°30'S 45°29'E
Mīāneh Iran 95 G7 .....37°24'N 47°40'E
Mianwali Pakistan 95 L6 .....32°32'N 71°34'E
Miass Russia 52 G3 .....54°58'N 60°05'E
Michigan d. U.S. 63 I6 .....46°12'N 88°00'W
Michigan, Lake U.S. 63 I5 .....43°02'N 87°18'W
Michipicoten Island Canada 63 I6 .....47°41'N 85°48'W
Michipicoten River town Canada 63 J6 .....47°57'N 84°50'W
Michoacán de Ocampo d. Mexico 66 D4 .....18°12'N 102°59'W
Michurinsk Russia 53 E3 .....52°55'N 40°30'E
Micronesia is Pacific Oc. 117 I3 .....11°40'N 147°31'E
Micronesia, Federated States of N. Pacific Oc. 103 K5 .....3°37'N 153°49'E
Mid and East Antrim d. Northern Ireland 20 B4 .....54°53'N 6°14'W
Middlesbrough England 13 F3 .....54°34'N 1°14'W
Middlesbrough d. England 21 E4 .....54°33'N 1°14'W
Middleton England 13 E2 .....53°33'N 2°12'W
Middleton-in-Teesdale England 13 E3 .....54°38'N 2°05'W
Middleton St George England 13 F3 .....54°31'N 1°28'W
Middlewich England 13 E2 .....53°12'N 2°27'W
Midhurst England 8 E1 .....50°59'N 0°44'W
Midi, Canal du France 44 E3 .....43°14'N 2°22'E
Midland U.S. 62 F3 .....32°01'N 101°58'W
Midleton Ireland 18 C1 .....51°55'N 8°10'W
Midlothian d. Scotland 20 D4 .....55°50'N 3°06'W
Mid Ulster d. Northern Ireland 21 B4 .....54°39'N 6°44'W
Miekojärvi l. Finland 43 F4 .....66°34'N 24°25'E
Mielec Poland 47 I4 .....50°17'N 21°26'E
Miercurea Ciuc Romania 50 F8 .....46°22'N 25°48'E
Mikhaylovka Russia 53 E3 .....50°04'N 43°15'E
Mikhaylovskiy Russia 98 D8 .....51°40'N 79°45'E
Mikkeli Finland 43 F3 .....61°41'N 27°17'E
Mikun' Russia 52 F4 .....62°22'N 50°05'E
Milan Italy 46 C1 .....45°28'N 9°11'E
Milas Turkey 51 G3 .....37°18'N 27°46'E
Milborne Port England 8 C1 .....50°58'N 2°28'W
Mildenhall England 9 F3 .....52°21'N 0°31'E
Mildura Australia 108 D3 .....34°12'S 142°11'E
Miles City U.S. 62 E6 .....46°25'N 105°47'W
Milford Haven Wales 10 B3 .....51°43'N 5°02'W
Milk r. U.S. 62 E6 .....48°03'N 106°19'W
Millárs r. Spain 45 E3 .....39°57'N 0°04'W
Millau France 44 E4 .....44°06'N 3°05'E
Mille Lacs lakes U.S. 63 H6 .....46°14'N 93°39'W
Milleur Point Scotland 14 D3 .....55°01'N 5°07'W
Millom England 12 D3 .....54°13'N 3°16'W
Millport Scotland 14 E3 .....55°45'N 4°56'W
Milnthorpe England 12 E3 .....54°14'N 2°46'W
Milos i. Greece 50 F3 .....36°39'N 24°25'E
Milton Keynes England 8 E3 .....52°01'N 0°44'W
Milton Keynes d. England 21 E3 .....52°00'N 0°44'W
Milwaukee U.S. 63 I5 .....43°01'N 87°55'W
Mimizan France 44 C4 .....44°12'N 1°14'W
Mīnāb Iran 95 I5 .....27°09'N 57°04'E
Minas Indonesia 97 J1 .....0°52'N 101°30'E
Minatitlán Mexico 66 F4 .....18°01'N 94°33'W
Mindanao i. Phil. 103 H5 .....7°48'N 125°06'E
Mindelo Cape Verde 84 B3 .....16°52'N 24°59'W
Mindoro i. Phil. 103 G6 .....13°05'N 120°52'E
Mindoro Strait Phil. 102 F6 .....12°47'N 119°59'E
Minehead England 11 D3 .....51°12'N 3°29'W
Mingäçevir Azerbaijan 53 E2 .....40°46'N 47°03'E
Mingulay i. Scotland 16 B1 .....56°49'N 7°37'W
Minna Nigeria 84 E2 .....9°38'N 6°32'E
Minneapolis U.S. 63 H5 .....44°59'N 93°18'W
Minnesota d. U.S. 63 H6 .....47°08'N 92°44'W
Minnesota r. U.S. 63 H5 .....44°55'N 93°11'W
Miño r. Portugal/Spain 45 A4 .....41°56'N 8°45'W
Minorca i. Spain 45 G4 .....40°06'N 3°51'E
Minot U.S. 62 F6 .....48°13'N 101°18'W
Minsk Belarus 47 L5 .....53°53'N 27°34'E
Minsterley England 8 C3 .....52°38'N 2°55'W
Mintlaw Scotland 17 H2 .....57°31'N 1°59'W
Miranda de Ebro Spain 45 D5 .....42°42'N 2°56'W
Mirandela Portugal 45 B4 .....41°29'N 7°10'W
Mirbāţ Oman 95 H3 .....17°02'N 54°43'E
Miri Malaysia 102 E4 .....4°27'N 114°01'E
Mirim, Lagoa l. Brazil/Uruguay 73 D3 .....32°40'S 52°59'W
Mirnyy Russia 55 M4 .....62°35'N 114°10'E
Mirpur Khas Pakistan 96 C6 .....25°32'N 69°04'E
Mirzapur India 96 F6 .....25°08'N 82°39'E
Miskitos, Cayos is Nicaragua 67 H3 .....14°24'N 82°44'W
Miskolc Hungary 46 I3 .....48°06'N 20°48'E
Misoöl i. Indonesia 103 I3 .....1°53'S 130°06'E
Miṣrātah Libya 84 F5 .....32°21'N 15°04'E
Missinaibi r. Canada 61 J3 .....50°45'N 81°31'W
Mississippi d. U.S. 63 I2 .....29°07'N 89°17'W
Mississippi r. U.S. 63 I2 .....29°07'N 89°17'W
Mississippi Delta U.S. 63 I2 .....29°03'N 89°06'W
Missoula U.S. 62 D6 .....46°53'N 113°58'W
Missouri d. U.S. 63 H4 .....38°27'N 92°10'W
Missouri r. U.S. 63 H4 .....38°49'N 90°08'W
Mistassini, Lac l. Canada 61 K3 .....51°01'N 73°34'W
Mistissini Canada 61 K3 .....50°24'N 73°48'W
Mitchell r. Australia 108 D5 .....15°14'S 141°37'E
Mitchell U.S. 62 G5 .....43°42'N 98°02'W
Mitchell, Mount U.S. 63 J4 .....35°51'N 82°20'W
Mitchelstown Ireland 18 C2 .....52°16'N 8°16'W
Mito Japan 104 D3 .....36°23'N 140°28'E
Mitrovicë Kosovo 50 D6 .....42°52'N 20°52'E
Mitsiwwa Eritrea 85 H3 .....15°36'N 39°27'E
Mittimatalik Canada 61 K5 .....72°41'N 77°46'W
Mitumba, Chaîne des mts Dem. Rep. Congo 83 B3 .....11°46'S 26°06'E
Miyako Japan 104 D3 .....39°38'N 141°57'E
Miyazaki Japan 104 B2 .....31°54'N 131°25'E
Mizdah Libya 48 F3 .....31°26'N 12°59'E
Mizen Head Cork Ireland 18 B1 .....51°26'N 9°49'W

Mizen Head Wick. Ireland 18 E2 .....52°51'N 6°03'W
Mizoram d. India 97 H5 .....23°27'N 92°50'E
Mjölby Sweden 43 C2 .....58°20'N 15°08'E
Mława Poland 46 I5 .....53°07'N 20°23'E
Mljet i. Croatia 50 B6 .....42°44'N 17°27'E
Mmabatho S. Africa 83 B2 .....25°47'S 25°37'E
Mobile U.S. 63 I3 .....30°40'N 88°04'W
Mobile Bay U.S. 63 I3 .....30°24'N 88°01'W
Mobridge U.S. 62 F6 .....45°32'N 100°25'W
Moçambique Mozambique 83 D3 .....15°05'S 40°41'E
Mocha Yemen 94 F2 .....13°20'N 43°12'E
Mochudi Botswana 83 B2 .....24°25'S 26°08'E
Mocuba Mozambique 83 C3 .....16°53'S 36°58'E
Modbury England 11 D2 .....50°21'N 3°53'W
Modena Italy 46 D1 .....44°39'N 10°56'E
Moelfre Wales 10 C5 .....53°21'N 4°14'W
Moel Sych hill Wales 10 D4 .....52°53'N 3°23'W
Moffat Scotland 15 F3 .....55°20'N 3°26'W
Mogadishu Somalia 85 I2 .....2°04'N 45°20'E
Mohawk r. U.S. 63 L5 .....42°46'N 73°44'W
Mohyliv-Podilskyi Ukraine 47 L3 .....48°27'N 27°48'E
Mo i Rana Norway 43 C4 .....66°19'N 14°10'E
Mold Wales 10 D5 .....53°10'N 3°08'W
Molde Norway 43 A3 .....62°44'N 7°10'E
Moldova Europe 49 I6 .....46°59'N 28°55'E
Moldoveanu, Vârful mt. Romania 50 F7 .....45°36'N 24°45'E
Molopo watercourse Botswana/S. Africa 83 B2 .....28°32'S 20°13'E
Moluccas is Indonesia 103 H3 .....0°30'S 127°20'E
Molucca Sea Indonesia 103 H3 .....1°08'S 125°11'E
Mombasa Kenya 85 H1 .....3°59'S 39°40'E
Møn i. Denmark 43 C1 .....55°00'N 12°22'E
Mona, Isla i. Puerto Rico 67 K4 .....18°04'N 67°52'W
Monach, Sound of str. Scotland 16 B2 .....57°33'N 7°39'W
Monach Islands Scotland 16 B2 .....57°32'N 7°41'W
Monaco Europe 44 G3 .....43°44'N 7°26'E
Monadhliath Mountains Scotland 17 E2 .....57°04'N 4°31'W
Monaghan Ireland 18 E4 .....54°15'N 6°57'W
Monaghan d. Ireland 18 E4 .....54°10'N 6°59'W
Mona Passage str. Dom. Rep./Puerto Rico 67 K4 .....18°01'N 68°06'W
Monar, Loch l. Scotland 16 D2 .....57°25'N 5°08'W
Monbetsu Japan 104 D4 .....44°21'N 143°21'E
Monchegorsk Russia 43 H4 .....67°57'N 32°56'E
Mönchengladbach Germany 42 F4 .....51°12'N 6°25'E
Monclova Mexico 66 D6 .....26°53'N 101°30'W
Moncton Canada 61 L2 .....46°04'N 64°47'E
Mondego r. Portugal 45 A4 .....40°10'N 8°39'W
Mondoví Italy 46 B1 .....44°23'N 7°49'E
Moneymore Northern Ireland 14 C2 .....54°41'N 6°40'W
Monforte de Lemos Spain 45 B5 .....42°32'N 7°30'W
Monga Dem. Rep. Congo 83 B5 .....4°11'N 22°50'E
Mongolia Asia 99 I7 .....46°59'N 103°48'E
Mongora Pakistan 95 L6 .....34°46'N 72°30'E
Mongu Zambia 83 B3 .....15°15'S 23°08'E
Moniaive Scotland 15 F3 .....55°12'N 3°55'W
Monmouth Wales 10 C3 .....51°49'N 2°43'W
Monmouthshire d. Wales 21 D2 .....51°47'N 2°58'W
Monnow r. U.K. 8 C2 .....51°49'N 2°43'W
Monroe U.S. 63 H3 .....32°30'N 92°06'W
Monrovia Liberia 84 C2 .....6°20'N 10°46'W
Mons Belgium 42 C3 .....50°27'N 3°57'E
Montana Bulgaria 50 E6 .....43°25'N 23°13'E
Montana d. U.S. 62 E6 .....46°44'N 109°17'W
Montargis France 44 E5 .....47°59'N 2°44'E
Montauban France 44 D4 .....44°01'N 1°21'E
Montbéliard France 44 G5 .....47°30'N 6°49'E
Mont-de-Marsan France 44 C3 .....43°53'N 0°30'W
Monte-Carlo Monaco 44 G3 .....43°44'N 7°25'E
Montego Bay town Jamaica 67 I4 .....18°28'N 77°54'W
Montélimar France 44 F4 .....44°33'N 4°45'E
Montemorelos Mexico 66 E6 .....25°11'N 99°49'W
Montería Colombia 72 B7 .....8°43'N 75°53'W
Monterrey Mexico 66 D6 .....25°42'N 100°18'W
Montes Claros Brazil 72 E5 .....16°42'S 43°49'W
Montevideo Uruguay 73 D3 .....34°54'S 56°13'W
Monte Vista U.S. 62 E4 .....37°36'N 106°09'W
Montgomery U.S. 63 I3 .....32°23'N 86°19'W
Montgomery Wales 10 D4 .....52°34'N 3°09'W
Mont-Joli Canada 63 M6 .....48°35'N 68°12'W
Montluçon France 44 E5 .....46°21'N 2°36'E
Montmagny Canada 63 L6 .....46°59'N 70°34'W
Montpelier U.S. 63 L5 .....44°16'N 72°35'W
Montpellier France 44 E3 .....43°37'N 3°53'E
Montréal Canada 61 K2 .....45°32'N 73°39'W
Montreuil France 9 G1 .....50°28'N 1°46'E
Montrose Scotland 17 G1 .....56°42'N 2°28'W
Montserrat i. Central America 67 L4 .....16°44'N 62°12'W
Monywa Myanmar 97 I5 .....22°05'N 95°13'E
Monza Italy 46 C1 .....45°35'N 9°17'E
Monzón Spain 45 F4 .....41°55'N 0°11'E
Moore, Lake Australia 108 A4 .....29°43'S 117°28'E
Moose r. Canada 61 J3 .....51°20'N 80°31'W
Moose Jaw Canada 60 H3 .....50°26'N 105°33'W
Moosomin Canada 62 F7 .....50°09'N 101°41'W
Moosonee Canada 61 J3 .....51°16'N 80°40'W
Mopti Mali 84 D3 .....14°30'N 4°11'W
Mora Sweden 43 C3 .....61°00'N 14°32'E
Morar, Loch l. Scotland 16 D1 .....56°57'N 5°43'W
Moray d. Scotland 20 D5 .....57°30'N 3°16'W
Moray Firth b. Scotland 17 E2 .....57°33'N 4°11'W
Morbach Germany 42 G2 .....49°48'N 7°06'E
Morden Canada 60 I2 .....49°12'N 98°07'W
More, Loch l. Scotland 16 E3 .....58°18'N 4°53'W
Morecambe England 12 E3 .....54°04'N 2°53'W
Morecambe Bay England 12 D3 .....54°07'N 3°04'W
Moree Australia 108 D4 .....29°28'S 149°52'E
Morehead P.N.G. 103 K2 .....8°44'S 141°39'E
Morelia Mexico 66 D4 .....19°39'N 101°12'W
Morelos d. Mexico 66 E4 .....18°47'N 98°59'W
Morena, Sierra mts Spain 45 B2 .....37°57'N 6°06'W
Moretonhampstead England 11 D2 .....50°39'N 3°46'W
Morgan City U.S. 63 H2 .....29°43'N 91°25'W
Mori Japan 104 D4 .....42°06'N 140°33'E
Morioka Japan 104 D3 .....39°42'N 141°08'E
Moriston r. Scotland 16 E2 .....57°13'N 4°36'W
Morlaix France 44 B6 .....48°35'N 3°50'W
Morley England 13 F2 .....53°45'N 1°36'W
Morocco Africa 84 D5 .....31°57'N 5°40'W
Morogoro Tanzania 83 C4 .....6°47'S 37°40'E
Moro Gulf Phil. 103 G5 .....6°59'S 123°2'E
Morombe Madagascar 83 D2 .....21°46'S 43°22'E
Morondava Madagascar 83 D2 .....20°18'S 44°17'E
Morón de la Frontera Spain 45 C2 .....37°08'N 5°22'W
Moroni Comoros 83 D3 .....11°39'S 43°41'E

Morotai i. Indonesia 103 H4 .... 2°23'N 128°27'E
Morpeth England 13 F4 .... 55°10'N 1°41'W
Morriston Wales 10 D3 .... 51°40'N 3°56'W
Morro, Punta pt Chile 73 B4 .... 27°07'S 70°59'W
Morrosquillo, Golfo de b. Colombia 67 I2 ... 9°33'N 75°39'W
Morshansk Russia 53 E3 .... 53°27'N 41°49'E
Morte Bay England 11 C3 .... 51°10'N 4°14'W
Mortehoe England 11 C3 .... 51°11'N 4°12'W
Morvern f. Scotland 16 D1 .... 56°36'N 5°53'W
Mosborough England 13 F2 .... 53°20'N 1°22'W
Moscow Russia 52 D3 .... 55°45'N 37°38'E
Moscow U.S. 62 C6 .... 46°44'N 116°58'W
Mosel r. Germany 42 G3 .... 50°22'N 7°36'E
Moselle r. France 44 G6 .... 49°27'N 6°22'E
Moshi Tanzania 83 C4 .... 3°23'S 37°20'E
Mosjøen Norway 43 C4 .... 65°51'N 13°12'E
Mosquitos, Golfo de los b. Panama 67 H2 ... 8°56'N 81°17'W
Moss Norway 43 B2 .... 59°26'N 10°39'E
Mossel Bay town S. Africa 83 B1 .... 34°11'S 22°08'E
Mossoró Brazil 72 F6 .... 5°08'S 37°15'W
Mostaganem Algeria 48 D4 .... 35°55'N 0°06'E
Mostar Bos. and Herz. 50 B6 .... 43°20'N 17°49'E
Mosul Iraq 94 F7 .... 36°18'N 43°05'E
Møsvatnet l. Norway 43 B2 .... 59°51'N 8°06'E
Motala Sweden 43 C2 .... 58°32'N 15°02'E
Motherwell Scotland 15 F3 .... 55°48'N 3°59'W
Motril Spain 45 D2 .... 36°45'N 3°31'W
Mouaskar Algeria 48 D4 .... 35°23'N 0°08'E
Moulins France 44 E5 .... 46°34'N 3°20'E
Moulmein Myanmar 97 I4 .... 16°30'N 97°40'E
Moundou Chad 84 F2 .... 8°34'N 16°05'E
Mount Gambier town Australia 108 D3 ... 37°52'S 140°48'E
Mount Isa town Australia 108 C4 .... 20°45'S 139°29'E
Mount Kazbek mt. Georgia/Russia 53 E2 ... 42°45'N 44°34'E
Mountmellick Ireland 18 D3 .... 53°07'N 7°20'W
Mountrath Ireland 18 D3 .... 53°00'N 7°28'W
Mount's Bay England 11 B2 .... 50°05'N 5°29'W
Mountsorrel England 8 D3 .... 52°44'N 1°08'W
Mourdi, Dépression du f. Chad 94 B3 ... 18°01'N 21°06'E
Mourne r. Northern Ireland 14 C2 .... 54°50'N 7°28'W
Mourne Mountains Northern Ireland 14 C2
.... 54°06'N 6°11'W
Mousa i. Scotland 17 H5 .... 60°00'N 1°11'W
Mouscron Belgium 42 C3 .... 50°44'N 3°13'E
Mouzon France 42 E2 .... 49°37'N 5°05'E
Moy r. Ireland 18 B4 .... 54°07'N 9°08'W
Moyale Ethiopia 85 H2 .... 3°32'N 39°03'E
Moyen Atlas mts Morocco 48 B3 .... 32°25'N 5°37'W
Mo'ynoq Uzbekistan 53 F2 .... 43°45'N 58°58'E
Mozambique Africa 83 F2 .... 20°09'S 34°14'E
Mozambique Channel Africa 83 D2 ...... 20°15'S 40°16'E
M'Saken Tunisia 48 F4 .... 35°43'N 10°35'E
Mtsensk Russia 47 Q5 .... 53°17'N 36°36'E
Mtwara Tanzania 83 D4 .... 10°19'S 40°09'E
Muar Malaysia 102 C4 .... 2°02'N 102°34'E
Muarabungo Indonesia 102 C3 .... 1°27'S 102°08'E
Much Wenlock England 8 C3 .... 52°36'N 2°33'W
Muck i. Scotland 16 C1 .... 56°50'N 6°14'W
Muckish Mountain hill Ireland 14 A3 ... 55°06'N 8°00'W
Muckle Roe i. Scotland 17 H5 .... 60°21'N 1°25'W
Mudanjiang China 99 N6 .... 44°32'N 129°34'E
Mudurnu Turkey 51 I5 .... 40°27'N 31°13'E
Mueda Mozambique 83 C3 .... 11°38'S 39°34'E
Muğla Turkey 51 H3 .... 37°12'N 28°21'E
Muhammad Qol Sudan 94 E4 .... 20°54'N 37°07'E
Mühlhausen/Thüringen Germany 46 D4 ... 51°13'N 10°27'E
Muhos Finland 43 F4 .... 64°48'N 25°58'E
Muine Bheag Ireland 18 E2 .... 52°42'N 6°58'W
Muirkirk Scotland 15 E3 .... 55°31'N 4°04'W
Muirneag hill Scotland 16 C3 .... 58°22'N 6°18'W
Mukacheve Ukraine 47 J3 .... 48°27'N 22°43'E
Mukalla Yemen 95 G2 .... 14°34'N 49°06'E
Mulanje, Mount Malawi 83 C3 .... 15°54'S 35°35'E
Mulde r. Germany 46 E4 .... 51°52'N 12°15'E
Mulhacén mt. Spain 45 D2 .... 37°02'N 3°18'W
Mulhouse France 44 G5 .... 47°45'N 7°20'E
Mull i. Scotland 14 D4 .... 56°27'N 5°58'W
Mull, Sound of str. Scotland 14 C4 .... 56°37'N 6°01'W
Mullaghareirk Mountains Ireland 18 B2 ... 52°22'N 9°17'W
Mullaghcleevaun hill Ireland 10 A5 .... 53°06'N 6°24'W
Mull Head Scotland 17 G4 .... 59°23'N 2°53'W
Mullingar Ireland 18 D3 .... 53°31'N 7°20'W
Mull of Galloway c. Scotland 14 E2 .... 54°38'N 4°52'W
Mull of Kintyre hd Scotland 14 D3 ...... 55°17'N 5°50'W
Mull of Oa hd Scotland 14 C3 .... 55°35'N 6°20'W
Multan Pakistan 96 D7 .... 30°12'N 71°35'E
Mumbai India 96 D4 .... 18°56'N 72°51'E
Mumbles Wales 10 C3 .... 51°34'N 4°00'W
Muna i. Indonesia 103 G2 .... 5°02'S 122°30'E
Muna r. Russia 55 N4 .... 67°51'N 123°04'E
Mundesley England 9 G4 .... 52°51'N 1°26'E
Mundford England 9 F3 .... 52°31'N 0°39'E
Munger India 96 G6 .... 25°22'N 86°28'E
Munich Germany 46 D3 .... 48°08'N 11°35'E
Münster Germany 46 B4 .... 51°57'N 7°38'E
Muojärvi l. Finland 43 G4 .... 65°55'N 29°38'E
Muonio Finland 43 E4 .... 67°57'N 23°40'E
Muonioälven r. Finland/Sweden 43 E4 ... 67°10'N 23°33'E
Murallón, Cerro mt. Chile 73 B2 .... 49°50'S 73°27'W
Murashi Russia 52 E3 .... 59°24'N 48°58'E
Murchison watercourse Australia 108 A4 ... 27°39'S 114°09'E
Murcia Spain 45 E2 .... 37°59'N 1°06'W
Mureș r. Romania 50 D8 .... 46°11'N 20°07'E
Muret France 44 D3 .... 43°28'N 1°20'E
Müritz l. Germany 46 E5 .... 53°25'N 12°43'E
Murmansk Russia 52 E4 .... 68°57'N 33°07'E
Murmanskiy Bereg f. Russia 52 D4 ...... 67°00'N 38°00'E
Murom Russia 52 E3 .... 55°34'N 42°04'E
Muroran Japan 104 D4 .... 42°19'N 140°58'E
Murray r. Australia 108 C3 .... 35°22'S 139°18'E
Murray Bridge Australia 108 C3 .... 35°07'S 139°17'E
Murrumbidgee r. Australia 108 D3 ...... 34°42'S 143°13'E
Murzuq Libya 84 F4 .... 25°54'N 13°55'E
Mürzzuschlag Austria 46 F2 .... 47°37'N 15°41'E
Musala mt. Bulgaria 50 E6 .... 42°11'N 23°35'E
Muscat Oman 95 I4 .... 23°36'N 58°35'E
Musgrave Ranges, The mts Australia 108 C4
.... 26°17'S 131°01'E
Muskogee U.S. 63 G4 .... 35°47'N 95°23'W
Musmar Sudan 94 E3 .... 18°13'N 35°40'E
Musoma Tanzania 83 C4 .... 1°32'S 33°47'E
Musselburgh Scotland 15 F3 .... 55°57'N 3°03'W
Mustafakemalpaşa Turkey 51 H5 ...... 40°02'N 28°23'E
Mût Egypt 85 G4 .... 25°28'N 28°58'E
Mut Turkey 51 J3 .... 36°39'N 33°26'E
Mutare Zimbabwe 83 C3 .... 18°58'S 32°39'E
Mutis, Gunung mt. Indonesia 103 G2 ... 9°35'S 124°14'E

Mutsu Japan 104 D4 .... 41°17'N 141°10'E
Mutuali Mozambique 83 C3 .... 14°52'S 37°01'E
Muyezerskiy Russia 52 D4 .... 63°57'N 32°01'E
Muzaffargarh Pakistan 95 L6 .... 30°03'N 71°14'E
Muzaffarpur India 96 G6 .... 26°05'N 85°28'E
Mwanza Tanzania 83 C4 .... 2°30'S 32°56'E
Mwene-Ditu Dem. Rep. Congo 83 B4 ... 7°01'S 23°27'E
Mweru, Lake Dem. Rep. Congo/Zambia 83 B4
.... 8°57'S 28°46'E
Myanmar Asia 97 I5 .... 22°37'N 95°02'E
Mykolaiv Ukraine 49 J6 .... 46°57'N 32°02'E
Myla Russia 52 F4 .... 65°27'N 50°52'E
Myronivka Ukraine 47 N3 .... 49°39'N 30°59'E
Myrtle Beach town U.S. 63 K3 .... 33°43'N 78°54'W
Mysuru India 96 E3 .... 12°16'N 76°36'E
My Tho Vietnam 102 D6 .... 10°20'N 106°23'E
Mytilini Greece 50 G3 .... 39°07'N 26°33'E
Mzuzu Malawi 83 C3 .... 11°27'S 34°00'E

N

Naas Ireland 18 E3 .... 53°13'N 6°40'W
Naberezhnyye Chelny Russia 52 F3 .... 55°42'N 52°21'E
Nabeul Tunisia 48 F4 .... 36°29'N 10°45'E
Nacala Mozambique 83 D3 .... 14°34'S 40°40'E
Nador Morocco 48 C4 .... 35°11'N 2°56'W
Nadvoitsy Russia 52 D4 .... 63°54'N 34°17'E
Nadym Russia 54 I4 .... 65°29'N 72°34'E
Næstved Denmark 43 B1 .... 55°14'N 11°46'E
Nafplio Greece 50 E3 .... 37°34'N 22°49'E
Naga Phil. 103 G6 .... 13°35'N 123°11'E
Nagaland d. India 97 H6 .... 26°03'N 94°37'E
Nagano Japan 104 C3 .... 36°38'N 138°11'E
Nagaoka Japan 104 C3 .... 37°26'N 138°51'E
Nagaon India 97 H6 .... 26°19'N 92°42'E
Nagasaki Japan 104 A2 .... 32°46'N 129°52'E
Nagercoil India 96 E2 .... 8°10'N 77°28'E
Nagha Kalat Pakistan 95 K5 .... 27°23'N 65°13'E
Nagorno-Karabakh d. Azerbaijan 53 E2 ... 40°00'N 46°30'E
Nagoya Japan 104 C3 .... 35°10'N 136°53'E
Nagpur India 96 E5 .... 21°09'N 79°05'E
Nagurskoye Russia 54 F6 .... 80°31'N 47°57'E
Nagykanizsa Hungary 46 G2 .... 46°28'N 16°59'E
Naha Japan 99 N3 .... 26°12'N 127°39'E
Nahāvand Iran 95 G6 .... 34°12'N 48°22'E
Na h-Eileanan Siar d. Scotland 20 B5 ... 57°54'N 6°48'W
Nailsworth England 8 C2 .... 51°42'N 2°13'W
Nain Canada 61 L3 .... 56°31'N 61°31'W
Na'in Iran 95 H6 .... 32°50'N 53°03'E
Nairn Scotland 17 F2 .... 57°35'N 3°52'W
Nairn r. Scotland 17 F2 .... 57°35'N 3°52'W
Nairobi Kenya 85 H1 .... 1°17'S 36°48'E
Najafābād Iran 95 H6 .... 32°37'N 51°20'E
Najd f. Saudi Arabia 94 F5 .... 26°14'N 40°21'E
Najrān Saudi Arabia 94 F3 .... 17°34'N 44°17'E
Nakhodka Russia 55 O2 .... 42°48'N 132°54'E
Nakhon Ratchasima Thailand 102 C6 ... 14°57'N 102°08'E
Nakhon Sawan Thailand 102 C7 .... 15°40'N 100°06'E
Nakhon Si Thammarat Thailand 102 B5 ... 8°25'N 99°58'E
Nakina Canada 61 J3 .... 50°10'N 86°43'W
Nakonde Zambia 83 C4 .... 9°21'S 32°42'E
Nakskov Denmark 43 B1 .... 54°49'N 11°09'E
Nakuru Kenya 85 H1 .... 0°16'S 36°05'E
Nal'chik Russia 53 E2 .... 43°29'N 43°38'E
Nālūt Libya 84 F5 .... 31°49'N 10°57'E
Namak, Kavīr-e f. Iran 95 I6 .... 34°26'N 57°32'E
Namakzar-e Shadad f. Iran 95 I6 ...... 30°44'N 58°01'E
Namangan Uzbekistan 98 C6 .... 40°59'N 71°38'E
Nam Co l. China 98 G4 .... 30°42'N 90°35'E
Nam Dinh Vietnam 102 D8 .... 20°22'N 106°11'E
Namib Desert Namibia 83 A2 .... 25°21'S 15°06'E
Namibe Angola 83 A3 .... 15°11'S 12°10'E
Namibia Africa 83 A2 .... 23°22'S 15°55'E
Namlea Indonesia 103 H3 .... 3°14'S 127°05'E
Nampo N. Korea 99 N5 .... 38°43'N 125°23'E
Nampula Mozambique 83 C3 .... 15°10'S 39°13'E
Namsos Norway 43 B4 .... 64°28'N 11°31'E
Namur Belgium 42 D3 .... 50°28'N 4°52'E
Namur d. Belgium 42 D3 .... 50°16'N 4°53'E
Nan Thailand 102 C7 .... 18°47'N 100°47'E
Nanaimo Canada 62 B6 .... 49°10'N 123°56'W
Nanao Japan 104 C3 .... 37°03'N 136°58'E
Nanchang China 99 L3 .... 28°42'N 115°58'E
Nanchong China 99 J4 .... 30°46'N 106°04'E
Nancy France 44 G6 .... 48°42'N 6°11'E
Nangan Dao i. Taiwan 99 M3 .... 26°13'N 120°00'E
Nanjing China 99 L4 .... 32°04'N 118°50'E
Nan Ling mts China 99 K2 .... 24°59'N 111°08'E
Nanning China 99 J2 .... 22°49'N 108°20'E
Nanortalik Greenland 61 N4 .... 60°09'N 45°15'W
Nanping China 99 L3 .... 26°41'N 118°09'E
Nantes France 44 C5 .... 47°13'N 1°33'W
Nantes à Brest, Canal de France 44 B5 ... 48°22'N 2°07'W
Nantong China 99 M4 .... 31°59'N 120°56'E
Nantucket Island U.S. 63 M5 .... 41°17'N 69°59'W
Nantwich England 13 E2 .... 53°04'N 2°31'W
Nant-y-moch Reservoir Wales 10 D4 ... 52°28'N 3°54'W
Nanyang China 99 K4 .... 33°01'N 112°35'E
Napaimiut U.S. 60 C4 .... 61°38'N 158°24'W
Napier New Zealand 109 G3 .... 39°30'S 176°53'E
Naples Italy 48 F4 .... 40°51'N 14°15'E
Narberth Wales 10 C3 .... 51°48'N 4°45'W
Narbonne France 44 E3 .... 43°11'N 3°01'E
Narborough Leics. England 8 D3 ...... 52°34'N 1°13'W
Narborough Norf. England 9 F3 .... 52°41'N 0°35'E
Nares Strait Canada/Greenland 61 K5 ... 79°12'N 71°28'W
Narmada r. India 96 D5 .... 21°43'N 73°06'E
Narodnaya, Gora mt. Russia 52 F4 .... 65°01'N 60°06'E
Naro-Fominsk Russia 47 Q6 .... 55°22'N 36°45'E
Närpes Finland 43 E3 .... 62°29'N 21°21'E
Narva Estonia 43 G2 .... 59°22'N 28°11'E
Narvik Norway 43 D5 .... 68°26'N 17°25'E
Nar'yan-Mar Russia 52 F4 .... 67°40'N 53°10'E
Naryn Kyrgyzstan 98 D6 .... 41°19'N 75°56'E
Nashik India 96 D5 .... 20°00'N 73°52'E
Nashville U.S. 63 I4 .... 36°11'N 86°46'W
Nassau Bahamas 67 I6 .... 25°05'N 77°22'W
Nasser, Lake resr Egypt 85 H4 .... 23°09'N 33°02'E
Nässjö Sweden 43 C2 .... 57°39'N 14°43'E
Nata Botswana 83 B2 .... 20°12'S 26°10'E
Natal Brazil 72 F6 .... 5°44'S 35°10'W
Natchez U.S. 63 H3 .... 31°35'N 91°24'W
Natron, Lake Tanzania 83 C4 .... 2°18'S 36°02'E

Natuna, Kepulauan is Indonesia 102 D4 ... 4°12'N 107°23'E
Natuna Besar i. Indonesia 102 D4 ...... 4°04'N 108°28'E
Nau, Cap de la r. Spain 45 F3 .... 38°44'N 0°15'E
Naujaat Canada 61 J4 .... 66°32'N 86°08'W
Nauru S. Pacific Oc. 109 F6 .... 0°30'S 166°56'E
Navalmoral de la Mata Spain 45 C3 ... 39°53'N 5°32'W
Navan Ireland 18 E3 .... 53°39'N 6°41'W
Navapolatsk Belarus 47 M6 .... 55°32'N 28°40'E
Naver r. Scotland 17 E3 .... 58°31'N 4°13'W
Naver, Loch l. Scotland 17 E3 .... 58°17'N 4°24'W
Navlya Russia 47 P5 .... 52°49'N 34°31'E
Navojoa Mexico 66 C6 .... 27°04'N 109°32'W
Navapolatsk → Navapolatsk
Nawabshah Pakistan 96 C6 .... 26°13'N 68°25'E
Naxçıvan Azerbaijan 95 G7 .... 39°13'N 45°24'E
Naxos i. Greece 50 F3 .... 37°02'N 25°35'E
Nayarit d. Mexico 66 D5 .... 22°07'N 104°45'W
Nay Pyi Taw Myanmar 97 I4 .... 19°44'N 96°13'E
Nazareth Israel 49 K3 .... 32°40'N 35°18'E
Nazas r. Mexico 66 D6 .... 25°34'N 104°55'W
Nazilli Turkey 51 H3 .... 37°55'N 28°19'E
Nazrēt Ethiopia 85 H2 .... 8°32'N 39°15'E
Nazwá Oman 95 I4 .... 22°56'N 57°31'E
Ndalatando Angola 83 A4 .... 9°18'S 14°56'E
Ndélé C.A.R. 85 G2 .... 8°24'N 20°38'E
Ndeni i. Solomon Is 109 F5 .... 10°41'S 166°07'E
N'Djaména Chad 84 F3 .... 12°08'N 15°03'E
Ndola Zambia 83 B3 .... 12°57'S 28°39'E
Neagh, Lough l. Northern Ireland 14 C2 ... 54°40'N 6°24'W
Nea Liosia Greece 50 E4 .... 38°04'N 23°42'E
Neapoli Greece 50 E3 .... 36°31'N 23°04'E
Neath Wales 10 D3 .... 51°39'N 3°48'W
Neath r. Wales 10 D3 .... 51°39'N 3°49'W
Neath Port Talbot d. Wales 21 D2 .... 51°43'N 3°49'W
Neblina, Pico da mt. Brazil 72 C7 ...... 0°49'N 66°13'W
Nebraska d. U.S. 62 F5 .... 41°30'N 100°06'W
Neckar r. Germany 44 H6 .... 49°31'N 8°27'E
Needham Market England 9 G3 .... 52°09'N 1°03'E
Needles U.S. 62 D3 .... 34°50'N 114°36'W
Neftekamsk Russia 52 F3 .... 56°06'N 54°14'E
Nefyn Wales 10 C4 .... 52°56'N 4°31'W
Negotin Serbia 50 E7 .... 44°13'N 22°33'E
Negra, Punta pt Peru 68 B4 .... 6°05'S 81°21'W
Negro r. Argentina 73 C2 .... 41°01'S 62°48'W
Negro r. Brazil 72 C6 .... 3°08'S 59°57'W
Negros i. Phil. 103 G5 .... 9°43'N 122°50'E
Neijiang China 99 J3 .... 29°35'N 105°04'E
Nei Mongol Zizhiqu d. China 99 I6 .... 40°12'N 103°26'E
Neisse r. Germany/Poland 46 F5 ...... 52°04'N 14°46'E
Neiva Colombia 72 B7 .... 2°55'N 75°15'W
Nek'emtē Ethiopia 85 H2 .... 9°06'N 36°32'E
Nelidovo Russia 47 O7 .... 56°14'N 32°47'E
Nellore India 96 E3 .... 14°29'N 79°59'E
Nelson Canada 60 G2 .... 49°29'N 117°17'W
Nelson r. Canada 61 I3 .... 56°58'N 92°45'W
Nelson England 13 E2 .... 53°50'N 2°13'W
Nelson New Zealand 109 G2 .... 41°17'S 173°15'E
Nelspruit S. Africa 83 C2 .... 25°28'S 30°59'E
Neman Russia 47 J6 .... 55°02'N 22°02'E
Neman r. Russia 47 J6 .... 55°03'N 22°14'E
Nementcha, Monts des mts Algeria 48 E3 ... 34°48'N 6°23'E
Nemuro Japan 104 E4 .... 43°17'N 145°30'E
Nenagh Ireland 18 C2 .... 52°52'N 8°12'W
Nene r. England 9 F3 .... 52°49'N 0°13'E
Nenjiang China 99 N7 .... 49°04'N 125°12'E
Nepal Asia 96 F6 .... 28°59'N 82°06'E
Nephin hill Ireland 18 B4 .... 54°01'N 9°22'W
Neris r. Lithuania 43 F1 .... 54°55'N 23°53'E
Ness r. Scotland 17 E2 .... 57°29'N 4°14'W
Ness, Loch l. Scotland 17 E2 .... 57°10'N 4°37'W
Neston England 12 D2 .... 53°17'N 3°04'W
Nestos r. Greece 50 F5 .... 40°51'N 24°48'E
Netherlands Europe 42 E5 .... 52°35'N 5°33'E
Netley Abbey England 8 D1 .... 50°52'N 1°19'W
Nettilling Lake Canada 61 K4 .... 66°30'N 70°39'W
Neubrandenburg Germany 46 E5 ...... 53°33'N 13°15'E
Neufchâteau Belgium 42 E2 .... 49°51'N 5°27'E
Neum Bos. and Herz. 50 B6 .... 42°55'N 17°37'E
Neumünster Germany 46 C6 .... 54°05'N 9°59'E
Neunkirchen Germany 42 F2 .... 49°21'N 7°10'E
Neuquén Argentina 73 C3 .... 38°57'S 68°03'W
Neuruppin Germany 46 E5 .... 52°56'N 12°48'E
Neustrelitz Germany 46 E5 .... 53°22'N 13°04'E
Neuwied Germany 46 B4 .... 50°26'N 7°28'E
Nevada d. U.S. 62 C4 .... 39°03'N 117°06'W
Nevada, Sierra mts Spain 45 D2 ...... 37°04'N 3°20'W
Nevada, Sierra mts U.S. 62 B5 .... 40°07'N 121°00'W
Nevel' Russia 47 M7 .... 56°01'N 29°55'E
Nevers France 44 E5 .... 47°00'N 3°09'E
Nevinnomyssk Russia 49 L5 .... 44°38'N 41°56'E
Nevis, Loch inlet Scotland 16 D2 ...... 57°00'N 5°42'W
Nevşehir Turkey 51 K4 .... 38°37'N 34°43'E
New Addington England 9 E2 .... 51°21'N 0°01'W
New Alresford England 8 D2 .... 51°05'N 1°10'W
Newark U.S. 63 L5 .... 40°44'N 74°24'W
Newark-on-Trent England 13 G2 ...... 53°04'N 0°48'W
New Bern U.S. 63 K4 .... 35°05'N 77°03'W
Newbiggin-by-the-Sea England 13 F4 ... 55°11'N 1°31'W
Newbridge Ireland 18 E3 .... 53°11'N 6°48'W
Newbridge Wales 10 D3 .... 51°40'N 3°09'W
New Britain i. P.N.G. 108 D6 .... 5°42'S 148°56'E
New Brunswick d. Canada 61 L2 ...... 46°41'N 66°28'W
Newburgh Scotland 15 F4 .... 56°21'N 3°14'W
Newbury England 8 D2 .... 51°24'N 1°19'W
New Cairo Egypt 85 H5 .... 30°03'N 31°30'W
New Caledonia is S. Pacific Oc. 109 F4 ... 21°45'S 164°17'E
Newcastle Australia 108 E3 .... 32°56'S 151°44'E
Newcastle Northern Ireland 14 D2 ...... 54°13'N 5°53'W
Newcastle Emlyn Wales 10 C4 .... 52°02'N 4°28'W
Newcastle-under-Lyme England 13 E2 ... 53°01'N 2°13'W
Newcastle upon Tyne England 13 F3 ... 54°59'N 1°37'W
Newcastle West Ireland 18 B2 .... 52°27'N 9°03'W
New Cumnock Scotland 14 E3 .... 55°23'N 4°11'W
New Delhi India 96 E6 .... 28°36'N 77°12'E
Newent England 8 C2 .... 51°56'N 2°24'W
New Forest nature res. England 8 D1 ... 50°52'N 1°37'W
Newfoundland i. Canada 61 M2 .... 48°30'N 56°04'W
Newfoundland and Labrador d. Canada 61 M3
.... 55°44'N 56°53'W
New Galloway Scotland 14 E3 .... 55°05'N 4°08'W
New Georgia Sound str. Solomon Is 108 E6 ... 7°21'S 156°36'E
New Glasgow Canada 63 N6 .... 45°35'N 62°35'W
New Guinea i. Indonesia/P.N.G. 103 K2 ... 5°26'S 140°49'E
New Hampshire d. U.S. 63 L5 .... 44°02'N 71°34'W
Newhaven England 9 F1 .... 50°48'N 0°03'E
New Haven U.S. 63 L5 .... 41°18'N 72°56'W
New Ireland i. P.N.G. 108 E6 .... 3°33'S 152°14'E

New Jersey d. U.S. 63 L4 .... 39°57'N 74°26'W
New Liskeard Canada 63 K6 .... 47°31'N 79°41'W
Newmarket England 9 F3 .... 52°15'N 0°25'E
Newmarket-on-Fergus Ireland 18 C2 ... 52°46'N 8°53'W
New Mexico d. U.S. 62 E3 .... 34°32'N 105°55'W
New Milton England 8 D1 .... 50°45'N 1°40'W
Newnham England 8 C2 .... 51°48'N 2°27'W
New Orleans U.S. 63 H2 .... 29°58'N 90°03'W
New Pitsligo Scotland 17 G2 .... 57°36'N 2°12'W
Newport Ess. England 9 F2 .... 51°59'N 0°13'E
Newport I. o. W. England 8 D1 .... 50°42'N 1°17'W
Newport New. Wales 10 E3 .... 51°35'N 2°59'W
Newport Pem. Wales 10 C4 .... 52°01'N 4°50'W
Newport Tel. Wre. England 8 C3 .... 52°46'N 2°22'W
Newport d. Wales 21 D2 .... 51°35'N 2°59'W
Newport Bay Wales 10 C4 .... 52°02'N 4°53'W
Newport News U.S. 63 K4 .... 37°00'N 76°26'W
Newport Pagnell England 8 E3 .... 52°05'N 0°43'W
New Providence i. Bahamas 67 I6 ...... 25°03'N 77°25'W
Newquay England 11 B2 .... 50°25'N 5°04'W
New Quay Wales 10 C4 .... 52°13'N 4°22'W
New Romney England 9 F1 .... 50°59'N 0°56'E
New Ross Ireland 18 E2 .... 52°23'N 6°57'W
Newry Northern Ireland 14 C2 .... 54°10'N 6°19'W
Newry Canal Northern Ireland 14 C2 ... 54°16'N 6°21'W
Newry, Mourne and Down d. Northern Ireland 21 B4
.... 54°10'N 6°18'W
New Siberian Islands Russia 55 P5 .... 76°08'N 149°21'E
New South Wales d. Australia 108 D3 ... 32°42'S 146°24'E
Newton Abbot England 11 D2 .... 50°32'N 3°37'W
Newton Aycliffe England 13 F3 .... 54°37'N 1°34'W
Newtonbutler Northern Ireland 14 B2 ... 54°10'N 7°21'W
Newtonhill Scotland 17 G2 .... 57°02'N 2°09'W
Newton-le-Willows England 12 E2 .... 53°27'N 2°38'W
Newton Mearns Scotland 14 E3 .... 55°46'N 4°20'W
Newtonmore Scotland 17 E2 .... 57°04'N 4°07'W
Newton St Cyres England 11 D2 ...... 50°46'N 3°35'W
Newton Stewart Scotland 14 E2 .... 54°58'N 4°29'W
Newtown Wales 10 D4 .... 52°31'N 3°19'W
Newtownabbey Northern Ireland 14 D2 ... 54°39'N 5°54'W
Newtownards Northern Ireland 14 D2 ... 54°35'N 5°41'W
Newtown St Boswells Scotland 15 G3 ... 55°35'N 2°40'W
Newtownstewart Northern Ireland 14 B2 ... 54°43'N 7°22'W
New York U.S. 63 L5 .... 40°41'N 73°59'W
New York d. U.S. 63 K5 .... 42°43'N 75°14'W
New Zealand Oceania 109 G2 .... 42°54'S 174°10'E
Nexø Denmark 46 F6 .... 55°03'N 15°08'E
Neyrīz Iran 95 H5 .... 29°12'N 54°19'E
Neyshābūr Iran 95 I7 .... 36°12'N 58°46'E
Ngaoundéré Cameroon 84 F2 .... 7°19'N 13°34'E
Ngerulmud Palau 103 I5 .... 7°30'N 134°39'E
Nguigmi Niger 84 F3 .... 14°14'N 13°05'E
Ngulu atoll Micronesia 103 J5 .... 8°28'N 137°37'E
Nha Trang Vietnam 102 D6 .... 12°11'N 109°11'E
Niamey Niger 84 E3 .... 13°31'N 2°07'E
Niangara Dem. Rep. Congo 83 B5 ...... 3°40'N 27°52'E
Nias i. Indonesia 102 B4 .... 1°11'N 97°04'E
Nicaragua Central America 67 G3 ...... 13°13'N 85°57'W
Nicaragua, Lake Nicaragua 67 G3 ...... 11°31'N 85°17'W
Nice France 44 G3 .... 43°42'N 7°17'E
Nicobar Islands India 97 H2 .... 8°00'N 93°53'E
Nicosia Cyprus 51 J2 .... 35°10'N 33°22'E
Nicoya, Golfo de b. Costa Rica 67 H2 ... 9°42'N 84°48'W
Nidd r. England 13 F3 .... 54°01'N 1°13'W
Nidzica Poland 46 I5 .... 53°22'N 20°26'E
Niedersachsen d. Germany 42 G5 ...... 52°43'N 8°53'E
Nienburg/Weser Germany 46 C5 ...... 52°38'N 9°13'E
Niers r. Germany 42 F4 .... 51°42'N 5°57'E
Nieuwpoort Belgium 42 B4 .... 51°08'N 2°45'E
Nieves, Pico de las mt. Canary Islands 45 Y1
.... 27°57'N 15°34'W
Niğde Turkey 51 K3 .... 37°59'N 34°41'E
Niger Africa 84 E3 .... 17°03'N 10°05'E
Niger r. Africa 84 E2 .... 4°17'N 6°05'E
Nigeria Africa 84 E2 .... 9°09'N 7°54'E
Nigg Bay Scotland 17 E2 .... 57°43'N 4°05'W
Niigata Japan 104 C3 .... 37°55'N 139°03'E
Nijmegen Neth. 42 E4 .... 51°50'N 5°52'E
Nikel' Russia 43 G5 .... 69°24'N 30°13'E
Nikol'sk Russia 52 E3 .... 59°32'N 45°27'E
Nikopol Ukraine 47 P2 .... 47°34'N 34°24'E
Niksar Turkey 51 L5 .... 40°35'N 36°57'E
Nikšić Montenegro 50 C6 .... 42°46'N 18°56'E
Nikumaroro atoll Kiribati 109 H6 ...... 4°43'S 174°31'W
Nile r. Africa 85 H5 .... 30°11'N 31°06'E
Nile Delta Egypt 94 D6 .... 30°50'N 31°00'E
Nilgiri Hills India 96 E3 .... 11°08'N 76°28'E
Nîmes France 44 F3 .... 43°51'N 4°22'E
Ningbo China 99 M3 .... 29°54'N 121°34'E
Ningxia Huizu Zizhiqu d. China 99 J5 ... 37°11'N 105°28'E
Niobrara r. U.S. 62 G5 .... 42°46'N 98°02'W
Nioro Mali 84 B3 .... 15°14'N 9°36'W
Niort France 44 C5 .... 46°20'N 0°28'W
Nipigon Canada 61 J2 .... 49°00'N 88°17'W
Nipigon, Lake Canada 61 J2 .... 49°43'N 88°33'W
Nipissing, Lake Canada 63 K6 .... 46°15'N 79°39'W
Niš Serbia 50 D6 .... 43°19'N 21°54'E
Nith r. Scotland 15 F3 .... 55°02'N 3°36'W
Nitra Slovakia 46 H3 .... 48°19'N 18°05'E
Niue i. S. Pacific Oc. 109 I5 .... 19°03'S 169°45'W
Nivelles Belgium 42 D3 .... 50°36'N 4°20'E
Nizamabad India 96 E4 .... 18°40'N 78°07'E
Nizhnekamsk Russia 52 F3 .... 55°38'N 51°55'E
Nizhneudinsk Russia 55 K3 .... 54°55'N 98°58'E
Nizhnevartovsk Russia 54 I4 .... 60°56'N 76°38'E
Nizhniy Tagil Russia 52 F3 .... 57°56'N 59°56'E
Nizhniy Novgorod Russia 52 E3 .... 56°17'N 43°54'E
Nizhnyaya Tura Russia 52 F3 .... 58°38'N 59°51'E
Nizhnyaya Tunguska r. Russia 55 J4 ... 65°47'N 87°59'E
Nizhyn Ukraine 47 N4 .... 51°02'N 31°53'E
Nizip Turkey 51 L3 .... 36°59'N 37°48'E
Nkongsamba Cameroon 84 E2 .... 4°58'N 9°57'E
Nobeoka Japan 104 B2 .... 32°34'N 131°41'E
Nogales Mexico 66 B7 .... 31°19'N 110°57'W
Nogent-le-Rotrou France 44 D6 .... 48°19'N 0°49'E
Nohfelden Germany 42 G2 .... 49°35'N 7°08'E
Noirmoutier, Île de i. France 44 B5 .... 46°58'N 2°16'W
Nok Kundi Pakistan 95 J5 .... 28°49'N 62°50'E
Nolinsk Russia 52 F3 .... 57°33'N 49°57'E
Nome U.S. 60 B4 .... 64°32'N 165°28'W
Nonthaburi Thailand 102 C6 .... 13°51'N 100°32'E
Noord-Brabant d. Neth. 42 E4 .... 51°32'N 5°01'E
Noord-Holland d. Neth. 42 D5 .... 52°37'N 4°55'E
Nordaustlandet i. Arctic Oc. 54 D5 .... 79°36'N 22°37'E
Norden Germany 42 G6 .... 53°36'N 7°12'E
Norderney i. Germany 42 G6 .... 53°44'N 7°19'E
Norderstedt Germany 46 D5 .... 53°44'N 10°00'E

Nordhausen Germany 46 D4 ....51°30'N 10°47'E
Nordhorn Germany 42 G5.....................52°26'N 7°05'E
Nordrhein-Westfalen d. Germany 42 G4...51°04'N 7°25'E
Nore r. Ireland 18 E2 ....52°25'N 6°58'W
Norfolk d. England 21 F3.......................52°44'N 0°59'E
Norfolk U.S. 63 K4...............................36°53'N 76°16'W
Norfolk Broads f. England 9 G3..............52°43'N 1°28'E
Norfolk Island S. Pacific Oc. 109 F4........28°59'S 167°59'E
Noril'sk Russia 55 J4.............................69°19'N 88°08'E
Normandy f. France 44 C6.....................48°53'N 0°32'W
Normanton Australia 108 D5.................17°41'S 141°05'E
Norra Storfjället mts Sweden 43 C4.........65°53'N 15°07'E
Norrköping Sweden 43 D2.....................58°36'N 16°12'E
Norrtälje Sweden 43 D2.........................59°45'N 18°41'E
Norseman Australia 108 B3....................32°14'S 121°47'E
Northallerton England 13 F3...................54°20'N 1°26'W
North America 56
North American Basin f. Atlantic Oc. 116 D3
....30°00'N 60°00'W
Northampton England 8 E3....................52°14'N 0°54'W
Northamptonshire d. England 21 E3........52°12'N 0°57'W
North Ayrshire d. Scotland 20 C4............55°44'N 4°44'W
North Battleford Canada 60 H3..............52°46'N 108°17'W
North Bay town Canada 61 K2................46°19'N 79°28'W
North Berwick Scotland 15 G4................56°04'N 2°43'W
North Cape New Zealand 109 G3............34°25'S 173°03'E
North Cape Norway 43 F5......................71°10'N 25°47'E
North Carolina d. U.S. 63 K4..................36°13'N 79°52'W
North Cave England 13 G2......................53°47'N 0°39'W
North Channel U.K. 14 C3......................55°23'N 6°13'W
North China Plain f. China 86 G3.............34°30'N 117°00'E
North Dakota d. U.S. 62 F6.....................47°19'N 100°24'W
North Dorset Downs hills England 8 C1....50°46'N 2°32'W
North Downs hills England 9 E2...............51°14'N 0°58'W
North East Lincolnshire d. England 21 E3..53°37'N 0°13'W
Northern Ireland d. U.K. 21 B4...............54°38'N 6°49'W
Northern Mariana Islands N. Pacific Oc. 103 K7
....17°15'N 143°32'E
Northern Territory d. Australia 108 C5.....17°40'S 133°30'E
North Esk r. Scotland 17 G1....................56°45'N 2°26'W
North European Plain f. Europe 34 G4......56°00'N 27°00'E
North Foreland c. England 9 G2..............51°23'N 1°27'E
North Frisian Islands Germany 46 C6........54°52'N 8°02'E
North Harris f. Scotland 16 C2.................57°59'N 6°48'W
North Hykeham England 13 G2...............53°11'N 0°35'W
North Island / Te Ika-a-Māui New Zealand 109 G3
....38°11'S 173°23'E
North Korea Asia 99 N6..........................40°01'N 126°39'E
North Lanarkshire d. Scotland 20 D4........55°53'N 3°57'W
North Lincolnshire d. England 21 E3.........53°37'N 0°35'W
North Macedonia Europe 50 D5...............41°31'N 21°46'E
North Platte U.S. 62 F5..........................41°09'N 100°46'W
North Platte r. U.S. 62 F5.......................41°10'N 100°48'W
North Ronaldsay i. Scotland 17 G4...........59°24'N 2°26'W
North Ronaldsay Firth str. Scotland 17 G4
....59°20'N 2°29'W
North Saskatchewan r. Canada 60 H3......53°13'N 105°11'W
North Sea Europe 34 E4.........................56°00'N 4°00'E
North Shields England 13 F4....................55°01'N 1°27'W
North Siberian Lowland f. Russia 55 L5.....73°26'N 103°17'E
North Somercotes England 13 H2............53°27'N 0°09'E
North Somerset d. England 21 D2............51°24'N 2°48'W
North Sunderland England 13 F4.............55°35'N 1°39'W
North Tidworth England 8 D2..................51°14'N 1°40'W
North Tyne r. England 13 E3...................54°59'N 2°08'W
North Ugie r. Scotland 17 H2..................57°32'N 1°55'W
North Uist i. Scotland 16 B2....................57°37'N 7°26'W
Northumberland d. England 20 D4...........55°09'N 2°35'W
Northumberland Strait Canada 63 N6.......46°50'N 64°43'W
North Walsham England 9 G3.................52°49'N 1°23'E
North West Cape Australia 108 A4...........21°49'S 114°12'E
Northwest Territories d. Canada 60 H4.....63°48'N 105°17'W
Northwich England 13 E2.......................53°16'N 2°31'W
North York Moors f. England 13 G3..........54°23'N 0°50'W
North Yorkshire d. England 21 E4.............54°12'N 1°59'W
Norton England 13 G3...........................54°08'N 0°47'W
Norton Fitzwarren England 11 D2...........51°02'N 3°08'W
Norton Sound str. U.S. 60 B4..................63°58'N 163°01'W
Norway f. Europe 43 B3.........................62°46'N 10°30'E
Norway House Canada 60 I3...................53°56'N 97°52'W
Norwegian Sea f. Atlantic Oc. 34 D5........66°00'N 2°00'E
Norwich England 9 G3...........................52°38'N 1°18'E
Noshiro Japan 104 D4............................40°12'N 140°01'E
Nosovaya Russia 52 F4...........................68°15'N 54°35'E
Noss, Isle of i. Scotland 17 H5................60°09'N 1°00'W
Nottingham England 8 D3......................52°57'N 1°09'W
Nottingham d. England 21 E3..................52°58'N 1°10'W
Nottinghamshire d. England 21 E3...........53°03'N 0°59'W
Nouadhibou Mauritania 84 C3................21°04'N 17°00'W
Nouakchott Mauritania 84 C3.................18°06'N 15°58'W
Nouméa New Caledonia 109 F4..............22°18'S 166°26'E
Noup Head Scotland 17 F4.....................59°20'N 3°04'W
Nova Gradiška Croatia 50 B7...................45°16'N 17°23'E
Novara Italy 46 C1................................45°27'N 8°37'E
Nova Scotia d. Canada 61 L2..................43°53'N 65°45'W
Novaya Sibir', Ostrov i. Russia 55 P5.......75°04'N 148°22'E
Novaya Zemlya is Russia 54 G5...............71°41'N 55°45'E
Nové Zámky Slovakia 46 H2....................47°59'N 18°09'E
Novi Pazar Serbia 50 D6........................43°08'N 20°30'E
Novi Sad Serbia 50 C7............................45°16'N 19°51'E
Novoanninskiy Russia 53 E3...................50°32'N 42°41'E
Novodvinsk Russia 52 E4........................64°25'N 40°50'E
Novo Hamburgo Brazil 73 D4................29°40'S 51°09'W
Novohrad-Volynskyi Ukraine 47 L4.........50°36'N 27°37'E
Novokuznetsk Russia 54 J3.....................53°45'N 87°09'E
Novo Mesto Slovenia 46 F1....................45°48'N 15°10'E
Novomoskovsk Russia 53 D3...................54°01'N 38°19'E
Novomoskovsk Ukraine 47 P3.................48°38'N 35°14'E
Novooleksiivka Ukraine 51 K8................46°14'N 34°39'E
Novorossiysk Russia 53 D2.....................44°43'N 37°47'E
Novosibirsk Russia 54 J3.........................55°03'N 83°02'E
Novovolynsk Ukraine 47 K4....................50°43'N 24°11'E
Novyy Port Russia 54 I4..........................68°13'N 73°02'E
Nowshera Pakistan 95 L6........................34°00'N 72°01'E
Nowy Sącz Poland 46 I3.........................49°38'N 20°42'E
Ntomba, Lac l. Dem. Rep. Congo 83 A4...0°52'S 18°05'E
Nuajaat town Canada 61 J4....................66°32'N 86°08'W
Nu'aym f. Oman 95 I4...........................23°14'N 55°59'E
Nuba Mountains Sudan 94 D2.................11°46'N 30°31'E
Nubian Desert Sudan 85 H4....................20°25'N 34°58'E
Nudo Coropuna mt. Peru 72 B5...............15°33'S 72°37'W
Nueva Casas Grandes Mexico 66 C7.........30°23'N 107°56'W
Nuevo Laredo Mexico 66 E6...................27°29'N 99°31'W
Nuevo León d. Mexico 66 E6..................25°51'N 99°50'W
Nui atoll Tuvalu 109 G6..........................7°12'S 177°12'E

Nuku'alofa Tonga 109 H4.......................21°07'S 175°12'W
Nukufetau atoll Tuvalu 109 G6.................8°03'S 178°25'E
Nukunonu atoll Tokelau 109 H6...............9°05'S 171°50'W
Nukus Uzbekistan 54 G2.........................42°27'N 59°36'E
Nullarbor Plain f. Australia 108 B3............31°01'S 129°03'E
Numazu Japan 104 C3............................35°05'N 138°52'E
Nunatsiavut f. Canada 61 L3...................56°30'N 62°30'W
Nunavut d. Canada 61 I4........................66°30'N 89°54'W
Nuneaton England 8 D3.........................52°31'N 1°28'W
Nunivak Island U.S. 60 B3......................59°58'N 166°18'W
Nuoro Italy 48 E5..................................40°19'N 9°20'E
Nuqrah Saudi Arabia 94 F5.....................25°36'N 41°26'E
Nuremberg Germany 46 D3....................49°27'N 11°06'E
Nurmes Finland 43 G3...........................63°33'N 29°07'E
Nusantara Indonesia 102 D3....................0°58'S 116°42'E
Nushki Pakistan 95 K5...........................29°34'N 66°02'E
Nyagan' Russia 52 G4............................62°09'N 65°24'E
Nyala Sudan 85 G3................................12°03'N 24°55'E
Nyasa, Lake Africa 83 C4.........................9°59'S 34°05'E
Nyborg Denmark 43 B1...........................55°19'N 10°47'E
Nybro Sweden 43 C2...............................56°44'N 15°55'E
Nyíregyháza Hungary 47 I2.....................47°57'N 21°43'E
Nykarleby Finland 43 E3.........................63°31'N 22°33'E
Nykøbing Falster Denmark 43 B1..............54°46'N 11°53'E
Nyköping Sweden 43 D2.........................58°45'N 17°01'E
Nynäshamn Sweden 43 D2.....................58°54'N 17°57'E
Nyrob Russia 52 F4................................60°43'N 56°42'E
Nyurba Russia 55 M4.............................63°17'N 118°17'E
Nyzhnohirskyi Ukraine 51 K7...................45°27'N 34°45'E

O

Oadby England 8 D3..............................52°36'N 1°05'W
Oahe, Lake U.S. 62 F5............................44°49'N 100°32'W
Oakengates England 8 C3.......................52°42'N 2°26'W
Oakham England 8 E3.............................52°40'N 0°44'W
Oakland U.S. 62 B4................................37°50'N 122°15'W
Oaxaca Mexico 66 E4..............................17°05'N 96°40'W
Oaxaca d. Mexico 66 E4..........................17°22'N 96°20'W
Ob' r. Russia 52 G4................................66°47'N 69°08'E
Oban Scotland 14 D4..............................56°25'N 5°28'W
Obi i. Indonesia 103 H3..........................1°33'S 127°41'E
Obihiro Japan 104 D4.............................42°55'N 143°11'E
Obninsk Russia 52 D3............................55°04'N 36°38'E
Oboyan' Russia 47 Q4.............................51°13'N 36°16'E
Obozerskiy Russia 52 E4.........................63°28'N 40°19'E
Obshchiy Syrt f. Russia 53 F3..................51°20'N 52°00'E
Ob"yachevo Russia 52 F4.......................60°20'N 49°37'E
Occidental, Cordillera mts Colombia 72 B7
....1°36'N 77°47'W
Occidental, Cordillera mts Peru 72 B5.....16°07'S 71°46'W
Ocean Falls town Canada 60 F3...............52°21'N 127°41'W
Oceania 106
Oceanside U.S. 62 C3.............................33°12'N 117°23'W
Ocher Russia 52 F3................................57°55'N 54°44'E
Ochil Hills Scotland 15 F4.......................56°12'N 3°49'W
Oda, Jebel mt. Sudan 85 H4....................20°20'N 36°39'E
Ódáðahraun f. Iceland 43 Y2...................64°48'N 17°37'W
Ōdate Japan 104 D4...............................40°16'N 140°34'E
Ōdemiş Turkey 51 G4.............................38°13'N 27°58'E
Odense Denmark 43 B1...........................55°24'N 10°23'E
Oder r. Germany 46 C4...........................51°43'N 9°56'E
Odesa Ukraine 49 J6..............................46°28'N 30°39'E
Odessa U.S. 62 F3..................................31°50'N 102°20'W
Odintsovo Russia 47 Q6.........................55°40'N 37°18'E
Odisha d. India 96 F5.............................20°57'N 84°15'E
Odra r. Germany/Poland 46 H3...............49°54'N 18°19'E
Offaly d. Ireland 18 D3..........................53°15'N 7°35'W
Offenbach am Main Germany 46 C4.........50°06'N 8°46'E
Offenburg Germany 46 B3......................48°29'N 7°57'E
Ogaden f. Ethiopia 85 I2.........................7°09'N 45°27'E
Ōgaki Japan 104 C3...............................35°21'N 136°37'E
Ogbomoso Nigeria 84 E2........................8°08'N 4°14'E
Ogden U.S. 62 D5..................................41°14'N 111°57'W
Ogilvie r. Canada 60 E4..........................65°50'N 137°13'W
Oglio r. Italy 46 D1................................45°01'N 10°40'E
Ogoki r. Canada 63 I7.............................51°40'N 85°58'W
Ogulin Croatia 50 A7..............................45°16'N 15°14'E
Ohio d. U.S. 63 J5..................................40°27'N 82°28'W
Ohio r. U.S. 63 I4...................................37°05'N 89°12'W
Ohrid North Macedonia 50 D5..................41°07'N 20°49'E
Ohrid, Lake Albania/North Macedonia 50 D5
....41°02'N 20°43'E
Oich r. Scotland 16 E2............................57°09'N 4°40'W
Oich, Loch l. Scotland 16 E2...................57°04'N 4°46'W
Oise r. France 44 E6...............................49°59'N 2°04'E
Ōita Japan 104 B2..................................33°13'N 131°37'E
Oiti mt. Greece 50 E4.............................38°48'N 22°16'E
Ojinaga Mexico 66 D6............................29°33'N 104°25'W
Ojos del Salado, Cerro mt. Argentina/Chile 73 C4
....27°06'S 68°35'W
Oka r. Russia 47 Q5...............................56°20'N 43°59'E
Okanogan r. U.S. 62 C6.........................48°06'N 119°41'W
Okavango Delta f. Botswana 83 B3...........19°42'S 23°02'E
Okaya Japan 104 C3...............................36°03'N 138°04'E
Okayama Japan 104 B2...........................34°39'N 133°55'E
Okeechobee, Lake U.S. 63 J2..................26°56'N 81°00'W
Okehampton England 11 C2....................50°44'N 4°00'W
Okha India 96 C5...................................22°26'N 69°08'E
Okha Russia 55 P3.................................53°33'N 143°01'E
Okhotsk Russia 55 P3............................59°22'N 143°22'E
Okhotsk, Sea of Japan/Russia 104 D4.......44°58'N 144°06'E
Okhtyrka Ukraine 47 P4.........................50°19'N 34°54'E
Okinawa Jima i. Japan 99 N3..................26°27'N 127°58'E
Oki Shotō is Japan 104 B3.......................36°07'N 133°26'E
Oklahoma d. U.S. 62 G4.........................35°41'N 97°24'W
Oklahoma City U.S. 62 G4......................35°31'N 97°31'W
Okovskiy Les f. Russia 52 D3...................56°10'N 34°20'E
Oksskolten mt. Norway 43 C4..................66°01'N 14°20'E
Oktyabr'skiy Russia 52 G3.......................61°05'N 43°07'E
Oktyabr'skiy Russia 53 F3.......................54°28'N 53°28'E
Oktyabr'skoye Russia 52 G4....................62°27'N 66°22'E
Oktyabr'skoy Revolyutsii, Ostrov i. Russia 55 K5
....79°00'N 96°42'E
Öland i. Sweden 43 D2...........................56°57'N 17°02'E
Olbia Italy 48 E5....................................40°55'N 9°30'E
Old Crow Canada 60 E4.........................67°36'N 139°54'W
Oldenburg Germany 46 C5......................53°09'N 8°14'E
Oldenzaal Neth. 42 F5............................52°19'N 6°54'E
Oldham England 13 E2...........................53°33'N 2°07'W
Old Head of Kinsale Ireland 18 C1............51°36'N 8°31'W
Old Leake England 13 H2........................53°02'N 0°06'E
Oldmeldrum Scotland 17 G2...................57°20'N 2°19'W

Olean U.S. 63 K5...................................42°05'N 78°26'W
Olekma r. Russia 55 N4...........................60°05'N 121°07'E
Olekminsk Russia 55 N4.........................60°24'N 120°21'E
Oleksandriia Ukraine 47 O3.....................48°41'N 33°07'E
Olenek Russia 55 M4.............................68°28'N 112°26'E
Olenek r. Russia 55 M5...........................72°58'N 119°45'E
Olenekskiy Zaliv b. Russia 55 N5.............73°22'N 121°09'E
Oléron, Île d' i. France 44 C4...................45°55'N 1°20'W
Olevsk Ukraine 47 L4.............................51°13'N 27°39'E
Olney England 8 E3................................52°09'N 0°42'W
Olomouc Czechia 46 G3..........................49°35'N 17°16'E
Olonets Russia 52 D4.............................60°58'N 32°59'E
Oloron-Ste-Marie France 44 C3................43°12'N 0°36'W
Olsztyn Poland 46 I5..............................53°47'N 20°29'E
Oltet r. Romania 50 F7...........................44°22'N 24°07'E
Olympia U.S. 62 B6................................47°02'N 122°53'W
Olympos mt. Cyprus 51 J2.......................34°56'N 32°51'E
Olympus, Mount Greece 50 E5................40°05'N 22°21'E
Olympus, Mount U.S. 62 B6...................47°45'N 123°42'W
Olyutorskiy Zaliv b. Russia 55 R3.............59°51'N 168°08'E
Omagh Northern Ireland 14 B2................54°36'N 7°17'W
Omaha U.S. 62 G5.................................41°17'N 95°58'W
Oman Asia 95 H3..................................18°15'N 53°34'E
Oman, Gulf of Asia 95 I5........................25°37'N 56°49'E
Ombersley England 8 C3........................52°16'N 2°14'W
Omdurman Sudan 85 H3........................15°38'N 32°28'E
Ommen Neth. 42 F5...............................52°32'N 6°25'E
Omolon r. Russia 55 Q4.........................68°44'N 158°43'E
Omono Gawa r. Japan 104 D3.................39°41'N 140°04'E
Omsk Russia 54 I3.................................55°00'N 73°22'E
Omsukchan Russia 55 Q4.......................62°25'N 155°43'E
Omulew r. Poland 46 I5..........................53°04'N 21°33'E
Ōmuta Japan 104 B2...............................33°02'N 130°28'E
Onchan Isle of Man 12 C3.......................54°11'N 4°27'W
Ondjiva Angola 83 A3.............................17°04'S 15°44'E
Onega Russia 52 D4..............................63°55'N 38°02'E
Onega r. Russia 52 D4............................63°55'N 38°07'E
Onega, Lake Russia 52 D4.......................62°05'N 35°21'E
Oneşti Romania 50 G8............................46°16'N 26°46'E
Ongole India 96 F4................................15°32'N 80°02'E
Onitsha Nigeria 84 E2............................6°08'N 6°48'E
Ono-i-Lau i. Fiji 109 H4...........................20°39'S 178°45'W
Ontario d. Canada 61 I3..........................51°51'N 91°22'W
Ontario, Lake Canada/U.S. 61 K2.............43°31'N 77°57'W
Ontong Java Atoll Solomon Is 109 E6.......5°24'S 159°34'E
Oosterschelde est. Neth. 42 C4................51°38'N 3°35'E
Oost-Vlaanderen d. Belgium 42 C3...........50°56'N 3°44'E
Opala Dem. Rep. Congo 83 B4................0°36'S 24°22'E
Opava Czechia 46 G3.............................49°56'N 17°54'E
Opochka Russia 43 G2............................56°43'N 28°41'E
Opole Poland 46 G4...............................50°40'N 17°56'E
Oporto Portugal 45 A4...........................41°11'N 8°36'W
Oradea Romania 47 I2............................47°04'N 21°57'E
Oral Kazakhstan 53 F3...........................51°11'N 51°24'E
Oran Algeria 84 D5................................35°42'N 0°38'W
Orange France 44 F4..............................44°09'N 4°49'E
Orange r. Namibia/S. Africa 83 A2............28°36'S 16°28'E
Orange, Cabo c. Brazil 72 D7..................4°22'N 51°17'W
Oranmore Ireland 18 C3.........................53°16'N 8°55'W
Orchila, Isla i. Venezuela 67 K3...............11°45'N 66°09'W
Orchy r. Scotland 14 D4.........................56°24'N 5°01'W
Ord, Mount hill Australia 108 B5.............17°19'S 125°29'E
Ordu Turkey 51 L5.................................40°59'N 37°53'E
Örebro Sweden 43 C2.............................59°16'N 15°14'E
Oregon d. U.S. 62 B5.............................43°43'N 120°32'W
Orël Russia 53 D3..................................52°58'N 36°05'E
Orenburg Russia 53 F3............................51°46'N 55°05'E
Orford Ness hd England 9 G3...................52°05'N 1°35'E
Orhei Moldova 47 M2............................47°22'N 28°50'E
Oriental, Cordillera mts Bolivia 72 C5........16°47'S 66°35'W
Oriental, Cordillera mts Colombia 72 B7....6°42'N 72°45'W
Oriental, Cordillera mts Peru 72 B5...........10°29'S 74°41'W
Orillia Canada 63 K5..............................44°36'N 79°25'W
Orinoco r. Col./Venez. 72 C7...................8°35'N 61°50'W
Orinoco Delta Venezuela 72 C7...............9°22'N 60°44'W
Oristano Italy 48 E4...............................39°55'N 8°35'E
Orivesi l. Finland 43 G3..........................62°14'N 29°27'E
Orizaba Mexico 66 E4.............................18°53'N 97°06'W
Örkelljunga Sweden 46 E7......................56°17'N 13°17'E
Orkney d. Scotland 20 D6.......................58°59'N 2°42'W
Orkney Islands Scotland 17 F4.................59°06'N 3°20'W
Orlando U.S. 63 J2.................................28°31'N 81°21'W
Orléans France 44 D5.............................47°55'N 1°54'E
Ormoc Phil. 103 G6................................11°00'N 124°37'E
Ormskirk England 12 E2.........................53°34'N 2°53'W
Orne r. France 44 C6..............................49°16'N 0°14'W
Örnsköldsvik Sweden 43 D3....................63°18'N 18°43'E
Oronsay i. Scotland 14 C4.......................56°01'N 6°12'W
Orrin r. Scotland 17 E2............................57°33'N 4°29'W
Orrin Reservoir Scotland 16 E2.................57°30'N 4°45'W
Orsha Belarus 47 N6..............................54°30'N 30°26'E
Orsk Russia 53 F3..................................51°07'N 58°33'E
Orşova Romania 50 E7............................44°42'N 22°25'E
Oruro Bolivia 72 C5...............................17°59'S 67°09'W
Osa, Península de pen. Costa Rica 67 H2...8°34'N 83°32'W
Ōsaka Japan 104 C2...............................34°42'N 135°30'E
Oshakati Namibia 83 A3.........................17°45'S 15°43'E
Oshawa Canada 61 K2............................43°54'N 78°51'W
Osh Uzbekistan 54 C5............................42°01'N 4°31'E
Osijek Croatia 50 C7...............................45°35'N 18°42'E
Ōsjön l. Sweden 43 C3............................63°11'N 14°39'E
Oskarshamn Sweden 43 D2.....................57°16'N 16°26'E
Öskemen Kazakhstan 54 J2.....................49°57'N 82°46'E
Oslo Norway 43 B2................................59°55'N 10°46'E
Osmancık Turkey 51 K5..........................40°58'N 34°48'E
Osmaniye Turkey 51 L3..........................37°04'N 36°15'E
Osnabrück Germany 46 C5......................52°17'N 8°04'E
Osorno Chile 73 B2................................40°35'S 73°09'W
Osorno Spain 45 C5................................42°25'N 4°21'W
Oss Neth. 42 E4....................................51°45'N 5°32'E
Ossa mt. Greece 50 E4............................39°48'N 22°41'E
Ossa, Mount Australia 108 D2..................41°56'S 146°12'E
Ostend Belgium 42 B4............................51°13'N 2°55'E
Österdalälven r. Sweden 43 C3................61°40'N 13°15'E
Österdalen f. Norway 43 B3.....................62°05'N 10°36'E
Östersund Sweden 43 C3........................63°11'N 14°39'E
Ostrava Czechia 46 H3...........................49°51'N 18°17'E
Ostróda Poland 46 H5............................53°42'N 19°59'E
Ostrov Russia 52 D4..............................53°42'N 26°32'E
Ostrowiec Świętokrzyski Poland 47 I4.......50°56'N 21°24'E
Ostrów Mazowiecka Poland 47 I5.............52°48'N 21°53'E
Ostrów Wielkopolski Poland 46 G4..........51°39'N 17°49'E
Ostrzeszów Poland 46 G4.......................51°25'N 17°56'E
Osŭm r. Bulgaria 50 F6...........................43°42'N 24°51'E
Ōsumi Kaikyō str. Japan 104 B2...............30°50'N 130°52'E

Ōsumi Shotō is Japan 104 B2...................30°32'N 130°36'E
Osuna Spain 45 C2.................................37°14'N 5°06'W
Oswestry England 8 B3..........................52°51'N 3°03'W
Otaru Japan 104 D4...............................43°12'N 140°59'E
Otjiwarongo Namibia 83 A2.....................20°28'S 16°40'E
Otley England 13 F2...............................53°54'N 1°41'W
Otranto Italy 50 C5................................40°09'N 18°30'E
Otranto, Strait of Albania/Italy 50 C5.......40°36'N 18°42'E
Otta Norway 43 B3................................61°46'N 9°31'E
Ottawa Canada 61 K2............................45°25'N 75°40'W
Ottawa r. Canada 61 K2.........................45°28'N 74°16'W
Ottawa Islands Canada 61 J3..................59°57'N 80°09'W
Otter r. England 11 D2...........................50°38'N 3°18'W
Otterburn England 13 E4........................55°14'N 2°11'W
Ottery r. England 11 C2..........................50°39'N 4°20'W
Ottignies Belgium 42 D3........................50°39'N 4°34'E
Otukpo Nigeria 84 E2.............................7°13'N 8°05'E
Ouachita r. U.S. 63 H3...........................31°50'N 91°49'W
Ouagadougou Burkina Faso 84 D3...........12°22'N 1°31'W
Ouargla Algeria 84 E5.............................31°59'N 5°20'E
Ouarzazate Morocco 84 D5......................30°56'N 6°54'W
Oudenaarde Belgium 42 C3......................50°51'N 3°36'E
Ouessant, Île d' i. France 44 A5................48°28'N 5°05'W
Ouezzane Morocco 48 B3........................34°46'N 5°32'W
Oughter, Lough l. Ireland 18 D4...............54°01'N 7°28'W
Ouistreham France 44 C6........................49°17'N 0°16'W
Oujda Morocco 84 D5.............................34°44'N 1°54'W
Oulainen Finland 43 F4...........................64°16'N 24°49'E
Oulton England 9 G3..............................52°30'N 1°43'E
Oulu Finland 43 F4.................................65°01'N 25°30'E
Oulujärvi l. Finland 43 F4.........................64°17'N 27°15'E
Oundle England 9 E3..............................52°29'N 0°28'E
Oupeye Belgium 42 E3............................50°42'N 5°39'E
Ourense Spain 45 B5.............................42°21'N 7°51'E
Ouse r. E. Sussex England 9 F1................50°48'N 0°03'E
Ouse r. E. Yorks. England 13 G2..............53°44'N 0°54'W
Outer Hebrides is Scotland 16 B2.............57°53'N 7°21'W
Outokumpu Finland 43 G3......................62°43'N 29°01'E
Out Skerries is Scotland 17 I5..................60°26'N 0°47'E
Ovamboland f. Namibia 83 A3.................17°50'S 15°41'E
Overijssel d. Neth. 42 F5.........................52°25'N 6°32'E
Overton Wales 10 E4..............................52°58'N 2°56'W
Övertorneå Sweden 43 E4.......................66°24'N 23°37'E
Oviedo/Uviéu Spain 45 C5......................43°22'N 5°50'W
Ovruch Ukraine 47 M4............................51°20'N 28°49'E
Owando Congo 84 F1.............................0°29'S 15°55'E
Owen Stanley Range mts P.N.G. 108 D6...8°59'S 147°57'E
Owyhee r. U.S. 62 C5.............................43°48'N 117°04'W
Öxarfjörður b. Iceland 43 Y2....................66°12'N 16°47'W
Oxelösund Sweden 43 D2........................58°40'N 17°05'E
Oxford England 8 D2..............................51°45'N 1°15'W
Oxfordshire d. England 21 E2..................51°54'N 1°27'W
Oxnard U.S. 62 C3.................................34°12'N 119°12'W
Oxted England 9 F2...............................51°16'N 0°01'E
Oyama Japan 104 C3..............................36°18'N 139°48'E
Oykel r. Scotland 16 E2...........................57°54'N 4°24'W
Ozark Plateau f. U.S. 63 H4.....................36°58'N 93°31'W
Ozarks, Lake of the U.S. 63 H4................38°14'N 93°08'W
Özd Hungary 46 I3.................................48°13'N 20°19'E
Ozernovskiy Russia 55 Q3......................51°30'N 156°35'E

P

Paamiut Greenland 61 N4.......................62°01'N 49°40'W
Pabbay i. Na h-E. S. Scotland 16 B1.........56°51'N 7°34'W
Pabbay i. Na h-E. S. Scotland 16 B2.........57°46'N 7°18'W
Pabianice Poland 46 H4..........................51°40'N 19°22'E
Pachuca Mexico 66 E5............................20°09'N 98°44'W
Pacific Ocean 116 B3
Padang Indonesia 102 C3.........................0°58'S 100°22'E
Paderborn Germany 46 C4......................51°43'N 8°45'E
Padiham England 13 E2..........................53°48'N 2°19'W
Padre Island U.S. 62 G2..........................26°57'N 97°22'W
Padstow England 11 C2...........................50°32'N 4°56'W
Padua Italy 46 D1..................................45°24'N 11°53'E
Pag i. Croatia 50 A7...............................44°31'N 14°53'E
Pagadian Phil. 103 G5.............................7°50'N 123°29'E
Pagai Selatan i. Indonesia 102 C3.............2°58'S 100°24'E
Pagai Utara i. Indonesia 102 C3................2°36'S 100°04'E
Pagan i. N. Mariana Is 103 L7..................18°08'N 145°49'E
Paget, Mount S. Atlantic Oc. 73 F1...........54°23'S 36°44'W
Paignton England 11 D2..........................50°26'N 3°34'W
Päijänne l. Finland 43 F3.........................61°30'N 25°26'E
Painswick England 8 C2..........................51°47'N 2°12'W
Paisley Scotland 14 E3............................55°51'N 4°26'W
Pakanbaru Indonesia 102 C4....................0°34'N 101°30'E
Pakaraima Mountains S. America 67 L1.....3°47'N 63°40'W
Pakistan Asia 96 C6...............................28°01'N 64°37'E
Pakokku Myanmar 97 I5..........................21°21'N 95°07'E
Pakxe Laos 102 D7................................15°04'N 105°50'E
Palana Russia 55 Q3...............................59°05'N 159°52'E
Palangkaraya Indonesia 102 E3................2°18'S 113°55'E
Palatka Russia 55 Q4..............................60°08'N 150°56'E
Palau N. Pacific Oc. 103 I5.......................7°23'N 134°07'E
Palawan i. Phil. 102 F5...........................8°50'N 117°43'E
Palembang Indonesia 102 C3....................2°56'S 104°46'E
Palencia Spain 45 C5.............................42°01'N 4°31'W
Palermo Italy 48 F4................................38°07'N 13°21'E
Pali India 96 D6....................................25°46'N 73°26'E
Palikir Fed. States of Micronesia 115 I3......6°55'N 158°09'E
Palk Strait India/Sri Lanka 96 E2..............9°36'N 79°18'E
Palma Spain 45 G3.................................39°35'N 2°40'E
Palmas Brazil 72 E5...............................10°20'S 48°14'W
Palmas, Cape Liberia 84 D2.....................4°22'N 7°32'W
Palmerston atoll Cook Is 109 J5................18°01'S 163°03'W
Palmira Colombia 72 B7..........................3°31'N 76°16'W
Palmerston North New Zealand 109 G2.....40°22'S 175°37'E
Palopo Indonesia 102 G3.........................3°01'S 120°11'E
Palos, Cabo de c. Spain 45 E2..................37°37'N 0°41'W
Palu Indonesia 102 F3.............................0°54'S 119°54'E
Pamiers France 44 D3.............................43°07'N 1°37'E
Pamirs mts Asia 95 L7.............................38°39'N 72°48'E
Pampas f. Argentina 73 C3......................36°23'S 64°07'W
Pamplona/Iruña Spain 45 E5....................42°49'N 1°39'W
Panagyurishte Bulgaria 50 F6..................42°30'N 24°11'E
Panaji India 96 D4.................................15°30'N 73°50'E
Panama Central America 67 H2................8°22'N 81°33'W
Panama, Gulf of Panama 67 I2..................7°38'N 79°19'W
Panama, Isthmus of f. C. America 56 F2.....9°00'N 80°00'W
Panama Canal Panama 67 I2.....................9°07'N 79°45'W
Panamá City Panama 67 I2......................8°56'N 79°36'W
Panama City U.S. 63 I3...........................30°10'N 85°40'W
Panay i. Phil. 103 G6..............................11°10'N 122°30'E
Pančevo Serbia 50 D7.............................44°52'N 20°40'E

anevėžys Lithuania 43 F1 .... 55°44'N 24°23'E
angkalanbuun Indonesia 102 E3 .... 2°40'S 111°38'E
angkalpinang Indonesia 102 D3 .... 2°08'S 106°06'E
angnirtung Canada 61 L4 .... 66°03'N 65°48'W
anjgur Pakistan 95 J5 .... 26°58'N 64°07'E
antelleria, Isola di i. Italy 48 F4 .... 36°47'N 12°04'E
anzhihua China 99 I3 .... 26°35'N 101°43'E
apa Stour i. Scotland 17 H5 .... 60°21'N 1°42'W
apa Westray i. Scotland 17 G4 .... 59°22'N 2°52'W
apenburg Germany 42 G6 .... 53°05'N 7°24'E
aphos Cyprus 51 J2 .... 34°47'N 32°25'E
apua, Gulf of P.N.G. 108 D6 .... 8°34'S 144°45'E
apua New Guinea Oceania 108 D6 .... 6°05'S 146°34'E
ar England 11 C2 .... 50°21'N 4°42'W
aracel Islands S. China Sea 102 E7 .... 16°46'N 112°39'E
araguai r. Brazil 72 D5 .... 22°06'S 57°57'W
araguay r. Argentina/Paraguay 73 D4 .... 27°12'S 58°39'W
araguay S. America 73 D4 .... 22°45'S 58°44'W
arakou Benin 84 E2 .... 9°22'N 2°36'E
aramaribo Suriname 72 D7 .... 5°51'N 55°17'W
araná Argentina 73 C3 .... 31°44'S 60°31'W
araná r. S. America 73 D3 .... 33°52'S 59°12'W
aranaguá Brazil 73 E4 .... 25°32'S 48°33'W
aranaíba r. Brazil 72 D5 .... 20°04'S 51°00'W
arângul Mare, Vârful mt. Romania 50 E7 .... 45°21'N 23°33'E
ardubice Czechia 46 F4 .... 50°03'N 15°47'E
arecis, Serra dos hills Brazil 72 C5 .... 11°28'S 63°12'W
arepare Indonesia 102 F3 .... 4°01'S 119°40'E
aria, Península de i. Venezuela 67 L3 .. 10°43'N 62°58'W
arima, Serra mts Brazil 67 L1 .... 2°57'N 64°15'W
aris France 44 E6 .... 48°52'N 2°21'E
arma Italy 46 D1 .... 44°48'N 10°19'E
arnaíba Brazil 72 E6 .... 2°56'S 41°45'W
arnaíba r. Brazil 72 E6 .... 3°02'S 41°51'W
arnassos mt. Greece 50 E4 .... 30°32'N 22°38'E
arnu Estonia 43 F2 .... 58°23'N 24°30'E
aropamisus mts Afgh. 95 J7 .... 35°06'N 61°20'E
aros i. Greece 50 F3 .... 37°06'N 25°08'E
arrett r. England 11 D3 .... 51°08'N 3°00'W
arry, Cape Canada 61 F5 .... 70°12'N 124°31'W
arry Islands Canada 60 G5 .... 76°50'N 111°03'W
arsęta r. Poland 46 F5 .... 54°11'N 15°34'E
arthenay France 44 C5 .... 46°39'N 0°15'W
artry Mountains hills Ireland 18 B3 .... 53°36'N 9°39'W
asadena U.S. 62 C3 .... 34°11'N 118°08'W
așcani Romania 47 L2 .... 47°15'N 26°44'E
asni Pakistan 95 J5 .... 25°13'N 63°31'E
assau Germany 46 E3 .... 48°34'N 13°25'E
asso Fundo Brazil 73 D4 .... 28°18'S 52°24'W
astavy Belarus 47 L6 .... 55°07'N 26°50'E
asto Colombia 72 B7 .... 1°11'N 77°17'W
atagonia f. Argentina 73 B1 .... 51°44'S 71°19'W
atchway England 8 C2 .... 51°32'N 2°34'W
aterson U.S. 63 L5 .... 40°54'N 74°09'W
athein Myanmar 97 H4 .... 16°45'N 94°44'E
atna India 96 G6 .... 25°35'N 85°16'E
atos U.S. 63 C5 .... 40°40'N 19°39'E
atos, Lagoa dos l. Brazil 73 D3 .... 30°39'S 50°58'W
atos de Minas Brazil 72 E5 .... 18°36'S 46°30'W
atraïkos Kolpos b. Greece 50 D4 .... 38°15'N 21°26'E
atras Greece 50 D4 .... 38°14'N 21°45'E
atrington England 13 G2 .... 53°41'N 0°01'W
au France 44 C3 .... 43°18'N 0°22'W
aulo Afonso Brazil 72 F6 .... 9°20'S 38°13'W
avia Italy 46 C1 .... 45°11'N 9°09'E
avlodar Kazakhstan 54 I3 .... 52°18'N 77°02'E
avlohrad Ukraine 47 P3 .... 48°31'N 35°53'E
avlovskaya Russia 49 K6 .... 46°09'N 39°47'E
ayapon Myanmar 97 I4 .... 16°16'N 95°41'E
y-Khoy, Khrebet hills Russia 52 G4 .... 69°17'N 62°13'E
ysandú Uruguay 73 D3 .... 32°19'S 58°05'W
azardzhik Bulgaria 50 F6 .... 42°12'N 24°20'E
ace r. Canada 60 G3 .... 58°54'N 111°50'W
acehaven England 9 E1 .... 50°48'N 0°00'W
ace River town Canada 60 G3 .... 56°15'N 117°17'W
ale, Mount U.S. 62 E4 .... 38°26'N 109°13'W
earl r. U.S. 63 I3 .... 30°10'N 89°37'W
chora Russia 52 F4 .... 65°09'N 53°54'E
chora r. Russia 52 F4 .... 68°13'N 53°54'E
chorskoye More sea Russia 52 F4 .... 69°00'N 55°00'E
cos U.S. 62 F3 .... 31°23'N 103°30'W
cos r. U.S. 62 F2 .... 29°50'N 101°28'W
cs Hungary 46 H2 .... 46°05'N 18°13'E
dro Juan Caballero Paraguay 73 D4 .... 22°29'S 55°44'W
ebbles Scotland 15 F3 .... 55°39'N 3°12'W
el r. Canada 60 E4 .... 68°03'N 134°26'W
el Isle of Man 12 C3 .... 54°13'N 4°41'W
gasus Bay New Zealand 109 G2 .... 43°20'S 172°49'E
gwell Bay England 9 G2 .... 51°19'N 1°21'E
ipus, Lake Estonia/Russia 43 F2 .... 58°38'N 27°28'E
jë Kosovo 50 D6 .... 42°39'N 20°17'E
kalongan Indonesia 102 D2 .... 6°54'S 109°38'E
lat, Mont m. France 44 E4 .... 44°16'N 6°43'E
leng i. Indonesia 103 G3 .... 1°15'S 123°29'E
llo Finland 43 E4 .... 66°47'N 23°59'E
lotas Brazil 73 D3 .... 31°46'S 52°19'W
lotas, Rio das r. Brazil 73 D4 .... 27°35'S 51°24'W
mba Mozambique 83 D3 .... 12°59'S 40°32'E
mba Zambia 83 B3 .... 16°33'S 27°22'E
mba Island Tanzania 83 C4 .... 5°25'S 39°46'E
mbrey Wales 10 C3 .... 51°41'N 4°17'W
mbroke Canada 63 K6 .... 45°49'N 77°06'W
mbroke Wales 10 C3 .... 51°40'N 4°55'W
mbroke Dock Wales 10 C3 .... 51°41'N 4°57'W
mbrokeshire d. Wales 21 C2 .... 51°55'N 4°48'W
mbury England 9 F2 .... 51°09'N 0°19'E
ñalara mt. Spain 45 D4 .... 40°51'N 3°56'W
ña Nevada, Cerro mt. Mexico 66 E5 .... 23°46'N 99°50'W
ñaranda de Bracamonte Spain 45 C4 .... 40°55'N 5°11'W
narth Wales 11 D3 .... 51°26'N 3°10'W
nas, Golfo de g. Chile 73 B2 .... 47°18'S 75°35'W
ndine Wales 10 C3 .... 51°45'N 4°34'W
ndlebury England 13 E2 .... 53°30'N 2°09'W
ndle Hill England 13 E2 .... 53°52'N 2°18'W
ndleton U.S. 62 C6 .... 45°39'N 118°48'W
nicuik Scotland 15 F3 .... 55°50'N 3°13'W
ninsular Malaysia Malaysia 102 C4 .... 3°59'N 102°43'E
nkridge England 8 C3 .... 52°43'N 2°07'W
nnines hills England 13 E3 .... 54°23'N 2°18'W
nny Icecap Canada 61 L4 .... 67°10'N 66°02'W
nrhyn Mawr pt Wales 10 C4 .... 52°51'N 4°43'W
nrith England 12 E3 .... 54°40'N 2°45'W
nsacola U.S. 63 I3 .... 30°27'N 87°13'W
nticton Canada 62 C6 .... 49°30'N 119°35'W
ntire Point England 11 B2 .... 50°35'N 5°00'W

Pentland Firth str. Scotland 17 F3 .... 58°43'N 3°16'W
Pentland Hills Scotland 15 F3 .... 55°43'N 3°30'W
Pentland Skerries is Scotland 17 G3 .... 58°41'N 2°54'W
Penygadair hill Wales 10 D4 .... 52°42'N 3°55'W
Pen-y-Ghent hill England 13 E3 .... 54°10'N 2°15'W
Penza Russia 53 E3 .... 53°12'N 45°01'E
Penzance England 11 B2 .... 50°07'N 5°32'W
Penzhinskaya Guba b. Russia 55 R4 .... 62°05'N 163°30'E
Peoria U.S. 63 I5 .... 40°41'N 89°37'W
Peregrebnoye Russia 52 G4 .... 62°59'N 65°11'E
Pereira Colombia 72 B7 .... 4°45'N 75°41'W
Périgueux France 44 D4 .... 45°11'N 0°43'E
Perijá, Sierra de mts Venezuela 67 J2 .... 9°09'N 73°12'W
Perito Moreno Argentina 73 B2 .... 46°36'S 71°02'W
Perlas, Punta de pt Nicaragua 67 H3 .... 12°24'N 83°31'W
Perm' Russia 52 F3 .... 58°01'N 56°14'E
Pernik Bulgaria 50 E6 .... 42°36'N 23°02'E
Péronne France 42 B2 .... 49°56'N 2°56'E
Perpignan France 44 E3 .... 42°42'N 2°54'E
Perranporth England 11 B2 .... 50°21'N 5°09'W
Pershore England 8 C3 .... 52°07'N 2°04'W
Perth Australia 108 A3 .... 31°56'S 115°47'E
Perth Scotland 15 F4 .... 56°24'N 3°26'W
Perth and Kinross d. Scotland 20 C5 .... 56°37'N 4°07'W
Peru S. America 72 B5 .... 5°50'S 77°14'W
Perugia Italy 48 F5 .... 43°07'N 12°23'E
Pervomaisk Ukraine 47 N3 .... 48°03'N 30°51'E
Pescara Italy 48 F5 .... 42°27'N 14°12'E
Pesebre, Punta pt Canary Islands 45 Y2 .... 28°07'N 14°29'W
Peshawar Pakistan 96 D7 .... 34°01'N 71°40'E
Peshkopi Albania 50 D5 .... 41°41'N 20°26'E
Peskovi mt. Serbia/North Macedonia 50 D6 .... 42°09'N 20°59'E
Peterborough Canada 61 K2 .... 44°18'N 78°20'W
Peterborough England 9 E3 .... 52°34'N 0°14'W
Peterborough d. England 21 E3 .... 52°36'N 0°16'W
Peterhead Scotland 17 H2 .... 57°31'N 1°47'W
Peterlee England 13 F3 .... 54°46'N 1°20'W
Petersfield England 8 E2 .... 51°00'N 0°56'W
Petersville U.S. 60 C4 .... 62°33'N 150°50'W
Petit Mécatina r. Canada 61 M3 .... 50°40'N 59°25'W
Petrich Bulgaria 50 E5 .... 41°24'N 23°12'E
Petropavl Kazakhstan 54 H3 .... 54°51'N 69°06'E
Petropavlovsk-Kamchatskiy Russia 55 Q3 .... 53°01'N 158°44'E
Petroșani Romania 50 E7 .... 45°25'N 23°23'E
Petrozavodsk Russia 52 D4 .... 61°48'N 34°19'E
Petworth England 9 E1 .... 50°59'N 0°36'W
Pevensey England 9 F1 .... 50°49'N 0°21'E
Pewsey England 8 D2 .... 51°20'N 1°46'W
Pforzheim Germany 46 C3 .... 48°53'N 8°42'E
Phan Thiet Vietnam 102 D6 .... 10°55'N 108°06'E
Phatthalung Thailand 102 C5 .... 7°39'N 100°06'E
Phayao Thailand 102 B7 .... 19°10'N 99°57'E
Phet Buri Thailand 102 B6 .... 13°06'N 99°56'E
Philadelphia U.S. 63 K4 .... 39°57'N 75°10'W
Philippeville Belgium 42 D3 .... 50°12'N 4°33'E
Philippines Asia 103 G6 .... 15°36'N 122°55'E
Phitsanulok Thailand 102 C7 .... 16°50'N 100°18'E
Phnom Penh Cambodia 102 C6 .... 11°33'N 104°57'E
Phoenix U.S. 62 D3 .... 33°31'N 112°07'W
Phoenix Islands Kiribati 109 H6 .... 2°43'S 173°22'W
Phongsali Laos 102 C8 .... 21°41'N 102°08'E
Phrae Thailand 102 C7 .... 18°07'N 100°12'E
Phuket Thailand 102 B5 .... 7°53'N 98°23'E
Piacenza Italy 46 C1 .... 45°03'N 9°42'E
Piatra Neamț Romania 47 L2 .... 46°56'N 26°22'E
Piave r. Italy 46 E1 .... 45°32'N 12°44'E
Picardy f. France 44 E6 .... 49°47'N 1°35'E
Pickering England 13 G3 .... 54°15'N 0°47'W
Pickering, Vale of f. England 13 G3 .... 54°13'N 0°45'W
Picos Brazil 72 E6 .... 7°05'S 41°20'W
Piedras Negras Mexico 66 D6 .... 28°40'N 100°34'W
Pieksämäki Finland 43 F3 .... 62°18'N 27°10'E
Pielinen l. Finland 43 G3 .... 63°14'N 29°41'E
Pierre U.S. 62 F5 .... 44°23'N 100°23'W
Pietermaritzburg S. Africa 83 C2 .... 29°36'S 30°23'E
Pietrosa mt. Romania 47 K2 .... 47°34'N 24°41'E
Pihlajavesi l. Finland 43 G3 .... 61°45'N 28°46'E
Pijijiapan Mexico 66 F4 .... 15°46'N 93°14'W
Piła Poland 46 G5 .... 53°09'N 16°45'E
Pilbara f. Australia 108 A4 .... 22°45'S 117°00'E
Pimperne England 8 C1 .... 50°53'N 2°08'W
Pinang i. Malaysia 102 C5 .... 5°21'N 100°11'E
Pınarbaşı Turkey 51 L4 .... 38°44'N 36°25'E
Pinar del Río Cuba 67 H5 .... 22°25'N 83°43'W
Pindus Greece 50 D4 .... 39°56'N 20°56'E
Pine Bluff U.S. 63 H3 .... 34°16'N 92°02'W
Pinega Russia 52 E4 .... 64°41'N 43°24'E
Pineios r. Greece 50 E4 .... 39°53'N 22°43'E
Pingdingshan China 99 K4 .... 33°45'N 113°18'E
Pingxiang Guangxi China 99 J2 .... 22°03'N 106°50'E
Pingxiang Jiangxi China 99 K3 .... 27°42'N 113°52'E
Pinsk Belarus 47 L4 .... 52°08'N 26°06'E
Pionerskiy Russia 52 G4 .... 61°08'N 62°51'E
Piotrków Trybunalski Poland 46 H4 .... 51°25'N 19°41'E
Pipmuacan, Réservoir Canada 63 L6 .... 49°37'N 70°33'W
Piraeus Greece 50 E4 .... 37°56'N 23°38'E
Pirot Serbia 50 E6 .... 43°09'N 22°34'E
Pisa Italy 48 F5 .... 43°42'N 10°24'E
Písek Czechia 46 F3 .... 49°19'N 14°10'E
Pisuerga r. Spain 45 C4 .... 41°34'N 4°50'W
Pisz Poland 47 I5 .... 53°38'N 21°48'E
Pitcairn Island S. Pacific Oc. 116 B2 .... 25°03'S 130°06'W
Pitcairn Islands S. Pacific Oc. 116 B2 .... 23°35'S 126°31'W
Piteå Sweden 43 E4 .... 65°19'N 21°30'E
Pitești Romania 50 F7 .... 44°52'N 24°53'E
Pitlochry Scotland 17 F1 .... 56°42'N 3°44'W
Pittsburgh U.S. 63 K5 .... 40°26'N 79°59'W
Piz Bernina mt. Italy/Switz. 46 C2 .... 46°23'N 9°54'E
Plasencia Spain 45 B4 .... 40°02'N 6°05'W
Platinum U.S. 60 B3 .... 58°59'N 161°48'W
Platte r. U.S. 62 G5 .... 41°04'N 95°53'W
Plauen Germany 46 E4 .... 50°30'N 12°08'E
Plavsk Russia 47 Q5 .... 53°42'N 37°18'E
Playa Blanca Canary Islands 45 Z2 .... 28°52'N 13°50'W
Plenty, Bay of g. New Zealand 109 G3 .... 37°37'S 176°59'E
Plesetsk Russia 52 E4 .... 62°43'N 40°18'E
Pleven Bulgaria 50 F6 .... 43°25'N 24°37'E
Płock Poland 46 H5 .... 52°33'N 19°43'E
Pločno mt. Bos. and Herz. 50 B6 .... 43°36'N 17°35'E
Ploiești Romania 50 G7 .... 44°56'N 26°02'E
Plomb du Cantal mt. France 44 E4 .... 45°03'N 2°46'E
Plovdiv Bulgaria 50 F6 .... 42°10'N 24°44'E
Plungė Lithuania 47 I6 .... 55°55'N 21°51'E
Plymouth England 11 C2 .... 50°22'N 4°08'W

Plymouth d. England 21 C2 .... 50°24'N 4°08'W
Plympton England 11 C2 .... 50°23'N 4°03'W
Plymstock England 11 C2 .... 50°21'N 4°06'W
Plynlimon hill Wales 10 D4 .... 52°28'N 3°47'W
Plzeň Czechia 46 E3 .... 49°45'N 13°23'E
Pô Burkina Faso 84 D3 .... 11°12'N 1°08'W
Po r. Italy 46 E1 .... 45°02'N 12°11'E
Pobeda, Gora mt. Russia 55 P4 .... 65°12'N 145°54'E
Pocatello U.S. 62 D5 .... 42°54'N 112°25'W
Pochep Russia 47 O5 .... 52°56'N 33°27'E
Pocklington England 13 G2 .... 53°56'N 0°47'W
Poços de Caldas Brazil 73 E4 .... 21°48'S 46°31'W
Podgorica Montenegro 50 C6 .... 42°27'N 19°17'E
Podkamennaya Tunguska r. Russia 55 K4 .... 61°36'N 90°08'E
Podol'sk Russia 52 D3 .... 55°25'N 37°34'E
Pohang S. Korea 104 A3 .... 36°01'N 129°22'E
Pointe-à-Pitre Guadeloupe 72 C8 .... 16°15'N 61°32'W
Pointe-Noire Congo 84 F1 .... 4°44'S 11°53'E
Poitiers France 44 D5 .... 46°35'N 0°20'E
Pokaran India 96 D6 .... 26°53'N 71°57'E
Pokrovsk Ukraine 49 K6 .... 48°17'N 37°10'E
Poland Europe 46 H4 .... 52°00'N 19°27'E
Polatlı Turkey 51 J4 .... 39°35'N 32°08'E
Polatsk Belarus 47 M6 .... 55°29'N 28°47'E
Polegate England 9 F1 .... 50°49'N 0°15'E
Pol-e Khomrī Afgh. 95 K7 .... 35°56'N 68°46'E
Polis Cyprus 51 J2 .... 35°01'N 32°25'E
Pollaphuca Reservoir Ireland 18 E3 .... 53°08'N 6°30'W
Polokwane S. Africa 83 B2 .... 23°54'S 29°27'E
Polperro England 11 C2 .... 50°20'N 4°31'W
Poltava Ukraine 47 P3 .... 49°36'N 34°34'E
Polygyros Greece 50 E5 .... 40°23'N 23°28'E
Polykastro Greece 50 E5 .... 40°59'N 22°34'E
Polynesia is Pacific Oc. 116 B2 .... 8°00'S 170°00'E
Pomhal Portugal 45 A3 .... 39°55'N 8°37'W
Ponce Puerto Rico 67 K4 .... 18°00'N 66°37'W
Ponferrada Spain 45 B5 .... 42°33'N 6°36'W
Ponta do Sol Cape Verde 84 B3 .... 17°10'N 25°05'W
Ponta Grossa Brazil 73 D3 .... 25°03'S 50°07'W
Pont-à-Mousson France 42 F1 .... 48°54'N 6°03'E
Pontardawe Wales 10 D3 .... 51°43'N 3°51'W
Pontefract England 13 F2 .... 53°41'N 1°18'W
Ponteland England 13 F4 .... 55°03'N 1°44'W
Pontevedra Spain 45 A5 .... 42°26'N 8°38'W
Pontianak Indonesia 102 D3 .... 0°03'S 109°18'E
Pontic Mountains mts Turkey 51 L5 .... 40°59'N 36°11'E
Pontoise France 44 E6 .... 49°03'N 2°06'E
Pontycymer Wales 10 D3 .... 51°37'N 3°35'W
Pontypool Wales 10 D3 .... 51°42'N 3°02'W
Pontypridd Wales 10 D3 .... 51°36'N 3°20'W
Poole England 8 D1 .... 50°43'N 1°59'W
Poole Bay England 8 D1 .... 50°40'N 1°55'W
Pooley Bridge England 12 E3 .... 54°37'N 2°49'W
Poopó, Lago de l. Bolivia 72 C5 .... 18°50'S 67°05'W
Popigay r. Russia 55 L5 .... 72°56'N 106°10'E
Poplar Bluff U.S. 63 H4 .... 36°47'N 90°23'W
Popocatépetl, Volcán vol. Mexico 66 E4 .... 19°02'N 98°38'W
Poprad Slovakia 46 I3 .... 49°04'N 20°18'E
Porbandar India 96 C5 .... 21°39'N 69°40'E
Pori Finland 43 E3 .... 61°29'N 21°48'E
Porlock England 11 D3 .... 51°13'N 3°36'W
Poronaysk Russia 55 P2 .... 49°16'N 143°03'E
Porsangerfjorden str. Norway 43 F5 .... 70°19'N 25°18'E
Porsangerhalvøya pen. Norway 43 F5 .... 70°45'N 25°01'E
Porsgrunn Norway 43 B2 .... 59°08'N 9°39'E
Porsuk r. Turkey 51 I4 .... 39°41'N 31°58'E
Portadown Northern Ireland 14 C2 .... 54°25'N 6°26'W
Portaferry Northern Ireland 14 D2 .... 54°23'N 5°32'W
Portage la Prairie Canada 60 I2 .... 49°58'N 98°19'W
Portalegre Portugal 45 B3 .... 39°18'N 7°25'W
Port Angeles U.S. 62 B6 .... 48°06'N 123°25'W
Port Arthur U.S. 63 H2 .... 29°51'N 93°58'W
Port Askaig Scotland 14 C3 .... 55°51'N 6°06'W
Port Augusta Australia 108 C3 .... 32°29'S 137°45'E
Port-au-Prince Haiti 67 J4 .... 18°33'N 72°19'W
Portavogie Northern Ireland 14 D2 .... 54°27'N 5°26'W
Port Blair India 97 H3 .... 11°41'N 92°42'E
Port-de-Paix Haiti 67 J4 .... 19°57'N 72°50'W
Port Elizabeth S. Africa 83 B1 .... 33°57'S 25°37'E
Port Ellen Scotland 14 C3 .... 55°38'N 6°11'W
Port Erin Isle of Man 12 C3 .... 54°05'N 4°45'W
Port-Gentil Gabon 84 E1 .... 0°46'S 8°49'E
Port Glasgow Scotland 14 E3 .... 55°56'N 4°41'W
Port Harcourt Nigeria 84 E2 .... 4°46'N 7°01'E
Porthcawl Wales 11 D3 .... 51°29'N 3°42'W
Port Hedland Australia 108 A4 .... 20°23'S 118°37'E
Porthleven England 11 B2 .... 50°05'N 5°19'W
Porthmadog Wales 10 C4 .... 52°56'N 4°08'W
Port Hope Simpson Canada 61 M3 .... 52°31'N 55°47'W
Portimão Portugal 45 A2 .... 37°08'N 8°32'W
Port Isaac Bay England 11 C2 .... 50°36'N 4°49'W
Portishead England 8 C2 .... 51°29'N 2°46'W
Portknockie Scotland 17 G2 .... 57°42'N 2°51'W
Portland Australia 108 D3 .... 38°21'S 141°34'E
Portland Me. U.S. 63 L5 .... 43°41'N 70°17'W
Portland Oreg. U.S. 62 B6 .... 45°29'N 122°38'W
Portland, Isle of pen. England 8 C1 .... 50°33'N 2°25'W
Portlaoise Ireland 18 D3 .... 53°02'N 7°18'W
Portlethen Scotland 17 G2 .... 57°04'N 2°08'W
Port Lincoln Australia 108 C3 .... 34°43'S 135°49'E
Port Louis Mauritius 79 C1 .... 20°10'S 57°30'E
Port Macquarie Australia 108 E3 .... 31°25'S 152°53'E
Port Moresby P.N.G. 108 D6 .... 9°28'S 147°13'E
Portnahaven Scotland 14 C3 .... 55°41'N 6°30'W
Porto Alegre Brazil 73 D3 .... 30°03'S 51°10'W
Porto Esperidião Brazil 72 D5 .... 15°50'S 58°32'W
Port of Ness Scotland 16 C3 .... 58°30'N 6°14'W
Port of Spain Trinidad and Tobago 67 L3 .... 10°37'N 61°30'W
Portogruaro Italy 46 E1 .... 45°46'N 12°50'E
Porto-Novo Benin 84 E2 .... 6°30'N 2°40'E
Porto-Vecchio France 44 H2 .... 41°35'N 9°16'E
Porto Velho Brazil 72 C6 .... 8°47'S 63°54'W
Portoviejo Ecuador 72 A6 .... 1°06'S 80°28'W
Portpatrick Scotland 14 D2 .... 54°51'N 5°07'W
Port Pirie Australia 108 C3 .... 33°10'S 138°02'E
Portree Scotland 16 C2 .... 57°25'N 6°12'W
Portrush Northern Ireland 14 C3 .... 55°12'N 6°39'W
Port Said Egypt 85 H5 .... 31°16'N 32°18'E
Portsmouth England 8 D1 .... 50°48'N 1°06'W
Portsmouth d. England 21 E2 .... 50°50'N 1°04'W
Portsmouth U.S. 63 J4 .... 38°44'N 82°59'W
Portsoy Scotland 17 G2 .... 57°41'N 2°41'W
Portstewart Northern Ireland 14 C3 .... 55°11'N 6°43'W
Port Sudan Sudan 85 H3 .... 19°36'N 37°12'E
Port Talbot Wales 10 D3 .... 51°36'N 3°48'W
Portugal Europe 45 B3 .... 39°41'N 7°57'W
Portumna Ireland 18 C3 .... 53°06'N 8°13'W

Port Vila Vanuatu 109 F5 .... 17°44'S 168°17'E
Port William Scotland 14 E2 .... 54°46'N 4°35'W
Posadas Argentina 73 D4 .... 27°23'S 55°52'W
Poso Indonesia 103 G3 .... 1°24'S 120°47'E
Potenza Italy 49 F5 .... 40°38'N 15°48'E
Poti Georgia 53 E2 .... 42°09'N 41°40'E
Potiskum Nigeria 84 F3 .... 11°42'N 11°04'E
Potosí Bolivia 72 C5 .... 19°36'S 65°47'W
Potsdam Germany 46 E5 .... 52°24'N 13°04'E
Poulton-le-Fylde England 12 E2 .... 53°51'N 2°59'W
Powell, Lake resr U.S. 62 D4 .... 37°34'N 110°37'W
Powick England 8 C3 .... 52°10'N 2°15'W
Powys d. Wales 21 D3 .... 52°23'N 3°25'W
Poyang Hu l. China 99 L3 .... 29°05'N 116°22'E
Požarevac Serbia 50 D7 .... 44°37'N 21°11'E
Poza Rica Mexico 66 E4 .... 20°35'N 97°26'W
Poznań Poland 46 G5 .... 52°25'N 16°56'E
Pozoblanco Spain 45 C3 .... 38°23'N 4°50'W
Prabumulih Indonesia 102 C3 .... 3°26'S 104°13'E
Prachuap Khiri Khan Thailand 102 B6 .... 11°49'N 99°49'E
Prague Czechia 46 F4 .... 50°04'N 14°26'E
Praia Cape Verde 84 B3 .... 14°55'N 23°29'W
Prapat Indonesia 102 B4 .... 2°41'N 98°57'E
Prawle Point England 11 D2 .... 50°12'N 3°44'W
Prayagraj India 96 F6 .... 25°25'N 81°52'E
Preparis Island Cocos Is 97 H3 .... 14°51'N 93°39'E
Přerov Czechia 46 G3 .... 49°27'N 17°27'E
Presidente Prudente Brazil 73 D4 .... 22°10'S 51°23'W
Prešov Slovakia 46 I3 .... 48°59'N 21°16'E
Prespa, Lake Europe 50 D5 .... 40°52'N 21°03'E
Presque Isle town U.S. 63 M6 .... 46°41'N 68°01'W
Prestatyn Wales 10 D5 .... 53°20'N 3°24'W
Presteigne Wales 10 D4 .... 52°16'N 3°00'W
Preston Dor. England 8 C1 .... 50°39'N 2°25'W
Preston Lancs. England 12 E2 .... 53°46'N 2°42'W
Prestonpans Scotland 15 G3 .... 55°58'N 2°59'W
Prestwick Scotland 14 E3 .... 55°30'N 4°37'W
Pretoria S. Africa 83 B2 .... 25°44'S 28°13'E
Preveza Greece 50 D4 .... 38°57'N 20°45'E
Prievidza Slovakia 46 H3 .... 48°47'N 18°38'E
Prijedor Bos. and Herz. 50 B7 .... 44°59'N 16°43'E
Prijepolje Serbia 50 C6 .... 43°23'N 19°39'E
Prilep North Macedonia 50 D5 .... 41°21'N 21°33'E
Primorsko-Akhtarsk Russia 51 M8 .... 46°03'N 38°10'E
Prince Albert Canada 60 H3 .... 53°12'N 105°44'W
Prince Alfred, Cape Canada 60 F5 .... 74°20'N 124°47'W
Prince Charles Island Canada 61 K4 .... 67°48'N 76°12'W
Prince Edward Island d. Canada 61 L2 .... 46°41'N 63°09'W
Prince Edward Islands Indian Oc. 117 F1 .... 47°00'S 37°00'E
Prince George Canada 60 F3 .... 53°55'N 122°46'W
Prince of Wales Island Australia 108 D5 .... 10°43'S 142°09'E
Prince of Wales Island Canada 61 I5 .... 72°27'N 99°08'W
Prince Patrick Island Canada 60 G5 .... 76°57'N 118°47'W
Prince Rupert Canada 60 E3 .... 54°19'N 130°19'W
Princes Risborough England 8 E2 .... 51°43'N 0°50'W
Príncipe i. São Tomé and Príncipe 84 E2 .... 1°39'N 7°22'E
Pripet r. Ukraine 47 N4 .... 51°59'N 30°16'E
Pripet Marshes Belarus/Ukraine 47 K4 .... 51°39'N 24°34'E
Priština Kosovo 50 D6 .... 42°40'N 21°10'E
Privas France 44 F4 .... 44°44'N 4°36'E
Prizren Kosovo 50 D6 .... 42°13'N 20°43'E
Probolinggo Indonesia 102 E2 .... 7°47'S 113°13'E
Probus England 11 C2 .... 50°18'N 4°57'W
Providence U.S. 63 L5 .... 41°50'N 71°25'W
Providence, Cape New Zealand 109 F2 .... 46°01'S 166°28'E
Providencia, Isla de i. Caribbean Sea 67 H3 .... 13°21'N 81°20'W
Provins France 44 E6 .... 48°34'N 3°18'E
Provo U.S. 62 D5 .... 40°17'N 111°41'W
Prudhoe Bay town U.S. 60 D5 .... 70°18'N 148°10'W
Prüm Germany 42 F3 .... 50°13'N 6°25'E
Pruszków Poland 46 I5 .... 52°10'N 20°49'E
Prut r. Europe 47 M1 .... 45°28'N 28°12'E
Pryluky Ukraine 47 O4 .... 50°35'N 32°24'E
Prypyat r. Ukraine 47 N4 .... 51°16'N 30°16'E
Przemyśl Poland 47 J3 .... 49°47'N 22°46'E
Psara i. Greece 50 F4 .... 38°37'N 25°35'E
Psebay Russia 51 N7 .... 44°07'N 40°47'E
Psel r. Russia/Ukraine 47 P4 .... 51°05'N 35°15'E
Pskov Russia 43 G2 .... 57°49'N 28°19'E
Pskov, Lake Estonia/Russia 43 F2 .... 58°02'N 27°56'E
Pucallpa Peru 72 B6 .... 8°22'S 74°35'W
Pudozh Russia 52 D4 .... 61°49'N 36°22'E
Pudsey England 13 F2 .... 53°48'N 1°40'W
Puducherry India 96 E3 .... 11°57'N 79°48'E
Puebla Mexico 66 E4 .... 19°02'N 98°12'W
Puebla d. Mexico 66 E4 .... 18°04'N 98°39'W
Pueblo U.S. 62 F4 .... 38°17'N 104°38'W
Puente-Genil Spain 45 C2 .... 37°23'N 4°46'W
Puerto Ángel Mexico 66 E3 .... 15°40'N 96°31'W
Puerto de la Estaca Canary Islands 45 X1 .... 27°47'N 17°54'W
Puerto del Rosario Canary Islands 45 Z2 .... 28°30'N 13°52'W
Puerto Deseado Argentina 73 C2 .... 47°45'S 65°55'W
Puertollano Spain 45 C3 .... 38°41'N 4°06'W
Puerto Montt Chile 73 B2 .... 41°27'S 72°58'W
Puerto Natales Chile 73 B1 .... 51°35'S 72°24'W
Puerto Peñasco Mexico 66 B7 .... 31°19'N 113°32'W
Puerto Princesa Phil. 102 F5 .... 9°45'N 118°45'E
Puerto Rico i. Central America 67 K4 .... 17°45'N 66°34'W
Puerto Vallarta Mexico 66 C5 .... 20°40'N 105°14'W
Pula Croatia 46 E1 .... 44°53'N 13°51'E
Pulborough England 9 E1 .... 50°57'N 0°30'W
Puławy Poland 46 I5 .... 51°25'N 21°05'E
Pune India 96 D4 .... 18°32'N 73°57'E
Puning China 99 L2 .... 23°17'N 116°09'E
Punjab d. India 96 E7 .... 30°17'N 75°18'E
Punta Arenas Chile 73 B1 .... 53°09'S 70°57'W
Punta Gorda Nicaragua 67 H3 .... 11°32'N 83°46'W
Punto Fijo Venezuela 67 J3 .... 11°39'N 70°11'W
Pur r. Russia 54 I4 .... 67°33'N 77°23'E
Purari r. P.N.G. 108 D6 .... 7°46'S 144°54'E
Purbeck, Isle of pen. England 8 C1 .... 50°39'N 2°01'W
Puri India 96 G4 .... 19°48'N 85°55'E
Purmerend Neth. 42 D5 .... 52°31'N 4°57'E
Pursat Cambodia 102 C6 .... 12°32'N 103°57'E
Purus r. Brazil/Peru 72 C6 .... 3°42'S 61°28'W
Pustoshka Russia 47 M7 .... 56°20'N 29°22'E
Putian China 99 L3 .... 25°26'N 119°00'E
Puting, Tanjung pt Indonesia 102 E3 .... 3°35'S 111°50'E
Putrajaya Malaysia 102 C4 .... 2°56'N 101°42'E
Puttalam Sri Lanka 96 E2 .... 8°01'N 79°50'E
Putumayo r. Colombia 72 B6 .... 2°43'S 70°03'W
Puuvuruntuq Canada 61 K4 .... 60°02'N 77°11'W
Puy de Dôme mt. France 44 E4 .... 45°46'N 2°58'E
Puy de Sancy mt. France 44 E4 .... 45°31'N 2°49'E
Pwllheli Wales 10 C4 .... 52°53'N 4°25'W
Pyaozero, Ozero l. Russia 43 G4 .... 66°11'N 30°47'E

Pyasina r. Russia 55 J5.....................................73°35'N 86°19'E
Pyatigorsk Russia 53 E2...................................44°02'N 43°03'E
Pyay Myanmar 97 I4...18°48'N 95°13'E
Pyhäjoki r. Finland 43 F4..................................64°28'N 24°15'E
Pyhäselkä l. Finland 43 G3.................................62°31'N 29°41'E
Pyinmana Myanmar 97 I4....................................19°44'N 96°13'E
Pyle Wales 11 D3..51°32'N 3°42'W
Pylos Greece 50 D3..36°55'N 21°42'E
P'yŏngyang N. Korea 99 N5................................39°01'N 125°44'E
Pyramid Lake U.S. 62 F5....................................40°09'N 119°37'W
Pyrenees mts Europe 45 G5.................................42°30'N 2°00'E
Pyrgos Greece 50 D3...37°40'N 21°27'E
Pyriatyn Ukraine 47 O4......................................50°14'N 32°30'E

Q

Qa'en Iran 95 I6..33°42'N 59°05'E
Qalbataū Kazakhstan 98 E7................................49°16'N 81°34'E
Qamanittuaq Canada 61 I4................................64°17'N 95°43'W
Qamdo China 98 H4...31°13'N 97°08'E
Qandyaghash Kazakhstan 53 F2..........................49°27'N 57°21'E
Qarabutaq Kazakhstan 54 H2.............................49°55'N 60°09'E
Qaraghandy Kazakhstan 54 I2.............................49°52'N 73°04'E
Qarshi Uzbekistan 95 K7....................................38°52'N 65°48'E
Qasigiannguit Greenland 61 M4...........................68°48'N 51°11'W
Qatar Asia 95 H5..25°25'N 51°57'E
Qattara Depression f. Egypt 85 G4......................29°48'N 27°06'E
Qazax Azerbaijan 53 E2.....................................41°06'N 45°21'E
Qazvīn Iran 95 G7...36°17'N 49°58'E
Qeshm Iran 95 I5...26°57'N 56°15'E
Qiemo China 98 F5...38°05'N 85°33'E
Qijiaojing China 98 G6......................................43°25'N 91°38'E
Qilian Shan mts China 98 H5..............................39°21'N 97°06'E
Qinā Egypt 85 H4...26°08'N 32°45'E
Qingdao China 99 M5..36°05'N 120°24'E
Qinghai China 98 H5...36°07'N 96°31'E
Qinghai Hu l. China 99 I5..................................36°49'N 100°06'E
Qinhuangdao China 99 L5..................................39°56'N 119°38'E
Qinzhou China 99 J2...21°57'N 108°31'E
Qionghai China 99 K1.......................................19°13'N 110°29'E
Qiqihar China 99 M7...47°13'N 123°58'E
Qom Iran 95 H6...34°38'N 50°51'E
Qo'ng'irot Uzbekistan 53 F2...............................43°04'N 58°51'E
Qornet es Saouda mt. Lebanon 51 L2...................34°18'N 36°06'E
Qostanay Kazakhstan 54 H3...............................53°12'N 63°40'E
Quang Ngai Vietnam 102 D7...............................15°04'N 108°50'E
Quantock Hills England 11 D3.............................51°10'N 3°15'W
Quanzhou China 99 K3.......................................25°57'N 111°05'E
Quba Azerbaijan 53 E2.......................................41°22'N 48°31'E
Quchan Iran 95 I7...36°59'N 58°29'E
Québec Canada 61 K2..46°48'N 71°15'W
Québec d. Canada 61 K3.....................................54°45'N 74°31'W
Queenborough England 9 F2................................51°25'N 0°45'E
Queen Charlotte Islands Canada 60 E3................53°59'N 133°20'W
Queen Charlotte Sound str. Canada 60 F3

....51°24'N 129°09'W
Queen Elizabeth Islands Canada 61 I4.................76°31'N 107°31'W
Queen Maud Gulf Canada 60 H4..........................68°13'N 102°08'W
Queensland d. Australia 108 D4............................22°37'S 144°17'E
Quelimane Mozambique 83 C3.............................17°53'S 36°53'E
Querétaro Mexico 66 D5.....................................20°37'N 100°22'W
Querétaro d. Mexico 66 E5..................................20°51'N 99°50'W
Quetta Pakistan 96 C7..30°14'N 67°03'E
Quetzaltenango Guatemala 66 F3.......................14°50'N 91°30'W
Quezon City Phil. 103 G6....................................14°36'N 121°01'E
Quibala Angola 83 A3...10°44'S 14°59'E
Quibdó Colombia 72 B7......................................5°39'N 76°38'W
Quimper France 44 A5...47°59'N 4°06'W
Quintana Roo d. Mexico 66 G4.............................18°44'N 88°47'W
Quito Ecuador 72 B6...0°14'S 78°30'W
Qulandy Kazakhstan 53 F2..................................46°03'N 59°32'E
Qulsary Kazakhstan 53 F2...................................46°56'N 54°00'E
Quoich, Loch l. Scotland 16 D2...........................57°03'N 5°18'W
Quoile r. Northern Ireland 14 D2.........................54°21'N 5°42'W
Quy Nhon Vietnam 102 D6..................................13°44'N 109°13'E
Quzhou China 99 L3..28°57'N 118°52'E
Qyzylorda Kazakhstan 54 H2...............................44°51'N 65°30'E

R

Raahe Finland 43 F4...64°41'N 24°29'E
Raalte Neth. 42 F5...52°23'N 6°17'E
Raasay i. Scotland 16 C2.....................................57°23'N 6°02'W
Raasay, Sound of str. Scotland 16 C2...................57°26'N 6°06'W
Raba Indonesia 102 F2.......................................8°32'S 118°46'E
Rabat Morocco 84 D5...34°01'N 6°47'W
Rābigh Saudi Arabia 94 E4..................................22°50'N 39°00'E
Race, Cape Canada 61 M2..................................46°38'N 53°09'W
Rach Gia Vietnam 102 D5...................................9°59'N 105°06'E
Radom Poland 46 I4...51°24'N 21°09'E
Radomsko Poland 46 H4.....................................51°04'N 19°27'E
Radstock England 8 C2.......................................51°17'N 2°27'W
Rafḥā' Saudi Arabia 94 F5...................................29°33'N 43°25'E
Rafsanjān Iran 95 I6...30°24'N 55°59'E
Raglan Wales 10 E3..51°46'N 2°51'W
Ragusa Italy 48 F4...36°55'N 14°44'E
Rahachow Belarus 47 N5.....................................53°05'N 30°03'E
Rahimyar Khan Pakistan 96 D6............................28°22'N 70°19'E
Raichur India 96 E4..16°13'N 77°18'E
Rainier, Mount vol. U.S. 62 B6............................46°54'N 121°44'W
Raipur India 96 F5...21°14'N 81°39'E
Rajamahendravaram India 96 F4.........................17°00'N 81°52'E
Rajanpur Pakistan 96 D6.....................................29°05'N 70°24'E
Rajasthan d. India 96 D6.....................................26°40'N 73°31'E
Rajkot India 96 D5...22°14'N 70°53'E
Rajshahi Bangl. 96 G5...24°22'N 88°36'E
Rakhiv Ukraine 47 K3...48°03'N 24°12'E
Rakitnoye Russia 47 P4.......................................50°50'N 35°50'E
Rakvere Estonia 43 F2..59°21'N 26°22'E
Raleigh U.S. 63 K4...35°47'N 78°37'W
Rame Head England 11 C2...................................50°19'N 4°15'W
Rāmhormoz Iran 95 G6......................................31°10'N 49°35'E
Râmnicu Vâlcea Romania 50 F7...........................45°07'N 24°22'E
Ramsbottom England 13 E2.................................53°39'N 2°19'W
Ramsey England 9 E3...52°27'N 0°06'W
Ramsey Isle of Man 12 C3...................................54°19'N 4°23'W
Ramsey Bay Isle of Man 12 C3.............................54°20'N 4°22'W
Ramsey Island Wales 10 B3.................................51°51'N 5°20'W
Ramsgate England 9 G2......................................51°20'N 1°25'E
Rancagua Chile 73 B3...34°11'S 70°44'W
Ranchi India 96 G5...23°22'N 85°20'E
Randers Denmark 43 B2......................................56°27'N 10°03'E
Rangoon Myanmar 97 I4.....................................16°49'N 96°08'E

Rangpur Bangl. 97 G6...25°46'N 89°16'E
Rankin Inlet Canada 61 I4...................................62°52'N 92°03'W
Rannoch, Loch l. Scotland 17 E1..........................56°41'N 4°23'W
Rannoch Moor f. Scotland 16 E1..........................56°38'N 4°46'W
Ranong Thailand 102 B5......................................9°57'N 98°38'E
Rantauprapat Indonesia 102 B4...........................2°06'N 99°47'E
Raoul Island Indian Oc. 109 H4............................29°16'S 177°57'W
Rapallo Italy 46 C1...44°21'N 9°14'E
Raphoe Ireland 14 B2...54°52'N 7°35'W
Rapid City U.S. 62 F5..44°04'N 103°14'W
Ras Dejen mt. Ethiopia 85 H3..............................13°12'N 38°23'E
Rasht Iran 95 G7...37°16'N 49°34'E
Ras Koh mts Pakistan 96 C6................................28°54'N 65°26'E
Ras Tannūrah Saudi Arabia 95 H5........................26°38'N 50°10'E
Rat Buri Thailand 102 B6.....................................13°31'N 99°50'E
Rathdrum Ireland 18 E2......................................52°56'N 6°14'W
Rathenow Germany 46 E5....................................52°37'N 12°20'E
Rathfriland Northern Ireland 14 C2.......................54°14'N 6°09'W
Rathkeale Ireland 18 C2......................................52°31'N 8°56'W
Rathlin Island Northern Ireland 14 C3...................55°17'N 6°10'W
Rathluirc Ireland 18 C2.......................................52°21'N 8°41'W
Ratne Ukraine 47 K4...51°40'N 24°32'E
Rattray Head Scotland 17 H2...............................57°37'N 1°48'W
Rättvik Sweden 43 C3...60°53'N 15°08'E
Rauma Finland 43 E3..61°08'N 21°31'E
Raunds England 9 E3..52°20'N 0°32'W
Ravenna Italy 46 E1..44°25'N 12°13'E
Ravensthorpe Australia 108 B3............................33°34'S 120°01'E
Rawaki i. Kiribati 109 H6....................................3°42'S 170°40'W
Rawalpindi Pakistan 96 D7..................................33°38'N 73°08'E
Rawicz Poland 46 G4..51°37'N 16°51'E
Rawlins U.S. 62 E5...41°48'N 107°13'W
Rawson Argentina 73 C2.....................................43°15'S 65°06'W
Rawtenstall England 13 E2..................................53°42'N 2°17'W
Rayleigh England 9 F2..51°35'N 0°36'E
Razgrad Bulgaria 50 G6......................................43°32'N 26°30'E
Ré, Île de i. France 44 C5....................................46°10'N 1°22'W
Reading England 8 E2...51°27'N 0°58'W
Reading d. England 21 E2....................................51°27'N 0°59'W
Reboly Russia 43 G3...63°50'N 30°48'E
Rechytsa Belarus 47 N5.......................................52°22'N 30°26'E
Recife Brazil 72 F6...8°02'S 34°48'W
Red r. U.S. 63 H3..31°05'N 91°44'W
Red Bluff U.S. 62 B5..40°11'N 122°14'W
Redcar England 13 F3...54°37'N 1°03'W
Redcar and Cleveland d. England 21 E4...............54°33'N 1°02'W
Redding U.S. 62 B5..40°36'N 122°29'W
Redditch England 8 D3..52°19'N 1°56'W
Redhill England 9 E2..51°14'N 0°10'W
Red Lake town Canada 61 I3................................51°01'N 93°50'W
Red Lakes U.S. 63 H6...48°03'N 94°44'W
Redruth England 11 B2.......................................50°14'N 5°14'W
Red Sea Africa/Asia 94 E4..................................26°30'N 34°42'E
Red Wharf Bay Wales 10 C5................................53°19'N 4°11'W
Ree, Lough l. Ireland 18 D3.................................53°32'N 7°59'W
Regensburg Germany 46 E3................................49°01'N 12°06'E
Reggane Algeria 84 E4..26°46'N 0°09'E
Reggio di Calabria Italy 49 G4.............................38°06'N 15°39'E
Reggio nell'Emilia Italy 46 D1..............................44°42'N 10°38'E
Regina Canada 60 H3...50°27'N 104°37'W
Rèidh, Rubha pt Scotland 16 D2..........................57°52'N 5°51'W
Reigate England 9 E2...51°14'N 0°12'W
Reims France 44 F6..49°15'N 4°03'E
Reindeer Lake Canada 60 H3...............................57°24'N 102°23'W
Reinosa Spain 45 C5...42°59'N 4°07'W
Reiphólsfjöll hill Iceland 43 X2............................65°41'N 22°20'W
Reliance Canada 60 H4.......................................62°43'N 109°06'W
Relizane Algeria 48 D4.......................................35°44'N 0°40'E
Rena Norway 43 B3..61°08'N 11°22'E
Renfrewshire d. Scotland 20 C4...........................55°50'N 4°33'W
Reni Ukraine 51 H7..45°27'N 28°18'E
Rennell i. Solomon Is 109 F5...............................11°40'S 160°18'E
Rennes France 44 C6..48°07'N 1°41'W
Reno r. Italy 46 E1...44°35'N 12°17'E
Reno U.S. 62 C4..39°32'N 119°48'W
Republican r. U.S. 62 G4.....................................39°06'N 96°52'W
Resistencia Argentina 73 D4................................27°24'S 58°59'W
Reşiţa Romania 50 D7..45°18'N 21°53'E
Resolute Canada 61 I5..74°41'N 94°46'W
Resolution Island Canada 61 L4...........................61°34'N 64°52'W
Retford England 13 G2.......................................53°19'N 0°57'W
Rethel France 42 F2...49°31'N 4°23'E
Rethymno Greece 50 F2......................................35°21'N 24°28'E
Réunion i. Indian Oc. 117 G2...............................20°00'S 55°00'E
Reus Spain 45 F4...41°09'N 1°06'E
Reutlingen Germany 46 C3..................................48°30'N 9°12'E
Rewa India 96 F5...24°32'N 81°18'E
Reykjavík Iceland 43 X2......................................64°08'N 21°55'W
Reynosa Mexico 66 E6..26°04'N 98°17'W
Rēzekne Latvia 43 F2..56°31'N 27°20'E
Rhayader Wales 10 D4..52°18'N 3°31'W
Rheine Germany 42 G5.......................................52°17'N 7°28'E
Rheinland-Pfalz d. Germany 42 G2.......................49°46'N 7°27'E
Rhine r. Europe 46 B4...51°53'N 6°03'E
Rhins of Galloway, The pen. Scotland 14 D2

....54°55'N 5°07'W
Rhode Island d. U.S. 63 L5..................................41°40'N 71°35'W
Rhodes Greece 51 I3..36°26'N 28°13'E
Rhodes i. Greece 51 H3......................................36°15'N 28°10'E
Rhodope Mountains Bulgaria/Greece 50 E5

....41°52'N 23°41'E
Rhondda f. Wales 10 D3......................................51°38'N 3°25'W
Rhondda Cynon Taff d. Wales 21 D2....................51°36'N 3°23'W
Rhône r. France/Switz. 44 F3................................43°37'N 4°40'E
Rhyl Wales 10 D5...53°19'N 3°29'W
Riau, Kepulauan is Indonesia 102 C4....................0°34'N 104°11'E
Ribble r. England 13 E2.......................................53°45'N 2°45'W
Ribe Denmark 43 B1...55°20'N 8°46'E
Ribeirão Preto Brazil 73 E4..................................21°12'S 47°48'W
Ribniţa Moldova 47 M2.......................................47°46'N 29°00'E
Richfield U.S. 62 D4...38°47'N 112°05'W
Richland U.S. 62 C6...46°19'N 119°17'W
Richmond England 13 F3....................................54°24'N 1°44'W
Richmond U.S. 63 K4...37°34'N 77°28'W
Riesa Germany 46 E4..51°19'N 13°17'E
Rifstangi pt Iceland 43 Y2...................................66°33'N 16°13'W
Rīga Latvia 43 F2...56°56'N 24°08'E
Riga, Gulf of Estonia/Latvia 43 E2.......................57°24'N 23°45'E
Rigside Scotland 15 F3.......................................55°36'N 3°47'W
Riihimäki Finland 43 F3.......................................60°44'N 24°47'E
Rijeka Croatia 50 A7..45°20'N 14°26'E
Rimini Italy 48 F5..44°04'N 12°34'E
Rimouski Canada 61 L2.......................................48°27'N 68°32'W
Rimsdale, Loch l. Scotland 17 F3.........................58°17'N 4°10'W
Ringkøbing Denmark 43 B2.................................56°05'N 8°15'E

Ringvassøya i. Norway 43 D5...............................69°55'N 18°56'E
Ringwood England 8 D1.....................................50°51'N 1°47'W
Riobamba Ecuador 72 B6....................................1°41'S 78°42'W
Rio Branco Brazil 72 C5......................................10°01'S 67°48'W
Río Cuarto Argentina 73 C3................................33°08'S 64°21'W
Rio de Janeiro Brazil 73 E4.................................22°55'S 43°17'W
Río Gallegos Argentina 73 C1.............................51°39'S 69°15'W
Rio Grande town Brazil 73 D3.............................32°04'S 52°08'W
Rio Grande r. Mexico/U.S. 67 E6.........................25°57'N 97°10'W
Riohacha Colombia 72 B8....................................11°32'N 72°58'W
Rio Verde Brazil 72 D5..17°48'S 50°55'W
Ripley England 13 F2..53°03'N 1°24'W
Ripon England 13 F3..54°08'N 1°32'W
Risca Wales 10 D3...51°37'N 3°06'W
Rishton England 13 E2..53°46'N 2°25'W
Riva del Garda Italy 46 D1...................................45°53'N 10°50'E
Riverside U.S. 62 C3..33°57'N 117°24'W
Rivière-du-Loup Canada 61 L2.............................47°50'N 69°32'W
Rivne Ukraine 47 L4...50°37'N 26°14'E
Riyadh Saudi Arabia 95 G4.................................24°43'N 46°41'E
Rize Turkey 51 N5..41°02'N 40°30'E
Rizhao China 99 L5..35°19'N 119°33'E
Rjukan Norway 43 B3...59°53'N 8°35'E
Rjuvbrokkene mt. Norway 43 A2.........................59°11'N 7°10'E
Roadford Reservoir England 11 C2.......................50°42'N 4°13'W
Roanne France 44 F5..46°03'N 4°05'E
Roanoke U.S. 63 K4...37°16'N 79°58'W
Roanoke r. U.S. 63 K4..36°02'N 76°22'W
Robert-Bourassa, Réservoir Canada 61 K3

....53°52'N 76°54'W
Robertsfors Sweden 43 E4..................................64°12'N 20°52'E
Roberval Canada 61 K2......................................48°31'N 72°14'W
Robson, Mount Canada 60 G3.............................53°07'N 119°06'W
Roca, Cabo da c. Portugal 45 A3..........................38°47'N 9°29'W
Rocha Uruguay 73 D3...34°30'S 54°19'W
Rochdale England 13 E2......................................53°37'N 2°10'W
Rochefort Belgium 42 E3.....................................50°10'N 5°13'E
Rochefort France 44 C4.......................................45°57'N 0°58'W
Rochester England 9 F2......................................51°23'N 0°30'E
Rochester Minn. U.S. 63 H5................................44°02'N 92°27'W
Rochester N. Y. U.S. 63 K5..................................43°09'N 77°38'W
Rochford England 9 F2..51°35'N 0°42'E
Rockford U.S. 63 I5..42°17'N 89°04'W
Rockhampton Australia 108 E4............................23°23'S 150°34'E
Rockingham Forest England 9 E3.........................52°31'N 0°32'W
Rocky Mountains Canada/U.S. 60 F3....................40°57'N 107°58'W
Rodel Scotland 16 C2...57°45'N 6°58'W
Rodez France 44 E4...44°22'N 2°34'E
Roe r. Northern Ireland 14 C3.............................55°06'N 6°58'W
Roermond Neth. 42 E4.......................................51°12'N 5°59'E
Roeselare Belgium 42 C3....................................50°56'N 3°08'E
Rokiškis Lithuania 43 F1.....................................55°57'N 25°35'E
Rolla U.S. 63 H4...37°56'N 91°46'W
Roma i. Indonesia 103 H2...................................7°31'S 127°25'E
Romain, Cape U.S. 63 K3....................................32°59'N 79°27'W
Roman Romania 47 L2..46°55'N 26°55'E
Romania Europe 49 H6.......................................46°07'N 24°36'E
Romanzof, Cape U.S. 60 B4................................61°49'N 166°06'W
Rombas France 42 F2..49°15'N 6°05'E
Rome Italy 48 F5...41°54'N 12°30'E
Romford England 9 F2..51°35'N 0°11'E
Romney Marsh f. England 9 F2.............................51°03'N 0°54'E
Romny Ukraine 47 O4...50°45'N 33°28'E
Romsey England 8 D1...50°59'N 1°30'W
Rona i. Scotland 16 D2.......................................57°33'N 5°57'W
Rona i. Scotland 16 D4.......................................59°07'N 5°49'W
Ronas Hill Scotland 17 H5..................................60°32'N 1°27'W
Ronda Spain 45 C2..36°44'N 5°10'W
Rondónopolis Brazil 72 D5..................................16°29'S 54°38'W
Rønne Denmark 43 C1..55°06'N 14°43'E
Ronse Belgium 42 C3..50°45'N 3°36'E
Roosendaal Neth. 42 D4.....................................51°31'N 4°28'E
Roque de los Muchachos vol. Canary Islands 45 X2

....28°45'N 17°51'W
Roquefort France 44 C4......................................44°02'N 0°19'W
Roraima, Monte Guyana 72 C7............................5°15'N 60°44'W
Røros Norway 43 B3..62°34'N 11°23'E
Rosario Argentina 73 C3.....................................32°56'S 60°41'W
Roscoff France 44 B6...48°43'N 3°59'W
Roscommon Ireland 18 C3..................................53°38'N 8°11'W
Roscommon d. Ireland 18 C3...............................53°49'N 8°16'W
Roscrea Ireland 18 D2..52°57'N 7°48'W
Roseau Dominica 67 L4......................................15°17'N 61°23'W
Roseburg U.S. 62 B5..43°13'N 123°21'W
Roseires Reservoir Sudan 94 D2..........................11°33'N 34°31'E
Rosenheim Germany 46 E2.................................47°51'N 12°08'E
Roșiori de Vede Romania 50 F7...........................44°07'N 25°00'E
Roslavl' Russia 47 O5...53°57'N 32°51'E
Rossan Point Ireland 18 C4.................................54°42'N 8°48'W
Rossel Island P.N.G. 108 F5................................11°24'S 154°10'E
Rossington England 13 F2...................................53°28'N 1°04'W
Rosslare Harbour Ireland 18 E2............................52°15'N 6°20'W
Rosso Mauritania 84 C3.....................................16°29'N 15°47'W
Ross of Mull pen. Scotland 14 C4.........................56°18'N 6°19'W
Ross-on-Wye England 8 C2.................................51°55'N 2°35'W
Rossosh' Russia 53 D3.......................................50°12'N 39°33'E
Røssvatnet l. Norway 43 C4................................65°46'N 14°19'E
Rostock Germany 46 E6......................................54°05'N 12°07'E
Rostov-na-Donu Russia 53 D2.............................47°13'N 39°44'E
Roswell U.S. 62 F3...33°21'N 104°30'W
Rota i. N. Mariana Is 103 L6................................14°09'N 145°17'E
Rote i. Indonesia 103 G1.....................................10°29'S 123°24'E
Rothbury England 13 F4......................................55°19'N 1°54'W
Rother r. England 8 E1.......................................50°57'N 0°32'W
Rotherham England 13 F2..................................53°26'N 1°21'W
Rothes Scotland 17 F2..57°31'N 3°13'W
Rothesay Scotland 14 D3....................................55°50'N 5°03'W
Rothwell England 8 E3.......................................52°25'N 0°48'W
Rotterdam Neth. 42 D4......................................51°55'N 4°30'E
Rotuma i. Fiji 109 G5..12°29'S 177°05'E
Roubaix France 44 E7...50°42'N 3°10'E
Rouen France 44 D6...49°26'N 1°06'E
Round Hill England 13 F3....................................54°24'N 1°05'W
Round Mountain Australia 108 E3.........................30°24'S 152°15'E
Rouyn-Noranda Canada 63 K6.............................48°14'N 79°02'W
Rovaniemi Finland 43 F4.....................................66°29'N 25°42'E
Rovigo Italy 46 D1..45°04'N 11°47'E
Rovinj Croatia 46 E1..45°05'N 13°38'E
Royale, Isle i. U.S. 63 I6....................................48°02'N 88°38'W
Royal Leamington Spa England 9 E3....................52°17'N 1°32'W
Royal Tunbridge Wells England 9 F2....................51°08'N 0°16'E
Royal Wootton Bassett England 8 D2...................51°32'N 1°54'W
Royan France 44 C4...45°38'N 1°01'W
Royston England 9 E3..52°03'N 0°01'W
Royton England 13 E2..53°34'N 2°07'W
Ruabon Wales 10 D4..52°59'N 3°02'W
Rub' al Khali des. Asia 95 G3..............................19°01'N 46°30'E

Rubtsovsk Russia 54 J3......................................51°33'N 81°09'E
Rudnya Russia 47 N6...54°57'N 31°06'E
Rüdnyy Kazakhstan 54 H3..................................52°57'N 63°07'E
Rufiji r. Tanzania 83 C4......................................8°02'S 39°17'E
Rugby England 8 D3..52°22'N 1°16'W
Rugby U.S. 62 F6..48°20'N 100°01'W
Rugeley England 8 D3..52°46'N 1°56'W
Rügen i. Germany 46 E6.....................................54°23'N 13°27'E
Ruhr r. Germany 42 F4.......................................51°26'N 6°43'E
Rukwa, Lake Tanzania 83 C4..............................8°09'S 32°25'E
Rum i. Scotland 16 C1..56°59'N 6°22'W
Ruma Serbia 50 C7..45°01'N 19°50'E
Rum Cay i. Bahamas 67 J5...................................23°42'N 74°48'W
Runcorn England 12 E2.......................................53°20'N 2°42'W
Rundu Namibia 83 A3...17°54'S 19°47'E
Ruoqiang China 98 F5..38°58'N 88°08'E
Ruse Bulgaria 50 F6...43°49'N 25°57'E
Rushden England 8 E3..52°17'N 0°36'W
Russia Asia/Europe 54 I4....................................57°12'N 40°44'E
Ruteng Indonesia 102 G2....................................8°33'S 120°25'E
Ruthin Wales 10 D5..53°07'N 3°19'W
Rutland d. England 21 E3....................................52°40'N 0°38'W
Rutland Water resr England 8 E3..........................52°39'N 0°40'W
Ruza Russia 47 Q6...55°42'N 36°13'E
Ruzayevka Russia 53 E3......................................54°03'N 44°58'E
Ružomberok Slovakia 46 H3................................49°05'N 19°17'E
Rwanda Africa 85 G1...2°16'S 29°58'E
Ryan, Loch b. Scotland 14 D3.............................55°01'N 5°05'W
Ryazan' Russia 53 D3...54°37'N 39°44'E
Rybachiy, Poluostrov f. Russia 52 D4..................69°40'N 32°32'E
Rybinsk Russia 52 D3...58°03'N 38°51'E
Rybinskoye Vodokhranilishche resr Russia 52 D3

....58°21'N 38°22'E
Rybnik Poland 46 H4..50°06'N 18°33'E
Ryde England 8 D1..50°44'N 1°10'W
Rye England 9 F1...50°57'N 0°44'E
Rye r. England 13 G3...54°10'N 0°56'W
Rye Bay England 9 F1..50°55'N 0°47'E
Ryōtsu Japan 104 C3...38°04'N 138°25'E
Ryukyu Islands Japan 99 M2...............................24°13'N 124°52'E
Rzeszów Poland 47 J4..50°02'N 22°01'E
Rzhev Russia 52 D3...56°16'N 34°20'E

S

Saale r. Germany 46 D4.....................................51°57'N 11°56'E
Saarbrücken Germany 46 B3...............................49°15'N 6°58'E
Saaremaa i. Estonia 43 E2..................................58°14'N 22°46'E
Saarland d. Germany 42 F2.................................49°28'N 6°53'E
Saarlouis Germany 42 F2....................................49°20'N 6°46'E
Sab' Ābār Syria 51 L1..33°42'N 37°47'E
Šabac Serbia 50 C7..44°46'N 19°42'E
Sabadell Spain 45 G4...41°33'N 2°05'E
Sabah d. Malaysia 102 F5...................................5°27'N 116°59'E
Sabana, Archipiélago de is Cuba 67 H5...............23°18'N 80°46'W
Sabhā Libya 84 F4...26°55'N 14°28'E
Sabinas Mexico 66 D6..27°52'N 101°07'W
Sable, Cape Canada 61 L2..................................43°25'N 65°39'W
Sable, Cape U.S. 63 J2.......................................25°08'N 81°10'W
Sable Island Canada 61 M2.................................43°57'N 59°55'W
Şabyā Saudi Arabia 94 F3...................................17°07'N 42°35'E
Sabzevār Iran 95 I7..36°12'N 57°37'E
Sacramento U.S. 62 B4.......................................38°34'N 121°25'W
Sacramento Mountains U.S. 62 E3.......................34°23'N 106°04'W
Sado r. Portugal 45 A3.......................................38°25'N 8°36'W
Sadoga Shima i. Japan 104 C3............................37°56'N 138°33'E
Säffle Sweden 43 C2..59°08'N 12°56'E
Saffron Walden England 9 F3..............................52°02'N 0°15'E
Safi Morocco 84 D5...32°22'N 9°15'W
Safonovo Russia 47 O6.......................................55°07'N 33°14'E
Safonovo Russia 52 E4.......................................65°41'N 48°08'E
Sagar India 96 E5..23°50'N 78°45'E
Sagra mt. Spain 45 D2.......................................37°58'N 2°35'W
Sagres Portugal 45 A2..37°01'N 8°57'W
Sahand, Kūh-e mt. Iran 95 G7.............................37°38'N 46°28'E
Sahara des. Africa 84 E4.....................................19°01'N 4°03'E
Saidpur Bangl. 96 G6...25°46'N 88°58'E
Saimaa l. Finland 43 G3......................................61°15'N 28°21'E
St Abb's Head Scotland 15 G3.............................55°55'N 2°09'W
St Agnes England 11 B2......................................50°19'N 5°12'W
St Agnes i. England 11 A1...................................49°53'N 6°21'W
St Albans England 9 E2.......................................51°45'N 0°20'W
St Aldhelm's Head England 8 C1..........................50°35'N 2°03'W
St-Amand-les-Eaux France 42 C3........................50°26'N 3°25'E
St-Amand-Montrond France 44 E5........................46°44'N 2°30'E
St Andrews Scotland 15 G4.................................56°20'N 2°48'W
St Anne Channel Is 11 Z9....................................49°43'N 2°12'W
St Ann's Head Wales 10 B3.................................51°41'N 5°12'W
St Anthony Canada 61 M3...................................51°20'N 55°23'W
St Asaph Wales 10 D5..53°15'N 3°27'W
St Austell England 11 C2....................................50°20'N 4°47'W
St Austell Bay England 11 C2..............................50°19'N 4°45'W
St-Barthélemy i. Central America 67 L4................17°54'N 62°49'W
St Bees England 12 D3.......................................54°30'N 3°35'W
St Bees Head England 12 D3...............................54°31'N 3°38'W
St Brelade Channel Is 11 Z8................................49°11'N 2°12'W
St Brides Bay Wales 10 B3..................................51°48'N 5°18'W
St-Brieuc France 44 B6.......................................48°31'N 2°45'W
St Catherine's Point England 8 D1.......................50°34'N 1°17'W
St Clears Wales 10 C3..51°49'N 4°30'W
St Cloud U.S. 63 H6...45°34'N 94°10'W
St Columb Major England 11 C2..........................50°26'N 4°56'W
St Davids Wales 10 B3.......................................51°53'N 5°16'W
St David's Head Wales 10 B3...............................51°54'N 5°20'W
St-Dié France 44 G6...48°17'N 6°57'E
St-Dizier France 44 F6..48°39'N 4°57'E
Saintes France 44 C4..45°45'N 0°37'W
St-Étienne France 44 F4......................................45°26'N 4°24'E
Saintfield Northern Ireland 14 D2........................54°27'N 5°49'W
St Gallen Switz. 46 C2..47°26'N 9°23'E
St-Gaudens France 44 D3....................................43°07'N 0°44'E
St George's Grenada 67 L3..................................12°04'N 61°45'W
St George's Channel Ireland/U.K. 18 E1...............51°58'N 6°08'W
St Germans England 11 C2..................................50°24'N 4°19'W
St Govan's Head Wales 10 C3..............................51°36'N 4°55'W
St Helena i. Atlantic Oc. 78 B2............................16°00'S 5°60'W
St Helena Bay S. Africa 83 A1..............................32°43'S 18°02'E
St Helens England 12 E2.....................................53°27'N 2°44'W
St Helens, Mount vol. U.S. 62 B6.........................46°08'N 122°13'W
St Helier Channel Is 11 Z8...................................49°11'N 2°06'W
St Ives Cambs. England 9 E3...............................52°20'N 0°04'W
St Ives Corn. England 11 B2................................50°13'N 5°29'W
St Ives Bay England 11 B2..................................50°13'N 5°28'W
St-Jean, Lac l. Canada 63 L6...............................48°37'N 72°07'W
St Joe r. U.S. 62 C6...47°25'N 116°45'W

aint John Canada 61 L2 .... 45°16'N 66°04'W
John Channel Is 11 Z8 .... 49°15'N 2°08'W
aint John r. U.S. 63 M6 .... 45°46'N 66°12'W
John's Antigua 67 L4 .... 17°05'N 61°51'W
John's Canada 61 M2 .... 47°28'N 52°18'W
John's Point Northern Ireland 14 D2 .... 54°13'N 5°39'W
John's Town of Dalry Scotland 14 E3 .... 55°06'N 4°10'W
Joseph U.S. 63 H4 .... 39°48'N 94°51'W
Joseph, Lake Canada 63 H7 .... 50°59'N 90°57'W
Just England 11 B2 .... 50°08'N 5°41'W
Keverne England 11 B2 .... 50°03'N 5°05'W
Kilda is Scotland 16 A2 .... 57°49'N 8°33'W
Kitts and Nevis Central America 67 L4 .... 17°17'N 62°35'W
Lawrence r. Canada 61 L2 .... 48°18'N 69°06'W
Lawrence, Gulf of Canada 61 L2 .... 48°20'N 61°29'W
Lawrence Island U.S. 60 B4 .... 63°05'N 169°50'W
-Lô France 44 C6 .... 49°07'N 1°05'W
-Louis Senegal 84 C3 .... 16°00'N 16°29'W
Louis U.S. 63 H4 .... 38°43'N 90°14'W
Lucia Central America 67 L3 .... 13°57'N 60°53'W
Magnus Bay Scotland 17 H5 .... 60°24'N 1°37'W
-Malo France 44 B6 .... 48°39'N 2°00'W
-Malo, Golfe de g. France 44 B6 .... 48°48'N 2°16'W
Margaret's Hope Scotland 17 G3 .... 58°49'N 2°57'W
Martin Channel Is 11 Y9 .... 49°26'N 2°33'W
Martin Channel Is 11 Z8 .... 49°13'N 2°03'W
-Martin i. Central America 67 L4 .... 18°08'N 62°59'W
Mary's i. England 11 A1 .... 49°58'N 6°17'W
Mary's i. England 11 A1 .... 49°56'N 6°16'W
Matthew Island U.S. 60 A4 .... 60°27'N 172°49'W
-Maurice r. Canada 63 L6 .... 46°22'N 72°32'W
Mawes England 11 B2 .... 50°09'N 5°01'W
Moritz Switz. 46 C2 .... 46°30'N 9°50'E
-Nazaire France 44 B5 .... 47°17'N 2°13'W
Neuts England 9 E3 .... 52°14'N 0°16'W
-Niklaas Belgium 42 D4 .... 51°10'N 4°10'E
-Omer France 42 B3 .... 50°45'N 2°16'E
Ouen Channel Is 11 Z8 .... 49°14'N 2°12'W
Paul U.S. 63 H5 .... 44°57'N 93°05'W
Peter Port Channel Is 11 Y9 .... 49°28'N 2°32'W
Petersburg Russia 53 E3 .... 59°56'N 30°18'E
Petersburg U.S. 63 J2 .... 27°45'N 82°42'W
Pierre and Miquelon is N. America 61 M2
   .... 46°42'N 56°29'W
-Pol-sur-Ternoise France 9 H1 .... 50°23'N 2°20'E
Pölten Austria 46 E2 .... 48°12'N 15°38'E
-Quentin France 44 E6 .... 49°51'N 3°17'E
Sampson Channel Is 11 Y9 .... 49°29'N 2°31'W
Vincent and the Grenadines Central America 67 L3
   .... 12°50'N 60°52'W
-Vith Belgium 42 F3 .... 50°17'N 6°07'E
Wendel Germany 42 G2 .... 49°28'N 7°09'E
aipan i. N. Mariana Is 103 L7 .... 15°15'N 145°49'E
aitama Japan 104 C3 .... 35°51'N 139°39'E
akai Japan 104 C2 .... 34°34'N 135°29'E
akākā Saudi Arabia 94 F5 .... 29°56'N 40°05'E
akawkawa, Lake U.S. 62 F6 .... 47°45'N 102°15'W
akarya r. Turkey 51 I5 .... 41°07'N 30°38'E
akata Japan 104 C3 .... 38°54'N 139°49'E
akhalin, Ostrov i. Russia 55 P3 .... 48°10'N 142°40'E
aki Azerbaijan 53 E2 .... 41°12'N 47°13'E
akura Japan 104 D3 .... 35°44'N 140°13'E
al i. Cape Verde 84 B3 .... 16°49'N 22°59'W
ala Sweden 43 D2 .... 59°55'N 16°36'E
alado r. Argentina 73 C3 .... 32°27'S 60°49'W
alado r. Mexico 66 E6 .... 26°45'N 99°26'W
alālah Oman 95 H3 .... 17°02'N 54°10'E
alamanca Spain 45 C4 .... 40°58'N 5°39'W
alawati i. Indonesia 103 I3 .... 1°05'S 130°53'E
alayar i. Indonesia 102 G2 .... 6°08'S 120°30'E
alčininkai Lithuania 47 K6 .... 54°18'N 25°23'E
alcombe England 11 D2 .... 50°14'N 3°46'W
aldanha S. Africa 83 A1 .... 33°01'S 17°57'E
ale Australia 108 D3 .... 38°06'S 147°06'E
ale England 13 E2 .... 53°26'N 2°19'W
alehurst England 9 F1 .... 50°59'N 0°30'E
alekhard Russia 52 G4 .... 66°31'N 66°43'E
alem India 96 E3 .... 11°37'N 78°08'E
alem U.S. 63 B5 .... 44°54'N 122°58'W
alerno Italy 48 F5 .... 40°40'N 14°47'E
alerno, Golfo di g. Italy 48 F5 .... 40°25'N 14°43'E
alford England 13 E2 .... 53°29'N 2°18'W
alihli Turkey 51 H4 .... 38°29'N 28°08'E
alihorsk Belarus 47 L5 .... 52°47'N 27°32'E
alinas U.S. 62 B4 .... 36°41'N 121°39'W
alisbury England 8 D2 .... 51°04'N 1°48'W
alisbury U.S. 63 K4 .... 38°22'N 75°36'W
alisbury Plain f. England 8 C2 .... 51°15'N 2°03'W
alluit Canada 61 K4 .... 62°11'N 75°42'W
almon r. U.S. 62 C6 .... 45°52'N 116°45'W
almon Arm Canada 62 C7 .... 50°42'N 119°17'W
almon River Mountains U.S. 62 C5 .... 44°46'N 115°01'W
alo Finland 43 F3 .... 60°23'N 23°08'E
alt r. U.S. 62 D3 .... 46°28'N 41°33'E
alta Argentina 73 C4 .... 24°45'S 65°25'W
altash England 11 C2 .... 50°24'N 4°13'W
altcoats Scotland 14 E3 .... 55°38'N 4°47'W
altillo Mexico 66 D6 .... 25°29'N 101°01'W
alt Lake City U.S. 62 D5 .... 40°42'N 111°54'W
alton Sea l. U.S. 62 C3 .... 33°28'N 115°58'W
alvador Brazil 72 F5 .... 12°57'S 38°25'W
alween r. China/Myanmar 97 I5 .... 24°06'N 98°35'E
alyan Azerbaijan 53 E1 .... 39°35'N 48°58'E
alzburg Austria 46 E2 .... 47°48'N 13°03'E
amandağ Turkey 51 K3 .... 36°04'N 35°58'E
amani Japan 104 D4 .... 42°08'N 142°54'E
amar i. Phil. 103 H6 .... 11°54'N 125°43'E
amara Russia 53 F3 .... 53°11'N 50°09'E
amarinda Indonesia 102 F3 .... 0°29'S 117°11'E
amarra' Iraq 94 F6 .... 34°12'N 43°54'E
amba Dem. Rep. Congo 83 B4 .... 4°38'S 26°20'E
ambalpur India 96 F5 .... 21°27'N 83°59'E
ambas Indonesia 102 D4 .... 1°22'N 109°19'E
ambir Ukraine 47 J3 .... 49°31'N 23°12'E
ambre r. Belgium/France 42 D3 .... 50°28'N 4°52'E
amer France 9 G1 .... 50°38'N 1°45'E
amoa S. Pacific Oc. 109 H5 .... 13°58'S 173°23'W
amos i. Greece 50 F5 .... 37°49'N 26°44'E
amothraki i. Greece 50 F5 .... 40°24'N 25°34'E
ampit Indonesia 102 E3 .... 2°34'S 112°55'E
amsun Turkey 51 L5 .... 41°17'N 36°19'E

San Mali 84 D3 .... 13°18'N 4°54'W
Sanaa Yemen 94 F3 .... 15°23'N 44°11'E
Sanandaj Iran 95 G7 .... 35°16'N 46°58'E
San Andrés, Isla de i. Caribbean Sea 67 H3
   .... 12°33'N 81°41'W
San Angelo U.S. 62 F3 .... 31°28'N 100°23'W
San Antonio U.S. 62 G2 .... 29°22'N 98°27'W
San Antonio, Cabo c. Cuba 67 H5 .... 21°51'N 84°55'W
San Benedicto, Isla i. Mexico 66 B4 .... 19°19'N 110°47'W
San Cristóbal Venezuela 72 B7 .... 7°45'N 72°15'W
San Cristóbal de la Laguna Canary Islands 45 X2
   .... 28°28'N 16°19'W
Sancti Spíritus Cuba 67 I5 .... 21°56'N 79°26'W
Sanda Island Scotland 14 D3 .... 55°16'N 5°35'W
Sandakan Malaysia 102 F5 .... 5°51'N 118°05'E
Sandane Norway 43 A3 .... 61°47'N 6°14'E
Sandanski Bulgaria 50 E5 .... 41°34'N 23°16'E
Sanday i. Scotland 17 G4 .... 59°15'N 2°29'W
Sanday Sound str. Scotland 17 G4 .... 59°12'N 2°34'W
Sandbach England 13 E2 .... 53°09'N 2°22'W
Sandhurst England 8 E2 .... 51°21'N 0°48'W
San Diego U.S. 62 C3 .... 32°43'N 117°05'W
Sandıklı Turkey 51 I4 .... 38°28'N 30°16'E
Sandnes Norway 43 A2 .... 58°51'N 5°44'E
Sandnessjøen Norway 43 C4 .... 66°01'N 12°39'E
Sandoway Myanmar 97 H4 .... 18°27'N 94°22'E
Sandown England 8 D1 .... 50°40'N 1°09'W
Sandpoint U.S. 62 C6 .... 48°16'N 116°33'W
Sandray i. Scotland 16 B1 .... 56°54'N 7°30'W
Sandviken Sweden 43 D3 .... 60°37'N 16°46'E
Sandwich England 9 G2 .... 51°16'N 1°20'E
Sandy England 9 E3 .... 52°08'N 0°18'W
Sandy Cape Australia 108 E4 .... 24°42'S 153°15'E
Sandy Lake town Canada 61 I3 .... 53°03'N 93°18'W
San Felipe Mexico 66 B7 .... 31°02'N 114°50'W
San Fernando Phil. 102 G7 .... 16°38'N 120°18'E
San Fernando Spain 45 B2 .... 36°28'N 6°11'W
San Fernando de Apure Venezuela 72 C7 .... 7°49'N 67°28'W
San Francisco U.S. 62 B4 .... 37°45'N 122°25'W
San Francisco de Paula, Cabo c. Argentina 73 C2
   .... 49°42'S 67°40'W
Sangir, Kepulauan is Indonesia 103 G4 .... 2°15'N 124°57'E
Sangkulirang Indonesia 102 F4 .... 0°55'N 117°58'E
Sangli India 96 D4 .... 16°53'N 74°38'E
Sangre de Cristo Range mts U.S. 62 E4 .... 38°19'N 106°01'W
Sanirajak (Hall Beach) town Canada 61 J4 .... 68°42'N 81°17'W
San Jorge, Golfo de g. Argentina 73 C2 .... 45°57'S 65°55'W
San José Costa Rica 67 H2 .... 9°57'N 84°02'W
San Jose U.S. 62 B4 .... 37°18'N 121°57'W
San José, Isla i. Mexico 66 B5 .... 24°54'N 110°33'W
San José del Cabo Mexico 66 C5 .... 23°04'N 109°44'W
San Juan Argentina 73 C3 .... 31°33'S 68°31'W
San Juan r. Costa Rica/Nicaragua 67 H3 .... 10°47'N 83°44'W
San Juan Puerto Rico 67 K4 .... 18°26'N 66°04'W
San Juan r. U.S. 62 D4 .... 37°15'N 110°30'W
San Juan Mountains U.S. 62 E4 .... 37°35'N 107°17'W
Şanlıurfa Turkey 51 M3 .... 37°09'N 38°49'E
San Lorenzo mt. Spain 45 D5 .... 42°14'N 2°58'W
Sanlúcar de Barrameda Spain 45 B2 .... 36°46'N 6°21'W
San Luis Obispo U.S. 62 B4 .... 35°18'N 120°40'W
San Luis Potosí Mexico 66 D5 .... 22°10'N 100°58'W
San Luis Potosí d. Mexico 66 D5 .... 22°51'N 100°48'W
San Marcos U.S. 62 G2 .... 29°51'N 97°56'W
San Marino Europe 48 F5 .... 43°58'N 12°27'E
San Marino San Marino 48 F5 .... 43°57'N 12°27'E
San Matías, Golfo g. Argentina 73 C2 .... 41°20'S 64°35'W
San Miguel r. Bolivia 72 C5 .... 13°52'S 63°54'W
San Miguel El Salvador 66 G3 .... 13°32'N 88°08'W
San Miguel de Tucumán Argentina 73 C4 .... 26°48'S 65°16'W
Sanming China 99 L3 .... 26°11'N 117°39'E
San Pablo Phil. 103 G6 .... 14°04'N 121°18'E
San Pedro Mezquital r. Mexico 66 D5 .... 21°52'N 105°29'W
San Pedro de Ycumandyyú Paraguay 73 D4
   .... 24°08'S 57°08'W
San Pedro, Sierra de mts Spain 45 B3 .... 39°31'N 7°15'W
San Pedro Sula Honduras 66 G4 .... 15°28'N 88°01'W
Sanquhar Scotland 15 F3 .... 55°22'N 3°56'W
San Quintín, Cabo c. Mexico 62 C3 .... 30°23'N 116°01'W
Sanremo Italy 44 G3 .... 43°49'N 7°47'E
San Salvador i. Bahamas 67 J5 .... 24°07'N 74°27'W
San Salvador El Salvador 66 G3 .... 13°43'N 89°11'W
San Salvador de Jujuy Argentina 73 C4 .... 24°10'S 65°20'W
San Sebastián de la Gomera Canary Islands 45 X2
   .... 28°05'N 17°06'W
Santa Ana El Salvador 66 G3 .... 14°00'N 89°31'W
Santa Ana U.S. 62 C3 .... 33°45'N 117°56'W
Santa Barbara U.S. 62 C3 .... 34°27'N 119°43'W
Santa Clara Cuba 67 I5 .... 22°24'N 79°56'W
Santa Cruz Bolivia 72 C5 .... 17°47'S 63°12'W
Santa Cruz de la Palma Canary Islands 45 X2
   .... 28°41'N 17°46'W
Santa Cruz de Tenerife Canary Islands 45 X2
   .... 28°27'N 16°15'W
Santa Cruz Islands Solomon Is 109 F5 .... 10°46'S 167°21'E
Santa Fé Argentina 73 C3 .... 31°37'S 60°42'W
Santa Fe U.S. 62 E4 .... 35°42'N 105°57'W
Santa Isabel i. Solomon Is 109 E6 .... 7°55'S 159°11'E
Santa Margarita, Isla i. Mexico 66 B5 .... 24°25'N 111°50'W
Santa Maria Brazil 73 D4 .... 29°41'S 53°48'W
Santa Maria U.S. 62 B3 .... 34°58'N 120°26'W
Santa Maria di Leuca, Capo c. Italy 50 C4 .... 39°47'N 18°21'E
Santa Marta Colombia 72 B8 .... 11°16'N 74°12'W
Santana Brazil 72 D6 .... 0°01'S 51°09'W
Santander Spain 45 D5 .... 43°28'N 3°48'W
Santarém Brazil 72 D6 .... 2°27'S 54°43'W
Santarém Portugal 45 A3 .... 39°15'N 8°41'W
Santa Rosa Argentina 73 C3 .... 36°37'S 64°17'W
Santa Rosalía Mexico 66 B6 .... 27°21'N 112°18'W
Santiago i. Cape Verde 84 B3 .... 15°19'N 23°45'W
Santiago Chile 73 B3 .... 33°25'S 70°39'W
Santiago Dom. Rep. 67 J4 .... 19°29'N 70°41'W
Santiago de Compostela Spain 45 A5 .... 42°53'N 8°32'W
Santiago de Cuba Cuba 67 I4 .... 20°00'N 75°49'W
Sant Jordi, Golf de g. Spain 45 F4 .... 40°49'N 0°56'E
Santo André Brazil 73 E4 .... 23°38'S 46°30'W
Santo Antão i. Cape Verde 84 B3 .... 17°01'N 25°21'W
Santo Domingo Dom. Rep. 67 K4 .... 18°31'N 69°52'W
Santoña Spain 45 D5 .... 43°27'N 3°27'W
Santos Brazil 73 E4 .... 23°58'S 46°20'W
San Valentín, Monte mt. Chile 73 B2 .... 46°35'S 73°27'W
São Francisco r. Brazil 72 E5 .... 10°19'S 36°31'W
São Gabriel da Cachoeira Brazil 72 C6 .... 0°06'S 67°02'W
São João do Rio Preto Brazil 73 E4 .... 20°49'S 49°22'W
São Luís Brazil 72 E6 .... 2°35'S 44°18'W
Saône r. France 44 F4 .... 45°44'N 4°49'E
São Paulo Brazil 73 E4 .... 23°35'S 46°36'W
São Tomé São Tomé and Príncipe 84 E2 .... 0°19'N 6°44'E

São Tomé i. São Tomé and Príncipe 84 E2 .... 0°21'N 6°35'E
São Tomé, Cabo de c. Brazil 73 E4 .... 22°00'S 40°59'W
São Tomé and Príncipe Africa 84 E2 .... 1°00'N 7°04'E
São Vicente, Cabo de c. Portugal 45 A2 .... 37°01'N 8°59'W
Sápmi f. Europe 43 E5 .... 67°12'N 18°37'E
Sapporo Japan 104 D4 .... 43°04'N 141°20'E
Sapri Italy 49 G5 .... 40°04'N 15°38'E
Saqqaq Greenland 61 M5 .... 70°01'N 51°56'W
Saqqez Iran 95 G7 .... 36°12'N 46°15'E
Sarāb Iran 95 G7 .... 37°55'N 47°31'E
Sara Buri Thailand 102 C6 .... 14°29'N 100°57'E
Sarajevo Bos. and Herz. 50 C6 .... 43°51'N 18°25'E
Sarandë Albania 50 D4 .... 39°53'N 20°01'E
Saransk Russia 53 E3 .... 54°11'N 45°12'E
Sarapul Russia 52 F3 .... 56°30'N 53°48'E
Sarasota U.S. 63 J2 .... 27°19'N 82°33'W
Saratov Russia 53 E3 .... 51°34'N 45°59'E
Saravan Iran 95 J5 .... 27°20'N 62°25'E
Sarawak d. Malaysia 102 E4 .... 1°46'N 111°55'E
Saray Turkey 51 G5 .... 41°26'N 27°55'E
Sardinia i. Italy 48 E4 .... 40°16'N 8°04'E
Sarektjåkkå mt. Sweden 43 D4 .... 67°27'N 17°43'E
Sar-e Pol Afgh. 95 K7 .... 36°15'N 65°57'E
Sargodha Pakistan 96 D7 .... 32°01'N 72°41'E
Sarh Chad 85 F2 .... 9°07'N 18°23'E
Sārī Iran 95 H7 .... 36°33'N 53°03'E
Sarigan i. N. Mariana Is 103 L7 .... 16°42'N 145°48'E
Sarıyer Turkey 51 H5 .... 41°10'N 29°03'E
Sark i. Channel Is 11 Y9 .... 49°24'N 2°24'W
Şarkışla Turkey 51 L4 .... 39°21'N 36°25'E
Şarköy Turkey 50 G5 .... 40°37'N 27°06'E
Särna Sweden 43 C3 .... 61°42'N 13°08'E
Sarny Ukraine 47 L4 .... 51°20'N 26°37'E
Saros Körfezi b. Turkey 50 G5 .... 40°34'N 26°36'E
Sarov Russia 53 E3 .... 54°56'N 43°20'E
Sarpsborg Norway 43 B2 .... 59°17'N 11°08'E
Sarrebourg France 44 G6 .... 48°44'N 7°03'E
Sarreguemines France 42 G2 .... 49°07'N 7°04'E
Sarria Spain 45 B5 .... 42°47'N 7°24'W
Sarthe r. France 44 C5 .... 47°34'N 0°31'W
Sasebo Japan 104 A2 .... 33°09'N 129°44'E
Saskatchewan d. Canada 60 H3 .... 53°08'N 106°03'W
Saskatchewan r. Canada 60 H3 .... 53°40'N 100°27'W
Saskatoon Canada 60 H3 .... 52°08'N 106°39'W
Sassandra Côte d'Ivoire 84 D2 .... 4°57'N 6°05'W
Sassari Italy 48 E4 .... 40°43'N 8°34'E
Sassnitz Germany 46 E6 .... 54°31'N 13°38'E
Satka Russia 52 F3 .... 55°04'N 58°58'E
Satpura Range mts India 96 D5 .... 21°47'N 74°23'E
Satu Mare Romania 47 J2 .... 47°48'N 22°53'E
Sauðárkrókur Iceland 43 Y2 .... 65°45'N 19°40'W
Saudi Arabia Asia 94 F4 .... 23°41'N 44°13'E
Sault Sainte Marie Canada 61 J2 .... 46°31'N 84°20'W
Saumlakki Indonesia 103 I2 .... 8°00'S 131°20'E
Saundersfoot Wales 10 C3 .... 51°43'N 4°42'W
Saurimo Angola 83 B4 .... 9°39'S 20°25'E
Sava r. Europe 50 D7 .... 44°50'N 20°28'E
Savai'i i. Samoa 109 H5 .... 13°25'S 172°39'W
Savannah U.S. 63 J3 .... 32°04'N 81°07'W
Savannah r. U.S. 63 J3 .... 32°02'N 80°53'W
Savannakhet Laos 102 C7 .... 16°32'N 104°46'E
Save r. Mozambique/Zimbabwe 83 C2 .... 20°56'S 35°03'E
Savinskiy Russia 52 E4 .... 62°56'N 40°09'E
Savona Italy 46 C1 .... 44°19'N 8°29'E
Savu Sea Indonesia 103 G2 .... 9°51'S 121°22'E
Sawel Mountain hill Northern Ireland 14 B2
   .... 54°49'N 7°02'W
Sawhāj Egypt 49 J2 .... 26°31'N 31°38'E
Sawston England 9 F3 .... 52°07'N 0°10'E
Sawtry England 9 E3 .... 52°26'N 0°17'W
Sawu i. Indonesia 103 G1 .... 10°32'S 121°58'E
Saxilby England 13 G2 .... 53°16'N 0°40'W
Saxmundham England 9 G3 .... 52°13'N 1°29'E
Sayhūt Yemen 95 H3 .... 15°15'N 51°19'E
Saylac Somalia 85 I3 .... 11°17'N 43°28'E
Saynshand Mongolia 99 K6 .... 44°46'N 110°12'E
Scafell Pike hill England 12 D3 .... 54°27'N 3°13'W
Scalasaig Scotland 14 C4 .... 56°04'N 6°11'W
Scalby England 13 G3 .... 54°18'N 0°27'W
Scalloway Scotland 17 H5 .... 60°08'N 1°17'W
Scalp hill Ireland 18 C2 .... 52°59'N 8°29'W
Scalpay i. High. Scotland 16 D2 .... 57°18'N 5°59'W
Scalpay i. Na h-E. S. Scotland 16 C2 .... 57°52'N 6°39'W
Scalp Mountain hill Ireland 14 B3 .... 55°06'N 7°22'W
Scampton England 13 G2 .... 53°18'N 0°34'W
Scandinavia f. Europe 34 F5 .... 65°00'N 18°00'E
Scapa Flow inlet Scotland 17 F3 .... 58°54'N 3°08'W
Scarba i. Scotland 14 D4 .... 56°10'N 5°45'W
Scarborough England 13 G3 .... 54°17'N 0°24'W
Scarp i. Scotland 16 B3 .... 58°01'N 7°11'W
Schaffhausen Switz. 46 C2 .... 47°42'N 8°38'E
Schagen Neth. 42 D5 .... 52°47'N 4°48'E
Schefferville Canada 61 L3 .... 54°47'N 66°48'W
Scheldt r. Belgium 42 D4 .... 51°21'N 4°15'E
Schiehallion mt. Scotland 17 E1 .... 56°40'N 4°06'W
Schiermonnikoog i. Neth. 42 F6 .... 53°28'N 6°09'E
Schleswig Germany 46 C6 .... 54°31'N 9°33'E
Schwäbische Alb mts Germany 46 C2 .... 47°59'N 8°43'E
Schwaner, Pegunungan mts Indonesia 102 E3
   .... 0°46'S 112°26'E
Schwarzer Mann hill Germany 42 F3 .... 50°15'N 6°21'E
Schwedt/Oder Germany 46 F5 .... 53°04'N 14°18'E
Schweinfurt Germany 46 D4 .... 50°03'N 10°13'E
Schwerin Germany 46 D5 .... 53°38'N 11°25'E
Scilly, Isles of England 11 A1 .... 49°55'N 6°17'W
Scioto r. U.S. 63 J4 .... 38°44'N 82°59'W
Scole England 9 G3 .... 52°22'N 1°09'E
Scone Scotland 15 F4 .... 56°25'N 3°24'W
Scotland d. U.K. 20 D5 .... 57°01'N 3°53'W
Scottish Borders d. Scotland 20 D4 .... 55°40'N 2°44'W
Scottsbluff U.S. 62 F5 .... 41°54'N 103°41'W
Scourie Scotland 16 D3 .... 58°21'N 5°09'W
Scranton U.S. 63 K5 .... 41°25'N 75°39'W
Scridain, Loch inlet Scotland 14 C4 .... 56°21'N 6°11'W
Scunthorpe England 13 G2 .... 53°35'N 0°38'W
Scuol Switz. 46 D2 .... 46°48'N 10°18'E
Scutari, Lake Albania/Montenegro 50 C6 .... 42°14'N 19°12'E
Seaford England 9 F1 .... 50°46'N 0°06'E
Seaham England 13 F3 .... 54°50'N 1°20'W
Seamer England 13 G3 .... 54°14'N 0°26'W
Seascale England 12 D3 .... 54°24'N 3°29'W
Seaton Cumb. England 12 D3 .... 54°40'N 3°31'W
Seaton Devon England 11 D2 .... 50°42'N 3°04'W
Seaton Delaval England 13 F4 .... 55°04'N 1°31'W
Seattle U.S. 62 B6 .... 47°36'N 122°20'W
Sebastián Vizcaíno, Bahía b. Mexico 66 B6
   .... 28°08'N 114°45'W

Sebeş Romania 50 E7 .... 45°58'N 23°34'E
Şebinkarahisar Turkey 51 M5 .... 40°17'N 38°25'E
Secunderabad India 96 E4 .... 17°25'N 78°27'E
Sedan France 44 F6 .... 49°42'N 4°57'E
Sedbergh England 13 E3 .... 54°19'N 2°31'W
Seefin hill Ireland 18 D2 .... 52°14'N 7°36'W
Segezha Russia 52 D4 .... 63°45'N 34°19'E
Segorbe Spain 45 E3 .... 39°51'N 0°28'W
Segovia Spain 45 C4 .... 40°57'N 4°06'W
Segura r. Spain 45 E3 .... 38°06'N 0°38'W
Segura, Sierra de mts Spain 45 D2 .... 37°59'N 2°46'W
Seiland i. Norway 43 E5 .... 70°28'N 23°18'E
Seim r. Russia/Ukraine 47 P4 .... 51°16'N 34°16'E
Seinäjoki Finland 43 E3 .... 62°47'N 22°51'E
Seine r. France 44 D6 .... 49°26'N 0°15'E
Seine, Baie de b. France 44 C6 .... 49°29'N 0°32'W
Sekondi-Takoradi Ghana 84 D2 .... 4°58'N 1°43'W
Selaru i. Indonesia 103 I2 .... 8°13'S 130°53'E
Selatan, Tanjung pt Indonesia 102 E3 .... 4°09'S 114°38'E
Selattyn England 8 B3 .... 52°54'N 3°05'W
Selawik U.S. 60 B4 .... 66°36'N 160°16'W
Selby England 13 F2 .... 53°47'N 1°04'W
Selkirk Canada 60 I3 .... 50°09'N 96°53'W
Selkirk Scotland 15 G3 .... 55°33'N 2°50'W
Sellindge England 9 F2 .... 51°06'N 0°59'E
Selsey England 8 E1 .... 50°44'N 0°47'W
Selsey Bill hd England 8 E1 .... 50°43'N 0°49'W
Selvas f. Brazil 72 B6 .... 6°29'S 71°47'W
Selwyn Mountains Canada 60 E4 .... 64°16'N 131°38'W
Selwyn Range hills Australia 108 C4 .... 21°14'S 139°54'E
Semarang Indonesia 102 E2 .... 6°55'S 110°29'E
Semenivka Ukraine 47 O5 .... 52°10'N 32°35'E
Seminoe Reservoir U.S. 62 E5 .... 42°06'N 106°51'W
Semipalatinsk Kazakhstan 54 J3 .... 50°25'N 80°19'E
Semnān Iran 95 H7 .... 35°30'N 53°21'E
Semois r. Belgium/France 42 D2 .... 49°53'N 4°45'E
Sendai Japan 104 D3 .... 38°15'N 140°53'E
Senegal Africa 84 C3 .... 14°29'N 14°41'W
Sénégal r. Mauritania 84 C3 .... 16°00'N 16°31'W
Senja i. Norway 43 D5 .... 69°20'N 17°14'E
Sennar Sudan 85 H3 .... 13°31'N 33°36'E
Sens France 44 E6 .... 48°12'N 3°17'E
Seoul S. Korea 99 N5 .... 37°32'N 127°00'E
Sepik r. P.N.G. 103 K3 .... 3°53'S 144°33'E
Sept-Îles Canada 61 L3 .... 50°13'N 66°23'W
Serang Indonesia 102 D2 .... 6°04'S 106°09'E
Serbia Europe 50 D6 .... 44°01'N 20°55'E
Serdar Turkmenistan 54 G1 .... 38°59'N 56°17'E
Şereflikoçhisar Turkey 51 J4 .... 38°56'N 33°33'E
Seremban Malaysia 102 C4 .... 2°41'N 101°54'E
Seret r. Ukraine 47 K3 .... 48°36'N 25°51'E
Sergino Russia 52 G4 .... 62°33'N 65°39'E
Sergiyev Posad Russia 52 D3 .... 56°19'N 38°08'E
Serhetabat Turkmenistan 95 J7 .... 35°15'N 62°17'E
Serik Turkey 51 I3 .... 36°57'N 31°07'E
Serov Russia 52 G3 .... 59°38'N 60°34'E
Serowe Botswana 83 B2 .... 22°24'S 26°42'E
Serpukhov Russia 53 D3 .... 54°55'N 37°25'E
Serra da Mesa, Represa resr Brazil 72 E5 .... 14°17'S 48°30'W
Serres Greece 50 E5 .... 41°06'N 23°33'E
Serui Indonesia 103 J3 .... 1°52'S 136°17'E
Sestroretsk Russia 43 G3 .... 60°05'N 29°57'E
Sète France 44 E3 .... 43°24'N 3°42'E
Sete Lagoas Brazil 72 E5 .... 19°28'S 44°13'W
Setesdal f. Norway 43 A2 .... 59°15'N 7°23'E
Sétif Algeria 84 E5 .... 36°11'N 5°25'E
Seto Naikai sea Japan 104 B2 .... 33°38'N 132°17'E
Settat Morocco 84 D5 .... 32°58'N 7°36'W
Settle England 13 E3 .... 54°04'N 2°17'W
Setúbal Portugal 45 A3 .... 38°32'N 8°53'W
Setúbal, Baía de b. Portugal 45 A3 .... 38°20'N 9°02'W
Seul, Lac l. Canada 63 H7 .... 50°21'N 92°29'W
Sevan Armenia 53 E2 .... 40°33'N 44°58'E
Sevastopol Ukraine 49 J5 .... 44°36'N 33°31'E
Seven Heads Ireland 18 C1 .... 51°34'N 8°42'W
Sevenoaks England 9 F2 .... 51°16'N 0°12'E
Severn r. Canada 61 J3 .... 55°59'N 87°36'W
Severn r. U.K. 8 C2 .... 51°51'N 2°21'W
Severnaya Zemlya is Russia 55 L6 .... 80°09'N 103°23'E
Severnyy Russia 52 G4 .... 67°36'N 64°13'E
Severnyy, Ostrov i. Russia 54 G5 .... 75°00'N 58°00'E
Severo-Kuril'sk Russia 55 Q3 .... 50°40'N 156°06'E
Sevier Lake U.S. 62 D4 .... 38°56'N 113°09'W
Seville Spain 45 C2 .... 37°24'N 5°58'W
Seward U.S. 60 D4 .... 60°09'N 149°24'W
Seward Peninsula U.S. 60 B4 .... 65°29'N 164°05'W
Seychelles Indian Oc. 79 E2 .... 4°40'S 55°43'E
Seydişehir Turkey 51 I3 .... 37°25'N 31°52'E
Seyðisfjörður Iceland 43 Z2 .... 65°16'N 14°02'W
Seyhan r. Turkey 51 K3 .... 36°44'N 34°54'E
Seymchan Russia 55 Q4 .... 62°50'N 152°20'E
Sfântu Gheorghe Romania 50 F7 .... 45°52'N 25°48'E
Sfax Tunisia 48 F3 .... 34°45'N 10°45'E
Sgurr Alasdair hill Scotland 16 C2 .... 57°12'N 6°13'W
Sgùrr Dhomhnuill hill Scotland 16 D1 .... 56°45'N 5°27'W
Sgùrr Mòr mt. Scotland 16 D2 .... 57°42'N 5°01'W
Shaanxi d. China 99 J4 .... 34°43'N 108°13'E
Shabeelle, Webi r. Ethiopia/Somalia 85 I2 .... 0°10'N 42°46'E
Shadrinsk Russia 52 G3 .... 56°07'N 63°37'E
Shaftesbury England 8 C2 .... 51°00'N 2°12'W
Shahr-e Kord Iran 95 H6 .... 32°19'N 50°49'E
Shahrezā Iran 95 H6 .... 32°00'N 51°52'E
Shāhrūd Iran 95 H7 .... 36°24'N 54°56'E
Shakhovskaya Russia 47 P7 .... 56°02'N 35°30'E
Shakhty Russia 53 E2 .... 47°42'N 40°12'E
Shakhun'ya Russia 52 E3 .... 57°40'N 46°36'E
Shalqar Kazakhstan 53 F2 .... 47°47'N 59°39'E
Shandong d. China 99 L5 .... 36°22'N 117°45'E
Shandong Bandao pen. China 99 M5 .... 37°05'N 121°02'E
Shanghai China 99 M4 .... 31°15'N 121°29'E
Shangqiu China 99 L4 .... 34°24'N 115°38'E
Shanklin England 8 D1 .... 50°38'N 1°10'W
Shannon r. Ireland 18 C2 .... 52°40'N 8°38'W
Shannon, Mouth of the Ireland 18 B2 .... 52°31'N 9°51'W
Shantarskiye Ostrova is Russia 55 O3 .... 55°00'N 137°36'E
Shantou China 99 L2 .... 23°24'N 116°42'E
Shanxi d. China 99 K5 .... 38°03'N 111°48'E
Shaoguan China 99 K2 .... 24°48'N 113°37'E
Shaoxing China 99 M4 .... 30°01'N 120°38'E
Shaoyang China 99 K3 .... 27°14'N 111°30'E
Shap England 12 E3 .... 54°32'N 2°41'W
Shapinsay i. Scotland 17 G4 .... 59°02'N 2°48'W
Shaqrā' Saudi Arabia 94 G5 .... 25°15'N 45°16'E
Sharjah U.A.E. 95 I5 .... 25°21'N 55°23'E
Shark Bay Australia 108 A4 .... 25°17'S 113°42'E
Shashta, Mount vol. U.S. 62 B5 .... 41°23'N 122°10'W
Shchigry Russia 47 Q4 .... 51°52'N 36°56'E

Sheberghān Afgh. 95 K7......36°42'N 65°45'E
Sheboygan U.S. 63 I5......43°45'N 87°43'W
Sheelin, Lough l. Ireland 18 D3......53°49'N 7°19'W
Sheep Haven b. Ireland 14 B3......55°12'N 7°55'W
Sheerness England 9 F2......51°26'N 0°46'E
Sheffield England 13 F2......53°23'N 1°28'W
Shelby U.S. 62 D6......48°29'N 111°48'W
Shelikhova, Zaliv g. Russia 55 Q4......60°40'N 157°23'E
Shelikof Strait U.S. 60 C3......57°27'N 155°17'W
Shenyang China 99 M6......41°46'N 123°24'E
Shenzhen China 99 K2......22°33'N 114°09'E
Shepetivka Ukraine 47 L4......50°11'N 27°04'E
Sheppey, Isle of i. England 9 F2......51°24'N 0°46'E
Shepshed England 8 D3......52°46'N 1°18'W
Shepton Mallet England 8 C2......51°11'N 2°33'W
Sherborne England 8 C1......50°57'N 2°31'W
Sherbrooke Canada 61 K2......45°24'N 71°54'W
Sheridan U.S. 62 E5......44°48'N 106°55'W
Sheringham England 9 G3......52°57'N 1°13'E
's-Hertogenbosch Neth. 42 E4......51°41'N 5°19'E
Sherwood Forest England 13 F2......53°04'N 1°07'W
Shetland d. Scotland 20 E7......60°14'N 0°57'W
Shetland Islands Scotland 17 I5......60°36'N 0°47'W
Shetpe Kazakhstan 53 F2......44°09'N 52°17'E
Sheyenne r. U.S. 62 G6......47°03'N 96°50'W
Shiant Islands Scotland 16 C2......57°53'N 6°25'W
Shibām Yemen 95 G3......15°59'N 48°57'E
Shiel, Loch l. Scotland 16 D1......56°47'N 5°35'W
Shieldaig Scotland 16 D2......57°31'N 5°39'W
Shifnal England 8 C3......52°40'N 2°22'W
Shihezi China 98 F6......44°14'N 86°03'E
Shijiazhuang China 99 K5......38°00'N 114°30'E
Shikarpur India 96 E3......14°14'N 75°18'E
Shikarpur Pakistan 95 K5......27°56'N 68°42'E
Shikoku i. Japan 104 B2......33°08'N 133°49'E
Shikoku Sanchi mts Japan 104 B2......33°26'N 132°53'E
Shildon England 13 F3......54°38'N 1°39'W
Shilega Russia 52 E4......64°04'N 44°06'E
Shillong India 97 H6......25°33'N 91°53'E
Shimonoseki Japan 104 B2......33°57'N 130°57'E
Shin, Loch l. Scotland 17 E3......58°09'N 4°38'W
Shingū Japan 104 C2......33°43'N 136°00'E
Shining Tor hill England 13 E2......53°16'N 2°00'W
Shipley England 13 F2......53°50'N 1°47'W
Shipston on Stour England 8 D3......52°04'N 1°37'W
Shīrāz Iran 95 H5......29°37'N 52°31'E
Shire r. Malawi 83 C3......17°41'S 35°19'E
Shivamogga India 96 E3......13°54'N 75°31'E
Shizuishan China 99 J5......38°58'N 106°27'E
Shizuoka Japan 104 C2......34°58'N 138°23'E
Shklow Belarus 47 N6......54°13'N 30°17'E
Shkodër Albania 50 C6......42°04'N 19°31'E
Shona, Eilean i. Scotland 16 D1......56°48'N 5°53'W
Sho'rchi Uzbekistan 95 K7......37°59'N 67°46'E
Shostka Ukraine 47 O4......51°51'N 33°29'E
Shpola Ukraine 47 N3......49°01'N 31°23'E
Shreveport U.S. 63 H3......32°29'N 93°46'W
Shrewsbury England 8 C3......52°42'N 2°45'W
Shropshire d. England 21 D3......52°45'N 2°38'W
Shuangjiang China 99 H2......23°28'N 99°49'E
Shubarqudyq Kazakhstan 53 F2......49°05'N 56°28'E
Shumagin Islands U.S. 60 C3......55°09'N 161°01'W
Shumen Bulgaria 50 G6......43°16'N 26°56'E
Shuqrah Yemen 95 G2......13°24'N 45°40'E
Shūshtar Iran 95 G6......32°01'N 48°49'E
Shwebo Myanmar 97 I5......22°34'N 95°43'E
Shwegyin Myanmar 97 I4......17°56'N 96°52'E
Shyhanaq Kazakhstan 54 I2......45°10'N 73°57'E
Shymkent Kazakhstan 54 H2......42°19'N 69°38'E
Siahan Range mts Pakistan 95 J5......27°13'N 63°38'E
Šiauliai Lithuania 43 E1......55°56'N 23°19'E
Šibenik Croatia 50 A6......43°44'N 15°54'E
Siberia f. Russia 55 M4......65°18'N 115°57'E
Siberut i. Indonesia 102 B3......1°23'S 98°41'E
Sibi Pakistan 95 K5......29°30'N 67°55'E
Sibiu Romania 50 F7......45°48'N 24°10'E
Sibolga Indonesia 102 B4......1°40'N 98°48'E
Sibsey England 13 H2......53°02'N 0°01'E
Sibu Malaysia 102 E4......2°17'N 111°51'E
Sibut C.A.R. 85 F2......5°44'N 19°05'E
Sichuan d. China 99 I4......30°05'N 103°11'E
Sicily i. Italy 48 F4......38°21'N 14°09'E
Sidi Bel Abbès Algeria 84 D5......35°12'N 0°38'W
Sidi Kacem Morocco 48 B3......34°12'N 5°39'W
Sidlaw Hills Scotland 15 F4......56°26'N 3°21'W
Sidmouth England 11 D2......50°41'N 3°14'W
Sidney U.S. 62 F5......41°12'N 103°09'W
Sidon Lebanon 49 K3......33°33'N 35°23'E
Siedlce Poland 47 J5......52°10'N 22°17'E
Siegen Germany 46 C4......50°52'N 8°01'E
Sierra Leone Africa 84 C2......8°35'N 11°58'W
Sighetu Marmaţiei Romania 47 J2......47°56'N 23°54'E
Sighişoara Romania 50 F8......46°14'N 24°47'E
Siglufjörður Iceland 43 Y2......66°08'N 18°52'W
Sigüenza Spain 45 D4......41°04'N 2°37'W
Siguiri Guinea 84 D3......11°28'N 9°10'W
Sihanoukville Cambodia 102 C6......10°38'N 103°34'E
Siilinjärvi Finland 43 F3......63°05'N 27°40'E
Siirt Turkey 94 F7......37°55'N 41°58'E
Sikar India 96 E6......27°36'N 75°13'E
Sikasso Mali 84 D3......11°19'N 5°40'W
Sikeston U.S. 63 I4......36°51'N 89°34'W
Sikhote-Alin' mts Russia 55 O2......43°58'N 133°53'E
Sikkim d. India 96 G6......27°31'N 88°27'E
Sil r. Spain 45 B5......42°28'N 7°42'W
Siletitengiz Köli l. Kazakhstan 98 C8......53°11'N 72°53'E
Silifke Turkey 51 J3......36°22'N 33°56'E
Siling Co l. China 98 F4......31°47'N 88°41'E
Silistra Bulgaria 50 G7......44°07'N 27°16'E
Silivri Turkey 51 H5......41°04'N 28°16'E
Siljan l. Sweden 43 C3......60°53'N 14°44'E
Šilutė Lithuania 47 I6......55°21'N 21°28'E
Silver City U.S. 62 E3......32°45'N 108°19'W
Silverstone England 8 D3......52°05'N 1°02'W
Silverton England 11 D2......50°49'N 3°29'W
Simanggang Malaysia 102 E4......1°12'N 111°30'E
Simav Turkey 51 H4......39°05'N 28°58'E
Simën mts Ethiopia 94 E2......13°16'N 57°00'E
Simeulue i. Indonesia 102 B4......2°41'N 96°08'E
Simferopol Ukraine 49 J5......44°57'N 34°00'E
Simojärvi l. Finland 43 F4......66°01'N 27°15'E
Simpson Desert Australia 108 C4......24°59'S 136°50'E
Simrishamn Sweden 46 F6......55°33'N 14°21'E
Sinai pen. Egypt 85 H4......29°13'N 33°47'E
Sinaloa d. Mexico 66 C6......25°12'N 108°11'W
Sincelejo Colombia 72 B7......9°17'N 75°24'W
Sinclair's Bay Scotland 17 F3......58°30'N 3°07'W

Sindor Russia 52 F4......62°52'N 51°54'E
Sines Portugal 45 A2......37°58'N 8°52'W
Singa Sudan 94 D2......13°09'N 33°54'E
Singapore Asia 102 C4......1°27'N 104°32'E
Singapore town Singapore 102 C4......1°19'N 103°51'E
Singaraja Indonesia 102 F2......8°06'S 115°06'E
Singida Tanzania 83 C4......4°50'S 34°45'E
Singkawang Indonesia 102 D4......0°57'N 108°59'E
Sinj Croatia 50 B6......43°42'N 16°38'E
Sinkat Sudan 94 E3......18°45'N 36°49'E
Sinop Turkey 51 K6......42°02'N 35°08'E
Sint Maarten i. Neth. Antilles 67 L4......18°02'N 63°04'W
Sion Mills Northern Ireland 14 B2......54°47'N 7°28'W
Sioux City U.S. 62 G5......42°32'N 96°23'W
Sioux Falls town U.S. 62 G5......43°32'N 96°43'W
Sioux Lookout Canada 61 I3......50°06'N 91°56'W
Sipacate Guatemala 66 F3......13°59'N 91°08'W
Siping China 99 M6......43°04'N 124°24'E
Sipura i. Indonesia 102 B3......2°12'S 99°42'E
Sira r. Norway 43 A2......58°16'N 6°24'E
Siret r. Romania 50 H7......45°25'N 28°02'E
Sīrjan Iran 95 I5......29°27'N 55°40'E
Sirte Libya 85 F5......31°09'N 16°40'E
Sirte, Gulf of Libya 85 F5......31°11'N 18°03'E
Şirvan Azerbaijan 53 E1......39°56'N 48°56'E
Sisak Croatia 50 B7......45°29'N 16°23'E
Sisimiut Greenland 61 M4......66°56'N 53°40'W
Sisophon Cambodia 102 C6......13°34'N 102°59'E
Sīstān, Daryācheh-ye marsh Afgh./Iran 95 J6......31°33'N 61°10'E
Sisteron France 44 F4......44°12'N 5°57'E
Siteia Greece 50 G2......35°12'N 26°06'E
Sitka U.S. 60 E3......57°03'N 135°18'W
Sittard Neth. 42 E3......50°59'N 5°51'E
Sittingbourne England 9 F2......51°20'N 0°44'E
Sittwe Myanmar 97 H5......20°08'N 92°54'E
Sivas Turkey 51 L4......39°43'N 37°00'E
Siverek Turkey 51 M3......37°44'N 39°21'E
Sivrihisar Turkey 51 I4......39°27'N 31°32'E
Sīwah Egypt 85 G4......29°09'N 25°30'E
Skadovsk Ukraine 51 J8......46°07'N 32°54'E
Skaftárós r. mouth Iceland 43 Y1......63°41'N 17°47'W
Skagen Denmark 43 B2......57°43'N 10°35'E
Skagerrak str. Denmark/Norway 43 B2......57°27'N 8°13'E
Skagway U.S. 60 E3......59°29'N 135°18'W
Skara Sweden 43 C2......58°23'N 13°26'E
Skarzysko-Kamienna Poland 46 I4......51°07'N 20°53'E
Skegness England 13 H2......53°09'N 0°20'E
Skellefteå Sweden 43 E4......64°45'N 20°57'E
Skellefteälven r. Sweden 43 E4......64°42'N 21°07'E
Skelmersdale England 12 E2......53°33'N 2°46'W
Skerries Ireland 18 E3......53°35'N 6°06'W
Ski Norway 43 B2......59°43'N 10°50'E
Skibbereen Ireland 18 B1......51°33'N 9°16'W
Skiddaw hill England 12 D3......54°39'N 3°09'W
Skien Norway 43 B2......59°12'N 9°36'E
Skikda Algeria 84 E5......36°54'N 6°57'E
Skipton England 13 E2......53°58'N 2°01'W
Skive Denmark 43 B2......56°34'N 9°02'E
Skokholm Island Wales 10 B3......51°41'N 5°16'W
Skomer Island Wales 10 B3......51°44'N 5°20'W
Skopje North Macedonia 50 D5......41°59'N 21°27'E
Skövde Sweden 43 C2......58°23'N 13°51'E
Skovorodino Russia 55 N3......54°05'N 123°52'E
Skye i. Scotland 16 C2......57°21'N 6°20'W
Skyros i. Greece 50 F4......38°53'N 24°35'E
Slagelse Denmark 43 B1......55°24'N 11°22'E
Slaney r. Ireland 18 E2......52°25'N 6°34'W
Slatina Romania 50 F7......44°26'N 24°22'E
Slave r. Canada 60 G4......61°17'N 113°31'W
Slave Lake town Canada 60 G3......55°17'N 114°47'W
Slavonski Brod Croatia 50 C7......45°10'N 18°01'E
Slavyansk-na-Kubani Russia 51 M7......45°16'N 38°08'E
Slawharad Belarus 47 N5......53°27'N 31°00'E
Sleaford England 9 E4......53°00'N 0°24'W
Sleat, Sound of str. Scotland 16 D2......57°07'N 5°53'W
Sleights England 13 G3......54°27'N 0°40'W
Slieve Anierin hill Ireland 14 B2......54°05'N 7°59'W
Slieve Beagh hill Ireland/U.K. 14 B2......54°20'N 7°12'W
Slievecallan hill Ireland 18 B2......52°51'N 9°16'W
Slieve Car hill Ireland 18 A4......54°04'N 9°40'W
Slieve Donard hill Northern Ireland 14 D2......54°11'N 5°55'W
Slievenamon hill Ireland 18 D2......52°26'N 7°34'W
Slieve Snaght hill Ireland 18 D5......55°12'N 7°20'W
Sligo Ireland 18 C4......54°17'N 8°28'W
Sligo d. Ireland 18 C4......54°17'N 8°28'W
Sligo Bay Ireland 18 C4......54°18'N 8°55'W
Sliven Bulgaria 50 G6......42°41'N 26°19'E
Slobozia Romania 50 G7......44°34'N 27°23'E
Slonim Belarus 47 K5......53°05'N 25°19'E
Slough England 9 E2......51°31'N 0°36'W
Slough d. England 21 E2......51°30'N 0°35'W
Slovakia Europe 46 H3......48°45'N 19°35'E
Slovenia Europe 46 F1......46°09'N 14°37'E
Sloviansk Ukraine 53 D2......48°51'N 37°37'E
Slovyechna r. Belarus 47 M4......51°39'N 29°43'E
Sluch r. Ukraine 47 L4......51°37'N 26°39'E
Słupsk Poland 46 G6......54°27'N 17°02'E
Slutsk Belarus 47 L5......53°01'N 27°33'E
Slyne Head Ireland 18 A3......53°24'N 10°14'W
Slyudyanka Russia 99 I8......51°38'N 103°36'E
Smallwood Reservoir Canada 61 L3......54°01'N 64°50'W
Smarhon' Belarus 47 L6......54°29'N 26°25'E
Smila Ukraine 47 N3......49°12'N 31°54'E
Smoky r. Canada 60 G3......56°08'N 117°20'W
Smøla i. Norway 43 A3......63°23'N 7°59'E
Smolensk Russia 53 D3......54°47'N 32°04'E
Smolikas mt. Greece 50 D5......40°05'N 20°56'E
Smolyan Bulgaria 50 F5......41°35'N 24°41'E
Snæfell mt. Iceland 43 Z2......64°48'N 15°35'W
Snaefell hill Isle of Man 12 C3......54°16'N 4°28'W
Snaith England 13 F2......53°41'N 1°01'W
Snake r. U.S. 62 C6......46°13'N 118°59'W
Snåsa Norway 43 B4......64°15'N 12°23'E
Sneek Neth. 42 E6......53°02'N 5°40'E
Snettisham England 9 F3......52°53'N 0°30'E
Snežnik mt. Slovenia 46 F1......45°35'N 14°26'E
Śniardwy, Jezioro l. Poland 47 I5......53°46'N 21°42'E
Snizort, Loch b. Scotland 16 C2......57°33'N 6°28'W
Snøtinden mt. Norway 43 C4......66°38'N 13°57'E
Snov r. Ukraine 47 N4......51°32'N 31°32'E
Snowdon mt. Wales 10 C5......53°04'N 4°04'W
Soay i. Scotland 16 C2......57°09'N 6°15'W
Sobradinho, Represa de resr Brazil 72 E5......10°14'S 42°40'W

Sobral Brazil 72 E6......3°41'S 40°19'W
Sochi Russia 53 D2......43°36'N 39°44'E
Society Islands is French Polynesia 116 B2......17°22'S 152°28'W
Socorro, Isla i. Mexico 66 B4......18°51'N 110°58'W
Socotra i. Yemen 95 H2......12°34'N 54°30'E
Sodankylä Finland 43 F4......67°25'N 26°34'E
Söderhamn Sweden 43 D3......61°18'N 17°04'E
Södertälje Sweden 43 D2......59°12'N 17°38'E
Sodo Ethiopia 85 H2......6°49'N 37°42'E
Sofia Bulgaria 50 E6......42°41'N 23°19'E
Sognefjorden inlet Norway 43 A3......61°05'N 5°33'E
Soham England 9 F3......52°20'N 0°20'E
Soignies Belgium 42 D3......50°35'N 4°04'E
Soissons France 44 E6......49°23'N 3°20'E
Söke Turkey 50 G3......37°45'N 27°23'E
Sokhumi Georgia 53 E2......43°00'N 41°02'E
Sokoto Nigeria 84 E3......13°05'N 5°15'E
Sokoto r. Nigeria 84 E3......11°23'N 4°09'E
Solapur India 96 E4......17°41'N 75°55'E
Solihull England 8 D3......52°25'N 1°45'W
Solikamsk Russia 52 F3......59°42'N 56°44'E
Sol'-Iletsk Russia 53 F3......51°06'N 54°58'E
Sollefteå Sweden 43 D3......63°10'N 17°17'E
Solomon Islands S. Pacific Oc. 109 F6......7°13'S 157°49'E
Solomon Sea S. Pacific Oc. 108 E6......7°01'S 152°18'E
Solway Firth est. Scotland 15 F2......54°48'N 3°33'W
Solwezi Zambia 83 B3......12°10'S 26°26'E
Soma Turkey 50 G4......39°10'N 27°36'E
Somalia Africa 85 I2......3°56'N 46°23'E
Sombor Serbia 50 C7......45°47'N 19°07'E
Somerset d. England 21 D2......51°04'N 2°56'W
Somerset Island Canada 61 I5......73°19'N 93°22'W
Somerton England 8 C2......51°03'N 2°44'W
Sommen l. Sweden 43 C2......58°00'N 15°17'E
Sønderborg Denmark 46 C6......54°55'N 9°48'E
Sondrio Italy 46 C2......46°10'N 9°52'E
Songea Tanzania 83 C3......10°39'S 35°38'E
Songkhla Thailand 102 C5......7°10'N 100°35'E
Songyuan China 99 M7......45°05'N 124°53'E
Son La Vietnam 102 C8......21°20'N 103°57'E
Sonora d. Mexico 66 B6......29°42'N 110°36'W
Sonora r. Mexico 66 B6......28°47'N 111°54'W
Soria Spain 45 D4......41°47'N 2°26'W
Soroca Moldova 49 I6......48°09'N 28°17'E
Sorochinsk Russia 53 F3......52°21'N 52°59'E
Sorol atoll Micronesia 103 K5......8°10'N 140°22'E
Sorong Indonesia 103 I3......0°54'S 131°17'E
Soroti Uganda 85 H2......1°42'N 33°37'E
Sørøya i. Norway 43 E5......70°34'N 22°32'E
Sorraia r. Portugal 45 A3......39°02'N 8°50'W
Sorsele Sweden 43 D4......65°31'N 17°33'E
Sortavala Russia 43 G3......61°42'N 30°41'E
Soshanguve S. Africa 83 B2......25°31'S 28°06'E
Sosna r. Russia 47 R5......52°41'N 38°54'E
Sosneado mt. Argentina 73 C3......34°44'S 69°59'W
Sosnogorsk Russia 52 F4......63°36'N 53°53'E
Sosnovka Russia 52 E4......66°30'N 40°34'E
Sosnowiec Poland 46 H4......50°17'N 19°08'E
Sos'va Russia 52 G3......59°08'N 61°48'E
Souk Ahras Algeria 48 E4......36°17'N 7°59'E
Souk el Arbaâ du Rharb Morocco 45 C1......34°40'N 5°58'W
Souris r. Canada 62 G6......49°41'N 99°40'W
Sousse Tunisia 48 F4......35°47'N 10°39'E
Soustons France 44 C3......43°45'N 1°20'W
South Africa Africa 83 B1......30°06'S 24°04'E
Southam England 8 D3......52°15'N 1°23'W
South America 72
Southampton England 8 D1......50°55'N 1°24'W
Southampton d. England 21 E2......50°56'N 1°24'W
Southampton Island Canada 61 J4......64°31'N 85°04'W
South Anston England 13 F2......53°21'N 1°13'W
South Australia d. Australia 108 C3......30°27'S 132°43'E
South Ayrshire d. Scotland 20 C4......55°09'N 4°47'W
South Bank England 13 F3......54°35'N 1°10'W
South Bend U.S. 63 I5......41°40'N 86°13'W
Southborough England 9 F2......51°09'N 0°16'E
South Carolina d. U.S. 63 J3......34°02'N 80°47'W
South Cave England 13 G2......53°46'N 0°36'W
South China Sea N. Pacific Oc. 102 F6......12°00'N 117°49'E
South Dakota d. U.S. 62 F5......44°27'N 100°14'W
South Dorset Downs hills England 8 C1......50°42'N 2°37'W
South Downs hills England 8 E1......50°53'N 0°28'W
South Dublin d. Ireland 18 E3......53°16'N 6°24'W
South East Cape Australia 108 D2......43°38'S 146°55'E
Southend-on-Sea England 9 F2......51°32'N 0°43'E
Southend-on-Sea d. England 21 F2......51°33'N 0°42'E
Southern Alps / Ka Tiritiri o te Moana mts New Zealand 109 G2......43°26'S 170°28'E
Southern Gilbert Islands is Kiribati 109 G6......1°37'S 175°52'E
Southern Ocean 116 E1
Southern Uplands hills Scotland 14 E3......55°14'N 4°32'W
Southery England 9 F3......52°32'N 0°24'E
South Esk r. Scotland 17 G1......56°43'N 2°33'W
South Georgia and South Sandwich Islands S. Atlantic Oc. 73 F1......53°50'S 36°30'W
South Gloucestershire d. England 21 D2......51°33'N 2°27'W
South Harris pen. Scotland 16 B2......57°49'N 7°03'W
South Island / Te Waipounamu New Zealand 109 G2......44°24'S 172°31'E
South Kirkby England 13 F2......53°36'N 1°19'W
South Korea Asia 99 N5......35°32'N 128°04'E
South Lanarkshire d. Scotland 20 D4......55°38'N 3°49'W
Southminster England 9 F2......51°40'N 0°50'E
South Molton England 11 D3......51°01'N 3°50'W
South Ockendon England 9 F2......51°31'N 0°18'E
South Ossetia d. Georgia 53 E2......42°00'N 44°06'E
South Platte r. U.S. 62 F5......41°08'N 100°47'W
Southport Australia 108 E4......27°56'S 153°23'E
Southport England 12 D2......53°39'N 3°00'W
South Ronaldsay i. Scotland 17 G3......58°47'N 2°54'W
South Saskatchewan r. Canada 60 H3......53°09'N 105°08'W
South Shields England 13 F3......54°59'N 1°26'W
South Sudan Africa 85 G2......7°01'N 30°00'E
South Tyne r. England 13 E3......54°59'N 2°08'W
South Uist i. Scotland 16 B2......57°17'N 7°22'W
South Walls pen. Scotland 17 F3......58°47'N 3°08'W
Southwell England 13 G2......53°05'N 0°58'W
Southwold England 9 G3......52°19'N 1°41'E
South Woodham Ferrers England 9 F2......51°39'N 0°37'E
South Wootton England 9 F3......52°46'N 0°26'E
South Yorkshire d. England 21 E2......53°28'N 1°16'W
Sovetsk Russia 47 I6......55°05'N 21°53'E
Sovetskiy Russia 52 G4......61°26'N 63°30'E
Soweto S. Africa 83 B2......26°15'S 27°50'E

Sozh r. Europe 47 N4......51°57'N 30°49'E
Spain Europe 45 D4......40°26'N 3°48'W
Spalding England 9 E3......52°47'N 0°09'W
Sparks U.S. 62 C4......39°32'N 119°46'W
Sparti Greece 50 E3......37°04'N 22°26'E
Spartivento, Capo c. Italy 48 E4......37°56'N 16°05'E
Spas-Demensk Russia 47 P6......54°25'N 34°03'E
Spatha, Akra pt Greece 50 E2......35°41'N 23°44'E
Spencer Gulf est. Australia 108 C3......34°54'S 136°27'E
Spennymoor England 13 F3......54°42'N 1°35'W
Sperrin Mountains hills Northern Ireland 14 B2......54°47'N 7°09'W
Spey r. Scotland 17 F2......57°39'N 3°06'W
Speyer Germany 44 H6......49°19'N 8°24'E
Spijkenisse Neth. 42 D4......51°50'N 4°19'E
Spilsby England 13 H2......53°10'N 0°06'E
Spitsbergen i. Arctic Oc. 54 C5......78°37'N 16°06'E
Split Croatia 50 B6......43°31'N 16°27'E
Spofforth England 13 F2......53°57'N 1°27'W
Spokane U.S. 62 C6......47°38'N 117°22'W
Spratly Islands S. China Sea 102 E6......10°01'N 114°21'E
Spree r. Germany 46 E5......52°32'N 13°13'E
Springfield Ill. U.S. 63 I4......39°48'N 89°39'W
Springfield Mass. U.S. 63 L5......42°05'N 72°35'W
Springfield Mo. U.S. 63 H4......37°16'N 93°18'W
Sprowston England 9 G3......52°39'N 1°19'E
Spurn Head England 13 H2......53°34'N 0°05'E
Srebrenica Bos. and Herz. 50 C7......44°07'N 19°19'E
Srednekolymsk Russia 55 Q4......67°32'N 153°38'E
Sretensk Russia 55 M3......52°08'N 117°41'E
Sri Jayawardenapura Kotte Sri Lanka 96 E2......6°56'N 79°54'E
Sri Lanka Asia 96 F2......7°29'N 80°42'E
Srinagar India 96 D7......34°08'N 74°51'E
Stadskanaal Neth. 42 F5......52°59'N 6°59'E
Staffa i. Scotland 14 C4......56°26'N 6°20'W
Stafford England 8 C3......52°48'N 2°07'W
Staffordshire d. England 21 D3......52°52'N 2°04'W
Staines-upon-Thames England 9 E2......51°26'N 0°31'W
Stalbridge England 8 C2......50°57'N 2°23'W
Stalham England 9 G3......52°46'N 1°31'E
Stalowa Wola Poland 47 J4......50°34'N 22°03'E
Stamford England 9 E3......52°39'N 0°29'W
Stamford Bridge England 13 G2......53°59'N 0°55'W
Standish England 12 E2......53°35'N 2°40'W
Stanley England 13 F3......54°52'N 1°42'W
Stanley Falkland Is 73 D1......51°43'S 57°52'W
Stanley, Mount Dem. Rep. Congo/Uganda 83 B5......0°25'N 29°56'E
Stannington England 13 F4......55°06'N 1°40'W
Stanovoy Khrebet mts Russia 55 N3......57°21'N 120°44'E
Stansted Mountfitchet England 9 F2......51°54'N 0°12'E
Stanton England 9 F3......52°19'N 0°53'E
Staraya Russa Russia 52 D3......57°59'N 31°22'E
Stara Zagora Bulgaria 50 F6......42°26'N 25°38'E
Stargard Szczeciński Poland 46 F5......53°20'N 15°03'E
Starogard Gdański Poland 46 H5......53°58'N 18°31'E
Starokostiantyniv Ukraine 47 L3......49°45'N 27°13'E
Start Bay England 11 D2......50°18'N 3°37'W
Start Point England 11 D2......50°13'N 3°38'W
Staryya Darohi Belarus 47 M5......53°02'N 28°17'E
Staryy Oskol Russia 53 D3......51°18'N 37°51'E
Stavanger Norway 43 A2......58°58'N 5°44'E
Staveley England 13 F2......53°16'N 1°21'W
Stavropol' Russia 53 E2......45°03'N 41°59'E
Stavropol'skaya Vozvyshennost' hills Russia 53 E2......45°05'N 42°35'E
Steenwijk Neth. 42 F5......52°47'N 6°07'E
Steep Holm i. England 8 B2......51°20'N 3°06'W
Stefansson Island Canada 60 H5......73°21'N 105°34'W
Steinfurt Germany 42 G5......52°09'N 7°21'E
Steinkjer Norway 43 B4......64°01'N 11°30'E
Stenness, Loch of l. Scotland 17 F4......59°00'N 3°16'W
Sterling U.S. 62 F5......40°39'N 103°09'W
Sterlitamak Russia 53 F3......53°36'N 55°53'E
Stevenage England 9 E2......51°54'N 0°12'W
Stewart Canada 60 F3......55°57'N 129°59'W
Stewart r. Canada 60 E4......63°18'N 139°26'W
Stewart Island / Rakiura New Zealand 109 F2......47°09'S 167°55'E
Stewarton England 14 E3......55°41'N 4°31'W
Steyning England 9 E1......50°53'N 0°20'W
Steyr Austria 46 F3......48°02'N 14°25'E
Stikine r. Canada 60 E3......56°41'N 132°19'W
Stilton England 9 E3......52°29'N 0°17'W
Stinchar r. Scotland 14 D3......55°06'N 5°01'W
Stirling Scotland 15 F4......56°07'N 3°56'W
Stirling d. Scotland 20 C5......56°17'N 4°23'W
Stjørdalshalsen Norway 43 B3......63°28'N 10°55'E
Stob Choire Claurigh mt. Scotland 16 E1......56°50'N 4°51'W
Stockholm Sweden 43 D2......59°20'N 18°04'E
Stockport England 13 E2......53°24'N 2°09'W
Stockton U.S. 62 B4......37°57'N 121°17'W
Stockton-on-Tees England 13 F3......54°34'N 1°19'W
Stockton-on-Tees d. England 21 E4......54°34'N 1°21'W
Stoer, Point of Scotland 16 D3......58°16'N 5°23'W
Stoke-on-Trent England 13 E2......53°00'N 2°11'W
Stoke-on-Trent d. England 21 D3......53°01'N 2°10'W
Stokesay England 8 C3......52°26'N 2°50'W
Stokesley England 13 F3......54°28'N 1°11'W
Stolin Belarus 47 L4......51°53'N 26°50'E
Stone England 8 C3......52°54'N 2°09'W
Stonehaven Scotland 17 G1......56°58'N 2°12'W
Stony Rapids town Canada 60 H4......59°15'N 105°50'W
Stora Lulevatten l. Sweden 43 D4......67°09'N 19°28'E
Storavan l. Sweden 43 D4......65°40'N 18°16'E
Støren Norway 43 B3......63°02'N 10°17'E
Stornoway Scotland 16 C3......58°13'N 6°23'W
Storrington England 9 E1......50°55'N 0°27'W
Storsjön l. Sweden 43 C3......63°13'N 14°16'E
Storskrymten mt. Norway 43 B3......62°22'N 9°03'E
Storuman Sweden 43 D4......65°05'N 17°09'E
Storuman l. Sweden 43 D4......65°11'N 16°54'E
Stotfold England 9 E3......52°01'N 0°14'W
Stour r. Dor. England 8 D1......50°44'N 1°46'W
Stour r. Kent England 9 G2......51°18'N 1°21'E
Stour r. Warwicks. England 8 D3......52°11'N 1°44'W
Stourbridge England 8 C3......52°27'N 2°09'W
Stourport-on-Severn England 8 C3......52°20'N 2°17'W
Stowbtsy Belarus 47 L5......53°28'N 26°44'E
Stowmarket England 9 F3......52°11'N 0°59'E
Stow-on-the-Wold England 8 D2......51°56'N 1°43'W
Strabane Northern Ireland 14 B2......54°50'N 7°27'W
Stradbroke England 9 G3......52°19'N 1°16'E
Stralsund Germany 46 E6......54°19'N 13°05'E
Stranda Norway 43 A3......62°18'N 6°57'E
Strangford Lough inlet Northern Ireland 14 D2......54°28'N 5°35'W

tranraer Scotland 14 D2......................54°54'N 5°02'W
trasbourg France 44 G6.....................48°35'N 7°44'E
tratford-upon-Avon England 8 D3...........52°11'N 1°43'W
trathaven Scotland 15 E3..................55°41'N 4°04'W
trathbeg, Loch of l. Scotland 17 H2.......57°37'N 1°54'W
trathbogie f. Scotland 17 G2..............57°26'N 2°53'W
trathmore r. Scotland 18 E3...............58°25'N 4°39'W
trathspey f. Scotland 17 F2...............57°11'N 3°47'W
trathy Point Scotland 17 E3...............58°36'N 4°01'W
tratton England 11 C2.....................50°50'N 4°31'W
tratton St Margaret England 8 D2..........51°35'N 1°45'W
traubing Germany 46 E3....................48°54'N 12°35'E
traumnes pt Iceland 43 X2.................66°26'N 23°10'W
treatley England 8 D2.....................51°32'N 1°09'W
treet England 8 C2........................51°07'N 2°44'W
trelka Russia 55 Q4.......................61°52'N 152°11'E
tretham England 9 F3......................52°21'N 0°13'E
trimonas r. Greece 50 E5..................40°48'N 23°51'E
troma, Island of Scotland 17 F3...........58°42'N 3°08'W
tromboli, Isola i. Italy 48 G4............38°45'N 15°14'E
tromness Scotland 17 F3...................58°58'N 3°18'W
trömsund Sweden 43 C3.....................63°52'N 15°34'E
tronsay i. Scotland 17 G4.................59°08'N 2°33'W
tronsay Firth str. Scotland 17 G4.........59°06'N 2°50'W
troud England 8 C2........................51°45'N 2°13'W
truer Denmark 43 B2.......................56°29'N 8°36'E
trule r. Northern Ireland 14 B2...........54°43'N 7°21'W
truma r. Bulgaria 50 E5...................41°23'N 23°20'E
trumble Head Wales 10 B4..................52°02'N 5°08'W
trumica North Macedonia 50 E5.............41°26'N 22°38'E
tryi Ukraine 47 J3........................49°15'N 23°51'E
tudley England 8 D3.......................52°16'N 1°54'W
tung Treng Cambodia 102 D6...........13°28'N 105°59'E
tupino Russia 47 R6.......................54°54'N 38°05'E
turry England 9 G2........................51°18'N 1°07'E
turt Stony Desert Australia 108 D4....28°20'S 141°15'E
tuttgart Germany 46 C3....................48°47'N 9°10'E
tyr r. Belarus/Ukraine 47 L5..............52°08'N 26°35'E
iakin Sudan 85 H3.........................19°06'N 37°18'E
ibotica Serbia 50 C8......................46°06'N 19°41'E
uceava Romania 47 L2......................47°40'N 26°16'E
uck r. Ireland 18 C3......................53°16'N 8°03'W
ucre Bolivia 72 C5........................19°05'S 65°18'W
udak Ukraine 51 K7........................44°51'N 34°59'E
udan Africa 85 G3.........................13°34'N 30°02'E
udbury Canada 61 J2.......................46°29'N 80°59'W
udbury England 9 F3.......................52°03'N 0°44'E
udd f. South Sudan 85 G2..................7°43'N 29°41'E
udety mts Czechia/Poland 46 F4............50°46'N 15°50'E
uez Egypt 85 H4...........................29°58'N 32°33'E
uez, Gulf of Egypt 85 H4..................28°03'N 33°33'E
uez Canal Egypt 49 J3.....................30°47'N 32°19'E
uffolk d. England 21 F3...................52°10'N 0°52'E
uḩār Oman 95 I4...........................24°22'N 56°44'E
uhl Germany 46 D4.........................50°36'N 10°42'E
uining China 99 J4........................30°29'N 105°33'E
uir r. Ireland 18 D2......................52°20'N 7°23'W
uizhou China 99 K4........................31°42'N 113°20'E
ukabumi Indonesia 102 D2.................6°58'S 106°53'E
ukadana Indonesia 102 D3.................1°12'S 109°59'E
ukhinichi Russia 47 P6....................54°07'N 35°22'E
ukkur Pakistan 96 C6......................27°42'N 68°55'E
ula i. Norway 43 A3.......................61°09'N 4°55'E
ulabesi i. Indonesia 103 H3..............2°12'S 125°58'E
ulina Romania 51 H7.......................45°09'N 29°39'E
ullana Port 72 A6.........................4°56'S 80°41'W
ully Wales 11 D3..........................51°24'N 3°13'W
ulu Archipelago is Phil. 103 G5..........6°55'N 123°10'E
ulu Sea N. Pacific Oc. 102 F5............8°20'N 119°46'E
umatra i. Indonesia 102 B4...............3°05'N 98°12'E
umba i. Indonesia 102 G2.................9°49'S 120°11'E
umbawa i. Indonesia 102 F2...............8°54'S 118°45'E
umburgh Scotland 17 H4....................59°52'N 1°17'W
umburgh Head Scotland 17 H4...............59°51'N 1°16'W
ummer Isles Scotland 16 D3................58°01'N 5°30'W
umqayit Azerbaijan 53 E2..................40°35'N 49°40'E
umy Ukraine 47 P4.........................50°55'N 34°48'E
unart, Loch inlet Scotland 16 D1..........56°40'N 5°51'W
unda, Selat str. Indonesia 102 C2.....6°32'S 104°55'E
underland England 13 F3...................54°54'N 1°23'W
undsvall Sweden 43 D3.....................62°24'N 17°17'E
ungurlu Turkey 51 K5......................40°11'N 34°22'E
uolijärvet l. Finland 43 G4..............66°14'N 28°04'E
uonenjoki Finland 43 F3...................62°37'N 27°07'E
uoyarvi Russia 52 D4......................62°06'N 32°22'E
uperior U.S. 63 H6........................46°41'N 92°01'W
uperior, Lake Canada/U.S. 61 J2.........47°46'N 87°14'W
uqian China 99 L4.........................33°55'N 118°18'E
uq ash Shuyūkh Iraq 95 G6................30°51'N 46°20'E
ur Oman 95 I4.............................22°34'N 59°31'E
urab Pakistan 95 K5.......................28°29'N 66°19'E
urabaya Indonesia 102 E2.................7°13'S 112°45'E
urakarta Indonesia 102 E2...............7°31'S 110°52'E
urat India 96 D5..........................21°11'N 72°53'E
urgut Russia 54 I4........................61°13'N 73°22'E
urigao Phil. 103 H5......................9°48'N 125°29'E
urin Thailand 102 C6.....................14°52'N 103°32'E
uriname S. America 72 D7.................4°05'N 56°22'W
urrey d. England 21 E2....................51°15'N 0°29'W
urtsey i. Iceland 43 X1...................63°18'N 20°36'W
usangerd Iran 95 G6.......................31°37'N 48°04'E
uşehri Turkey 51 M5.......................40°10'N 38°04'E
usuman Russia 55 P4.......................62°47'N 148°02'E
usurluk Turkey 51 H4......................39°55'N 28°09'E
utak India 96 E7..........................30°07'N 77°34'E
utherland f. Scotland 17 E3...............58°16'N 4°24'W
utlej r. India/Pakistan 96 D6............29°24'N 71°08'E
utterton England 9 F3.....................52°54'N 0°06'W
utton England 9 F3........................52°23'N 0°07'E
utton Bridge England 9 F3.................52°46'N 0°11'E
utton Coldfield England 8 D3..............52°34'N 1°49'W
utton in Ashfield England 13 F2...........53°08'N 1°16'W
uva Fiji 109 G5..........................18°07'S 178°28'E
uvorov Russia 47 Q6.......................54°07'N 36°31'E
uwałki Poland 47 J6.......................54°07'N 22°55'E
uwarrow atoll Cook Is 109 I5............13°11'S 162°57'W
uzhou Anhui China 99 L4..................33°34'N 116°59'E
uzhou Jiangsu China 99 M4...............31°18'N 120°40'E
uzu Japan 104 C3..........................37°26'N 137°15'E
uzuka Japan 104 C2........................34°53'N 136°35'E
valbard is Arctic Oc. 54 C5..............79°47'N 16°13'E
vapa r. Russia 47 P4......................51°44'N 34°57'E
veg Sweden 43 C3..........................62°02'N 14°22'E
vendborg Denmark 43 B1....................55°04'N 10°37'E
vetlogorsk Russia 43 G3...................45°20'N 42°51'E
vetogorsk Russia 43 G3...................61°07'N 28°51'E
vahnúkar vol. Iceland 43 Y2..............64°25'N 17°09'W

Svitavy Czechia 46 G3.....................49°45'N 16°28'E
Svitlovodsk Ukraine 47 O3.................49°03'N 33°15'E
Svobodnyy Russia 55 N3...................51°23'N 128°04'E
Svyetlahorsk Belarus 47 M5................52°38'N 29°46'E
Swadlincote England 8 D3..................52°46'N 1°33'W
Swaffham England 9 F3.....................52°39'N 0°41'E
Swains Island atoll American Samoa 109 H5
                                      11°01'S 171°03'W
Swakopmund Namibia 83 A2..................22°41'S 14°32'E
Swale r. England 13 F3....................54°05'N 1°21'W
Swanage England 8 D1......................50°36'N 1°58'W
Swanley England 9 F2......................51°24'N 0°11'E
Swan River town Canada 62 F7..............52°06'N 101°16'W
Swansea Wales 10 D3.......................51°37'N 3°57'W
Swansea d. Wales 21 D2....................51°39'N 3°57'W
Swansea Bay Wales 10 D3...................51°34'N 3°54'W
Swaziland Africa 83 C2....................26°29'S 31°30'E
Sweden Europe 43 C3.......................61°48'N 15°08'E
Sweetwater r. U.S. 62 E5..................42°27'N 106°55'W
Świdnica Poland 46 G4.....................50°50'N 16°29'E
Świdwin Poland 46 F5......................53°47'N 15°47'E
Swift Current Canada 60 H3................50°17'N 107°47'W
Swilly, Lough inlet Ireland 18 D5........55°15'N 7°34'W
Swindon England 8 D2......................51°33'N 1°47'W
Swindon d. England 21 E2..................51°35'N 1°45'W
Swineshead England 9 E3...................52°57'N 0°10'W
Świnoujście Poland 46 F5..................53°54'N 14°15'E
Switzerland Europe 48 E6..................46°44'N 8°18'E
Swords Ireland 18 E3......................53°27'N 6°13'W
Sybil Point Ireland 18 A2.................52°11'N 10°28'W
Sychevka Russia 47 P6.....................55°49'N 34°17'E
Sydney Australia 108 E3...................33°54'S 151°11'E
Sydney Canada 61 L2.......................46°06'N 60°08'W
Syktyvkar Russia 52 F4....................61°41'N 50°48'E
Sylarna mt. Norway/Sweden 43 C3..........63°01'N 12°12'E
Sylt i. Germany 43 B1.....................54°49'N 8°15'E
Syracuse U.S. 63 K5.......................43°04'N 76°11'W
Syr Darya r. Asia 98 A7...................46°05'N 60°55'E
Syria Asia 94 E6..........................35°25'N 39°17'E
Syrian Desert Asia 94 E6..................32°02'N 39°22'E
Syros i. Greece 50 F3.....................37°27'N 24°53'E
Syzran' Russia 53 E3......................53°10'N 48°29'E
Szczecin Poland 46 F5.....................53°26'N 14°34'E
Szczecinek Poland 46 G5...................53°42'N 16°42'E
Szczytno Poland 46 I5.....................53°34'N 20°59'E
Szeged Hungary 46 I2......................46°16'N 20°09'E
Székesfehérvár Hungary 46 H2.............47°12'N 18°25'E
Szekszárd Hungary 46 H2...................46°22'N 18°42'E
Szolnok Hungary 46 I2.....................47°10'N 20°12'E
Szombathely Hungary 46 G2................47°15'N 16°38'E

T

Ṭabas Iran 95 I6..........................33°35'N 56°52'E
Tabasco d. Mexico 66 F4...................18°03'N 92°59'W
Tábor Czechia 46 F3.......................49°24'N 14°42'E
Tabora Tanzania 83 C4.....................5°00'S 32°47'E
Tabrīz Iran 95 G7.........................38°04'N 46°17'E
Tabūk Saudi Arabia 94 E5.................28°22'N 36°38'E
Täby Sweden 43 D2.........................59°27'N 18°04'E
Tacheng China 98 E7.......................46°43'N 83°01'E
Tacloban Phil. 103 H6.....................11°12'N 125°01'E
Tacna Peru 72 B5..........................18°01'S 70°15'W
Tacoma U.S. 62 B6.........................47°15'N 122°27'W
Tacuarembó Uruguay 73 D3..................31°42'S 55°59'W
Tadcaster England 13 F2...................53°53'N 1°16'W
Tadjoura Djibouti 94 F2...................11°46'N 42°48'E
Tadmur Syria 94 E6........................34°34'N 38°17'E
Taf r. Wales 10 C3........................51°47'N 4°27'W
Taganrog Russia 49 K6.....................47°14'N 38°55'E
Taganrog, Gulf of Russia/Ukraine 49 K6...47°00'N 38°31'E
Tagbilaran Phil. 103 G5..................9°38'N 123°53'E
Tagula Island P.N.G. 108 E5..............11°33'S 153°23'E
Tagus r. Portugal 45 A3...................38°59'N 8°56'W
Tahat, Mont mt. Algeria 84 E4............23°18'N 5°37'E
Tahiti i. French Polynesia 114 B2........17°49'S 149°15'W
Taichung Taiwan 99 M2.....................24°09'N 120°42'E
Tain Scotland 17 E2.......................57°49'N 4°03'W
Tainan Taiwan 99 M2.......................23°01'N 120°13'E
Tainaro, Akra pt Greece 50 E3............36°23'N 22°29'E
Taipei Taiwan 99 M3.......................25°04'N 121°33'E
Taiping Malaysia 102 C4...................4°55'N 100°42'E
Tairbeart, Loch An inlet Scotland 16 C2..57°51'N 6°46'W
Taitung Taiwan 99 M2......................22°45'N 121°08'E
Taivalkoski Finland 43 G4................65°34'N 28°14'E
Taivaskero hill Finland 43 F5............68°04'N 24°02'E
Taiwan Asia 99 M2.........................23°34'N 121°32'E
Taiwan Strait China/Taiwan 99 L2........23°49'N 119°16'E
Taiyuan China 99 K5.......................37°48'N 112°38'E
Taizhou China 99 M3.......................28°39'N 121°32'E
Ta'izz Yemen 94 F2........................13°35'N 43°59'E
Tajikistan Asia 87 E3.....................38°54'N 71°08'E
Tak Thailand 102 B7.......................16°51'N 99°08'E
Takamatsu Japan 104 B2....................34°19'N 134°03'E
Takaoka Japan 104 C3......................36°45'N 137°01'E
Taklimakan Desert China 98 E5............38°25'N 80°50'E
Talagang Pakistan 95 L6..................32°55'N 72°29'E
Talaud, Kepulauan is Indonesia 103 H4....4°05'N 127°24'E
Talavera de la Reina Spain 45 C3.........39°58'N 4°49'W
Talca Chile 73 B3.........................35°26'S 71°39'W
Talcahuano Chile 73 B3....................36°44'S 73°07'W
Taldyqorghan Kazakhstan 54 I2............44°59'N 78°22'E
Talgarth Wales 10 D3......................51°59'N 3°14'W
Taliabu i. Indonesia 103 G3..............1°47'S 124°43'E
Tallahassee U.S. 63 J3....................30°26'N 84°17'W
Tallinn Estonia 43 F2.....................59°27'N 24°45'E
Taloyoak Canada 61 I4.....................69°27'N 93°22'W
Talsi Latvia 43 E2........................57°15'N 22°35'E
Taltson r. Canada 60 G4..................61°24'N 112°43'W
Tamale Ghana 84 D2........................9°25'N 0°51'W
Tamanrasset Algeria 84 E4................22°48'N 5°33'E
Tamar r. England 11 C2....................50°29'N 4°13'W
Tamaulipas d. Mexico 66 E5...............24°21'N 99°13'W
Tambacounda Senegal 84 C3................13°47'N 13°40'W
Tambelan, Kepulauan is Indonesia 102 D4
                                      1°03'N 107°03'E
Tambov Russia 53 E3.......................52°43'N 41°26'E
Tambre r. Spain 45 A5.....................42°49'N 8°51'W
Tâmega r. Portugal 45 A4.................41°05'N 8°17'W
Tamiahua, Laguna lagoon Mexico 66 E5....21°39'N 97°36'W
Tamil Nadu d. India 96 E3................11°11'N 78°08'E
Tamiš r. Serbia 50 D7.....................44°50'N 20°39'E
Tampa U.S. 63 J2..........................27°57'N 82°29'W
Tampere Finland 43 E3.....................61°30'N 23°48'E
Tampico Mexico 66 E5......................22°16'N 97°52'W

Tamsweg Austria 46 E2.....................47°08'N 13°47'E
Tamworth Australia 108 E3................31°06'S 150°56'E
Tamworth England 8 D3.....................52°38'N 1°41'W
Tana r. Kenya 85 I1.......................2°31'S 40°30'E
Tana, Lake Ethiopia 85 H3................11°59'N 37°16'E
Tanafjorden inlet Norway 43 G5...........70°32'N 28°13'E
Tanami Desert Australia 108 C5..........19°26'S 131°26'E
Tanana U.S. 60 C4.........................65°12'N 152°04'W
Tanaro r. Italy 46 C1.....................45°01'N 8°47'E
Tando Adam Pakistan 96 C6................25°43'N 68°40'E
Tandragee Northern Ireland 14 C2.........54°21'N 6°24'W
Tanega Shima i. Japan 104 B2............30°28'N 130°58'E
Tanga Tanzania 83 C4......................5°06'S 39°05'E
Tanganyika, Lake Africa 83 B4............5°00'S 29°26'E
Tangier Morocco 84 D5.....................35°47'N 5°49'W
Tangshan China 99 L5......................39°34'N 118°13'E
Tanimbar, Kepulauan is Indonesia 103 I2..7°29'S 131°40'E
Tanjay Phil. 103 G5.......................9°29'N 123°09'E
Tanjungpandan Indonesia 102 D3...........2°46'S 107°37'E
Tanjungredeb Indonesia 102 F4............2°09'N 117°27'E
Tank Pakistan 95 L6.......................32°14'N 70°29'E
Tanna i. Vanuatu 109 F5..................19°32'S 169°14'E
Tanout Niger 84 E3........................14°56'N 8°53'E
Ţanţa Egypt 85 H5.........................30°47'N 31°00'E
Tanzania Africa 83 C4....................6°14'S 34°03'E
Taonan China 99 M7........................45°12'N 122°48'E
Taourirt Morocco 48 C3....................34°25'N 2°55'W
Tapachula Mexico 66 F3...................14°56'N 92°15'W
Tapajós r. Brazil 72 D6..................2°23'S 54°48'W
Tapti r. India 96 D5......................21°13'N 72°58'E
Taquarí r. Brazil 72 D5..................19°05'S 57°22'W
Tar r. Ireland 18 D2......................52°17'N 7°50'W
Tara r. Bos. and Herz./Montenegro 50 C6
                                      43°20'N 18°53'E
Tarakan Indonesia 102 F4.................3°20'N 117°37'E
Taranaki, Mount vol. New Zealand 109 G3
                                      39°18'S 174°03'E
Tarancón Spain 45 D4......................40°01'N 3°00'W
Taransay i. Scotland 16 B2...............57°55'N 7°02'W
Taranto Italy 49 G5.......................40°28'N 17°14'E
Taranto, Gulf of Italy 49 G5.............40°07'N 17°20'E
Tarbat Ness pt Scotland 17 F2............57°52'N 3°46'W
Tarbert A. and B. Scotland 14 D3.........55°58'N 5°50'W
Tarbert A. and B. Scotland 16 C2.........55°52'N 5°25'W
Tarbert Na h-E. S. Scotland 16 C2........57°54'N 6°48'W
Tarbes France 44 D3.......................43°14'N 0°05'E
Târgovişte Romania 50 F7.................44°56'N 25°27'E
Târgu Jiu Romania 50 E7..................45°03'N 23°17'E
Târgu Mureş Romania 47 K2................46°32'N 24°34'E
Târgu Secuiesc Romania 50 G8.............46°00'N 26°08'E
Tarija Bolivia 73 C4......................21°36'S 64°47'W
Tarīm Yemen 95 G3.........................16°08'N 49°23'E
Tarim Basin China 98 E5..................39°41'N 80°53'E
Tarleton England 12 E2....................53°41'N 2°50'W
Tarn r. France 44 D4......................44°05'N 1°03'E
Tarnica mt. Poland 47 J3.................49°05'N 22°46'E
Tarnobrzeg Poland 47 I4..................50°34'N 21°40'E
Tarnów Poland 46 I4.......................50°01'N 20°59'E
Tarragona Spain 45 F4.....................41°07'N 1°15'E
Tarsus Turkey 51 K3.......................36°54'N 34°53'E
Tartu Estonia 43 G2.......................58°23'N 26°43'E
Ṭarṭūs Syria 51 K2........................34°54'N 35°53'E
Tashk, Daryācheh-ye l. Iran 95 H5.......29°32'N 53°29'E
Tashkent Uzbekistan 54 H2................41°16'N 69°15'E
Tasiilaq Greenland 61 O4.................65°37'N 37°42'W
Tasikmalaya Indonesia 102 D2.............7°19'S 108°17'E
Tasmania d. Australia 108 D2.............42°27'S 145°20'E
Tasman Sea S. Pacific Oc. 108 G2.........40°31'S 170°54'E
Tatabánya Hungary 46 H2...................47°34'N 18°26'E
Tatarbunary Ukraine 51 H7................45°50'N 29°37'E
Tatarsk Russia 54 I3......................55°13'N 75°59'E
Tatarskiy Proliv str. Russia 55 P3.......50°29'N 141°05'E
Tatvan Turkey 94 F7.......................38°29'N 42°17'E
Taunggyi Myanmar 97 I5...................20°49'N 97°05'E
Taunton England 11 D3.....................51°01'N 3°06'W
Taunus hills Germany 46 B4...............50°10'N 7°59'E
Tauragė Lithuania 47 J6..................55°15'N 22°17'E
Taurus Mountains Turkey 51 J3............37°00'N 32°09'E
Tavda Russia 52 G3........................58°05'N 65°19'E
Taverham England 9 G3.....................52°41'N 1°12'E
Tavira Portugal 45 B2.....................37°08'N 7°38'W
Tavistock England 11 C2...................50°33'N 4°08'W
Tavşanlı Turkey 51 H4.....................39°32'N 29°28'E
Tavy r. England 11 C2.....................50°27'N 4°09'W
Taw r. England 11 C3......................51°04'N 4°03'W
Tawau Malaysia 102 F4.....................4°16'N 117°54'E
Tawe r. Wales 10 D3.......................51°37'N 3°55'W
Tawitawi i. Phil. 102 F5.................5°14'N 119°57'E
Tay r. Scotland 15 F4.....................56°25'N 3°24'W
Tay, Firth of est. Scotland 15 F4........56°25'N 3°07'W
Tay, Loch l. Scotland 14 E4..............56°30'N 4°11'W
Taymā' Saudi Arabia 94 E5................27°39'N 38°28'E
Taymura r. Russia 55 K4..................63°43'N 98°05'E
Taymyr, Ozero l. Russia 55 L5...........74°20'N 101°51'E
Taymyr Peninsula Russia 55 J5............73°54'N 89°12'E
Tayport Scotland 15 G4....................56°27'N 2°53'W
Taytay Phil. 102 F6.......................10°49'N 119°30'E
Taz r. Russia 54 I4.......................67°34'N 78°36'E
Taza Morocco 48 C3........................34°16'N 3°56'W
Tbilisi Georgia 53 E2.....................41°42'N 44°48'E
Tczew Poland 46 H6........................54°06'N 18°48'E
Te Anau, Lake New Zealand 109 F2.........45°18'S 167°48'E
Tébessa Algeria 48 E4.....................35°23'N 8°12'E
Tebingtinggi Indonesia 102 B4............3°19'N 99°08'E
Tecuci Romania 50 G7......................45°51'N 27°26'E
Tees r. England 13 F3.....................54°34'N 1°15'W
Tees Bay England 13 F3....................54°41'N 1°09'W
Tegal Indonesia 102 D2...................6°51'S 109°07'E
Tegucigalpa Honduras 66 G3...............14°05'N 87°12'W
Tehrān Iran 95 H7.........................35°39'N 51°23'E
Tehuantepec, Gulf of Mexico 66 F4........15°47'N 94°53'W
Teide vol. Canary Islands 45 X2..........28°16'N 16°37'W
Teifi r. Wales 10 C4......................52°05'N 4°40'W
Teign r. England 11 D2....................50°32'N 3°35'W
Teignmouth England 11 D2.................50°33'N 3°30'W
Teith r. Scotland 14 E4...................56°09'N 3°59'W
Tejen Turkmenistan 95 J7.................37°22'N 60°25'E
Tekirdağ Turkey 50 G5.....................40°59'N 27°30'E
Telangana d. India 96 E4.................18°00'N 79°00'E
Telavi Georgia 53 E2......................41°55'N 45°29'E
Tel Aviv-Yafo Israel 49 J3...............32°04'N 34°46'E
Teles Pires r. Brazil 72 D6..............7°20'S 58°03'W
Telford England 8 C3......................52°41'N 2°27'W
Telford and Wrekin d. England 21 D3......52°43'N 2°29'W
Telpoziz, Gora mt. Russia 52 F4.........63°54'N 59°16'E
Tembenchi r. Russia 55 K4................64°35'N 99°49'E
Teme r. England 8 C3......................52°10'N 2°13'W

Temirtaü Kazakhstan 54 I3................50°03'N 72°57'E
Temple Ewell England 9 G2................51°09'N 1°16'E
Templemore Ireland 18 D2.................52°48'N 7°50'W
Temryuk Russia 51 L7......................45°17'N 37°23'E
Temuco Chile 73 B3........................38°44'S 72°35'W
Tenasserim Myanmar 97 I3.................12°02'N 98°58'E
Tenbury Wells England 8 C3...............52°18'N 2°36'W
Tenby Wales 10 C3.........................51°40'N 4°42'W
Ten Degree Channel India 97 H2...........9°57'N 92°51'E
Tendō Japan 104 D3........................38°21'N 140°22'E
Tenerife i. Canary Islands 45 X2.........28°28'N 16°39'W
Tengiz, Ozero l. Kazakhstan 54 H3.......50°09'N 68°23'E
Tennessee d. U.S. 63 I4..................36°12'N 85°01'W
Tennessee r. U.S. 63 I4..................37°08'N 88°25'W
Tenterden England 9 F2...................51°04'N 0°41'E
Tentudia mt. Spain 45 B3.................38°03'N 6°19'W
Teófilo Otoni Brazil 72 E5...............17°52'S 41°31'W
Tepic Mexico 66 D5........................21°31'N 104°55'W
Teplice Czechia 46 E4.....................50°38'N 13°50'E
Terebovlia Ukraine 47 K3.................49°18'N 25°42'E
Teresina Brazil 72 E6.....................5°07'S 42°44'W
Terme Turkey 51 L5........................41°12'N 36°59'E
Términos, Laguna de lagoon Mexico 66 F4
                                      18°30'N 91°37'W
Termiz Uzbekistan 95 K7..................37°15'N 67°17'E
Tern r. England 8 C3......................52°40'N 2°40'E
Ternate Indonesia 103 H4.................0°49'N 127°20'E
Terneuzen Neth. 42 C4.....................51°19'N 3°50'E
Terni Italy 48 F5.........................42°33'N 12°39'E
Ternopil Ukraine 47 K3...................49°33'N 25°36'E
Terrace Canada 60 F3......................54°32'N 128°37'W
Terrassa Spain 45 G4......................41°34'N 2°00'E
Terre Haute U.S. 63 I4...................39°28'N 87°24'W
Terrington Marsh England 9 F3............52°47'N 0°16'E
Terschelling i. Neth. 42 E6..............53°27'N 5°28'E
Teseney Eritrea 94 E3....................15°07'N 36°39'E
Teslin Canada 60 E4.......................60°12'N 132°39'W
Test r. England 8 D1......................50°56'N 1°29'W
Tetas, Punta pt Chile 73 B4..............23°28'S 70°34'W
Tetbury England 8 C2......................51°38'N 2°09'W
Tete Mozambique 83 C3....................16°10'S 33°36'E
Tetney England 13 G2......................53°29'N 0°01'W
Tétouan Morocco 84 D5.....................35°34'N 5°23'W
Tetovo North Macedonia 50 D6.............42°00'N 20°58'E
Teuco r. Argentina 73 C4.................25°39'S 60°11'W
Teviot r. Scotland 15 G3.................55°36'N 2°26'W
Teviothead Scotland 15 G3................55°20'N 2°56'W
Tewkesbury England 8 C2..................51°59'N 2°09'W
Texarkana U.S. 63 H3......................33°25'N 94°08'W
Texas d. U.S. 62 G3.......................31°58'N 99°13'W
Texel i. Neth. 42 D6......................53°09'N 4°46'E
Texoma, Lake U.S. 62 G3..................33°59'N 96°53'W
Tezpur India 97 H6........................26°36'N 92°49'E
Thabana Ntlenyana mt. Lesotho 83 B2.....29°29'S 29°16'E
Thai Binh Vietnam 102 D8.................20°24'N 106°19'E
Thailand Asia 102 C7.....................16°14'N 101°59'E
Thailand, Gulf of Asia 102 C6............11°08'N 101°06'E
Thai Nguyen Vietnam 102 D8...............21°31'N 105°52'E
Thal Desert Pakistan 95 L6...............31°25'N 71°33'E
Thame England 8 E2........................51°45'N 0°58'W
Thame r. England 8 D2.....................51°38'N 1°10'W
Thames est. England 9 F2.................51°30'N 0°31'E
Thames r. England 9 F2....................51°27'N 0°21'E
Thandwe Myanmar 97 H4.....................18°27'N 94°22'E
Thanet, Isle of pen. England 9 G2........51°22'N 1°17'E
Thanh Hoa Vietnam 102 D7.................19°47'N 105°49'E
Thar Desert India/Pakistan 96 C6.........25°48'N 69°50'E
Thasos i. Greece 50 F5...................40°40'N 24°31'E
Thatcham England 8 D2.....................51°24'N 1°16'W
Thaton Myanmar 97 I4......................16°54'N 97°23'E
Thaxted England 9 F2......................51°57'N 0°21'E
The Bahamas Central America 67 I6........24°55'N 77°44'W
The Calf hill England 13 E3..............54°22'N 2°31'W
The Cheviot hill England 13 E4...........55°29'N 2°09'W
The Cuillin Scotland 16 C2...............57°14'N 6°17'W
The Fens f. England 9 E3.................52°42'N 0°08'W
The Gambia Africa 84 C3..................13°22'N 16°25'W
The Great Oasis Egypt 94 D4..............24°52'N 30°42'E
The Gulf Asia 95 H5.......................28°03'N 50°06'E
The Hague Neth. 42 D5.....................52°04'N 4°18'E
Thelon r. Canada 60 I4...................64°17'N 96°18'W
The Marsh England 9 F3....................52°50'N 0°10'E
The Minch str. Scotland 16 C3............58°02'N 6°02'W
The Mullet b. Ireland 18 A4..............54°10'N 10°07'W
The Naze p England 9 G2..................51°52'N 1°17'E
The Needles f. England 8 D1..............50°40'N 1°37'W
The North Sound str. Scotland 17 G4......59°17'N 2°43'W
Theodore Roosevelt r. Brazil 72 C6.......7°35'S 60°21'W
The Old Man of Coniston hill England 12 D3
                                      54°22'N 3°07'W
The Pas Canada 60 H3......................53°49'N 101°16'W
Thermaïkos Kolpos g. Greece 50 E5........40°11'N 22°54'E
The Solent str. England 8 D1.............50°45'N 1°23'W
The Sound est. England 11 C2.............50°21'N 4°09'W
Thessaloniki Greece 50 E5................40°38'N 22°57'E
The Storr hill Scotland 16 C2............57°31'N 6°11'W
Thet r. England 9 F3......................52°24'N 0°45'E
Thetford England 9 F3.....................52°25'N 0°45'E
The Trossachs hills Scotland 14 E4.......56°13'N 4°26'W
The Wash b. England 9 F3.................52°55'N 0°11'E
The Weald f. England 9 F2................51°05'N 0°18'E
Thiers France 44 E4.......................45°51'N 3°33'E
Thiès Senegal 84 C3.......................14°48'N 16°56'W
Thimphu Bhutan 97 G6......................27°29'N 89°42'E
Thionville France 44 G6..................49°22'N 6°10'E
Thira i. Greece 50 F3.....................36°27'N 25°27'E
Thirlmere resr England 12 D3.............54°33'N 3°04'W
Thirsk England 13 F3......................54°14'N 1°20'W
Thiruvananthapuram India 96 E2...........8°30'N 76°57'E
Thisted Denmark 43 B2.....................56°57'N 8°41'E
Thomastown Ireland 18 D2.................52°31'N 7°07'W
Thompson Canada 60 I3.....................55°48'N 97°55'W
Thornaby-on-Tees England 13 F3...........54°32'N 1°17'W
Thornbury England 8 C2....................51°36'N 2°31'W
Thorne England 13 G2......................53°37'N 0°58'W
Thornhill Scotland 15 F3.................55°15'N 3°46'W
Thornton England 12 D2...................53°52'N 3°00'W
Thrakiko Pelagos sea Greece 50 F5........40°22'N 24°46'E
Thrapston England 9 E3....................52°24'N 0°32'W
Thuin Belgium 42 D3.......................50°20'N 4°17'E
Thule Greenland 61 L5.....................77°28'N 69°11'W
Thunder Bay town Canada 61 J2............48°26'N 89°15'W
Thurles Ireland 18 D2.....................52°41'N 7°49'W
Thurrock d. England 21 F2................51°31'N 0°22'E
Thursby England 12 D3.....................54°51'N 3°03'W
Thurso Scotland 17 F3.....................58°36'N 3°31'W
Thurso r. Scotland 17 F3.................58°36'N 3°31'W

Thurso Bay Scotland 17 F3 ....58°38'N 3°32'W
Tianjin China 99 L5 ....39°04'N 117°15'E
Tianshui China 99 J4 ....34°30'N 105°37'E
Tiaret Algeria 48 D4 ....35°20'N 1°19'E
Tibati Cameroon 84 F2 ....6°26'N 12°35'E
Tibesti f. Chad 85 F4 ....20°53'N 17°03'E
Tibet, Plateau of f. China 98 E4 ....33°48'N 84°16'E
Tiburón, Isla i. Mexico 66 B6 ....29°08'N 112°29'W
Ticehurst England 9 F2 ....51°03'N 0°25'E
Tidjikja Mauritania 84 C3 ....18°31'N 11°26'W
Tiel Neth. 42 E4 ....51°52'N 5°25'E
Tielt Belgium 42 C3 ....50°59'N 3°20'E
Tienen Belgium 42 D3 ....50°48'N 4°56'E
Tien Shan mts China/Kyrgyzstan 98 D6 ....40°48'N 76°25'E
Tierra del Fuego i. Argentina/Chile 73 C1 .....54°11'S 68°48'W
Tiétar r. Spain 45 C3 ....39°56'N 5°54'W
Tigre r. Venezuela 72 C7 ....9°26'N 62°25'W
Tigris r. Iraq/Syria 95 G6 ....30°59'N 47°25'E
Tihāmah f. Saudi Arabia 85 I3 ....17°18'N 42°25'E
Tijuana Mexico 66 A7 ....32°29'N 117°02'W
Tikhoretsk Russia 53 E2 ....45°52'N 40°06'E
Tikhvin Russia 52 D3 ....59°39'N 33°32'E
Tikrīt Iraq 94 F6 ....34°33'N 43°37'E
Tiksi Russia 55 N5 ....71°38'N 128°36'E
Tilburg Neth. 42 E4 ....51°33'N 5°05'E
Tilbury England 9 F2 ....51°28'N 0°22'E
Tilehurst England 8 D2 ....51°27'N 1°02'W
Tillabéri Niger 84 E3 ....14°13'N 1°29'E
Tillicoultry Scotland 15 F4 ....56°09'N 3°44'W
Til'tim Russia 52 G4 ....65°12'N 63°13'E
Timā Egypt 49 J2 ....26°53'N 31°25'E
Timanskiy Kryazh f. Russia 52 F4 ....65°00'N 50°00'E
Timashëvsk Russia 53 D2 ....45°37'N 38°56'E
Timbuktu Mali 84 D3 ....16°46'N 2°59'W
Timiş r. Romania 50 D7 ....45°27'N 20°52'E
Timişoara Romania 50 D7 ....45°46'N 21°14'E
Timmins Canada 61 J2 ....48°29'N 81°21'W
Timor i. East Timor/Indonesia 103 H2 ....8°49'S 126°02'E
Timor-Leste Asia 103 H2 ....8°55'S 125°59'E
Timor Sea Australia/Indonesia 108 B5 ....11°23'S 126°22'E
Timrå Sweden 43 D3 ....62°30'N 17°20'E
Tindouf Algeria 84 D4 ....27°42'N 8°07'W
Tinian i. N. Mariana Is 103 L6 ....14°58'N 145°41'E
Tinos i. Greece 50 F3 ....37°40'N 25°12'E
Tintagel England 11 C2 ....50°40'N 4°45'W
Tinto hill Scotland 15 F3 ....55°36'N 3°40'W
Tipperary Ireland 18 C2 ....52°28'N 8°10'W
Tipperary d. Ireland 18 D2 ....52°43'N 7°54'W
Tiptree England 9 F2 ....51°49'N 0°45'E
Tirana Albania 50 C5 ....41°19'N 19°49'E
Tiraspol Moldova 49 I6 ....46°51'N 29°37'E
Tiree i. Scotland 14 C4 ....56°30'N 6°57'W
Tirga Mòr hill Scotland 16 C2 ....57°59'N 6°59'W
Tiruchchirappalli India 96 E3 ....10°49'N 78°41'E
Tiruppur India 96 E3 ....11°06'N 77°18'E
Tisa r. Serbia 50 D7 ....45°08'N 20°17'E
Tisza r. Hungary 47 I2 ....46°09'N 20°04'E
Titicaca, Lake Bolivia/Peru 72 C5 ....15°49'S 69°40'W
Tiverton England 11 D2 ....50°54'N 3°29'W
Tizi Ouzou Algeria 48 D4 ....36°41'N 4°05'E
Tiznit Morocco 84 D4 ....29°41'N 9°43'W
Tiztoutine Morocco 45 D1 ....34°58'N 3°09'W
Tlaxcala Mexico 66 E4 ....19°21'N 98°13'W
Tlaxcala d. Mexico 66 E4 ....19°35'N 98°20'W
Tlemcen Algeria 84 D5 ....34°54'N 1°19'W
Toamasina Madagascar 83 D3 ....18°09'S 49°22'E
Toba, Danau l. Indonesia 102 B4 ....2°32'N 98°59'E
Tobago i. Trinidad and Tobago 67 L3 ....11°17'N 60°38'W
Tobelo Indonesia 103 H4 ....1°44'N 127°57'E
Tobermory Scotland 16 C1 ....56°38'N 6°04'W
Toboali Indonesia 102 D3 ....2°59'S 106°30'E
Tobol r. Kazakhstan/Russia 54 H3 ....58°10'N 68°13'E
Tobol'sk Russia 54 H3 ....58°14'N 68°16'E
Tocantins r. Brazil 72 E6 ....1°49'S 49°13'W
Todmorden England 13 E2 ....53°43'N 2°06'W
Toft Scotland 17 H5 ....60°28'N 1°13'W
Togian, Kepulauan is Indonesia 103 G3 ....0°06'S 121°53'E
Togo Africa 84 E2 ....8°27'N 1°11'E
Tok U.S. 60 D4 ....63°21'N 143°01'W
Tokat Turkey 51 L5 ....40°19'N 36°32'E
Tokelau is S. Pacific Oc. 109 H6 ....8°30'S 171°28'W
Tokushima Japan 104 B2 ....34°04'N 134°34'E
Tōkyō Japan 104 C3 ....35°40'N 139°46'E
Tōkyō d. Japan 104 C3 ....35°22'N 139°03'E
Tôlañaro Madagascar 83 D2 ....25°02'S 46°58'E
Toledo Spain 45 C3 ....39°52'N 4°01'W
Toledo U.S. 63 J5 ....41°39'N 83°33'W
Toledo, Montes de mts Spain 45 C3 ....39°39'N 4°54'W
Toledo Bend Reservoir U.S. 63 H3 ....31°38'N 93°43'W
Toliara Madagascar 83 D2 ....23°22'S 43°39'E
Tolitoli Indonesia 103 G4 ....1°05'N 120°50'E
Tollesbury England 9 F2 ....51°45'N 0°50'E
Tolsta Head Scotland 16 C3 ....58°21'N 6°10'W
Toluca Mexico 66 E4 ....19°18'N 99°39'W
Tol'yatti Russia 53 E3 ....53°31'N 49°26'E
Tomakomai Japan 104 D4 ....42°38'N 141°36'E
Tomanivi mt. Fiji 109 G5 ....17°37'S 178°00'E
Tomaszów Lubelski Poland 47 J4 ....50°28'N 23°25'E
Tomaszów Mazowiecki Poland 46 I4 ....51°32'N 20°01'E
Tombigbee r. U.S. 63 I3 ....31°11'N 87°57'W
Tômbwa Angola 83 A3 ....15°50'S 11°50'E
Tomelloso Spain 45 D3 ....39°09'N 3°00'W
Tomini, Teluk g. Indonesia 102 G3 ....0°21'S 120°54'E
Tomsk Russia 54 J3 ....56°30'N 85°01'E
Tomtabacken hill Sweden 43 C2 ....57°30'N 14°29'E
Tonbridge England 9 F2 ....51°12'N 0°17'E
Tondano Indonesia 103 G4 ....1°21'N 124°56'E
Tønder Denmark 46 C6 ....54°57'N 8°52'E
Tone r. England 8 C2 ....51°04'N 2°56'W
Tonelagee hill Ireland 10 A5 ....53°03'N 6°24'W
Tonga S. Pacific Oc. 109 H4 ....20°05'S 173°45'W
Tongatapu Group is Tonga 109 H4 ....21°07'S 174°45'W
Tongeren Belgium 42 E3 ....50°47'N 5°28'E
Tonghua China 99 N6 ....41°43'N 125°57'E
Tongliao China 99 M6 ....43°31'N 122°14'E
Tongling China 99 L4 ....30°55'N 117°52'E
Tongue Scotland 17 E3 ....58°29'N 4°25'W
Tongue, Kyle of b. Scotland 17 E3 ....58°29'N 4°25'W
Tonk India 96 E6 ....26°10'N 75°50'E
Tonkin, Gulf of China/Vietnam 99 J2 ....20°29'N 108°15'E
Tonle Sap l. Cambodia 102 C6 ....13°04'N 103°51'E
Tonopah U.S. 62 C4 ....38°04'N 117°14'W
Tønsberg Norway 43 B2 ....59°17'N 10°23'E
Toowoomba Australia 108 E4 ....27°33'S 151°58'E
Topeka U.S. 63 G4 ....39°04'N 95°36'W
Topozero, Ozero l. Russia 43 H4 ....65°42'N 32°00'E

Torbay d. England 21 D2 ....50°26'N 3°34'W
Tor Bay England 11 D2 ....50°25'N 3°32'W
Tordesillas Spain 45 C4 ....41°31'N 4°59'W
Torenberg hill Neth. 42 E5 ....52°14'N 5°52'E
Torfaen d. Wales 21 D2 ....51°44'N 3°05'W
Tormes r. Spain 45 B4 ....41°18'N 6°27'W
Tornealven r. Sweden 43 F4 ....65°49'N 24°09'E
Torneträsk l. Sweden 43 D5 ....68°23'N 18°56'E
Tornio Finland 43 F4 ....65°50'N 24°11'E
Toronto Canada 61 K2 ....43°40'N 79°23'W
Toropets Russia 47 N7 ....56°30'N 31°38'E
Torpoint England 11 C2 ....50°22'N 4°12'W
Torquay England 11 D2 ....50°28'N 3°31'W
Torre mt. Portugal 45 B4 ....40°20'N 7°35'W
Torremolinos Spain 45 C2 ....36°36'N 4°30'W
Torrens, Lake Australia 108 C3 ....30°32'S 137°28'E
Torreón Mexico 66 D6 ....25°31'N 103°27'W
Torres Islands Vanuatu 109 F5 ....13°08'S 166°17'E
Torres Strait Australia 108 D6 ....9°50'S 142°31'E
Torres Vedras Portugal 45 A3 ....39°06'N 9°15'W
Torrevieja Spain 45 E2 ....37°59'N 0°40'W
Torridge r. England 11 C2 ....50°59'N 4°11'W
Torridon Scotland 16 D2 ....57°33'N 5°31'W
Torridon, Loch b. Scotland 16 D2 ....57°37'N 5°50'W
Tórtolas, Cerro de las mt. Chile 73 C4 ....29°56'S 69°52'W
Tortosa Spain 45 F4 ....40°50'N 0°32'E
Toruń Poland 46 H5 ....53°01'N 18°37'E
Tory Island Ireland 18 C5 ....55°16'N 8°13'W
Torzhok Russia 52 D3 ....57°02'N 34°57'E
Tosno Russia 43 G2 ....59°33'N 30°54'E
Tosya Turkey 51 K5 ....40°59'N 34°04'E
Totland England 8 D1 ....50°41'N 1°32'W
Tot'ma Russia 52 E3 ....59°59'N 42°46'E
Totnes England 11 D2 ....50°26'N 3°41'W
Totton England 8 D1 ....50°55'N 1°29'W
Tottori Japan 104 B3 ....35°29'N 134°14'E
Toubkal, Jebel mt. Morocco 84 D5 ....31°03'N 7°57'W
Touggourt Algeria 84 E5 ....33°06'N 6°04'E
Toulon France 44 F3 ....43°08'N 5°56'E
Toulouse France 44 D3 ....43°37'N 1°26'E
Toungoo Myanmar 97 I4 ....18°55'N 96°25'E
Touraine f. France 44 D5 ....47°14'N 0°21'E
Tournai Belgium 42 C3 ....50°36'N 3°24'E
Tournon-sur-Rhône France 44 F4 ....45°04'N 4°50'E
Tours France 44 D5 ....47°23'N 0°42'E
Tove r. England 8 E3 ....52°05'N 0°50'W
Towada Japan 104 D4 ....40°36'N 141°12'E
Towcester England 8 E3 ....52°08'N 0°59'W
Townsville Australia 108 D5 ....19°15'S 146°49'E
Towori, Teluk b. Indonesia 103 G3 ....2°02'S 121°57'E
Toyama Japan 104 C3 ....36°41'N 137°13'E
Toyama Wan b. Japan 104 C3 ....36°54'N 137°14'E
Toyota Japan 104 C3 ....35°05'N 137°10'E
Tozeur Tunisia 48 E3 ....33°55'N 8°07'E
Trabzon Turkey 51 M5 ....40°59'N 39°44'E
Trafalgar, Cabo c. Spain 45 B2 ....36°11'N 6°02'W
Tralee Ireland 18 B2 ....52°16'N 9°42'W
Tralee Bay Ireland 18 B2 ....52°18'N 9°57'W
Tramore Ireland 18 D2 ....52°10'N 7°09'W
Trangan i. Indonesia 103 I2 ....6°35'S 134°16'E
Transnistria Europe 47 M2 ....47°45'N 29°03'E
Transylvanian Alps mts Romania 47 J1 ....45°35'N 24°40'E
Trapani Italy 48 F4 ....38°01'N 12°31'E
Traunsee l. Austria 46 E2 ....47°54'N 13°47'E
Traverse City U.S. 63 I5 ....44°46'N 85°37'W
Travnik Bos. and Herz. 50 B7 ....44°14'N 17°40'E
Trawsfynydd, Llyn resr Wales 10 D4 ....52°55'N 3°59'W
Trebišov Slovakia 47 I3 ....48°38'N 21°44'E
Tredegar Wales 10 D3 ....51°46'N 3°15'W
Tregaron Wales 10 D4 ....52°13'N 3°56'W
Treig, Loch l. Scotland 16 E1 ....56°48'N 4°44'W
Trelleborg Sweden 43 C1 ....55°22'N 13°10'E
Tremadog Bay Wales 10 C4 ....52°52'N 4°15'W
Trenčín Slovakia 46 H3 ....48°53'N 18°02'E
Trent r. England 13 G2 ....53°38'N 0°43'W
Trento Italy 46 D2 ....46°04'N 11°08'E
Trenton U.S. 63 L5 ....40°13'N 74°47'W
Treorchy Wales 10 D3 ....51°39'N 3°30'W
Tresco i. England 11 A1 ....49°57'N 6°19'W
Tres Puntas, Cabo c. Argentina 73 C2 ....47°08'S 65°53'W
Treviso Italy 46 E1 ....45°40'N 12°15'E
Trevose Head England 11 B2 ....50°33'N 5°06'W
Trier Germany 46 B3 ....49°45'N 6°38'E
Trieste Italy 46 E1 ....45°39'N 13°46'E
Trikala Greece 50 D4 ....39°33'N 21°46'E
Trim Ireland 18 E3 ....53°33'N 6°47'W
Trincomalee Sri Lanka 96 F2 ....8°37'N 81°13'E
Trindade, Ilha da i. S. Atlantic Ocean 68 E2
     ....20°31'S 29°19'W
Tring England 8 E2 ....51°48'N 0°39'W
Trinidad i. Trinidad and Tobago 67 L3 ....10°27'N 61°13'W
Trinidad U.S. 62 F4 ....37°11'N 104°30'W
Trinidad and Tobago Central America 67 L3
     ....10°49'N 61°00'W
Tripoli Greece 50 E3 ....37°31'N 22°23'E
Tripoli Lebanon 49 K3 ....34°26'N 35°52'E
Tripoli Libya 84 F5 ....32°52'N 13°08'E
Tripolitania f. Libya 48 F3 ....30°39'N 13°17'E
Tripura d. India 97 H5 ....23°50'N 91°35'E
Tristan da Cunha i. Atlantic Oc. 116 E2 ....38°00'S 12°00'W
Trnava Slovakia 46 G3 ....48°23'N 17°35'E
Trobriand Islands P.N.G. 108 E6 ....8°33'S 151°09'E
Troisdorf Germany 42 G3 ....50°49'N 7°09'E
Trois-Rivières Canada 61 K2 ....46°21'N 72°35'W
Troitsk Russia 53 G3 ....54°08'N 61°36'E
Trollhättan Sweden 43 C2 ....58°16'N 12°18'E
Tromsø Norway 43 D5 ....69°39'N 18°57'E
Trondheim Norway 43 B3 ....63°25'N 10°22'E
Troon Scotland 14 E3 ....55°32'N 4°40'W
Trostan hill Northern Ireland 14 C3 ....55°03'N 6°09'W
Troup Head Scotland 17 G2 ....57°41'N 2°18'W
Trout Lake Canada 63 H7 ....51°15'N 93°06'W
Trowbridge England 8 C2 ....51°19'N 2°12'W
Troyes France 44 F6 ....48°18'N 4°05'E
Trubchevsk Russia 47 O5 ....52°35'N 33°47'E
Trujillo Peru 72 B6 ....8°07'S 79°02'W
Truro Canada 61 L2 ....45°22'N 63°13'W
Truro England 11 B2 ....50°16'N 5°03'W
Tsaratanana, Massif du mts Madagascar 83 D3
     ....13°44'S 48°59'E
Tsetserleg Mongolia 99 I7 ....47°19'N 101°29'E
Tshchikskoye Vodokhranilishche resr Russia 51 M7
     ....44°57'N 39°28'E
Tsimlyanskoye Vodokhranilishche resr Russia 53 E2
     ....48°00'N 43°00'E
Tsna r. Belarus 47 L5 ....52°09'N 27°01'E

Tsu Japan 104 C2 ....34°43'N 136°31'E
Tsuchiura Japan 104 D3 ....36°04'N 140°12'E
Tsugaru Kaikyō str. Japan 104 D4 ....41°16'N 140°21'E
Tsumeb Namibia 83 A3 ....19°14'S 17°43'E
Tsumis Park Namibia 83 A2 ....23°47'S 17°31'E
Tsuruga Japan 104 C3 ....35°38'N 136°04'E
Tsu Shima is Japan 104 A2 ....34°24'N 129°23'E
Tuam Ireland 18 C3 ....53°31'N 8°51'W
Tuamotu Archipelago is French Polynesia 116 B2
     ....14°29'S 142°50'W
Tuapse Russia 53 D2 ....44°06'N 39°04'E
Tuban Indonesia 102 E2 ....6°55'S 112°02'E
Tubbercurry Ireland 18 C4 ....54°03'N 8°43'W
Tübingen Germany 46 C2 ....48°31'N 9°04'E
Tubruq Libya 85 G5 ....32°04'N 23°57'E
Tucson U.S. 62 D3 ....32°14'N 110°54'W
Tucumcari U.S. 62 F4 ....35°12'N 103°44'W
Tucuruí Brazil 72 E6 ....3°42'S 49°44'W
Tucuruí, Represa resr Brazil 72 E6 ....4°26'S 49°07'W
Tudela Spain 45 E5 ....42°04'N 1°36'W
Tuela r. Portugal 45 B4 ....41°38'N 7°08'W
Tuguegarao Phil. 103 G7 ....17°37'N 121°43'E
Tui Spain 45 A5 ....42°03'N 8°38'W
Tukangbesi, Kepulauan is Indonesia 103 G2
     ....5°40'S 123°55'E
Tukums Latvia 43 E2 ....56°58'N 23°10'E
Tula Russia 53 D3 ....54°12'N 37°37'E
Tulcea Romania 51 H7 ....45°10'N 28°48'E
Tulchyn Ukraine 47 M3 ....48°41'N 28°50'E
Tulit'a Canada 60 F4 ....64°55'N 125°31'W
Tullamore Ireland 18 D3 ....53°17'N 7°30'W
Tulle France 44 D4 ....45°16'N 1°46'E
Tullow Ireland 18 E2 ....52°48'N 6°44'W
Tullybrack hill Northern Ireland 14 B2 ....54°23'N 7°52'W
Tulsa U.S. 62 G4 ....36°09'N 95°58'W
Tumaco Colombia 72 B7 ....1°48'N 78°49'W
Tumakuru India 96 E3 ....13°19'N 77°06'E
Tummel r. Scotland 17 F1 ....56°39'N 3°40'W
Tummel, Loch l. Scotland 17 F1 ....56°42'N 3°58'W
Tump Pakistan 95 J5 ....26°06'N 62°26'E
Tumucumaque, Serra hills Brazil 72 D7 ....1°59'N 56°09'W
Tunceli Turkey 51 M4 ....39°06'N 39°33'E
Tundzha r. Bulgaria 50 G5 ....41°39'N 26°33'E
Tunis Tunisia 48 F4 ....36°46'N 10°16'E
Tunisia Africa 48 E3 ....34°52'N 9°24'E
Tunja Colombia 72 C7 ....5°30'N 73°22'W
Tunnsjøen l. Norway 43 C4 ....64°42'N 13°24'E
Tuolumne r. U.S. 62 B4 ....37°36'N 121°10'W
Tura Russia 55 L4 ....64°16'N 100°15'E
Turabah Saudi Arabia 94 F4 ....21°14'N 41°37'E
Turbat Pakistan 96 B6 ....26°01'N 63°07'E
Turbo Colombia 67 I2 ....8°05'N 76°43'W
Turda Romania 47 J2 ....46°34'N 23°47'E
Turgutlu Turkey 50 G4 ....38°29'N 27°42'E
Turhal Turkey 51 L5 ....40°23'N 36°04'E
Turia r. Spain 45 E3 ....39°26'N 0°18'W
Turin Italy 46 B1 ....45°04'N 7°41'E
Turinsk Russia 52 G3 ....58°04'N 63°42'E
Turkana, Lake Ethiopia/Kenya 85 H2 ....3°59'N 35°57'E
Turkey Asia/Europe 51 I4 ....39°19'N 34°21'E
Turkmenabat Turkmenistan 54 H1 ....39°05'N 63°34'E
Turkmenbaşy Turkmenistan 53 F2 ....40°02'N 52°59'E
Turkmenistan Asia 87 D4 ....40°00'N 60°00'E
Turks and Caicos Islands Central America 67 J5
     ....21°59'N 71°36'W
Turks Islands Turks and Caicos Is 67 J5 ....21°25'N 71°09'W
Turku Finland 43 E3 ....60°27'N 22°15'E
Turnhout Belgium 42 D4 ....51°19'N 4°57'E
Turnu Măgurele Romania 50 F6 ....43°45'N 24°51'E
Turpan China 98 F6 ....42°52'N 89°12'E
Turquino, Pico mt. Cuba 67 I5 ....20°02'N 76°51'W
Turriff Scotland 17 G2 ....57°32'N 2°28'W
Tuscaloosa U.S. 63 I3 ....33°11'N 87°30'W
Tutbury England 8 D3 ....52°51'N 1°41'W
Tuticorin India 96 E2 ....8°48'N 78°08'E
Tuttlingen Germany 46 C2 ....47°59'N 8°49'E
Tutuila i. American Samoa 109 H5 ....14°16'S 170°33'W
Tuvalu S. Pacific Oc. 109 G6 ....7°24'S 178°20'E
Tuxford England 13 G2 ....53°14'N 0°54'W
Tuxpan Mexico 66 E5 ....20°58'N 97°22'W
Tuxtla Gutiérrez Mexico 66 F4 ....16°46'N 93°08'W
Tuz, Lake Turkey 51 J4 ....38°42'N 33°24'E
Tuzla Bos. and Herz. 50 C7 ....44°33'N 18°42'E
Tver' Russia 52 D3 ....56°50'N 35°54'E
Tweed r. U.K. 13 E4 ....55°45'N 2°06'W
Twin Falls town U.S. 62 D5 ....42°35'N 114°27'W
Twyford England 8 E2 ....51°29'N 0°52'W
Tyler U.S. 63 G3 ....32°22'N 95°18'W
Tynda Russia 55 N3 ....55°07'N 124°44'E
Tyne r. Scotland 15 G4 ....55°58'N 2°35'W
Tyne and Wear d. England 20 E4 ....54°56'N 1°16'W
Tynemouth England 13 F4 ....55°01'N 1°25'W
Tynset Norway 43 B3 ....62°16'N 10°47'E
Tyre Lebanon 49 K3 ....33°15'N 35°14'E
Tyrrhenian Sea France/Italy 48 F5 ....40°13'N 10°15'E
Tyumen' Russia 54 H3 ....57°09'N 65°28'E
Tywi r. Wales 10 C3 ....51°48'N 4°20'W
Tzia i. Greece 50 F3 ....37°38'N 24°24'E

U

Ubangi r. C.A.R./Dem. Rep. Congo 85 F1 ......0°25'S 17°44'E
Úbeda Spain 45 D3 ....38°01'N 3°22'W
Uberaba Brazil 73 E4 ....19°46'S 47°53'W
Uberlândia Brazil 72 E5 ....18°56'S 48°14'W
Ubon Ratchathani Thailand 102 C7 ....15°14'N 104°53'E
Ucayali r. Peru 72 B6 ....4°28'S 73°29'W
Uchur r. Russia 55 O3 ....57°19'N 131°17'E
Uckfield England 9 F1 ....50°58'N 0°06'E
Uda r. Russia 55 O3 ....54°41'N 135°28'E
Udaipur India 96 E6 ....24°35'N 73°47'E
Uddevalla Sweden 43 B2 ....58°21'N 11°57'E
Uddjaure l. Sweden 43 D4 ....65°56'N 17°52'E
Udine Italy 46 E2 ....46°04'N 13°14'E
Udon Thani Thailand 102 C7 ....17°22'N 102°50'E
Udupi India 96 D3 ....13°20'N 74°46'E
Ueda Japan 104 C3 ....36°24'N 138°15'E
Uele r. Dem. Rep. Congo 83 B5 ....3°32'N 25°16'E
Uelzen Germany 46 D5 ....52°58'N 10°34'E
Ufa Russia 53 F3 ....54°44'N 55°58'E
Uganda Africa 85 H2 ....2°34'N 32°37'E
Uglegorsk Russia 55 P2 ....49°02'N 142°02'E
Uig Scotland 16 C2 ....57°35'N 6°22'W
Uíge Angola 83 A4 ....7°36'S 15°05'E
Uinta Mountains U.S. 62 D5 ....40°36'N 110°59'W

Ukhta Russia 52 F4 ....63°33'N 53°46'
Ukiah U.S. 62 B4 ....39°09'N 123°13'
Ukmergė Lithuania 47 K6 ....55°15'N 24°46'
Ukraine Europe 47 N3 ....49°23'N 31°18'
Ulaangom Mongolia 98 G7 ....49°57'N 92°09'
Ulan Bator Mongolia 99 J7 ....47°48'N 106°58'
Ulanhot China 99 M7 ....46°04'N 122°03'
Ulan-Khol Russia 53 E2 ....45°26'N 46°51'
Ulan-Ude Russia 55 L3 ....51°49'N 107°38'
Uliastay Mongolia 98 H7 ....47°36'N 96°48'
Ulithi atoll Micronesia 103 J6 ....10°07'N 139°40'
Uljin S. Korea 104 A3 ....36°59'N 129°23'
Ullapool Scotland 16 D2 ....57°54'N 5°10'
Ulleungdo i. S. Korea 104 B3 ....37°30'N 130°55'
Ullswater l. England 12 E3 ....54°34'N 2°54'
Ulm Germany 46 C2 ....48°25'N 9°59'
Ulsan S. Korea 104 A3 ....35°32'N 129°19'
Ulster Canal Ireland/U.K. 14 B2 ....54°14'N 7°01'
Uludağ mt. Turkey 51 H5 ....40°06'N 29°17'
Ulundi S. Africa 83 C2 ....28°19'S 31°25'
Uluru / Ayers Rock hill Australia 108 C4 ....25°20'S 131°05'
Ulva i. Scotland 14 C4 ....56°28'N 6°13'
Ulverston England 12 D3 ....54°12'N 3°05'
Ul'yanovsk Russia 53 E3 ....54°18'N 48°23'
Uman Ukraine 47 N3 ....48°45'N 30°14'
Umba Russia 52 D4 ....66°41'N 34°23'
Umboi i. P.N.G. 108 D6 ....5°42'S 147°50'
Umeå Sweden 43 E3 ....63°50'N 20°17'
Umeälven r. Sweden 43 D4 ....63°46'N 20°19'
Umm Keddada Sudan 94 C2 ....13°35'N 26°42'
Umm Ruwaba Sudan 94 D2 ....12°52'N 31°10'
Umm Sa'ad Libya 85 G5 ....31°34'N 25°03'
Umtata S. Africa 83 B1 ....31°35'S 28°47'
Umuarama Brazil 73 D4 ....23°46'S 53°19'
Una r. Bos. and Herz./Croatia 50 B7 ....45°16'N 16°56'
'Unayzah Saudi Arabia 94 F5 ....26°05'N 43°57'
Unecha Russia 47 O5 ....52°51'N 32°41'
Ungava, Péninsule d' pen. Canada 61 K4 ....60°46'N 74°25'
Ungava Bay Canada 61 L3 ....59°16'N 67°29'
Unimak Island U.S. 60 B3 ....54°58'N 164°02'
United Arab Emirates Asia 95 H4 ....23°30'N 52°25'
United Kingdom Europe 20 ....54°35'N 1°53'
United States N. America 62 G4 ....38°59'N 99°57'
Unst i. Scotland 17 I5 ....60°46'N 0°53'
Upa r. Russia 47 Q6 ....54°01'N 36°20'
Upavon England 8 D2 ....51°18'N 1°48'
Upemba, Lac l. Dem. Rep. Congo 83 B4
     ....8°39'S 26°29'
Upernavik Greenland 61 M5 ....72°48'N 56°09'
Upington S. Africa 83 B2 ....28°28'S 21°15'
Upolu i. Samoa 109 H5 ....14°04'S 171°39'
Upper Klamath Lake U.S. 62 B5 ....42°22'N 121°53'
Upper Lough Erne l. Northern Ireland 14 B2
     ....54°15'N 7°34'
Upper Tean England 8 D3 ....52°57'N 1°59'
Uppingham England 8 E3 ....52°35'N 0°43'
Uppsala Sweden 43 D2 ....59°51'N 17°38'
Upton upon Severn England 8 C3 ....52°04'N 2°13'
Ural r. Kazakhstan/Russia 53 F2 ....46°55'N 51°46'
Ural Mountains Russia 54 H4 ....66°50'N 63°48'
Uranium City Canada 60 H3 ....59°31'N 108°43'
Ure r. England 13 F3 ....54°05'N 1°20'
Urengoy Russia 54 I4 ....65°55'N 78°23'
Urganch Uzbekistan 54 H2 ....41°32'N 60°39'
Urie r. Scotland 17 G2 ....57°16'N 2°22'
Urla Turkey 50 G4 ....38°17'N 26°46'
Urmia, Lake Iran 94 G7 ....37°57'N 45°17'
Uruapan Mexico 66 D4 ....19°25'N 102°04'
Urubamba r. Peru 72 B5 ....10°46'S 73°47'
Uruguaiana Brazil 73 D4 ....29°45'S 57°03'
Uruguay r. Argentina/Brazil/Uruguay 73 D4
     ....33°52'S 58°25'
Uruguay S. America 73 D3 ....32°45'S 55°56'
Ürümqi China 98 F6 ....43°44'N 87°34'
Urziceni Romania 50 G7 ....44°43'N 26°37'
Usa r. Russia 52 F4 ....66°00'N 57°24'
Uşak Turkey 51 H4 ....38°40'N 29°24'
Ushuaia Argentina 73 C1 ....54°45'S 68°19'
Usinsk Russia 52 F4 ....66°01'N 57°36'
Usk Wales 10 E3 ....51°42'N 2°54'
Usk r. Wales 10 E3 ....51°34'N 2°59'
Usk Reservoir Wales 10 D3 ....51°56'N 3°44'
Usogorsk Russia 52 E4 ....63°26'N 48°42'
Usol'ye-Sibirskoye Russia 55 L3 ....52°40'N 103°30'
Ussuriysk Russia 55 O2 ....43°48'N 131°57'
Ust'-Ilimsk Russia 55 L3 ....58°02'N 102°42'
Ust'-Ilych Russia 52 F4 ....62°33'N 56°43'
Ústí nad Labem Czechia 46 F4 ....50°40'N 14°03'
Ust'-Kamchatsk Russia 55 R3 ....56°15'N 162°32'
Ust'-Kara Russia 52 G4 ....69°13'N 64°59'
Ust'-Kulom Russia 52 F4 ....61°41'N 53°42'
Ust'-Kut Russia 55 L3 ....56°45'N 105°42'
Ust'-Maya Russia 55 O4 ....60°27'N 134°33'
Ust'-Olenek Russia 55 M5 ....72°55'N 119°44'
Ust'-Tsil'ma Russia 52 F4 ....65°26'N 52°10'
Ustyurt Plateau f. Kazakhstan/Uzbekistan 53 F2
     ....43°29'N 56°13'
Utah d. U.S. 62 D4 ....39°34'N 111°34'
Utena Lithuania 47 K6 ....55°30'N 25°36'
Utica U.S. 63 K5 ....43°06'N 75°15'
Utiel Spain 45 E3 ....39°34'N 1°11'
Utqiagvik U.S. 60 C5 ....71°18'N 156°43'
Utrecht Neth. 42 E5 ....52°06'N 5°07'
Utrecht d. Neth. 42 E5 ....52°07'N 5°12'
Utrera Spain 45 C2 ....37°11'N 5°46'
Utsunomiya Japan 104 C3 ....36°34'N 139°53'
Utta Russia 53 E2 ....46°26'N 46°02'
Uttaradit Thailand 102 C7 ....17°37'N 100°06'
Uttarakhand d. India 96 E7 ....30°11'N 79°09'
Uttar Pradesh d. India 96 E6 ....27°37'N 79°11'
Uttoxeter England 8 D3 ....52°54'N 1°52'
Uusikaupunki Finland 43 E3 ....60°48'N 21°22'
Uvs Nuur l. Mongolia 98 G8 ....50°20'N 92°33'
Uwajima Japan 104 B2 ....33°13'N 132°33'
Uxbridge England 9 E2 ....51°33'N 0°29'
Uyuni, Salar de f. Bolivia 73 C4 ....20°13'S 67°36'
Uzbekistan Asia 87 E4 ....40°00'N 60°00'
Uzhhorod Ukraine 47 J3 ....48°37'N 22°17'
Užice Serbia 50 C6 ....43°51'N 19°52'
Uzlovaya Russia 53 D3 ....53°59'N 38°12'
Uzunköprü Turkey 50 G5 ....41°15'N 26°4'

V

Vaal r. S. Africa 83 B2 ....29°05'S 23°3'
Vaasa Finland 43 E3 ....63°06'N 21°3'

ic Hungary 46 H2 ....47°47'N 19°09'E
ododara India 96 D5 ....22°16'N 73°14'E
dsø Norway 43 G5 ....70°05'N 29°44'E
aduz Liechtenstein 46 C2 ......47°08'N 9°32'E
ærøy i. Norway 43 C4 ....67°39'N 12°36'E
aganski Vrh mt. Croatia 50 A7 ..44°22'N 15°30'E
áh r. Slovakia 46 H2 ....47°46'N 18°08'E
aiaku Tuvalu 109 G6 ....8°28'S 179°10'E
itupu i. Tuvalu 109 G6 ....7°27'S 178°43'E
ldai Hills Russia 34 H4 ....57°10'N 33°00'E
ldepeñas Spain 45 D3 ....38°46'N 3°22'W
ldés, Península pen. Argentina 73 C2 ...42°31'S 63°25'W
ldez U.S. 60 D4 ....61°07'N 146°16'W
al-d'Or Canada 61 K2 ....48°06'N 77°47'W
ldosta U.S. 63 J3 ....30°51'N 83°18'W
ldres f. Norway 43 B3 ....60°56'N 9°13'E
alence France 44 F4 ....44°56'N 4°54'E
alencia Spain 45 E3 ....39°29'N 0°21'W
alencia Venezuela 72 C8 ....10°10'N 67°59'W
alencia, Golfo de g. Spain 45 F3 ...39°28'N 0°02'E
alencia de Alcántara Spain 45 B3 ...39°25'N 7°14'W
alenciennes France 44 E7 ......50°21'N 3°32'E
ale of Glamorgan d. Wales 21 D2 ...51°26'N 3°21'W
alier, Mont mt. France 44 D3 ..42°48'N 1°05'E
alinco, Golfe de g. France 44 H2 ...41°40'N 8°50'E
aljevo Serbia 50 C7 ....44°17'N 19°55'E
alka Latvia 43 F2 ....57°46'N 26°00'E
alkeakoski Finland 43 F3 ......61°15'N 24°03'E
alkenswaard Neth. 42 E4 ....51°21'N 5°27'E
alladolid Spain 45 C4 ....41°39'N 4°43'W
alle de la Pascua Venezuela 67 K2 ...9°10'N 65°57'W
alledupar Colombia 72 B8 ......10°30'N 73°16'W
alletta Malta 48 F4 ....35°54'N 14°30'E
alley Wales 10 C5 ....53°17'N 4°34'W
lparaíso Chile 73 B3 ....33°03'S 71°36'W
als, Tanjung c. Indonesia 103 J2 ...8°26'S 137°40'E
ammala Finland 43 E3 ....61°20'N 22°56'E
an Turkey 94 F7 ....38°30'N 43°22'E
n, Lake Turkey 94 F7 ....38°37'N 42°47'E
nadzor Armenia 53 E2 ....40°49'N 44°28'E
ncouver Canada 60 F2 ....49°16'N 123°08'W
ncouver Island Canada 60 F2 ...49°28'N 125°39'W
nern l. Sweden 43 C2 ....59°05'N 13°36'E
nersborg Sweden 43 C2 ....58°23'N 12°20'E
ngaindrano Madagascar 83 D2 ...23°22'S 47°34'E
nimo P.N.G. 103 K3 ....2°42'S 141°20'E
nnäs Sweden 43 D3 ....63°55'N 19°46'E
nnes France 44 B5 ....47°39'N 2°45'W
ntaa Finland 43 F3 ....60°18'N 24°57'E
nua Levu i. Fiji 109 G5 ....16°10'S 179°40'E
nuatu S. Pacific Oc. 109 F5 ...16°05'S 167°04'E
an Diemen Gulf Australia 103 I1 ...11°54'S 132°00'E
ranasi India 96 F6 ....25°20'N 83°04'E
rangerfjorden str. Norway 43 G5 ...70°04'N 29°07'E
raždin Croatia 46 G2 ....46°19'N 16°22'E
rberg Sweden 43 C2 ....57°07'N 12°16'E
rdar r. North Macedonia 50 E5 ..41°07'N 22°32'E
réna Lithuania 47 K6 ....54°13'N 24°35'E
rese Italy 46 C1 ....45°49'N 8°50'E
rkaus Finland 43 F3 ....62°19'N 27°54'E
rna Bulgaria 51 G6 ....43°12'N 27°54'E
rnamo Sweden 43 C2 ....57°11'N 14°03'E
rpalota Hungary 46 H2 ....47°12'N 18°08'E
sterås Sweden 43 D2 ....59°37'N 16°33'E
sterdalälven r. Sweden 43 C3 ..60°32'N 15°07'E
stervik Sweden 43 D2 ....57°45'N 16°39'E
sylkiv Ukraine 47 N4 ....50°11'N 30°19'E
tersay i. Scotland 16 B1 .....56°56'N 7°38'W
tican City Europe 35 F3
tnajökull ice cap Iceland 43 Y2 ...64°28'N 16°37'W
ttern l. Sweden 43 C2 ....58°05'N 14°21'E
va'u Group is Tonga 109 H5 ...18°24'S 174°21'W
wkavysk Belarus 47 K5 ....53°09'N 24°27'E
xjö Sweden 43 C2 ....56°53'N 14°49'E
ygach, Ostrov i. Russia 52 F5 ...69°59'N 59°05'E
chte r. Germany 42 F5 ....52°37'N 6°43'E
endam Neth. 42 E4 ....53°06'N 6°53'E
enendaal Neth. 42 E5 ....52°01'N 5°33'E
ga i. Norway 43 B4 ....65°39'N 11°53'E
jle Denmark 43 B1 ....55°43'N 9°32'E
en Germany 42 F4 ....51°53'N 6°59'E
les North Macedonia 50 D5 ....41°42'N 21°47'E
lika Morava canal Serbia 50 D7 ...44°43'N 21°03'E
likaya r. Russia 47 M7 ....57°50'N 28°15'E
likaya r. Russia 55 S4 ....64°32'N 176°06'E
likiye Luki Russia 52 D3 .....56°20'N 30°32'E
likiy Novgorod Russia 52 D3 ..58°33'N 31°16'E
likiy Ustyug Russia 52 E4 ....60°46'N 46°18'E
liko Tarnovo Bulgaria 50 F6 ..43°05'N 25°39'E
lizh Russia 47 N6 ....55°36'N 31°12'E
llore India 96 E3 ....12°56'N 79°07'E
l'sk Russia 52 E4 ....61°03'N 42°05'E
ndôme France 44 D5 ....47°48'N 1°04'E
nezuela S. America 67 K2 .....7°35'N 66°30'W
nezuela, Golfo de g. Venezuela 72 B8
.........................11°32'N 71°03'W
nice Italy 46 E1 ....45°26'N 12°20'E
nice, Gulf of Europe 46 E1 ...45°19'N 12°43'E
nray Neth. 42 E4 ....51°31'N 5°58'E
nta r. Latvia/Lithuania 43 E2 ...56°24'N 22°14'E
ntnor England 8 D1 ....50°36'N 1°12'W
ntspils Latvia 43 E2 ....57°23'N 21°36'E
ra Spain 45 E2 ....37°15'N 1°52'W
racruz Mexico 66 E4 ....19°11'N 96°09'W
racruz d. Mexico 66 E5 ....20°54'N 97°46'W
rcelli Italy 46 C1 ....45°19'N 8°26'E
rdalsøra Norway 43 B3 ....63°47'N 11°29'E
rde r. Portugal 72 D5 ....21°10'S 51°58'W
rde r. U.S. 62 D3 ....33°33'N 111°39'W
rdun France 44 F6 ....49°10'N 5°24'E
rín Spain 45 B5 ....41°56'N 9°25'W
rkhnevilyuysk Russia 55 N4 ...63°26'N 120°12'E
rkhoyansk Russia 55 O4 ....67°32'N 133°27'E
rkhoyanskiy Khrebet mts Russia 55 N5
.........................70°07'N 128°50'E
rmont d. U.S. 63 L5 ....43°53'N 72°42'W
roia Greece 50 E5 ....40°32'N 22°13'E
rona Italy 46 D1 ....45°26'N 10°59'E
rsailles France 44 E6 ....48°48'N 2°08'E
t, Cap c. Senegal 84 C3 ......14°44'N 17°31'W
rviers Belgium 42 E3 ....50°35'N 5°52'E
wood England 8 D1 ....50°53'N 1°52'W
elaya, Gora mt. Russia 53 F3 ...54°34'N 57°59'E

Vesoul France 44 G5 ....47°38'N 6°09'E
Vesterålen is Norway 43 C5 ....68°43'N 13°59'E
Vestfjorden str. Norway 43 C4 ..67°40'N 13°54'E
Vestmannaeyjar is Iceland 43 X1 ...63°24'N 20°13'W
Vesturhorn hd Iceland 43 Z2 ...64°17'N 14°59'W
Vesuvius vol. Italy 48 F5 .....40°50'N 14°26'E
Veszprém Hungary 46 G2 ....47°06'N 17°54'E
Vetluga Russia 52 E3 ....57°52'N 45°48'E
Veurne Belgium 42 B4 ....51°04'N 2°40'E
Vézère r. France 44 D4 ....44°53'N 0°53'E
Vezirköprü Turkey 51 K5 ....41°09'N 35°28'E
Viana do Castelo Portugal 45 A4 ...41°42'N 8°49'W
Viborg Denmark 43 B2 ....56°27'N 9°24'E
Vic Spain 45 G4 ....41°56'N 2°15'E
Vicenza Italy 46 D1 ....45°33'N 11°33'E
Vichy France 44 E5 ....46°08'N 3°26'E
Victoria d. Australia 108 D3 ..36°56'S 144°52'E
Victoria r. Australia 108 C5 ..15°23'S 130°17'E
Victoria Canada 60 F2 ....48°25'N 123°22'W
Victoria Seychelles 79 E2 .....4°38'S 55°28'E
Victoria U.S. 62 G2 ....28°49'N 96°59'W
Victoria, Lake Africa 83 C4 ...0°59'S 32°51'E
Victoria, Mount Myanmar 97 H5 ..21°11'N 93°56'E
Victoria, Mount P.N.G. 108 D6 ..8°49'S 147°30'E
Victoria Falls Zambia/Zimbabwe 83 B3 ...17°49'S 25°42'E
Victoria Island Canada 60 H5 ..70°42'N 106°38'W
Viedma Argentina 73 C2 ....40°50'S 63°00'W
Viedma, Lago l. Argentina 73 B2 ...49°35'S 72°49'W
Vienna Austria 46 G2 ....48°12'N 16°23'E
Vienne France 44 F4 ....45°31'N 4°53'E
Vienne r. France 44 D5 ....47°13'N 0°05'E
Vientiane Laos 102 C7 ....17°58'N 102°37'E
Vierzon France 44 E5 ....47°14'N 2°04'E
Vieste Italy 50 B5 ....41°53'N 16°11'E
Vietnam Asia 102 D7 ....19°20'N 104°48'E
Vignemale mt. France 44 C3 ....42°46'N 0°09'W
Vigo Spain 45 A5 ....42°14'N 8°43'W
Vijayapura India 96 E4 ....16°49'N 75°48'E
Vijayawada India 96 F4 ....16°33'N 80°39'E
Vík Iceland 43 Y1 ....63°26'N 19°02'W
Vikna i. Norway 43 B4 ....64°53'N 10°50'E
Vilagarcía Spain 45 A5 ....42°36'N 8°45'W
Vilaine r. France 44 B5 ....47°35'N 2°16'W
Vila Real Portugal 45 B4 ......41°18'N 7°44'W
Vilcabamba, Cordillera mts Peru 72 B5 ...12°30'S 73°27'W
Vilhelmina Sweden 43 D4 ....64°37'N 16°41'E
Vilhena Brazil 72 C5 ....12°42'S 60°07'W
Viljandi Estonia 43 F2 ....58°22'N 25°35'E
Vilkaviškis Lithuania 47 J6 ...54°39'N 23°03'E
Vilkitskogo, Proliv str. Russia 55 K5 ...77°30'N 98°42'E
Villach Austria 46 E2 ....46°37'N 13°50'E
Villahermosa Mexico 66 F4 .....18°00'N 92°53'W
Villarrobledo Spain 45 D3 .....39°16'N 2°36'W
Villavicencio Colombia 72 B7 ..4°07'N 73°36'W
Villefranche-sur-Saône France 44 F4 ...45°59'N 4°44'E
Villena Spain 45 E3 ....38°38'N 0°51'W
Villeneuve-sur-Lot France 44 D4 ...44°25'N 0°42'E
Villeurbanne France 44 F4 .....45°46'N 4°54'E
Vilnius Lithuania 43 F1 ....54°40'N 25°16'E
Vilvoorde Belgium 42 D3 ....50°55'N 4°27'E
Vilyuy r. Russia 55 N4 ....64°24'N 126°28'E
Vindelälven r. Sweden 43 D3 ...63°56'N 19°51'E
Vinh Vietnam 102 D7 ....18°38'N 105°42'E
Vinkovci Croatia 50 C7 ....45°17'N 18°49'E
Vinnytsia Ukraine 47 M3 ....49°14'N 28°30'E
Viranşehir Turkey 51 M3 ....37°13'N 39°47'E
Virden Canada 62 F6 ....49°51'N 100°56'W
Vire France 44 C6 ....48°50'N 0°53'W
Virginia d. U.S. 63 K4 ....37°47'N 78°19'W
Virgin Islands (U.K.) Central America 67 L4 ...18°37'N 64°37'W
Virgin Islands (U.S.) Central America 67 L4 ...18°14'N 64°53'W
Virovitica Croatia 50 B7 ......45°50'N 17°23'E
Virton Belgium 42 E2 ....49°34'N 5°33'E
Vis i. Croatia 50 B6 ....43°05'N 16°06'E
Visaginas Lithuania 47 L6 .....55°36'N 26°26'E
Visby Sweden 43 D2 ....57°38'N 18°18'E
Viscount Melville Sound str. Canada 60 G5
.........................73°50'N 112°57'W
Viseu Portugal 45 B4 ....40°40'N 7°55'W
Vishakhapatnam India 96 F4 ....17°42'N 83°22'E
Vistula r. Poland 46 H5 ....54°18'N 18°55'E
Viterbo Italy 48 F5 ....42°24'N 12°07'E
Viti Levu i. Fiji 109 G5 ......18°05'S 177°19'E
Vitim r. Russia 55 M3 ....59°26'N 112°35'E
Vitória Brazil 73 E4 ....20°19'S 40°21'W
Vitória da Conquista Brazil 72 E5 ...14°50'S 40°47'W
Vitoria-Gasteiz Spain 45 D5 ...42°51'N 2°39'W
Vitsyebsk Belarus 47 N6 ....55°12'N 30°10'E
Vittel France 44 F6 ....48°12'N 5°57'E
Vizianagaram India 96 F4 ......18°08'N 83°31'E
Vlaams-Brabant d. Belgium 42 D3 ...50°56'N 4°36'E
Vlaardingen Neth. 42 D4 ....51°54'N 4°21'E
Vlădeasa, Vârful mt. Romania 47 J2 ...46°45'N 22°50'E
Vladikavkaz Russia 53 E2 ......43°02'N 44°41'E
Vladimir Russia 52 E3 ....56°08'N 40°24'E
Vladivostok Russia 55 O2 ......43°07'N 131°56'E
Vlieland i. Neth. 42 D6 ....53°16'N 4°57'E
Vlissingen Neth. 42 C4 ....51°27'N 3°34'E
Vlorë Albania 50 C5 ....40°28'N 19°30'E
Vltava r. Czechia 46 E4 ....50°19'N 14°29'E
Voe Scotland 17 H5 ....60°21'N 1°16'W
Vohimena, Tanjona c. Madagascar 83 D2
.........................25°36'S 45°12'E
Volda Norway 43 A3 ....62°08'N 6°05'E
Volga r. Russia 53 E2 ....45°47'N 47°34'E
Volga Uplands hills Russia 34 I4 ...53°15'N 45°45'E
Volgodonsk Russia 53 E2 ....47°32'N 42°08'E
Volgograd Russia 53 E2 ....48°44'N 44°30'E
Völklingen Germany 42 F2 .....49°15'N 6°51'E
Volodymyr-Volynskyi Ukraine 47 K4 ...50°51'N 24°20'E
Vologda Russia 52 D3 ....59°13'N 39°54'E
Volos Greece 50 E4 ....39°22'N 22°57'E
Vol'sk Russia 53 E3 ....52°02'N 47°22'E
Volta, Lake resr Ghana 84 E2 ..6°23'N 0°05'E
Volta Redonda Brazil 73 E4 ....22°30'S 44°07'W
Volzhskiy Russia 53 E2 ....53°24'N 50°05'E
Voreioi Sporades is Greece 50 E4 ...39°15'N 23°27'E
Vorkuta Russia 52 G4 ....67°29'N 64°05'E
Voronezh Russia 53 D3 ....51°38'N 39°12'E
Vorskla r. Russia 47 P3 ....48°55'N 34°08'E
Vosges mts France 44 G5 ......48°06'N 6°41'E
Voss Norway 43 A3 ....60°38'N 6°27'E
Vostochnyy Sayan mts Russia 55 K3 ...54°43'N 94°48'E
Votkinsk Russia 52 F3 ....57°03'N 53°58'E
Vouziers France 42 D2 ....49°24'N 4°42'E

Voznesensk Ukraine 47 N2 ......47°33'N 31°21'E
Vranje Serbia 50 D6 ....42°33'N 21°54'E
Vratsa Bulgaria 50 E6 ....43°12'N 23°33'E
Vrbas r. Bos. and Herz. 50 B7 ..45°07'N 17°31'E
Vršac Serbia 50 D7 ....45°07'N 21°17'E
Vuktyl Russia 52 F4 ....63°52'N 57°19'E
Vung Tau Vietnam 102 D6 ....10°22'N 107°05'E
Vuollerim Sweden 43 E4 ....66°26'N 20°37'E
Vyaz'ma Russia 47 P6 ....55°13'N 34°18'E
Vyborg Russia 43 G3 ....60°42'N 28°46'E
Vychegda r. Russia 53 E4 ......61°15'N 46°28'E
Vygozero, Ozero l. Russia 52 D4 ...64°40'N 35°00'E
Vyrnwy, Lake Wales 10 D4 ......52°46'N 3°29'W
Vyshniy-Volochek Russia 52 D3 ..57°35'N 34°33'E
Vytegra Russia 52 D4 ....61°00'N 36°26'E

W

Wa Ghana 84 D3 ....10°04'N 2°30'W
Wabasca r. Canada 60 G3 ....58°18'N 115°23'W
Wabash r. U.S. 63 I4 ....37°50'N 88°01'W
Wabush Canada 61 L3 ....52°51'N 66°49'W
Waco U.S. 62 G3 ....31°34'N 97°08'W
Wad Pakistan 96 C6 ....27°20'N 66°30'E
Waddān Libya 84 F4 ....29°09'N 16°09'E
Waddenzee str. Neth. 42 D5 ....52°51'N 4°51'E
Waddington England 13 G2 ......53°10'N 0°32'W
Waddington, Mount Canada 60 F3 ...51°21'N 125°18'W
Wadebridge England 11 C2 ......50°31'N 4°50'W
Wadhurst England 9 F2 ....51°04'N 0°20'E
Wadhwan India 96 D5 ....22°42'N 71°41'E
Wadi Halfa Sudan 85 H4 ....21°48'N 31°20'E
Wad Madani Sudan 85 H3 ....14°22'N 33°30'E
Wagga Wagga Australia 108 D3 ..35°08'S 147°23'E
Wāhāt Jālū Libya 49 H2 ....29°14'N 21°04'E
Wahpeton U.S. 62 G6 ....46°15'N 96°50'W
Waigeo i. Indonesia 103 I3 ....0°11'S 130°59'E
Wainfleet All Saints England 13 H2 ...53°06'N 0°14'E
Waingapu Indonesia 102 G2 .....9°38'S 120°15'E
Waini Point Guyana 72 D7 ......8°22'N 59°44'W
Wainwright U.S. 60 C5 ....70°39'N 159°51'W
Wakasa Wan b. Japan 104 C3 ....35°45'N 135°36'E
Wakayama Japan 104 C2 ....34°13'N 135°10'E
Wakefield England 13 F2 ......53°41'N 1°30'W
Wakkanai Japan 104 D5 ....45°24'N 141°40'E
Wałbrzych Poland 46 G4 ....50°46'N 16°18'E
Wałcz Poland 46 G5 ....53°17'N 16°29'E
Wales d. U.K. 21 D3 ....52°04'N 3°41'W
Wallasey England 12 D2 ....53°26'N 3°04'W
Wallingford England 8 D2 ......51°36'N 1°08'W
Wallis and Futuna is S. Pacific Oc. 109 H5
.........................13°24'S 177°57'W
Walls Scotland 17 H5 ....60°14'N 1°33'W
Walney, Isle of i. England 12 D3 ...54°04'N 3°16'W
Walsall England 8 D3 ....52°35'N 1°59'W
Waltham on the Wolds England 8 E3 ...52°49'N 0°49'W
Walton-on-Thames England 9 E2 ...51°23'N 0°25'W
Walvis Bay town Namibia 83 A2 ..22°58'S 14°30'E
Wandsworth England 9 E2 ......51°27'N 0°12'W
Wantage England 8 D2 ....51°35'N 1°25'W
Wanzhou China 99 J4 ....30°47'N 108°22'E
Warangal India 96 E4 ....17°59'N 79°35'E
Warboys England 9 E3 ....52°24'N 0°05'W
Warburton watercourse Australia 108 C4 ...27°54'S 137°19'E
Ward Hill Scotland 17 F3 .....58°54'N 3°22'W
Ward's Stone hill England 12 E3 ...54°02'N 2°38'W
Wareham England 8 C1 ....50°41'N 2°07'W
Waremme Belgium 42 E3 ....50°42'N 5°15'E
Warlingham England 9 E2 ......51°19'N 0°03'W
Warminster England 8 C2 ......51°12'N 2°11'W
Warrego r. Australia 108 D3 ...30°24'S 145°21'E
Warrenpoint Northern Ireland 14 C2 ...54°06'N 6°15'W
Warri Nigeria 84 E2 ....5°35'N 5°45'E
Warrington England 12 E2 .....53°23'N 2°36'W
Warrington d. England 21 D3 ...53°24'N 2°33'W
Warsaw Poland 46 I5 ....52°15'N 21°01'E
Warta r. Poland 46 F5 ....52°35'N 14°37'E
Warwick England 8 D3 ....52°17'N 1°35'W
Warwickshire d. England 21 E3 ..52°19'N 1°32'W
Washington England 13 F3 .....54°54'N 1°31'W
Washington d. U.S. 62 B6 ......47°36'N 120°19'W
Washington D.C. U.S. 63 K4 ....38°54'N 77°01'W
Washington, Mount U.S. 63 L5 ..44°18'N 71°18'W
Waskaganish Canada 61 K3 .....51°28'N 78°46'W
Wast Water l. England 12 D3 ...54°26'N 3°18'W
Watampone Indonesia 102 G3 ....4°31'S 120°21'E
Watchet England 11 D3 ....51°11'N 3°20'W
Waterford Ireland 18 D2 ......52°15'N 7°07'W
Waterford d. Ireland 18 D2 ....52°10'N 7°53'W
Watergate Bay England 11 B2 ...50°27'N 5°05'W
Waterlooville England 8 D1 ....50°53'N 1°02'W
Water of Saughs r. Scotland 17 G1 ...56°47'N 2°37'W
Watertown U.S. 62 G5 ....44°53'N 97°07'W
Watford England 9 E2 ....51°39'N 0°23'W
Watlington England 8 D2 ......51°39'N 1°01'W
Watson Lake town Canada 60 F4 ...60°05'N 128°42'W
Watten, Loch l. Scotland 17 F3 ...58°29'N 3°21'W
Watton England 9 F3 ....52°34'N 0°50'E
Wau South Sudan 85 G2 ....7°40'N 27°59'E
Wausau U.S. 63 I5 ....44°58'N 89°37'W
Waveney r. England 9 G3 ......52°29'N 1°41'E
Wear r. England 13 F3 ....54°54'N 1°27'W
Wedmore England 8 C2 ....51°14'N 2°49'W
Weener Germany 42 G6 ....53°10'N 7°21'E
Weert Neth. 42 E4 ....51°15'N 5°43'E
Weifang China 99 L5 ....36°42'N 119°03'E
Weihai China 99 M5 ....37°30'N 122°07'E
Weinan China 99 J4 ....34°27'N 109°33'E
Weipa Australia 103 K1 ....12°37'S 141°55'E
Weldiya Ethiopia 85 H3 ....11°49'N 39°36'E
Welkom S. Africa 83 B2 ....27°59'S 26°44'E
Welland r. England 9 E3 ......52°52'N 0°03'W
Wellesley Islands Australia 108 C5 ...16°18'S 139°33'E
Wellingborough England 8 E3 ...52°18'N 0°42'W
Wellington New Zealand 109 G2 ..41°18'S 174°46'E
Wellington Som. England 11 D2 ..50°59'N 3°13'W
Wellington Tel. Wre. England 8 C3 ...52°42'N 2°31'W
Wells England 8 C2 ....51°13'N 2°39'W
Wells, Lake Australia 108 B4 ..26°40'S 123°16'E
Wells-next-the-Sea England 9 F3 ...52°57'N 0°51'E
Wels Austria 46 F2 ....48°10'N 14°01'E
Welshpool Wales 10 D4 ....52°40'N 3°09'W
Welwyn Garden City England 9 E2 ...51°48'N 0°12'W
Wem England 8 C3 ....52°51'N 2°44'W
Wembley England 9 E2 ....51°33'N 0°18'W

Wemyss Bay town Scotland 14 E3 ...55°53'N 4°53'W
Wenchi Ghana 84 D2 ....7°45'N 2°07'W
Wendo Ethiopia 85 H2 ....6°35'N 38°25'E
Wendover England 8 E2 ....51°46'N 0°44'W
Wenlock Edge f. England 8 C3 ..52°27'N 2°49'W
Wensleydale f. England 13 E3 ..54°09'N 2°02'W
Wensum r. England 9 G3 ....52°37'N 1°20'E
Wenzhou China 99 M3 ....27°59'N 120°41'E
Wesel Germany 42 F4 ....51°40'N 6°38'E
Weser r. Germany 46 C5 ....53°15'N 8°29'E
Wessel, Cape Australia 108 C5 ..11°03'S 136°46'E
Wessel Islands Australia 108 C5 ...11°19'S 136°26'E
West Australian Basin f. Indian Oc. 117 H2
.........................17°42'S 102°36'E
West Bank Asia 49 K3 ....31°52'N 35°19'E
West Bengal d. India 96 G5 ....22°34'N 87°20'E
West Berkshire d. England 21 E2 ...51°28'N 1°20'W
West Bridgford England 8 D3 ...52°56'N 1°08'W
West Bromwich England 8 D3 ....52°31'N 1°59'W
Westbury England 8 C2 ....51°15'N 2°11'W
West Calder Scotland 15 F3 ....55°51'N 3°34'W
West Dunbartonshire d. Scotland 20 C4 ...55°59'N 4°31'W
Western Australia d. Australia 108 B4 ...24°24'S 121°53'E
Western Desert Egypt 49 I2 ....26°42'N 29°45'E
Western Dvina r. Europe 47 N6 ..55°28'N 30°54'E
Western Ghats mts India 96 D3 ..14°19'N 74°54'E
Western Isles d. Scotland 20 B5 ...57°54'N 6°48'W
Western Sahara Africa 84 C4 ...22°14'N 15°05'W
Wester Ross f. Scotland 16 D2 ..57°39'N 5°20'W
Westerschelde est. Neth. 42 C4 ...51°27'N 3°27'E
West Falkland i. Falkland Is 73 C1 ...51°16'S 61°32'W
West Fen f. Cambs. England 9 F3 ...52°32'N 0°00'E
West Fen f. Lincs. England 13 G2 ...53°04'N 0°05'W
West Frisian Islands Neth. 42 D6 ...53°11'N 4°37'E
Westhill Scotland 17 G2 ......57°09'N 2°17'W
West Kirby England 12 D2 .....53°22'N 3°11'W
West Lavington England 8 D2 ...51°17'N 1°59'W
West Linton Scotland 15 F3 ....55°45'N 3°21'W
West Loch Roag b. Scotland 16 C3 ...58°15'N 6°57'W
West Lothian d. Scotland 20 D4 ...55°54'N 3°31'W
West Malling England 9 F2 .....51°18'N 0°25'E
Westmeath d. Ireland 18 D3 ....53°34'N 7°24'W
West Mersea England 9 F2 .....51°47'N 0°56'E
West Midlands d. England 21 E3 ...52°28'N 1°49'W
Weston-super-Mare England 8 C2 ...51°21'N 2°59'W
West Palm Beach town U.S. 63 J2 ...26°40'N 80°09'W
Westport Ireland 18 B3 ....53°48'N 9°31'W
Westray i. Scotland 17 F4 .....59°18'N 3°02'W
Westray Firth str. Scotland 17 F4 ...59°16'N 3°07'W
West Siberian Plain f. Russia 54 J4 ...62°39'N 80°21'E
West Sussex d. England 21 E2 ..51°00'N 0°18'W
West Virginia d. U.S. 63 J4 ...38°45'N 80°27'W
West-Vlaanderen d. Belgium 42 B3 ...50°59'N 2°56'E
Westward Ho! England 11 C3 ...51°02'N 4°14'W
West Yorkshire d. England 21 D3 ...53°46'N 2°04'W
Wetar i. Indonesia 103 H2 .....7°49'S 126°13'E
Wetherby England 13 F2 ....53°56'N 1°23'W
Wetzlar Germany 44 H7 ....50°34'N 8°30'E
Wexford Ireland 18 E2 ....52°20'N 6°28'W
Wexford d. Ireland 18 E2 ......52°37'N 6°32'W
Wexford Bay Ireland 18 E2 .....52°25'N 6°19'W
Weybridge England 9 E2 ....51°22'N 0°27'W
Weyburn Canada 62 F6 ....49°40'N 103°52'W
Weymouth England 8 C1 ....50°37'N 2°27'W
Whalsay i. Scotland 17 I5 .....60°21'N 0°57'W
Whangarei New Zealand 109 G3 ..35°43'S 174°19'E
Wharfe r. England 13 F2 ......53°50'N 1°08'W
Wheeler Peak Nev. U.S. 62 D4 ..38°57'N 114°17'W
Wheeler Peak N. M. U.S. 62 E4 ..36°33'N 105°24'W
Whernside hill England 13 E3 ..54°14'N 2°24'W
Whitburn Scotland 15 F3 ......55°52'N 3°41'W
Whitby England 13 G3 ....54°29'N 0°37'W
Whitchurch England 8 C3 ......52°58'N 2°41'W
Whitchurch Wales 11 D3 ....51°31'N 3°13'W
White r. U.S. 63 H3 ....33°59'N 91°09'W
White, Lake Australia 108 B4 ..21°03'S 129°07'E
Whitecourt Canada 60 G3 ......54°08'N 115°43'W
Whitehaven England 12 D3 .....54°33'N 3°35'W
Whitehead Northern Ireland 14 D2 ...54°45'N 5°42'W
Whitehill England 8 E2 ....51°06'N 0°52'W
Whitehorse Canada 60 E4 ......60°43'N 135°03'W
White Nile r. Sudan/South Sudan/Uganda 85 H3
.........................15°38'N 32°30'E
White Sea Russia 52 D4 ....65°51'N 36°58'E
White Volta r. Burkina Faso/Ghana 84 D2 ...9°07'N 1°10'W
Whitfield England 9 G2 ....51°09'N 1°17'E
Whithorn Scotland 14 E2 ......54°44'N 4°25'W
Whitland Wales 10 C3 ....51°49'N 4°37'W
Whitley Bay town England 13 F4 ...55°03'N 1°27'W
Whitney, Mount U.S. 62 C4 .....36°35'N 118°16'W
Whitsand Bay England 11 C2 ...50°20'N 4°20'W
Whitstable England 9 G2 ......51°22'N 1°01'E
Whittlesey England 9 E3 ......52°34'N 0°08'W
Whyalla Australia 108 C3 .....33°03'S 137°31'E
Wichita U.S. 62 G4 ....37°42'N 97°20'W
Wichita Falls town U.S. 62 G3 ..33°55'N 98°29'W
Wick Scotland 17 F3 ....58°26'N 3°06'W
Wick r. Scotland 17 F3 ....58°26'N 3°05'W
Wickford England 9 F2 ....51°37'N 0°31'E
Wickham England 8 D1 ....50°54'N 1°11'W
Wickham Market England 9 G3 ...52°09'N 1°22'E
Wicklow Ireland 18 E2 ....52°59'N 6°02'W
Wicklow d. Ireland 18 E3 ......53°02'N 6°27'W
Wicklow Head Ireland 18 E2 ....52°58'N 5°59'W
Wicklow Mountains Ireland 18 E2 ...52°53'N 6°34'W
Widecombe in the Moor England 11 D2 ...50°34'N 3°49'W
Wide Firth str. Scotland 17 F4 ...59°01'N 3°02'W
Widnes England 12 E2 ....53°21'N 2°44'W
Wieluń Poland 46 H4 ....51°13'N 18°34'E
Wiener Neustadt Austria 46 G2 ..47°49'N 16°15'E
Wiesbaden Germany 46 C4 ......50°05'N 8°14'E
Wiesmoor Germany 42 G6 ....53°25'N 7°45'E
Wigan England 12 E2 ....53°33'N 2°38'W
Wight, Isle of i. England 8 D1 ...50°37'N 1°20'E
Wigston England 8 D3 ....52°35'N 1°06'W
Wigton England 12 D3 ....54°49'N 3°10'W
Wigtown Scotland 14 E2 ....54°52'N 4°27'W
Wigtown Bay Scotland 14 E2 ....54°48'N 4°19'W
Wijchen Neth. 42 E4 ....51°48'N 5°43'E
Wildhorn mt. Switz. 46 B2 .....46°22'N 7°22'E
Wilhelm, Mount P.N.G. 108 D6 ..5°46'S 144°52'E
Wilhelmshaven Germany 46 C5 ...53°32'N 8°08'E
William, Mount Australia 108 D3 ...37°19'S 142°35'E
Williams Lake town Canada 60 F3 ...52°08'N 122°09'W
Willingdon England 9 F1 ......50°48'N 0°15'E

Williston U.S. 62 F6 ....48°10'N 103°37'W
Williston Lake Canada 60 F3 ....55°51'N 123°43'W
Williton England 11 D3 ....51°10'N 3°19'W
Wills, Lake Australia 108 B4 ....21°20'S 128°37'E
Wilmington Del. U.S. 63 K4 ....39°43'N 75°38'W
Wilmington N. C. U.S. 63 K3 ....34°13'N 77°58'W
Wilmslow England 13 E2 ....53°20'N 2°14'W
Wilson's Promontory pen. Australia 108 D3
....38°55'S 146°27'E
Wilton England 8 D2 ....51°05'N 1°52'W
Wiltshire d. England 21 E2 ....51°24'N 1°53'W
Wiltz Lux. 42 E2 ....49°58'N 5°56'E
Wimblington England 9 F3 ....52°31'N 0°05'E
Wimborne Minster England 8 D1 ....50°48'N 1°59'W
Wimereux France 9 G1 ....50°46'N 1°37'E
Wincanton England 8 C2 ....51°03'N 2°25'W
Winchester England 8 D2 ....51°04'N 1°19'W
Windermere England 12 E3 ....54°23'N 2°54'W
Windermere l. England 12 E3 ....54°18'N 2°57'W
Windhoek Namibia 83 A2 ....22°34'S 17°04'E
Windrush r. England 8 D2 ....51°43'N 1°25'W
Windsor Canada 63 J5 ....42°18'N 83°01'W
Windsor England 9 E2 ....51°29'N 0°37'W
Windsor and Maidenhead d. England 21 E2
....51°28'N 0°40'W
Windward Islands Caribbean Sea 67 L4 ...15°42'N 60°03'W
Windward Passage str. Cuba/Haiti 67 J4 ...19°40'N 74°11'W
Wingate England 13 F3 ....54°44'N 1°23'W
Winisk r. Canada 61 J3 ....55°01'N 85°22'W
Winkleigh England 11 D2 ....50°51'N 3°57'W
Winnebago, Lake U.S. 63 I5 ....44°00'N 88°28'W
Winnemucca U.S. 62 C5 ....40°59'N 117°44'W
Winnipeg Canada 60 I2 ....49°53'N 97°10'W
Winnipeg, Lake Canada 60 I3 ....51°31'N 96°40'W
Winnipegosis, Lake Canada 60 H3 ......53°05'N 100°40'W
Winsford England 13 E2 ....53°12'N 2°31'W
Winslow England 8 E2 ....51°57'N 0°53'W
Winslow U.S. 62 D4 ....35°02'N 110°42'W
Winston-Salem U.S. 63 J4 ....36°07'N 80°17'W
Winterswijk Neth. 42 F4 ....51°58'N 6°42'E
Winterthur Switz. 46 C2 ....47°30'N 8°43'E
Winterton England 13 G2 ....53°39'N 0°36'W
Wirksworth England 13 F2 ....53°05'N 1°34'W
Wirral pen. England 12 D2 ....53°22'N 3°07'W
Wisbech England 9 F3 ....52°40'N 0°10'E
Wisconsin d. U.S. 63 I5 ....44°30'N 89°32'W
Wishaw Scotland 15 F3 ....55°46'N 3°55'W
Wismar Germany 46 D5 ....53°53'N 11°28'E
Witham England 9 F2 ....51°48'N 0°38'E
Witham r. England 9 F3 ....52°56'N 0°05'E
Witheridge England 11 D2 ....50°55'N 3°42'W
Withernsea England 13 H2 ....53°44'N 0°02'E
Witney England 8 D2 ....51°47'N 1°29'W
Wittenberge Germany 46 D5 ....52°59'N 11°45'E
Wittlich Germany 42 F2 ....49°59'N 6°53'E
Wittmund Germany 42 G6 ....53°35'N 7°47'E
Wiveliscombe England 11 D3 ....51°03'N 3°19'W
Wivenhoe England 9 F2 ....51°51'N 0°58'E
Wkra r. Poland 46 I5 ....52°27'N 20°45'E
Władysławowo Poland 46 H6 ....54°47'N 18°25'E
Włocławek Poland 46 H5 ....52°39'N 19°05'E
Wokam i. Indonesia 103 I2 ....5°45'S 134°31'E
Woking England 9 E2 ....51°19'N 0°34'W
Wokingham England 8 E2 ....51°25'N 0°50'W
Wokingham d. England 21 E2 ....51°24'N 0°53'W
Wolfsberg Austria 46 F2 ....46°50'N 14°51'E
Wolfsburg Germany 46 D5 ....52°25'N 10°48'E
Wollaston Lake Canada 60 H3 ....58°16'N 103°22'W
Wollongong Australia 108 E3 ....34°25'S 150°51'E
Wolsingham England 13 F3 ....54°44'N 1°53'W
Wolvega Neth. 42 F5 ....52°53'N 6°00'E
Wolverhampton England 8 C3 ....52°35'N 2°08'W
Wolverton England 8 E3 ....52°03'N 0°48'W
Wombwell England 13 F2 ....53°31'N 1°24'W
Wŏnsan N. Korea 99 N5 ....39°09'N 127°27'E
Woodbridge England 9 G3 ....52°06'N 1°19'E
Woodcote England 8 D2 ....51°32'N 1°04'W
Woodhall Spa England 13 G2 ....53°09'N 0°13'W
Woodlark Island P.N.G. 108 E6 ....8°58'S 152°47'E
Woods, Lake of the Canada/U.S. 61 I2 ...49°22'N 94°50'W
Woodstock England 8 D2 ....51°51'N 1°21'W
Wooler England 13 E4 ....55°33'N 2°01'W
Worcester England 8 C3 ....52°12'N 2°13'W
Worcester S. Africa 83 A1 ....33°38'S 19°27'E
Worcester U.S. 63 L5 ....42°16'N 71°48'W
Worcestershire d. England 21 D3 ....52°12'N 2°12'W
Wörgl Austria 46 E2 ....47°29'N 12°05'E
Workington England 12 D3 ....54°39'N 3°32'W
Worksop England 13 F2 ....53°19'N 1°07'W
Worms Germany 44 H6 ....49°38'N 8°21'E
Worms Head Wales 10 C3 ....51°34'N 4°21'W
Worth England 9 E2 ....51°07'N 0°09'W
Worthing England 9 E1 ....50°49'N 0°22'W
Wowoni i. Indonesia 103 G3 ....4°09'S 123°13'E
Wragby England 13 G2 ....53°17'N 0°18'W
Wrangel Island Russia 55 T5 ....71°07'N 178°56'W
Wrangell U.S. 60 E3 ....56°28'N 132°22'W
Wrangle England 13 H2 ....53°02'N 0°07'E

Wrath, Cape Scotland 16 D3 ....58°38'N 5°00'W
Wreake r. England 8 D3 ....52°42'N 1°06'W
Wrexham Wales 10 E5 ....53°03'N 2°59'W
Wrexham d. Wales 21 D3 ....53°01'N 2°59'W
Wrigley Canada 60 F4 ....63°12'N 123°24'W
Wrocław Poland 46 G4 ....51°06'N 17°02'E
Wuhai China 99 J5 ....39°36'N 106°53'E
Wuhan China 99 K4 ....30°37'N 114°18'E
Wuhu China 99 L4 ....31°21'N 118°25'E
Wuppertal Germany 42 G4 ....51°16'N 7°09'E
Würzburg Germany 46 C3 ....49°48'N 9°55'E
Wuvulu Island P.N.G. 103 K3 ....1°43'S 142°50'E
Wuwei China 99 I5 ....37°52'N 102°38'E
Wuxi China 99 M4 ....31°31'N 120°18'E
Wuzhou China 99 K2 ....23°28'N 111°22'E
Wye England 9 F2 ....51°11'N 0°56'E
Wye r. Wales 10 E3 ....51°37'N 2°40'W
Wylye r. England 8 D2 ....51°04'N 1°48'W
Wymondham England 9 G3 ....52°34'N 1°07'E
Wyndham Australia 108 B5 ....15°29'S 128°05'E
Wynyard Canada 62 F7 ....51°46'N 104°12'W
Wyoming d. U.S. 62 E5 ....42°57'N 107°30'W
Wythall England 8 D3 ....52°23'N 1°53'W

X

Xai-Xai Mozambique 83 C2 ....25°02'S 33°41'E
Xankändi Azerbaijan 53 E2 ....39°49'N 46°46'E
Xanthi Greece 50 F5 ....41°09'N 24°53'E
Xiamen China 99 L2 ....24°29'N 118°11'E
Xi'an China 99 J4 ....34°12'N 108°59'E
Xiangkhoang Laos 102 C7 ....19°21'N 103°25'E
Xiangtan China 99 K3 ....27°52'N 112°47'E
Xiangyang China 99 K4 ....32°03'N 112°07'E
Xichang China 99 I3 ....27°55'N 102°11'E
Xigazê China 98 F3 ....29°17'N 88°45'E
Xi Jiang r. China 99 K2 ....22°23'N 113°20'E
Xilinhot China 99 L6 ....43°54'N 116°08'E
Xingtai China 99 K5 ....37°01'N 114°33'E
Xingu r. Brazil 72 D6 ....1°37'S 52°12'W
Xining China 99 I5 ....36°35'N 101°40'E
Xinjiang Uygur Zizhiqu d. China 98 D6 ...40°15'N 78°50'E
Xintai China 99 L5 ....35°55'N 117°45'E
Xinxiang China 99 K5 ....35°14'N 113°54'E
Xinyang China 99 K4 ....32°08'N 114°04'E
Xizang Zizhiqu d. China 98 F4 ....31°26'N 88°12'E
Xun Jiang r. China 99 K2 ....23°27'N 111°25'E
Xuwen China 102 E8 ....20°18'N 110°09'E
Xuzhou China 99 L4 ....34°12'N 117°14'E

Y

Yablonovyy Khrebet mts Russia 55 L3 ...50°48'N 108°47'E
Yakima U.S. 62 B6 ....46°36'N 120°29'W
Yakumo Japan 104 D4 ....42°15'N 140°15'E
Yaku Shima i. Japan 104 B2 ....30°15'N 130°36'E
Yakutsk Russia 55 N4 ....61°59'N 129°40'E
Yala Thailand 102 C5 ....6°32'N 101°17'E
Yalova Turkey 51 H5 ....40°39'N 29°17'E
Yalta Ukraine 51 K7 ....44°30'N 34°11'E
Yamagata Japan 104 D3 ....38°15'N 140°20'E
Yamal Peninsula Russia 54 H5 ....70°40'N 69°23'E
Yambol Bulgaria 50 G6 ....42°29'N 26°30'E
Yamoussoukro Côte d'Ivoire 84 D2 .....6°48'N 5°15'W
Yamuna r. India 96 F6 ....25°26'N 81°57'E
Yana r. Russia 55 O5 ....71°09'N 135°57'E
Yanbu' al Baḥr Saudi Arabia 94 E4 ....24°05'N 38°06'E
Yancheng China 99 M4 ....33°22'N 120°09'E
Yangon Myanmar 97 I4 ....16°49'N 96°08'E
Yangquan China 99 K5 ....37°52'N 113°33'E
Yangzhou China 99 L4 ....32°23'N 119°25'E
Yanji China 99 N6 ....42°54'N 129°31'E
Yanskiy Zaliv g. Russia 55 O5 ....71°55'N 135°13'E
Yantai China 99 M5 ....37°30'N 121°21'E
Yany Kapu Ukraine 51 J7 ....45°57'N 33°49'E
Yaoundé Cameroon 84 F2 ....3°51'N 11°30'E
Yap i. Micronesia 103 J5 ....9°30'N 138°12'E
Yapen i. Indonesia 103 J3 ....1°46'S 136°12'E
Yaqui r. Mexico 66 B6 ....27°36'N 110°36'W
Yare r. England 9 G3 ....52°35'N 1°38'E
Yaren Nauru 115 J2 ....0°33'S 166°54'E
Yarm England 13 F3 ....54°30'N 1°21'W
Yarmouth Canada 61 L2 ....43°50'N 66°07'W
Yarmouth England 8 D1 ....50°42'N 1°30'W
Yarono Russia 52 G4 ....68°11'N 69°23'E
Yaroslavl' Russia 52 D3 ....57°37'N 39°53'E
Yartsevo Russia 47 O6 ....55°04'N 32°41'E
Yasawa Group is Fiji 109 G5 ....16°56'S 177°18'E
Yasyel'da r. Belarus 47 L5 ....52°08'N 26°27'E
Yatağan Turkey 51 H3 ....37°20'N 28°09'E
Yate England 8 C2 ....51°32'N 2°25'W
Yatton England 8 C2 ....51°23'N 2°49'W
Yavari r. Brazil/Peru 72 B6 ....4°18'S 69°59'W

Z

Zaandam Neth. 42 D5 ....52°26'N 4°51'E
Zabīd Yemen 94 F2 ....14°11'N 43°15'E
Zacatecas Mexico 66 D5 ....22°46'N 102°38'W
Zacatecas d. Mexico 66 D5 ....23°56'N 102°42'W
Zadar Croatia 50 A7 ....44°07'N 15°14'E
Zafra Spain 45 B3 ....38°26'N 6°25'W
Zagreb Croatia 50 A7 ....45°48'N 15°58'E
Zagros Mountains Iran 95 G6 ....34°02'N 47°10'E
Zāhedān Iran 95 J5 ....29°30'N 60°52'E
Zahlé Lebanon 49 K3 ....33°50'N 35°55'E
Zaječar Serbia 50 E6 ....43°54'N 22°16'E
Zākhū/Zaxo Iraq 94 F7 ....37°08'N 42°42'E
Zakynthos Greece 50 D3 ....37°47'N 20°54'E
Zakynthos i. Greece 50 D3 ....37°45'N 20°42'E
Zalaegerszeg Hungary 46 G2 ....46°51'N 16°53'E
Zalău Romania 47 J2 ....47°11'N 23°04'E
Zambezi r. Africa 83 C3 ....15°41'S 30°25'E
Zambia Africa 83 B3 ....14°13'S 27°30'E
Zamboanga Phil. 103 G5 ....6°56'N 122°05'E
Zamora Spain 45 C4 ....41°31'N 5°44'W

Zamość Poland 47 J4 ....50°43'N 23°16'E
Zanjān Iran 95 G7 ....36°40'N 48°27'E
Zanzibar Tanzania 83 C4 ....6°08'S 39°14'E
Zanzibar Island Tanzania 83 C4 ....6°17'S 39°32'E
Zaoyang China 99 K4 ....32°10'N 112°46'E
Zaozhuang China 99 L4 ....34°52'N 117°34'E
Zapadnaya Dvina Russia 47 O7 ....56°16'N 32°06'E
Zapadnyy Sayan f. Russia 55 J3 ....51°41'N 88°08'E
Zapolyarnyy Russia 43 G5 ....69°26'N 30°50'E
Zaporizhzhia Ukraine 47 P2 ....47°50'N 35°10'E
Zara Turkey 51 L4 ....39°54'N 37°45'E
Zaragoza Spain 45 E4 ....41°40'N 0°51'W
Zarand Iran 95 I6 ....30°49'N 56°34'E
Zaraza Venezuela 67 K2 ....9°21'N 65°18'W
Zaria Nigeria 84 E3 ....11°07'N 7°43'E
Żary Poland 46 F4 ....51°38'N 15°08'E
Zarzis Tunisia 48 F3 ....33°30'N 11°05'E
Zawiercie Poland 46 H4 ....50°29'N 19°26'E
Zawīlah Libya 48 G2 ....26°08'N 15°08'E
Zaysan Kazakhstan 54 J2 ....47°27'N 84°55'E
Zaysan Köli Kazakhstan 54 J2 ....48°05'N 83°34'E
Zealand i. Denmark 43 B1 ....55°23'N 11°46'E
Zeebrugge Belgium 42 C4 ....51°20'N 3°16'E
Zeeland d. Neth. 42 C4 ....51°31'N 3°49'E
Zeil, Mount Australia 108 C4 ....23°24'S 132°24'E
Zelenodol'sk Russia 52 E3 ....55°49'N 48°32'E
Zelenograd Russia 47 Q7 ....56°00'N 37°12'E
Zémio C.A.R. 85 G2 ....5°00'N 25°05'E
Zenica Bos. and Herz. 50 B7 ....44°11'N 17°55'E
Zerah, Gowd-e f. Afgh. 95 J5 ....29°50'N 62°27'E
Zeya Russia 55 N3 ....53°47'N 126°54'E
Zêzere r. Portugal 45 A3 ....39°28'N 8°20'W
Zgierz Poland 46 H4 ....51°51'N 19°24'E
Zhalpaqtal Kazakhstan 53 E2 ....49°40'N 49°28'E
Zhambyl Kazakhstan 98 C6 ....42°50'N 71°25'E
Zhangaarqa Kazakhstan 54 I2 ....48°42'N 71°37'E
Zhangaözen Kazakhstan 53 F2 ....43°18'N 52°53'E
Zhangjiakou China 99 K6 ....40°41'N 114°55'E
Zhangping China 99 L3 ....25°21'N 117°28'E
Zhangshu China 99 L3 ....28°04'N 115°30'E
Zhanjiang China 99 K2 ....21°10'N 110°22'E
Zhaotong China 99 I3 ....27°22'N 103°41'E
Zhashkiv Ukraine 47 N3 ....49°15'N 30°08'E
Zhejiang d. China 99 M3 ....29°21'N 120°06'E
Zhel*znogorsk Russia 47 P5 ....52°19'N 35°23'E
Zhengzhou China 99 K4 ....34°41'N 113°41'E
Zhenjiang China 99 L4 ....32°10'N 119°25'E
Zheshart Russia 52 E4 ....62°04'N 49°34'E
Zhezqazghan Kazakhstan 54 H2 ....47°45'N 67°44'E
Zhitiqara Kazakhstan 53 G3 ....52°08'N 62°09'E
Zhlobin Belarus 47 N5 ....52°54'N 30°02'E
Zhmerynka Ukraine 47 M3 ....49°03'N 28°06'E
Zhob Pakistan 95 K6 ....31°21'N 69°32'E
Zhongshan China 99 K2 ....22°31'N 113°20'E
Zhovti Vody Ukraine 47 O3 ....48°21'N 33°30'E
Zhukovskiy Russia 47 R6 ....55°35'N 38°08'E
Zhuzhou China 99 K3 ....27°49'N 113°07'E
Zhytkavichy Belarus 47 L5 ....52°13'N 27°52'E
Zhytomyr Ukraine 47 M4 ....50°15'N 28°40'E
Zibo China 99 L5 ....36°47'N 118°06'E
Zielona Góra Poland 46 F4 ....51°57'N 15°30'E
Ziġhan Libya 49 H2 ....25°27'N 22°07'E
Zigong China 99 I3 ....29°24'N 104°49'E
Žilina Slovakia 46 H3 ....49°14'N 18°44'E
Zillah Libya 49 G2 ....28°32'N 17°33'E
Zima Russia 99 I8 ....53°54'N 101°59'E
Zimbabwe Africa 83 B3 ....22°06'S 30°59'E
Zimmi Sierra Leone 84 C2 ....7°16'N 11°17'E
Zimnicea Romania 50 F6 ....43°40'N 25°22'E
Zinder Niger 84 E3 ....13°48'N 8°59'E
Zlatoust Russia 52 F3 ....55°10'N 59°35'E
Zlín Czechia 46 G3 ....49°13'N 17°41'E
Zmiyevka Russia 47 Q5 ....52°40'N 36°23'E
Znamianka Ukraine 47 O3 ....48°43'N 32°41'E
Znojmo Czechia 46 G3 ....48°51'N 16°04'E
Zolochiv Ukraine 47 K3 ....49°48'N 24°54'E
Zolotonosha Ukraine 47 O3 ....49°42'N 32°02'E
Zonguldak Turkey 51 I5 ....41°27'N 31°46'E
Zouar Chad 85 F4 ....20°27'N 16°35'E
Zouérat Mauritania 84 C4 ....22°46'N 12°29'W
Zrenjanin Serbia 50 D7 ....45°23'N 20°25'E
Zugdidi Georgia 53 E2 ....42°30'N 41°52'E
Zugspitze mt. Austria/Germany 46 D2 ...47°26'N 10°59'E
Zuid-Holland d. Neth. 42 D4 ....51°57'N 4°28'E
Zújar r. Spain 45 C3 ....39°01'N 5°46'W
Zülpich Germany 42 F3 ....50°41'N 6°40'E
Zunyi China 99 J3 ....27°40'N 106°54'E
Zürich Switz. 46 C2 ....47°23'N 8°32'E
Zutphen Neth. 42 F5 ....52°09'N 6°12'E
Zuwārah Libya 48 F3 ....32°56'N 12°05'E
Zvolen Slovakia 46 H3 ....48°35'N 19°08'E
Zvornik Bos. and Herz. 50 C7 ....44°24'N 19°07'E
Zwickau Germany 46 E4 ....50°43'N 12°30'E
Zwolle Neth. 42 F5 ....52°30'N 6°06'E
Zyryanovsk Kazakhstan 98 E7 ....49°46'N 84°02'E